D0225668

NEVILLE CHAMBERLAIN
A Biography

Released from
Samford University Library

To Katie – as always

Released from
Samford University Library

Neville Chamberlain
A Biography

ROBERT SELF

ASHGATE

Samford University Library

© 2006 R.C. Self

All rights reserved. No part of this publication may be reproduced, stored in a retrieval system, or transmitted in any form or by any means, electronic, mechanical, photocopied, recorded or otherwise without the prior permission of the publisher.

R.C. Self has asserted his moral right under the Copyright, Designs and Patents Act, 1988, to be identified as the author of this work.

Published by
Ashgate Publishing Limited
Gower House
Croft Road
Aldershot
Hants GU11 3HR
England

Ashgate Publishing Company
Suite 420
101 Cherry Street
Burlington, VT 05401-4405
USA

Ashgate website: http://www.ashgate.com

British Library Cataloguing-in-Publication Data

Self, Robert C., 1953–
  Neville Chamberlain : a biography
    1. Chamberlain, Neville, 1869–1940 2. Prime ministers – Great
    Britain – Biography 3. Great Britain – Politics and
    government – 1901–1936 4. Great Britain – Politics and
    government – 1936–1945
    I. Title
    941'.083'092

Library of Congress Cataloging-in-Publication Data

Self, Robert C., 1953–
  Neville Chamberlain: a biography / Robert Self.
      p. cm.
    Includes bibliographical references and index.
    ISBN 0-7546-5615-2 (alk. paper)
    1. Chamberlain, Neville, 1869–1940. 2. Great Britain – Politics
and government – 1910–1936. 3. Great Britain – Politics and government
– 1936–1945. 4. Great Britain – Foreign relations – 1936–1945.
5. Great Britain – Foreign relations – 1910–1936. 6. Prime ministers
– Great Britain – Biography.   I. Title.
    DA585.C5S43   2006
    941.084'092–dc22

2005020535

ISBN 0 7546 5615 2

This volume is printed on acid-free paper

Typeset in Palatino by J.L. & G.A. Wheatley Design, Aldershot, Hampshire.

Printed and bound in Great Britain by MPG Books, Bodmin, Cornwall.

Contents

DA
585
.C5
S43
2006

Preface		vii
Acknowledgements		ix
List of plates		xi
1.	The Chamberlain Enigma	1
2.	Formative Influences: From Highbury to Andros	19
3.	Birmingham and National Service, 1911–August 1917	39
4.	The Frustrated Backbencher, August 1917–October 1922	65
5.	A Rising Star, October 1922–October 1924	87
6.	The Ministry of Health, November 1924–May 1929	105
7.	Opposition and the Financial Crisis, June 1929–October 1931	137
8.	The Treasury, Tariffs and Economic Diplomacy, 1931–1934	163
9.	Depression and Recovery, 1931–1935	193
10.	Unemployment, Special Areas and Lloyd George's 'New Deal', 1932–1937	213
11.	Foreign and Defence Policy, 1934–1937	235
12.	A New Style of Prime Minister, May 1937–February 1938	261
13.	The Road to Munich, March–September 1938	291
14.	Betrayal, October 1938–March 1939	327
15.	The Coming of War, March–September 1939	351
16.	'The Bore War', September 1939–January 1940	383
17.	Decline and Fall, February–May 1940	411
18.	Epilogue, May–November 1940	431
Notes and references		453
A Guide to Sources		539
Index		553

Preface

It is now exactly 60 years since Keith Feiling completed the first biography of Neville Chamberlain written with full access to his private papers and diaries. Yet as Feiling acknowledged at the time, without the ability to consult either government records or the papers of other politicians, the work could claim only a 'provisional character'.[1] In reality, under Cabinet Office rules established in October 1934, Feiling actually possessed an extremely strong claim to see the relevant official papers in his capacity as an authorised biographer seeking 'to vindicate the memory of a deceased person'. As he remained unaware of this provision, however, the Cabinet Secretary fobbed off his repeated requests for access and Feiling's defence of Chamberlain's record was substantially weaker and less complete as a result.[2] Little wonder that he complained privately in August 1944 that 'contemporary history strikes me as a pretty hard business, when everything of final value is under ground or not yet revealed'.[3] Other biographies of Chamberlain inevitably followed – although there have been astonishingly few given the length, prominence and self-evident importance of his career. Most notable among these efforts was that written (at least in part) by Iain Macleod, the Conservative politician who detected in his own career at the Conservative Research Department and then the Ministry of Health, a direct parallel with that of Chamberlain a generation earlier. Despite these perceived affinities, however, Macleod's biography added little to Feiling's account, prompting A.J.P. Taylor's observation that 'Chamberlain is now beyond defence or condemnation. He needs a biographer who will try to understand him. Probably none will be found. Neville Chamberlain is fated to go on being the man with no luck.'[4]

Unlike either Feiling or Macleod, H. Montgomery Hyde did meet Chamberlain from time to time while serving as private secretary to Lord Londonderry during the 1930s. He also enjoyed the far greater benefits bestowed by the introduction of the 'thirty year rule' in 1967, which gave him access to Cabinet and other official papers of the Chamberlain era. Nonetheless, the relatively slim volume which appeared in 1976 was never intended as the ultimate definitive biography.[5] Conversely, while Professor David Dilks published a formidably lengthy first volume of his biography in 1984, it drew on a relatively limited range of the available archival material beyond the Chamberlain papers and the volume only covered the period up to 1929. Unfortunately, despite the passage of two decades, there is still no sign of its eagerly awaited companion.[6] As a result, as David Dutton notes in his excellent recent assessment of Chamberlain's historical reputation, no satisfactory study of the life of this vitally important figure in inter-war history yet exists.[7] Against this background, the case for a new single volume biography to fill this crucial lacuna in our historical understanding is so compelling as to be absolutely overwhelming.

In preparing such a study, the author has been fortunate in having access to a vast body of research published since Feiling and Macleod first approached the subject. But notwithstanding these scholarly debts, the principal assumption underlying this work has been that any reassessment of Chamberlain's life and career should be based as far as possible upon an exhaustive examination of the almost overwhelming body of archival evidence currently available to historians in over 150 collections of private papers and countless official files at the National Archives. By adopting this approach, it is hoped that Chamberlain's own authentic tones, emotions and perspectives can be faithfully reproduced as he explains, justifies and rationalises unfolding events and his responses to them. In this respect, at least, this volume can claim the distinction of being the first to draw upon an extremely high proportion of the existing primary source material on both sides of the Atlantic written by or to Neville Chamberlain as well as a very substantial quantity of that which his contemporaries wrote about him. Readers should be under no illusion that in the selection and juxtaposition of this material, the interpretation of its meaning and the construction of the contemporary 'reality' as perceived by Chamberlain, the author is largely responsible for the picture presented. It is also the case that any assessment of Chamberlain's career, whether as Lord Mayor of Birmingham or as Prime Minister, involves any biographer in a critical evaluation of achievements, failures and missed opportunities. But ultimately, like Keith Feiling some 60 years ago, the principal intention is not to excuse or condemn, but rather to 'let N.C. speak for himself' in order to understand more clearly why he acted as he did and what he hoped to achieve during a long and important career of service to his country.[8]

Acknowledgements

A large number of debts are incurred during the preparation of a biography of this sort. First and most obvious, I owe an immense debt of gratitude to the generosity of the University of Birmingham for granting its kind permission to draw so extensively upon the letters and diaries of Neville Chamberlain and to quote from other Chamberlain family correspondence in their care. Thanks are due particularly to Christine Penney, the Head of Special Collections and Archivist at Birmingham University Library, who cheerfully provided so much valuable assistance during this research. Martin Killeen and Anne Clarke also deserve special mention for their efforts in dealing with increasingly frantic requests for further boxes of papers and in deciphering my now almost illegible scrawl. By the same token, the editor is indebted to the owners, custodians and archivists of the many other collections of private papers and diaries used in the preparation of the text. For access and permission to quote from material in privately owned collections I am grateful to Viscount Addison, the Countess of Avon, the Earl of Derby, Mr John Grigg, Captain J. Headlam, Vice-Admiral Sir Ian Hogg, the Syndics of Cambridge University Library, the Warden and Fellows of New College Oxford, the Marquess of Salisbury, Mr John Simon, Mrs A. Stacey and the Trustees of the Bridgeman family archive, Mrs R.M. Stafford, the Clerk of Records of the House of Lords acting on behalf of the Beaverbrook Foundation Trust, the Masters and Fellows of Churchill College and Trinity College, Cambridge and the Conservative Party. Transcripts of Crown copyright records at the National Archives at Kew appear by permission of the Controller of H.M. Stationery Office. I have also consulted archive collections held by a large number of other libraries and institutions listed in the bibliography and my thanks are due to the keepers, librarians and curators of these institutions and their staff. Every effort has been made to trace the copyright holders of unpublished documents from which quotations have been made. To anyone whose copyright I have unwittingly infringed I offer my sincere apologies.

Debts of a more personal kind also exist. I am particularly deeply indebted to Mr James Lloyd, Neville Chamberlain's grandson, for his kind hospitality and assiduous detective work in answering many questions about his family and to Dr Stuart Ball for all the practical and scholarly advice and assistance he has so freely given during the course of the five volumes I have now produced on Neville Chamberlain. By the same token, Professors John Ramsden, Iwan Morgan, Peter Marsh and Peter Waite all provided valuable advice or assistance on various aspects of this work, while my old friend (and former supervisor)

Alan Beattie deserves much credit for firing my passion for the inter-war years in general and the Chamberlains in particular through his inspired teaching, his vast knowledge and his generous hospitality. I also wish to record my appreciation for the support and professionalism supplied by Tom Gray and all the staff at Ashgate over an association of eight years during which they have produced four substantial volumes of Neville Chamberlain's diary letters to his sisters before embarking upon this biography. Without their vision and indulgence this project would never have come to fruition in the desired form. Christine Craig also provided invaluable professional insights into the painful process of abridgment. Finally, there is the vast debt of gratitude I owe to Katie for all she has contributed to this project – and for just being there.

Author's Note

Neville Chamberlain's punctuation and use of capital letters is erratic and inconsistent but the quotations are produced exactly as he wrote them. Unless otherwise stated, the term 'Unionist' is employed in the text to describe the alliance of the Conservative and Liberal Unionist parties until the end of the Union with Ireland in December 1921, after which the term 'Conservative' or 'Conservative and Unionist' gradually returned to general usage.

List of plates

between pages 212 and 213

1. Neville Chamberlain, April 1938

2. The family at Highbury

3. The dominant patriarch and his wife and children, *c* 1890s

4. Histed portrait of Neville Chamberlain, May 1905

5. Lord Mayor of Birmingham

6. Chamberlain opening the ninth branch of the Birmingham Municipal Bank, 1923

7. Neville and Anne Chamberlain with their children, *c* 1920

8. Westbourne, Chamberlain's home after his marriage in 1911

9. The orchid house, Westbourne, 1926

10. Inspecting new houses in Roehampton, mid-1920s

11. On the way to the Imperial Economic Conference at Ottawa, July 1932

12. Budget Day, 17 April 1934

13. Fishing for trout, 1939

14. Shooting was Chamberlain's other great weekend pursuit

15. Boarding the Electra for his first meeting with Hitler, 1938

16. After a stormy meeting with Hitler, 22–23 September 1938

17. Broadcasting after his triumphant return from Munich, 30 September 1938

18. Downing Street, 30 September 1938

19. Visit to Rome in January 1939 to meet Mussolini

20. The War Cabinet, September 1939

21. On the way to the Commons, 8 May 1940

List of plates

between pages 212 and 213

Chapter 1

The Chamberlain Enigma

'There is nothing Neville would have hated more, with his sort of candour and integrity, than the "stained glass window" type of biography.'
Keith Feiling to Anne Chamberlain, 27 October 1941, NC11/1/15/2

'Few men can have known such a tremendous reverse of fortune in so short a time', Neville Chamberlain reflected bitterly three weeks before his death.[1] He had every reason for such a lament. In September 1938 his political prestige had soared to its zenith. Standing on the tarmac at Heston aerodrome after his triumphant return from the Munich conference, he read to the waiting crowds and newsreel cameras the famous document signed by Hitler that morning. When he reached the passage about the determination of 'our two peoples never to go to war with one another again', his voice was almost lost amidst the jubilant cheers. He then boarded the royal car to be transported slowly through the ecstatic crowds to an official welcome. 'Even the descriptions of the papers gives no idea of the scenes in the streets as I drove from Heston to the Palace', he wrote to his sisters. 'They were lined from one end to the other with people of every class, shouting themselves hoarse, leaping on the running board, banging on the windows & thrusting hands in to the car to be shaken.' At Buckingham Palace he acknowledged the acclamation of the assembled throng from the floodlit balcony flanked by his wife and the royal couple. After this unique honour, Lord Zetland and the rest of the Cabinet watched in amazement as mounted police slowly forced a path for Chamberlain's car 'through a surging mass of people singing patriotic songs and roaring their applause at him' as he made his way to Downing Street.[2] Despite the cold, damp and blustery conditions, the crowd shouted deliriously until he appeared at a first floor window to proclaim that he had returned with 'Peace for our time'. It was one of the defining moments of the twentieth century and it was certainly Neville Chamberlain's finest hour.

Yet in little under a year his star had plunged to its nadir. 'I am speaking to you from the Cabinet Room at 10 Downing Street', he solemnly intoned at 11.15 on the morning of Sunday 3 September 1939:

This morning the British Ambassador in Berlin handed the German Government a final note stating that, unless we heard from them by 11 o'clock that they were prepared at once to withdraw their troops from Poland, a state of war would exist between us.
I have to tell you now that no such undertaking has been received, and that consequently this country is at war with Germany.

You can imagine what a bitter blow it is to me that all my long struggle to win peace has failed. Yet I cannot believe that there is anything more or anything different that I could have done and that would have been more successful.[3]

Devastated by the defeat of all his hopes for peace, within eight months he had fallen from the Premiership after a substantial parliamentary revolt. 'Politics are an uncertain career', Viscount Mersey recorded with commendable understatement on the day of Chamberlain's fall. 'A man who one year is hailed as the epitome of all that is best in England or even as the saviour of his country may be execrated the next as an example of lethargy and surrender.'[4] Exactly six months later Neville Chamberlain was dead.

Despite the immense potency of these two defining images of illusory triumph and tragic failure, there was far more to Neville Chamberlain's career than his ultimately unsuccessful quest for peace during the final three years of his life. After a remarkably effective term as Lord Mayor of Birmingham in 1915–16 and a much less successful period as Director-General of National Service in 1917, Chamberlain entered the House of Commons in 1918 at the age of almost fifty. Having swiftly established a formidable claim to advancement, the fall of the Lloyd George Coalition in October 1922 provided him with a golden opportunity to begin his meteoric rise from Postmaster-General, via the Ministry of Health, to the Treasury and the second place within the government in the space of only ten months. Thereafter, Chamberlain occupied a pivotal position in national politics until his death. The principal architect of a brand of 'New Conservatism' in Opposition during 1924, as Minister of Health between 1924 and 1929 he gave policy substance to the promise of Tory progressivism. As Conservative chairman during the party crisis of 1930–31 he played a central role in defending Stanley Baldwin's leadership from attack, while as the economic slump deepened he emerged as the principal protagonist in the drama which led to the fall of the Labour government and its replacement with an all-party coalition. After the 1931 election, he rapidly emerged as the dominant personality within the National Government as Chancellor of the Exchequer and then as Prime Minister. Even after his fall from the Premiership in May 1940, Chamberlain still exercised considerable influence and authority within both the party and the Churchill coalition until his sudden death from cancer in early November. By any standard, this was a record of remarkable prominence and achievement.

Yet for all that was achieved, Neville Chamberlain still remains a profoundly underrated, misjudged and misunderstood figure. Indeed, ultimately, there can be no more depressing commentary on Chamberlain's exile to the margins of popular and historical attention than the fact that historians generally agree the most penetrating and balanced complete account of his life is still that written by Keith Feiling at the request of Chamberlain's family in the immediate aftermath of his death. As a result, it is perhaps scarcely surprising that when a number of prominent historians and commentators were asked to rate the

Prime Ministers of the twentieth century on the eve of the new millennium, Neville Chamberlain was ranked in eighteenth place – located above only Anthony Eden whose reputation remains indelibly stained by his disastrous mishandling of the Suez crisis in 1956.[5]

One obvious explanation for this neglect and misunderstanding is that perceptions of Chamberlain's long career have been fundamentally blighted by the ultimate failure of his policy of appeasement. Ministers, and even more Prime Ministers, are judged on their record and few could pretend that Chamberlain's very personal form of diplomacy in pursuit of peace was anything other than an abject failure in its primary objective – whatever the crucial secondary benefits it conferred upon a nation gravely ill-prepared for war. As he confessed to the Commons on the outbreak of war: 'Everything I have worked for, everything that I have hoped for, everything that I have believed in during my public life, has crashed into ruins.'[6] Contemporaries and posterity have judged him accordingly. A more balanced evaluation of the man and his broader career has thus inevitably been obstructed by the fact that Chamberlain's name has become synonymous with the ambivalent and rapidly changing emotions generated by 'Munich' and the disastrous drift into total war. As Lord Salter observed almost thirty years after Chamberlain's death, he presents 'a problem of personal assessment of unusual difficulty. The personality is so deeply submerged under the policy for which he bore the first responsibility ... and the opinions about him of his contemporaries, were so divergent and so passionate that the man himself, his real nature and quality, will be hard to recapture and convey.'[7]

By common consent, had Chamberlain retired or died in 1937 instead of just three years later, he would have gone down in history as a great peacetime minister – a radical but realistic social reformer, a supremely talented administrator and the driving force behind many of the National Government's under-estimated successes of the early and middle-1930s. Instead, at the age of sixty-eight, he became Prime Minister, to be dismissed by posterity as 'an outstanding example of the leader whom the current of world events carried out of his depth'.[8] Although as Chancellor of the Exchequer from 1931 Chamberlain must bear a heavy responsibility for the lamentable state of national defence when he succeeded to the Premiership in May 1937, he led a nation with singularly few realistic policy options open to it. The skill with which he played the limited cards dealt to him has been the subject of intense controversy ever since. Yet too often, the contemporary critics who rose to power after his defeat and who survived to denigrate his memory, preferred to suggest that he could have been playing with an alternative, imaginary deck of cards, in which there were nothing but aces. Moreover, they often did so to conceal their own share in the errors and failures of these years whether from the Opposition benches or from Chamberlain's own. Either way, the final three years of his life tend to dominate perceptions of the man and his reputation. 'It has been Neville Chamberlain's fate', one anti-appeaser noted with an atypical generosity of spirit, 'to be first obsequiously praised and then extravagantly abused.'[9]

Chamberlain was acutely aware that the failure of his policy towards the dictators would overshadow his many other achievements. Such fears were well-founded. 'Poor Neville will come badly out of history', Churchill is once supposed to have quipped, 'I know, I will write that history.' In his deeply coloured but highly influential account of *The Gathering Storm* (1948), Churchill characterised Neville Chamberlain as 'an upright, competent, well meaning man' possessed of 'a narrow, sharp edged efficiency within the limits of the policy in which he believed' but fatally handicapped by limited vision, inexperience of the European scene and a deluded confidence in his own omniscience. Churchill's critical verdict has proved remarkably persistent. In the aftermath of mass unemployment, appeasement and total war, Chamberlain was castigated as the most culpable of all the 'Guilty Men' of Munich – a naively complacent blunderer whose failure of imagination, vision and nerve at the Treasury, and later in the conduct of foreign affairs, helped to sustain the pessimistic mood of collective self-doubt which supposedly characterised this decisive stage in national decline.[10] For many even today, the abiding popular image of a man whose public career spanned three decades, from the eve of the Great War to the first year of an even greater one, thus remains that of a tragi-comic figure standing at Heston airport with a rolled umbrella and a worthless piece of paper inscribed with the legend 'Peace in our Time'. As such, Chamberlain remains misunderstood and underrated; to be written off as a vain, self-opinionated and deluded mediocrity whose true stature and reputation are too easily dismissed with Lloyd George's malicious jibe that he was 'a good Lord Mayor of Birmingham in a lean year'.[11]

Although the layman's preconceptions of Chamberlain's place in history have remained largely impervious to the passage of time, since the mid-1960s much scholarly research has been devoted to an exhaustive re-examination of the foundations and guiding logic behind the policy of appeasement with which his name has become indissolubly associated. As Professor Dutton skilfully recounts in his penetrating study of Chamberlain's evolving historical reputation, a wave of sustained and sympathetic 'revisionism' during the 1960s has been followed since the 1980s by various species of 'post-revisionist' criticism, which in its most extreme form 'completes a somewhat bizarre full circle, returning in the minds of at least some scholars very much to the point of departure in 1940'.[12] Yet although these alternative perspectives throw much light upon the determinants of British foreign policy in this period, they contribute rather less to a better understanding of the character of its principal architect. On the contrary, by viewing his personality and career through the prism of his conduct during the final three years of his life, such a perspective often obscures, even distorts, as much as it illuminates about this complex man – not least because during this period many of the most negative and less attractive features of Chamberlain's personality were at their most conspicuous.

During his Premiership, Chamberlain often did appear autocratic, excessively secretive, inordinately sensitive to criticism and ruthlessly intolerant of all opposition – however well intentioned and constructive. He was also certainly at his most arrogant and complacently self-sufficient in his own omniscience. But it is misleading to assume that such characteristics reflect the entire picture of the man over a long and varied career of public service. On the contrary, there seems ample evidence to suggest that his accession to the Premiership and the decision to assume direct personal control of foreign policy marked a distinct watershed in Chamberlain's leadership style. Certainly as he emerged as the rising star of the Conservative frontbench during the 1920s, Neville Chamberlain was widely perceived to be 'immeasurably superior' to his half-brother both 'in ability and in general attractiveness': a man 'better liked in the House than Austen', with 'greater promise' and a 'superior head-piece'. 'I like what I have seen of Neville Chamberlain', one Conservative backbencher noted in 1926, 'he seems simple and unpretending and is not boring despite his amazing efficiency and complete mastery over subjects which to me are boring *a mourir*.'[13] Yet even at this stage, more negative personality traits were evident. Looking back on the 1924–29 government, one Cabinet colleague noted presciently that Chamberlain 'suffers from a rather close habit of reserve which is the one drawback which might prevent him being a good leader'. Among his other defects was a tendency to be 'a little too easily offended and [he] occasionally appears petulant'.[14]

II

The preoccupation of contemporaries and later historians with appeasement is only one explanation for the enigma surrounding Neville Chamberlain. At the heart of the problem lies Chamberlain's own deliberate attempt throughout his life to obscure the very existence of a deeper and more complex personality. This was a striking family characteristic. Although in some crucial respects very different personalities, Joseph Chamberlain's two sons were both shy, reserved and deeply sensitive men who acquired a hard defensive shell in order to protect themselves from the all too easily inflicted wounds of public life. Austen Chamberlain certainly possessed a 'dual personality'. Concealed beneath the stiff, cold, formal exterior of frock coat, monocle and pompous persona there lurked a very different individual which few outside the immediate family ever glimpsed.[15] Precisely the same can be said of Neville Chamberlain, although in his case the public persona was more abrasive and the gulf between appearance and reality inflicted far greater damage upon his reputation. To the few who knew him well, there was a 'strange contradiction in his character and personality ... Contrary to all appearances, Neville was in fact warm of heart; but this warmth and his shyness were concealed behind a cold manner as though he were viewing everybody with distant disdain.' As Chamberlain's Parliamentary Private Secretary during his Premiership noted, his political master was 'a rare complex person, half of him hidden from the world'.[16]

The origins of this self-sufficient defensive mentality can be traced to a variety of mutually-reinforcing influences in his early life. In large part, the development of a hard protective shell was simply a natural defence for a profoundly reserved and diffident personality. Despite his combative confidence in public, Neville Chamberlain was painfully aware of his own 'accursed shyness'.[17] Perhaps it was also a habit of mind learned from a remote father who, after the death of two wives in childbirth, turned away from his young family and channelled all his passion and force into politics. An unhappy time at Rugby School, desolate solitude in the Bahamas for six years and a return to an almost equally lonely existence at Highbury before the Great War reinforced Neville's natural reticence. Equally plausibly, the aloof detachment of this essentially solitary man could be attributed to an acute consciousness of being the less favoured son. While his half-brother was extravagantly groomed for political greatness vicariously to fulfil their father's own frustrated ambitions, Neville was consigned to Mason College and a career in business to finance a political dynasty in which he was not intended to play a direct part. Such feelings were reinforced still further by the early sensation of failure and self doubt as he laboured in the wretched isolation of the Bahamas to rebuild the family fortune with an ill-conceived sisal venture.[18] These experiences undoubtedly instilled a habit of robust self-sufficiency, but they also encouraged the development of a 'compartmentalised' mind in which the private emotions and feelings of the inner man were carefully concealed behind an impenetrable public facade of cold invulnerability.[19] Ultimately, this attempt at deliberate deception lies at the very core of the problem when attempting to disentangle Chamberlain's essential personality from the mythology he consciously chose to promote.

Within the immediate family circle of his wife, the children he adored and the sisters he loved, Neville Chamberlain revealed a very different side of his character which was warm, affectionate and far more likeable. Above all, in the confessional security of his diary letters to his maiden sisters, Ida and Hilda, he was able to expose that more vulnerable side of his personality and to unburden himself of his most private hopes, fears and disappointments.[20] Yet few ever got sufficiently close to Neville Chamberlain to see past the austerely forbidding defensive mask. Even with his own half-brother, a mutual reticence obstructed real intimacy.[21] To suggest that he was a supremely 'unclubbable' individual would be a substantial understatement. At Rugby 'he made practically no friends' and throughout his subsequent career there were astonishingly few real intimates with whom he felt sufficiently confident to share his innermost thoughts.[22] 'He does not seem to care whether he has friends or not' one colleague noted after five years in the same Cabinet, 'yet every now & then he seems strangely grateful for any show of friendship from a colleague.' A few perceptive observers recognised that 'his reserved nature made it difficult for him to become intimate with anyone, and undoubtedly much of his outward frigidity was due to a disturbing self-consciousness'.[23] But for the vast majority of his contemporaries this more complex dual personality only became apparent after his death when Feiling's biography published brief extracts from his diaries and family letters. For many, such an insight into the inner man provided a disconcerting revelation. As Harold Macmillan acknowledged with striking candour: 'Now that I have read the lives that have been written of him, and especially the quotations from his diaries, I realise that underneath this stern exterior was a warm, sympathetic, and sensitive heart. But this was not apparent then to me, or indeed to any but his most intimate friends.'[24]

For all those excluded from this charmed circle of intimates, everything about the public face which Neville Chamberlain presented to the world confirmed the impression of stern superiority and 'Brahminical aloofness'.[25] His physical appearance and demeanour were seemingly contrived to reinforce the harsh public persona. 'His voice is high pitched, his face hard and stern. He seldom smiles', Labour's J.R. Clynes noted in 1937. He reminded many of 'an eagle with his hooked nose and piercing dark eyes. He was always carefully dressed and wore a stiff winged collar and a full tie. Tall of figure and wearing usually a swallow-tailed coat, he possessed a commanding appearance.'[26] Spare, even ascetic in figure, with a small head, gaunt in form and more corvine than aquiline, the effect was forbidding and intimidating. To the unsympathetic, he looked every inch like the model of a 'provincial undertaker'.[27] Similarly, although clear and resonant, his thin dry voice had 'a quality of harshness and was without seductive charm'. Although never a classical parliamentary orator like his half-brother, in debate Chamberlain was lucid, precise and relentless in the force with which his points were driven to their logical conclusion. In contrast, fanciful flourishes of rhetoric, showmanship and displays of emotion which detracted from the inexorable logic of his closely-knit argument were banished and disdained. Such qualities conferred 'a sense of mastery'.[28]

Yet, as so often with Neville Chamberlain, even his virtues could easily appear to be vices. Sir Robert Vansittart came close to the perceived truth in this verdict:[29]

> A Personality without *allure*; no orator but a better debater than any of the party leaders, he breathed prose without wings but smartened it with the asperity which Baldwin expelled. Neville Chamberlain's bark was as bad as his bite, and often gave the impression of harshness greater than he intended. He riled the more because he seldom slipped; he had command of himself and exercised it sharply.

The unfortunate impression created by this sober precision of speech was compounded by the hint of a sardonic, even contemptuous, tone and demeanour. Although a sneer was always perilously close to his lips, by the late-1930s the tendency had developed into an instinctive reflex response towards all critics. Even his closest friends and most loyal allies conceded 'Chamberlain's great fault was that he sneered at people; he sneered at the Labour Members and they never forgave him.'[30]

These outward characteristics confirmed the view that Chamberlain was wholly devoid of instinctive warmth, sympathy and even humanity. His demeanour often suggested (as Harry Snell put it) that he had been 'weaned on a pickle'. Or as a disgruntled Birmingham constituent is supposed once to have complained, 'if the b— was cut in half neither part would bleed'. To Lord Balfour, something of a cold fish himself, Chamberlain 'always seemed to have a heart like stone'. For those on the Labour benches in particular, it appeared that 'the coldness of his character encompassed him like an aura'.[31] Given the sombre countenance and austere manner, it was little wonder that many backbenchers habitually referred to Chamberlain as 'the Coroner'.[32] Equally important, he had far too much personal integrity to feign a convenient show of emotions he did not possess. Nor would he contemplate blatant self-advertisement or the projection of a more favourable image simply for public consumption. Similarly, his life-long contempt for Lloyd George was unquestionably reinforced by disdain for the theatrically-contrived histrionics he cynically employed to manipulate opinion.[33] The one great exception to this instinctive desire to conceal his emotions came in February 1932 when his speech introducing the Import Duties Bill carried the Commons with a poignant sense of the historic fulfilment of his father's frustrated dreams – but such displays were astonishingly rare. 'I never saw any emotional reaction whatever except an annoying twitch of the moustache', Labour's Herbert Morrison recalled after many years of dealing with Chamberlain.[34] Never a man to wear his heart on his sleeve, many on both sides of the political divide came to assume that he simply did not possess one.

During Chamberlain's lifetime the mask rarely slipped to reveal anything of what lay beneath – even to those with whom he worked closely for many years. After a dinner at Admiralty House in mid-October 1939 at which Chamberlain became animated when describing his six years of struggle in the Bahamas, Churchill recalled: 'This was really the only intimate social conversation that I can remember with Neville Chamberlain amid all the business we did together over nearly twenty years.'[35] Duff Cooper who served under Chamberlain at the Treasury during the early 1930s and then as a fellow Cabinet member from 1935 to 1938, recorded that 'relations with Neville Chamberlain were friendly but never intimate. He was not a man whom it was easy to get to know well.' Similarly, his ministerial aide when Prime Minister remembered that although there was mutual regard, 'if one went in at the end of the day for a chat or a gossip, he would be inclined to ask "What do you want?" He was a very difficult man to get to know. Few of his colleagues were at ease with him.'[36]

While ministerial colleagues found Chamberlain reserved, distant and difficult to know, the humble backbencher rarely caught more than a glimpse of the great man outside the Commons chamber. When they did, his manner was invariably 'glacial rather than genial' because he possessed 'neither the spontaneous ease of intercourse of some of his colleagues nor the *fausse bonhomie* of others'.[37] In this respect, Neville Chamberlain was as much of an anti-social figure as his half-brother and his leadership suffered accordingly. Unlike Austen, however, this failing was compounded by a complete lack of sentimental affinity with the House of Commons. While Austen revelled in Parliament and its arcane rituals, for the more austerely pragmatic Neville it was always a place of business rather than a spiritual home.[38] For this reason he made it an invariable practice to avoid the distinctive social camaraderie of the Smoking Room. Assuming that he had been appointed as Chamberlain's PPS in the hope that his easy manner would help to 'humanise' the Prime Minister, Lord Dunglass (later Sir Alec Douglas-Home) strove valiantly to improve his social contact with MPs. Unfortunately, when efforts were made to lure Chamberlain into the Smoking Room to meet a few carefully selected backbenchers, the outcome was an awkwardly uncomfortable conversation saved only by a brief discussion about fly fishing. Neither man repeated the error. As the organiser of this embarrassing exercise in enforced sociability later recalled:[39]

> It was absolute murder trying to get him *in* to the smoking room, or to talk out of school at all, he was so shy. He was charming to work for, in that he was most considerate to one as an individual, but was very difficult in the sense that he would never expand – never gossip. He made no effort to put himself across and no one could really do it for him.

As a young MP in the 1920s, Harold Macmillan considered that a talk with Churchill lavishly accompanied by alcohol and cigars was like young men at Oxford arguing with dons. In contrast, being summoned to Neville Chamberlain's room was 'more like an interview with the headmaster'.[40] By the same token, despite tireless exertions to cultivate and encourage his constituency activists, after the October 1924 general election an evidently anxious Austen reported to his sisters the unsatisfactory situation in Ladywood where party workers felt unappreciated and unloved. 'N's manner freezes people ...' he lamented. 'Everyone respects him & he makes no friends.'[41]

Neville Chamberlain undeniably possessed a shy personal charm and even some magnetism. Such qualities earned him genuine affection as well as respectful admiration.[42] Yet he had relatively little interest in either exercising or developing his social skills with a wider audience. He was largely devoid of small talk and impatient and disdainful of those who excelled in it and nothing else. The social acquaintances with whom he felt comfortable were always those 'genuine' people who said what they meant and who acted accordingly. He liked the Tryons because, 'though neither of them is brilliant, [they] are really "nice" people, straightforward & honest.' A mutual regard developed with Lord Weir because he was also 'very simple & straightforward ... and the sort of man on whom you can always rely to help you in a difficulty'. Chamberlain's later affection for the Stanhopes and the Forbes and the hosts of his other most regular weekend retreats all fitted the same profile. 'Atholl Forbes isn't very "brainy",' he noted in 1937, but 'he is a real good fellow who improves always as he gets over his hampering shyness.' Even Nancy Astor, the pushy socialite hostess of Cliveden, eventually earned 'the tolerant affection one feels for a warmhearted merry and sometimes naughty child'. As Chamberlain put it revealingly in February 1925, 'though she jars upon me dreadfully I can't help a sneaking liking for her because she *is* genuine'.[43]

Outside the tightly-knit Chamberlain-Kenrick family 'Click', his only real social contacts were those actively cultivated by his more gregarious wife. Even here, he was perhaps only at his best in a relaxed small party after dinner when he demonstrated both a talent for broad-ranging discussion and a quiet sense of humour. He was even capable of wry self-mockery in reporting the astonishment of fellow guests at one such weekend house party who 'hadn't realised [he] had a sense of humour'.[44] Yet fundamentally, Neville Chamberlain was a confirmed loner. His off-duty pastimes were essentially solitary and contemplative. Above all, he loved the outdoor pleasures of the countryside – botany, ornithology, entomology, hill-walking, fishing for salmon and trout and shooting almost anything. These were the real pleasures which lured him from his political labours to an increasingly endless round of country house weekends as he ascended the ladder of ministerial prominence. Even in familiar haunts like Nancy Astor's Cliveden and Lord Stanhope's Chevening, however, to some eyes he had 'a curiously stiff appearance, like those old daguerreotypes of the host's father or grandfather which hung about the passages and gun-rooms of country houses'.[45]

III

Historical understanding of the Chamberlain enigma is rendered the more complex by the fact that the personality which he sought to conceal was in itself 'a curious mixture of qualities and defects'.[46] Worse still, many contemporaries and subsequent historians have often chosen to interpret his virtues as indications of even greater flaws and weaknesses in order to explain the ultimate failure of his Premiership. Among his great strengths were an encyclopaedic knowledge, a prodigious memory and an astonishing capacity for hard work. He also possessed spectacular reserves of physical and mental resilience. Unlike his temperamentally more lethargic and highly-strung half-brother who often appeared to be on the verge of physical and mental breakdown, Neville far more closely resembled their father in his robust constitution, restless activity and remorseless drive. 'I can't help always trying to find a way out of or round a difficulty', he told his sisters in April 1921. 'If I am not actively working at *something*, tho it be only weeding the garden an uneasy sensation creeps into my mind & I become restless.' Where work did not obviously exist, Chamberlain believed it a family trait to create it.[47] Given the sheer magnitude of the burden he often assumed, Chamberlain was extremely fortunate in needing little sleep while possessing the capacity to recoup his strength and spirits by immersing himself in the simple distractions of the garden and the countryside. He was also skilled at 'switching off' from the stresses of politics, often staying up late playing patience to clear his mind and dispel his worries.[48] Remarkably, he retained these qualities until shortly before his final illness in 1940.

In many ways this capacity for sustained hard work was one of the great sources of Neville Chamberlain's political strength. He was undoubtedly a great exponent of the proposition that political effectiveness, like all forms of success, depended far more upon perspiration than inspiration:

> He had no belief in sudden inspirations or sensational short cuts: everything must be patiently thought out. Steely persistence – some might say obstinacy – in the course he had adopted was a strong element in his character. He had so often found the right solution, in municipal affairs or at the Treasury, by the hard labour of his own brains, that he was inwardly confident that world problems would in the end yield to his treatment.[49]

Although not the most intellectually gifted member of the Conservative governments of these years, he made himself their most formidable member through an unparalleled mastery of the detail of departmental policy and administration. Soon after his entry to the Commons, Chamberlain learned that it was possible to build a reputation through sheer hard work and 'mugging up'. Thereafter he emerged swiftly within Conservative ranks as the man who 'knew his case better than anyone else in the country'.[50] Like Margaret Thatcher, this was one of the principal weapons used to assert mastery over Cabinet colleagues until the end of his career. 'The P.M. is standing the strain wonderfully well and is an assiduous reader of all memoranda', Thomas Jones, the former Deputy Cabinet Secretary, noted in January 1940. 'He masters them in a way no other member of the Cabinet does and by his thorough knowledge of each item of the agenda dominates his colleagues.'[51]

Even at the time, such qualities were easily caricatured by critics and detractors as fundamental flaws of character, method and approach. Hard work and mastery of detail were dismissed as the hallmarks of a worthy but uninspired pedant wholly devoid of imagination and vision. Listening to any speech by Chamberlain, Aneurin Bevan once quipped, 'was like paying a visit to Woolworths: everything in its place and nothing above sixpence'. For this lifelong adversary, Chamberlain possessed 'the lucidity which is the by-product of a fundamentally sterile mind'.[52] Significantly, such criticisms were not confined either to Labour opponents or to his period as Prime Minister. Even before 1937 a Conservative critic noted that Chamberlain was 'a very clear-headed man but certainly lacks imagination: he is a machine and his outlook is strangely circumscribed'. Thomas Jones, for many years the Deputy Cabinet Secretary, was equally damning: 'Give Chamberlain a file of documents on a certain subject and he would be excellent in deciding what should be done *within the limits of the file*, but he would see nothing at all beyond the file, nor be able to view the problem in the light of the surrounding conditions, direct and indirect.'[53]

In retrospect, such perceptions provided a recurrent explanation for Chamberlain's failure to avert war with the dictators. He is thus repeatedly accused of managing foreign policy like the municipal business of the Birmingham City Council. Although Lloyd George can claim considerable credit for fostering such a reputation, Churchill helped reinforce the myth with the allegation that Chamberlain 'viewed world affairs through the wrong end of a municipal drain-pipe'.[54] Among the opponents of appeasement this was swiftly elevated into a central explanation for failure. Duff Cooper, who resigned a ministerial job he loved and a salary he dearly needed in protest at the Munich agreement in 1938, spoke for many when he lamented that for Chamberlain the Continent of Europe was 'a closed book':

> Chamberlain had many good qualities but he lacked experience of the world, and he lacked also the imagination which can fill the gaps of experience … He had been a successful Lord Mayor of Birmingham, and for him the Dictators of Germany and Italy were like the Lord Mayors of Liverpool and Manchester, who might belong to different political parties and have different interests, but who must desire the welfare of humanity, and be fundamentally reasonable, decent men like himself.[55]

The more such interpretations were repeated, the greater became the plausibility of the underlying proposition. 'I didn't like Chamberlain', an otherwise remarkably sympathetic Harold Macmillan told his official biographer some forty years after Chamberlain's death, 'he was a nice man, but I thought he was very, very middle class and very, very narrow in view.'[56]

In reality there was something in these criticisms, but they were a long way from the complete truth. Contrary to the image of a dull but worthy mediocrity whose hard work and pedantic mastery of boring detail concealed a profound lack of vision and inspiration, Chamberlain's approach to policy problems reflected a constructive mind, an incisive penetrating intelligence and imaginative vision which enabled him swiftly to separate the wood from the trees. On this basis, Sir Samuel Hoare contrasted MacDonald the 'romanticist' and Baldwin the 'humanist' with 'Chamberlain the analyst', whose sharp mind 'broke down problems of government into their constituent parts and fixed on the points that really mattered'. Lord Swinton, who worked closely with Chamberlain throughout the interwar period, also rated him extremely highly on the analytical clarity of his mind: 'I knew no one who could listen to a long discussion and sum up a situation better than Chamberlain. Such men have a mind like a searchlight.'[57] Painstaking, grimly methodical, confident that hard work and systematic thinking would produce the right answer, Chamberlain appeared to others to have 'a mind like a chisel'.[58] Whatever the defects of his understanding and approach to foreign affairs, this ability to discern the quintessential core of the problem and (in modern management parlance) to 'think outside the box', lay at the heart of his constructive, often radical, approach to policy problems throughout his career.

Another aspect of Chamberlain's character in which virtues gave rise to allegations of vice concerned his supposed conceit and obstinacy. Although in the privacy of his correspondence to his sisters there is scarcely a hint of self-criticism or doubt at any time, in public Chamberlain often gave the impression of a becoming modesty – at least during his earlier parliamentary and ministerial career. Again, in practice, the allegation of vanity rests heavily upon the disproportionate focus on the final three years of his career when as Prime Minister he ignored all opinions which conflicted with his own. More important, critics were too often apt to forget that smugness and conceit are not quite the same thing. And given his abilities and application, Neville Chamberlain often had something to be smug about. As Donald Watt shrewdly observes, 'It was not so much that he was conceited as that, as Scottish parlance has it, he had a good conceit of himself; but the English rarely succeed in distinguishing between the two qualities.'[59] In precisely the same manner, the virtues of self-belief and 'steely persistence' in pursuit of his goals are often translated by critics into 'self-sufficient obstinacy'. Significantly, this phrase also first became public currency after the publication of Lloyd George's *War Memoirs* in 1934, with their malice-ridden account of Chamberlain's failure at the National Service Department in 1917.[60] Thereafter, precisely the same phrase became an accepted part of many subsequent accounts of Chamberlain's leadership style in the approach to another world war.

Beyond the simple prejudice of the observer, perceptions of arrogance, obstinacy and conceit often stemmed largely from Chamberlain's approach to all problem-resolution. Having developed from youth the habit of patiently assembling and considering all of the facts before methodically reasoning through the best line to adopt, Chamberlain inevitably tended to trust his own judgement above that of all others. As his sister recalled, 'he very seldom moved away from that solution once found ... The very fact he had given so much thought to the subject before coming to any conclusion made it difficult to shake his mind when it was made up.'[61] This made him appear inflexible and 'cock-sure'. To those who adopted a different view it also made him insufferable. Embittered by her experience under Chamberlain at the National Service Department in 1917, the strong-willed Violet Markham caustically observed, 'His mind, once made up, was ringed round by a barrier so hard and so unimaginative that no argument could penetrate it'; a verdict echoed by Sir Herbert Samuel who recalled that as a Cabinet colleague in the National coalition during 1931–32, Chamberlain 'was always willing to listen to arguments with a friendly spirit – but a closed mind'.[62] There was even less open-minded flexibility when challenged over foreign affairs in the late-1930s.

When taken together, self-belief and steely determination only increased Chamberlain's propensity for intolerance and impatience towards those lesser mortals who either failed to understand the facts as he saw them or who drew different conclusions from them. Throughout his career, Chamberlain's own precision of thought and expression made him a ferocious scourge of woolly-minded romantics moved principally by instinct and emotion. He was even more contemptuous of those who deliberately preferred to avoid unpleasant realities by retreating behind facile party slogans or sentimental prescriptions. 'He did not suffer fools gladly and made no attempt to conceal it', one Conservative MP recalled. 'He was always ready to put a questioner in his place, and he was quite ready to make him feel a fool.' Although this tendency always lay just beneath the surface, as his experience, confidence and stature increased, so did his propensity to reveal his authoritarian tendencies.

> His instinctive attitude to a critic was to resist and bear down, not to conciliate or compromise. An opponent must be crushed; and a supporter who showed signs of independence must be disciplined. In the choice of his own Cabinet, and in dealing with its members, he regarded unquestioning loyalty and obedience as giving better claims to his favours than personal initiative or judgement ... he seemed to prefer the even running of the boat to the vigour of an individual oar.[63]

By the time he became Prime Minister in May 1937, such characteristics fully justified the complaint of backbench anti-appeasers like Ronald Cartland that 'they had a Führer now in the Conservative Party. The Prime Minister was becoming more and more dictatorial.'[64]

Nowhere was this intolerance of dissent more obvious, or the lash of his caustic tongue more painful, than when directed towards the Labour party and its allies. 'He always knew his case, but I felt that he showed little generosity in his attitude towards anyone whom he felt was a political opponent' an atypically sympathetic trade unionist recalled. 'He was adept at veiled sarcasm when he replied to trade union people, and his own precision in the use of language made him rather impatient with others less gifted.' Or as Clement Attlee later put it more bluntly: 'He always treated us like dirt.'[65] While Baldwin's essential human decency and fair play inspired affection and respect from the Labour benches, Chamberlain's capacity for unflinching scorn provoked only loathing and hatred. Such tensions were already severe when Chamberlain was confined to the domestic policy arena, but as the international crisis deepened during the 1930s, Chamberlain became progressively less restrained in both his private disgust and public contempt at Labour's retreat into what he believed to be cynically contrived fantasies. Often sitting next to Chamberlain on the Treasury bench, 'Rab' Butler recalled that he 'would fidget and fume expletives in a manner which brought to mind the famous physical eccentricities of Dr Johnson'. Moreover, having banished many of the customary civilities of parliamentary life from his own political style, Chamberlain had no compunction about rebuking fellow ministers when he felt they were 'not sharp enough with the Opposition'.[66]

Yet even in this respect, Chamberlain's personality and motives are too often misunderstood and misjudged. To explain Chamberlain's intolerance and hostility towards opponents in terms of intellectual arrogance, misplaced self-belief or partisanship fails to capture the full complexity of his nature and the impact of his chosen profession upon his political style. Despite his pivotal role in political manoeuvre during his long career, Chamberlain never regarded politics as an end in itself. 'My pleasure is in administration rather than the game of politics' he confessed after electoral defeat had ended his reforming tenure at the Ministry of Health in 1929.[67] Above all, he appeared to loath the posturing, mock emotions, 'humbug' and blind obstructionism demanded by a profoundly adversarial political system in which ritualised party warfare predominated over good sense, sincerity and an honest approach towards problem-resolution.

In this context, it is important to recognise that Chamberlain's understanding of politics was rooted fundamentally in a set of technocratic managerial values, strongly influenced by his father's Liberal heritage and his own early years of public service in Birmingham. The art of governance was less about political point-scoring for facile electoral advantage than the establishment of an effective managerial regime capable of directing the collective resources of State and community towards national improvement for the benefit of all.[68] From this perspective, what mattered was an empirical approach towards the definition of policy goals and outcomes. 'Mr Chamberlain is the plain man in politics', one commentator noted in the late 1920s, 'his yea is yea and his nay is nay ... He would have the business of state carried on in the same orderly manner as Birmingham business ... he is the statesman for the counting house.'[69] Neither misplaced sentimentality, woolly-minded wishful thinking nor slavish adherence to irrelevant ideological prescriptions should be permitted to deflect policy-makers from the 'right' course of action dictated by due regard for the facts, public economy and the moral well-being of the individual. Having served Chamberlain for most of the 1930s at the Treasury and then as Cabinet Secretary, Sir Edward Bridges later recalled, 'the dominating feature of his make-up was not merely his power of analysis but also the ruthlessly realistic judgement of ... the action to be taken which followed the analysis'.[70] In the application of such an approach, Chamberlain was characteristically unemotional, undeviating and remorseless. His administrative cast of mind reduced politics to a matter of efficient administration to be earnestly undertaken by men of good will in pursuit of self-evidently desirable goals.

Such a perspective helps to resolve the paradox of a man who possessed deep and sincere social sympathies for the plight of the 'less fortunate' but who also became the most ferocious tormentor of the Labour Party and its principal *bête noire*. As Lord Mayor of Birmingham there was relatively little of the asperity towards Labour councillors and local trade unionists which later became his hallmark. On the contrary, he prided himself upon his ability to work with moderate Labour men in order to achieve necessary reforms in which they had a common interest. Similar attitudes prevailed at National Service in 1917. Chamberlain's contempt towards Labour opponents only really emerged powerfully after his entry to the Commons – and particularly after becoming a minister in 1922. Ultimately, perhaps this suggests that detestation of Labour had less to do with the perceived ideological fallacies of socialism *per se* than with Chamberlain's revulsion towards what he saw as the idiotic ritualised abuse and cant they consistently hurled at the government for no better reason than that this was the principal function of His Majesty's Opposition in an adversarial system. For a sensitive man who was easily bruised and offended, Chamberlain hated and resented the brazen injustice and fraudulent passion behind Opposition attacks. As a technocrat with a Benthamite view of 'politics as administration', he detested their waste, inefficiency and hypocrisy even more. As he complained revealingly of his Labour opponents in 1928, 'their gross exaggerations, their dishonesty in slurring over facts that tell against them, and their utter inability to appreciate a reasonable argument, do embitter my soul sometimes, and if I seem hard and unsympathetic to them, it is the reaction brought about by their own attitude'.[71]

This same distaste for the adversarial rituals of British politics and admiration for the virtues of rational administration also explains Chamberlain's often far more comfortable relations with officials than with his political colleagues. Chamberlain embodied precisely those qualities most admired by Whitehall officials, insofar as he was industrious, diligent, precise and decisive, while his tendency to lead from the front made him extremely effective in advancing departmental policy and claims for resources within the broader Whitehall community. Little wonder that he rapidly acquired the reputation of being the 'ideal minister'.[72] But for all that, the warmth of feeling and his ability to inspire loyalty and respect was real enough. When Chamberlain was forced out of the National Service Department, his Assistant Director encapsulated the view of many senior officials throughout his career when he wrote that 'No one could ever wish for a kindlier chief to work under and I have never come into contact with any man that I respected so much.'[73]

Unfortunately, beyond the Birmingham Council House, the Whitehall department and the immediate family, the existence of any more endearing qualities was little understood – or even really suspected. Given his ability to conceal at least half of the inner man from the outside world, it was scarcely surprising that many concluded there was something fundamentally lacking in Chamberlain's personality and emotional composition. 'It is not any lack of ability in which he fails', one disgruntled junior minister complained in March 1927: 'it is the spark of humanity ... He is more of a machine than a man – at least that is how he strikes the ordinary individual.'[74] Although Chamberlain did not recognise it until the end, there was a high price to be paid for this pretence of bloodless invulnerability. Lloyd George carefully nurtured a passionate loathing for his life-long adversary and on 8 May 1940 he finally took his revenge. Although his speech denouncing Chamberlain's Premiership lasted only twenty minutes, Dingle Foot in a nearby seat felt it contained 'all the accumulated dislike and contempt of twenty-five years!' Labour hated Chamberlain like poison and on the following day they also paid him back for all the sneers, condescension and abuse with their pointed refusal to join any coalition of which he was leader. Even among his own loyal supporters and colleagues this profoundly unlovable man often elicited admiration and respect without evoking much human warmth or affection. As one of his best friends is alleged to have remarked in the 1920s, 'Neville is a man to die with, but not a man to die for.'[75] Posterity has often followed where Chamberlain's contemporaries led, by focusing too much on an outwardly smug persona which, in Donald Watt's view, makes it 'extremely difficult to like Neville Chamberlain. ... He remains cold and distant, and his gift for arousing hostility among those who study him has outlived his death.'[76] In order to understand the strengths – and even more the weaknesses – of this most enigmatic politician, it is first necessary to comprehend the profound influence of those formative years before he took up his chosen profession.

Chapter 2

Formative Influences:
From Highbury to Andros

'If ever a proper life of me is written there will still I suppose be 20 years during which my doings were of no intrinsic public interest except insofar as they might give some clue to the training which carried me so quickly into administration after I entered politics.'

Neville to Ida Chamberlain, 20 January 1940

Arthur Neville Chamberlain was born in Birmingham on 18 March 1869, the second son of Joseph Chamberlain. It was the beginning of Britain's greatest political dynasty of the twentieth century. With only two brief intervals of a few months, there was at least one Chamberlain in every Unionist Cabinet from 1895 to 1940. Of this remarkable triumvirate, Joseph Chamberlain's elder son Austen was twice Chancellor of the Exchequer before rising to become Conservative leader in 1921–22. Like his half-brother, Neville also had the distinction of serving two terms as Chancellor before attaining the supreme political prize in May 1937. Yet although their father never achieved the elevated Cabinet rank of his sons, there can be little dispute that Joseph Chamberlain was by far the greatest of the Chamberlains. 'Pushful Joe' was arguably the most dynamic statesman of his era; a towering presence so elemental that many believed he made the political weather, while to those around him he appeared 'almost like one of the forces of nature in his power'.[1]

The Chamberlain connection with Birmingham began in 1854 when the eighteen year old Joseph was sent to the city to watch over the family investment in the screw-manufacturing enterprise of Nettlefold & Chamberlain. Having rapidly amassed a fortune through hard work and a shrewd entrepreneurial spirit, Joseph Chamberlain was first drawn into politics by his radical and Unitarian sympathies during the great campaigns for franchise reform and a national system of state-funded, non-denominational education in the late 1860s. As Lord Mayor from 1873 to 1876, his passionate civic pride, boundless energy and desire for social improvement ensured that Birmingham was 'parked, paved, assized, marketed, Gas-and-Watered and *improved* – all as a result of three years active work'.[2] Elected as Liberal MP for Birmingham in 1876, Chamberlain rose to the Cabinet within four years before breaking with Gladstone and the Liberals over Irish Home Rule in 1886. By 1895 he had returned to office as Colonial Secretary, but this time as the leader of a Liberal Unionist wing of the Unionist alliance under a Conservative Prime Minister. Convinced

19

of the urgent need for tariffs to strengthen the bonds of Empire, however, by 1903 he decided to resign from the Cabinet to carry the tariff crusade to the country. Having split the Liberal party in 1886, in less than two decades Joseph Chamberlain had inflicted the same fate upon the Unionist party. Whatever else it was, life around 'Pushful Joe' was anything but dull.

Despite the political turmoil of their father's career at Westminster, at their Birmingham home of Highbury, the impressive Italianate Gothic mansion in Edgbaston to which they moved in 1880, the Chamberlains were always a close and 'extraordinarily united family'.[3] Yet although Neville Chamberlain enjoyed a relatively happy childhood, the household in which he grew to maturity was scarred by a domestic grief which profoundly influenced the relationship between a caring but austerely remote father and adoring children who regarded him with a God-like reverence throughout their lives. In 1863 Joseph Chamberlain's first wife died giving birth to her second child, Austen. Five years later, he married her first cousin, Florence Kenrick, and although her health was never robust she gave birth to Neville and his three sisters, Ida, Hilda and Ethel in just five years, only to die herself before delivering her fifth child in February 1875. Aged only six at the time, Neville later claimed that his mother had died before he was 'hardly able to understand what had happened'.[4] This second tragedy, however, had a devastating effect upon his father. As Neville recounted for his own children, although his father's love for his mother was never overtly passionate, 'it was so profound that when she died it destroyed all his pleasure in life and altered his whole being'. As a result, the distraught father turned away from his young family to repress private grief in active public service – but at the cost of becoming a somewhat stern and distant force to children who loved and worshipped him from afar. Certainly Neville came to believe that the result of this dreadful blow was to 'harden' his father 'so that for a good many years I respected and feared him more than I loved him'.[5] After this double tragedy, Joseph Chamberlain abandoned his Unitarian faith and his younger son never developed one.

Within the family it was always a solemn article of faith that 'father never made favourites amongst his children'. As Hilda Chamberlain recalled many years later, 'each one had his or her individual place, and there was never any feeling amongst us that one was favoured or loved more than another'.[6] Yet while this might be true, it is equally clear that the paths sketched out by the dominant patriarch for his two sons were very different and this fact alone had a definite bearing upon Neville's early life, his perceptions of his 'individual place' in the greater scheme of family life and upon his relationship with his more fortunate elder half-brother. Austen Chamberlain was destined from birth to be his father's political heir. No statesman since Chatham had done more to mould the career of his son or invested greater hopes and dreams in their eventual success in reaching the pinnacle of political power. From Rugby School, Austen progressed to Trinity College, Cambridge. After taking his degree in 1885, he spent nearly two years in Germany and France developing the breadth of experience necessary for a future statesman of the top rank.

Upon his return, Austen acted as a confidential aide to his revered father. From 1892 they sat together in the Commons and for three years served in the same Cabinet. After Joseph Chamberlain's resignation from the government in 1903 and his paralysing stroke three years later, Austen increasingly assumed the role of principal lieutenant and spokesman for his stricken father.[7]

'If it could be said that early life was made too easy for Austen, the same could not apply to Neville', his sister later recalled with remarkable understatement. While the elder son was destined to achieve all the frustrated ambitions of his much greater father, it was decided from an early age that the younger son 'must make his own way in the world'. While Austen flourished at Rugby, Neville's time there 'left a most unhappy impression on his mind'. Beside being spitefully victimised by an older boy, the younger Chamberlain suffered under a housemaster who was 'a bully or worse'. At his father's insistence, he was also uprooted from the Classical Sixth and a peer group with whom he was settled and transferred to the newly-established 'Modern Side' of the school to study subjects more relevant to the planned career in business, but as the only senior boy it left him feeling 'alone and *déclassé*'. Little wonder, perhaps, that an already diffident child retreated further into his shell or that 'he gave Papa a good deal of anxiety by his continual bad reports'.[8] Equally unsurprising, he did not return to the school for another 35 years and was determined never to send his own son there. After Rugby, his father decided that Neville should attend Mason College, the forerunner of Birmingham University, undertaking a course of metallurgy, mathematics and engineering for two years as a preparation for a career in the Birmingham metal industry. Unfortunately, as his lecturer at the time recalled, the young Neville Chamberlain approached the study of metallurgy with the substantial dual disadvantage that he had little background in science and even less enthusiasm for the subject.[9] As a result, he was apprenticed in 1889 to a leading firm of Birmingham chartered accountants where he demonstrated rather greater application and within six months he was promoted to become a salaried employee.

II

Although Joseph Chamberlain had entered politics as an extremely wealthy man after the sale of his interest in the family screw manufacturing business, he was a prodigal spender. Worse still, after heavy losses in the South American securities crash of the late-1880s, the value of his investments had fallen so substantially that he was forced to live off his capital; a depressing financial situation which still further reinforced his determination that his younger son should go into business to sustain himself. In the autumn of 1890, however, these plans took a new and critical twist during a visit to Montreal when Joseph Chamberlain met the Governor of the Bahamas, Sir Ambrose Shea. Shea convinced Chamberlain that a fortune could be made in his neglected colony by growing sisal; a product apparently 'growing like a weed' on the islands but capable of producing excellent hemp which could be sold for a good price.[10] Entranced by Shea's confident assurances of a substantial return on his investment, the idea fired Joseph Chamberlain's dreams of both restoring the family fortunes while exploiting the great 'undeveloped estates' of Empire to which his imperialist mind had turned since a family visit to Egypt in the previous autumn. On 10 November 1890 Chamberlain's two sons thus arrived in the Bahamas with orders to explore the possibilities of sisal production. By Christmas they had concluded that the venture was viable and expected a 50 per cent net profit on capital, although they estimated that it would require the investment of £13,000 over the first three years.[11] On this basis, their father decided to act boldly and on a large scale to develop an unexploited opportunity and obtain the best possible prices before selling out for a fortune on a rising market as others entered to share in the profits.[12]

Although Joseph Chamberlain would later talk in visionary terms of the great potentialities of Britain's imperial possessions, it was his younger son who he consigned to the hardships of life as a pioneer on the fringes of Empire in order to turn this dream into a reality. As Neville later recalled, it was a formidable burden of responsibility 'entrusted solely to a boy just out of his teens with no experience of the world whatsoever'. Barely 22 years old when he returned to the Bahamas in April 1891, by early June Chamberlain had taken an option on 20,000 acres on Andros island. 'I am confident that I have secured the best site available in the Bahamas', he assured his father after methodically surveying all the other islands. Beside plenty of good level ground, sufficient labour, a cart-road and sheltered harbour, at Mastic Point he found an ideal location for a house on a hill with shade trees and a beautiful view over the sea.[13]

Today Andros is a reef diver's paradise, but in the 1890s it was a God-forsaken backwater of Empire. For a young man alone, separated by an ocean from his family and friends and remote from what passed for civilised society in Nassau, Chamberlain inevitably at times found this a heavy and extremely lonely burden. As he complained to his family in November 1891:

> Just now I am feeling rather low spirited and depressed ... Besides that everything seems to have gone wrong lately. I wrote to New York for a Union Jack & they sent me some miserable American ensign, my safe is too small, the furniture man has sent quantities of stuff that I didn't order and left out the weights and cords for my windows, the glass in the latter is like tissue paper. I have nearly quarrelled with my Nassau agent and sent him the nastiest letter I can politely concoct, & finally the vessel I sent for plants stopped in Nassau because the Captain was afraid to go out in a little blow. The consequence is that I have piles of land ready for planting & no plants. Perhaps also the continued roughing tells on my spirits. My cot is so uncomfortable that I cannot sleep at nights and I have had to resort to sleeping draughts ... I think I have been through enough roughing to last a lifetime and I am heartily sick of it & long for civilization and comfort.

To add to his miseries, the weather was oppressively hot, he could find no convenient supply of fresh water and he was tormented by vast swarms of mosquitoes and the undisciplined habits of his local labourers.[14]

Despite these difficulties, frustrations and hardships, Chamberlain's spirits rapidly improved as he lost himself in hard physical work. For six days a week he typically rose before dawn, walked for over an hour across rough ground to work all day and then wearily trudged home again after dusk, while in the evenings he tended to the accounts. By mid-September 1891, some 300 acres had been cleared. As he reported home proudly, all observers were 'dumbfounded' by his progress and declared that 'no one in the Bahamas would have made the progress we have in the face of difficulties which would have deterred many altogether'. In addition, Chamberlain supervised the construction of his comfortable new house, a kitchen and accommodation for the workforce, a long deep water jetty and a road linking it to the plantation. In time, these feats extended to the opening of a bank for his labourer's wages, an improved range of provisions in the shop and eventually the erection of seven miles of railway track to transport the harvest. Within five months he was also able to report with some satisfaction that 'I keep tightening the rein of discipline on the people and though they grumble a good deal to each new rule they begin to understand that they have got to work according to my ideas and not according to theirs.'[15]

On his return to Andros after a three month visit to England during the summer of 1892, Chamberlain was delighted to find that 'over the whole plantation the plants have put on such a growth during the rainy season that our most sanguine hopes of early cutting seem likely to be realised'. Three months later, with almost 2000 acres cut and 1835 planted, it appeared that everything was 'going on very satisfactorily'. Unfortunately, in the same month he obtained the first indications of later problems. Although they always knew the plants would only produce their first crop in their fourth season, he now learned that they would be useless for further production after their sixth year – thus seriously threatening their earlier profit projections.[16] Nevertheless, after a personal tour of inspection late in 1893, Joseph Chamberlain told his son that he was 'much encouraged by all that I saw and heard'.[17]

Despite the progress of the plants and the confidence of the family, the continued fall in the value of their investments placed an ever greater reliance upon the success of their Andros venture at precisely the moment when Neville began to nurture private concerns about its viability. In November 1893, he reported home anxiously that the necessary machinery to process the crop and the railway to transport it from the fields would cost a good deal more than expected. A year later, there was also the dawning realisation that it would take longer than anticipated before they could begin large-scale harvesting of the leaves.[18] More immediately distressing was the death of his manager's wife in November 1894. This delivered a double blow, as the invaluable Knowles took refuge in a bout of heavy drinking which eventually drove him half out of his mind, while Neville lamented that 'what little social life I had is gone absolutely and I see myself condemned for an indefinite period to a life of total solitude, mentally if not physically'. After being deserted by his drunken crew in Nassau a week later, he confessed to his sisters he was 'in the most wretched state of mind you can imagine'.[19]

After this misfortune, problems followed thick and fast. The railway tracks proved more difficult to lay than expected and while almost 6000 acres had been cut and planted, without Knowles to supervise them the labourers grew lazy. Worse still, the price of sisal on the world market plummeted to a 'sickening' level which the young Chamberlain gloomily concluded was likely to 'remain low for some time yet' at a time when the venture consumed even larger quantities of cash with little hope of immediate returns.[20] Throughout this period, his torment at adversity was intensified by the even more depressing realisation that the crop was not flourishing on any except the best tracts of land and this accounted for only a fifth of the total plantation. Depressed and lonely, he finally confessed his fears to Austen in January 1895. Oppressed by the vast burden of family expectations, he declared that 'Sometimes when I think of what failure means for Father ... I can hardly hold up my head.' Such feelings were aggravated by the acutely painful awareness of the personal implications of failure. 'What is to become of me in the future if this thing fails I don't know. The mere sense of failure after so much hard work and sacrifice in other ways is enough to crush a man by destroying self-confidence.'[21] Although his father attempted to accept the news with stoicism in the hope that his son was being unduly pessimistic, nine months later Neville repeated the same doubts. 'I confess I do not feel very sanguine about the future', he wrote home in November 1895, 'but I think for the present we can make it pay very well to reap what we have ready, keeping down expenses while waiting to see how the rest turns out.'[22]

When Chamberlain began to harvest and process the leaves in January 1896, new disappointments followed. First, the baling shed burned down destroying the machinery and all of the bales of fibre they had accumulated after so much labour. His spirits were crushed still further when the fibre samples sent out to his prospective American buyers were the subject of complaint, forcing him to reject a large portion of the crop as unsuitable and then washing the remainder at still greater expense. Yet despite his best endeavours to overcome these problems, the fundamental difficulty remained intractably the same. As he confessed to his father in February 1896:

> The plants don't grow & I am again feeling very low and despondent about the whole concern ... I don't see how we can possibly last out longer than the end of March & then we must wait till the plants are ready to cut again ... Meanwhile everything will be disorganised. All the order & discipline that I have worked up will be lost, all the people will go away for I shall have nothing for them to do & I myself shall be at a loose end. I should not mind so much if I could see any prospect of a speedy increase in the leaf supply but I do not ... In spite of all that you and Austen said before this is

my failure. I can't bear to think of it, only it is impossible to shut one's eyes to the possibilities.

With fixed expenses running at £100 a month, Chamberlain gloomily concluded that he should harvest what they could, pay off the men and survey the estate because 'unless we really have cause to hope that an immense difference will make itself felt in a few years it is folly for me to go on wasting your money & my own time here'.[23]

Unfortunately, the survey suggested that the situation was worse than anticipated. 'It seems to me', he reported home in late April, 'that there is only one conclusion to be drawn from it which I do with the greatest reluctance and with the most bitter disappointment. I no longer see any chance of making the investment pay.' Perhaps more as a penance than a serious proposition, he even suggested further efforts to salvage something from the better tracts of land, adding plaintively that 'I should be much more than willing to spend another ten years here, if by so doing I could make a success out of the business in which I have failed.' By this stage, however, everyone recognised that the only realistic option was simply to cut their losses. After a much-needed holiday in England, he intended to return to Andros in October 1896 to dispose of their property and 'then sever my connection with the Bahamas for ever. It will be like coming from the dentist after having a tooth drawn.' In the event, even this proved a bitter disappointment. After baling the remaining 27 tons of sisal, he was unable to sell either Mastic Hall or the land and he raised a meagre £560 from the disposal of the machinery.[24]

The failure of the Andros Fibre Company represented a 'catastrophe' for Joseph Chamberlain who until the end had continued to nurture vague hopes of some financial return in the relatively near future. In the event, although he declared that it was to 'be faced courageously if there is no alternative', the loss amounted to some £50,000 – considerably more than a third of the total proceeds from the sale of his interest in Nettlefold & Chamberlain in 1874 and the modern equivalent of over £3,500,000 on the basis of the retail price index.[25] Yet the psychological impact of Andros upon his son was far more devastating. 'I cannot blame myself too much for my want of judgement', Neville protested to his father in late April. 'I have been here all the time & no doubt a sharper man would have seen long ago what the ultimate result was likely to be.'[26] Despite repeated assurances from his father and half-brother to the contrary, this sensitive 27 year old judged himself harshly for the outcome and he continued to regard it as the most intensely personal failure for many years to come. Indeed, 20 years later, when confronted with the equally humiliating failure of his efforts at the National Service Department – again for reasons largely beyond his control – he noted bitterly that 'I am in a position that reminds me of the Bahamas when the plants didn't grow.'[27]

In later years, Neville Chamberlain's recollections of the Bahamas to his children were ones of 'great affection' for a personal adventure rather than rancour at the waste of six years of his life. 'I seem to myself to have been an even more timid reserved self conscious boy than Frank', he wrote to his sisters in 1928. 'Yet all the time there was a hard core in me that only appeared when circumstances for the time cut away the covering. My experiences in the Bahamas must have exercised a great effect in showing me this core and giving me more self confidence.'[28] His father and sisters also regarded it as a truly character-building experience – although the character it formed was the curious mixture of the strengths and weaknesses which perplexed all who later encountered him. In particular, Andros confirmed the tendency of an already naturally reserved young man to turn in upon himself. The qualities it developed were those of hard-work, complete self-reliance and steely determination to succeed.[29] The absence of anyone considered to be an equal or a potential friend also encouraged a broad streak of egotism and aloof condescension behind a hard defensive shell which concealed from the outside world all signs of human emotion or distress. In later life, these became both his most effective political weapons and the least attractive aspects of an outwardly cold persona. Little wonder that many biographers have subscribed to the view that, 'If there is a name, like Rosebud, which will help unravel his life story it is surely Andros.'[30]

Yet the influence of such an experience should not be exaggerated in the quest for revelation and understanding. Andros was not a uniquely traumatic watershed. Rather, it could be argued that it conformed with the pattern of 'emotional deprivation' which characterised Neville Chamberlain's formative first quarter century.[31] The death of his mother when Neville was only six affected him far more acutely than Austen's loss of his own mother – particularly as his distraught father then erected an emotional barrier which distanced him from his children. Indeed, within the family it was generally agreed that it was not until after his third marriage in 1888 to Mary Endicott, the American daughter of President Cleveland's Secretary for War, that Joseph Chamberlain really became 'human' to his children.[32] Although Mary was only six years older than Neville, like his siblings he welcomed her warmly into the family and rejoiced at the influence of her youthful buoyancy on their father and the atmosphere at Highbury. By then, however, he had endured the unhappiness of Rugby, while his return to Birmingham and Mason College meant an equally dull and solitary life with few friends outside the Chamberlain-Kenrick clan, consigned to a lonely existence in uncomfortable rooms in the 'bachelor wing' at Highbury when the rest of the family were away at Westminster. Against this background, Andros was perhaps less a traumatic character-forming discontinuity in the life of the young Neville Chamberlain than a continuation and reinforcement of an established pattern.

In much the same way, the experience on Andros confirmed the profound ambivalence in the relationship between Joseph Chamberlain's two sons which remained with them for the rest of their lives. According to Neville's daughter, they had 'a good brotherly relationship'. Given his greater age and status as the chosen political heir, Austen habitually treated his younger brother with an unintended air of barely disguised condescension. As Hilda later recalled,

'Austen never lost his elder brother sense with regard to Neville.' In his turn, Neville deeply resented such pretensions and in the Commons together during the 1920s they had remarkably little personal or social contact – a distance reinforced by an enduring lack of sympathy between their wives.[33] Indeed, it was not until Neville's emergence as heir-apparent to Baldwin that he 'noted a new attitude on Austen's part. He has never before quite abandoned the elder brother manner', he told his sisters in May 1931. 'But now he treats me as an equal and as a result I feel much more sympathetic than at any time since we have been in the House together.' Yet even as late as 1936, a year before his belated elevation to the Premiership, Neville Chamberlain was still complaining privately in his diary that Austen 'always finds it difficult to realise that I am no longer his little brother'.[34] Underlying such feelings was the awareness that from an early stage in their lives he was the less favoured son marked down for a life of commerce and toil to build the family fortune, while his half-brother was destined for a glittering political career as the focus for family admiration and public success.[35] Almost inevitably, this recognition ensured that an already diffident young man suffered from something of an inferiority complex which made him distrustful of his own powers in early life.[36] It is also scarcely plausible that at times he should not have felt keenly the fact that while he endured loneliness and hardships on the fringes of the Empire, his half brother had become an MP in 1892 before rising to the rank of a junior minister within only three years and to the Exchequer by 1903.

III

'It's no use crying over spilt milk', Chamberlain recorded upon his return to England during the summer of 1896. 'I have got to try and forget and settle down to something else over here.'[37] In the event, he took up the life of a competent Midland businessman and compassionate employer. With the assistance of his uncle, a directorship was obtained with Elliott's Metal Company producing copper and brass at nearby Selly Oak. In November 1897 he also took over the entirely family-owned business of Hoskins & Company which manufactured metal cabin berths for ships at Bordesley. In each of these ventures he demonstrated all of those qualities of diligence, meticulous attention to detail and a keen eye for practical improvements which became the hallmarks of his later ministerial career.[38]

Chamberlain's management style contained a strong streak of benevolent paternalism which won him considerable popularity with his workers. On a work's outing to New Brighton in June 1914 he announced a profit-sharing bonus scheme for Hoskins which was worth an extra week's wages per employee at the cost of £200–300 a year, but as he explained to the family, 'if it saves us from a strike or even from having our men drawn into a Union it may save us many thousands in a single year'. This was the forerunner of many other innovations such as a pension scheme at Hoskins and a welfare officer and well-equipped surgery at Elliotts which dealt with a thousand cases a week by 1916. Characteristically, he also derived considerable pride from the fact that there had never been a strike in any of the works at which he was a director.[39] Contrary to the later sneers of his opponents that his failure at Andros was matched by a corresponding lack of talent and success as a businessman, under Chamberlain's management both Hoskins and Elliotts soon prospered – to the considerable relief of both father and son. Moreover, this Midland business background was always a source of considerable personal pride to Chamberlain. As he later declared, 'I come from the middle classes, and I am proud of the ability, the shrewdness, the industry and providence, the thrift by which they are distinguished.'[40]

Despite his dedication to this work, the life of a relatively prosperous local businessman left Chamberlain with plenty of time for leisure pursuits and alone at Highbury for much of the year he often felt the need for distraction. Most Sundays were devoted to his father's garden and orchid house from which he sent detailed reports on progress to London or Cannes. Chamberlain had first developed his passion for orchids shortly before leaving for Andros. Having talked about flowers with his uncle one day, he returned home and characteristically 'resolved that then and there I *would* care about them. Being young and enthusiastic I threw myself into the new interest with extraordinary energy and thoroughness.' After spending many hours in the orchid houses, he soon acquired an outstanding knowledge of all aspects of their cultivation, to the 'intense pleasure' of his father with whom he inspected their vast collection every Sunday morning.[41] After his marriage, Chamberlain equally lovingly devoted himself to the restoration of the derelict garden at his Edgbaston home of Westbourne, where he developed an outstanding orchid collection of his own. This remained a source of pride and distraction until a shortage of time and money compelled him to dispose of it in November 1936.

Chamberlain's love of natural history remained a burning passion throughout his life. Although he remained active in collecting new entomological specimens well into the Great War, when his son Frank suddenly developed an enthusiasm for the subject in 1921 he could sympathise with his excitement at seeing a Hummingbird Hawk Moth in the garden for the first time but confessed 'it no longer gives me the thrill & the intense longing for its possession'.[42] On the other hand, Chamberlain's interest in bird life always remained one of his greatest passions. As a child, his characteristic inability to do anything by halves encouraged him to rise before dawn in order to learn by heart the songs of all the local birds. After his return from Andros, he meticulously recorded the birdlife of Highbury and surrounding area and throughout his life he was always capable of being thrilled by the return of migrants every spring, while watching for evidence of breeding activity or the appearance of new species in the garden. In March 1922 he thus reported with unaffected simplicity his 'great excitement' over the visit of a Great Spotted Woodpecker to the coconut shell outside his drawing room window – a 'very remarkable occurrence' which he felt obliged to share with the readers of the *Birmingham Daily Mail*, just as many years later he wrote to *The Times* whenever he recorded the presence of an unusual species in St James Park.[43] Even at the pinnacle of his career in the late 1930s, he was still contributing articles on natural history and botany to journals like *The Countryman*, while as Prime Minister he was not above summoning his PPS to witness the discovery of a Scaup on St James Park lake during his morning constitutional.[44]

Chamberlain's skills as a field botanist, entomologist and ornithologist were all symptomatic of a far more profound love of the great outdoors and all it had to offer. The beauty of the British countryside always thrilled and exhilarated him. Long walks across remote hillsides, mountains and moorlands are often recorded in evocative detail, with graphic descriptions of the vistas and the flora and fauna encountered along the way. As he noted after one mountain walk at Llanfairfechan in 1916:

> The sun shone brilliantly and the gorse was full of birds, whinchats and yellow hammers as well as blackbirds, thrushes and occasional willow wrens. They all sang joyfully to the chorus of larks above and we lay and basked in the sun, enjoying the view of the imposing mountains and the sea sparkling in the sunlight. There were lots of interesting flowers too – thymes and sedums, rock roses and occasionally a deliciously scented wild rose, Rosa Pimpinellifolia.

Twenty years later, he was still capable of being thrilled in the same unaffected manner by his annual summer visits to Dalchosnie in the Scottish highlands. 'I can't tell you what a joy it is to be here again', he told his sisters in 1934. 'When I walked up the hill … and saw the heather and the rocks and the burn again I could have shouted for joy, and the rest of the family feel the same.'[45]

Another aspect of this passion was the enduring enthusiasm for shooting and fishing which he developed during this Highbury period and which continued to fill a large part of his leisure time throughout his adult life. Fishing for trout (and salmon from 1914) provided him with his most thrilling and all-consuming pleasure – but as much for the peace of the river bank as the hope of eventually capturing his quarry. 'I really can't consent to die', he declared in 1931, 'until they arrange some fishing in the next world.' Chamberlain's Fishing Diary, detailing weather and water conditions, catch and equipment continues until a final entry on 22 June 1940 records him catching two trout before being recalled to the War Cabinet to consider the collapse of French resistance.[46] The annual visits to the Dee with his old friend Arthur Wood every Easter between 1921 and 1935 and his fortnight in September spent at Loubcroy Lodge with his uncle George were among the highlights of his year. Despite inclement weather, fierce biting midges, elusive salmon and difficult grouse, he waxed eloquent about his 'joy to be on the hills among such magnificent sky and landscapes'. Even a day spent pheasant shooting around Birmingham had great therapeutic powers as 'a mental change of a complete kind' which refreshed his mind, dispelled his worries and helped him sleep.[47] Moreover, in later years,

Chamberlain clearly delighted in the sense of paternal bonding as his son followed literally in his father's footsteps with a shotgun or fishing rod. As they started on the path to Loch Rannoch together for the last time, he confessed to his sister that 'he could have shouted with joy!'[48] Ironically, therefore, this supposedly quintessential 'Brummagen' businessman was in every respect the complete countryman. As Chamberlain himself once remarked, 'I know every flower; S[tanley] B[aldwin] knows none. I know every tree; S.B. knows none. I shoot and fish; S.B. does neither. Yet he is known as the countryman; and I am known as the townsman.'[49]

After his return from Andros, Chamberlain also fed his appetite for literature, art and music so starved during his years in the Bahamas. Moreover, contrary to the frequently repeated claim that this amounted to nothing more than a bourgeois provincial's liking for Shakespeare and Beethoven, Chamberlain had catholic tastes and informed opinions on all of these subjects. His knowledge of Shakespeare's work was broad and detailed and in later years he conducted an informed correspondence with one of the foremost experts on the subject.[50] Although Beethoven always remained 'his main love, his musical passion', throughout his life he attended a wide variety of concerts and recitals and when time permitted he was an avid reader of musical reviews.[51] He was far less enthusiastic about the theatre or opera, but informed critiques on performances and individual actors were not uncommon, while his frequent visits to private galleries and public exhibitions often provoked strong reactions – particularly towards modern art. Augustus John's etchings were thus commended for their technical excellence but he found the subjects 'mostly repellent', while Chamberlain observed of Epstein's Christ that it was 'certainly an impressive figure though it strikes me as audacious to call it Christ'. As he later concluded, 'He must have done it for the cynical satisfaction of hearing fools exhaust their vocabulary of admiration over it.' Similarly, he was utterly appalled by Stanley Spencer's 'hideous, distorted, grotesque productions' at Burlington House: 'It rouses me to fury to think that imposters should have the impudence to fob off such stuff as "art" or that any otherwise intelligent person should be fool enough to try to admire it.'[52] Despite the condescendingly dismissive image of Neville Chamberlain as the boorish bourgeois provincial, therefore, his metropolitan pastimes were diverse, cultured and well-informed. Indeed, it was a measure of the man's breadth that there were simply far too many such distractions. As he complained in 1922, 'Life is really not long enough to follow up more than 5 or 6 "interests" properly.'[53]

Contrary to another much favoured myth, that Chamberlain's ultimate failure in foreign affairs was attributable to a provincial mentality limited by a lack of exposure to the world at large, Chamberlain travelled extensively during this period – both in Europe and North Africa and in a five month tour of Ceylon, Burma and India in 1904–5. Rather than being one of the least travelled Prime Ministers of the period, in many respects he could claim to be one of those with most personal experience of foreign countries. Similarly, long before his entry to national politics, Chamberlain displayed an informed interest in defence and foreign policy and he played an active role in re-invigorating the Navy League in Birmingham as a direct result.[54]

IV

Despite the apparently relaxed tenor of Chamberlain's life during these years at Highbury, not all of his time was given over to either work or recreation. On the contrary, while he conceded that he derived 'lots of interest and enjoyment out of the struggle for the filthy lucre', from an early stage it was clearly not sufficient to satisfy his restless personality. Indeed, the more his business interests thrived, the more he found himself drawn into a closer engagement with civic affairs. As he told an old friend: 'Partly the tradition of the family & partly my own incapacity to look on and see other people mismanage things drives me on to take up new and alas! unremunerative occupations.' One of the earliest of these civic distractions involved Chamberlain in the development of the new Birmingham University, partly because it was one of his father's great local causes, but also because he confessed to being 'painfully and increasingly conscious of the defects of my own education & should like to do something to give the younger ones ... a chance of doing something better'.[55]

Chamberlain's personal impact was far greater with regard to the long-term provision of medical treatment for the citizens of Birmingham. As a sharp-eyed Official Visitor and then a member of the management board of the General Hospital from 1898, Chamberlain had been assiduous in noting all manner of defects in the system of care and administration. In particular, he devoted vast efforts to the problem of 'out-patient abuse' and possible methods of improving both the efficiency and quality of service offered by the city's hospitals.[56] At the heart of the problem was the fact that far too many patients had become accustomed to using hospital facilities for treatment which should have been administered elsewhere by a local doctor. Chamberlain's response to this problem was ingenious and the full novelty and breadth of vision has not always been fully appreciated by biographers. Put simply, he proposed the introduction of an out-patient 'filtration scheme' in which both of the city's hospitals would cooperate to assess cases according to need, with the most serious attended by highly qualified doctors and surgeons rather than by junior housemen at the hospital. Those cases turned away as too minor were to be directed to an enhanced medical service offered by the existing Birmingham General Dispensary with its many branches across the city. Here patients would be attended by doctors in return for a small monthly subscription to a provident fund at a cost far below that of private practice and well within the means of many workers. On this basis, Chamberlain hoped to educate the public and encourage thrift, while promoting cooperation between the hospitals in order to improve the quality and range of medical care within the reach of far more people than ever before; a complementary and decentralised structure of provision which he expected would eventually become a model to be emulated elsewhere.[57] In order to carry through this controversial scheme, however, Chamberlain was obliged reluctantly to add further to his existing civic burden by joining the Hospital's House Committee while becoming President of the Provident Dispensary.

Beyond these reforms which came into operation in 1908–9, Chamberlain's experience with the General Hospital convinced him of the need for a new and much larger hospital complex in the suburbs, away from their cramped quarters in the city centre; a vision he privately encouraged when he returned to the Ministry of Health in November 1924.[58] As a result, largely at Chamberlain's instigation, a plan emerged for a new teaching hospital on a 150 acre site adjacent to the University. This, he hoped, would prove large enough eventually to 'swallow up the minor and special Hospitals of the City', while he anticipated that a new spirit of cooperation between the medical school and the University would be beneficial to both medical care and education. With a characteristic note of civic pride, he also believed it would 'put Birmingham right in the front among teaching hospitals'.[59] Although building did not begin until 1934, it was a visionary scheme for which Chamberlain deserves considerable credit and even as late as May 1938 he was still soliciting the last of the funds necessary to complete the project.[60]

Beyond this local and municipal work, Chamberlain was also increasingly drawn into national politics during this period – particularly after his father resigned from the Cabinet in 1903 to unfurl the banner of tariff reform and imperial preference. Although free trade had acquired the status of a secular religion by this juncture, as a Midland businessman, a keen imperialist and his father's son, Neville Chamberlain was by instinct and conviction an ardent protectionist. As a result, after 1903 he increasingly assumed the role of 'son-apprentice' representing his father on the Tariff Reform Committee; a body affiliated to the Birmingham Liberal Unionist Association and which soon became Joseph Chamberlain's command centre in the battle to convert the entire Unionist party to tariff reform.[61]

This involvement with Unionist politics increased dramatically after 1906. Since the launch of the tariff campaign, Joseph Chamberlain had carried an extremely heavy burden and by the end of 1905 he manifested alarming signs of exhaustion and failing health. Although this prompted Neville to have a 'serious talk' with his father in January 1906, his warning only drew the reply that as he could not go at 'half speed' he preferred to accept the risk.[62] A few days after Birmingham's spectacular civic celebrations marking Joseph Chamberlain's seventieth birthday on 7 July, Neville's worst fears were realised when his father suffered a devastating stroke which paralysed his entire right side, seriously impaired his speech and effectively ended his political career. Despite this disability, however, his father simply refused publicly to admit the seriousness of the condition – with the result that Neville's sisters sacrificed their social lives and any hope of marriage in order to nurse their father, while his sons were compelled to fill the political void left by his withdrawal. While Austen became his father's mouth-piece on the Unionist front bench at

Westminster, Neville increasingly found himself in a pivotal position as his father's principal representative in Birmingham until his death on 2 July 1914 brought a blessed release from a humiliating and demoralising ordeal.[63]

Always overawed by the towering presence of a dominant father, Joseph Chamberlain's sons lived out the rest of their lives under his shadow, constantly attempting to measure up to his greater image and achievements. Although Austen more closely resembled his father in appearance, with the characteristic monocle and frock coat which he wore long after it had gone out of fashion, as everyone within the family recognised, Neville was far closer to his father in his robust physical and mental constitution, his constructive outlook and radical approach to policy problems.[64] As a measure of his devotion, in later life Neville Chamberlain was the principal force in pressing for a permanent tribute to their father's memory, both by nurturing the idea of a memorial library at Highbury (eventually opened in July 1934 after a long struggle with a sceptical Austen) and in the quest for a worthy biography of the great man – a dream only partially fulfilled during his lifetime, despite his constant and infuriated prodding designed to force the exasperating J.L. Garvin to complete the task.

V

Despite the satisfaction derived from useful work and rising local prominence, Neville Chamberlain was painfully aware of the vast gap in his personal life left by the absence of a wife and children of his own. During the summer of 1903 he had fallen in love with Rosalind Craig Sellor, a friend of his sister Hilda and a professional singer. By the time he revealed this courtship to his family in October, he was in the grip of an almost adolescent infatuation. His letters home from his tour of Italy during this period thus reveal a man afflicted by intense pangs of separation, with a consequent loss of appetite and sleep as he fretted about potential rivals and spent every hour 'revolving [his] chances'. Although the 'affair' continued into the spring of 1904, by the end of April all his hopes had been crushed. 'I must and do look upon her as dead, for I do not expect ever to see her again', he wrote bitterly. 'I have been taken up to the top of the mountain & had my glimpse of the Promised land, and now I must descend again into the wilderness.' Resigned to 'grinding through the weary round with all the spur & hope taken out of it', he unconvincingly spoke of the possibility of finding someone else in time – but for the present, he confessed, 'I have the animal instinct and cannot bear to let my agony be seen, so you will all help me best by never speaking to me of this again.'[65] After this grievous blow, the hard outer shell of reserve developed yet another layer. 'He longed intensely for his own home and children', his sister later recalled, 'but with his nature he would never put up with second best, or choose a wife with a view only to have children.'[66]

At the age of 41, Chamberlain appears almost to have resigned himself to a lonely bachelorhood. When he visited the home of his aunt Lilian Cole over the Whitsun holiday in 1910, however, he did so in the hope of resuming his acquaintanceship with her niece by marriage, the 29-year-old Anne Vere Cole. Having done so, 'he fell head over heels in love with her from the first moment'. Utterly captivated, Chamberlain pursued his courtship of his 'dearest best & sweetest girl' with a truly astonishing private intensity and passion.[67] It was a classical case of the attraction of opposites. From an Irish 'county' family with military connections and cousin to Lord Monteagle, Annie possessed in abundance all of those qualities her tightly-buttoned suitor so conspicuously lacked but so much admired – the poise and assurance of her class, a vivacious enthusiasm, emotional exuberance and a gift for sociability which enabled her to get on with everyone. Less fortunate was her tendency to vagueness and a maddening habit of failing to respond to his affectionate letters. According to less charitable observers, she was also rather less than well endowed with brain power.[68]

None of this mattered to Neville. 'Everything that went before seems only to have been the introduction to this absolute contentment for I no longer have a care in the world', he wrote home from his honeymoon.[69] Annie appeared in every respect to be the perfect complement. Above all, her unstinting affection, loyalty and pride in her husband's achievements provided this privately sensitive man with a valued soul-mate, the emotional bedrock of companionship and the family life he so desperately craved. Equally important, marriage completed Neville Chamberlain as a man without ever creating a gulf with the younger sisters to whom he was utterly devoted and upon whom he relied throughout his life for a crucial source of support and affirmation. 'It is a great happiness to me', Neville wrote to his sisters in 1928, 'that you & Ida have not been pushed out of my life by marriage' and he attributed this good fortune largely to Annie's 'genius for friendship'. Many years later, Hilda also confessed in a memoir for her late brother's children that although she was happy at Neville's marriage, she 'secretly felt that the best would have gone out of my life, for … I should lose that intimate knowledge, that delightful response and ever-present sympathy and love which Neville has given me for so many years'. That this did not occur she also attributed to Annie, 'who never tried to separate us or to shut us out, but opened her heart to us, and was willing to share him with us, as very few wives would have done'.[70]

By November 1910 the couple were engaged and two months later they were married. The arrival of two children, Dorothy on Christmas Day 1912 and Frank in January 1914, completed the picture of family bliss which provided this truly domestic man with such a source of emotional security and personal joy throughout his life.[71] Having 'long felt miserable at the thought of a childless old age', he declared this was 'the only thing needed to perfect my married life'. The news of Annie's first pregnancy was thus 'the crowning joy and though it comes very late to me I am so thankful that it should come at all that I have no room for regret. I want *lots*!'[72] Although he privately wished for a son, he declared himself 'very delighted with my little girl'. After the arrival of Frank, however, he confessed that 'I am at perhaps the happiest time of my life and it all seems sometimes too good to last.' The devoted husband with an intense pride in his wife's beauty, charm and achievements was now accompanied by a new role as the doting father. As his daughter later explained, he 'felt he'd missed so much in having no mother that he must make that up to his own children'.[73]

To ensure they enjoyed this 'complete family life', Neville Chamberlain took endless pains to entertain his two children in the nursery with 'the animal book', with regular visits to the zoo, instructive walks in the countryside, building sand-castles on the beach and as a talented story-teller regaling them with a thrilling Sunday serial of his own devising about pirates and the 'Spanish King' which ran over two years. Moreover, his letters to his family are full of endearing accounts of the winning ways and charming little escapades of his 'nice couple of imps'.

> Dorothy is fearfully busy these days; she has so many important works on hand. One morning I found her with a square of canvas and a needleful of blue wool. 'What are you doing, Dorothy' I asked. 'Makin a wexkit for Papa'says Dorothy too busy even to look up. And the next minute she coolly sewed it, canvas & all, to the side of my coat and stepping back to admire the effect she remarked in a tone of immense satisfaction '*Dere*! Dere's a wexkit for Papa'.

Despite the ostensibly cold and austere exterior, the intensity of this affection never abated. 'They certainly are loveable little mortals', he wrote in April 1920. 'When I got in Dorothy almost choked with emotion and Frank clung to me for a long time kissing my face and declaring that I was a "dear" ...'[74] Ultimately, these abundant accounts of his love for his wife and his pride in the achievements of their two 'wunderkind', refute the absurd allegations of those historians offering 'psychological' insights which seek to present Chamberlain as a man of 'passionless rigidity' whose supposedly loveless marriage reflected 'an arid wasteland devoid of personal satisfaction'.[75]

Despite their unquestioning mutual devotion, there was a less happy side to this seemingly ideal relationship. Always emotionally volatile and highly strung, Annie was a poor delegator and prone to chronic over-exertion. The risk of physical and nervous collapse was thus an omnipresent concern throughout their marriage. Fears that Annie would 'overtire' herself emerged even before Chamberlain became Lord Mayor of Birmingham in November 1915. In the mid-1920s, however, he was becoming increasingly anxious about the state of Annie's 'nerves'. In March 1926, he reported confidentially to his sisters, 'the strain acting on a highly strung temperament' had led to 'a condition which borders on a nervous breakdown and she reacts upon herself so powerfully that she falls into the extreme of depression and actually prevents herself from getting the repose which is what she needs'.[76]

As time went on, such fears became a recurrent and deepening source of anxiety and distress. Moreover, by the early 1930s a difficult and protracted menopause only increased the tendency to 'fits of jangling nerves and depression', with its accompanying nervous debility and intense 'inferiority complex'. After receiving one particularly distressing account of her condition in May 1933, which he destroyed at her insistence, her anxious husband could only offer the now customary reassurance: 'When you get down like that you must give yourself a chance to get up and *if* you do you *will* get up again. But perpetual mental strain prevents the natural elasticity from making a beginning.' Yet as he also recognised all too clearly from bitter experience, to press her too hard would only lead to a reaction in the opposite direction.[77] These 'crippling' attacks of nerves continued throughout their marriage, although ironically, during the darkest days of 1938–39 Annie proved herself 'wonderfully good in a crisis'. 'You might suppose that with her temperament she would become hysterical', Chamberlain told his sisters in the aftermath of Hitler's invasion of Prague in March 1939, 'but on the contrary the blacker the outlook the calmer she grows and where many women would be an additional burden she helps me because she can stand anything I tell her.'[78]

All of this was in the future. In the short-term, Annie was the ideal wife for an aspiring politician. Her unaffected simplicity and Celtic charm made her a successful hostess and an accomplished platform speaker capable of captivating any audience, while her indefatigable labours on behalf of innumerable good causes won her much admiration and many hearts throughout the city.[79] As wife of a Birmingham MP, she was a tireless constituency worker touring Ladywood on her bicycle, assiduously cultivating a poor working class seat while becoming a central figure in the development of the Unionist women's organisation in the West Midlands. When her husband was first promoted to the front bench, she soon busied herself with regular afternoon 'at homes' at which MPs met their leaders and these continued for fifteen years. Many years later, these parties were still recalled with affection by those who had attended them.[80] In all of these roles, Annie committed herself wholeheartedly to the advancement of her husband's career. Even those who did not succumb to her supposed beauty and charm were compelled to concede that she was an undoubted asset to an aspiring public figure. 'His wife is rather heavy in the hand', the churlish Cuthbert Headlam observed in 1926, 'but no doubt splendidly useful and worthy.'[81] At an objective level, Chamberlain's private secretary during the 1920s was almost certainly correct in arguing that her inability to believe that her husband could ever be wrong 'was a slightly bad influence on him ... because he was very self-confident and it was extremely difficult to shift him out of any preconceived ideas that he had'.[82] Yet in this (like so much else) Annie also proved a personal tower of strength.

Although perhaps rarely consulted on policy, he 'talked everything over with her' and genuinely respected her judgement as a critic and commentator. As he told his sisters, 'her mind works like that of the typical man in the street & as she doesn't in the least mind saying what she thinks I have to writhe under very plain comments'. [83] It was thus not an exaggeration when Chamberlain publicly declared on their 25th wedding anniversary that 'She has rejoiced in my successes: she has encouraged me in my disappointments: she has guided me with her counsel: she has never allowed me to forget the humanity which underlies all politics.' A year later, when he became Prime Minister in May 1937, he was equally sincere in saying that 'I should never have been P.M. if I hadn't had Annie to help me. It isn't only that she charms every one into good humour & makes them think that a man can't be so bad who has a wife like that ... But besides all this she has softened & smoothed my natural impatience and dislike of anything with a whiff of humbug about it and I know she has saved me from making an impression of hardness that was not intended.'[84]

Chapter 3

Birmingham and National Service, 1911–August 1917

'I am very well in spite of a restless and nightmary night. I kept dreaming about the Lord Mayoralty and seeing Brooks' bald head in my seat and half awake kept wishing and wishing I were back again. I thought how I had been for a little while the "first citizen" of Birmingham and how I should never again be first anything anywhere and it all seemed a bitter pill to swallow.'

Neville Chamberlain to his wife, 2 January 1917

There are few clues in Neville Chamberlain's early life to suggest that he would embark upon a career in municipal politics at the age of 42 and that this would carry him to the Premiership within a quarter of a century. The shadow cast by a dominant father and over-privileged half-brother apparently deterred the shy, younger Chamberlain from a more active interest in politics during his youth. At Rugby he took no interest in debating and claimed to detest politics, while at home, 'where politics always had pride of place', his preference for Darwinism and natural science gained him 'little sympathy from Papa'.[1] Despite repeated rumours that he was about to enter Parliament for every Midland constituency that became vacant, such suggestions were always rejected with disdain. As he told an old friend from Andros during the election campaign of 1900:

> The fact is, I was intended by nature to get through a lot of money. I should never be satisfied with a cottage, and having chucked away a competence – you know where – I am going to toil and moil till I grub it back again. Of course that doesn't prevent my taking some part in a contest like this and speaking as often as my nervousness and laziness permits me (which is not much) but I haven't begun to think of politics as a career.

Ten years later, he was equally adamant in protesting after his part in the January 1910 election that 'if ever I had thought of offering myself as a sacrifice to Parliamentary "honours" ... that experience would have sickened me of it'.[2]

On the other hand, given a long family tradition of municipal service, as early as 1901 Chamberlain was already entertaining thoughts of eventually joining the Council. But as he also recorded, 'I have quite made up my mind not to attempt it till I can afford to work at it to some purpose and that won't be for some time yet.' By the end of the decade, however, all of these conditions had been fulfilled. As Hoskins no longer needed his constant supervision, he confessed that he found himself 'spending less and less time at the works ... as I get more and more drawn into public life.'³ Against this background, Annie immediately provided a powerful new impetus behind her husband's career. Within two months of their marriage she had instructed him to sever his unproductive connection with the local Territorial Army 'but I may do as much as I like in Birmingham and in politics generally. The fact is that she thinks politics great fun and can't have too much of them.'⁴ For an aspiring civic reformer seeking a sense of purpose, 1911 was a particularly propitious year to enter municipal politics because this was precisely the moment at which sprawling industrial Birmingham truly came into its own as 'the second city of the Empire'.

It is an eloquent testimony to Chamberlain's fundamentally technocratic attitude towards politics that his decision to stand for Birmingham City Council in November 1911 was prompted less by personal ambition or partisan zeal than an enthusiasm for rational town planning and the opportunities it offered for social improvement. In 1910, Chamberlain had given evidence to assist the legislative progress of the Birmingham Extension Bill, arguing strongly in favour of a 'Greater Birmingham' and the benefits of a single unified authority. In June 1911, the Act received Royal Assent. At a stroke, a city of 13,500 acres was enlarged by another 30,000 acres to make Birmingham the second city of the Empire, encompassing a population of 840,202 citizens previously artificially fragmented into nine separate local authorities. At an emotional level, Chamberlain had always shared his father's enormous sense of civic pride in his native city and he rejoiced in its newly elevated status. But what most appealed to Chamberlain's reforming instincts were the advantages for coherent policy planning. As he told the voters of All Saints Ward in the ensuing council elections, these developments afforded vast scope for new forms of municipal activity for the benefit of the entire community and he wished to play his part. In particular, his election address dwelt upon the opportunities offered by the Town Planning Act of 1909 to control the growth of undeveloped districts in order to make proper provision for open spaces and parks, along with the prevention of overcrowding and the construction of more salubrious dwellings.⁵ This was the authentic voice of the progressive municipal reformer, anxious to tackle the urban evils of the late Victorian era into which he had been born and for whom there was a strong causal connection between housing, environment, health, crime and morals.

After his election, Chamberlain immediately plunged into a lifetime's crusade for better town planning and the related themes of health and housing. In November 1911 the Town Planning Sub-Committee became a separate entity and Chamberlain became its first chairman. Under his very personal supervision, four major development schemes were prepared covering some 15,000 acres around the city. These were designed to allow planned suburban expansion while safeguarding open spaces, designating specific land use and controlling building type and density within developments intended to be self-contained communities rather than mere city dormitories. Through the Birmingham General Survey Sub-Committee, an ambitious 'skeleton plan' was eventually prepared for the development of the entire city.

In July 1913 Chamberlain also became chairman of a special committee to investigate the housing conditions of the poor in Birmingham. As Gordon Cherry rightly notes, this was 'work which revealed him at his best: a patient collector of evidence, a sharp, succinct report writer, realistic in policy, incremental but determined in reform'. The picture presented in its interim report in October 1914 reflected the endemic urban problems of insanitary housing and chronic overcrowding in a city with 42,000 properties with no internal water supply and 58,028 with no separate toilet facilities. As Chamberlain noted in the report, 'a large proportion of the poor in Birmingham are living under conditions of housing detrimental both to their health and morals'. Perhaps predictably, Chamberlain's proposed remedy was for a 'gradual reconstruction of the old city on better lines', within the framework of a 'pre-arranged and carefully thought out plan' which outlined amended street lines and zoning for dwellings, industry and open spaces. 'In the last resort', the report thundered, 'if private enterprise failed, the Corporation must step in' with municipal ownership of land and housing estates in better planned suburbs.[6] Although the Great War intervened to prevent the implementation of Chamberlain's vision, the ideals and the value system which underpinned them remained a constant feature of his entire public career.

Diligence and enterprise on this scale soon won Chamberlain a deserved prominence on the Council. It also gained him a new respect and status within the family. By this stage, it was apparent that Austen had inherited none of his father's dynamism, constructive radical mind or sheer pugnacious enjoyment of a fight; deficiencies of ambition and sheer grit which became painfully obvious during Austen's unsuccessful contest for the party leadership in 1911 and which prompted 'criticism at home'.[7] Indeed, shortly before his death in 1914, their father is alleged to have acknowledged that he had 'greater faith in Neville's future as a politician than Austen's, and had summed up Austen's limitations by saying that he had been born in a red box, brought up in one, and would die in one'.[8] Even within Birmingham, the younger Chamberlain derived some modest satisfaction from 'a turning of the tables' in terms of the two brothers' public reputation and esteem.[9]

II

When war broke out in August 1914 Neville Chamberlain was 45 years old. Too old to enlist, he immediately threw himself into active support for the war effort both as a civic leader and as a director of several local firms engaged in munitions production. In November 1914 he became an Alderman and seven months later he was formally invited to become the next Lord Mayor; a considerable honour after four years on the Council, but one due less to the 'pull' of the Chamberlain name than his personal 'push' and proven 'sound business capacity, his grasp of big facts, his tactful direction of delicate negotiations'.[10] In reality, however, Chamberlain always recognised this was his ineluctable destiny, determined by history as well as ability. In accepting the mayoralty, Neville Chamberlain followed in a strong family tradition. No fewer than ten of his direct relatives had been Lord Mayor before him and in the 40 years since his father's first mayoralty in 1873, he was the eighth member of the family to hold the office. Although deeply gratified by the many comments on the apparent similarity between his speaking style and that of his father when installed as Lord Mayor, in a family with more than its share of filial piety, Chamberlain was suitably impressed by the difficulty of measuring up to his father's legend. 'At the moment of putting on my armour I feel how far short of what Father's son should be', he wrote to his step-mother. 'I have often thought lately how pleased and interested he would have been in my new office and it will be my endeavour not to disgrace him.' Yet for all the tone of modesty and self doubt, he also felt himself ready for the task and more than a match for its challenges.[11]

In accepting the mayoralty during wartime Chamberlain knew he could never hope to emulate the dramatic record of constructive reforms associated with his father. On the contrary, war demanded retrenchment and a conscientious approach to the essential but mundane business of a great city in abnormal times and Chamberlain soon declared there was 'a good deal of scope for an active Lord Mayor'. At the same time, his sisters predicted that their brother had the opportunity to emerge as one of the strong men of the war effort exerting the same influence over the West Midlands as Lord Derby, the so-called 'King of Lancashire', did over his native county.[12] Both expectations were soon fully vindicated. From the outset, Chamberlain injected a new dynamism into the conduct of affairs in Birmingham; his practical mind proving as swift at identifying problems and deficiencies as it was inventive and bold in devising suitable new remedies. By leading from the front, by example and practical inspiration, he also displayed all of the hallmarks of his future ministerial style. Not sparing himself a vast burden of work, he demanded similar sacrifices from his officials and colleagues and soon rejoiced that he had 'very much strengthened my position with members of the Council who did not know me very well previously'.[13]

One of Chamberlain's greatest contributions to the municipal war-effort was his reinvigoration and coordination of the Corporation's various committees. Aware that virtually all these bodies were either 'lamentably weak' or engaged in wasteful rivalries, Chamberlain intervened immediately to take charge of the weakest committee, responsible for the electricity supply essential to the town's munition works. Having instilled a new sense of purpose in its members, he moved on to coordinate the activities of various other committees to maximise efficiency and eliminate waste. As the beneficial results became evident, Chamberlain derived predictable satisfaction from the knowledge that both councillors and officials were receptive to his leadership and that he had '"got" them and that they will be ready to follow my lead in other matters'. As the Town Clerk declared at a dinner for officials in October 1916: 'They had never in their experience been treated by any Ld Mayor as I treated them; they were all conscious of how much their several departments had improved by the way in which I had entered into their work & I had linked them all up together in a fashion which had been to the greatest benefit to the City.' Even allowing for the normal pleasantries of the occasion, there was much truth in the verdict.[14]

Many other vital, but essentially unglamorous, opportunities for civic improvement were seized with equal alacrity. A coal purchase committee was formed and supplies were stockpiled around the city to be sold at cost price to the poor when shortages arose – a precaution which paid handsome dividends when fuel became scarce after April 1917. In response to complaints about the quality, price and supply of milk, a commission was established which reported (after Chamberlain's resignation) in favour of municipalisation. As some 24,000 of the 43,601 acres within the city were under cultivation to help the war effort, during the spring of 1916 Chamberlain devised a scheme for women to work on the land to boost food production.[15] He also played a prominent role in the promotion of social welfare. Always painfully conscious of the death of his own mother in childbirth, as Lord Mayor Chamberlain built on his earlier work as a member of the Health Committee to improve ante-natal care. Nursing mothers received an allowance to provide extra nutrition for themselves and their child, while through its fourteen infant welfare centres the council ensured that 85 per cent of all babies born in Birmingham were visited soon after birth and provided with assistance; an innovation which earned the praise of the government's Chief Medical Officer.[16] In March 1916 Chamberlain also launched his idea of crèches for the children of war workers.[17]

Like the mayors of many other towns, in January 1916 Chamberlain began work as chairman of the new local tribunal reviewing appeals for exemption from military service. This was initially 'the most tiring work', when sitting for up to six hours a day on three days every week, but the creation of a second tribunal in March quickly eased the burden on the Lord Mayor.[18] Significantly, although a strong supporter of conscription, Chamberlain soon noted that he was more lenient than some members of the Tribunal. 'My position' he declared, 'is that I carry out the instructions to the best of my ability. If they are wrong they should be altered, but it is not for us to alter them.'[19] Ultimately, perhaps this experience on the local tribunal influenced the more liberal attitude towards conscientious objectors contained in the Military Training Bill which Chamberlain himself introduced in May 1939.[20]

In addition to his municipal duties, from June 1915 Chamberlain was also a member of the newly formed Central Control Board designed to regulate the liquor trade. When the war broke out, the Government had acted swiftly to control the sale of alcohol. When complaints continued about drunkenness among munitions workers, servicemen and their wives, the government intervened decisively in June 1915 by establishing the Central Control Board (Liquor Trade) with powers to control licensing and reduce opening hours in areas where drunkenness was demonstrably impeding vital war production. From his own experience in the Birmingham engineering trade, Chamberlain was directly aware of these labour problems and, like many of his contemporaries, he was particularly concerned about drunkenness among women and its consequences for child neglect, despite evidence from the CCB's own Women's Advisory Committee that there had been no increase in female drunkenness.[21] Yet while disdainful of the cynical self-interest of the brewers, Chamberlain was largely free from the dogmatic 'faddist' opposition to the drink trade so prevalent among many of those prominent in the alcohol control campaign. Indeed, his concern about the threat to war production was always balanced by a practical recognition of the positive value of pubs to the morale and the social life of the industrial working classes in Birmingham and elsewhere. Perhaps for this reason, one member of the Board soon reported he was 'rather disappointed' with Chamberlain because he began with the belief 'there is very little to be done'.[22] Whatever the reason, within two months of joining the CCB Chamberlain was talking of resignation because his duties in Birmingham simply prevented him from active participation on the Board. Rather than provide assent to decisions in which he was not directly involved, he thus tendered his resignation in December 1915. Despite the chairman's determined efforts to decline it, Chamberlain finally severed his connection in February 1916.[23]

Within Birmingham, however, Chamberlain remained a fierce opponent of 'the Trade' throughout his mayoralty. In particular, he continued to harry the brewers in a fierce battle of wills over the serving of young women and girls.[24] In a more constructive spirit, he also launched a Civic Recreation League in November 1916, designed to bring together the various social and youth organisations in the city to improve opportunities for wholesome leisure activity in alcohol-free social centres which he anticipated would eventually be municipally funded.[25] Although by no means an abstainer himself, Chamberlain continued to speak for the Temperance Legislation League into the early 1920s when advocating his father's idea of municipalisation as the first step toward the complete state purchase and control of the liquor trade.

Another municipal problem which brought Chamberlain to national attention concerned the threat from air raids. In January and April 1915 Zeppelins bombed various coastal towns before making their first raid on London's East End at the end of May. Nine further night raids followed between June and October. When the raids resumed on 31 January 1916, considerable damage was inflicted on the Black Country towns, but the strict enforcement of Chamberlain's unpopular lighting restrictions enabled Birmingham to escape relatively unscathed. Although the death toll was relatively modest, these attacks created vast disruption to war production out of all proportion to their actual scale or frequency. They also generated a tidal wave of public and press fury at the complete absence of effective warning or defence.[26]

Having been caught in a Zeppelin raid on the Midlands in January 1916, Chamberlain shared this general sense of outrage. By 4 February he was at the Home Office with a plan to coordinate early warnings and after 'the great wise and eminent hummed and hawed a good deal' they agreed to support the scheme. As his letter to the press on the subject created 'quite a nine-days wonder', Chamberlain then led a high-powered delegation of Midland leaders to press their case upon Lord French and the Home Office, while the Railways Executive was persuaded to provide spotters to cascade the information of impending raids to local authorities along the Zeppelin's expected path. As a direct result, Birmingham's lighting restrictions were extended to other Midland towns and arrangements were made for the more effective location of guns and searchlights. Meanwhile, to restore public confidence, the citizens of Birmingham were issued with instructions as to what to do on hearing the warning signal, while a large number were each fined £10 for breaches of the lighting restrictions.[27]

The creation of a Birmingham Municipal Savings Bank was undoubtedly the most enduring monument to Chamberlain's mayoralty.[28] Although the government had floated war loans in November 1914 and June 1915 to help finance the war, Chamberlain regarded the schemes as ill-conceived and unattractive to ordinary working men in receipt of high wages but without any previous habit of regular saving. Instead he proposed to establish a municipal savings association, collecting graduated contributions to be deducted painlessly from wages. The municipality lay at the core of the scheme by guaranteeing the interest, lending its prestige to the scheme and by enlisting strong local loyalties in a manner in which the remoteness of government's War Bonds could not. Indeed, such was his faith in the value of the local connection that Chamberlain even anticipated the opportunity for healthy competition between municipalities in their attempts to raise money for the war effort.[29]

Chamberlain first outlined his scheme in late-November 1915 but it was soon almost overwhelmed by opposition and discouragement from a variety of sources. First, Austen poured cold water on the plan. Then the Treasury decided to reject it on the grounds that the Birmingham Corporation would become a competitor to its own War Loans, before Chamberlain's concerted pressure and force of argument moved it into a position of tepid detachment. At this point, the objections of the joint stock banks to a potential rival reinforced Treasury faintheartedness before parliamentary procedure raised further complications. It was 'enough to make the angels weep' Chamberlain declared in April, 'dishearten[ed] to find that one can expect no help from the very people who profess to be anxious to get savings established'.[30] Finally, in mid-May the scheme appeared doomed after a surprise rebuff by an unrepresentative meeting of local trade unionists apparently denied him the support of organised labour which he recognised to be crucial and which he had striven so hard to secure. 'Being Lord Mayor is dust and ashes and I should like to resign and return to obscurity', he protested. 'I'm beat, and the Savings Bank is dead!'[31]

Despite all the obstruction, indifference, departmental rivalry and complacency, Chamberlain barely faltered in his determination. Using all his prodigious powers of persuasion, diplomacy and cajolery, with the aid of his trusty Town Clerk, the problems were each gradually and painstakingly overcome. Eventually even the Treasury was forced to concede defeat, but only after Chamberlain blatantly blackmailed the bankers into withdrawing their opposition with the threat of being exposed for 'opposing a great patriotic movement for purely selfish reasons'. To his great surprise, on 23 June 1916 Chamberlain arrived at the Treasury to find the draft bill ready for presentation to Parliament. 'You could have knocked me down with a feather but I preserved an air of composure', he wrote to his sisters. 'I pinched myself all the way down the Treasury steps to make sure it was true.' The War Loan Investment Act received Royal Assent on 23 August 1916.

In practice, the final legislation was significantly more restrictive in scope and vision than Chamberlain's original scheme. Only boroughs with a population of over a quarter of a million inhabitants could exercise these new powers; deposits could only be made through employers rather than through other associations (a restriction Chamberlain opposed until the final moment); withdrawals were limited to £1 without seven days notice; maximum deposits were restricted to £200; and the investment of funds and rates of interest were controlled by the government. Such amendments were 'not nice' and they certainly hampered the wartime growth of the Bank, but as Chamberlain recognised, the very fact that it had come into existence at all against such formidable opposition represented a substantial personal triumph. Even the stipulation that these new institutions should be wound up within three months of the end of the war, Chamberlain accepted with sanguine pragmatism because 'if the scheme is a failure I shan't care what becomes of it; if it is a success no Chancellor dare shut it up'.[32]

As Birmingham was the only municipality to take advantage of the legislation, Chamberlain was absolutely determined to ensure that the Bank did succeed after it opened for business on 29 September 1916. Above all, convinced 'that it is not enough to offer our working people a good thing', he was determined to 'shove it down their throats'.[33] He thus played a leading role in a campaign of mass factory meetings to recruit new depositors. Within two months there had been some 266 meetings and nearly a thousand were held in total. By the end of the war, almost 35,000 depositors had invested £350,000 – of which some 80 per cent was loaned to the State to support the war effort.[34] Always convinced that it was 'a scheme which may have a profound effect on the habits of the working classes during the next 50 years', some years later he proudly proclaimed that 'its foundation was the most important development in the Corporation since Father's day'.[35]

Chamberlain's other great constructive legacy as Lord Mayor related to his passion for music and uplifting public recreation. At a Hallé Orchestra concert at Birmingham in March 1916, he 'dropped a little bombshell' by suggesting that the city should have a first-class local orchestra, supported from the rates.[36] Although he had nurtured the idea as a private ambition for some time, he had two reasons for believing it a propitious moment to start the ball rolling. First, while the dullness and restrictions of wartime life created a vast appetite for less elevated forms of leisure, serious music also enjoyed a considerable renaissance in popularity. Secondly, Chamberlain's forceful leadership conferred a new sense of unity and common purpose upon the city's musical community, previously notorious for its acute jealousies and bitter internecine struggles. As President of the newly-established Midland Concert Promoter's Association, in February 1917 Chamberlain persuaded the wealthy, if temperamental, Sir Thomas Beecham to become musical adviser to the Association. Despite early financial losses which prompted some to doubt the viability of the New Philharmonic Society, Chamberlain persisted, 'convinced that if we can keep things going for a little longer we shall see great advances in the near future'. Hopes of municipal support eventually came to fruition in March 1919 when the Corporation agreed to support a City of Birmingham Symphony Orchestra, the first of its kind in Britain.[37]

With this record of solid achievement behind him, Chamberlain felt justifiably satisfied with his performance as Lord Mayor. 'I think my position has been still further strengthened in the town', he confided in his diary in June 1916; 'it is generally recognised that a new atmosphere of initiative and energy has been imparted into the administration.' From the outset, a central theme of his mayoralty had been the determination to ensure that Birmingham obtained its proper recognition as 'the first of the provincial towns' and the 'second city of the Empire'. Despite continual complaints about the failure of the two Birmingham newspapers adequately to report his activities, Chamberlain undoubtedly derived considerable satisfaction from the degree of attention his activities attracted further afield. For example, in April 1916 the *Sunday Chronicle* proclaimed 'The Revival of Birmingham', arguing that under his influence the city was once more 'regaining its place in the sun' after lingering under a 'regime of stereotyped lack of enterprise' since his father's mayoralty. In commenting upon his new national prominence, Chamberlain's schemes for air raid precautions, the infant welfare centres and the municipal savings bank were all widely praised.[38] Given the scale of achievement and the national recognition earned for Birmingham, it was little wonder that he was invited to accept a second term as Mayor in July 1916. In private too, Chamberlain confessed to a new sense of confidence. As he told his sisters at the end of October, 'I have a patient temperament & a certain habit of persistence & after the Bank I feel that there is nothing one can't get if one goes on long enough.'[39]

During this final phase of his mayoralty Chamberlain increasingly came to national attention by expounding his views on post-war reconstruction. In July 1916 he lead a powerful deputation of local authorities to press upon the Chancellor the need for adequate pensions funded from direct taxation and paid as of right.[40] In the same month, he also outlined a positive vision of inter-imperial relations couched in terms of a new Commonwealth constitution. More important, Chamberlain had equally radical views about the domestic impact of war. As early as February 1916 he had spoken boldly to a Birmingham audience about 'the changes in England that were coming about through the war[,] State Socialism, the sinking of old party divisions, the new position of women and the altered relations between employers and employed'.[41] Sentiments of this sort had led him to join the Industrial League in July 1915; a new Midland organisation established to promote 'a more complete understanding' between the two sides of industry.[42]

Building on these themes, Chamberlain's welcoming speech to the Trade Union Congress at Birmingham in September 1916 was among the first pronouncements by a prominent figure in support of Lord Milner's idea that the wartime industrial truce should become the basis for a permanent new alliance between Capital and Labour. Warning the TUC of the difficulties of the post-war transition arising from demobilisation and the revival of foreign competition, Chamberlain proposed a united front in which both sides made sacrifices for the greater good in peacetime as they had during the military struggle. In return for an abandonment of their restrictive practices to promote greater productivity and competitiveness, Chamberlain proposed clear benefits for the workers, including a 'greater share in the distribution of wealth they help to produce, regularity of employment, and improved conditions in the factory and in their homes, so that they could preserve their health and spirit and bring up their children in cheerful and healthy surroundings'. Beside the retention of war-time administrative controls, he contemplated some form of limited industrial democracy, with the eventual goal of worker directors to enable local union leaders 'to see a little bit more of the game from inside'.[43]

Such radical views were scarcely those of an orthodox Conservative. Yet as Chamberlain had confessed to his sister Beatrice six months earlier, 'I have really ceased to think of myself as a Party man but that doesn't mean that I have ceased to care about the causes which were associated with it … so if Unionist principles have now become National principles lets be thankful for that and never mind what they are called.'[44] After the TUC dispersed, even Chamberlain confessed, 'I rather smile at my own cheek in departing from the usual banal speech of welcome and coolly addressing a T.U.C. on the question on which its susceptibilities are supposed to be most delicate. But it came off because I said what a great many people are thinking and what no one has yet found quite the right opportunity to say.'[45] Four months later, Chamberlain was pressed strongly to preside over the first meeting of the 'Capital and Labour' movement at Birmingham designed to further these goals.[46] Therefore, despite Iain Macleod's claim that Chamberlain 'emerged … from his "Birmingham" period as a Tory Democrat', it is more accurate to characterise him as an advocate of a popular brand of Milnerite social imperialism in which domestic themes of social reform were fused with his father's enthusiasm for Empire federation, imperial development and tariff reform to provide a solid foundation both for post-war reconstruction and a new ideological cleavage between socialism and its opponents.[47]

Throughout these battles Chamberlain was clearly in his element, enjoying to the full the 'most interesting and exciting life' of a busy Lord Mayor. Yet as his confidence in his own abilities increased, he began to show signs of a later intolerance towards the well-meaning interference of others derived from a conviction that he needed 'to run the whole show myself'.[48] Alongside this growing administrative competence, Chamberlain also sharpened his political skills. Above all, in his battles with the brewers and the bankers he demonstrated that acute awareness of the importance of effective media management which became the hallmark of his later ministerial methods. Having groomed his journalistic contacts assiduously, in May 1916 he rejoiced that, 'the press birds are becoming quite tame in consequence of the care I have taken to feed them regularly through the winter & even the Post is learning to do a few tricks quite prettily'.[49]

Despite his municipal success and rising national prominence, two anxieties blighted this period. At a personal level, Annie suffered the first of two miscarriages in late November 1916 which left her unwell for much of the following year. Although her husband attempted to accept it philosophically as 'one of the sacrifices you have to make if you do public service', it was a 'bitter disappointment' to the Chamberlains who both desperately wanted a larger family.[50] Chamberlain's second source of anxiety related to the conduct of the war and the incompetence of its political leadership. Like many of his fellow countrymen, Chamberlain was relatively slow to acknowledge that the war would not be 'over by Christmas' and that it would not be won by conventional means. Yet when he recognised the full magnitude of the challenge, he instinctively demanded a radical solution. 'The more I think it over and the more I hear and see of the attitude of men in the factories the more certain I feel that National Service is the only solution to the present situation which is rapidly becoming intolerable', he wrote to his wife in May 1915 soon after Herbert Asquith replaced his Liberal government with a coalition involving Conservative and Labour participation.

> It must however be accompanied by a surtax on or a limitation on profits for all, because workmen will never consent to restrictions which would have the effect of putting money into their employer's pockets. Personally I hate the idea of making profits out of the war when so many are giving their lives and limbs and I hope and pray that the new government will have the courage and the imagination to deal with the situation promptly and properly.[51]

When these hopes failed to materialise, Chamberlain became more convinced than ever that the ineffectual and dilatory Asquith needed to be removed and that the entire ministry should be reconstructed under more vigorous leadership. As he told his sisters in October 1915, 'I only wish I had the mixing of the P.M.'s rum and water.' After the gradual slide into conscription five months later, he still bitterly lamented that 'the "Squiffery" of the Government is past belief. Every pit they fall into is of their own digging and ... it all comes of trying to please everyone.'[52]

Chamberlain had never nurtured any admiration for David Lloyd George, the radical Liberal firebrand and 'Welsh Wizard'. Indeed, he was already a *bête noire* within the Chamberlain household by the turn of the century as the vociferous 'Pro-Boer' who denounced 'Joe's war' in South Africa while impugning the entire family's personal honour with allegations that they had corruptly profited from government armaments contracts. After this, the intense partisan passions engendered by his aggressive free trade, his 'People's Budget' and the ensuing constitutional crisis between 1909 and 1911 only confirmed Chamberlain's visceral hatred for this 'degraded little skunk'.[53] Despite Lloyd George's support for conscription and the remarkable dynamism he injected into the war effort, these old partisan animosities were never completely dispelled. On the contrary, as a Midland engineering employer, Chamberlain rapidly became disillusioned with Lloyd George's posture as the 'Saviour of his country' at the Ministry of Munitions, given personal experience of its inefficient profligacy and reports that it was in 'a state of absolute chaos' by the time Lloyd George left for the War Office in July 1916. He was equally doubtful about the quality of Lloyd George's political judgement, concluding in March 1916 that he had 'no balance and that's why he would be a very dangerous Prime Minister'.[54] Yet for all his mistrust and doubts, Chamberlain recognised that Lloyd George possessed an unshakeable determination to win the war whatever the cost or physical sacrifice. As such, he differed sharply from his half-brother in the belief that Lloyd George represented the lesser evil when compared with the failure, lethargy and indecision of the Asquith regime.[55]

'Thank God', Chamberlain wrote to Milner soon after the fall of Asquith in December 1916. '"Wait and See" is over and though the change has come too late to save us from a long list of blunders and lost opportunities it is not too late to retrieve the situation.'[56] The outcome of this political crisis radically transformed Neville Chamberlain's career and the horizons within which it would be pursued. For some time it had been apparent that the Lord Mayor of Birmingham was 'a coming man … bound to make his mark'.[57] Less than two weeks after Lloyd George became Prime Minister, Chamberlain was plucked reluctantly from a world of municipal administration he knew well and thrust into a maelstrom of national politics and Whitehall intrigue in which he appeared like an innocent abroad. Like his lonely failure on Andros, his first brief taste of national politics as Director-General of National Service would be a truly formative experience in the making of this politician. It also left the most enduring scars.

III

Although the First World War swiftly developed into a mortal struggle between entire nations at arms, British war planning had been conceived within the parameters of the nineteenth century strategy of 'business as usual'. On this basis, it was expected that the military effort would be confined to a small expeditionary force sent to France, while relying upon the Royal Navy and economic power to bring about German defeat with only modest strains on either the domestic economy or the civilian population. Given these underlying assumptions there was little which could be dignified with the label of manpower policy prior to 1914.[58] Compared with a German army of 4,300,000 trained men, in August 1914 the total strength of the British regular and territorial army (plus reservists) stood at a meagre 707,466. In response to Kitchener's personal appeal for recruits, some 1,342,647 men had enlisted by January 1915 but the supply of volunteers dwindled thereafter as the slaughter and stalemate of trench warfare increased; a trend which forced the Asquith government reluctantly to introduce the principle of conscription in January 1916 to meet the apparently insatiable need for military recruits. Yet as the scale and expected duration of the military effort increased, vast new problems of manpower allocation on the home front also emerged as the government struggled to find an acceptable means of satisfying the demands of the army without impeding war production. Confronted by this crucial challenge, by 30 November 1916 the Asquith coalition had finally accepted the principle of compulsory National Service for all men up to the age of 55, for civil as well as military purposes. Before such a radical scheme could be piloted past Parliament and hostile trade unions, however, the government collapsed.[59]

This was the problem which Neville Chamberlain inherited in December 1916. His appointment as Director-General of the new Department of National Service owed most to the efforts of his half-brother. Having decided to establish such a department, Lloyd George pressed the office strongly on Edwin Montagu whose prior experience at the Ministry of Munitions and the Man-Power Distribution Board, combined with his reluctance to join Asquith on the Opposition benches, made him a valuable potential recruit to Lloyd George's Liberal following. When Montagu declined, Austen Chamberlain proposed his half-brother to Lord Curzon, who together with Milner, put his name forward to the War Cabinet 'and everyone *jumped* at it'.[60] Intercepted at Paddington Station as he boarded a train for Birmingham, Neville was thus hurried away to hear the news from Austen before being whisked off to meet the Prime Minister who pressed him for an immediate answer. Within minutes an announcement was made to an enthusiastic House of Commons.

Lloyd George did not exaggerate when he told the Commons on 19 December that it was 'with very great difficulty that we induced him to take this very onerous duty'.[61] Certainly the offer came upon him 'like a thunderclap' and it was the subject of much heart-searching.[62] 'What a bombshell!' exclaimed Hilda, '… it obviously can't have struck us more suddenly than it did you, but it has devastated us. We don't know whether to congratulate or to condole!'[63] Chamberlain was equally ambivalent. He had great plans for Birmingham in his second mayoralty which he feared would now be abandoned because – rather characteristically – he doubted whether there was anyone else on the council with the vision or drive to promote them. The break was all the harder because he recognised more clearly than anyone else that this probably signalled the effective end of his municipal career. There were also family considerations. Besides the pain of enforced separation from his young children, he was gravely concerned about Annie after her miscarriage only days before Asquith's fall. 'I don't suppose there is a more miserable man in Birmingham tonight than I', he declared the same evening. Yet for all these regrets, he understood that it was 'no time for shilly shallying' and he recognised that he could not deny a Prime

Minister who emphasised so vigorously the imperative significance of the task and his patriotic duty to subordinate personal desires to the greater need.[64]

On the face of it, Chamberlain had much to commend him as a candidate for this vast new task. His proven record of successful municipal administration had conferred a national prominence and reputation. He enjoyed the advantage of a half-brother in the government and the respect and support of Lord Milner, an old ally of his father's who now sat in the War Cabinet. Despite their later bitter mutual antagonism, he also had the inestimable benefit of commanding the trust of organised labour, whose goodwill would be indispensable when dealing with sensitive questions of manpower allocation and trade union prerogatives.[65] For a Prime Minister so acutely sensitive to matters of presentation, the warm reception in the press given to his appointment was equally beneficial. Above all, Chamberlain appeared ostensibly to be precisely the sort of practical 'man of push and go' that Lloyd George had promised to introduce into a government organised on business lines. Yet ironically, despite all these qualifications, Neville Chamberlain remained Director-General of National Service for only eight turbulent months, sustained for much of this period largely by the Prime Minister's greater fear of giving the appearance of having made a mistake.[66]

The scale of the task Chamberlain confronted was little short of breathtaking, for not only did he have direct responsibility for a problem he later claimed was 'big enough to satisfy the most super-eminent of supermen', but he did so while having to construct a completely new department to implement a plan which no one had yet conceived.[67] Little wonder that he confessed to 'a very sick feeling in my tummy' or that he felt 'exactly like a boy on the last day of the summer holidays again with the additional drawback that I was going to a new school'.[68] He didn't realise it at the time, but it would be the school of hard knocks. Despite his past administrative successes, the environment in which he operated as Lord Mayor was better-natured, more cooperative, less partisan and more amenable to strong personal control than anything he would encounter in Whitehall. Although Austen breezily declared that the lack of such experience did not constitute a major disadvantage, this was not a confidence endorsed by some of Chamberlain's senior staff.[69] Above all, Violet Markham, the *de facto* head of his Women's Section, believed her chief to be 'utterly devoid of instinct or experience' and she rapidly became contemptuous of both Chamberlain's weakness in dealing with other departments and his arrogance in handling his own. From her perspective, the department's ineffectiveness in these battles was to be blamed entirely on 'Chamberlain's series of surrenders which seem to me to have cut the ground completely away from beneath our feet.'[70] Unfortunately, this was not an indictment confined solely to one fiery malcontent. 'With an able chief, not afraid to assert his position, the history of the N.S. Dept. might have been quite different', another critic inscribed as a departmental obituary after Chamberlain's resignation. 'Its fatal initial mistakes would have been avoided and it would at least have secured the respect of other Govt Depts.'[71]

It cannot be denied that some of the problems confronting the NSD stemmed directly from Chamberlain's innocence and inexperience in the black arts of Whitehall politics. As Lord Mayor observing from outside, he had been highly critical of departmental duplication and backstairs politics in which the 'only thing … is to keep Tom out and Dick in or to see that Harry's little schemes don't come off for fear he should get too much credit'.[72] Yet nothing prepared him for the game he would be compelled to play. Among the early errors and miscalculations which contributed to his later difficulties was the practice of surrounding himself with men he knew from Birmingham rather than with seasoned heavyweights capable of compensating for his own lack of knowledge and understanding of Whitehall. Above all, Chamberlain placed vast faith in Ernest Hiley, the recently retired Town Clerk of Birmingham, who he had always considered 'the most devoted and loyal servant & friend'; a man upon whose judgement he always relied and who he commended to Lloyd George as 'simply invaluable'.[73] After rejecting or being rejected by experienced Whitehall officials like Auckland Geddes and James Stevenson, Lloyd George intervened personally to persuade the reluctant Hiley to become Chamberlain's deputy on 1 February. Within a fortnight, however, criticisms were already being expressed about his suitability.[74]

The presence of these two Whitehall outsiders served to reinforce the mistrust of other government departments towards an unwelcome interloper in an unusually contentious policy arena and when the NSD failed in its task, it was easy for critics to attribute it to errors of this sort. At their final acrimonious meeting (and later in his *War Memoirs*), Lloyd George dwelt at length on the 'vein of self-sufficient obstinacy' behind Chamberlain's rejection of Geddes, Stevenson and later Kennedy Jones as the root cause of his failure.[75] Yet it also needs to be remembered that unlike the other new ministries of Shipping, Mines and Food Production, the NSD was not able to draw upon the personnel or experience of the departments which formerly held the responsibility. Moreover, critics of Chamberlain's choice of Deputy Director often conveniently chose to forget that Lord Derby, the War Minister, opposed the transfer of General Auckland Geddes to become Chamberlain's Chief of Staff at the NSD just as vigorously as Christopher Addison repeatedly resisted Prime Ministerial demands that he should transfer James Stevenson from his own Ministry of Munitions on the grounds that 'it would be too great a loss'.[76]

In retrospect, a more damaging error of judgement was the failure to insist upon a seat in the Commons, a ministerial title and direct access to the War Cabinet in order to defend his department and policy against better placed opponents. But in fairness, such an indictment ignores the assurances of both Lloyd George and his own half-brother that this would be an unnecessary and undesirable distraction from his principal responsibilities. Even less convincing is the criticism that Chamberlain allowed himself to be too easily placed in an impossible position when he should have demanded all the powers he needed from the outset while he enjoyed the greatest leverage in making such demands.[77] Undeniably, Chamberlain soon complained to his sisters that he 'never had even a scrap of paper appointing me or giving me any idea of where my duties begin and end', but in reality the problem was less one of Chamberlain's failure to demand powers than Lloyd George's consistent reluctance to honour his initial promise because of more pressing pledges already given to organised labour.[78]

The magnitude and fundamental nature of these problems soon became apparent. Three days after his appointment, Lloyd George demanded a workable scheme within a few days. After this, Chamberlain confessed to 'feeling rather downhearted' because he 'didn't really know where or how to begin'. Yet having rejected the plan already conceived by his half-brother and Montagu at the now defunct Man-Power Distribution Board as 'wrong in all the essential particulars', within a week Chamberlain had 'already evolved an "Idea"' which he believed capable of development into 'rather a good scheme'.[79] This conception drew on his established belief that industrial compulsion was an inevitable corollary to military conscription. To this end, he had already spoken publicly in favour of a disciplined 'industrial army' capable of being centrally directed to where it was most needed and employed at comparable rates of pay to soldiers.[80] Profoundly sceptical of the value of the voluntary principle, at the NSD Chamberlain began to develop plans along these lines despite warnings from senior officials that 'the Unions wouldn't stand it for a minute'.[81] More to the point, nor would the Prime Minister.

Although Lloyd George had risen to supreme power as the champion of war *à outrance*, he was not prepared to countenance such a policy if it threatened to provoke either industrial unrest or the resignation of Labour members from his coalition government. Indeed, in the full knowledge that the Labour movement considered 'industrial conscription' to be anathema, at his first Prime Ministerial meeting with Labour MPs and trade unionists on 7 December, Lloyd George had pledged 'that just as the enforcement of military conscription had been preceded by a period ... of voluntary enrolment with a time limit, so a similar procedure might be adopted in the present case'. Despite Lloyd George's later allegation that Chamberlain's 'narrow spirit of unimaginative officialism' had bound the NSD 'in a tangle of red tape which kept it from getting ahead with its job', this crucial undertaking fundamentally hobbled the new department from the outset.[82] Montagu's plans for industrial conscription produced at the MPDB were thus to be achieved implausibly through patriotic voluntarism in circumstances very different from those of August 1914. Little wonder that Chamberlain should have lamented in early January that 'the difficulties literally bristle. At every turn one is held up by somebody's pledge & the pledges have always been in the direction of bribes to the proletariat.'[83]

These problems were intensified still further by Lloyd George's consistent lack of support, sympathy or even understanding for his new appointment. At the heart of these difficulties lay the most profound differences of personality, leadership style and approach to policy-making. As an enthusiastic phrenologist who believed himself capable of judging people by the shape of their heads, Lloyd George left his first meeting with Chamberlain convinced he had appointed the wrong man. 'When I saw that pin-head, I said to myself he won't be any use' the

Prime Minister is alleged to have remarked; an explanation for prejudice which might appear fanciful were it not for the fact that he continued talking about the shape of his skull and its 'big bumps of conceit' until Chamberlain's death.[84] Even before Chamberlain presented his plans to the War Cabinet, therefore, Lloyd George was confiding to intimates that this was 'one of the very few cases in which I have taken a pig in a poke, and I am not very sure of the pig!'[85] Thereafter his disappointment with Chamberlain became a recurrent theme.

Unfortunately, Prime Ministerial doubts about Chamberlain's personal dynamism were apparently substantiated by fundamentally different approaches towards policy-making. Having served in Cabinet with both men at different times, Viscount Simon later concluded that 'Lloyd George and he were not likely to pull together. His demand for precision and his patient working out of detail seemed to the Prime Minister to show a lack of imaginative treatment while Chamberlain at no time had any use for wizardry.'[86] By instinct and temperament, Lloyd George was a born showman and innovator, only truly in his element when playing the role of a visionary man of action. For him, the 'big idea' was crucial, but as Lord Riddell noted in an astonishingly shrewd analysis of the Prime Minister's character during this period:[87]

> His chief defects are: (1) Lack of appreciation of existing institutions, organisations, and solid dull people, who often achieve good results by persistency, experience, and slow, but sound, judgement. It is not that he fails to understand them. The point is that their ways are not his ways and their methods are not his methods. (2) Fondness for a grandiose scheme in preference to an attempt to improve existing machinery. (3) Disregard of difficulties in carrying out big projects. This is due to the fact that he is not a man of detail.

This assessment offers a sharp insight into the problems confronting Chamberlain and his fledgling Department. The creation of new ministries of Food, Shipping, Labour and National Service in December 1916 reflected Lloyd George's supreme faith in the efficacy of dramatic gestures, charismatic leadership and extemporised structural responses to complex policy problems. Hence his insistence upon the immediate acceptance of the post from a man whom he had never previously met. To enhance the dramatic impact of this announcement, the Prime Minister misleadingly suggested to Parliament that a plan already existed to produce 'a sufficiently large industrial army to mobilise the whole of the labour strength of this country for war purposes'.[88] In arousing these false expectations in pursuit of grandiose rhetoric, Lloyd George chose to ignore all of Montagu's warnings about the substantial practical problems, just as he had overlooked those obstructing his vision of dramatic increases in munitions production in 1915.[89]

In this context, it was particularly unfortunate that the man charged with honouring this rash promise had a style of policy-making diametrically opposed to the flashy brilliance of his chief. Chamberlain was a methodical cautious planner who reached policy decisions only after long and careful deliberation of all the available facts. As his scheme evolved, he tended to remain silent, listening to the views of others while continually refining his own. Such a method had served him well when devising schemes to combat Zeppelins and to launch the Savings Bank. As he assured his sisters: 'It all takes a long time but when you are working out an absolutely new idea time spent at the beginning is time saved afterwards.' But, as even they conceded, such methods were often unnerving for more impetuous souls.[90] Certainly they were scarcely calculated to impress a Prime Minister with a penchant for the sort of intellectual pyrotechnics capable of commanding newspaper headlines. Nor did they impress Christopher Addison, Lloyd George's closest Liberal ally and a major employer of industrial labour at the Ministry of Munitions. Within nine days of his appointment Chamberlain was already damned. 'I must say that nothing more feeble than Neville Chamberlain's attitude have I witnessed for a long long time', Addison noted scornfully in his diary. 'He seems not to know even now what it is he is going to do and does not appear to have the remotest notion of how he is going to do it and leans up against me or Stevenson or anyone else who will help him like a helpless man against a wall.' Lord Riddell also came away from a similar meeting at this time with the impression that Chamberlain 'cannot make up his mind and is afraid to act'.[91]

Unfortunately, the problem was that Chamberlain never enjoyed the luxury of time for ruminative contemplation to resolve a problem which had eluded the best minds for two years. 'Lloyd George launched it without ever having thought out or understood what its functions were to be', Chamberlain complained to a friend after it was all over. 'He gave me just a fortnight to collect a staff, arrange their administrative functions, make myself acquainted with the outlines of one of the most difficult of problems, settle my relations with other Depts. & invent a scheme!'[92] Although determined not 'to be rushed into anything half digested', as his difficulties mounted, Chamberlain increasingly attributed his problems to the pressure to act before he had developed the scheme fully.[93]

Within a month of his appointment, this clash of style and method had already doomed Chamberlain to failure. At a conference of relevant departments on 12 January, the Prime Minister suddenly insisted that Chamberlain should outline his scheme – despite assurances before the meeting that such a demand would not arise.[94] His failure to do so 'made a very bad impression on all concerned' and Lloyd George declared himself 'very much depressed' and 'very angry with Neville Chamberlain who, he consider[ed], is not getting ahead'.[95] Moreover, when Chamberlain did present his first plan to the War Cabinet a week later, Lloyd George again concluded the Director-General was inadequate for the task. In reality, Lloyd George mistook cautious deliberation for a failure of imagination. Once damned, however, Chamberlain was unable to do anything to retrieve his position because this would have required powers which Lloyd George's pledge to organised labour had effectively precluded. In these circumstances, it was perhaps fortunate that Chamberlain never told Lloyd George he was 'revolving vast and revolutionary notions of turning the whole war industry of the country into State owned concerns in which every one should be only an officer or a private and all the surplus should go to the State!!!'[96]

To make matters worse, an equally characteristic feature of Chamberlain's policy-making style was that having carefully decided on the best course, he was utterly remorseless and undeviating in advocating it. Confronted by Army demands for 450,000 extra recruits in the first quarter of 1917, Chamberlain argued that 'drastic measures' were necessary and that 'some risks must be run'. In his first report to the War Cabinet, dated 13 January, he proposed a 'clean cut' with the cancellation of virtually all exemptions from military service for men up to the age of 22 – except for the most skilled whose talents could not be employed fully in the army. In addition, a patriotic appeal would enlist volunteers in an 'Industrial Army' to fill the gaps left by men called into the services; a force to be deployed solely by the NSD's own district commissioners while the Labour Exchanges should be transferred to his department to assist with their allocation. Chamberlain also requested powers to inspect all factories to ensure that men were properly employed. Given Lloyd George's prior undertakings to labour and Addison's vociferous protests about the devastating effect upon munitions output, the War Cabinet rejected the scheme on 19 January.[97]

At this juncture Chamberlain was convinced he 'shouldn't last much longer', although he conceded he 'wasn't quite certain whether I should be "sacked" or resign but there seemed no third alternative'.[98] Despite this unequivocal rebuff, however, two weeks later Chamberlain's second report urged reconsideration of precisely the same plan, on the grounds that the War Cabinet's decisions would not provide sufficient men and that only 'prompt and drastic measures' would resolve the problem. Questioning the degree of industrial disruption likely to arise, he argued 'that if these measures were universal in character they would have a very much better chance of acceptance than any half-hearted attempts to deal with a critical situation'. Equally predictably, the War Cabinet refused to consider the scheme because it conflicted with the Prime Minister's earlier pledge to the unions.[99] The same process of entreaty and rejection was repeated in late June.

Forced to abandon the only option he believed truly capable of achieving the objective, Chamberlain was compelled to fall back upon patriotic exhortation and voluntarism. In a speech at Birmingham on 20 January, he first announced his ideas about an 'Industrial Army', describing his role as that of 'a dentist to the nation' charged with the task of 'extracting teeth with as little inconvenience to the victim as possible and providing a reasonably satisfactory set of artificial ones'. The national campaign was then launched in a blaze of publicity at Central Hall, Westminster, on 6 February. Flanked by Lloyd George, the Archbishop of Canterbury and Arthur Henderson, the Labour leader, Chamberlain appealed for men aged 18 to 61 in non-essential trades to register as National Service Volunteers prepared to replace fit men withdrawn from key industries. 'I would say to my critics', Chamberlain declared, 'here is a scheme; there is no other; let us not waste precious time in destructive criticism but let us resolve with one accord to make it work, and it will work.'[100]

To help the appeal on its way, Chamberlain had already carefully briefed the editors and proprietors of the press on 26 January.[101] Although he conspicuously declined to comment on whether voluntarism represented the best means of achieving his goal, the press responded well to his plea for support, with the result that Chamberlain found that 'LL.G. smiles upon me most benevolently' because 'nothing succeeds in the Cabinet like success'.[102] Unfortunately for Chamberlain, however, his national appeal fell on deaf ears. Aiming for 500,000 recruits by the end of March, only 206,000 actually enrolled. Of these 92,489 were subsequently processed by the Employment Exchanges, but half were already in protected trades and among the others were two Admirals and a Governor of the Bank of England. Ultimately, a depressingly meagre 388 National Service Volunteers were directed into new employment.[103]

In reality, Chamberlain was almost certainly not the best man to organise a campaign of public exhortation. He frankly admitted that 'he loathed public speaking' and the departmental files are filled with refusals to attend public meetings to propagate the appeal.[104] In these circumstances, it was not unreasonable for Lloyd George to urge Chamberlain 'to put a good deal more life' into the public campaign. Nor is it surprising that the press engaged in sustained ridicule of Chamberlain's 'Palace of Make-Believe' at the St Ermins Hotel, while the parliamentary Select Committee on National Expenditure produced a damning indictment of the excessive cost of producing so little reward.[105] Confronted by all of these obstacles and frustrations, Chamberlain was fully justified in claiming that he had endured 'a pretty rotten time' and in many ways, the wonder is less that he survived for only eight months than that he lasted as long as he did in conditions of almost continuous crisis.[106]

Underlying all of Chamberlain's problems was the fact that his fledgling department was handicapped by intense departmental rivalries and jealousies from its inception and it was not long before the great labour-using ministries recognised the NSD's impotence and exploited it to the full. As his far from supportive Deputy Head of the Women's Section later recalled, the other ministries 'proceeded in their own ineffable way to show the contempt they felt for the newcomer. I wish I could compare the latter to the cuckoo in the nest. Unfortunately it was the legitimate birds who saw to it that the unwelcome fledgling was ousted.'[107] Indeed, despite the efforts of Milner and the War Cabinet, even their pleas for greater inter-departmental harmony fell on deaf ears.[108]

The problem was exacerbated by the fact that at least six government departments had powerful sectional interests in the recruitment and allocation of labour and these conflicting claims had already generated fierce inter-departmental disputes before Chamberlain came on the scene. The addition of his new department as an arbiter between ministries competing for labour thus only aggravated such tensions while providing a common target for collective antagonism – particularly as the new department was consistently handicapped by 'the lack of any clear conception of its place in the general scheme of things'.[109] Despite Lord Derby's initially encouraging and cooperative personal utterances,[110] his War Office officials successfully fought off all efforts to interfere with their autonomy, while the Army Council refused even to acknowledge the importance of industry to the overall war effort, preferring to see their labour demands simply as an unwarranted competition for men. In order to achieve their target of 450,000 army recruits during the first quarter of 1917, the War Office thus simply circumvented the NSD altogether with a series of bilateral arrangements with the Ministry of Munitions and the Board of Agriculture. There was an equally evident 'undercurrent of reserve and hostility' with regard to the NSD's role as recruiting agent for the Women's Army Auxiliary Corps.[111]

Worse still, this high-handed policy to defend the War Office's sectional interests from NSD 'interference' only encouraged the other labour-using departments to follow suit. This was particularly true at the Ministry of Munitions. Convinced that Chamberlain was a 'nuisance', Addison dismissed his national appeal as 'altogether too silly ... for words' and refused to allow any of his personnel to enrol in Chamberlain's expensive 'Stage Army'.[112] Furthermore, during April he tried to persuade Milner to end this 'hopeless duplication of effort' by substantially curtailing the NSD's role with the threat of resignation unless he got his way.[113] As Lloyd George's closest Liberal ally during the December 1916 crisis, Addison's strictures proved profoundly corrosive of Prime Ministerial confidence in his new Director-General.

The scope for departmental rivalry was further compounded by the creation of a Ministry of Labour in December 1916 under Labour's John Hodge. Although covering only seven trades, this shared responsibility created an insecure new rival fiercely jealous of any attempt to impinge on its embryonic role and ill-defined territory. Above all, its responsibility for the 400 Employment Exchanges proved a source of continual conflict and animosity throughout 1917, given the absence of any local organisation controlled directly by the NSD through which to operate Chamberlain's scheme; problems exacerbated by the deep hostility of both labour and employers towards any voluntary scheme operated through the Exchanges.[114] Yet while even the Minister of Labour later conceded the Exchanges were notoriously inefficient and unpopular, the War Cabinet insisted that this unsuitable vehicle should be the agency through which Chamberlain operated his scheme for fear of upsetting Hodge and the Labour Party.[115] Beyond institutional and bureaucratic problems of this sort, Chamberlain's difficulties with the Ministry of Labour were compounded by the astonishing personal antipathy of Colonel Sir Charles Rey, the Director of its Employment Department. From the outset, Rey not only encouraged the obstructionism of the Exchanges under his control, but also vigorously fuelled the hostility of other government departments, while instigating a press vendetta against the NSD 'unequalled in the annals of journalism'. Little wonder that Chamberlain denounced Rey as 'a man who makes trouble everywhere & is universally disliked because he is a mischievous chatterbox always boasting, lying and intriguing'.[116]

Within this extremely hostile policy environment, Chamberlain soon recognised he was 'not universally beloved'. Only a month after his appointment he complained he was suffering 'an awful time, with recurring periods of the most harrowing anxiety', but he persisted because of an overwhelming sense of public service. 'What a *beast* of a time we are all having' he complained in late January. 'The only consolation is that if we didn't we should feel guilty – like enjoying yourself on Sunday in Scotland!' By early March he still felt 'rather low' because 'there are intrigues going on all the time and one has no fair chance'. After 'a short & very unsatisfactory interview' with the Cabinet a fortnight later, he declared himself 'very much inclined to stick my hat on and go back to Westbourne' until he had a 'more soothing talk' with Milner – although even then he confessed 'there are times when one would give anything to be free of this nightmare'.[117] Confronted by 'the perpetual jealousy' of the Labour Exchanges, by the end of March Chamberlain resolved to circumvent them by creating his own local committees under Substitution Officers until thwarted by external rivals and critics within his own department who complained of the wasteful duplication of effort when the real solution lay in reform of existing machinery over which he had no control.[118]

This frustrating administrative limbo continued throughout the summer. By the end of May Chamberlain again complained of the Cabinet's failure 'to warn Depts against ignoring me'. But convinced that 'no one cares to kill me in order to make Hodge King', he resigned himself to 'just go on fighting and scrapping with the other Departments in the hope of gradually acquiring the powers that ought to have been handed over to me at first'.[119] Despite some success in placing 100,000 volunteers in agriculture and helping to bring another 20,000 acres under cultivation in 1917, by the summer it was reported that Chamberlain's department was living 'on the brink of a chronic volcano and ... may blow up at any time'.[120] To make matters worse, in late May, Hiley resigned as Deputy Director. This was ostensibly because of his pressing financial need to return to his business career, but when the news leaked to the press, it was inevitably presented as a vote of no-confidence in Chamberlain's policy and leadership.[121] At the same time, Chamberlain's relations with Violet Markham had almost completely broken down. After a series of perceived retreats and snubs, she prepared an angry indictment of the department's policy under 'a Chief who lets you down at every turn and corner'. Unable to influence a leader whose personal attitude filled her only with 'irritation and contempt', she reported her concerns behind Chamberlain's back directly to Derby, Milner, the Prime Minister and the editor of *The Times*.[122]

Matters came to a head in late June when it became apparent that the munitions industry was not releasing any men for military service – with the result that there were no vacancies to be filled by National Service Volunteers. In a final effort to force the issue and restore some sort of *raison d'être* for the NSD, Chamberlain's Tenth Report on 22 June outlined all of the constraints and problems confronting the Department as a prelude to pressing his initial plan which had twice before been rejected by the War Cabinet. If accepted, he argued, this would provide the necessary men for the Army, compel employers to respond, generate demand for his National Service Volunteers as substitutes and create a viable long-term role for the Department while being accepted by the country as the 'fairest all round'. If not, he declared defiantly, there was no obvious future for it as a separate entity.[123] Underlying Chamberlain's challenge was a determination to extricate himself from an increasingly hopeless and humiliating position. 'I hate the idea of resignation under present circumstances' he explained to his sisters on 1 July:

> You know I like to stick to things even after there seems no chance of success but when I have made up my mind that the thing is hopeless I generally cut the loss with rapidity and determination. Now I am in a position that reminds me of the Bahamas when the plants didn't grow. With all the Departments against me and a chief who wont help I see no chance of success and if so it would be folly to let slip an opportunity of getting out on a principle.[124]

When his report on the future of the NSD was left undiscussed by the War Cabinet for a month, Chamberlain saw his opportunity and he was determined to seize it. In reality, the Cabinet's delay was less a deliberate rebuff than a consequence of Lloyd George's 'horribly unbusinesslike methods' in the War Cabinet, which by mid-July was reportedly three weeks behind with their agenda and deeply preoccupied with more pressing matters.[125] Nevertheless, after the perceived discourtesy with which his Parliamentary Secretary was replaced without any consultation in early July and then rumours of private breakfast meetings about his department to which he was not invited, Chamberlain was in no mood 'to be treated like a doormat'. After protesting to the Prime Minister in terms expected to 'paralyse him with fury',[126] Chamberlain's conversation with Lloyd George on 11 July concluded with the warning that he 'could not remain in office unless the false position in which I found myself was promptly rectified'. When nothing happened, on 17 July Chamberlain obtained the support of the War Minister, the President of the Local Government Board and the Food Controller for a joint memorandum commending his original scheme. Feeling 'somewhat strengthened', two days later he despatched another robust letter to Lloyd George protesting at his 'intolerable' position and demanding definite Cabinet support or he would resign the next day and state publicly the reasons for it.[127] Although forestalled by the Prime Minister's request for more time to consider an alternative plan from Geddes, which proposed the release of industrial manpower by occupation rather than age, a week later Chamberlain again demanded a 'speedy decision'.[128]

The outcome was never in doubt. Lloyd George was determined to replace a man in whom he had lost all faith, while the War Cabinet had resolved to 'prevent the present muddle and eternal friction' with the Exchanges by unifying military and civilian recruitment in a single department under new civilian leadership. The NSD, it concluded, was now 'so much discredited that the transference of a very difficult task to Neville Chamberlain would rather shake the confidence of the Army in the change'.[129] At the same time, Chamberlain was equally adamantly opposed to such a merger and resolved to extricate himself from an impossible position on this (or any other) point of principle. Suspecting that renewed press attacks were a cynically engineered prelude to ignominious dismissal, he was thus resolved to resign before being manoeuvred into this final humiliation.

On 7 August a candid talk with the sympathetic Milner ended with the advice that Chamberlain should 'get out of it'. After this, he despatched a bitter letter of resignation expressing his grievances and his refusal to accept the new scheme which would turn the NSD into a military recruiting office in civilian clothes. In an even more acrimonious final interview on 9 August he again rebuked Lloyd George for his consistent lack of support. But as he later complained, it was 'quite impossible to make him understand or even listen to my causes of complaint' because Lloyd George retorted that departmental battles had always existed; that Milner had 'always acted with the most perfect fairness and impartiality'; and that the root of the problem was Chamberlain's failure to recruit suitable senior staff.[130] The same day Lloyd George wrote in Welsh to his family in Wales, 'Neville Chamberlain has resigned and thank God for that.'[131] As a petulant parting shot Chamberlain only signed the final statement on the work of the NSD for the War Office with 'very bad grace', while refusing either to sign or send copies to the Prime Minister, Hodge or the War Cabinet.[132]

Despite the torment of these months and the abject public humiliation of his Department, Chamberlain was inundated by sympathetic letters from his closest officials, lamenting the passing of a respected chief, while a member of the Labour Advisory Committee assured him that he stood 'higher today … in the estimation of labour than ever before'.[133] At an emotional final dinner at the Savoy on 16 August, Chamberlain was 'overwhelmed' by the many personal tributes to 'a "straight" man' and the presentation of a silver cigar box inscribed with the NSD's badge. After another touching presentation from the entire junior staff next day, he took his leave of the now defunct Department, 'greatly encouraged and heartened by the thought that I had made a definite impression on those with whom I had worked and that they knew I was not a "colourless incompetent" as one of those idiotic papers called Austen'.[134]

In retrospect, historians agree that it is 'tempting to sneer' at the efforts of the NSD. Arguably, it was 'a considerable fiasco'.[135] Yet even severe contemporary critics like Addison later conceded that Chamberlain 'never really had a fair chance' given the almost insuperable accumulation of obstacles.[136] Moreover, as his ministerial successor tersely conceded after Chamberlain's resignation, 'He was asked to use a department which did not exist to solve a problem which had never been stated.' Milner was equally close to the mark when he noted, 'How hard it is to get things right, when once they have been *started* on the wrong lines!'[137] Moreover, Chamberlain was by no means the only casualty of Lloyd George's zeal for administrative improvisation. During 1917 the First Lord of the Admiralty, the Food Controller and even Addison were also replaced. In this context, it is reasonable to conclude that Chamberlain became 'a convenient scapegoat for a plan never meant to succeed'.[138]

This danger was evident from the outset. During the parliamentary debate on the National Service Bill on 27 February 1917, a Labour MP had denounced the government's 'blind confidence' that a single man could solve the problem, noting presciently that 'if that one man is not a Member of this House and he fails in his mission ... the Government will put all the responsibility on that man, and they will escape altogether'.[139] This was precisely Lloyd George's logic in seeking to resolve a peculiarly difficult policy dilemma. On one hand, the Army were demanding more men for another massive offensive in 1917 and the new Prime Minister needed to make a dramatic gesture to demonstrate his support. On the other hand, however, he was appalled by the prospect of a repetition of the pointless slaughter on the Somme during the summer of 1916 and he sought to restrain Haig by limiting the flow of men to the army.[140] By creating the public expectation that Chamberlain could achieve the results of industrial conscription armed only with the power of exhortation and patriotic voluntarism, Lloyd George achieved his own political objectives at the direct cost of Chamberlain's reputation.

There would always have been a vast temperamental gulf between the passionate Celtic visionary and the reserved tight-buttoned Midland businessman. Yet the experience of National Service embittered the relationship between the two men for the rest of their lives. As Austen Chamberlain later told Lloyd George, he had treated his half-brother 'very badly, never giving [him] a chance at Nat. Service & ... he had never forgiven [him] for it'.[141] By the same token, Neville Chamberlain 'could not forget nor forgive Ll. G's treatment' and the experience left him with an implacable hatred for a man whom he afterwards denounced, at his most charitable moments, as a duplicitous 'little beast'.[142] In later years Chamberlain proved a formidable adversary whose antipathy effectively prevented Lloyd George's return to office in 1931, 1935 and 1940. Yet in the longer term, these events were even more unfortunate for Neville Chamberlain's historical reputation. In the aftermath of his fall from office in 1940, his failure at National Service would be misleadingly presented as a paradigm of all his later failings as a supposedly rigid and unimaginative policy-maker and an incompetent political leader.[143]

Chapter 4

The Frustrated Backbencher, August 1917–October 1922

'I have to fight very hard against a growing depression & disinclination to put my head again in the noose. Every now & then a feeling of almost irrepressible nausea & repulsion comes over me at the thought of all the drudgery, the humiliations the meanness & pettinesses of that life & of the hopeless impossibility of getting things done. And then I grind my teeth & think if it hadn't been for my d—d well meaning brother I might still have been Lord Mayor of Birmingham practically in control of the town & about to enter upon my third year in office. Oh Lord but it is hard. Only I couldn't do anything else & even now when I often feel so "down" about my future it does not occur to me as possible that I should change my mind & keep out of the House … What a d-mn-bl- world it is.'

Neville to Hilda Chamberlain, 21 October 1917

In accepting the Department of National Service, Chamberlain had been genuinely distressed at having to leave Birmingham only six weeks after the commencement of his second term as Lord Mayor. His apprehension was all the greater because he sensed that it signalled the effective end of his municipal career.[1] As he reflected on the imminent prospect of resignation or dismissal during the summer of 1917, he was thus inevitably oppressed by the difficulties in picking up the threads of his former business and civic life.[2] To ease the pain of his transition back to life in Birmingham, immediately after his resignation Chamberlain retired to Rowfant near Crawley, a magnificent Elizabethan house which the two Chamberlain brothers and their families had taken for the summer. Given Austen's own resignation after criticism in the Mesopotamia Commission's report in mid-July, it proved 'very handy as a retreat for two ministers out of a job'.[3]

Despite efforts to lose himself in the pleasures of the garden, the Sussex countryside and later shooting in Scotland, Chamberlain felt a burning sense of injustice at his public humiliation in a job he never wanted. 'Although you have not dwelt upon it I see that you have perceived the intense bitterness of a failure which is not my fault but with which I must inevitably be associated', he wrote to his step-mother a few days after his resignation. 'I feel I ought to have a gold stripe as one wounded in the war, but seriously it is only by thinking of those who have had their causes broken by wounds that I can reduce my own misfortunes to their proper proportions.' Despite these efforts at stoicism, however, the intensity of the stigma was so great that he regularly confessed a desire 'to flee away and hide ... in a South Sea Island. Of course people naturally don't suspect how sensitive one is – in fact I do my best to prevent their seeing it & the consequence is that they unintentionally tread unmercifully on one's corns. Even the sympathy which is freely & generally expressed hurts like the devil.'[4]

Some private malicious consolation was derived from the difficulties of his successor and the eventual vindication of his own policy. Three days after his resignation, General Auckland Geddes, the War Office Director of Recruiting, became the new civilian Minister of National Service. The transformation was far more fundamental than simply a change in personnel and departmental title. Determined to avoid Chamberlain's errors, Geddes obtained a seat in the Commons, a ministerial title, precise written instructions and a place on the newly-established War Priority Committee. Nevertheless, as Chamberlain rightly anticipated, Geddes had 'cut a stick for his own back and ... will be black and blue before he has done'.[5] Despite the institutional reforms, the underlying problems of departmental friction and inefficiency remained as stubbornly intractable as ever. In the event, the Military Service (No 1) Act in February 1918 finally introduced the bulk release from exemptions which Chamberlain had sought thirteen months earlier. When the German offensive broke through the British lines on 21 March 1918, the threat of imminent military disaster completed Chamberlain's vindication when the Military Service (No 2) Act in April finally implemented his principle of the 'clean cut', by removing the exemption from men in the 18–50 age groups. At one point, Chamberlain even contemplated the possibility that he would be called-up for military service with the grim satisfaction that at least he would have felt that he had 'done his bit'.

Despite the apparent triumph of his own manpower strategy and Geddes' 'sincere tribute of respect' for all his predecessor's efforts,[6] little could assuage Chamberlain's bitterness. In public he gave vent to his private feelings only once, at a meeting of the Grand Committee of the Birmingham Liberal Unionist Association on 18 December 1917. Although the meeting was 'scantily attended' and Chamberlain's remarks were not reported in the London press, his 40-minute speech offered a carefully prepared defence of his record at National Service, while at Annie's insistence, his rousing peroration declared that the Unionists had new sympathies and progressive new ideas on social issues. According to Austen, his half-brother spoke 'very easily and fluently with perfect command of his voice'. He was 'above all impressed by the skill and force with which he stated his case ... Such a speech delivered in the House of Commons would have put the Government on their trial and I think they would have found it hard to answer it.'[7] The effort of unburdening himself was undoubtedly cathartic, but the 'stigma of failure' remained indelibly etched upon Chamberlain's consciousness.[8] At the end of the same month further satisfaction was derived from the opportunity to reject Lloyd George's characteristically ungracious offer of a knighthood.[9] In September 1918 Chamberlain then set about preventing Lloyd George from receiving the Freedom of the City of

Birmingham and although he succeeded only in delaying it until February 1921, he conspicuously absented himself from the ceremony.

Beyond engendering a lifelong animus towards Lloyd George, the experience at National Service convinced Chamberlain that his future career must lie in the House of Commons. As a Councillor, there was always the vague public expectation that he would automatically succeed to his father's old seat of West Birmingham after the war, but while he remained Lord Mayor the prospect of Parliament exercised little real appeal. 'I confess I see little use or profit in the H. of C.' he told a friend in May 1916, 'you won't readily get me to leave my job while I feel I can be of use, for the sake of beating my head against a wall in London.'[10] After his experiences at National Service, however, Chamberlain resolved that he would never accept government office again without having first served his apprenticeship in the Commons. He also recognised that for all the bitterness at his recent treatment, he could not settle down to business and the selfish pursuit of money when one cousin had already been killed at the Front and another was still in danger in France. Encouragement from his siblings brushed aside all remaining doubts, for as he told his sisters, 'although I know that half of what you say is exaggerated and three-quarters of what Annie says is exaggerated … if I didn't try people would always think I could have done something if I had tried'.[11]

By 22 August Chamberlain was sufficiently resolved to write a revealingly ruminative letter to Charles Vince, the veteran Secretary of the Birmingham Liberal Unionist Association. Explaining 'the impossibility of my taking up life again where I left it', Chamberlain stated bluntly that his only options were to give up public life altogether or to enter Parliament. Although conceding that he was now perhaps too old, he requested Vince to make discreet enquiries about likely Birmingham vacancies as he could never represent anywhere else.[12] While the speed of the decision was not perhaps surprising, what is remarkable about this letter is its implicit assumption that he would again hold ministerial office – probably under this own half-brother; a confident tone and language which runs directly counter to the repeated expressions of melancholy self-doubt and uncertainty he employed within the family circle for much of the next year. But as Hilda shrewdly concluded only two days later, 'I feel pretty sure that you *do* mean to go into Parliament in your inner mind, and have known it for some time, however much the outward man protesteth'; a verdict Chamberlain conceded was 'abominably clear sighted & brutal in pulling off all the clothes under which I had crawled'.[13]

The Chamberlain sisters were less accurate in their prediction that once Neville's intentions were known one of the sitting Members would soon cheerfully make way for him. Despite a public hint in early September that he did not want to wait for a general election before entering the Commons, none of the incumbent Birmingham Members were prepared to stand aside.[14] The possibility of succeeding the 74-year-old John Middlemore in Birmingham North was ruled out by the prior claim of Eldred Hallas, Chamberlain's old ally in the campaign to launch the Savings Bank and a candidate for the British

Workers' League with whom he hoped to collaborate in attracting working class votes to the anti-socialist cause. Even the frail 86-year-old Jesse Collings, who had worked closely with Joseph Chamberlain for 30 years and who had previously declared his willingness to stand down for Neville, now had a prospective candidate at Bordesley. While Vince's soundings prompted local assurances that it had been 'the dream of Bordesley for years that *you* should follow Mr Collings', the constituency association warned that the difficulty would be with John Dennis, who as Collings' adopted successor, was rumoured to be more eager than ever to enter the Commons in order to satisfy an ambitious wife.[15]

Despite tactful efforts by both Chamberlain brothers to encourage Dennis to stand aside, he attempted to play 'rather a deep game' in the hope of placing the local and national party machine under such an obligation that he could obtain a more attractive agricultural constituency in return.[16] At the same time, efforts to circumvent Dennis by direct overtures to the ailing Collings were obstructed by his son-in-law who equivocated until Collings health had deteriorated to such a state that a personal approach was impossible. The resulting frustrations provoked Chamberlain to further outpourings of bitter self-doubt about his chosen path:

> My career is broken. How can a man of nearly 50, entering the House with this stigma upon him, hope to achieve anything? The fate I foresee is that after mooning about for a year or two I shall find myself making no progress … I shall perhaps be defeated in an election, or else shall retire, and that will be the end. I would not attempt to re-enter public life if it were not war-time. But I can't be satisfied with a purely selfish attention to business for the rest of my life.

In the event, another Liberal Unionist intermediary coaxed Ebenezer Parkes into accepting retirement from Birmingham Central at the next election, much to the chagrin of the scheming Dennis who Chamberlain rejoiced had tried to be 'just a bit too clever and has cooked his own goose!'[17]

Having finally secured a seat, for the remainder of 1918 Chamberlain turned his mind to the task of reviving the local party machine from its wartime atrophy. Even before the war Chamberlain had expressed alarm that since the removal of his father's 'very personal' influence, their supporters 'had fallen more and more out of touch with party politics', with a corresponding decline in organisational vigour at a time when the Unionists were being strongly challenged by rival parties.[18] These anxieties were highlighted and exacerbated by the 1918 Representation of the People Act, with its prospect of wholesale constituency redistribution and a mass democratic franchise. In Birmingham, the Act increased the electorate from 95,000 to 427,000 voters while the number of constituencies rose from seven to twelve. To prepare for this turmoil, Chamberlain sought to revitalise, reorganise and, above all, centralise the party's organisation within the city.

Although a joint committee had considered the fusion of Conservative and Liberal Unionist organisations within Birmingham in March 1914, the war had prevented the implementation of its plan and old animosities still remained strong. When the committee reconvened in December 1917, however, it soon reported in favour of complete amalgamation within a structure proposed by Chamberlain for a single central office in new premises under joint presidents and with committees composed of equal representation from the two wings of the party.[19] In proposing this plan, Chamberlain's principal practical objective was the creation of a strong centralising authority. As a result, after a brief but determined battle with Sir Arthur Steel-Maitland, the Conservative joint chairman of the new Birmingham Conservative and Unionist Association, Chamberlain almost immediately asserted his ascendancy over the new organisation. As he wrote to his sisters after a meeting of Birmingham MPs and candidates had almost unanimously agreed to his plans, 'this decision practically places the direction of Unionist politics in Birm. in my hands. I am not quite sure whether all those present perceived this; I didn't mention it!'[20] At the same time, Chamberlain threw himself with equal vigour into the 'very difficult' task of doing the same for the Midland Union. As the Central Office District Agent recalled over a decade later, 'the credit of steering the Unionist Party successfully through it, leaving no trace of old time animosities, is a tribute to your extraordinary skill, tact and foresight'.[21]

Rather less satisfactory from Chamberlain's perspective was the party's relationship with the British Workers' League. Established in March 1916 to rally the forces of 'patriotic labour' against the Labour Party, the League had signed an electoral agreement with the Unionists in February 1917. Chamberlain was initially 'very anxious' to promote an alliance with local BWL leaders like Eldred Hallas, as a means of giving substance to the wartime movement towards class cooperation and to undermine the sectional appeal of the Labour Party.[22] To this end, he publicly expressed sympathy with their ideas, while behind the scenes he struggled against Central Office indifference to reach a satisfactory arrangement over seats in the Midlands, including intervening personally to assist the selection of Hallas at Duddeston in face of 'disgruntled' local opposition.[23]

Yet despite this personal loyalty to Hallas, Chamberlain soon became disillusioned with the 'confoundedly aggressive' tactics of Victor Fisher, the BWL's leader, which he feared would 'alienate everyone and in particular the very Labour section we want to attract'.[24] Convinced the BWL had now 'destroyed its usefulness', in February 1918 Chamberlain urged Conservative Central Office to reconsider the electoral pact – a warning it appeared to ignore despite its own evident misgivings.[25] In retaliation, after protests from the Stourbridge constituency association at having Fisher foisted upon them in June 1918, Chamberlain led the Midland Union's attack upon Central Office high-handedness in defence of local autonomy. When the party managers retorted that they were only acting in accordance with the party's rules, Chamberlain replied that 'it was not the rules we wanted to change but the spirit in which

they were administered' and he reinforced Midland protests with the threat
that if they did not achieve progress they 'must seriously consider whether
[they] were prepared to go on as an organisation'. The ensuing battle rumbled
on until April 1919, when Central Office grudgingly conceded a greater degree
of autonomy over candidate selection to the provincial organisation.[26]

Beyond these political activities, Chamberlain settled down to make the
most constructive use of the time at his disposal. On the City Council he
became Deputy Mayor in November 1917 but declined a third term as Lord
Mayor, given his determination to enter the Commons and the conviction that
'"sequels" are notoriously apt to be disappointing'.[27] He also pressed on with
the plans to modernise facilities in the Council House and associated himself
with radical new proposals for city development 'pointing the way to a higher
conception of Civic dignity and Civic responsibility'. These included plans
for a new Town Hall on the 'skyscraper' model and the building of a Civic
Recreation Hall to provide Birmingham's now more prosperous workers with
'an opportunity of forming fresh tastes', rather than driving them back 'to
coarse or degrading forms of pleasure for lack of something more wholesome'.[28]
Sensing that 'the psychological moment for something of the kind has arrived',
plans for the creation of a city orchestra, a new school of music, opera house
and concert hall also took much energy. In time, he had even more ambitious
plans:

> Every club & every big works should have its own orchestra and glee society
> and competitions should be held under the auspices of the City Council.
> Thus you would help to educate the public, you would introduce a new
> & engrossing interest into the lives of the working & lower middle classes
> and incidentally you would make it possible for a more educated & highly
> trained people with musical taste to get high class concerts & opera at a
> comparatively cheap rate.[29]

At the University, Chamberlain proved an equally visionary promoter of a
free course of general education for trade unionists, designed to attract more
popular sympathy for the institution within the city. Despite an initially cool
reception, Chamberlain's drive and his excellent relations with organised
labour ensured the scheme was in operation by the autumn of 1917.[30] By 1919
this partnership was expanded into a diploma programme of 'Education for
citizenship' although only the Workers' Union participated – and even they
proved 'very unbusinesslike' in meeting their obligation to pay the wages of
students attending the courses. By the end of the first year, the University thus
warned Chamberlain that unless the experiment achieved a better response in
the 1920/21 session the scheme must lapse.[31] In the event, the onset of the post-
war economic slump finally doomed the scheme in 1923 as the unions were
unable to subsidise the students selected to attend the course. By then, however,
Chamberlain's increasing ministerial burdens had forced him to resign from the
University's Council.[32]

In his business affairs, Chamberlain had almost immediately resumed his duties at Hoskins, Elliotts and BSA and these took up much of his time. During this period, Chamberlain reinforced his credentials as a clear-sighted businessman and a paternalistic employer anxious to give practical substance to the nascent corporatist ideas he had expounded to the TUC in 1916. At a national level, he warmly applauded the Federation of British Industry's support for Whitley Councils drawn from both sides of industry to settle disputes as 'broad-minded and farsighted', while after a threatened strike at BSA in November 1917 he established a work's labour committee under his chairmanship to bring directors and men into closer personal contact to help overcome the alienating anonymity and class conflict inherent in mass production. He even talked to Austen about his ideas for compulsory registration of all workers in each trade, with joint committees of employers and employees to regulate wages and improve trade conditions.[33]

At the same time, within his own businesses, Chamberlain actively promoted a wide-ranging package of social reforms designed to improve conditions for employees while consolidating their relationship with management. A well-equipped out-patients department was established at BSA and plans were put in progress for permanent recreation grounds with gymnasia and an elaborate new meeting hall. At Hoskins a scheme for paid holidays was introduced in June 1918 along with pensions for those disabled or killed in action. He even floated the idea of a model village of worker's houses at Selly Oak which could eventually be purchased by their tenants. At a rather different level, to 'show the men ... that they were not regarded merely as machines for turning out work but that the Board take a human interest in them & their amusements', the Chamberlains regularly attended works sports events and ceremonies to award medals and long-service certificates to employees. In order to secure his future finances for a career in politics, Chamberlain also took steps to strengthen the management of both Hoskins and Elliotts, while actively seeking amalgamations to create a new metal combine capable of commanding the sort of dominant market position necessary to succeed in what he gloomily anticipated would be difficult post-war trading conditions.[34]

Despite the prudent preparations and the welter of constructive reforms, this was a difficult transitional period in Chamberlain's life. Uncertainty about the timing of his entry to Parliament left him easy prey to nagging doubts about the future and these were compounded by acute anxieties in his family life. In March 1918, hopes that Annie would have a third child faded after a second miscarriage, a gynaecological operation and a long period of convalescence. Even more devastating was the loss of his cousin, Norman Chamberlain. Reports that he was missing in action after ferocious street-to-street fighting during the Battle of Cambrai in early December 1917, prompted Chamberlain to lament that 'we are all going through one of the black times, when everything seems to be against us'. Despite an obstinate refusal to be pessimistic, however, on 10 February news finally arrived that Norman's body had been found. The formal confirmation of his worst fears came as a devastating blow. He had endured the loss of his cousin John in May 1917 with characteristic stoicism, but this news left him 'sick at heart' at the loss of a man whom he regarded as a brother and one of 'the most intimate friends' he ever had. As fellow members of Birmingham Council, Neville always admired the constructive moral purpose behind Norman's social work on behalf of boys' clubs, juvenile employment exchanges, playing fields and assisted emigration to Canada. As he noted in his diary after the memorial service, 'Strange that we do not fully realise men's characters while they are alive. Only now do I begin to see the extraordinary beauty of his. His life was devoted to others, and I feel a despicable thing beside him.'[35] In order that 'future generations of the family should realise how greatly Norman had contributed to the family fame', Chamberlain laboured sporadically throughout his first parliament at a memoir of his cousin – the only book he ever wrote.[36] More important, while he strove throughout the rest of his career to fulfil much of Norman's social reform programme, the memory of a constructive life extinguished in its prime unquestionably remained a potent force behind Chamberlain's revulsion against war and his tireless quest for peace during the late 1930s.

Despite all of these worries, distractions and demands upon his time, worse was to follow. Although for some time Chamberlain had tentatively predicted that the war would not last into 1919, the speed with which the Central Powers collapsed surprised him along with virtually everyone else. But when the moment finally arrived, the taste of national triumph was embittered by the death of his sister Beatrice from influenza a week after the Armistice was signed. Exhausted by her war work for the Red Cross and other causes, she fell easy prey to the pandemic which killed between 150,000 and 230,000 people in Britain and 21,500,000 worldwide. Although some solace was derived from the fact that she had lived to see victory and died without pain, this was another severe blow to the entire Chamberlain family. 'She was a wonderfully gifted woman of brilliant intellect and the highest moral character', Chamberlain recorded in his diary immediately afterwards. 'She had the warmest heart ... It is an awful gap in our family circle. I cannot write more now.'[37]

Fortunately before he could brood over the loss of Beatrice, Chamberlain was thrown into the turmoil of his first general election campaign as a candidate for the constituency of Ladywood; an all-absorbing burden which he embraced as 'a good thing ... for it has forced me to put a sort of crust over my emotions'.[38] Despite his public assertion that the peace negotiations and domestic reconstruction could best be achieved 'by setting aside old party divisions and by the continued cooperation of those who have stood side by side in the war', he conspicuously declined to use the notorious 'Coupon' sent jointly by Lloyd George and Bonar Law, the Conservative leader, to all government-supported candidates.[39] Instead, he campaigned on a radical reforming manifesto declaring that 'we could best show our gratitude to those who have fought and died for England by making it a better place to live in. My sole reason for wishing to enter Parliament is my desire to assist in bringing about this transformation.' To this end, he advocated a minimum wage to ensure the worker 'a decent standard of comfort for himself and his family', shorter hours to permit more recreation, cooperation between Capital and Labour and more expenditure on State-funded social reform delivered by local authorities – particularly with regard to housing, maternity and infant welfare. In true Chamberlain tradition, he also called for industrial protection and a preferential tariff structure to help develop the resources of the Empire.[40] In the ultra-patriotic circumstances of December 1918, there was little doubt about the outcome against a Labour opponent fighting on an unequivocal socialist programme including wholesale nationalisation, conscription of wealth to pay for the war, the abolition of the Lords and 'drastic treatment' for profiteers.[41] On a turnout of only 50.5 per cent, Chamberlain obtained almost 70 per cent of the vote and a majority of 6,833.

II

The Parliament elected in December 1918 has been immortalised as 'a lot of hard-faced men, who look as if they had done well out of the war'.[42] In an assembly in which nearly half of all Unionist Members were newly elected and the same proportion were businessmen, Chamberlain was a typical representative of the transformation which was taking place within the Conservative Party in Parliament and during his backbench period he worked hard to increase the links between Birmingham's MPs and its industrial and business community.[43] Yet unlike most of these new colourless backbenchers, Chamberlain entered Parliament convinced by Austen's verdict that he possessed 'both the special ability & special experience which would make ... a career in the House' at 'a formative & creative time when old ties are loosening, new ideas and policies are forming'.[44] Moreover, despite the apprehensions of the past year, Chamberlain entered immediately into the spirit and work of the Commons, immersing himself in its practices, studying its ways and assiduously lunching and dining there to meet his fellow Members. All of this soon made him 'feel much more at home in the House' and by late-February he was compelled to 'confess (rather reluctantly) that I begin to feel something of the fascination of the House of Commons'. After a complimentary response to his maiden speech on an important amendment to the Rent Restrictions Bill on 11 March, he declared he felt 'distinctly more satisfied with the House than I did'.[45]

Although Chamberlain caught the Speaker's eye with remarkable regularity, this was often only achieved only through sheer persistence by staying in the Chamber late into the night or speaking to largely deserted benches. Like his father, public speaking did not come easily and the effort of preparing and delivering speeches caused him much anxiety during the early years of his parliamentary career. 'You have no idea how I have to force myself to get up and face the House', he confessed after eighteen months in the Commons. 'I feel like Henri IV at Cahors!' Yet through sheer hard work he had trained himself to speak without detailed notes by early 1922, although it was not until the election campaign of October 1924 that this stern discipline finally produced any substantial benefit.[46] To make matters worse, the personal satisfaction at having overcome these obstacles was often undermined the following morning when he found that even the Birmingham press had failed to report his words adequately, if at all. Nevertheless, looking back over his first session in Parliament he concluded with some justice that 'without creating any sensation, a thing to be avoided like the plague in these days of journalistic stunts, I have yet made a certain position there for myself and, in short, have now the "ear of the House". So I am satisfied.'[47]

Beyond the floor of the Commons, Chamberlain was also extremely active through his membership of a multitude of parliamentary committees. He was soon appointed to an important Standing Committee which during his first parliamentary session dealt with a variety of vexed and complex legislative issues such as the Docks & Harbour, Ministry of Transport, Railway and Electricity Supply Bills and on the latter, Chamberlain's amendments radically changed the nature of the legislation in favour of greater local authority control. Having taken the lead in the formation of the Association of Local War Pension Committees, in January 1919 he was immediately appointed its President; expert knowledge which assured him a seat on another committee dealing with Bills on the future administration of police and war pensions. In addition, he served as chairman of a lengthy and unglamorous joint committee of both Houses examining three Private Bills designed to increase the charges paid by London for water from the Rivers Lee and Thames. Beyond these legislative commitments, Chamberlain was also a member of various departmental investigations as well as advisory committees on health and transport.[48] Indeed, such was the accumulation of commitments that when Austen invited him to join the Select Committee on War Profits in November 1919, Chamberlain declined with the message that he 'really cannot undertake another big job like that unless they are prepared to sit between midnight and 7.30am'. Beyond the sheer time such activities consumed, however, what troubled Chamberlain and his wife most was the fear that these commitments prevented him from speaking in debates where the real parliamentary reputations were made.[49] Ultimately, it was a measure of his burden that Chamberlain voted in only 95 of the 166 divisions in the 1919 Session and he made only one major speech in the next Session.

Yet for a late middle-aged man in a hurry to make his mark, Chamberlain was remarkably fortunate that his special knowledge and experience coincided closely with the policy areas which most preoccupied Lloyd George's post-war coalition. During these debates, Chamberlain revealed the essential radicalism of his political vision and his willingness to employ the power of the State to achieve his goals. The development of inland waterways was one such issue. Before the war, Chamberlain had been a strong supporter of canal transport and as president of the Waterways Association he had advocated an integrated transport policy under a single State authority controlling roads, railways, canals, harbours and terminals.[50] The introduction of the Ways and Communications Bill early in 1919, with its bold initial plan for a Ministry of

Transport capable of nationalising any transport undertaking simply by Order in Council, thus enabled Chamberlain to emerge as a staunch champion of canals and their nationalisation against a domineering and deeply unpopular minister apparently determined to overlook them. As a result, in February 1920 Chamberlain agreed to chair a committee to consider canal improvement in the hope of achieving some progress. The report inevitably echoed Chamberlain's long-standing conclusions. While nationalisation was rejected on cost grounds, all waterways were to be unified into seven regional Public Trusts to be protected from unfair railway competition during their early years. In order to demonstrate the viability of the scheme, the committee proposed that the experiment should be confined to canal improvements along the River Trent – a development which finally came to fruition in 1925.[51]

Housing played a far more prominent part in the work of both Chamberlain and the Coalition. On the eve of the Armistice, he shared the widespread view that 'housing was one of the most urgent of all problems to be solved & that unless people were shown that something big was actually in preparation there would be serious trouble'. Given his pessimism about the ability of private enterprise to respond sufficiently swiftly to the challenge, Chamberlain again demonstrated his radical faith in State intervention by proposing large sums of money for public housing with powers for local authorities to buy and develop sites and to administer the properties on the State's behalf. Encouragement would also be given to the tenant to purchase their own home with the aid of Municipal Housing Banks, although the State should retain the first option to re-purchase and the obligation to buy back if no one else came forward.

> In this way you would strike popular imagination with a big scheme, you would have all the advantages of collecting information about housing at the centre which could help and advise Local Authorities, you would bring in all the savings of the working classes to ease the financial situation & you would offer the strongest possible incentive to save. Moreover you would have a good landlord who could afford to keep his property in good order & you would give the proletariat a stake in the country.[52]

Alongside his direct involvement in scrutinising the government's housing legislation, in October 1919 Chamberlain was appointed chairman of a Ministry of Health committee on the clearance and reconstruction of 'unhealthy areas'. Again, this proved an ideal vehicle to promote his earlier ideas on town planning and the need for a more active role for local authorities in the regeneration of slum districts. The interim report in March 1920 focused largely on London and proposed that the chronic congestion in the city could be most effectively addressed by the dispersal of part of its population. To this end, local authorities should have wider powers to control land use and industrial development in congested areas, while garden cities of between 30–50,000 inhabitants with better living conditions and more open spaces should be established around London, surrounded by a green belt of agricultural land to ensure that 'the inhabitants

will live close to their work under the best possible conditions'. Although
often largely ignored by Chamberlain's biographers, this was a truly landmark
document. Indeed, as Gordon Cherry argues, it 'is difficult to overestimate the
importance of this report in the history of strategic land-use planning' as the
unacknowledged forerunner of the Barlow Report of 1940, which did so much
to influence post-war official attitudes and policy towards the subject. In order
to prepare the necessary general plan and to coordinate the activities of the
122 local authorities within the Greater London area, the report recommended
another enquiry to consider the scope and powers of a proposed new authority
to control housing and transport for the city and its surrounding districts. As a
result, in June 1921 Chamberlain and his former Town Clerk, Sir Ernest Hiley,
became members of the Royal Commission under Lord Ullswater established
to resolve these broader questions. Although little tangible reform resulted
from these deliberations, in October 1926 Chamberlain again took the initiative
as Minister of Health when he convened a conference of the relevant authorities
to prepare a Greater London Regional Plan; a document which eventually
proposed a 'green girdle' around London with decentralisation to garden cities,
greater playing field provision and the planned dispersal of industrial and
residential development.[53]

In contrast, the final report of the Unhealthy Areas Committee in April 1921
focused on general policy for dealing with slums, but it also foreshadowed
many of Chamberlain's later policy ideas. Given the likely shortage of material
and skilled labour, combined with the sheer magnitude of the problems, he
had always been convinced that the only short-term solution lay in a bold use
of Part II of the 1890 Housing Act. This enabled local authorities to acquire and
repair existing slum dwellings in order to render them habitable for another
ten years until eventual clearance and reconstruction to a carefully balanced
town plan.[54] Although these ideas were ahead of their time and the concept of
municipalisation raised many practical and political objections, Chamberlain
continued to promote the idea of slum 'reconditioning' in a variety of forms
throughout the inter-war years both as Minister of Health and as Chancellor of
the Exchequer.

While wrestling with these major national problems, Chamberlain was
also busy trying to guarantee the future of Birmingham's Municipal Savings
Bank. Having rejoined the Bank's management committee in June 1918 and
then elected President five months later, Chamberlain soon evolved a plan to
turn it into a Municipal Loan Bank for the purpose of assisting working men
to buy their own houses; a plan which came to fruition in June 1919 when the
Birmingham Corporation Act removed all of the onerous conditions in the 1916
legislation and established it permanently as a savings and housing bank with
extended powers and greater access to local savers.[55] On 1 September 1919 the
new enterprise opened for business with headquarters at the Council House,
seventeen branches and some £300,000 of voluntary transfers from the soon to
be defunct existing institution. Within two and a half years, the new bank had
25 branches, £1,800,000 on deposit, over 76,000 investors and had advanced

1200 mortgages. By March 1943 deposits had risen to £50,797,006 from a total of 537,030 customers. The Birmingham Municipal Bank finally closed for business in its existing form in 1976 with £137 million on deposit and three-quarters of a million accounts.[56] Despite his formal retirement from the Bank's board in November 1919, Chamberlain retained a direct personal influence over its work and policy for much longer and in July 1927 he gave evidence to a Treasury committee in the hope of encouraging the extension of the idea, but to no avail.[57] As a sincere believer in the notion of a 'property owning democracy', however, his sister later recalled that 'one of the happiest moments of his official life' was the day he opened the ten thousandth house built by Birmingham's bank. Proud of his achievement and glad that others now fully recognised his role in its creation, Chamberlain declared in June 1923 that he regarded it as the greatest monument to his municipal career.[58]

Chamberlain was equally tireless in his efforts to sustain the vitality of the Ladywood, Birmingham and Midland Unionist organisations. In Ladywood, the number of Unionist political meetings and social gatherings increased sharply while Chamberlain launched a Unionist Workers' League in January 1921 to recruit and train committed canvassers who could be deployed across the constituency at election times; a development which fully justified the effort in the increasingly close election contests of 1922, 1923 and 1924. In September 1921, a branch of 'Junior Unionists' was established by the Chamberlains 'to provide an opportunity for young people of both sexes to become properly instructed in political questions'.[59] Within a month of her husband's election, Annie also floated the idea of a Women's Unionist Association in Ladywood 'to impress upon all that a woman's political duty is not only to exercise her right to vote, but to understand for what she is voting'. Although initially the idea aroused male suspicions that this was simply an effort 'to develop a smart set in Ladywood', within a year the body had achieved some degree of acceptance and by the spring of 1922 the four Women's Unionist Institutes in Ladywood were acknowledged 'to be the most useful adjuncts to the organisation of the Party in the constituency'.[60]

Always far more conscientious as a constituency MP than Austen and more sensitive to the challenge of the new mass electorate, in September 1919 Chamberlain also began the novel experiment of 'slumming'; a process which involved visits to Ladywood several nights a week to chat with constituents in their own homes, both to gratify the voters and to obtain a clearer impression of the changing mood of public opinion. Less appealing, but equally necessary, were the grim 'tripe suppers' with loyal supporters in smoky pothouses around the constituency. 'What an evening' he wrote after one such meeting in Austen's West Birmingham constituency:

First, soup, cold & very nasty. Then an enormous piece of frozen beef red, ragged, and calculated to blunt the sharpest knife. It was accompanied by a mass of very watery potato and very strong smelling cabbage. The third course was the celebrated scrag of boiled mutton which the chairman devoured without winking … but I fainted completely away and was only revived when they thrust beneath my nose a powerful mass of mouse-trap cheese … Well, it was got over and I delivered (without notes) a 'magnificent address' which was received with great applause & satisfaction.[61]

Under Chamberlain's active personal leadership, similar organisational advances were made within the Unionist organisation across the entire city. In order 'to counteract the insidious propaganda of the Socialists', a newspaper, entitled *Straightforward*, was launched in May 1920 to report on local party activity and general politics. Two months later a Unionist Propaganda Society was established to train supporters wishing to become party speakers, while a new Secretaries' Guild brought together all Ward Secretaries and Staff Agents to stimulate activity, improve communication and coordinate resource deployment within the City. At Chamberlain's suggestion, a new Press Sub-Committee was also created in April 1921 to keep the Birmingham editors in touch with the activities of local MPs; a reflection of Chamberlain's earlier recognition of the importance of 'feeding' the press with favourable stories while Lord Mayor and a prelude to his spectacular efforts at media manipulation while Prime Minister.[62] Within the Midland Union the improvement of organisation and propaganda also became increasingly prominent themes after 1918.[63] Without exaggerating the degree of Unionist domination in Birmingham during the inter-war years, therefore, there can be little doubt that these organisational reforms, undertaken largely at Chamberlain's instigation and often under his direct supervision, made a significant contribution to the party's vitality within the city and enabled it to build upon a relatively solid foundation.

III

It is easy to be dismissive of Chamberlain's worthy but essentially humdrum efforts during this period on the backbenches and in many respects he was his own harshest critic. 'In the House itself I have spoken occasionally but have done nothing to increase my reputation with the public' he reported despondently in December 1919. 'At present I feel very little inclination to try and perhaps I shan't make any progress unless something comes along to stir me to more vigorous action.'[64] From the spring of 1920, however, Chamberlain's progress and success in his parliamentary apprenticeship was palpable. By the end of the year no fewer than seven parliamentary and departmental committees plus the backbench Reconstruction Committee vied for the time and attention of a man who rightly considered himself to be 'the "handy man" of the House as regards committees'.[65] Success in the Private Members ballot also enabled him to introduce a Bastardy Bill (later renamed the Children of Unmarried Parents Bill) in May 1920, designed to legitimise the children of unmarried mothers on their subsequent marriage and to increase the financial support from absent fathers; a measure blocked in 1920 and 1921 but eventually adopted by the Home Office in 1922 and which passed into law in the following year. On the floor of the House too there was a new confidence that he had 'a steadily growing position as a man of judgement among MPs' – even on issues beyond his traditional areas of expertise.[66] One signal recognition of this new parliamentary status was the fact that the editor of the *Birmingham Post* began to treat him as the leader of the local Unionist party, with the result that his every word was reported with large headlines on the front page.

A more important recognition of his achievement came in the form of offers of parliamentary and ministerial office. First, in March 1920 he was offered the chairmanship of the Unionist Reconstruction Committee. This was the direct lineal descendant of the Unionist War Committee, which under Sir Edward Carson's leadership had rapidly emerged as the largest and most influential backbench 'ginger group' after its formation in January 1916 and it continued to act as the guardian of Unionist principles against coalition compromise throughout the post-war Lloyd George ministry.[67] In the event, Chamberlain was denied the chairmanship by the petty jealousy of Sir Frank Lowe, a fellow Birmingham MP who had become increasingly pompous in asserting his nominal seniority since Chamberlain's emergence as the effective leader of Birmingham Unionism. To circumvent this difficulty, Chamberlain, Carson and Lord Midleton were appointed as joint vice-chairmen under John Gretton, the Diehard leader of the overlapping Unionist Business Committee. After Gretton resigned the post in July 1921, Chamberlain served as chairman for the remainder of the session, although Austen's succession to the party leadership four months earlier precluded the possibility of more permanent control. Nevertheless, over issues such as tariffs, anti-dumping and Irish Home Rule, Chamberlain's position on the committee enabled him to raise his profile as an influential and independently-minded backbencher who was occasionally prepared to be critical of the Coalition.[68]

A second and more significant indication of Chamberlain's rising status was a tentative offer of junior ministerial office from an evidently embarrassed Bonar Law in March 1920. It was a difficult moment for both men. With 'some diffidence' Law explained that he understood that Chamberlain might not be content to become an Under-Secretary at the Ministry of Health having once been head of a 'great department'. He also conceded Chamberlain 'was worth more but didn't see how anything more could be offered'. For his part, Chamberlain had 'a very kindly feeling towards Bonar who has always been very nice' and so he 'did not want to say anything that might seem ungracious'. He thus declared he would positively prefer a junior position, but that he 'could not forget nor forgive Ll.G's treatment' while at National Service. To his sisters he was rather more forceful: 'I should be miserable with my head under the Goat's arm again and am not so enamoured of office that I would sell my peace of mind for it.' But while such a principled stand brought personal satisfaction, it also highlighted the profoundly depressing dilemma with which Chamberlain had been wrestling for some time. Indeed only a month before Law's offer, he informed his sisters that he had 'personally never felt

more depressed about politics'. Had these private musings not been sufficient
to demoralise him, the nature of his dilemma was brutally illuminated when
Bonar Law pointedly enquired about Chamberlain's age. As Lloyd George was
likely to remain Prime Minister for 'a very long time', Law explained that to
decline an offer of junior office at 50 would probably ensure that Chamberlain
did not get another chance. Despite the warning, however, he wrote back
politely to the effect that he 'couldn't, wouldn't, couldn't, wouldn't, *wouldn't*
join the dance'.[69]

At the heart of Chamberlain's problem was the almost complete absence of
any acceptable strategy for personal and political advancement. Although he
periodically supported the positions adopted by Tory Diehards, Chamberlain
never shared any of their ultra-reactionary credo or blind resistance to change.
On the contrary, his acceptance of the enduring nature of wartime transformation
encompassed an expectation of fundamental party realignment. 'No one can
foretell what will happen after the war in domestic politics', he wrote to his half-
brother in June 1917. 'Parties will be disrupted, new cries and new men very
likely will be coming to the front.' Six months later he warned the Birmingham
Liberal Unionist Association that 'the old shibboleths have gone for ever, and it
may be that when the war is over we shall find new groupings of parties on new
lines'.[70] In many respects, such language conformed well with Lloyd George's
own plans to carry wartime unity into peacetime, as the foundation upon which
to realign the party system in pursuit of a bold policy of national reconstruction
and in opposition to the burgeoning threat from the Labour Party. However,
although he initially considered the Coalition's reconstruction programme 'a
very fine one on paper', Chamberlain swiftly became disillusioned with both
the Coalition and its leaders.[71]

Unlike his half-brother who gradually came to develop a real respect
for Lloyd George after the war, Chamberlain's own observation from the
backbenches did nothing to soften his loathing for Lloyd George's methods or
personality. 'I suppose I am prejudiced', he told his sisters in June 1920, 'but the
little Welshman always leaves me completely cold.'[72] Yet there were far more
fundamental and principled objections to the idea of coalition and the price
it demanded from the Unionists. This was particularly so when rumours of
party 'fusion' abounded after November 1919, at a time when Chamberlain
detected 'a strong feeling of dissatisfaction with the position of the Unionists in
the Coalition and a desire to have something in the nature of a Unionist policy
defined'. Like many others on the government benches, Chamberlain was most
'afraid of being cozened into accepting a Lloyd Georgian policy which would
sacrifice Unionist principles'.[73]

On the other hand, he was almost equally swiftly repelled and disillusioned
by Unionist opponents of the Coalition like Sir Arthur Steel-Maitland and
Lord Robert Cecil. Although initially willing to attend a luncheon meeting of
declared critics in November 1919, Chamberlain was not prepared to join a cave
of rebellious irreconcilables. Moreover, it did not take him long to conclude that
'Bob Cecil is not the stuff leaders are made of ... he is too cranky to command

a following.' In consequence, Chamberlain declined to join a weekly dinner of Cecil's supporters and during 1920 he found himself increasingly out of sympathy with Cecil's patrician temperament and negative carping about government failures without offering any constructive alternative proposals of his own.[74] By the end of the year he had broken off all effective contact and when Cecil's 'Independent Group' issued its manifesto, signed by 71 Tory MPs and Peers in February 1922, Chamberlain's name was conspicuously absent from the list.[75]

Despite satisfaction at the progress he had made in his new career, therefore, after the spring of 1920 Chamberlain confronted the most depressing personal and political dilemma. As he lamented in his diary in December 1920, he had 'plenty of friendly acquaintances in the House but no one whose views accord sufficiently closely with my own to tempt me into joining forces'. In the absence of any acceptable alternative, Chamberlain resentfully resigned himself to the life of a useful but unfulfilled backbencher doomed to carry the burden of mundane and thankless work without any encouraging prospect of ministerial advancement. 'My Committees have occupied all my mornings, many afternoons and frequently part of my nights ... with the result that I have been able to put in but little time in the House and have only spoken once', he noted with weary resignation in a private review of 1920. 'This is very bad for a Parliamentary career, for a man soon gets forgotten and I have done nothing to increase my reputation with the public.'[76]

IV

The depth of Chamberlain's gloom about his personal position during 1921–22 was intensified by two further factors. First, his half-brother's emergence as leader of the Unionist party in March 1921 raised a variety of difficulties. In part, these stemmed from a rapidly increasing awareness that Austen had fallen under the mesmeric spell of the 'Welsh Wizard', whose plans to turn the Coalition into a new party under his leadership were likely to split the Conservatives and place the two brothers on opposite sides. Beyond fundamental strategic dilemmas of this sort, however, Austen's leadership also inhibited Chamberlain's ability to maintain his own independent influence within the parliamentary party. Such constraints became apparent almost immediately when he felt obliged to decline the chairmanship of the Unionist Reconstruction Committee because 'there is the difficulty that I could not agree to head a revolt against Austen & a revolt might be wanted. There's where the handicap is always coming in.'[77] Secondly, these political frustrations were compounded by deepening financial anxieties. Already living off his capital after only two years as an MP, as the severity of the post-war slump increased during 1921, his income from Elliotts collapsed while he confessed that BSA had 'gone down hill so rapidly as to cause me very serious anxiety'. Only Hoskins proved 'a little gold mine' with its bulging order book and record dividends, but even here he correctly predicted that this would not last much longer.[78] As a result of these combined trials, Chamberlain lamented in his review of 1921, that it had been 'a very trying year'. 'Sometimes' he complained bitterly, 'I wish I were out of the House altogether but I am not sure that I should be any happier if I were. But it is a great handicap to be the son of my father and the brother of my brother for every success is discounted and every failure is counted double. Moreover when one's brother is leader all independence goes unless one is prepared to quarrel and I am nowhere keen enough about politics for that.'[79]

Ironically, at the very moment that Chamberlain was penning these melancholy reflections, the fortunes of both Lloyd George and the Coalition suffered a major blow from which they never recovered. Flushed with success over the Irish Treaty in December 1921, Lloyd George decided that the Coalition should snatch another election victory in January in order to achieve by stealth the party merger which could not be achieved through direct appeals for 'fusion'. As the effective leader of Midland Unionism, however, Chamberlain's response to Austen's formal soundings on the question endorsed the almost unanimous opposition towards the idea of an early election, arguing that the government would be severely handicapped by the fact that Ireland, Second Chamber reform and economies were unsettled, while unemployment remained a major source of vulnerability at a time when 'the Coalition has no friends to speak of'. Against this background, he pessimistically predicted that 'if an Election were held now, half the seats ... might be swept away'. He was equally sceptical about the prospects for 'fusion' between the two wings of the Coalition as 'there are a number of Unionists who would not agree to give up the old name and scrap the old machine and enter a new combination under a new name and with Lloyd George accepted as Leader of their party'. Conceding that he might himself be among the rebels, Chamberlain thus emphasised privately that his own preference was 'to dissolve the Coalition and go to the country as a Unionist Party', adding cheerfully that 'I fully realise that this is out of the question until somebody has the happy idea of "poisoning Lloyd George's rum and water".'[80]

Although plans for an early election were abandoned, the tensions unleashed by Lloyd George's underhand manoeuvre engendered a mood of escalating crisis which blighted the Coalition's final months. After the failure of the election kite in January 1922, Chamberlain derived malicious comfort from the belief that 'whatever line Ll.G. takes ... the mischief is done and that the Coalition won't be the same again'. In order to drive the lesson home, at the Midland Union, he warned publicly that 'some of the Liberal members of the Coalition should be made to realise the weight the Unionist Party was carrying ... The Unionists had put loyalty to their Country first and unless that was recognised they would refuse to be dragged at the tail of the Liberal Wing of the Party.' When these tensions culminated in a divisive battle over tariff protection for fabric gloves in the summer, it confirmed all of Chamberlain's frustrations with the limitations of Coalition and stiffened his determination 'to adopt a very firm attitude' towards these nominal allies should the matter come to a crisis.

He was equally adamant in refusing to contemplate any prospect of electoral concessions to Coalition Liberals in Birmingham.[81]

Although Chamberlain regularly confessed that he 'should like to be rid of the Goat' during 1922, the evident decay of the coalition did little to dispel his underlying anxieties. At an inter-party level, this was because he still gloomily anticipated that 'the little Welshman' would remain in control for some time – particularly given doubts about Diehard influence and the surprising strength of pro-Coalition Unionist sentiment. Above all, the widely-shared assumption that his own party could not win an overall electoral majority without Lloyd George implied the need for another coalition after the next election to keep Labour out of office; an arrangement which required Lloyd George's return to power, if not necessarily to the Premiership.[82] Worse still, the apparent decline of the Coalition forced Chamberlain to confront the ambivalent feelings with which he had wrestled for some time. On one hand, during the spring of 1922, Chamberlain became increasingly critical of Austen and the Unionist leadership on the grounds that 'not one of them has any original ideas and that is where both Ll.G. & Winston have the pull':

> I find there is a good deal of dissatisfaction in the Party more or less connected with the Coalition. The fact is that they miss anything in the nature of a constructive policy among the Unionist leaders and though the latter are on safe ground when they say they can't break with Ll.G. unless there is something to break about, there is a sort of feeling, hardly definite enough to express, that if only they had a few ideas there soon would be something to break about, or alternatively that we should be then leading the Coalition instead of trailing after the Libs.[83]

Such criticisms of Austen's lack of originality and constructive thought were not new. Within days of his election to Parliament, a snub from Austen over policy prompted a revealing outburst: 'The fact is I always said that if I went into the House we should differ and we are bound to do so because our minds are differently trained. He thinks me wild and I think him unprogressive and prejudiced.'[84] But on the other hand, for all his defects, Austen was still leader of the party and however much Chamberlain loathed Lloyd George and the Coalition, he was extremely reluctant to participate actively in a rebellion against his own half-brother as its joint leader.

Torn between a political desire to end the Coalition and personal feelings of fraternal loyalty, Chamberlain was thus compelled to remain silent to avoid providing ammunition for critics of the government, while tactfully attempting to nudge Austen towards a constructive programme encompassing legislation for women and trade unions and reform of unemployment insurance, the Poor Law, slums, housing and agriculture.[85] Ultimately, it was symptomatic of the depth of Chamberlain's accumulated political and financial worries, that during the autumn of 1922 his doctor diagnosed his extreme tiredness over the past few months as a 'condition arising from excessive mental strain'.[86]

Given the complications of his position, Neville Chamberlain was astonishingly fortunate to be abroad during the final crisis of the Coalition. As the Conservative revolt began to take definite shape during July, the Chamberlains decided to visit Canada. After a fortnight taking the waters at Harrogate and a week fishing in Scotland, they sailed for Canada on 7 September for a six week tour. From Quebec, Chamberlain travelled to Montreal and Toronto before crossing the vast prairies and spectacular Rocky Mountains to British Columbia and Vancouver Island. Already elated by the thought that he was following in the footsteps of his father's visit in 1889, the scale and grandeur of the scenery clearly exhilarated him. As his father's son and an ardent advocate of imperial unity, he was also 'surprised and delighted ... to find the most intense British feeling'.[87]

From what he learned from the press, Chamberlain was confident that at the Carlton Club meeting of Unionist MPs on 19 October, Austen would declare in favour of an election fought as separate parties, with their own leaders and programmes, but in the expectation of a further coalition after the poll. Moreover, he assumed unquestioningly that as the party could not win an overall majority alone it would endorse such a stance – particularly as it implied that Austen rather than Lloyd George would become Prime Minister if the balance of parties shifted still further in favour of the Unionists. He was thus utterly astonished when he heard that this momentous meeting had voted decisively to end the Coalition and that Lloyd George and most of the Unionist leadership (including his own half-brother) had resigned rather than submit to the rebels.

Although naturally sorry that Austen had lost the party leadership to Bonar Law for a second time, Chamberlain's principal initial impulse was to offer 'profound thanks to Providence for delivering us from the Goat'. Second thoughts then appeared briefly to intensify the acute personal dilemma with which he had grappled since the spring of 1920. As never before, he confronted the stark choice between either loyalty to Austen (and the hated Lloyd George) or to his own career with the majority of the Conservative party. Yet if any doubt ever really existed in his mind, it was swiftly dispelled. Two days out from New York he had already excluded the possibility of going out of politics because of Austen's difficulties on the grounds that 'with no fundamental difference of policy but only of personalities I could not see myself following Ll.G. and that if Austen were out of the question I would have no hesitation in remaining with the Unionists & even, if I were asked, joining the new Govt'. Knowing that Leo Amery was sufficiently close to Bonar Law to be well placed to advance his claims to office, Chamberlain reminded his old friend and fellow Birmingham MP of his previous desire to serve as his junior minister if Amery ever became Colonial Secretary.[88]

Delayed by a howling gale in the Channel, Chamberlain did not arrive in London until late on 29 October. Next morning over breakfast, Amery informed him that Law wished him to become Postmaster-General and Chamberlain made it clear that he 'was in every way anxious to give ... support and come in'.[89] His uncharacteristically acrimonious meeting with his over-wrought half-brother later in the day, however, was a considerable trial for both men as they each sought to exert moral blackmail to achieve their own personal goals. Austen 'took the idea very badly evidently feeling that if [Neville] accepted it would be the last drop of bitterness in the cup' and such was Neville's distress at the thought of a permanent breach in their relations that when Amery met him later in the day he had 'to work very hard to get him not to acquiesce in [Austen's] ultimatum'.[90] When the brothers met over dinner, Neville again attempted to assure Austen that his acceptance would not put them in opposite camps, but rather would serve 'as a link between him and the new Govt, making relations easier & facilitating his acceptance as one of the leaders if not the leader in the event of B.L.'s being unable to carry on'. When Austen bitterly refused to be convinced, however, Neville angrily played his emotional ace by threatening to refuse office in deference to Austen's feelings, but making it clear that if he did so he would withdraw from politics altogether as 'one cannot go on refusing office when one does not differ on principles' and because it would be unfair to his constituency and supporters. Confronted explicitly with such a heavy personal responsibility, Austen withdrew his objection and urged his half-brother to accept Law's offer.[91] Nevertheless, as Neville progressed rapidly up the ministerial ladder over the next year, these private tensions over their divergent paths remained painfully evident and stretched fraternal goodwill to its limits.[92]

V

Bonar Law's motives for including Neville Chamberlain in his government are open to question, but they could not have been entirely without thought of its impact upon Austen and his disaffected coalitionist supporters lurking in self-imposed exile. Certainly Law's closest associates assured him that 'one additional good result' of Chamberlain's acceptance was that it might help heal the rift – but that even if it did not, it would undermine the unity of the Chamberlainite ex-ministers because, with Neville in the government, Austen could not decently prevent his followers from joining if asked to do so.[93] In accepting Law's invitation, Chamberlain had himself stressed that his presence in the Government 'may help to heal the wounds left by recent differences in the party and that as time goes on all members of the party may feel themselves to be a happy family again'.[94] Yet notwithstanding Neville's repeated efforts to act as an intermediary and conciliator, Maurice Cowling overstates the cynicism of Law's motivation when asserting that Chamberlain was initially 'used as a disposable pawn' in this game.[95] The far more likely explanation for Chamberlain's appointment in October 1922 was Law's urgent need to fill portfolios with men of proven ability at a time when the majority of the party's most experienced talent refused to join his government. As a result, while Law declared that he hoped 'it will not be long before we are all in the same boat again', he was almost certainly sincere when he assured Chamberlain that it was 'a real pleasure to have you in the Government and in saying this I am not thinking of the political advantage of your having joined us'.[96]

In the ensuing general election in November 1922, Chamberlain was confident of a comfortable majority in Ladywood given his organisational reforms in the constituency since 1918, the high morale of his party workers and Annie's assiduous efforts to cultivate this poor, largely working class constituency. In the Chamberlain archives two leather-bound volumes detail all of her social work visits to constituents between October 1919 and November 1922, accompanied by notes of their appearance, domestic circumstances and the remedial assistance provided, along with reminders for future reference about any flowers or Christmas cards subsequently despatched or received. With characteristic frenetic zeal, she threw herself wholeheartedly into the 1922 election campaign, touring Ladywood on her bicycle in a hat with a large orange plume 'talking encouraging scolding cajoling charming and converting the multitude' with house visits, street corner meetings and mass rallies.[97] As one local party official remarked, 'There wasn't a dog-hanging ... they didn't attend.'[98]

Yet despite all of these efforts, the electoral climate had become distinctly more hostile in Birmingham as the economic slump increased in severity. Labour's advance in the municipal elections of November 1921 was attributed to the fact that they 'unscrupulously exploited the grave condition of the moment' in a city with 90,000 unemployed and as their prospects improved, the intensity of Labour opposition increased. Moreover, given the poverty and vulnerability of Chamberlain's constituency, it was inevitable that Ladywood became one of the main battlegrounds in an election characterised by 'systematic door to door misrepresentation about Unionist candidates, flagrant exploitation of the miseries of the unemployed, organised rowdyism ... and a great deal of literature which would not have commended itself to George Washington'.[99] In the event, while Chamberlain attributed Unionist victory in all twelve Birmingham seats largely to his efforts at strengthening the party's organisation throughout the city, his confident prediction that his own seat was 'as safe as houses' proved excessively optimistic.[100] Ladywood produced the second smallest majority on an increased turnout. Chamberlain was back in Parliament and in office, but his majority had been reduced to an uncomfortable 2443, while Dr Dunstan proved a far more formidable Labour challenger than his predecessor.

Chapter 5

A Rising Star,
October 1922–October 1924

'[Baldwin] said he had felt the need of a colleague ... with whom he could discuss affairs as he had formerly discussed them with Bonar. It was an immense help to have someone at hand in whose judgement he could have confidence and hitherto it had been as though he were deprived of one of his hands. From this point of view, he said, there was no satisfactory alternative to myself. He liked me personally & he thought my judgement good ... Everyone respected me and if he had to be away there was no one he could have in charge with the same feeling of comfort as myself.'

Neville to Hilda Chamberlain, 26 August 1923

The fall of the Lloyd George Coalition on 19 October 1922 marked the decisive watershed in Neville Chamberlain's political career. Like so many Conservative leaders between the wars, Chamberlain was a major beneficiary of the unique situation created by the Carlton Club revolt. When the bulk of the party's most experienced leadership resigned rather than submit to the wishes of rebellious subordinates, Bonar Law was forced 'to depend upon the under-secretaries and bottle-washers of the late Government' to form his administration.[1] Within the ranks of this so-called 'Second Eleven', Chamberlain had undoubtedly established a strong claim to ministerial preferment, but few could have predicted the meteoric rise that these developments made possible. Appointed as Postmaster-General outside the Cabinet in October 1922, within ten months he had risen, via the Ministry of Health, to become Chancellor of the Exchequer and one of Baldwin's closest ministerial confidants. Thereafter, he remained at the pinnacle of national and Conservative politics until his death in 1940. Moreover, beyond its direct implications for Chamberlain's career advancement, October 1922 marked an equally significant personal watershed. With Austen stranded in the political wilderness while he rapidly rose to prominence on the Conservative frontbench, Neville Chamberlain swiftly moved out of the shadow of his older half-brother. Perhaps for the first time in his life, he was now his own man, standing on terms of equality with his more fortunate and privileged sibling. The rise to office even induced a heady sense of walking in the footsteps of his remote but revered father. Having both become Lord Mayor after four years on the Council, Chamberlain noted with particular satisfaction that they had also both achieved ministerial office only four years after entering the Commons.[2]

As a member of Law's government, Chamberlain swiftly established a formidable reputation as a minister of imagination and outstanding administrative competence with a real talent for parliamentary debate. After his disastrous experience at National Service in 1917, he was grateful for the 'comfortable obscurity' of the Post Office in order to serve a proper ministerial apprenticeship before advancing to more exalted positions and his policy responsibilities were relatively modest.[3] Nevertheless, Chamberlain had the distinction of granting the first operating licence to the newly-established British Broadcasting Company in January 1923, although he was less sympathetic to its request to transmit the King's Speech on the grounds that it may be used as a precedent for airing parliamentary debates – 'a prospect which makes one shudder'.[4] A more important departmental achievement related to the development of a chain of wireless stations across the Empire, over which Chamberlain carried his proposal for a government monopoly through Cabinet against the initial scepticism of the Prime Minister and Chancellor of the Exchequer. As Lord Curzon concluded after Chamberlain's detailed and persuasive exposition of the case to Cabinet, 'Capital cost small, commercial prospects good, object excellent, decision immediate and affirmative.'[5]

Although the Post Office offered a sound apprenticeship in the arts of ministerial leadership and parliamentary management, it was scarcely the place to earn a great reputation. Yet from the outset, Chamberlain rapidly acquired broader opportunities to demonstrate his abilities. Perhaps because of the kindred spirit felt by men of similar character and temperament, a warm mutual regard soon developed between Law and Chamberlain.[6] Given Chamberlain's 'affectionate feeling' for Law since his National Service days, it was no mere conventional expression of deference when he accepted office with the assurance that he would serve 'with real pleasure for … I have long felt a special personal regard for you'.[7] For his own part, Law evidently had considerable confidence in Chamberlain's judgement and he was soon keen to sound his private opinions on a variety of issues ranging over domestic politics and foreign affairs.[8] Indeed, it was indicative of Law's increasing respect for his judgement that when he resigned as Prime Minister, Chamberlain's name was apparently the first to be considered when asked for someone to advise the King about a successor, before Law eventually suggested Lord Salisbury.[9] It is even possible that Bonar Law genuinely did confide in one intimate friend that with a little more parliamentary experience Chamberlain would have been the right man to have succeeded him in May 1923.[10] In any event, it was scarcely surprising that Chamberlain should have rejoiced at 'what a relief & *contrast* it is to have colleagues who want to help you and a P.M. who treats you like a friend'.[11]

Given his proven expertise on housing, Chamberlain was widely acknowledged as the obvious candidate to succeed the unfortunate Griffith-Boscawen as Minister of Health after his humiliating failure to be re-elected at the Mitcham by-election in March 1923.[12] Despite his initial determination not to leave the Post Office before he 'had a chance of doing something there', when

Sir Robert Horne's rejection of the portfolio removed any immediate prospect of party reunion with Austen's estranged coalitionist following, Chamberlain bowed to Law's insistent pressure to accept the post in the belief that 'it would not be playing the game' to refuse.[13] But as he also frankly confessed, his elevation to the Cabinet 'moves me singularly little ... The fact is ... I have felt conscious of an influence in the Govt beyond what my office warranted and ascribable to a general respect for my experience and judgement.' Deeply gratified by the enthusiastic public and press response to his appointment, Chamberlain immediately threw himself into his formidable task with a characteristic energy and imagination, already armed with 'a good many ideas' he hoped to put into practice.[14] 'I never knew a man who gave such meticulous care to every detail in his department', his Under-Secretary later recalled. 'Perhaps this was a fault and it would have been better if he had been able to separate the important from the unimportant, but his mind was extraordinarily able and accurate and he never seemed to find himself over-burdened. In some way, perhaps, he was like his father.'[15] This was a perceptive judgement which highlights one of Chamberlain's greatest weaknesses, but in the short-term it also reflected a vital strength in difficult circumstances.

The sheer scale of the political and administrative challenge posed by housing policy was truly formidable given the existence of two fundamental and interlocking problems. First, the pressure of unfulfilled demand during the war had created an estimated deficit of 822,000 units (excluding the replacement need for unfit dwellings) by the time Chamberlain became Health Minister in March 1923, despite the construction of 252,000 houses since 1919.[16] Second, these shortages were compounded by the effects of the Increase of Rent and Mortgage Interest (War Restrictions) Act in 1915, which had fixed most rents at the level prevailing at the outbreak of war or their first wartime letting. Although these restrictions successfully defused discontent and rent strikes in centres of war production, they also trapped later governments in a vicious spiral which militated against any easy resolution of the housing problem. Thus, on one hand, it was politically impossible to repeal rent restrictions because the acute shortage of houses would immediately produce a catastrophic increase in rents. On the other hand, however, by removing all prospect of a reasonable profit, rent controls acted as a major disincentive to speculative builders and investors who might otherwise have entered the market to satisfy the demand for low cost working class housing for rent. Little wonder that soon after becoming Minister of Health Chamberlain had compared housing to 'a skein of wool inextricably entangled so that they could not find the end to begin unwinding'.[17] Against a background of severe electoral discontent about the uncertainty of future policy towards rent restrictions, Chamberlain was thus scarcely exaggerating when he claimed that 'it seems my fate to be given the most dangerous and responsible position in the front line and probably the fate of the Govt will depend upon poor me'.[18]

Far from being daunted by the task, Chamberlain rejoiced that 'at the moment I hold the key position and they are bound to give me a pretty free hand'.

Moreover, given a high level of parliamentary ignorance about the complexities of the housing problem he expected 'to be able to do as well as most & better than Bosky (which isn't saying much)'.[19] Although conceited, this was no more than the truth. Since its creation in December 1922, the Cabinet's housing committee had been far more strongly influenced by Chamberlain's perceptions of problems and responses than by those of Boscawen, the nominal Minister of Health, who Chamberlain suspected was 'grasping about without any fixed ideas and always to be influenced by the last person who has spoken to him'.[20] Sweeping aside Boscawen's doubts about the reintroduction of a subsidy for new houses at their first meeting on 8 December, within a month Chamberlain had persuaded the committee that the subsidy should take the form of a fixed financial liability for the State over a set period because, whatever the economic and political objections, 'the Government cannot simply allow things to remain as they are, trusting to private enterprise and the unaided effort of local authorities gradually to right the problem'.[21] The Cabinet formally endorsed the Chamberlain proposals at the end of January, although it was agreed they should lay 'as much stress as possible on the importance of stimulating private enterprise'.[22]

The Housing Bill which Chamberlain introduced to the Commons on 11 April was a financially far more conservative measure than that championed by Addison in 1919. It also clearly reflected Chamberlain's belief that the housing shortage was an essentially temporary problem created by the dislocation of private building caused by the war and the effects of Lloyd George's 'People's Budget' in 1909.[23] Although Chamberlain's Act retained Addison's principle of subsidised house building, its central objective was to 'get rid of the unlimited liability of the State for all losses exceeding the produce of a 1d rate on housing schemes ... carried out by Local Authorities' with which Addison had saddled the Coalition.[24] The Treasury subsidy was thus fixed at £6 per house per annum for 20 years, without requiring any accompanying rate subsidy and it applied to all houses built before October 1925, whether by local authorities or private enterprise and whether for rent or sale. Although the new subsidy was available on dwellings built within specified parameters of size and amenity, in practice the severity of these limitations led critics like Labour's John Wheatley to condemn Chamberlain's houses as squalid 'rabbit hutches' with rooms smaller than the desk on which the Bill had been drafted. In his own defence, however, Chamberlain replied that he had focused the subsidy on the cheapest housing to meet the greatest need within the community and in a manner which allowed local authorities 'a free hand as to the plans and construction'.[25]

Although the 1923 Housing Act represented an important legislative landmark by establishing the principle of fixed annual subsidies as the dominant method of central government support until the Housing Finance Act of 1972, it is important not to exaggerate its novelty – particularly as the underlying idea had first been proposed by Sir Alfred Mond, Addison's successor at the Ministry of Health. On the other hand, however, Chamberlain can claim considerable credit for persuading the Cabinet and the Treasury to accept this approach at all rather than Boscawen's alternative policy which rejected a subsidy in favour of rate-exemption. Furthermore, at his first Cabinet as Minister of Health Chamberlain also persuaded his colleagues of the political benefits of accepting the local authority demand for an annual subsidy of £6 over 20 years to win their goodwill rather than the £4 basis on which negotiations had previously been conducted.[26]

The 1923 Housing Act embodied some eminently Conservative principles – albeit reflecting a significantly less radical solution than Chamberlain had advocated during the housing debates of 1919–20. Above all, the emphasis was now upon the restoration of private enterprise as the principal source of working class housing, while the Act equally resolutely closed the door on Addison's fundamental objective of making public housing a species of social service to be met principally by local authority provision. To this end, local authorities were permitted to build only if they could convince the Minister that they could do so better than private enterprise or to meet an unfulfilled need. The Act was also designed to promote the vision of owner-occupation which Chamberlain had championed with the Housing Bank concept in Birmingham and as a lifelong supporter of the building societies movement. As he had famously written in 1920, 'every spadeful of manure dug in, every fruit tree planted converted a potential revolutionary into a citizen'.[27] To make owner-occupation possible, local authorities were empowered to provide payment guarantees and loans to those unable to provide the initial deposit necessary to obtain a building society mortgage. On this basis, by 1925 he was already rejoicing that the Act was 'building up a whole new class of good citizens'.[28] As such, it did much to give substance to the Conservative notion of a 'property-owning democracy' popularised by Anthony Eden after 1945.

More vexatious and intractable problems arose over the future of the wartime rent controls which were due to expire in 1923. In the hope of influencing three ministerial by-elections in which the issue appeared crucial, in February 1923 the Cabinet had agreed hastily to end all rent controls by June 1925.[29] Dissatisfied with this rash commitment formulated in panic, Chamberlain had insisted on a free hand to reconsider this policy as a condition for his acceptance of the post.[30] As he recognised that rent restrictions could never be abolished until a sufficient increase in the housing stock rendered such controls unnecessary in a free market, this implied the need for a short-term method of stabilising the rent situation until his Housing Act expanded the supply of working class housing. His initial preference was thus for a gradual relaxation of restrictions over a five or possibly ten year period, in the belief that this offered some degree of certainty about the future, while progressively reducing the scope of the controls until they could finally be abolished; a measure which represented an 'equitable compromise' between the interests of the landlord seeking free market rents and tenants anxious to avoid exploitation and hardship.[31] The Rent and Mortgage Interest Restrictions Bill introduced on 20 May thus extended the existing legislation until mid-1925 with certain modifications. Although he expected a further extension of five years before a complete return to free market rents, in the event, the persistence of the housing problem obliged the Conservatives to continue the Act periodically until the entire scheme was revised in 1933.

II

Chamberlain's brief term at the Ministry of Health was one of frenetic activity and remarkable legislative success. Beside highly controversial Bills on housing and rent restrictions, others dealt with agricultural rates, the abatement of smoke nuisance and the regulation of the manufacture, sale and importation of vaccines liable to dangerous contamination. In addition, Chamberlain wrestled with the equally complex and contentious problems of rating and valuation reform, the refusal to provide additional grants for the relief of Poor Law Unions in 'necessitous areas' and the most effective response to the overspending of the Poplar Board of Guardians in flagrant disregard of government instructions. He also maintained a heavy burden of visits to hospitals and sanatoria, promoted a visionary scheme for medical education which eventually came to fruition a decade later in a postgraduate medical school in London and discussed all manner of other health issues with his Chief Medical Officer.[32] With such experience came a greater feeling of authority. 'He has gained in confidence and speaks in a stronger voice and with an ease which ensures the comfort of the listener', Austen noted after one 'admirable' speech in June. 'I hear on all hands that his management of the Housing Bill in Comtee, has been perfect. We can all be very happy in his success.'[33] At a more general level, Chamberlain also rightly believed he could claim much of the personal credit for having dispelled the sense of crisis, failure and despondency which had blighted the early months of the Conservative government.[34]

Ultimately, it was a perverse indication of this proven success that during the parliamentary recess in August Chamberlain was unceremoniously plucked from a job he loved to become Chancellor of the Exchequer. This represented an astonishingly rapid promotion and a great personal tribute, but it was also a profoundly unwelcome personal development. Soon after his election in 1918, Chamberlain had declined a seat on the prestigious parliamentary committee on national expenditure on the grounds that his 'forte [was] more in construction than in critical work'.[35] Similarly, in May 1923, press speculation about his appointment to the Exchequer again prompted the confession that 'it is an office which I should particularly dislike, quite apart from my objection to be continually pulled up by the roots. I never could understand finance, and moreover I should hate a place whose main function was to put spokes in other people's wheels.'[36] When Reginald McKenna, a former Liberal Chancellor, finally declined to accept the Exchequer in mid-August, however, Baldwin immediately offered it to a despondent Chamberlain.

'What a day!' Chamberlain replied to Baldwin's request by return of post from Scotland. 'Two salmon this morning, and the offer of the Exchequer this afternoon!' But while thanking him for 'the greatest compliment I ever received in my life', he firmly declined with the protest that 'I do not feel that I have any gifts for finance … and I fear that as Chancellor I should not fulfil your expectations.'[37] Despite this very definite refusal, however, Baldwin persisted in a telegram which acknowledged Chamberlain's reasons but stressed that his own were 'overwhelming'.[38] Rather than risk the discourtesy of a further refusal by telegram, Chamberlain reluctantly gave up the last two days of his fishing holiday to meet Baldwin at Downing Street on the morning of 24 August. After brushing aside all objections, Baldwin declared that as Chamberlain enjoyed the confidence and respect of both the Commons and the City he was the ideal candidate. He then put the decisive argument:

> Baldwin had felt very much the absence of a colleague living under the same roof with whom he could discuss affairs at any time and every moment. An association of this kind had always been customary and to be deprived of it was like losing one hand. Its success depended on personal qualities and he would rather have me than any of his colleagues in the Cabinet.

As Chamberlain later explained, if it had simply been a matter of promotion and glory he would have refused in an instant, but when put in these personal terms, 'it appeared to me that I should be acting contrary to the principles which have hitherto always guided me in public matters if I declined to accept the responsibility'.[39]

By any standard, Chamberlain's rise from the backbenches to Chancellor and second place in the government in little more than nine months was truly meteoric. As a former colleague from Birmingham and National Service quipped, his congratulations on Chamberlain's successive promotions 'follow each other so rapidly now that I am thinking of having a letter printed!'[40] To some degree, this advancement was undoubtedly assisted by the fortuitous circumstances created by the Carlton Club revolt and the absence of many more experienced ministerial candidates. Yet this should not obscure the importance of Chamberlain's personal achievement in winning this promotion. Baldwin was almost certainly unaware that Chamberlain had privately favoured Curzon's claims to the Premiership over his own in May; a preference which rested largely on the belief that Curzon would allow his ministers a free hand in domestic policy rather than because he favoured the return of Austen and his coalitionist following to the Cabinet.[41] But whether Baldwin knew this or not, he had already formed a high opinion of Chamberlain's abilities and his 'admirable' parliamentary performance.[42] Countering Chamberlain's protests about his desire to remain at Health, Baldwin thus pointed out that he had brought this predicament upon himself through this proven skill over recent months. As Lord Curzon encapsulated the prevailing view, during his short ministerial career Chamberlain had demonstrated 'qualities and abilities which would be a source of strength to any Government and indeed raise you by a natural process to the highest responsibilities'.[43]

Since being uprooted from the Post Office, Chamberlain had resigned himself 'to put aside all regrets for what might have been and only to look forward to the possibilities of my new office'. Nevertheless, this did not prevent a brief lament about the 'unkind fate' which denied him the opportunity to implement any constructive reforms; regrets widely echoed by despondent officials at the Ministry of Health. 'The blow to us is a very heavy one', declared his Permanent Secretary, who felt that he had been deprived of a minister who was genuinely capable of achieving the great programme of reform Chamberlain had sketched out shortly before leaving for Scotland. 'We all loved working under you and to a man we are grateful to you for leading us so splendidly and giving us that measure of appreciation which makes work so much easier and pleasant. I was often reminded of your father under whom I was fortunate enough to learn the first lessons in statecraft.'[44]

III

Although keenly aware of his 'privileged position vis-à-vis the P.M.', Chamberlain freely confessed that he was '*very* frightened at the financial part and that my knees knock together when I think of addressing "City men"!'[45] In the event, however, Chamberlain's brief first period at the Treasury between August 1923 and January 1924 was remarkable only for its lack of any significant departmental achievement. Excluding Iain Macleod, whose tenure of the office was cut short by his sudden death after less than a month, Chamberlain's was the shortest Chancellorship since Sir Robert Peel in 1834–35 and he was one of only four Chancellors not to introduce a Budget; perhaps a fortunate outcome given the 'extremely unpromising' budgetary situation. 'We are not yet out of the wood', he gloomily informed a Birmingham audience in mid-October. 'We have in front of us a weary, perhaps an exhausting struggle, and you have got to set your teeth and go through with it as you went through bad times in the war.'[46]

Yet despite the paucity of departmental initiatives, Chamberlain did play a significant, if sometimes misunderstood, role in Baldwin's ill-fated decision to resurrect tariff reform in October 1923. Standing amid the ruins of Bonar Law's majority for 'tranquillity' after the December 1923 election, stunned observers inevitably searched for scapegoats for the disaster which had befallen them. Curzon and the Earl of Crawford believed the 'evil geniuses' were 'the whipper snappers in the Cabinet, Amery, Lloyd-Greame, and I believe N. Chamberlain'.[47] George Younger in a 'graphic ac[count]' for Herbert Gladstone made 'Davison [sic] the real villain of the piece with Neville Chamberlain as a leading actor, Amery and others chipping in.'[48] Given his past antipathy it was not surprising that Auckland Geddes also named Chamberlain as the principal instigator and Lord Derby subsequently concurred.[49] In retrospect, it is easy to understand why suspicion fell on Chamberlain and the other leading ministerial tariff reformers with whom Baldwin had closeted himself in the fortnight leading up to his disastrous declaration to the party conference at Plymouth on 25 October. In the case of Amery and Sir Philip Lloyd-Greame, there was some substance in the allegation. In contrast, however, Chamberlain represented a consistent brake upon Baldwin's ill-considered ambitions for an early election and he played a curiously indirect role in the disaster which befell the party.

Contrary to David Dilks' supposition that 'it is scarcely conceivable that Baldwin would have pressed Neville Chamberlain so hard to take the Treasury without some thought of the consequences for tariff reform',[50] there is absolutely no evidence to confirm either that Baldwin had decided on such a policy departure at this juncture or that Chamberlain's fiscal predilections were a substantial factor in his appointment. Like the free trade McKenna to whom Baldwin had offered it previously, Chamberlain's principal claim to the Treasury rested upon his proven ability and the public confidence this was likely to inspire in the absence of any other credible alternative. Although Amery had certainly 'rubbed in a bit of protection *à propos* of Neville's appointment' during a long walk with Baldwin at Aix-les-Bains in late August, in reality, Baldwin only gradually came to recognise that tariff reform offered a potential solution to his political problems.[51] Indeed, he probably did not embrace it privately until quite suddenly on 6 or 7 October when he crystallised his thoughts in some notes on unemployment.[52] As a result, Chamberlain was as surprised as everyone else when Baldwin suddenly made it clear what he had in mind.

On the night of 5 October Chamberlain had a 'lot of interesting talks' with Baldwin and was 'much encouraged' to find him 'very seriously considering the party policy and disposed to go a long way in the direction of new duties with preferences designed to help the Dominions to develop Empire cotton, sugar and tobacco'; a policy departure which Chamberlain 'warmly welcomed' as the 'salvation of the country & incidentally of the party'. At this stage, however, both men agreed that Bonar Law's 1922 election pledge against any radical fiscal change without a further mandate precluded food taxes but not a gradual extension of selective protective duties on manufactured goods.[53] As a result, Chamberlain was given to understand that Baldwin wanted to 'go in for a few extra duties in Nov[embe]r but to lead up by an education campaign to a more thorough going policy by the time we were ready for an election'. But less than two days after this conversation, Baldwin informed Stanley Jackson, the party chairman, that 'he thought it might be necessary to go in for general protection wh. wd. necessitate an early appeal to the country' and he enquired about his preparedness for a November election. When Jackson informed Chamberlain of these developments on 10 October, he thus found him more than a little surprised because Baldwin 'had not intended to go nearly as fast' five days earlier.[54]

It is possible that Baldwin had pursued a characteristically circumlocutory method of sounding Chamberlain about his plans on 5 October and that Chamberlain, already thinking in terms of an extended education campaign, simply misunderstood Baldwin's intentions. Yet this seems implausible – and the fact remains that Chamberlain learnt of these developments indirectly some two days after Baldwin had confided in Amery and Jackson; a curious oversight when Baldwin lived next door to Chamberlain, knew him to be an ardent tariff reformer and had less than two months before assured him that his judgement made him 'the "one man" to whom he felt he could entrust the Treasury'.[55] Nevertheless, having finally learned of the plan, Chamberlain became one of the 'inner circle' concerting strategy, although perhaps less intimately involved with Baldwin than either Amery or Lloyd-Greame.[56]

Although enthusiastic about the adoption of tariff protection, from the outset Chamberlain consistently urged the need to avoid any declaration at the party conference which would provoke speculation about an early election before either an education campaign could be conducted or the details of the policy were agreed. Moreover, despite pressure from Amery and Lloyd-Greame who wanted 'a tariff declared at once', virtually unanimous pleas for caution soon induced 'a very worried' Baldwin 'to water down the proposals considerably' along the lines suggested by Chamberlain.[57] At Cabinet on 23 and 29 October, the Chamberlain strategy was thus enshrined in the agreement 'to confine action during the Autumn Session to an extension of the McKenna duties ... but to take the verdict of the country within six months'.[58] As Chamberlain told his half-brother, without food taxes it was 'not the *whole* hog but it is the major part of the animal and the only way of getting a fair bite at what remains'.[59]

Baldwin's speech for the Conservative party conference at Plymouth on 25 October had been consciously designed with this objective in mind. As Baldwin told Winston Churchill shortly before the speech and Sir William Bull immediately after it, he was simply putting out a 'feeler'.[60] Moreover, if the eye-witness testimony of the 'inner circle' is to be believed, Baldwin succeeded in relation to his own supporters. As Chamberlain encapsulated the general view, Baldwin had been 'sufficiently definite to please our people but ... vague enough to leave the country undisturbed at the thought of an election in the very near future'.[61] But, ironically, the free trade parties almost immediately interpreted the Plymouth speech as a breach of Bonar Law's pledge and the prelude to an election campaign. Moreover, despite David Dilks' claim to the contrary, in many ways it was Chamberlain's speech to a simultaneous overflow meeting at Plymouth in which he 'dotted the i's on T[ariff] R[eform]' which fuelled most speculation about an early election.[62] In an otherwise cautious speech, Chamberlain's declaration that an adequate response to unemployment over the next winter would require the government to be released from Bonar Law's pledge, unwittingly negated the effect of Baldwin's carefully worded personal declaration and contributed significantly to the revival of tariff reform as an immediate focus for political controversy. Indeed, although he believed his speech 'has pleased our people & not frightened the country', even *The Times*, which had been remarkably authoritative in its pronouncements throughout, interpreted Chamberlain's speech to mean 'a definite decision on the part of the Cabinet to go to the country on the question of Tariff Reform'.[63] After this, it swiftly became apparent that the government was losing the initiative. Convinced that the policy could only be saved by snatching victory before the free trade parties could mobilise fully, on 11 November it was decided to hold an election in early December.

In Ladywood, Chamberlain's appeal was deliberately contrived to be reminiscent of his father's pre-war tariff campaign with its slogans about 'keeping British work for British workers' and the need to 'Make the Foreigner Pay'.[64] In contrast, Dr Dunstan, Chamberlain's left-wing Labour opponent, preferred to fight the election on the class war. In particular, he pointed to the adverse effects of the Rent Restrictions Act on Ladywood's working class voters and blamed Chamberlain personally for large rent increases and mass evictions; a campaign theme accompanied by organised Labour rowdyism worse than that witnessed in any other Birmingham constituency except Deritend.[65] As a result, on the eve of the poll, Chamberlain confessed that his agent had 'got the wind up badly'. In the event, Chamberlain held the seat with a reduced majority of only 1554; an outcome which convinced him that it was 'almost impossible to hold that seat much longer'.[66] Although Birmingham remained true to its Chamberlainite protectionist heritage by returning Conservatives for all twelve seats for the third time in succession, in the country as a whole the Conservatives remained the largest party but they were deprived of both their overall majority and their mandate for fiscal change.

IV

Chamberlain attributed defeat to the inadequacies of the voters rather than to the government's poor strategy. 'The new electorate contains an immense number of very ignorant voters … whose intelligence is low and who have no power of weighting evidence', he recorded in his diary. 'These voters could not grasp the idea of better employment & wages as springing from a tariff. All they could understand was that a tariff would increase the cost of what they had to buy and they repeated in their dull way that they couldn't afford to pay more.' Although defeat came as an unwelcome surprise and a painful personal blow, however, Chamberlain did not subscribe to general fears about the prospect of a minority Labour government supported by Liberal votes in the Commons. On the contrary, he positively favoured the idea on the grounds that 'they would be too weak to do much harm but not too weak to get discredited'. Convinced that nothing would more effectively undermine Labour's electoral appeal or the credibility of its propaganda about unemployment than a prophylactic dose of Labour government, he thus confidently reassured the faint-hearted that 'The country has asked for it and now it must see what it tastes like.' As he told the Birmingham Conservative and Unionist Association, a Labour government was regrettable but unavoidable and it 'could not have come in under less advantageous circumstances to themselves' because office would be likely to split Labour and damage Liberal credibility, while the absence of an overall majority effectively precluded a capital levy or other dangerously radical reforms.[67]

While in many respects this was a prudent judgement, the loss of power and the transition to Opposition brought with it some distinctly adverse consequences for Neville Chamberlain. This was particularly so with regard to his relationship with Baldwin, which became progressively more remote and strained as the year progressed. In mid-January, Sir Warren Fisher, Chamberlain's very supportive Permanent Secretary at the Treasury, had a revealing conversation with both men which throws much light upon their relationship. First, he impressed upon Baldwin 'the necessity of having in Opposition a lieutenant on whom he could rely' and pressed the claims of Chamberlain as 'the one man whose motives were disinterested & whose judgement could be relied upon'. Convinced that Baldwin agreed but would not act upon this suggestion, Fisher then urged Chamberlain 'to go against your own inclinations and operate on him or you will find him with his inability to make up his mind vacillating till the last moment & then having it made up for him by the coarse fibred energetic selfseekers'. Most instructive about this incident is the fact that Chamberlain recognised that Fisher was right in both assessments. 'I feel myself so totally unable to follow his advice', he recorded in his diary. 'I am not and never can be a pusher though I might act for a brief period like one by a great effort.' Unfortunately, having resolved to act on Fisher's advice to persuade Baldwin to call a party meeting, his efforts were received 'without any comment' and a bemused Chamberlain was left unable to determine whether he had made any impression at all. After this, however, while he noted that Baldwin appeared 'rather depressed', it also became increasingly apparent that he deeply resented Chamberlain's reluctant efforts to galvanise him into decisive leadership. Whatever the reason, by June Chamberlain complained that 'I see a good deal less of him than I did & he doesn't seem so much in need of council [sic] as when he was in office.'[68]

In the immediate aftermath of defeat, Chamberlain was also compelled to make some unpalatable doctrinal compromises about the future of tariff reform. By the time the Cabinet met to discuss the King's speech on 18 December, only Chamberlain, Amery and Bridgeman continued to believe 'it would be the greatest mistake in the world to show anything like weakening on protection'. At this juncture, Chamberlain confidently anticipated 'SB will declare his continued belief in Protection and his readiness to make way for someone else if the Party does not agree.'[69] Instead, however, the 'three Cabinet extremists',[70] found themselves isolated by more pragmatic ministerial protectionists who argued that the Conservatives could not win another election on the existing tariff programme. Despite his initial resistance to this retreat, over the next month Chamberlain's soundings of party opinion also led him to the reluctant conclusion that 'Education must … precede resurrection', because they did not want 'to be tied up to putting it in the foreground having got a bad scare at the last election.' Although disappointed by the prospect of a more limited commitment to the piecemeal protection of individual industries, Chamberlain recognised that this was the most they could achieve if they were to 'satisfy everyone sufficiently to keep the party together'.[71] On the other hand, however, he still joined Amery and Sir Henry Page Croft in attempting to launch the

Fair Trade Union as a new propagandist organisation designed to educate the country on lines similar to the Tariff Reform League; a body which eventually became the Empire Industries Association.

Despite this policy defeat, Chamberlain simultaneously scored a notable success when he single-handedly engineered the party's reunion with his half-brother and his coalitionist supporters. After Baldwin's disastrous meeting with Austen on the subject in May, Chamberlain had impressed upon him that 'if he ever did wish to approach A[usten] again he might remember that I was at his service, that I understood A. & might perhaps save such needless wounding of feelings again'.[72] When a second attempt at reunion failed on the eve of the election because of party opposition to the return of the despised Lord Birkenhead, Austen had lapsed into a sullen and uncooperative mood. Nevertheless, he played little active part in coalitionist plots to oust Baldwin in the immediate aftermath of defeat, while the 'concentrated bitterness' of his speech denouncing Liberal support for a Labour government when Parliament reassembled on 21 January placed him 'once again in the odour of sanctity' with the party.[73] On this basis, Chamberlain impressed upon his frontbench colleagues that the time had come for reunion and that as Austen remained loyal to the detested Birkenhead 'there was a general feeling that if it were necessary it was better to have FE [Smith, Lord Birkenhead] in than A[usten] or Horne out'.[74] After privately conciliating the principal opponents of reunion, Chamberlain then arranged a secret dinner at his own house on 5 February to consummate the reunion. Having 'carefully coached SB as to what to say' to avoid further offence and misunderstanding, to Chamberlain's 'great satisfaction' Baldwin then said 'what he had to say without any beating about the bush and after one moment's hesitation A[usten] frankly accepted the invitation. After that all went like clockwork and very soon it was My dear Stanley and My dear Austen as if they had ne'er been parted.' Two days later, the Tory coalitionist ex-ministers returned to the Conservative Shadow Cabinet in an atmosphere of 'marked affability'.[75]

Despite his satisfaction at the achievement of Conservative reunion, Chamberlain was much less happy with the consequences of his half-brother's political rehabilitation. At the frontbench meeting on 7 February, Baldwin almost immediately abdicated control of the discussion to Austen who then declared that outright protectionism should be abandoned on the grounds that their first objective should be to 'smash the Liberal Party' and 'repeat the history of Liberal-Unionism' by absorbing those sympathetic Liberals who remained.[76] Neville Chamberlain was even less pleased to find that Austen and his allies intended to give substance to this strategy by supporting Churchill's candidature as an 'Independent Anti-Socialist' in the Westminster Abbey by-election against an official Conservative candidate in one of the safest Tory seats in Britain. Sensitive to the prospect of a further dilution of Conservative doctrinal purity after his defeat over tariffs in January, Chamberlain was adamantly opposed to Austen's general strategy and he specifically denounced Churchill's candidature as 'a great mistake'. 'It would be said by our party, we always knew what "taking in"

F.E. would mean. Here comes Winston; Lloyd George will be after him directly & we shall be back in Coalition again.' As Churchill was 'intensely unpopular' in the country and 'profoundly mistrusted by the working class', his return to the Conservative fold also threatened to 'drive the Labour moderates into the arms of the extremists'. Anyway, he feared that the still nominally Liberal Churchill had little real sympathy with Conservative ideas and was 'such a pronounced Free Trader' that he would be a 'disturbing and disruptive force' likely to 'push his own ideas aggressively' to the detriment of party cohesion. Above all, Chamberlain recognised that Churchill's return was likely to 'drive a wedge under the Protection door which would fasten it up hermetically and finally he would begin inevitably to intrigue for the leadership'.[77]

When Chamberlain told his sisters that Baldwin had 'not been fortunate in his handling' of the Abbey candidature he was exercising a remarkable degree of self-control. Throughout these chaotic events, Chamberlain believed the only proper course was to support the official Conservative candidate. Instead, he complained bitterly that 'S.B. has been at his worst in this business – incapable of making up his mind and continuously vacillating'; a failure of leadership he attributed to Baldwin's evident depression and the fact he 'was so anxious lest he should divide the party that he hesitated to commit himself in public'.[78] If this was Baldwin's intention, his strategy collapsed in disarray at a frontbench meeting on 6 March at which Austen became 'angry and excited' and threatened to speak for Churchill if Neville or Amery spoke for his official Conservative opponent.[79] After Churchill's narrow defeat Chamberlain resolutely opposed any working arrangement with either him or his Liberal following except as formal converts to Conservatism; an intransigence which provoked further sharp words between the two brothers. Coming so soon after his defeat over the retention of the tariff, however, Chamberlain's inability to uphold his view over Churchill's candidacy compelled him briefly to recognise the limitations on his own influence within the leadership.

Despite these disappointments and rebuffs, Chamberlain emerged from this Opposition period during 1924 stronger than he had gone into it. In the Commons, he certainly consolidated his rising stature as a parliamentary leader and tactician of formidable talents. In practice, this often simply meant a devastating attack on the Labour government to the delight of Conservative backbenchers. On 2 April he thus launched a ferocious assault on the capital levy, denouncing it as 'the biggest electoral bribe that has ever been offered'. At the same time, Wheatley's Bill to prevent evictions where these were due to unemployment was subjected to withering sarcasm when Chamberlain claimed the principle that 'My need is greater than thine' could be extended by unemployed workers to the produce of the baker, butcher, grocer and even to Wheatley's own coat.[80] At the end of May Chamberlain further heartened his own backbenchers by attacking Philip Snowden's Finance Bill for the 'narrow pedantry that adheres to doctrinaire opinion divorced from reality'. 'He spoke of my "superabundance of spite & spleen" and my "vitriolic rhetoric" till I felt quite above myself', Chamberlain cheerfully recorded of the Chancellor's remarks after the debate. At other times, however, the objective was more subtle as the Conservatives continued to make a show of trying to expel the Labour government while tacitly ensuring it did not fall; a strategy designed to place all the odium for keeping Labour in power firmly upon the Liberals in the hope of splitting their parliamentary party and producing a disastrous collapse in their electoral support.[81]

In marked contrast with his usual tactics, Chamberlain's response to Wheatley's Housing Bill was rather more complex. Wheatley had savaged Chamberlain's Housing Act for its short duration, the niggardly scale of its subsidy and for its focus on private building for sale rather than to let at rents the working class could afford. At the heart of Wheatley's own Housing Bill was a larger subsidy of £9 per house per annum for 40 years for houses to let. He also extended Chamberlain's scheme until 1939. Contrary to the claim that Wheatley's Act was really Chamberlain's except for the finance,[82] however, it crucially reversed Chamberlain's retreat from Addison's 1919 emphasis by restoring the position of local authorities as the principal provider of working class council housing as a social service; a principle reaffirmed in Chamberlain's consolidating Housing Act of 1925 and which no subsequent government was prepared openly to challenge until the 1980s.

Contemptuous of Wheatley's intelligence, his ministerial competence and the underlying objectives of his legislation, Chamberlain subjected his Housing Bill to such a devastating forensic critique on 4 June that Wheatley was forced to concede that he could not 'undergo a catechism' on the precise details of his own legislation; a fatal admission which prompted Chamberlain to remark acidly that Wheatley was 'in need of sympathy, for the minister does not himself seem to know what is the type of house on which he has based the most fundamental part of his scheme'. He was equally dismissive of the market logic underpinning Wheatley's Building Materials (Charges and Supply) Bill on the same day designed to prevent profiteering; an attack hailed by *The Times* as 'a deadly analysis of his proposals ... by one who knew the subject from the first to last letter of the alphabet'.[83] But rather than alienate public opinion by negative parliamentary criticism and obstructionism on a crucial national issue, Chamberlain believed the only safe course was to kill the Wheatley Housing Bill with kindness. Convinced that it was 'fundamentally rotten and the sooner it fails the better', he thus cynically posed as a reasonable critic in the hope of highlighting the Bill's defects while refusing to improve it through amendments or constructive dialogue with the minister.[84] In the event, 15,800 private and 504,500 local authority houses were built under the Wheatley Act between 1924 and 1934 compared with 362,700 private and 75,300 council houses constructed under Chamberlain's Act during its shorter life from 1923–29. As many of these houses were beyond the pockets of those most in need, however, neither Act really resolved the central problem they sought to overcome.[85]

Alongside his success in demolishing the keystone of Labour's legislative programme, Chamberlain simultaneously played a far more constructive role in outlining the 'new Conservatism' which emerged during 1924 to fill the void left by the suspension of tariff reform. Pressure for a restatement of the party's programme was already apparent when the Conservatives went into Opposition. Above all, Chamberlain noted the party was 'getting very impatient at our lack of a social programme'.[86] To satisfy these demands a Leaders' Conference met for the first time on 2 April to 'decide larger questions of policy', while a parallel Standing Conference of ex-ministers from the Commons organised sub-committees on the Cabinet committee model. The statement of *Aims and Principles* which emerged from these deliberations was in gestation for only two months and overwhelmingly reflected Chamberlain's policy dominance and social reforming preoccupations. On 15 April in Chamberlain's absence, the Commons Standing Committee had agreed that a draft statement prepared by Curzon 'would serve admirably for a comprehensive review of policy'.[87] Chamberlain, however, had other ideas. Rejecting all the earlier drafts as unsatisfactory, he then produced his own 'authoritative statement of the attitude of the Unionist Party towards the main political questions of the day' which the Leaders' Conference accepted on 1 May after 'the usual somewhat desultory discussion'.[88]

Chamberlain's statement was as comprehensive as it was deliberately unspectacular. Abroad, it committed the Party to strengthen and develop the Empire, to work towards gradual Indian self-government, to protect Irish Loyalists and to defend British interests in Egypt and the Sudan. There were also declarations in favour of honouring the post-war treaties, support for the League of Nations and a vague suggestion of arms limitation, although again only insofar as was compatible with British interests. At home, there were references to co-partnership in industry, abolition of the trade union political levy to the Labour party, greater assistance for agriculture, housing, pensions, temperance without compulsion and the cause of ex-servicemen and Lords reform.[89] In short, therefore, *Aims and Principles* provided a statement of good intentions skilfully appropriated as the exclusive preserve of Conservatism.

Chamberlain was pleased with the public response to *Aims and Principles*, but many other Conservatives despaired that there 'never was a more colourless document'. The veteran tariff reformer, William Hewins, thought it 'deplorable' and symptomatic of the party's decline into 'a sort of amiable dotage'. From the other end of the fiscal spectrum, Lord Robert Cecil was equally pessimistic when he declared, 'I hope it pleases someone but I really don't know who.'[90] Yet in drafting *Aims and Principles* Chamberlain had never intended to excite political histrionics. At the Hotel Cecil in February the general tariff had been abandoned as the central plank in the Conservative platform in favour of something less disruptive; *Aims and Principles* spelt out in simple terms Chamberlain's vision of this alternative foundation for popular Conservatism defined in terms of political stability, financial prudence and social reform. With it, the age of modified 'tranquillity' had dawned, with Baldwin as its articulator and living expression and Neville Chamberlain as its principal architect and policy inspiration.

V

Despite these plans for a return to government, throughout 1924 the vigour of Labour campaigning in Ladywood ensured that Chamberlain remained anxious about the next election. As he warned the Birmingham Unionist Association after the 1922 election, 'conditions were now very different to what they had been in the days of his father, when his personal influence had been so overwhelming that there was really no need for organisation'. They now faced more determined socialist opponents whose remorseless propaganda 'exploited the sufferings of the poor, setting class against class, and particularly appealed to the out-of-works who were in such a hopeless state that they were ready to believe that their sufferings were due to political causes'.[91] As one of the poorer constituencies in the city, Ladywood was particularly vulnerable to this sort of Labour campaigning. Alarmed by the narrowness of Chamberlain's majority in 1922 and 1923, in January 1924 the constituency executive confessed it 'was looking with a certain amount of anxiety to the next election'.[92] It was a measure of Chamberlain's own alarm that early in 1924 he seriously considered the possibility of switching to the far safer middle class Edgbaston constituency, but the inevitable allegation of 'desertion in the face of the enemy' precluded the option.[93]

The defection of Dr Dunstan to the Communist Party in July and the collapse of the Labour government in October, briefly encouraged Chamberlain's hopes that the election would come before a new Labour challenger had time to dig in. Unfortunately, the ambitious Oswald Mosley proved a formidable Labour adversary and Ladywood became the cockpit of a particularly dirty campaign. After disappointing indications earlier in the day, Chamberlain attended the count prepared 'to face the worst with calmness', for although he 'hated the thought of being beaten ... by that viper', there was the consolation that he could fall back upon Edgbaston. In the event, however, after five recounts Chamberlain was finally declared the victor by 77 votes amidst scenes of exceptional rowdiness stirred up by Mosley.[94] Convinced that next time the seat would be lost, Chamberlain accepted the Edgbaston invitation when it was formally offered by his cousin in July 1926. At the next general election in 1929, Ladywood was lost to Labour by eleven votes.

In the wake of the Conservative electoral landslide in October 1924, Chamberlain rejoiced at the return to office and the resumption of a relatively lucrative ministerial salary to dispel increasing financial worries at a time when even Hoskins now recorded a substantial loss; a development which caused 'a certain amount of anxiety' as it provided 'a considerable share of the family income'.[95] On a strictly commercial basis he had even agreed in September to write an article for a Harmsworth encyclopaedia on 'Personality and the Equipment for Success' simply to earn the proffered 'thirty pieces of silver', although he soon concluded that it would take a lot of writing to generate a significant contribution to income at a time when he was forced to pay supertax out of capital.[96] Confronting the prospect of 'a very lean period for some little while ahead' at Hoskins, Chamberlain confessed 'I am thankful to have got a salary or I should be in the soup.'[97]

Yet relief at his ministerial salary was nothing compared with the reinvigorating opportunity to achieve worthwhile reforms. 'Lord!' he wrote to his sisters shortly afterwards, 'it is interesting being in office again and everyone tells me how remarkably fit I look!' Although aware that his supporters wanted him to accept the Treasury and that Baldwin would feel obliged to offer it to him, Chamberlain was determined that he should decline it in the belief that he 'might be a great Minister of Health but ... not likely to be more than a second rate Chancellor'.[98] In the event, when Baldwin offered Chamberlain the Treasury on 5 November, he was deeply touched by his leader's 'personal loyalty ... in that he actually did offer what he hoped but did not expect I should refuse'. Unfortunately, this affection soon turned to fury when he learned of Baldwin's 'incredible bungling' in appointing Churchill as Chancellor of the Exchequer without any further consultation with anyone. 'He is unfit to be leader, that is the long and short of it and I foresee splits in the Cabinet, resignations and the destruction of our great power before long!'[99] For his own part, however, while friends commended his 'public spirit and self-sacrifice', Chamberlain rejoiced in returning to his first love. Convinced that 'unless we leave our mark as social reformers the country will take it out of us hereafter', he immediately settled down to plan a four year programme of comprehensive social reform to give substance to the promise of the 'new Conservatism' he had formulated in Opposition.[100]

Chapter 6

The Ministry of Health,
November 1924–May 1929

'I haven't sacrificed anything that I care about [by declining the Treasury];
on the contrary I am grateful to you for letting me try my hand at solving
some very difficult but intrinsically interesting problems. With time, &
patience on the part of the public, I believe I may do something to improve
the condition for the less fortunate classes – and that's after all what we are
in politics for.'

> Chamberlain to Baldwin, 7 November 1924, Baldwin MSS 42/256

Neville Chamberlain's commitment to social reform was lifelong and sincere.
In his own terms, it was also privately passionate. Undoubtedly, the austere
persona suggested little love for his fellow man and Chamberlain's reforms
were often couched in the language of the bureaucratic rationaliser seemingly
more concerned with efficiency than the relief of human suffering – and many
at the time (and ever since) have taken him at face value. Yet beneath the harsh
exterior, Chamberlain was his father's son; a late-Victorian reformer motivated
by genuine humanitarian impulses and within whom individualism and
collectivism were in a state of continuous creative interaction. Such sympathies
had drawn him into association with the Unionist Social Reform Committee
before the Great War and they provided the moving spirit behind his social
programme during the inter-war period. Deeply touched by a tribute to his
many achievements in this field a month before his death, Chamberlain declared
that 'it was the hope of doing something to improve the conditions of life for the
poorer people that brought me at past middle life into politics, and it is some
satisfaction to me that I was able to carry out some part of my ambition'.[1] It was
undoubtedly the happiest and most fulfilling period of his ministerial career
and the culmination of everything for which he had previously striven.

Although the decision to sacrifice his claim to the most important ministerial
portfolio in the Cabinet for a far less important office appears to be a noble
and quixotic gesture, it never caused Chamberlain a moment's regret. It is true
that the Ministry of Health had experienced a rather chequered history since
its establishment in 1919 – not least because it had six ministers in only five
years before Chamberlain's return in November 1924. It is equally true that
Chamberlain had initially been deeply sceptical about the need for such a new
department when the idea was first mooted late in 1917.[2] By 1924, however,
Chamberlain recognised better than anyone else, the Ministry's vast potential

as an agency for radical reform. Moreover, it needs to be remembered that the Ministry of Health in the 1920s was a very different and far more broad-ranging department than its modern namesake. Indeed, in some respects it was the first modern 'super-ministry' long before Edward Heath conceived the notion in the early 1970s. The department which Chamberlain inherited thus encompassed not just every aspect of health, hospitals, sanitation, welfare and nursing but also old age pensions, health insurance, roads, housing and town planning along with the vast apparatus of the Poor Law and local government. It was a massive responsibility and during the 1920s Neville Chamberlain was perhaps uniquely qualified to make the most of the opportunities it offered.

Soon after the Conservative 1924 election landslide Lord Beaverbrook claimed that 'Britain has at last attained Bonar Law's ideal of tranquillity – under Baldwin. As long as the Conservative Government do nothing, they can go on for a very long time.'[3] Yet the idea that 'tranquillity' could be equated with legislative inertia had no part in Chamberlain's vision. At the Hotel Cecil meeting in February 1924, Baldwin had declared the Conservatives were 'not going to beat Labour on a policy of tranquillity, negation or sitting still. There is vitality in Labour … and unless we can share a vitality of that kind we shall be unable to conquer.'[4] Chamberlain was determined to provide much of the dynamic legislative force needed to make this a reality. Within two weeks of his appointment, he had presented a provisional programme to the Cabinet outlining 25 measures covering everything from reform of pensions, housing, rent restrictions, rating, the Poor Law and local government to legislation dealing with milk hygiene, the control of therapeutic substances, smoke abatement, the regulation of maternity homes and the registration of births, marriages and deaths.[5] By the time the second Baldwin government left office in May 1929 no fewer than 21 of these proposals had been passed. On these legislative foundations, Chamberlain rightly deserves his reputation as 'the most effective social reformer of the interwar years'.[6] As his private secretary later recalled, while Chamberlain actually did nothing that 'was not … in the stocks already', only his skill, determination and coherent vision of the larger picture enabled them to 'weld the whole lot of things together into a policy' capable of being carried in such a short time and with such far-reaching effects.[7]

Perhaps the most immediately popular of Chamberlain's social reforms was introduced during his first parliamentary session in the shape of the Widows', Orphans' and Old Age Contributory Pensions Act of 1925. Against a background of mounting pressure for some form of unified social insurance scheme, shortly before leaving office the first Baldwin government had established a committee of senior civil servants under Sir John Anderson to consider the options, including the idea of an 'all-in' scheme under which a flat-rate national insurance contribution covered not merely sickness and unemployment but old age, industrial accidents and support for widows and orphans. Their report in July 1924, dismissed ideas of 'all-in' insurance and a non-contributory scheme as too costly, but it proposed a less ambitious scheme of compulsory contributory pensions to cover widows, orphans and old age to which the State should be the principal contributor.[8] By this stage, however, in Opposition Chamberlain had already reached a similar conclusion as chairman of a party sub-committee on social insurance. Indeed, as early as March 1924 he argued there were 'four essentials for a satisfactory scheme. (1) It must be contributory (2) it must be compulsory (3) it must cover the 4 main needs for security, unemployment, sickness, old age & death leaving widows & dependents (4) the provision for old age must offer sufficient to induce the old men to retire.' Moreover, while he recognised the scheme 'bristles with difficulties', he was confident of its electoral potential and hoped that his draft for Baldwin's speech at Edinburgh on 24 March would at least 'peg out our claim to the ground before the others have had time to get in'.[9] Although the actuarial provisions still remained unresolved, therefore, in their October 1924 manifesto the Conservatives were committed to a contributory scheme integrating pensions for old age, widows and orphans 'as a right, for which payment has been made, instead of as a dole or a charity'.[10] Within a fortnight of entering office, Chamberlain had obtained Cabinet approval to translate his work in Opposition into an outline scheme.

Although Chamberlain had initially scheduled pension reform for 1926, at Churchill's instigation the measure was moved forward to 1925 on the grounds that it was 'a fence to jump at a gallop'.[11] In part, this was because it appeared to be a popular measure with the working class, capable of balancing the income tax cuts for the middle class planned for Churchill's first Budget. Yet pensions also satisfied Churchill's more fundamental desire for the government to leave behind it a number of 'big landmarks'; a priority which required it to 'concentrate on a few great issues in the social sphere … rather than fritter away our resources on a variety of services which, though possibly good in themselves, were not of vital national importance'. As he had to finance the scheme, within three weeks of coming to office he thus confidentially approached Chamberlain to 'enter partnership & work the plan with him'. In return, he promised to 'scratch & scrape & claw up everything he could in the way of money to help'. For the first, but by no means the last time, Chamberlain submitted to Churchill's implied blackmail in order to ease the passage of the measure. But as a worrying foretaste of future complications, Chamberlain also noted:

> It was curious how all through he showed how he was thinking of personal credit & it seemed plain to me that he regretted still that he was not Minister of Health. He spoke of the position. 'You are in the van. *You* can raise a monument. *You* can have a name in history etc …' A man of tremendous drive & vivid imagination but obsessed with the glory of doing something spectacular which should erect monuments to him.[12]

Although these ambitions would create almost insuperable obstacles for Chamberlain's plans for Poor Law reform in 1927–28, in the short term it proved a fruitful and harmonious union and by the end of March Chamberlain was convinced he had 'a good scheme' which was capable of making 'something of a sensation'.[13] Despite opposition from employer's organisations and the

Ministry of Labour who were both concerned about increased contributions while unemployment remained high, Chamberlain persisted for fear that their favourable political opportunity would be lost and the Cabinet Committee agreed to the final plan on 4 April.[14]

At the heart of Chamberlain's plan was a compulsory contributory scheme encompassing all those already covered by National Health Insurance. It offered old age pensions of ten shillings (50p) a week to insured men and their wives between 65 and 70 before they passed into the 1908 non-contributory scheme; widows also received ten shillings a week plus five shillings for their eldest child and three shillings for each subsequent child under 14. These pensions for existing widows and orphans came into force on 1 January 1926, but to spare the Treasury further cost, regular contributors were scheduled to receive the other benefits two years later, while the gradual shift of pension finance to a contributory basis was to be achieved through a decennial increase in contributions. Although a non-contributory scheme was excluded on strictly financial grounds, Chamberlain had inherited from his father the conviction that the principle itself was morally undesirable on the grounds that doles carried the stigma of pauperisation and undermined personal responsibility. Conversely, by 'rounding off the great insurance plan of 1911', he declared that his Bill completed what he called 'the circle of security for the worker'.[15]

Throughout the long and difficult passage of the Bill, Chamberlain demonstrated an unfailing mastery of the Commons and the complexities of the legislation. As Baldwin reported to the King, his speech on the Second Reading was 'a model in the art of exposition' and Chamberlain's references to his father's involvement with the subject 'struck a very happy note'. At other times, however, Chamberlain 'showed that when it comes to making war upon his opponents he is a keen and vigorous debater'. Having rejoiced when the Labour Opposition appeared 'thoroughly sick' at the announcement, Chamberlain savagely refuted Wheatley's false allegation that Labour planned a far more generous non-contributory scheme with a damning quotation from the former Labour Chancellor; a devastating attack resented all the more when delivered 'in those quiet and velvety tones which add effectiveness to his taunts'.[16] Similarly, when confronted by constant Labour obstructionism in early July, Chamberlain repeatedly exploited the Conservative majority to force the measure through while effectively blackmailing Labour to desist with the threat of blaming them for the postponement of the Bill and its benefits.[17] Despite further heated exchanges and much vexatious opposition, in the end Chamberlain's 'bland persuasiveness and unfailing courtesy and tact' combined with prudent concessions helped to create 'an atmosphere of conciliation and goodwill' which soothed the doubts of opponents on both sides of the House while winning the considerable admiration of Conservative MPs, the Cabinet and the Palace.[18]

Chamberlain's pension scheme was still far from an integrated and unified insurance scheme, but it was linked directly to National Health Insurance and it was sufficiently close to Beveridge's own 'all-in' plan for him to commend the Bill.[19] Yet although the measure made contributory insurance the customary vehicle for future social welfare, the final scheme introduced fewer radical changes than Chamberlain had initially intended. While it partially amalgamated two schemes of social security and extended it to widows, orphans and those aged 65–70, it excluded most employed women and all casual workers not covered by health insurance and it completely abandoned his initial hope to substitute a contributory scheme for its non-contributory predecessor. Accepting that ten shillings was 'the highest figure admissible on financial grounds', Chamberlain was also compelled to jettison his original proposal for pensions of 25 shillings.[20] As a result, the scheme was far from successful in alleviating economic hardship among the aged poor who were barely able to exist on pension rates which were not increased until 1940. But as the pragmatic Chamberlain always maintained, this was all national finances could stand and the only other option was nothing at all. Despite its deficiencies, therefore, Sam Hoare hailed the measure as 'Not only ... a great personal triumph for you but ... also a historic event in the development of Conservative policy.'[21]

II

Although the pensions legislation encountered opposition both in the Commons and from vested interests outside it, Chamberlain experienced far more difficulty with his other major measure of 1925. The Conservatives had planned to reform the machinery of rating and valuation while leaving the principles unchanged in 1923, but the government had fallen before it had time to do more than pass an Agricultural Rating Act in August. By March 1925, however, Chamberlain was pressing for immediate action to introduce essentially the same Rating and Valuation Bill given the length and complexity of its over seventy clauses and eight schedules. Part I of the Bill proposed the abolition of parochial rating in order to reduce the number of rating authorities from 12,844 to 648 in rural districts and from 2550 to 1148 in urban areas. In future, rating was to be concentrated in the larger local authorities as the 'real living bodies of today', while consolidating up to 20 different charges in some rural districts into a single 'general rate' for all local purposes. Part II sought to simplify the process of assessment and to introduce uniformity of practice without which it would be 'impossible to formulate any practicable scheme for the settlement of the vexed question of the relations between national and local taxation'.[22] By 29 April the Cabinet had approved the introduction of the Bill given the 'desirability of passing it during the present session of Parliament as an indispensable preliminary to the reform of the Poor Law and other portions of the Government's social reform policy'.[23]

While Chamberlain was convinced that 'when it has time to work the Party will point to it as one of the great reforms of which it can be proud', he always anticipated stiff opposition. Such fears were fully justified. Indeed, by the summer recess, he complained of 'unexpectedly fierce opposition in the country districts where all the vested interests of overseers & guardians & farmers who have up to now successfully wangled their own assessment in their own favour have now combined against us'.[24] Worse still, this resistance only encouraged the repeated faint-heartedness of the whips who regularly employed their almost unlimited 'powers of passive resistance' to obstruct a measure they rightly feared was unpopular with core supporters in the country. As a result, after a 'series of excursions and alarums' in April and May, efforts to force its complete withdrawal were only averted when Chamberlain stood firm with Baldwin's resolute support. In July, however, a meeting with anxious Conservative MPs persuaded Chamberlain to make significant concessions to save a measure essential for his planned reform of the Poor Law and local government. Only after further concessions to agricultural interests in October and a final appeal to a mass meeting of government backbenchers in late November was Chamberlain able to steady nerves sufficiently for the Bill to complete its passage in December.[25] It had been a severe ordeal, but given the heavy burden of steering this measure through the Commons in parallel with the Pensions Bill, Chamberlain had every right to feel considerable satisfaction at his success.

Rather less satisfactory progress was made with efforts to solve the housing shortage. By offering his subsidy over two years in the 1923 Housing Act, Chamberlain had acknowledged that it was essentially an interim measure designed to prevent the situation getting any worse until the government developed new methods of stimulating private enterprise to bridge the gap between construction costs and an economic rent that poor tenants could afford.[26] Always anxious to avoid any unnecessary interference with private enterprise, Chamberlain was reluctant to intervene directly to tackle the problems of labour and material shortages which had driven up building costs since the Armistice. On the other hand, however, he agreed with Churchill that such considerations did not preclude the promotion of alternative materials and techniques to reduce construction costs 'for the housing of the classes who cannot afford to pay at the existing prices'.[27] Ultimately, this quest led Chamberlain into a frustrating campaign to encourage the widespread acceptance of prefabricated timber-framed steel-clad houses mass-produced in factories and assembled on-site by unemployed unskilled labour working for engineering rates of pay and conditions.

The principal exponent of this concept was Lord Weir, a self-confident, aggressively anti-union Glasgow industrialist and technocratic problem-solver whose successful steamship engineering business had been founded upon the principles of standardisation in production and payment by results. By building cheap prefabricated steel houses with standardised fittings, Weir hoped to apply the same ideas to solve the housing shortage, reduce expenditure on unemployment relief and undermine the stranglehold of the National Federation of Building Trades Operatives in order to force down building costs and wage rates in an exploitative sheltered trade.[28] Contrary to claims that Churchill was the enthusiastic driving force behind the Conservative government's entanglement with steel houses while Chamberlain remained cautious,[29] within two weeks of becoming Minister of Health in March 1923 Chamberlain began discussions with Weir on his proposals and after examining a demonstration model in July 1924 he was even more convinced that it offered a cheap and viable solution.[30]

Unfortunately for the government, there were two major problems with such a commitment. First, Chamberlain recognised that the novelty of the method and materials would inevitably deter local authorities from placing the necessary bulk orders before extensive and protracted trials were completed. To overcome this problem, one of his first actions on returning to office was to arrange a subsidy for various demonstration models in order to popularise the concept. A second, and more immediately damaging problem was that Weir had a reputation as an aggressive class warrior and there was little doubt that his direct challenge to the craft unions owed as much to political motives as to an entrepreneurial desire to generate profits.[31] As a result, Weir's plans inevitably provoked the determined opposition of the building unions who contended that the 'fair wages clause' in Wheatley's Housing Act demanded that Weir's men should be paid at the higher rates of pay prevailing in the building trade rather than in engineering. To make this demand effective, in December 1924 the union withdrew its labour from Glasgow Corporation in order to halt the erection of 20 experimental Weir houses by unemployed men.

While this politically explosive threat remained unresolved Chamberlain recognised that other councils would not place orders and that steel houses would never be an economic proposition if constructed at skilled rates of pay. Despite the pessimism of his officials, however, he refused to accept defeat because there was far too much at stake in political as well as policy terms. 'Cheap houses were wanted', he told the Cabinet Committee considering Weir houses in February 1925:

> not only with a view to reducing the gap between the rent which the occupiers could pay and the subsidy to be found by the State and the Local Authorities, but also with a view to breaking the existing building trade monopoly. The building trade had been subjected to appeals and threats, neither of which had had the least effect. At present the Trade had the country entirely at its mercy and cheap steel houses in large quantities afforded the only possible escape.

Moreover, once cheap steel houses were under construction, Chamberlain believed this would force down the cost of brick houses, while Weir contended that 'until costs of production had been reduced there could be no healthy industrial revival'. Indeed, he assured the government that his present proposals were merely 'a first step toward reorganising British industry on American lines'.[32]

Despite Weir's pressure for an unequivocal government declaration that nothing would be allowed to obstruct the programme, by late February 1925

Chamberlain had decided 'to risk everything on a Court of Enquiry'. He did so in the confident expectation that it would recommend a modification to the 'fair wages clause' in such a way as to absolve the government from direct involvement or any 'reasonable suspicion that we are making an attack upon trade union standards'.[33] In the event, the enquiry did find in favour of Weir, but as Chamberlain feared, the unions simply refused to surrender and the position in Scotland remained deadlocked. Alarmed that both the Scottish Secretary and Minister of Labour appeared 'vague & wild' on the subject, in late September Chamberlain seized the initiative by persuading a ministerial conference that the greater need for Weir houses north of the border made Scotland 'a far more favourable battleground for the fight with the T.U.'s than England'. He thus proposed an additional subsidy of £40 per home over the Wheatley terms for the first 4000 steel houses erected in Scotland as a means of breaking the deadlock.[34] When this incentive failed to overcome local authority reluctance to defy the building unions, in early November ministers were obliged to accept Chamberlain's further proposal that the government should intervene directly to construct these houses through the Scottish National Housing Company.[35] Ultimately, it was a measure of Chamberlain's determination and ascendancy, that although these developments were technically outside the remit of his department, he became the principal driving force in shaping Scottish housing policy during 1925 on the grounds that he did not trust the relevant ministers and it was 'too important to be allowed to go wrong'.[36]

By early 1926, Weir had effectively lost interest in a project which was meeting neither its commercial nor political objectives.[37] By this juncture, however, Chamberlain was also less enthusiastic about the concept given the satisfactory progress of building south of the border and the relatively high cost of Weir houses. Indeed, progress with conventional construction was sufficiently impressive that in July 1926 he proposed a reduction in the house building subsidies under both the Chamberlain and Wheatley Acts as a first step towards their eventual abolition and in the hope of further forcing down buildings costs. As these continued to fall and output rose to record levels, in December 1928 a further cut was announced in the Wheatley subsidy along with the total abolition of the Chamberlain subsidy on all houses completed after September 1929.[38]

Despite this frustration over steel houses, Chamberlain's first full year at the Ministry of Health was one of remarkable achievement. Beside contributory pensions and rating reform, Bills were passed to regulate the manufacture and distribution of proprietary medicines and therapeutic substances, along with important consolidation Acts for public health, town planning and housing – the latter providing new powers to inspect and force repairs upon the private owners of unfit habitations, although the problems of forging a viable scheme for slum 'reconditioning' continued to defeat him for the remainder of the decade. Having achieved so much in such a short period, Chamberlain already talked of 'the Golden Age at the Ministry' and his hope that although he was never likely to become a favourite of the press like his father or Churchill, 'if

I have 4 or 5 years of office I may leave behind as ... great a reputation as Minister of Health as Father did as Colonial Secretary'.[39]

Chamberlain's plans for 1926 were equally impressive and included eight further pieces of legislation, of which the most important was the Housing (Rural Workers) Bill, influenced to a considerable degree by his sister Ida. This measure applied Chamberlain's earlier enthusiasm for the 'reconditioning' of slum housing to rural areas by providing Exchequer grants to cover half the cost of local authority loans to those owners engaged in improvements to sub-standard housing in return for controls over future rent levels. In a tactic employed regularly thereafter, Chamberlain briefed the press on the proposal before obtaining the agreement of a hesitant Cabinet in order to create such a groundswell of support that its adoption became unavoidable.[40] Although to Chamberlain's intense frustration these new powers generated relatively little response from either the local authorities or rural landlords, they represented a minor victory for his commitment to the concept of subsidised property 'reconditioning' over those like Churchill who preferred to demolish and build new and better houses. The Act was renewed by the ensuing Labour government and was only allowed to lapse by Attlee's Labour government after 1945. In addition, measures were passed to register and inspect midwives, maternity homes and dairies and to protect against lead paint poisoning. In 1927–28 more worthwhile legislation was added with regard to the registration and supervision of nursing homes and the sale of drugs along with a humane reform of the definition of 'mental deficiency' to assist the treatment and care of those suffering from the 'sleepy sickness' epidemic which swept across Europe in the 1920s.[41]

Yet despite the scope of all this useful activity, the middle period of Chamberlain's term at the Ministry of Health did not live up to the confident constructive optimism of 1925. In part this change in tone can be attributed to the long shadow cast by the General Strike in May 1926 and the devastating effects of the coal stoppage which continued until the end of the year. Not entirely without reason, these events cast Chamberlain in an essentially negative role as the rigidly bureaucratic upholder of harsh Poor Law regulations over local Boards of Guardians inclined to be more generous and humane. Equally inevitably, this posture provoked ferocious Labour condemnation of the 'Minister of Death', whose policies were alleged to have contributed to the near-starvation of entire mining communities – particularly as Chamberlain made little effort to disguise his contempt for the 'sentimental sob-stuff' uttered by Labour MPs or his disbelief in the existence of any abnormal hardship. But in practice, acrimonious partisan tensions of this sort were already evident before the strike since Chamberlain's leading role in the passage of the deeply unpopular Economy (Miscellaneous Provisions) Bill in March–April 1926 which introduced a wide range of cuts in social expenditure. Moreover, while the substance of the Bill ensured that he was 'cursed and abused for a thief, a cad and a bully', his tough-minded tactics in dealing with persistent Labour obstructionism aroused still more violent denunciations and hostility.[42]

In reality, not all of these Labour accusations were well founded. On the contrary, after a 'strenuous fight' with the Chancellor over the Economy Bill, Chamberlain successfully defeated attempts to cut the health and housing budget.[43] Similarly, despite his apparent indifference to the plight of the miners during the protracted coal stoppage, the Ministry prided itself upon its neutrality in curbing both the excessively punitive actions of local Conservative Poor Law authorities as well as the 'extravagance' of their Labour counterparts.[44] Moreover, Chamberlain played a largely conciliatory role during the discussions leading up to the General Strike in May 1926 and after its defeat he urged the need 'to show generosity and to establish new relations of mutual confidence and trust'.[45] As his contribution to that spirit, in the formulation of the otherwise punitive Trade Disputes Bill, he opposed any restrictions on the right of trade unions to pay a political levy to the Labour Party and equally unsuccessfully attempted to include provisions for an industrial court to provide compulsory arbitration before strikes commenced.[46]

Whatever the reality of Chamberlain's policy position in the secrecy of the Cabinet, however, in Parliament his political tone and condescending manner infuriated his Labour opponents during this period. Those who knew him well invariably emphasised the crucial but frequently overlooked distinction between Chamberlain's impatient sharpness towards ill-informed and partisan opposition which 'sometimes goaded him beyond all endurance' and the conspicuous courtesy and consideration he showed towards informed critics.[47] Yet for all that, his ability to put his case 'with such brutal candour, such cold-blooded frankness and such telling force' made the Labour Opposition hate and despise him all the more fervently. As Baldwin noted in December 1926:

> There are few Ministers or ex-Ministers in the House who are so supremely efficient or so devastating to their opponents as Mr Chamberlain. He starts with the most complete knowledge of his subject than any Minister can possess. Allied to that are his faculty for clear and precise reasoning, a severely practical mind which prevents his judgement from being warped by sentimental considerations, and a most ruthless logic which enables him to set out his arguments in such a convincing manner that he usually reduces his opponent to impotent wrath. Nevertheless, the angry abuse in which his political opponents are sometimes driven to indulge through sheer inability to fight him on his own grounds is equally to no avail against that cold emotionless demeanour and calm determination which Mr Chamberlain possesses.

Little wonder that even the most neutral observers considered that he often seemed 'unnecessarily dictatorial and insulting' to opponents in the conduct of parliamentary business.[48]

In part, this increased political animosity during 1926 was simply a reflection of a rise in the general political temperature. Beyond his aggressive conduct during the Economy Bill and the coal dispute, the bitterness of Labour attacks was intensified by Chamberlain's unswerving determination to deal effectively with what he saw as the pervasive abuse and corruption of the Poor Law by 'extravagant' Labour Boards of Guardians. Yet personal factors also played a significant part in sharpening Chamberlain's tone and manner. First, he experienced deep personal alarm and anxiety at his wife's slide into something approaching a nervous breakdown in March 1926 and then the pain of protracted separation during her convalescence.[49] Secondly, Chamberlain's contempt for his Labour opponents was further intensified in July 1926 by their highly personal allegations of corruption and impropriety regarding his directorship of Hoskins; an unfounded smear which impugned his personal honour and which he resented all the more bitterly because it was widely regarded as vindictive retaliation for his punitive action against Labour Boards of Guardians.[50] Always acutely sensitive to attacks of this nature since they had been levelled against the family at the turn of the century, after 1926 Chamberlain's invective became more bitter and vitriolic than ever before.

The supreme irony of Neville Chamberlain's social reforming period was thus that his endeavours on behalf of the 'less fortunate classes' actually intensified the animus which existed between him and the party which claimed to represent this section of society. As a result, Clement Attlee's recollection that Chamberlain 'always treated us like dirt' precisely described his actual attitude and he made little effort to conceal it.[51] 'More and more do I feel an utter contempt for their lamentable *stupidity*', he wrote of Labour opposition to his Audit Bill in June 1927:

> They cannot see the futility of their own arguments, and to see them wisely wagging their heads and observing that 'its a funny thing that all these bills are only aimed at places where there is a Labour majority' really makes me tired … Stanley [Baldwin] begged me to remember that I was addressing a meeting of gentlemen. I always gave him the impression, he said, when I spoke in the H. of C. that I looked on the Labour Party as dirt. The fact is that intellectually, with a few exceptions, they *are* dirt.

Many Conservative colleagues might have shared this view, but few ever came close to displaying it so brazenly or so provocatively. Indeed, Chamberlain privately rejoiced at his unique skill in baiting the Opposition. 'I believe they hate me most', he boasted to his sisters in April 1927. 'I fancy its because of my nasty sarcastic way. Very few people can stand sarcasm; the Socialists so far lose control that they have taken to hissing me. No wonder people say its like old times!'[52]

III

Of all the policy problems confronted by Chamberlain at the Ministry of Health, none was more problematical or capable of arousing greater opposition than that posed by the Poor Law. As a safety net for the relief of poverty and destitution it dated back to the Poor Laws of 1598 and 1601, but the system Chamberlain inherited had its roots in the Poor Law Amendment Act of 1834. This measure transferred the burden of relief from the parish to larger Poor Law Unions within which ratepayers elected a Board of Guardians to administer local poor relief supervised by a central department intended to ensure uniformity of standards. Each Union operated a workhouse with a grim regime of 'indoor relief' designed to deter all except the absolutely desperate, while 'outdoor relief' within the home was confined to those whose poverty was not deemed to be their own fault; a category which included the aged poor but which was specifically intended to exclude the able-bodied unemployed. In practice, the need for radical reform was well-established long before Chamberlain returned to the Ministry of Health. Despite piecemeal tinkering in the late nineteenth century, in 1909 a Royal Commission on the Poor Law had condemned this ramshackle edifice for both its underlying philosophy and its wasteful duplication of functions with local authorities; a proposal for the 'break-up of the Poor Law' echoed by another Royal Commission under Sir Donald Maclean in 1917–18. In the event, however, the opposition of the Poor Law authorities prevented reform during the war, while the onset of economic slump and long-term unemployment after 1921 simply overwhelmed the entire structure with problems beyond its capacity to resolve or even manage.[53]

Against this background, it has rightly been argued that Poor Law reform was one of the oldest and most complex problems of social politics and one 'easier to deplore than to discuss intelligently, let alone to try and solve'. Indeed, after the failure of Addison's efforts immediately after the Great War, the matter had effectively been allowed to lapse until Chamberlain emerged determined to act where all others lacked the knowledge, enthusiasm and the political courage to reform effectively. Yet it is often alleged that the principal difference between Chamberlain and his reforming antecedents like Addison, the Fabian socialists Sidney and Beatrice Webb and the Maclean Committee, was that while the latter were all moved by active humanitarian concern for the victims of the Poor Law, Chamberlain's 'top-down' approach to reform was motivated by a far narrower bureaucratic desire simply to improve the functional efficiency of 'a broken piece of administrative apparatus'. On this basis, Chamberlain's achievements at the Ministry of Health are too often dismissed as simple matters of 'administrative rationalisation' concerned 'less with what was to be done than how it was to be done'.[54]

In reality, such verdicts are neither accurate nor fair when considering Chamberlain's radical programme to 'break-up the Poor Law' while extending the role of local government as the welfare service arm of the State. Indeed, ultimately, such judgements often stem from a fundamental failure to differentiate between Chamberlain's pragmatically bureaucratic emphasis upon *means* and his longer-term hopes as to the *end* to which that effort was directed. Without doubt, Chamberlain's bureaucratic cast of mind was offended by the wasteful overlap and untidy confusion of administrative boundaries and responsibilities at a time when no fewer than seven public authorities might provide financial assistance in the home, six supplied various forms of medical treatment and five supported the able-bodied unemployed.[55] It is equally undeniable that Chamberlain's unrivalled knowledge of local government meant that he dwelt at length upon the institutional obstacles and bureaucratic details in a manner in which Churchill's febrile imagination unencumbered by any practical understanding never did. But what the critics often fail to recognise is that it was precisely because Chamberlain possessed this direct personal understanding of means and machinery that he was able to see, as very few others did, both the need for unified local authority services and the importance of a programme of interlocking stages of reform to achieve this ultimate objective. As his private secretary later recalled, from the outset Chamberlain 'saw the whole thing as none of us in the Ministry saw it, as just part of a single great problem'.[56]

From this perspective, reform of rating and valuation in 1925 was an essential prerequisite for any progressive change in the system of central government grants to local authorities. In their turn, such reforms were a necessary prelude to the eventual abolition of the Poor Law, the fundamental restructuring of central-local finances and the emergence of a properly organised and efficient health service based on suitably sized administrative districts. Even his essentially negative and punitive battle to curb the 'extravagant' expenditure and 'lax' administration of some Poor Law Unions arose to some extent from a recognition that sustained post-war economic depression had exposed fundamental weaknesses in the existing provision for the able-bodied unemployed which threatened to undermine the entire structure. By forcing these men on to the Poor Law, Chamberlain believed that government had demoralised both the Guardians and the recipients of their relief because it ended 'in pushing them down in the scale, instead of pulling them up to something better'. Against this background, his efforts to control expenditure on outdoor relief stemmed less from a mean-spirited, bureaucratic concern about the primacy of punitive regulations than a more radical recognition that the national and international causes of unemployment implied the need to accept State responsibility for unemployment relief as a national charge, rather than permitting it to remain an inequitable burden on local authorities dispensed by corrupted institutions.[57]

The roots of Chamberlain's battle for control over the administration of the Poor Law can be traced back to the 'Revolt of Poplar' in the autumn of 1921. Although the practice of granting relief to able-bodied men was scarcely new, when Poplar Borough Council refused to pay its annual precept to the London County Council because of its own abnormally high cost of poor relief, 30 councillors were imprisoned. When confronted by a surge of public sympathy, however, the LCC and the government backed away from confrontation by releasing the councillors after an apology. More important, a Local Authorities (Financial Provisions) Act was hastily passed in November 1921, increasing the Metropolitan Common Poor Fund contribution for 'indoor relief' (in workhouses) and took over the entire cost of 'outdoor relief' (outside the workhouses) to ensure that the wealthier parts of London heavily subsidised those poorer Labour-controlled Unions with highest levels of unemployment and pauperism.

The 'extravagance' and 'lax' administration of Poplarist Boards of Guardians in blatant defiance of Poor Law principles and central government direction offended Chamberlain's cardinal Benthamite belief that 'local government can only be kept efficient and vigorous if it is made to exercise responsibility, and if necessary, suffer the consequences of its own mistakes'.[58] Equally important, the cynical exploitation of these powers by Labour-controlled Guardians to win elections added a further political outrage to administrative delinquency. In particular, substantial Labour gains in the Guardian elections in London in April 1925 highlighted the financial and political dangers of allowing paupers to vote for those who decided their relief scales, in circumstances in which this was often the only issue at such elections.[59] Although it is difficult conclusively to establish the impact of the pauper vote, such evidence as does exist suggests that Chamberlain had some justification for his concern. Certainly in his own mind he had no doubt that the willingness of the Poplar Guardians to pay generous scales of relief to their constituents at the expense of wealthy ratepayers in other areas of London represented the high road to political corruption of the very worst sort.[60]

Before leaving office in 1923 the Conservatives had already decided to obtain powers to replace defaulting Boards of Guardians with Ministry nominees. After returning to power in November 1924 the problem was soon brought into sharp focus by the predicament of the West Ham Guardians, who by 31 March 1925 had accumulated a debt of £1,975,000 and were expending £500–600,000 a year more than they raised from rates within the Union.[61] When West Ham applied to the Committee on Necessitous Areas for yet another advance of £350,000 in June 1925, therefore, Chamberlain refused to sanction any further loans unless accompanied by strict limitations on outdoor relief. When they refused, he ignored warnings about the very real risk of communist-inspired disorder and sternly informed the Cabinet that 'the best way of inducing these Guardians to see reason is to remain absolutely firm and to make them understand that we are quite prepared, if need be, to supersede them'.[62] Despite the grave reservations of his senior officials, by the end of September the Guardians had surrendered to Chamberlain's demands.[63]

Despite this localised victory, Chamberlain recognised that West Ham was only the tip of a very large and menacing iceberg and that effective central control was the only means of avoiding the financial collapse of the entire structure of local relief. Analysis of different types of Poor Law Unions in November 1925 suggested that while domiciliary relief had risen 15 per cent since April in England and Wales as a whole, it had risen by 77 per cent in mining areas. Indeed, in Durham, an aggregate increase of 141 per cent concealed the fact that four of its 15 Unions between them contributed an increase of 254 per cent. Alarmed by this evidence and confronted by continual demands for additional funds to assist with Poor Law relief in the 'necessitous areas', in April 1926 Chamberlain finally dug in his heels. There would be no special assistance to these authorities on the grounds that their own 'incompetence or deliberate policy' was largely responsible for these difficulties and that further assistance would only encourage others to follow their delinquent example.[64]

In order to remove the fundamental causes of the problem, Chamberlain also prepared what he called a 'Guardian Coercion Bill'. As he explained to the Cabinet in February 1926, in London, Durham and South Wales, Guardians had often now 'adopted a definite policy of transforming Poor Law administration into a system of providing maintenance in lieu of work' on an automatic (and sometimes illegal) basis. As current controls over their actions were 'limited and unsatisfactory', legislation was needed to provide for the replacement of defaulting Guardians with Ministry nominees, to disenfranchise recipients of poor relief (other than medical assistance) from voting in Guardian elections and to disqualify from service those Guardians who refused to obey restraining injunctions.[65] As Chamberlain claimed he was not deeply committed to the disenfranchisement proposal, this was soon abandoned when his officials 'got cold feet' and Conservative backbenchers protested at the likely disenfranchisement of ex-servicemen – but this did not prevent him resurrecting the idea as 'right in principle' in his Poor Law reform Bill six months later until further protests and the imminent abolition of Guardians forced its abandonment for a second time in February 1928.[66]

When West Ham requested a further loan in July 1926, Chamberlain was now 'determined to stand no nonsense' and the resulting Board of Guardians (Default) Act received Royal Assent on 15 July 1926.[67] The West Ham Guardians were superseded by Chamberlain's Commissioners on 20 July and outdoor relief lists and payments were cut dramatically. Six weeks later the Guardians in Chester-le-Street (Durham) were also superseded, according to the Webbs 'not so much because of their bankruptcy, or even of the excessive amount of the Out-Relief, as because of their recalcitrancy in defying the Orders of the Ministry'. In February 1927 the bankrupt Guardians of Bedwellty were also displaced.[68] In addition to the imposition of direct control in these three cases, Chamberlain also instituted an intrusive but highly effective 'Campaign of Inspection of Outdoor Relief' in other Unions during 1927–28. Although these measures further reduced both scales of relief and the numbers of those relieved in the most insolvent Unions, in their classic study of the Poor Law the Webbs denounced these harsh practices as the replacement of local self-government with 'local dictatorship'; a view echoed by many modern historians of social policy who condemn the legislation as 'a violent and much resented corruption of the English tradition that the care of the poor was the responsibility of the locality'.[69] Yet while critics denounced Chamberlain's callous inhumanity and authoritarianism, from the ministerial perspective such actions were regarded as no more than simply a long overdue reassertion of elementary financial discipline to restore the probity of a corrupted and irresponsible local institution.

Despite the cumulative effect of all these piecemeal controls, the fundamental problem remained unchanged. A ramshackle deterrent system of workhouses and labour yards devised a century earlier to drive rural malingerers back to work had simply been overwhelmed by the very different challenges posed by long-term unemployment after 1921. Chamberlain always fully recognised the compelling case for radical reform, but what his critics often fail to grasp is that his increasing emphasis upon the corruption and incompetence of the Guardians was part of 'a deliberate plan of campaign designed to awaken public opinion' in order to provide the ammunition needed to justify the complete abolition of the entire structure. Indeed, as his private secretary later recalled, the Ministry already possessed long forgotten powers to deal with West Ham – but Chamberlain chose not to use them because this did not suit his broader strategic purpose.[70] But by the same token, it also needs to be acknowledged that when adopting these tactics, Chamberlain never fully grasped the individual human consequences of his actions. This was demonstrated most depressingly in December 1928 when even he was finally forced to concede that in mining areas 'the guardians generally are not failing to do what they can within the limits of their powers and responsibilities under the law, but that it is necessary to supplement their efforts by special action' because the diet was 'insufficient to keep the workers in a fit condition to take up work when this is made available, or to keep the population generally in a condition of ordinary health'. The Minister thus accepted the need for Treasury-funded communal feeding stations in the 'distressed areas' over the winter of 1928–29 to stave off further suffering.[71] It was a sad but telling comment on Chamberlain's earlier dismissal of the complaints of these economically blighted areas and upon his own inability sometimes to see the human trees for the administrative wood.

IV

Constructive reform of the Poor Law had been a major feature of Chamberlain's thinking on social reform since 1921 and it figured prominently in his four year legislative programme outlined in November 1924. As he told the Cabinet, such a measure was justified on four main grounds. First, the overlap in the health functions of the Poor Law and the local authorities caused administrative confusion and retarded 'real advance in the direction of a properly organised Health Service'. Second, to implement the anticipated conclusions of the Royal Commission on National Health Insurance it was necessary to create a single unified health authority of an appropriate size in each area. Third, the gradual decrease in the number of recipients of Poor Law relief, as a result of extended unemployment and pension benefits, also indicated the need and opportunity for reform. Finally, at a pragmatic level, he warned that unless reform was undertaken in 1926 the need to renew the legislation centralising the cost of outdoor relief in London, 'would revive in an acute form the problem of London government'.[72]

At the heart of Chamberlain's bold plan was the desire to implement the findings of the Maclean commission of January 1918. This had proposed the abolition of the Boards of Guardians and the break up of the entire system of parochial relief by devolving all of its existing functions and institutions to the appropriate sub-committees of the county and county borough councils which would then develop specialised services for all categories of need within a uniform national structure.[73] Soon convinced that the best approach to reform should be 'a gradual process than a drastic uprooting of present arrangements', Chamberlain envisaged implementing these recommendations in two stages; the first, to transfer the administrative functions of the local authorities, with 'the alteration of the Poor Law itself being postponed until actual experience of unified administration results in a demand for unified services'.[74] In May 1925, the Cabinet agreed to this two-stage approach and by October of the same year Chamberlain was authorised to begin negotiations with the local authorities.[75]

Chamberlain's problem was that his own carefully elaborated plan of advance almost immediately became entangled in Churchill's far more grandiose vision in which Poor Law reform would form only part of a wholesale restructuring of rating and local government finance. Locked in the uncomfortable embrace of reciprocal need and dependency without any hint of mutual understanding or sympathy, it was a frustrating and unhappy union for both partners – particularly as fundamental differences in style and habits of mind became apparent from the outset. Churchill lamented Chamberlain's lack of vision in adhering so rigidly to his own more limited scheme, but he recognised that he could not carry his own plans without the support of the Cabinet's expert on local government and the minister directly responsible for it.[76] Conversely, Chamberlain recognised the desirability of introducing both derating and Treasury block grants for health and necessitous areas in order to relate central government's financial support to local need rather than current levels of expenditure, but he was profoundly sceptical about the practicality of Churchill's broader scheme. Moreover, his orderly, fastidious mind and faith in careful preparation were outraged by Churchill's febrile flights of imagination and regular brainstorms. 'There is too deep a difference between our natures for me to feel at home with him or to regard him with affection', Chamberlain confessed after the battle was over. 'He is a brilliant wayward child who compels admiration but who wears out his guardians with the constant strain he puts upon them.'[77] Worse still, it was painfully apparent that not only did Churchill envy Chamberlain's ability to achieve 'the glory of doing something spectacular' at Health, but that as Chancellor he was determined to make the Treasury 'an active instrument of Government social policy instead of a passive concomitant or even, as it sometimes was, an active opponent'.[78] At this stage, however, Chamberlain believed the Chancellor's ambitions to hijack his own plans for Poor Law reform were just a passing fancy. In this expectation, he wearily resigned himself to the need to allow Churchill 'to splash about for a bit till he gets some water in his mouth'. [79]

A year later, convinced that opposition to Poor Law reform was 'bunkum', Chamberlain returned to the Cabinet claiming that consultation with the various local authorities was now complete. On this basis, he sought authority to introduce a Bill in the next Session to transfer the work of the Guardians to the local authorities, while replacing the complicated and obsolete system of Treasury grants to local authorities with a unified block grant calculated on the basis of local need and efficiency. 'The effect of the Bill', Chamberlain assured the Cabinet, 'will be to bring about the most important reorganisation of local government which has been attempted since 1902 ... and possibly since County Councils were established by the Local Government Act of 1888.'[80] By this stage, however, Churchill had prepared his own far more spectacular scheme for recasting local government finances and he again urged the Cabinet not to allow its implementation to be prejudiced by the passage of Chamberlain's proposals because they represented only 'a comparatively small part of the whole field of Government subventions to Local Authorities'. Put simply, he was prepared to support Chamberlain's proposal, but only if it was synchronised with 'the adoption of a complete scheme of block grants for local services'. Beside the administrative desirability of such a strategy, Churchill also tempted the Cabinet with the political advantage that 'to proceed simultaneously with two first class measures of this kind would tend to divide and confuse any opposition to the Government's proposals, without adding seriously to the volume of Parliamentary business'.[81]

Although the Chancellor's demands clearly represented a major obstacle, at the Cabinet on 24 November Chamberlain was initially heartened by the 'not unsatisfactory reception' given to his own proposals when compared with the 'rather chilly atmosphere' created by Churchill's grander scheme – particularly when he highlighted 'the importance of the time factor' and the absence of any agreed block grant formula because of ministerial concerns about the problems of relating it to education, agriculture, Scotland and the police.[82] After 'a full discussion' of Chamberlain's proposals at two further meetings on 16–17 December, the Cabinet finally agreed to the preparation of a Bill while work continued on the block grant formula.[83] The decision was then postponed until the New Year.

'This is the critical moment for my administration', Chamberlain wrote to a friend, 'for if I am turned down now, I shall have failed to carry out the biggest reform of all.' Although at this stage he did not seriously believe he would fail, party opposition rapidly mounted against any measure of controversial reform. Soundings among the whips and ministers over Christmas suggested that 'the political effect of the Poor Law Bill would be disastrous and that the danger of the general block grant system could not be exaggerated' because 'it opens a door to a Socialist Government going to the country on a promise of endless financial assistance to local authorities – West Ham, in fact, on a large scale'.[84] At Cabinet on 2 February, the subject occupied most of the meeting before it was agreed to include a general statement on Poor Law reform in the King's Speech, but only on the specific understanding that it 'must be regarded as associated with the adoption of a system of block grants'. If an acceptable formula for this new financial structure could not be devised, however, the case for Poor Law reform would have to be completely re-examined. To make matters worse, when the Chief Whip omitted the measure from the parliamentary timetable for the coming session, an unenthusiastic Cabinet cheerfully agreed to postpone it until November. With little support in the Cabinet, the whips office, Parliament or the country, Chamberlain was 'desperately disappointed', but he had no option other than to accept the delay in the certain knowledge that 'all the critics & the diehards and the fainthearts will croak in chorus' to kill his Bill.[85]

At this point, everything began to unravel. First, the proposed abolition of the rural Guardians inevitably alarmed their many friends at a time of great nervousness about the loyalty of the rural vote.[86] Secondly, there were increasing signs of opposition from interested parties within the Cabinet. Chamberlain strongly favoured a new general block grant to local authorities to fund health, police, education and roads on the grounds that it would make for greater economy in local and national expenditure, ease the rate burden on industry in the necessitous areas and pave the way for his own reforms. But there was determined resistance at the Home Office and the Board of Education.[87] Chamberlain was equally frustrated by Churchill's behaviour as chairman of the committee considering the block grant when it appeared he wanted to drop the idea completely in late March.[88] Finally, to make matters worse, Baldwin collapsed through sheer exhaustion in early April and two months later Chamberlain was still complaining that 'since his fainting fit … his indisposition to take a lead has been more marked than ever'.[89]

Confronted by all these obstacles, even Chamberlain's Permanent Secretary and junior minister began to despair of progress, but he resolutely continued his 'lonely struggle' against the odds.[90] First, he attempted to persuade Churchill that he should proceed with block grants, but to apply them only to the Ministry of Health in the first instance, in order to achieve something before the general election.[91] While busily mollifying Churchill, he also attempted to appease rural discontent by redrafting his proposals and then playing a 'masterstroke' by meekly persuading the anxious backbench Agriculture Committee to establish a negotiating sub-committee to search for an agreement. After this, Chamberlain skilfully bamboozled them into proposing what he himself privately wanted for the revised plan and by mid-June he had scored a 'remarkable success'.[92]

Unfortunately for Chamberlain, no sooner had these obstacles been cleared from the path than another far greater one presented itself in the form of Churchill's new and still more elaborate scheme of rating relief. This, he claimed, 'would enable us to make Neville Chamberlain's Bill the greatest measure of the Parliament'.[93] On 7 June Churchill sent a six page summary to Chamberlain arguing that a reduction in rates would help 'every class, all parts of the country, every town, every constituency' while establishing 'a sound relation between national and local finance, with proper incentive to economy and real responsibility for the local bodies'. In reply, Chamberlain cautiously warned that to spend £30 million on the plan 'would provoke quite as much criticism as approval', but undeterred, the Chancellor argued that this was 'fundamental' to the scheme's merits.[94] Not for the first time, Chamberlain privately lamented that 'Winston has gone off the deep end and is in full cry after a new and … fantastic plan … I fear in pursuing these imaginative flights he will lose interest in really practical proposals.'[95]

At this juncture, Chamberlain's conception of what constituted 'practical proposals' was confined to Poor Law reform, with a new block grant for health and necessitous areas and more money for slum improvement because it 'would be a better electoral stunt than Winston's & it is only as an election cry that he wants it'.[96] In secret, a senior Treasury official frankly conceded that Chamberlain's new scheme was 'excellent, and if the scheme could be regarded merely as an isolated piece of reform, I doubt whether we could suggest any improvement'. But as he also warned the Chancellor, the introduction of this more limited scheme of block grants would obstruct their own more ambitious plans by removing much of the existing pressure for wholesale reform. As a result, the Treasury decided to oppose Chamberlain's revised proposal unless subsumed within their own larger scheme.[97]

By the autumn of 1927, the position had thus reached a stalemate. Chamberlain was convinced that he 'had one advantage over Winston of which he was painfully conscious. He could not go on without me.'[98] Churchill, however, believed that precisely the same situation applied to Chamberlain. To escape from this impasse, the Chancellor attempted to persuade him to cooperate in a bolder scheme to achieve their mutual objectives with a combination of flattery, coaxing and the omnipresent hint of blackmail – but as he told his officials, if Chamberlain refused, 'we must go on alone'.[99]

Chamberlain's efforts to persuade Churchill to separate their two schemes in October 1927 in order to permit him to proceed immediately with his more limited reforms, thus prompted the ominous retort that 'joint action is indispensable for success' because 'you really must not expect me to produce 3 or 4 millions a year for a partial scheme of modest dimensions. That wd. only hurt the Finances without helping the Govt.'[100] Little wonder that Sir Philip Cunliffe-Lister, the President of the Board of Trade, later told Churchill that 'the truth is that you and Neville are out for two quite different things … Neville wants to keep as much in the rate areas as he can, and treat your policy as an exception grafted on to that rule. You want the opposite.'[101]

Even more frustrating for Chamberlain was Churchill's assumption that the power of the purse gave him the decisive upper hand. As Chamberlain complained petulantly on 6 December, Churchill 'talked of "our" rating scheme. I protested & said he must not say "our". I hadn't even seen the scheme.' In order to escape from this unwelcome entanglement, two days later Chamberlain 'solemnly warned' Baldwin that they 'were heading for a Cabinet crisis. Winston was getting so obsessed with his scheme that soon he wd be unable to go back while I had the gravest doubts as to whether I could go forward with him.' When Baldwin declined to commit himself, however, Chamberlain declared that if Poor Law reform was to be postponed 'it wd be kinder to tell me so before I had committed myself so far that I shd have to resign if I didn't get it'. Having obtained assurances of 'a prominent position' for the policy in their election programme, Chamberlain quite astonishingly agreed 'not to press for it in this Parlt'. It was a remarkably high price to pay, but trapped between a Chancellor seeking to go much further than he believed practicable and the collective opposition of the Guardians, local authorities, party managers and backbenchers, perhaps Chamberlain briefly appeared to recognise the limits of his own influence.[102]

In contrast, Churchill remained in confident and ebullient mood, despite rumours of Treasury 'despair over Winston's wildcat schemes'.[103] By mid-December, his plan for wholesale derating was complete and he was ready to resume the offensive. Unveiling the plan to Chamberlain he thus repeated his earlier subtle warning that 'without [your] aid I do not believe it will be possible to carry this scheme through. In that case I shall be saved an immense amount of risk & trouble, & shall have to recast my finances on purely negative but highly orthodox lines. "Think well, think wisely, think not for the moment but for the years that are to come", before you reject this Bill.'[104] This threat placed Chamberlain in an extremely delicate position. While Churchill held the purse strings he had no choice but to humour him, but in private Chamberlain was appalled by Churchill's 'unwise, immoral and dangerous' scheme. He was equally cynical about Churchill's motives, believing he had taken it up after 'looking around for some new thing to ornament and illuminate his next Budget'.[105] On the other hand, however, Chamberlain derived comfort from the knowledge that Churchill had already received 'some vy knobbly criticisms' from friendly industrialists and his own Treasury officials. Convinced that Churchill 'doesn't want another Gallipoli', Chamberlain thus drafted an unanswerable critique of Churchill's scheme intended to mobilise the language of cautious support and constructive criticism while demolishing any prospect of the plan being ready for the 1928 Budget or being tied to his own scheme for Poor Law reform.[106]

To this end, Chamberlain pointed to the need for 'careful and perhaps prolonged negotiations' with the many vested interests, the probable underestimate of the cost of rate relief and the likely criticism that the necessary additional taxation would both injure national credit and prove electorally unpopular. He expressed even more alarm at the adverse implications for local government. By removing any direct financial interest in its expenditure, Chamberlain warned that industrial derating would reduce still further the supply of practical men of business coming forward as candidates, with the result that local government would become dominated by 'those representatives of "Labour" who regard office as a means of advancing Socialist theories and benefiting their own particular supporters at the expense of the community'.[107] He also objected that it would so drastically reduce the income of many local authorities that they would have no resources from which to meet the cost of new services other than by demanding progressively larger block grants. While posing as a sympathiser, therefore, Chamberlain concluded that 'the subject is so complicated that prolonged examination would be necessary and I am doubtful whether it could be completed in time for legislation next year'. He then personally typed out his comments on Christmas Eve and sent them to

Baldwin with a covering note saying 'My attitude, though cautious, is not wholly unfriendly.'[108]

Chamberlain briefly appeared to have won this first round. After a preliminary conversation with Churchill on 20 December, he noted cheerfully that he had 'never seen him so low spirited about his scheme before'. Baldwin also appeared to be persuaded by Chamberlain's arguments for caution and postponement.[109] Yet by 2 January Churchill had substantially amended his proposals by abandoning the proposed profits tax and full rating exemption for industry in favour of a two-thirds remission to meet Chamberlain's principal objections. He then bombarded Baldwin with a powerful counter-barrage, arguing that with partial remission he was 'defacing the classical purity of the conception for the sake of an easier passage!', but that 'it is this year or never' and that the Health Ministry 'should not feel they have the power of veto'.[110] Moreover, when the Chancellor outlined his revised proposals to Cabinet on 20 January, Chamberlain was alarmed to note that they received 'very favourable consideration'.[111]

In the Policy Committee established to examine the new scheme further, the battle was largely fought over two key issues, relating to the timing of implementation and the more important question of whether local or central government should receive the product of the fixed national rate to be levied on largely derated properties. Although Chamberlain had reluctantly accepted the idea of a fixed rate, he argued strongly for the proceeds to go to the local authorities rather than the Exchequer and he was supported by most of the committee on 5 March.[112] Without notice to the others, however, Churchill then issued a paper repeating his objections in such forceful terms that Chamberlain went to the next meeting 'in a state of high indignation and hit back as hard as [he] could'. This angry demonstration concluded with a blank refusal to undertake any negotiations on such lines; a 'bombshell' which forced an embarrassed committee hastily to move on to other matters.[113]

Churchill responded to Chamberlain's outburst with the now customary combination of coaxing and veiled threats. He thus protested that he was 'rather startled by the air of antagonism wh you seemed … to show yesterday morning, & I shd be vy sorry indeed if I have done anything to justify it'. But his acknowledgement that Chamberlain was 'the master' and that he could 'make no progress in the face of yr opposition', was accompanied by the warning that as Chancellor 'my only remedy if I find the task too hard or too wearisome will be to withdraw the scheme'.

> Without it there cd be no Poor Law reform in this Parliament … With it the whole system of Local Govt can be the subject of a reform as famous as that of 1834. I always expected that you wd be eager for this opportunity, & wd supply at least half the driving power. Instead of this, I have felt extremely lonely in the shafts. Without yr active aid, not merely acquiescence, I am sure I cannot drag the cart up the hill – nor shall I try.[114]

This polite but menacing threat provoked another 'rather strong' reply from Chamberlain next day in which he declared coldly that he 'had no alternative but to speak plainly' after Churchill's underhand behaviour because 'if we are to work together there must be give and take on both sides. Up to now I have done all the giving, but very little weight has been attached to my views if they have differed from yours.' This uncharacteristically angry letter, blazing with pent-up wrath and righteous indignation, had a chastening effect upon Churchill who was 'almost elaborately forthcoming and friendly' at their meeting next day at which Chamberlain again 'seized the opportunity to do some plain talking'. The result, he believed, was that he had left Churchill 'with a clearer understanding of my difficulties and perhaps of my character'.[115]

Although David Dilks dismisses the Treasury's allegation that Chamberlain was 'sulkily negative' in his conduct during these negotiations, there is ample evidence to suggest more than a hint of the 'not invented here' syndrome in his attitude and he admitted as much to Churchill.[116] 'The plan is a gamble', he confessed more revealingly to his sisters in mid-March. 'I am trying at least to reduce the risks but I cannot be as enthusiastic about it as about my own scheme which it supersedes.' In private, Chamberlain also conceded the truth of the allegation when he confessed in his diary that his real problem was that he 'never found the ground on which [he] could take a definite stand, except that of the retention of the flat rate'.[117] In an effort to extend the ground on which to make such a stand, he consequently re-opened the battle over the derating of railways, canals, harbours and docks; provisions which Churchill regarded as fundamental but which Chamberlain opposed as an additional burden on the Exchequer for what he correctly believed to be a barely 'camouflaged subsidy' to ailing staple industries which could be more effectively dealt with directly. This conflict rumbled on in the Policy Committee until 26 March when, in the absence of officials, the contestants agreed to exclude railways and docks.[118]

Two days after this momentary success, Chamberlain finally unburdened himself of his frustrations to Baldwin in such a way as to increase his leverage in Cabinet. Declaring that he 'had an unhappy week facing up to resignation', he professed himself 'determined to withdraw rather than assent to a scheme which [he] believed to be dangerous to the future of local government'. After Baldwin assured him that the Cabinet would not allow him to resign, Chamberlain effectively laid out his terms – the exclusion of railways from the scheme and the retention of the fixed rate by the local authorities. At this juncture Baldwin appeared to accept the force of Chamberlain's argument. After three full meetings devoted to the issue on 2–3 April, within the Cabinet there was also 'general agreement that, in order to carry so comprehensive a scheme, a united Cabinet and a united Party was essential, and above all, that the Minister of Health and the Secretary of State for Scotland, as the Ministers mainly concerned, must be in cordial agreement with the policy'.[119]

'The Plan has at last been settled', Chamberlain rejoiced prematurely on 4 April.[120] Despite Churchill's attempts to reopen the railway exemption issue three days later, this time the opposition of Cabinet colleagues and senior

Treasury officials persuaded him to abandon the plan. Baldwin also initially advised against reopening the issue. 'For a Tory Cabinet they have successfully and pretty contentedly swallowed a large morsel', he assured Churchill, 'and the inevitable cud-chewing must follow before they are ready for more.'[121] Within days, however, Baldwin had changed his mind. As he told Chamberlain over dinner on 18 April, he had endured intense and prolonged pressure to return to the original scheme from Walter Guinness, the Agriculture Minister, Cunliffe-Lister and Churchill – the latter so much overwrought that he 'marched about the room shouting and shaking his fist and had launched out a tremendous tirade' against Chamberlain for his constant cold water and jealousy. Although Chamberlain dismissed Churchill's tantrums as 'too childish & contemptible ... to be upset over', Baldwin then crucially revealed his own doubts over the exclusion of railways and asked him to reconsider.[122]

By the following morning Chamberlain had already decided to surrender to Baldwin's appeal 'on account of [his] personal affection for him & because ... he had a real flair for the way things would appear to the man in the street'. After another long talk with Baldwin 'to liberate [his] soul' about the many frustrations endured in his dealings with Churchill, Chamberlain agreed that he would not obstruct Cabinet agreement – a remarkably magnanimous gesture given Baldwin's own admission that Chamberlain still commanded a majority in Cabinet, but one which reflected his responsiveness to Baldwin's personal appeal in circumstances in which no major personal or departmental issues were perceived to be at stake.[123] Next day, the 'fateful meeting of the Cabinet' went as planned. After Chamberlain's opening statement of his case and 'a very long discussion', Baldwin went round the table and Chamberlain's supporters withdrew their opposition to railway, dock and canal derating while Chamberlain got his way on the departmentally far more important issue of the variable rather than national flat rate. He also derived some consolation from the belief that his Cabinet position had been strengthened by a gesture which made it correspondingly less easy for Baldwin to evade his commitment to Poor Law reform.[124]

V

Events soon fulfilled Chamberlain's gloomy prediction that he had 'a horrible session' ahead in which 'Winston will do all the prancing and I shall do all the drudgery.' The derating scheme figured prominently in Churchill's Budget speech delivered on 24 April to an admiring Parliament. Conversely, Chamberlain was immediately left to steer the complex Rating and Valuation (Apportionment) Bill through Parliament to pave the way for the full measure in the next session. At the same time, he was busily engaged in drafting the 'great memorandum' which eventually became the Local Government Bill, meticulously going through every clause and contingency with his officials to remove all possible objections. When the White Paper was published on

29 June to a warm reception he congratulated himself on 'a very good document'.[125]

After four months of intense negotiations with the various local authority associations, the Bill of 115 clauses and twelve schedules covering 127 closely printed pages was introduced to Parliament on 13 November. As the *Annual Register* noted, by any standard, it was 'a stupendous measure' with many of its clauses as long as an ordinary Act of Parliament.[126] It represented a massive personal triumph. As one of Chamberlain's former officials noted in congratulation, 'it will go down to history – and your name deservedly in association with it – as the greatest piece of local government legislation in our long record'. He was almost certainly correct in the view that 'no one else ... could have carried so far reaching & complicated a measure through the House'.[127] On 26 November Chamberlain moved the Second Reading of the Local Government Bill in a compelling two and a half hour speech in which he set out his plan for the reform of the entire structure of local government within the context of its historic evolution since the Poor Law Amendment Act of 1834. Explaining the trends of population, shifting patterns of industry and the development of new services which had occurred to render that machinery obsolete, he summed up the deficiencies of the existing structure under the five headings which had changed little since he outlined his provisional programme of legislation in November 1924. In one striking passage he declared:

> Local government comes so much nearer to the homes, and therefore to the hearts of the people, than any national government can. To them it is something friendly, something familiar, something accessible ... They regard it as standing as a guardian angel between them and ill-health or injustice, and they look upon it, too, as something ... of a benefactor and a teacher in want ... They come to it for advice. They feel confidence in its integrity. They look to it because it has ideals which they understand, and that they approve, and because it is helping and teaching them to rise to higher things.

In a stirring peroration which drew upon his own personal experiences and pride in Birmingham, he thus explained that 'it is just because I have seen for myself what local government can do, what I think it ought to do ... and because to my mind local government reform means social reform, that I rejoice that today the opportunity has been given to me to bring forward this measure'.[128]

This 'masterly piece of exposition and argument' earned him 'unstinting praise from all sides of the House'.[129] According to one observer, the speech was 'listened to in almost complete silence and the closest attention ... which [he] had seen since the war given to a speech of this character'. Moreover, its appeal to the collective sentiment of the Commons was increased by the fact that it contained 'more human touches and humour than is customary with Neville's speeches';[130] personal embellishments about local government as it appeared to the people of Birmingham, introduced at his wife's instigation 'to put in something human lest the speech shd appear to be devoted too exclusively to the coldly mechanical efficiency of administration'. When he sat down, he did so to vigorous and enthusiastic cheering from all parts of the House for longer than Worthington-Evans could recall in his 18 years in the Commons. Certainly Chamberlain confessed himself to be well satisfied with the speech and gratified by its results – particularly the fact that his lucid exposition enabled MPs to recognise, for perhaps the first time, that this represented 'a great help towards a happy result at the Gen. Election'.[131] Despite the now customary Opposition filibuster and obstructionism, under Chamberlain's skilled and meticulously prepared guidance, the Bill had an easy passage through Parliament and received Royal Assent on 27 March 1929. As Baldwin told the King after it was all over, 'there was something to stir the imagination in the spectacle of the son incorporating in his Bill proposals made by his father forty years ago'.[132]

In financial terms, the Act relieved industry of three-quarters of its rate burden while agricultural land and buildings (already three-quarters exempt since 1923) were now freed from all rates. Remaining assigned revenues and percentage grants for public health were all abolished and replaced with an annual Exchequer block grant fixed for each authority for five years and at least equal in value to their losses from derating and discontinued grants. A bonus of £5 million (which could be increased in subsequent quinquennial periods), would be distributed on the basis of need as calculated by reference to population and weighted to allow for low rateable value, unemployment and the proportion of children.[133]

At the heart of this immensely complex and broad-ranging measure was the formal separation of the highly problematic, often blurred and demoralising, dual responsibility of the Poor Law for both the able-bodied unemployed and those confined largely to the institutions. Henceforth, the former were to be administered by newly established Public Assistance Committees appointed by local authorities and funded jointly from the rates and the Exchequer. In contrast, the Poor Law Unions, Boards of Guardians and Scottish parochial boards were abolished and the care of the non-able-bodied poor was transferred to the county and county borough councils while the powers, duties, assets and institutions of the 625 Poor Law Unions were assigned to specialist council committees in order to improve the quality of provision. Under this arrangement, workhouse infirmaries were assigned to council health committees where they were intended to develop into general and municipal hospitals but without their previous stigma of destitution and pauperism, while responsibility for the education of Poor Law children was transferred to local education committees. In this manner, the major local authorities were finally empowered to 'break up the Poor Law', to end the wasteful duplication of services which had so appalled reformers since the Poor Law Commission in 1909 and to unify provision for the destitute and able-bodied unemployed on the same terms as the rest of the community. On this basis, the measure was hailed by reformers of all persuasions as 'a sentence of death' on the century old Boards of Guardians, the concept of 'less eligibility' and the other principles of 1834.[134]

The actual impact of the Local Government Act is difficult to assess fairly – particularly given the almost immediate onset of the Great Depression which inhibited local authorities from grasping the opportunities offered by the measure, while the outbreak of the Second World War effectively uprooted the entire structure. Nevertheless, while some contend that in the longer-term 'both the structural and the financial reforms were improvements of great importance',[135] many other commentators follow Sidney and Beatrice Webb in lamenting that although the administrative structures and titles changed, the old Poor Law remained largely untouched in its fundamentals with regard to the notion of relief and the stigma of pauperism. As Bentley Gilbert contends, 'beyond the disappearance of the guardians themselves, the expansion of hospital facilities by some ... local authorities, turned out to be almost the only notable change in the durable apparatus of local welfare functions'. Yet as he also concedes, although such changes were slow to come in many areas, the Act did enable local authorities to make improvements where they chose to act and this was always Chamberlain's intention.[136] As Chamberlain told a Cabinet Committee as early as 1925, the eventual reform 'involved very considerably decentralisation. In future the State would prescribe a minimum standard of efficiency, and subject to that standard being reached, Local Authorities would be allowed within fairly wide limits to experiment.'[137]

Unfortunately, Chamberlain's decision to rely upon ministerial exhortations to persuade councils to make imaginative use of these new powers had little effect in the absence of much financial incentive to do so – particularly as the economic crisis of the early 1930s inevitably deterred local government from assuming new responsibilities or undertaking the costly reorganisation so urgently required. As a result, outside London, the following decade witnessed a continuation of the previous pattern of 'rudderless drifting towards specialised institutions'.[138] All of this fell considerably short of Chamberlain's optimistic vision of a national hospital service, with local government leading the way towards greater coordination in health provision and the translation of general workhouse institutions into public hospitals.[139] For the poor receiving indoor relief the picture was very similar. As one historian of the workhouse notes, 'Chamberlain had laid the foundations of a more specialised system of residential institutions, but a corresponding social investment was not made until the more prosperous 1950s.' At a practical level, the physical legacy of the Poor Law endured for still longer in the continued use of old workhouse buildings, while the extremely hierarchical administrative structures and authoritarian attitudes acquired in Poor Law years too often persisted into the newly-created PACs and even under the NHS after 1948.[140]

For all its deficiencies and unfulfilled promise, however, the Local Government Act of 1929 represented a fitting culmination of Neville Chamberlain's record of structural reform at the Ministry of Health and he rightly anticipated that it would 'prove ... my magnum opus when my obituary is written'.[141] Although in many respects its sheer scope gave it the appearance of a consolidation Act, the measure combined three central themes of Chamberlain's long-term thinking about local government in Britain. First, its radical approach to the problems of the Poor Law completed his comprehensive review of local government services and provision. He thus sought finally to 'break up the Poor Law' by subsuming it within a unified system of provision for all citizens under the direct democratic control of local councils. Secondly, the Act involved the fundamental restructuring of a system of local government finance largely untouched since the establishment of the county councils in 1888. Ultimately, this had been a problem which required radical attention even without the parallel reform of the Poor Law both because of its distorting effects upon the distribution of central government support and because these inequitable financial burdens fell most heavily upon those depressed areas and industries least able to bear them and for whom they represented a major cause of their own lack of competitiveness. The final aspect of continuity concerned the enlargement of local government units which Chamberlain had favoured since advocating the Birmingham Extension Bill in 1910–11. Like the Poor Law and Maclean Commissions before him, Chamberlain was convinced of the benefits of poor relief and public health services administered by larger units able to spread the financial burden more evenly to ensure that richer areas assisted poorer ones. The Poor Law Unions, which replaced the parish as the geographical unit for relief in 1834, were thus in their turn replaced by the county and country borough councils.

While much of real value was achieved under Chamberlain's dynamic leadership at the Ministry of Health, it is important not to exaggerate the scale of that achievement in order to juxtapose it all the more poignantly with the supposed failure of his later foreign policy. Despite a steady increase in the annual construction of houses, significantly more were built under the Wheatley Act than under Chamberlain's while the hope of solving the housing problems of the poor through steel houses proved to be a chimera. Similarly, while his imaginative and broad-ranging slum 'reconditioning' scheme was intended to improve the quality of the tenants as well as the standard of their accommodation, the outline plan did not actually see the light of day until shortly before he left office.[142] Even his bold application of subsidised reconditioning to the problems of rural housing left him 'a good deal disappointed' by the modest and tardy response of country landlords.[143]

It also needs to be recognised that if Baldwin's 'New Conservatism' can be defined as 'social idealism tied to sound finance', the policy record of Neville Chamberlain at the Ministry of Health gave substance to precisely this balance.[144] Contributory pensions were a significant policy development, but whatever Chamberlain said about the encouragement of thrift and self-help, their eventual financial basis was fashioned far more with a practical eye on the needs of the Treasury and the taxpayer than those of the aged poor often consigned to a miserable existence below the level of subsistence. Not until July 1939, when the government faced a general election and when 10 per cent of pensioners were on public assistance, did Chamberlain concede that 10 shillings a week was insufficient to live on, while the evidence suggests the

Ministry deliberately ignored and suppressed embarrassing reports of physical suffering and health deterioration in the distressed areas.[145] And while the Local Government Act was a spectacular administrative achievement, Chamberlain's reliance upon local authorities taking advantage of permissive powers without either central direction or adequate finance meant that the measure would probably always have failed to deliver against the expectations of its principal architect.

But for all the missed opportunities, failures and caveats, when the broader record of these years is considered as a whole, Neville Chamberlain still undoubtedly deserves a very significant chapter in the history of social welfare in Britain. Despite his contempt for 'sentimental sob-stuff', he was sincere and deeply committed to improving the lot of the 'less fortunate classes' and he contributed a great deal to this cause within the parameters defined by persistent economic slump, party doctrine and that particular brand of Victorian philanthropic individualism he had inherited from his father. There was little searing emotional content in the crusade and he conceptualised the problem far more in terms of the abstract mass than as an accumulation of individual personal tragedies. Yet despite the repeated indictment, Chamberlain's pursuit of coldly rational administrative solutions to large structural problems achieved substantial and valuable advances towards his intended goal.

It also needs to be noted that beyond the many reforms already outlined, Chamberlain's hope when he returned to the Ministry that he would 'be allowed to do something for "Health" as well as "Housing"',[146] was to some degree fulfilled – most notably through the broad-ranging public health implications of the Local Government Act, but also through improved registration and inspection of a wide range of services and the appointment of special departmental committees in 1928 on midwives and maternal mortality – always a subject close to his heart since the death of his own mother in childbirth. These inquiries led directly to substantial improvements in ante-natal and post-natal care and culminated in the Midwives Act of 1936 which introduced a national salaried midwifery service.[147] Contrary to some claims, under Chamberlain's aegis, the Ministry also took a significant step towards the coordination of curative and preventative medical services of a sort proposed by the Dawson Committee in 1920.[148] Tragically, as Chamberlain rightly recalled on his death bed, the demands of rearmament had deprived him of his greatest opportunity to 'enter on a new era of social improvement' when the economy boomed during the mid-1930s.[149] For all the criticisms, therefore, the fact remains that in 1939 the social services in Britain were 'taken all in all, … the most advanced in the world' and Neville Chamberlain contributed more to that improved state of affairs than any single interwar figure. As his private secretary noted: 'I felt that I was working for someone who really could do things that needed to be done, & that made my work seem worth doing.'[150]

VI

Although valuable reforms still remained to be achieved at the Ministry of Health, on the eve of the 1929 election Chamberlain resolved that he needed a fresh challenge for fear 'one might well get oneself and the office into a groove'.[151] Baldwin expected to make him Chancellor when he returned to office, but Chamberlain thought more of following in his father's footsteps to become Colonial Secretary. In reality, the Colonial Office was as much of a ministerial backwater in 1929 as when Joseph Chamberlain unexpectedly requested it in 1895, but his son's decision was not entirely a matter of 'filial piety'.[152] Increasingly convinced that 'our future lies in the Empire', during his final months at the Ministry of Health, Chamberlain confessed that he felt 'ashamed of our record of ineffectiveness' on imperial development and confidently looked forward to the fulfilment of the other half of his father's vision by developing the vast resources of the colonial empire while binding the Dominions to the destiny of the mother country.[153] In order to do so, however, the government needed to win the forthcoming general election and in this respect his view of the vote winning potential of derating and local government reform was somewhat ambivalent. At the annual party conference at Yarmouth in September 1928, Chamberlain enjoyed 'the success of [his] life', and he sat down to 'a perfect hurricane of cheers' before the audience sang 'For he's a jolly good fellow'. Yet despite this 'very gratifying tribute', at other times he more soberly reflected that the measure was 'too technical and too involved ever to make much appeal to the man in the street' and he reconciled himself to the belief that it would be 'remembered to our credit hereafter'.[154] The latter judgement came far closer to the truth – particularly as the new higher rating assessments were despatched to householders only a few weeks before the election.

Yet since the defeat of the General Strike in 1926, the government had increasingly demonstrated the symptoms of a debilitating *malaise d'ennui* which carried them listlessly into the 1929 general election. Without the electoral fillip of Cabinet reconstruction or any radical commitment to tariffs, the Conservatives fell back upon a sound but unexciting record of domestic legislation and an uninspiring employment policy firmly rooted in Treasury orthodoxy and derating. But despite these problems, like most other observers, Chamberlain never really doubted their ability to achieve an overall working majority. In Birmingham, his heavy departmental burden had not prevented him from keeping a close eye on the party's organisation and he anticipated that the Conservatives would lose Yardley but hold all eleven other seats in the city.[155] In the event, while Chamberlain enjoyed a far less rowdy contest in the middle class safety of Edgbaston, within the city as a whole the election was a near disaster for the Conservatives. Since 1886 the Unionists had never lost more than one seat in Birmingham. In 1929 Labour took no fewer than six of its twelve seats, including that of a Cabinet Minister in Erdington, while in West Birmingham Austen only just scraped in by 43 votes in a seat held continuously by a Chamberlain for almost half a century. Among the fallen was Geoffrey Lloyd who, despite vast exertions to cultivate Chamberlain's former constituency, was defeated in Ladywood by eleven votes.

Initial explanations for defeat tended to vary in emphasis, but the 'natural swing of the pendulum' was believed to have been aggravated by specific discontents. Certainly Chamberlain was convinced that the key factor had been 'the ceaseless propaganda that has been going on for years among the working classes to the effect that things would never be right for them till a "Labour" Govt came in ... There is no conversion to Socialism. It is merely the present discontents showing themselves in a desire for change.'[156] Nevertheless, he also recognised his own reforms had partly contributed to defeat because his pensions and housing policies probably won no new votes while the radical tone of other reforms alarmed the party faithful. Indeed, at a more general level, nothing contributed more in tangible policy terms to the government's disquieting reputation for 'socialistic tendencies' than Chamberlain's record at the Ministry of Health.[157]

Despite the electoral unpopularity of some of his policies, throughout the 1924–29 government Chamberlain had progressively strengthened his position as Baldwin's principal lieutenant and as a future leader of the party. Certainly there were many who shared Lord Salisbury's view that he was 'the man who has most influence with the P.M.' and there was much speculation about his likely succession 'if ... a street omnibus were to misconduct itself at Baldwin's expense'.[158] Even Baldwin believed that if 'anything happened to me, the best men are Neville and Hogg' and although both he and Chamberlain favoured the latter, after Baldwin removed Douglas Hogg from the running by forcing him to become Lord Chancellor in March 1928 it left Chamberlain the most likely successor.[159] But while well placed, the inevitability of Chamberlain's advance at this stage should not be overstated. Chamberlain genuinely had very little burning desire for the leadership and to his relief Baldwin made it clear that he 'did not want to go out for he doubted if the Party was ripe for a successor'.[160] This is not to deny Chamberlain's regular frustration and his disappointment at the indolence of Baldwin's leadership style. As he complained in October 1925: 'He always gives you the feeling that he is not opening his mind and the fear that that is because there is very little there.' A month later, these suspicions were amply confirmed during an important presentation to the Economy Committee, when Chamberlain was appalled to see Baldwin pass a note to Churchill bearing the message:[161]

MATCHES
lent at 10.30am
Returned
?

Whatever Baldwin's failings as leader, however, Chamberlain was sincere in telling him in July 1927 that 'his ... disappearance wd be a disaster for the party. For myself I wanted nothing – I was happy where I was.' As he explained the complex nature of their relationship a year later: 'For myself I often criticise him, and he often vexes me by what seems to me timidity or lethargy when rapid and vigorous action is wanted. But I have an immense respect and admiration for him. It means a tremendous lot to have absolute faith in the single-mindedness of your chief and I have long since become aware of a certain simple shrewdness about him which seems to provide him with an instinctive knowledge of the common man.'[162] In these circumstances, it was not surprising that in the immediate aftermath of their electoral defeat in June 1929, Chamberlain's transition to the leadership was generally assumed to be a long way off. If nothing else, he was rightly believed to be 'too loyal to S.B. to attempt to dislodge him'.[163] During the next two years, however, a ferocious period of internecine warfare shook Baldwin's leadership to its foundations and brought Chamberlain almost to the point of succession.

Chapter 7

Opposition and the Financial Crisis, June 1929–October 1931

'It is astonishing to me to see the amount of time that Max [Beaverbrook] devotes to searching with a fine-toothed comb for defeatist propaganda in the Conservative press. If he would only spend one-hundredth part of his energies on a similar attention to the real enemies of his policy, it seems to me he would be more usefully employed ... I am very tired of Max's continual complaints.'
Chamberlain to Patrick Hannon, 2 May 1930, Hannon MSS 17/1

Depression, distaste for politics and gloomy forebodings about the future are natural emotional responses to electoral defeat among those so rudely deprived of office, status and worthwhile occupation. Chamberlain was no exception. Indeed, for a man who could more genuinely claim than most of his colleagues that his 'pleasure is in administration rather than in politics', the transition to the Opposition benches was a painful and traumatic experience. Within days of the election, Chamberlain predicted that Labour would spend two years establishing their credibility in office, before introducing a popular budget as a prelude to a general election designed to usher in a full term of majority government and the socialist millennium. As a result, he was soon dismally contemplating the prospect of seven years in Opposition – by which time he would be 67, with his powers in decline and with a new generation of leaders emerging to obstruct any future claim he might have to office. 'It is hard to bear & it will take time to recover spirits', he confessed to his sisters, consoling himself with the thought that 'there is no certainty in politics and that is why one does not go out in despair. The most unexpected things may happen and we may return to office sooner than seems possible now.'[1]

In political terms, the prospects were equally cheerless. As in 1924, Chamberlain remained convinced that 'the only way to check the advance of Socialism ... is to give the country a dose of Socialist Government' and he derived malicious comfort from thoughts of the Cabinet's intellectual deficiency and internal jealousies.[2] Yet for the Conservatives to benefit from the situation, a united Opposition with strong combative leadership and a clear constructive vision were essential requirements and even in the immediate aftermath of defeat Chamberlain lamented privately that 'Baldwin lacks the qualities of a leader in that he has no power of rapid decision and consequently no initiative.'[3] Worse still, Baldwin's retreat into depressed inertia coincided with a crisis in party discipline and morale as long-suppressed tensions over tariffs boiled to the surface almost immediately the Conservatives left office.

The first signs of trouble came from Lord Beaverbrook, the self-made Canadian proprietor of the mass-circulation Express Newspapers group. Widely perceived to be the *eminence grise* behind Bonar Law and a close associate of Lloyd George, during the 1920s Beaverbrook's unenviable reputation as an unscrupulous adventurer and maverick ensured that under Baldwin's very different style of leadership he was banished to the margins of Conservative politics as a detested pariah. Despite an unobtrusive role in the 1929 election, however, on 30 June Beaverbrook launched his press campaign for 'Empire Free Trade' with a savage indictment of those politicians who believed in Empire but withdrew from the fulfilment of 'Imperial Fiscal Union' for reasons of electoral expediency. Although supremely ambiguous and opportunistic as both a policy and a movement, at the heart of Beaverbrook's Empire Crusade was an aggressive exaltation of food taxes and a direct assault upon the 'outworn fallacy of the "Dear Loaf"'.[4] To make matters worse, in the Commons on 9 July, Amery finally gave vent to his protectionist fury at Churchill's free trade obstructionism when in office while Chamberlain's own speech to the Empire Industries Association extolling an explicitly protectionist policy reinforced the alarm of Conservative free traders that this was all part of a concerted *demarche* to foist tariffs and food taxes upon the Conservative Party.[5] Indeed, such was the party's mood that by early October close associates warned Chamberlain that 'things are moving so fast that unless something happens quickly, everything and everybody will collapse like a pack of cards'.[6]

Mounting party disenchantment with Baldwin's leadership placed Chamberlain in an invidious and frustrating position for two reasons. First, increasing speculation about leadership distracted attention from his primary objective of committing the party to a radical change in its fiscal policy. For Chamberlain, the first priority was to jettison all past limiting pledges on tariffs in favour of a 'free hand' to deal with trade and imperial needs as circumstances suggested; a position which included the possibility of food taxes. Moreover, his urgency in pressing this policy was substantially increased by fears that J.H. Thomas, the new Dominion Secretary, would persuade Labour to steal the Conservative clothes on imperial preference.[7] Secondly, Chamberlain recognised that his proven ability combined with his well-known commitment to tariffs increasingly made him appear the obvious successor to a position he did not particularly crave. As Baldwin was his friend as well as his leader, therefore, he hoped that Baldwin's lethargy was just a 'passing phase'. But as he confessed in October 1929 it 'is all very depressing and particularly embarrassing for me because everyone I meet tells me of S.B.'s failings and many suggest that I should do better in his place. Heaven knows I don't want the job. It is a thankless one at any time & never more so than now when the party is all to pieces.' To make matters worse, the fear that Baldwin's distaste for Opposition might prompt his retirement confronted Chamberlain with the possibility of having to contest the succession with Churchill who was 'shoving very hard with an eye to the leadership'; a choice which prompted the confession that 'I don't know which I should dislike most!' Reluctant to assume the leadership himself, but adamantly opposed to Churchill's succession, Chamberlain thus became even more firmly committed to the defence of Baldwin's position. In late October, he warned Baldwin of the poor state of party morale and urged him to 'do violence to his instincts, give a lead and attack the enemy'. He also attempted to persuade him that tariffs were 'the only thing which could pull [our] people together and that an advance there was the thing to work for'.[8]

This logic implied the need to achieve an accommodation with Beaverbrook, despite the fact that Chamberlain believed Empire Free Trade was 'obsolete, impracticable and mischievous' and so 'woolly' that it would be 'riddled with criticisms' if adopted as a party commitment. He also feared that it was likely to jeopardise his own plans to 'make tariffs ... only part of a larger Imperial trade policy'. Until the end of October Chamberlain refused to negotiate with Beaverbrook, partly because of his evident vendetta against Baldwin and partly because he suspected 'the Beaver [was] trying to queer our pitch by setting an impossible standard and then crabbing everyone who does not come up to it'.[9] Yet encouraged by Harold Macmillan into believing that 'with a "few kind words" he might be won over', Chamberlain and Hoare met Beaverbrook on 4 November. Although discouraged by Beaverbrook's equivocation, his 'strong personal hostility to S.B.' and intransigence over food taxes, however, on the following morning Beaverbrook informed Hoare that after Chamberlain's forthcoming East African tour if they went to him 'meaning business he would be prepared to do a deal ... and ... his personal feelings about S.B. wd not stand in the way as he cared much more about Empire Free Trade than he did about his vendetta'.[10] On this basis, the accommodation was consummated at a meeting between Baldwin and Beaverbrook followed by a few sympathetic words in the leader's Albert Hall speech on 21 November.

Chamberlain was pleased by Baldwin's speech as the first step towards the adoption of the 'free hand', but although he believed him 'quite sound on the merits' he complained that he 'wavers backwards and forwards on the expediency according to the last person who talked to him'. As a result, Chamberlain (loyally aided by his close friend and ally, Sir Samuel Hoare) worked to maintain the protectionist pressure on Baldwin. 'He is like a top' Chamberlain told his sisters, 'You must keep whipping him or he falls over!'[11] Everything now depended on sustaining the new *modus vivendi* with the press lords while Chamberlain formulated a new and practicable tariff policy of his own. To assist him in this task, in November it was announced that Joseph Ball would become Director of a new Conservative Research Department. Although temporarily headed by Lord Eustace Percy, the Central Office press release made it clear that 'it is Mr Chamberlain's intention, on his return from South [sic] Africa, to associate himself actively with the work of the Department'.[12] Almost immediately Chamberlain arranged for an enquiry to consider the most effective method of support for domestic and Dominion farmers, while Cunliffe-Lister began work on an industrial tariff enquiry. Although he recognised the scale of the problem in converting the party and country to a policy of Empire development and the 'free hand', on tariffs, Chamberlain declared himself 'very well satisfied with our beginning'.[13] He then set off for 'the great adventure' in East Africa on 11 December, confident that the worst was now behind them and that a period of constructive Opposition lay ahead.

II

Chamberlain's three month tour of East Africa early in 1930 was intended both as a much needed holiday and as a necessary preparation for his future term as Colonial Secretary. Accompanied by his wife and daughter, he arrived at Mombasa on 30 December. Travelling first to Nairobi, Chamberlain dutifully inspected schools, hospitals and research laboratories, met officials, coffee planters and local chiefs and fished for rainbow trout in Lake Nyeri. From there he moved on to the Rift Valley to stay with the pioneering Lord Delamere, where he thrilled at the abundant wildlife and marvelled at vast flocks of flamingos on Lake Naivasha which appeared 'like a snow storm of pink snowflakes'. 'I have quite lost my heart to the country', he wrote home in mid-January. 'To begin with there is the most marvellous variety of scenery & climate & one is always coming on something totally unlike what one has seen before.' He was also gratified to feel that he was 'beginning to know something about the problems of the country' and that he had 'won the complete confidence of … the settlers [who] would do anything for me!'[14] From Kenya the family travelled to Uganda, although flooding prevented the continuation of their tour through Tanganyika. Embarking at Zanzibar on 16 February, Chamberlain arrived back in England on 8 March 'looking very well' and restored in vigour only to find that all his carefully prepared plans were in chaos.[15]

The rapprochement which Chamberlain had carefully negotiated with Beaverbrook before his departure proved as short-lived as it was superficial. This was largely a result of Beaverbrook's new alliance with Lord Rothermere, the extremely wealthy proprietor of the rival *Daily Mail*, then the largest selling daily newspaper in Britain. Rothermere's reactionary yellow press populism defied conventional party labels, but his intense hatred for Baldwin and the 'undisguised socialism' of his government fuelled Rothermere's determination to destroy his leadership and 'bring the Conservative Party back to Conservatism'.[16] Always convinced that control of the popular press was tantamount to political power in a mass democracy, Rothermere saw in Beaverbrook's Empire Crusade a vehicle to achieve these ends. Urged on by Rothermere's demands for a more aggressive strategy to contest by-elections with an organisation similar to his own Anti-Waste League which had inflicted so much damage on Lloyd George's coalition in 1921–22, Beaverbrook dispensed with official Conservative support and launched the United Empire Party on 18 February with the intention of carrying the fight to the constituencies. Having done so, he then almost immediately abandoned Rothermere after becoming 'really frightened at the utter lack of statesmanship and knowledge of politics' displayed by his fellow press baron.[17] At a private meeting on 3 March, Baldwin then agreed to a referendum on food taxes after the next general election as the price of reunion with the erratic Beaverbrook; an expedient Baldwin announced as official party policy in his Hotel Cecil speech next day.

When Chamberlain arrived home from Africa four days later, these unsatisfactory new circumstances soon forced him to overcome his 'strong distaste for politics' and to assert himself. As a result, within a few days, he had persuaded Baldwin to establish a 'Committee of Business' as 'a sort of inner Shadow Cabinet' and took up the reins of his new domain at the Conservative Research Department through which he expected to keep his 'fingers on the springs of policy'. He also renewed his cordial relations with an evidently discontented Beaverbrook.[18] During a long talk on 11 March, Beaverbrook gave vent to his renewed suspicions of the sincerity of J.C.C. Davidson, the party chairman, and announced that he hoped the referendum would soon be dropped; an opinion Chamberlain begged him to suppress for fear of alarming fiscally less advanced opinion in Parliament and the constituencies. By the end of this meeting, Beaverbrook expressed his gratitude for Chamberlain's candour and understanding. On both sides, it appeared a new relationship was developing on the foundations of a growing sense of mutual respect. As Beaverbrook declared next day, it was 'the best political discussion he had had, free from any kind of reserve, with any kind of politician since Bonar's death'. To consolidate the bond, Chamberlain persuaded a reluctant Baldwin to accept Austen's idea of inviting Beaverbrook to become a member of a weekly Fiscal Policy Committee 'to discuss ways and means of promoting "Empire Free Trade"'; a device which would place Beaverbrook in an apparently influential position without the obvious disadvantage of formally admitting him to the Shadow Cabinet.[19]

Despite Chamberlain's soothing influence, within a fortnight the volatile Beaverbrook had rebelled again. Already in 'rather an irritable frame of mind' because he suspected the Conservatives were 'letting him down', the publication of an aggressively free trade letter from Lord Salisbury in *The Times* left him 'very restless and angry'.[20] At an unpleasant meeting with Davidson and Chamberlain on 25 March, Beaverbrook retaliated by announcing his intention to revive the Empire Crusade. After this meeting, Davidson noted prophetically that Beaverbrook 'wants everything and will give nothing. He will take every opportunity which is given by the luke-warm or clumsy advocacy … of Empire Free Trade as a reason why he should be critical of our sincerity, and at the same time find some excuse for not giving any support whatever to our campaign in the country.' As it would be 'intolerable' for Beaverbrook to 'call the tune and write the slogans', an evidently outraged Davidson urged Chamberlain to ascertain the limits of his support for the forthcoming 'Home and Empire' campaign and for Conservative candidates fighting on the Hotel Cecil policy.[21] Unfortunately, the direct consequence of this hardening attitude was to drive Beaverbrook back into the arms of Rothermere as a prelude to renewed hostilities against the Conservative party – and in particular directed against Davidson, in the belief that his 'destruction would be a deadly blow to Baldwin'.[22]

Whatever Beaverbrook liked to believe about this threat, he only represented an indirect danger to Davidson by illuminating his shortcomings. The principal challenge to his continued influence came from Chamberlain. By March 1930 Chamberlain had resolved to remove Davidson from the party chairmanship because he was 'a fool and a danger in his post' and he said as much to Beaverbrook.[23] Having suggested to Davidson on 3 April that 'he had better go before he was fired out', Davidson's position became untenable a month later when Robert Topping, the Principal Agent, produced a calculated memorandum of concern about the 'extremely disturbing' deterioration of party morale since the dismal failure of the 'Home and Empire' campaign. If another electoral disaster was to be avoided, Topping warned, the party needed a lasting accommodation with Beaverbrook.[24] As Davidson was manifestly incapable of repairing the breach, Topping's memorandum was thus of considerable importance in undermining his intra-party position and after press reports about the formation of a backbench 'ginger group' to remove Davidson, Chamberlain decided to act before there was a parliamentary 'explosion'.[25]

Chamberlain initially planned that Geoffrey Ellis should succeed Davidson as he was already familiar with Central Office and his ideas generally accorded very closely with his own – particularly about the need for 'clearing out … some of the old gang of Palace Chambers'. Discreetly trying to avoid the appearance of a plot, Chamberlain began to canvass support for Ellis during April and at one point even hoped to induce Davidson to propose Ellis himself. In the event, however, the prevarication of Baldwin and Davidson aroused fears that they intended to leave Topping in effective control of Central Office behind the façade of a management committee; a suspicion which forced Chamberlain to decide that he should himself become party chairman for a limited period with Ellis as his 'understudy'.[26] After some further equivocation, Baldwin eventually agreed and Chamberlain's appointment was formally announced on 23 June.

Chamberlain was only too well aware of the sacrifices which the chairmanship entailed, having previously rejected any idea of accepting such 'a soulless job' in 1921 and 1924.[27] Despite his palpable lack of enthusiasm, however, the decision offered a variety of advantages for the party and even for Chamberlain himself. First, he rightly believed that Beaverbrook respected his intentions and sincerity and 'at the Central Office I may have perhaps a better chance of convincing him where the true interests of his policy lie'.[28] Second, although a less than ideal solution for Chamberlain, it had the merit of averting a greater evil, namely that Baldwin's retirement might force him reluctantly to become leader to prevent Churchill from doing so.[29] Third, from Baldwin's perspective, it effectively neutralised the party's most likely alternative leader by inextricably associating Chamberlain's reputation and future with Baldwin's own; a risk of which Chamberlain and his family were all too keenly aware. Finally, in the short-term, Chamberlain's appointment served to infuse the leadership with a new sense of purpose and direction when challenging its critics at a party meeting at Caxton Hall on 30 June. Indeed, the Chief Whip hailed the idea as 'too good to be true' and even the reluctant Chamberlain recognised 'it would buck the party up though it might ultimately break me!'[30]

More than ever, Chamberlain now wanted permanent reconciliation with Beaverbrook because he could 'be equally a very valuable friend and a very formidable enemy'. Within three weeks of becoming chairman, therefore, Chamberlain invited Beaverbrook 'to settle whether we are to be at peace or war'. On 18 July at a private dinner at his Eaton Square home, Chamberlain, Cunliffe-Lister and Hoare 'profoundly impressed and depressed' Beaverbrook with warnings that Labour's rumoured plans for import boards, quotas and bulk purchase from the Empire would sabotage Empire Free Trade. Chamberlain then played his 'trump card' when he 'brought ... home to Max the absolute folly of quarrelling with [the] Party and the necessity of finding some way of destroying the Labour Party before they destroyed his policy'. On this basis, Beaverbrook agreed to cease his attacks and rival candidatures in return for official toleration towards Conservative candidates sympathetic to his policy. Although Baldwin appeared 'half disappointed' by the possibility of agreement, Chamberlain believed that they would be 'in clover' if it materialised and Topping rejoiced at 'the first gleam of light after many months of gloom'.[31]

Chamberlain's satisfaction was short-lived. Indeed, on the following day Beaverbrook told Amery that he was reluctant to abide by his agreement given the possibility of several by-elections in the next few weeks. Despite Chamberlain's strenuous efforts to avoid it, therefore, less than a week after their meeting, another split occurred over Beaverbrook's decision to support Rothermere and the UEP against the Conservative candidate at the Bromley by-election; a rift widened by the resumption of attacks in the *Daily Express* and Chamberlain's discovery that Beaverbrook had not only 'been playing a double game ... all through' the Bromley negotiations, but that he had told a group of MPs he was only cooperating 'to keep Neville sweet'.[32] In language very similar to that later employed about Hitler after the betrayal of his hopes at Munich, Chamberlain recorded that 'I had given my trust and it had been abused and I was bitterly humiliated and outraged.' This he considered to be 'one of [Beaverbrook's] biggest blunders. He has destroyed my confidence in him', he told his sisters bitterly, 'and when that has happened I won't readily give it up again, *vide* Lloyd George.' Now 'very bitter and resolved to fight tooth and nail whatever the consequences', within hours Chamberlain had effectively thwarted the UEP in Bromley and he again awaited a Conservative by-election defeat 'for the compensation in the moral it would point'.[33]

This fiasco over Bromley was symptomatic of Beaverbrook's fundamental inability to choose between Rothermere and the Conservative party as the best means to achieve his desired end. It also brutally exposed his chronic political unreliability. Within days of the breach with Chamberlain, Beaverbrook had quarrelled with Rothermere, withdrawn from further participation in the by-election and in September began conciliatory overtures to Chamberlain through

Lord Bridgeman.[34] By now, however, Chamberlain was in an altogether less forgiving mood. Warning Bridgeman that he was 'on the wrong tack trying to separate Max from Rothermere' because 'R. has got Max by the short hairs', Chamberlain's decision to 'let him stew in his own juice' reflected the conviction that unless Beaverbrook was forced finally to choose between his two allies, lasting accommodation would never be possible.[35] While this assessment was largely correct, these events also highlighted the invidious nature of Chamberlain's own position. As he was forced to concede in late July, 'the tragedy is that – most reluctantly – I have come to the conclusion that if S.B. would go the whole party would heave a sigh of relief … yet it looks as if I will have to go down fighting for S.B. when my desire is, as it has always been, to go for the free hand'.[36]

III

Political anxieties about Beaverbrook's erratic behaviour were compounded by Chamberlain's increasing alarm about his wife's physical and mental condition. In April 1930, her doctors had diagnosed 'nervous exhaustion' due to the menopause and overwork and they recommended a complete rest in Switzerland over the summer.[37] While Annie rested at Chateau D'Oex in mid-July, Chamberlain decided to spend his summer holiday travelling across Europe to escort her back to England. Accompanied by his son and daughter, he travelled to Brussels where he saw his first performance of Madame Butterfly but concluded 'I don't really care about opera.' He was more impressed by Waterloo, the Ypres Salient, the war graves and the early Flemish painters. After a week in Germany, he confidently declared that 'though there are places in this country which are charming … and individuals who are likeable … on the whole I loathe Germans and detest all their habits & customs'.

> To begin with they are a revoltingly ugly race. I have seen only one woman who was not positively repulsive and I think she … must have been Swiss. As for the men with their great shining bald skulls, their little rolls of fat at the back of their necks, and their huge paunches, they are fit mates for their womankind … German beds infuriate me … And the food! No wonder Germans always seem to suffer from indigestion.

In this choleric mood, Chamberlain arrived in Chateau D'Oex on 26 August where he found his wife 'looking much better though still complaining of pains'. On the day after his arrival, however, she suffered a complete relapse and 'crumbled even more completely than … expected' until the arrival of Chamberlain's sisters, summoned from their own holiday to act as 'good Samaritans'. Even three days later Chamberlain was distressed to find that Annie was still 'very disturbed in mind', but next day she appeared much better and they returned to London.[38] Despite some initial optimism, however, her physical and psychosomatic condition evidently deteriorated. Although Chamberlain's diary letter to his sisters is missing for the following week and part of the next one was later destroyed by his wife, it is clear from what remains that Annie suffered a 'puzzling' fainting attack (and other 'women's troubles') in mid-September after which she consulted innumerable doctors about her gynaecological condition. Meanwhile, her somewhat exasperated husband was 'convinced that what she wants is to get her mind off herself … But I know by experience that you can't press her beyond a point or she only goes back on you.'[39] In June 1931 the problem returned, prompting Annie's renewed censorship of her husband's letters to his sisters.

Amidst this domestic anxiety and turmoil, Chamberlain returned from Germany to find yet another political crisis. As he noted gloomily, confidential reports of 'general dissatisfaction with the leadership' represented 'only the echo of a refrain that reaches me from every quarter with a dreary monotony'. By now, Chamberlain had been driven to despair by the manner in which Baldwin staunchly resisted the abandonment of the referendum at a time when the party overwhelmingly shared his own desire for a far more aggressive tariff commitment. Worse still, he knew that the more Baldwin offended party sensibilities, the greater would be the pressure on him to succeed to the leadership. Indeed, in August, Lord Camrose, the proprietor of the *Daily Telegraph*, urged Chamberlain to assume the leadership while Amery noted the increasing numbers of MPs who 'were already treating Neville with the deference due to the future leader'.[40] Acutely aware that he was now regarded as Baldwin's 'natural successor' and gravely concerned by the extent and intensity of party discontent, Chamberlain was forced to recognise that ultimately he would need 'to have it out with S.B.'.[41]

In the event, Chamberlain's solution to the problem was to kill two birds with one stone. From the outset, his interpretation of his role of party chairman was very different from that of Davidson and Baldwin's other close associates. While Davidson was content to be a loyal secretary to the leader offering 'a means of sounding the feeling in the country', Chamberlain was determined to exploit his position to initiate policy.[42] Despite influential backbench warnings that 'any policy which Baldwin launches as leader is doomed as a damp squib because he has lost the confidence of the Party and will never regain it', Chamberlain concluded that only by committing Baldwin to a far more radical tariff policy could he ever hope to restore party confidence in his leadership.[43] With this in mind, he had already prepared the ground for Baldwin's public conversion to the new policy by launching his own 'unauthorised programme' in a speech at Crystal Palace on 20 September calling for drastic economy (especially on unemployment insurance), an emergency tariff, a wheat – and possibly meat – quota and the abandonment of the referendum to permit a 'free hand' on other imports to improve imperial economic relations. As one of Baldwin's closest political associates, Bridgeman was also persuaded to impress upon their leader the urgent need to abandon the referendum, adopt the 'free hand' on protection and to call another party meeting to silence the malcontents.[44]

Unfortunately, when Bridgeman attempted to do this on 1 October, Baldwin gave the distinct impression that 'his heart did not seem to be in the business'. This response left Chamberlain 'very depressed' because he realised that if Baldwin failed to '"get it across" at the Party meeting they would have fired [their] last shot'.[45] Furthermore, as Chamberlain's supporters understood all too clearly, the defeat of Baldwin's leadership in these circumstances would place his successor 'in the most difficult position'.[46] Despite his apparent relief at Baldwin's determined acceptance of the new tariff programme at the Business Committee on 7 October, therefore, there is evidence to suggest that later that evening Chamberlain consulted his half-brother and Hoare about the possibility of calling a front bench meeting in Baldwin's absence to discuss a change of leadership in his own favour. By the following day, however, Chamberlain had abandoned the plan because 'if any move is made, it should really come from the House of Commons – the body which makes, and can presumably unmake, leaders'.[47]

Beyond a desire to avoid accusations of treachery, Chamberlain's change of heart on 8 October was assisted by dramatic developments at the Imperial Economic Conference in London. At its second plenary session that morning, the Canadian Premier proposed 'to the Mother Country and to all other parts of the Empire, a preference in the Canadian market in exchange for a like preference in theirs'.[48] The moment Chamberlain heard of Bennett's offer, he recognised that it provided a 'Heaven-sent opportunity' of attaching Baldwin to the 'unauthorised programme' in such a way as 'to tide us over the immediate difficulties, and to give an opportunity to those who are still loyal, to renew their allegiance'.[49] After brief consultations, Chamberlain immediately issued a statement over Baldwin's name accepting the offer on behalf of the next Conservative government.[50] In the long-term, this public declaration represented a personal triumph and a crucial reorientation of the party's tariff position. The referendum had been 'buried without loss of credit' and Chamberlain's 'unauthorised programme' had become official policy. Indeed, his triumph was almost completed when Churchill informed the Business Committee on 14 October of his refusal to accept Chamberlain's policy before bidding his colleagues 'a sort of formal farewell'. During an 'awkward pause' Chamberlain breathed a sigh of relief and passed a note to the Chief Whip saying 'Vex not his ghost. Oh! Let him pass.' Unfortunately, at this point Austen ruined everything by imploring their overwrought colleague to reconsider. 'It seemed too good to be true', Chamberlain told his sisters, but to his intense frustration the opportunity for ridding themselves of 'a dangerous liability' had already passed.[51]

In the short-term, Chamberlain's policy initiative radically transformed perceptions of the threat posed by Beaverbrook and the forthcoming party meeting. Chamberlain drafted a second public letter for Baldwin in the following week reaffirming their commitment to the 'unauthorised programme', but this was designed merely to 'save S.B.'s bacon long enough to enable him to go later without a triumph for R[othermere] and B[eaverbrook]'. Convinced that it was now only a matter of time before the inevitable backbench revolt, Chamberlain was content to 'await events'. Should Baldwin recover his position then no harm would be done: if he did not, then the parliamentary party could disown him without directly implicating Chamberlain in his downfall. Assured from all sides that 'the whole party has been heartened up and feels that it has a policy once more', Chamberlain believed that everything now depended on Baldwin's willingness to use his opportunity. He also noted that it was 'curiously characteristic of him that he hasn't said a word of thanks to me or even shown any sense that he realises what has happened'.[52]

During October Baldwin emerged briefly from his morose apathy to demonstrate a new vigour and determination. His short speech to the party meeting at Caxton Hall on 30 October unveiled the new policy and obtained its endorsement with only one dissident – Beaverbrook. Baldwin then withdrew to enable the attack on the leadership to be defeated by 462 to 116 votes. In such a highly charged atmosphere, the news that an Empire Crusader had narrowly defeated the official Conservative in the South Paddington by-election by 914 votes was recognised on both sides to be 'a Pyrrhic victory' and Beaverbrook soon sued for peace. Indeed, when Chamberlain met Beaverbrook a week later, he was surprised to find 'a New Max' with all his assurance gone and 'at times almost humble in manner'.[53] In the belief that 'he really does mean, this time, to come in' Chamberlain arranged a public exchange of letters between Beaverbrook and Baldwin on 21 November as the basis for a resumption of full cooperation.[54]

Again, however, the promise of accommodation proved illusory as Beaverbrook exploited Conservative defensiveness over food taxes in the Commons debate on 27 November as a pretext 'to drift for a bit until we see how things are developing'.[55] Although a now depressingly familiar pattern of behaviour, it was a worrying portent of his later dealings with Hitler that Chamberlain proved remarkably easy prey to Beaverbrook's duplicity during late November and early December despite their stormy past relationship. Nevertheless, the resumption of the press and by-election offensive in December finally disabused Chamberlain of his last illusions about Beaverbrook. 'He is as unstable as water, without patience, balance or self-control', Chamberlain lamented. 'He can never wait, and his restless vanity impels and compels him always to keep himself in the limelight.' Moreover, his encouragement to the Norfolk branch of the National Farmers' Union to form an 'Agricultural Party' to run candidates on a food tax platform against the Conservatives forced Chamberlain 'reluctantly ... to the conclusion that it was impossible to work with him' – although ironically, he still considered the possibility of an arrangement with Rothermere, 'who if a bigger scoundrel is at least less unreliable'.[56]

IV

Although Chamberlain successfully undermined the UEP campaign at the East Islington by-election in January, the crisis of confidence in Baldwin's leadership reached a climax in February 1931. Since October he had relapsed once more into depressed lethargy, while his lack of enthusiasm for his new tariff policy was painfully apparent. Inundated with letters from all over the country informing him 'that people have lost all trust in his ability or will to carry anything', Chamberlain finally concluded that his succession was the 'natural outcome'. As in October, however, his problem was that while he was the only person able to bring about Baldwin's retirement, he could not act without the damaging appearance of self-seeking disloyalty.[57] Fortunately, this potentially compromising dilemma was once more resolved by the decisive intervention of Robert Topping, now General Director at Central Office. In a brutally uncompromising memorandum in late February 1931, Topping reported that support for Baldwin's leadership had declined so dramatically that even his most loyal supporters now shared the widespread feeling that 'in the interests of the Party ... the Leader should reconsider his position'. While conceding that Churchill's policy on India was more popular with the party than Baldwin's, Topping crucially expressed the view that they 'would prefer ... that if a new Leader is to be chosen, he should be elected on broad policy and not on any one single issue'. In short, by claiming to speak for the bulk of party sentiment, Topping had provided Chamberlain with a weapon to unseat Baldwin, to exclude Churchill from the succession and put himself forward as the only natural leader. Moreover, he precipitated the crisis in such a way as to leave Chamberlain uncompromised by allegations of self-interest.[58]

Confident that Topping's memorandum would finally dislodge Baldwin, Chamberlain betrayed an unmistakable note of disappointment when a UEP candidate almost immediately emerged in the St George's by-election to fight purely on the leadership question. As he noted in his diary, 'it is in accord with the irony of politics that just as I was about to take the step which must have resulted in the speedy retirement of S.B. Max comes in with a move which must cause him to dig his toes in and will rally to him many who wish for a change. This is the 2nd time Max has spoiled his own game by his precipitation.'[59] Nevertheless, the crisis he had predicted since October had finally arrived and Chamberlain seized his opportunity with alacrity. Despite his best efforts to save Baldwin, he now convinced himself that these had failed and that while Baldwin remained as leader the party would never be united or politically effective.

When Chamberlain consulted senior colleagues separately about the best course of action, they unanimously agreed that Baldwin should be shown Topping's report although Lord Hailsham prevailed in delaying its disclosure until after Baldwin's Newton Abbott speech on 6 March; a proposal Chamberlain accepted against his own better judgement because although 'afraid of missing the bus' he 'did not relish the prospect of hearing ... that [he] had shown indecent haste in pushing S.B. off the throne'. In the event, Chamberlain's dilemma was resolved for him on 28 February with the news that the official Conservative candidate had withdrawn from the St George's by-election rather than defend Baldwin's leadership. Armed with this compelling pretext for immediate action, Chamberlain ordered the removal of some phrase 'too wounding for S.B. to read' and despatched Topping's memorandum next day. Archly explaining that he had been 'rather torn between my affection for you as a friend and my duty to you as Chairman of the Party', Chamberlain informed Baldwin that senior colleagues agreed he should be shown it because he would have 'some ground for complaint if hereafter a situation were to arise in which any action taken by you might have been different if you had been fully aware of the feeling described by Topping'.[60]

Having read the document, a dejected Baldwin summoned Chamberlain to announce that he had decided to resign immediately and that he would help him to obtain the leadership to prevent Churchill seizing it. Baldwin concluded their meeting by asking Chamberlain to summon a front bench meeting for the following morning to 'say goodbye'. Later that evening, however, the leadership was effectively snatched from Chamberlain's grasp when Bridgeman 'rolled in like an old Admiral' to protest against Baldwin's resignation 'in so ignominious a fashion', while Davidson reported alternative Central Office sources which suggested Topping's memorandum was 'giving vent to his own personal hostility' towards Baldwin.[61] In this context, Bridgeman declared that Baldwin should 'challenge the right of the press millionaires to dictate procedure to the Party' by contesting the St George's by-election himself. Even if defeated, he argued, Baldwin could then retire 'with honour and dignity as the champion of a cause which 99% of the people knew in their hearts was right'. Baldwin found it rather less easy to convince Chamberlain about the wisdom of this course. Indeed, he appeared 'very cold' when Baldwin broached the idea next morning and pointed to the difficulties which Baldwin's defeat would create for his successor 'in having to treat with 2 victorious generals'; a far from disinterested calculation which prompted Baldwin's curt reply, 'I don't give a damn about my successor, Neville.'[62]

Baldwin's new determination did not significantly modify Chamberlain's perception of the situation or its likely outcome. In the belief that Baldwin could not remain leader much longer, Hoare and Amery mobilised support, while Chamberlain and Hailsham agreed privately on 5 March that they were prepared to serve under each other as a 'partnership', but never under Churchill. Baldwin's reaction to these rather premature arrangements was predictably brusque and he soon made it known that he was 'very angry with "some of his colleagues"', particularly Hailsham who had he believed been plotting against him'. Although Chamberlain was not among 'the chief sinners', Baldwin was known to be 'sore against [him] for not having supported him more stoutly' – an accusation which Chamberlain understandably found 'difficult to stomach without resentment'.[63]

In this atmosphere of mutual suspicion and recrimination, the final act in the drama was precipitated by Chamberlain's half-brother. Austen had always opposed Neville's decision to accept the party chairmanship and by March 1931 he believed Baldwin was so 'heavily waterlogged' that this association was severely jeopardising his chances of the succession.[64] At the Business Committee on 11 March Austen bluntly enquired when Baldwin was going to relieve his half-brother at Central Office as his debating talents were desperately required on the front bench.[65] He had not warned Neville in advance, probably because of his earlier veto of a similar scheme in October and the closeness of the family connection. Nevertheless, to all present it was 'pretty plain what [Austen] had in mind' and 'even SB could hardly miss the underlying implication that it was to free Neville for the successorship'.[66] By this stage, however, Austen didn't care what Baldwin thought and even Chamberlain inclined to the view that Austen was correct. In an icy conversation with Baldwin two days later Chamberlain thus explained his desire to resign as party chairman, only to be astonished and wounded to hear absolutely no word of surprise, regret or appreciation. After this, he curtly completed the explanatory letter to accompany his formal resignation, denying foreknowledge of Austen's plans, explaining his own 'singularly painful and embarrassing position' when confronted by the Topping memorandum and objecting that it was 'intensely disagreeable' to feel his motives were regarded as self-interested.[67]

Chamberlain's anger and frustration at Baldwin's behaviour were intensified by the activities of the press lords whose impudent intervention in the St George's by-election represented both the climax of their campaign against Baldwin and the end of Chamberlain's hopes of replacing him before he was ready to go. During an often scurrilous and abusive campaign, Baldwin easily subordinated questions of policy to the moral right of the party to choose its own leader without dictation from an 'insolent and irresponsible plutocracy' seeking 'power without responsibility – the prerogative of the harlot throughout the ages'.[68] After Duff Cooper's comfortable victory in holding the seat for the Conservatives, all that remained was to resolve outstanding difficulties. Although Baldwin soon let it be known that he was 'anxious to avoid a rift' with Chamberlain, there were further angry scenes before their breach was finally healed on 24 March, after a 'frank not to say brutal talk' which enabled them to part 'shaking hands with the clouds removed'. On the same day, Chamberlain reluctantly reopened negotiations with a chastened Beaverbrook and an agreed exchange of letters was published on 31 March – but only after Chamberlain thwarted a last-ditch effort to give the appearance that the Conservatives had changed their policy to accommodate Beaverbrook.[69] Two weeks later Chamberlain left Central Office to the evidently genuine regret of its senior staff, although he crucially retained complete control over the Conservative Research Department until his death. Under the direction of his close confidant and fishing friend, Joseph Ball, the CRD increasingly served as 'Neville Chamberlain's private army' during the 1930s, while Ball progressively moved into the centre of Chamberlain's web of personal advisers in his role as a shadowy but accomplished political 'fixer'.[70]

In retrospect, the Empire Crusade was a farcical episode. The tariff policies which Chamberlain introduced less than a year after the St George's by-election borrowed nothing in their conception from Beaverbrook or Empire Free Trade. Despite constant lobbying by trade associations and organisations like the Empire Industries Association during the 1920s, the contention that the tariff was largely the product of pressure group politics is also utterly without foundation.[71] The principal impetus was provided by Chamberlain and his front bench protectionist associates. Upon going into Opposition in 1929, a party committee had been established to make proposals on 'the general industrial policy which the Party should adopt'.[72] Here, and in Chamberlain's Conservative Research Department, the tariff policy had been in gestation since early 1930. When Cunliffe-Lister's committee produced its hundred-page report in June 1931, the Conservatives were armed with an all-embracing protectionist policy and 'a definite, practical working plan, which can be put into operation without delay'.[73] All that was needed was the opportunity to put these plans into effect.

V

In the immediate aftermath of defeat in 1929, Chamberlain had anticipated seven years in Opposition. Eighteen months later he was doubtful whether the Labour government could survive much longer and talked more in terms of months rather than years.[74] To accelerate this process of government collapse, since November 1930 Chamberlain had been planning to destroy it from within by encouraging sympathetic Liberal MPs to join with the Conservatives to oust Labour in return for suitable guarantees about their own position. In early December, he was encouraged to find Sir John Simon vehemently hostile to the government and 'by no means irreconcilable' to tariff protection because 'though he was not a convinced Protectionist he was ready to take any risks to get the Govt out'. Simon also let it be known that he and Lord Reading were prepared to join a 'hybrid' Conservative Ministry and that although 'he could not control many votes in the House ... he believed he had a considerable following in the country'.[75] By the spring of 1931, Chamberlain had made the necessary deals over seats and induced Sir Edward Grigg to organise a 'Liberal Unionist' wing to act in alliance with the Conservatives.[76] It was a measure of his anxiety to eject Labour from office that during July 1931 Chamberlain even half-heartedly authorised secret negotiations with Lloyd George in order to defeat the government in return for some limited measure of electoral reform.[77] In the event, the arrival of the European financial crisis in London at the end of the same month rendered all such arrangements unnecessary.

Chamberlain was the principal architect of the Conservative Party's evolving response towards the emerging financial and political crisis during the summer of 1931. In practice, Baldwin clearly did envisage an ideal outcome from the crisis when he consistently declared that he would assist the Labour government with economies but would never join another coalition and 'preferred the "Gamble" of a General Election'.[78] Yet in reality, Baldwin abdicated any influence he might have had early in the negotiations by appearing 'not ... to have a strong view one way or the other' and by returning to his holiday in France after only six hours in London for crisis meetings on 13 August. Chamberlain's failure to remonstrate betrayed a deeper relief. '[T]he decisions are left to me as S.B. is not coming back', Chamberlain recounted to his sister three days later.

> I think he would agree that crises of this kind are not his forte. He had apparently given no thought to the situation, asked no intelligent question, made no helpful suggestions and indeed was chiefly anxious to be gone before he was 'drawn into something'. He left a final message for me that he was most grateful to me for sparing him the necessity of returning and would 'back me to the end'![79]

Free from interference and surveillance, Chamberlain conducted negotiations as he desired. Certainly his clarity of mind and grasp of detail ensured he was almost alone in knowing precisely what he wanted from the rapidly developing situation. As such, his thoughts and motives are central to the principal remaining controversy surrounding the events of 1931, relating to the allegation that the crisis was a 'Conservative ramp' and that Chamberlain 'displayed unique qualities of leadership and foresight' in deliberately exploiting the financial situation to pursue 'a strategy that ensured the downfall of Labour and prepared the way for a National Government under Conservative control'.[80]

In recent years this view of a Conservative conspiracy has been subjected to vigorous and effective scholarly rebuttal, principally on the grounds that the formation of the National Government was 'neither sought nor desired' by the Conservatives, but rather something into which they were 'stampeded' by the panic atmosphere of August 1931 and then accepted out of national duty and an ardent desire for economy. As a result, the allegation that 'any Conservatives were principally concerned ... with cunning notions of wrecking the Labour party' is dismissed as 'patently absurd'.[81] As one recent study notes, 'Despite playing a prominent role in the negotiations which led up to the establishment of the National Government, [Chamberlain] neither foresaw the manner of the crisis's outcome nor tried to direct the discussion against the trend of events.'[82] Yet while this counter-view has now undoubtedly become the established orthodoxy, the problem with rebuttals based on a close examination of the events of August 1931 is that they often obscure the partisan dimension underlying Chamberlain's longer-term strategy. In this context, the creation of a National Government may not have been the outcome that Chamberlain initially anticipated or consistently desired, but in a crucial sense it was the logical outcome of the strategy he had pursued throughout the preceding year. As such, in a very important respect, he was the principal arbiter of the Labour government's fortunes and the outcome of the crisis.

In Opposition, Chamberlain had consistently condemned the government's allegedly irresponsible finance and demanded economy, particularly in relation to borrowing for the Unemployment Insurance Fund. Indeed, soon after the 1929 election he had predicted that unemployment insurance 'would be the "Achilles heel" of the Labour Government'. As the slump deepened and the cost of unemployment benefits spiralled upwards, Chamberlain had beaten the economy drum with increasing vigour. The once zealous reformer at the Ministry of Health thus informed a Birmingham audience in January 1931 that social expenditure had risen by 450 per cent in 20 years and that the 'first duty' of the next Conservative government must be to reduce public expenditure to a level the nation could afford.[83] By February he was confidently predicting that 'the Government cannot maintain themselves in office for many more months' because their 'policy of spending will have its effect in the money market and public opinion will make itself felt in condemnation'. On precisely this basis, Chamberlain countered Baldwin's vehement objections to the widely rumoured idea of a National Government in July with a remarkably prescient assessment of the crisis as it eventually developed:

> What I foresaw the possibility of was a panic in the City a hundred million deficit in the Budget, a flight from the £ & industry going smash; such a position that it could only be met by such drastic steps as Germany & Austria were taking. It was then that R.M[acDonald, the Labour Prime Minister] would come to him because he would not be able to count on his own people to support him.

At this juncture, Chamberlain loathed the idea of National Government, but he was sufficiently realistic to recognise that in panic circumstances such a demand 'might be very hard to refuse'.[84]

It is undeniable that Chamberlain passionately and sincerely believed that it was crucial to balance the budget and reduce public expenditure – particularly with regard to the increasingly heavy borrowing of the Unemployment Insurance Fund. Warned that the Royal Commission on Unemployment Insurance was about to recommend an increase in benefits, in May Chamberlain declared that this 'would be more than [he] could stand' and that he 'would rather run the risk of losing the election than giving way on what seems to me a really vital matter'. From Chamberlain's perspective, unemployment benefit was the key to everything and 'unless they can straighten out Un[employmen]t. In[suran]ce the whole Budget crumples up and its falsity is exposed'. As he warned the Commons on the eve of the summer recess, foreign confidence had been shaken by the growth in public expenditure and it could only be restored 'when the foreigner is convinced, first, that the people of this country realise the situation; and, secondly, that they are going to have the courage to take the necessary steps to deal with it'.[85]

In order to achieve these goals, Chamberlain was prepared to sacrifice much in the national interest. Indeed, as the financial crisis erupted, Amery was not alone in being 'afraid that even Neville may be influenced by City panic and by the idea that it is our duty to "save the pound" at the risk of weakening the only policy that can save the pound'.[86] It is also clear that the Conservatives stood every chance of winning the next election with an overall majority, even without the devastating effects of either a political crisis or a schism within Labour ranks. But the truth of these propositions should not obscure the equally fundamental fact that Chamberlain clearly perceived that the situation offered an opportunity to achieve a massive and enduring partisan advantage while pursuing these vital national goals and that he actively manipulated the crisis discussions in order to bring this about. As he boasted privately to his wife on the eve of the final Cabinet crisis, 'We have got the Govt into a most difficult position and by concentrating on economy have preserved our rights on taxation completely.'[87]

In this context, Chamberlain's calculations and strategy as the crisis unfolded during August 1931 were guided by two central assumptions. First, he was rightly convinced that '[f]rom the party point of view the chance of getting "economy" out of the way before a General Election and of destroying the enemy's most dangerous weapon by identifying the present Government with "economy" is so important that it would be worth much to obtain it'.[88] This was particularly true because since the New Year his optimism about the imminent fall of the Labour government had been accompanied by the grim realisation that they had 'left us a *damnosa hereditas* and I don't look forward to any share I may have in cleaning up the mess'.[89] Any attempt to resolve this problem thus inevitably implied immediate action and profound electoral unpopularity because, as he noted in his diary, 'we could never escape from economies at the election by shirking them beforehand since every candidate would be asked to pledge himself against individual cuts and probably would do so'. In these circumstances, he believed the obvious and most prudent course was simply to enter an election saying to the electorate, 'Now you know the worst; the cuts have been made the nation has roused itself and made its sacrifice now we come with the only remedy which can ever make it possible to bring back prosperity.'[90] But to extract the maximum benefit from this strategy, Chamberlain needed either to assist a Labour government to implement such economies or, if absolutely unavoidable, to create an all-party emergency government to do so in such a way as to blame Labour for the crisis while gaining Conservative credit for its resolution. Allied to this conviction, Chamberlain's second guiding assumption was that, if successful in this immediate objective, there would be either 'a new alignment of parties' or 'an appeal to the country in conditions offering the utmost advantage, seeing that we could no longer be saddled with the unpopularity of economy, but could concentrate on tariffs and Imp[erial] Preference as the restorer of prosperity'.[91]

In the event, Chamberlain did not have to wait long for his opportunity. On 31 July the report of the May Committee on National Expenditure gloomily predicted a £120 million budget deficit and proposed drastic retrenchment of £97 million – including £66.5 million from unemployment insurance. This provided Chamberlain with precisely the weapon he needed to saddle Labour with all the opprobrium of passing such drastic measures while undermining both its electoral support and Cabinet unity. In response, Chamberlain immediately made it clear to Bank of England officials that the Conservatives would 'back up the Chancellor if he will squarely face the issues, ... *even if his own side should go against him*'.[92] He then left London when the Commons went into recess and remained in Scotland on his fishing holiday convinced that 'one can best leave things to go on simmering for the present'.[93] As the May Report had fully confirmed foreign pessimism about British solvency and the government's ability to restore it, the rapidly dwindling credits from New York and Paris did not halt the flight from sterling. In these circumstances, the Bank of England made it clear to Ramsay MacDonald, that 'we were on the edge of the precipice and unless the situation changed radically we should be over it directly' because 'the cause of the trouble was not financial but political & lay in the complete want of confidence in HMG existing among foreigners'. After this blood-curdling warning, it was little wonder that Chamberlain was 'agreeably surprised to note the extent to which the Bankers had succeeded in frightening Ramsay' when he attended their first crisis meeting on 13 August.[94]

Chamberlain 'had done some pretty hard thinking' before this meeting with MacDonald and Philip Snowden, the Labour Chancellor. After it, he was astonished to find that they were determined to balance the budget on the basis of 'equality of sacrifice' and that 'so perilous has the state of the national finance grown ... that a Socialist Govt. is actually contemplating a cut of £100 millions a year! To secure such a measure of relief and to do so through a Socialist Govt seems to me so important in the national interest that we *must* give it our support.' Convinced that 'the Govt do mean business at last and that provided they get the requisite assurances from us they will face the music', Chamberlain was greatly relieved and prepared to 'give the assurances and hope that we shall not as a party suffer for it'.[95] To help dispel the crisis atmosphere, he then returned to Scotland. At this juncture, while Chamberlain knew precisely what he wanted in both financial and political terms, he lacked the means to bring it about. As he complained to the editor of the *Morning Post* on 13 August, when his City editor 'speaks of our "insisting" on this or that I am not sure that he realises our limitations'. As the Conservatives were not being asked to join the government, 'our only "sanction" may be to withdraw support from proposals which both on National and Party grounds we may very anxiously desire to see forwarded'.[96]

As it happened, this latter scenario precisely outlined the turn of events. On the same day, with French and American loans almost exhausted, Bank of England soundings in New York confirmed that there was no prospect of any further credits unless the Labour Government obtained the support of the other parties for their economy programme. Chamberlain now had the fulcrum upon which the leverage supplied by the May Committee could be exerted. From this moment, MacDonald effectively became the prisoner of the Opposition parties.[97] All that remained was for Chamberlain to offer terms for Opposition support which the Cabinet could not accept and remain either united or electorally credible. By the time he was summoned back to London from Scotland on 18 August, Chamberlain was able to crystallise his strategy:

> The problem was to restore foreign confidence in British credit. This could only be done by announcing such a cut in natl. expenditure as would convince him (the foreigner) that we had sufficient courage to tackle the situation. I put the figure at 100 millions and I knew that that could not be obtained unless there was a substantial reduction in unempl[oymen]t insurance benefit. I proposed therefore to concentrate on reduction leaving all questions of taxation (including tariffs) to be dealt with hereafter.

This was the line to which Chamberlain adhered single-mindedly during a succession of crisis meetings with the Labour leaders between 20 and 23 August. By sticking rigidly to the argument 'that retrenchment was the vital thing', and particularly by making a 10 per cent cut in unemployment benefit the acid test of the Labour Cabinet's economic responsibility and willingness to 'squarely face the issues', Chamberlain sought to balance the budget and save sterling while detaching those ministers committed to 'responsible government' from the rest of the Cabinet committed primarily to the defence of sectional class interests and Labour party unity. As he predicted on 20 August, 'one of two things may happen. Either R.M. may surrender to his malcontents & put forward inadequate proposals in which case I am told he will lose Snowden and the flight from the £ will set in, or he will part with Henderson & others and open negotiations for a National Govt.'[98]

Later that morning, Chamberlain informed the Labour leaders that their reduced calculation of the possible savings on unemployment benefit was hopelessly inadequate to restore confidence. He repeated the same view privately that afternoon and again on the following evening, although he prudently refused to be drawn by MacDonald's efforts on 21 August to put an exact figure on the level of economies he would accept – largely for fear of being drawn into a bargaining process which would end in less than he thought either acceptable on national grounds or capable of achieving his partisan expectations. At the same time, he equally consistently emphasised that unless the Opposition parties' terms were met they 'would combine to kick him out as soon as Parlt met', but that it was 'the P.M.'s bounden duty to avoid [the] crash' and that they 'were ready to give him any support in our power for that purpose either with his present or in a reconstructed Govt'. 'Nothing was said about a Nat. Govt.', Chamberlain confided to his sisters, 'but it was obviously not excluded' and MacDonald was clearly heartened by the intimation.[99] Given the clarity of Chamberlain's objectives and the undeviating determination with which he pursued them, it was little wonder that when his colleagues re-assembled in London on 21 August they agreed that 'Neville is handling the situation admirably.' As Cunliffe-Lister recorded after this briefing, 'everything turns on whether the Government will cut the dole – without that you can't get the necessary economies, and ... the other economies hang on it. Nor can you justify taxation. A tariff is no alternative. First and foremost you must have drastic economy. That alone will save the situation. Whatever happens there will be a political crisis.'[100]

Against this background, the principal flaw in the 'Conservative ramp' thesis lies not in the assertion that Chamberlain manipulated the crisis to achieve conveniently overlapping national and party goals, but rather in the claim that this crucially involved an outcome defined in terms of a Conservative-dominated National Government. In reality, the successful pursuit of Chamberlain's objectives did not necessarily imply a National Government and historians too often overstate and pre-date the moment at which the idea of such an arrangement began to germinate in Chamberlain's mind as a convenient outcome to the crisis.[101] Chamberlain's initial intention had certainly been to force the Labour government to shoulder all of the opprobrium for economies while giving them all necessary external support to achieve this goal short of actually joining a coalition. Rumours of MacDonald's desire for a National Government in early July had thus been dismissed because the party 'would not stand it for a moment'.[102] By the end of the month, however, the crisis had deepened sufficiently for a meeting of the two Chamberlains, Hailsham, Hoare and Cunliffe-Lister to agree that coalition could still be averted, but 'might be unavoidable'. At this juncture, Chamberlain dismissed talk of a coalition with the prediction that 'if it came at all it would be much more probable that R.M. would resign and that a certain number of the present Government would come into an administration under S.B.'.[103]

Yet three weeks is a long time in crisis politics. Having hinted at a National Government to MacDonald and Snowden on 21 August, when the final crisis erupted on 23 August after the Labour Cabinet failed to agree to the economies demanded by Opposition leaders, Chamberlain and Hoare had 'already come to the conclusion that a National Government was inevitable'.[104] Confronted by the prospect of MacDonald's resignation and a minority Conservative ministry, Chamberlain thus urged Baldwin 'to try and get Ramsay, Snowden & one or two other members of the Govt in even if they brought no one with them'. Moreover, later that day, when MacDonald dismissed the idea on the grounds that he would be 'a ridiculous figure unable to command support and would bring odium on us as well as himself', Chamberlain swiftly retorted that his adhesion would substantially strengthen any National combination because of the electoral support he commanded and (more important) because of the beneficial effects on foreign confidence. Shifting from flattery to cajolery, he also warned of the criticism likely to follow if MacDonald refused to join such a government when he supported its policy.[105]

The outcome of the political crisis of August 1931 represented a major personal triumph for Chamberlain. The formation of a National Government was never one of his primary goals, and until the last moment he thought the Labour Cabinet would accept his terms and avert it – but only at the cost of being 'shaken to its foundations'. But when a National Government emerged as the option most likely to deliver his central objectives, he accepted it as 'the best thing that could have happened' and declared himself 'much happier'. Ultimately, its adoption did not necessitate a fundamental reappraisal of his broader strategy and certainly does not substantiate the claim that during the August crisis the Conservative Party was blown off course at least as much as Labour. After all, the Labour Cabinet had been split down the middle; MacDonald was persuaded to remain as Prime Minister in an all-party combination pledged to execute essential but unpopular economies; and this interim coalition was committed to deal only with the financial emergency before a dissolution and a party election held in circumstances of the utmost advantage of the Conservatives. At the same time, Chamberlain's will had decisively prevailed over Baldwin's instinctive antipathy towards the idea of joining another coalition. By the time he returned to London on 22 August, Baldwin still undoubtedly 'hoped and prayed that he might not have to join a National Government', but when he attempted to express these doubts Chamberlain became 'very impatient with S.B.'. By then, even Baldwin was compelled to accept that he had little real option but to acquiesce in the logical outcome which Chamberlain had engineered.[106]

It is scarcely surprising that when looking back on the outcome of the crisis, Chamberlain felt that he had 'nothing to regret & no reason to be dissatisfied with the part I have played'.[107] As Chamberlain's principal lieutenant throughout the crisis, Sam Hoare also assured him that 'if you had not at the very outset of the negotiations adopted not only the right line but also the right tone the country might have been plunged into an irrevocable catastrophe. It is such crises that really test a man's judgement.' Throughout the drama Chamberlain had repeatedly remarked 'the mercy of God was vouchsafed in three ways, Lloyd George was in bed: Winston was in Biarritz and S.B. was at Aix'. Yet as Hoare noted, 'The greatest of all [good luck] … was the series of events that left you in full control of a situation that particularly demanded your qualities of quick decision and consistent action.' Certainly looking back in amazement in the aftermath of their election landslide two months later, Central Office believed 'that but for [Chamberlain] the Conservative Party would not be where it is to-day'.[108] There would appear to be far more substance in this verdict than the prevailing historical orthodoxy would suggest.

VI

At noon on 24 August, MacDonald returned from the Palace to inform an astonished Labour Cabinet that as they were unable to agree on economies he intended to tender their resignation to permit the 'formation of a National Government on a comprehensive basis for the purpose of meeting the present emergency'.[109] The National Government, created as a temporary expedient to balance the budget and restore foreign confidence, remained in power until Chamberlain's fall from the Premiership in May 1940. By the terms of the Buckingham Palace concordat agreed between the party leaders that day, it was 'not a coalition in the ordinary sense of the term but a cooperation of individuals' and the Cabinet should be 'reduced to a minimum'.[110] In the ten-man Cabinet, MacDonald remained Prime Minister and he was supported by three other Labour men – Snowden, Thomas and Sankey, the Lord Chancellor. With Lloyd George still recovering from a prostate operation, the Liberals were represented by Sir Herbert Samuel and Lord Reading, while Baldwin was accompanied by Cunliffe-Lister, Hoare and Chamberlain. Although Baldwin was soon 'in very good spirits & ... happier than he has been for a long time', in practice it was Chamberlain who dominated the Conservative contingent by force of mental agility. 'Chamberlain is an acute critic of proposals but has a constructive mind as well', MacDonald noted in his diary after a week together in Cabinet. 'Baldwin almost a dead weight but reliable – listens and leaves discussions to others.'[111]

Economy dominated the Cabinet's labours during its first month and Chamberlain proved characteristically punctilious in seeking to deliver the full figure of £1,250,000 required from his own departmental budget at the Ministry of Health. Indeed, in deference to the political and electoral concerns of fellow ministers he was actually obliged to abandon his more draconian proposals.[112] Although an Economy Bill was passed on 8 September, it was soon overtaken by further disasters. Newly-obtained credits were almost exhausted when the Home Fleet at Invergordon staged its famous 'mutiny' in protest at unannounced pay cuts. The consequent loss of confidence in sterling provoked a dramatic outflow of gold from London which largely negated the Cabinet's frenetic exertions of the past month. On 21 September, after a 'terrible week' in which Chamberlain reported 'the atmosphere has been as depressing as it is possible to imagine', a Bill suspending the gold standard was hastily passed.[113]

Even before the defence of sterling had failed, it was apparent to Chamberlain that 'the task of setting our house in order will not be fulfilled unless measures are taken to redress the unfavourable balance of trade'.[114] Initial expectations that the parties could fight an election when sterling had been saved were destroyed with the abandonment of the gold standard. After this, the bankers warned MacDonald that such a course would disastrously undermine foreign confidence unless fought on an agreed programme to restore the balance of trade. The need for agreement upon such measures thus became inextricably associated with Conservative clamour for an election and the implementation of tariff protection at a time when the party's leadership recognised that 'pressure from the Conservative rank and file for an election is so overwhelming that the members of the Cabinet "would be left high and dry" if it does not come off'.[115]

Yet rather than rank and file pressure redirecting Chamberlain's intentions, it actually permitted the realisation of his long-term strategy. By mid-September he was already saying that 'Nothing but a protective tariff of the kind ... worked out in the last six months, would ... be effective and ... any attempt to buy Liberal support by compromising on this all-important matter would [not] be in the interests either of the Party or the Country.' As such, he was determined that 'the Liberal Party will have to face up to the fiscal decision ... The decision will split it from top to bottom, and ... will end it, the two sections going off in opposite directions; and bring us back nearly to the two party system.'[116] Even at this juncture, Chamberlain anticipated that this would necessitate an immediate general election and despite pressure from his own 'idiotic party' to fight on party lines, Chamberlain was convinced that 'the only way to secure the sort of majority which would give confidence is to go as a National Government, perhaps even as a National Party carrying MacDonald and his colleagues with as many Liberals as we could get'. In order to achieve this goal, Chamberlain resolved to make 'the Prime Minister ... face up to [the tariff], to decide by a majority to adopt it, to accept Samuel's resignation and after filling his place ... go to the country as a National Government on a programme of the full tariff and a free hand to save the country'. After his colleagues endorsed this strategy, Chamberlain noted with more than a touch of malicious irony, 'Truly the Conservative Party is a wonderful embodiment of good sense, patriotism and honesty.'[117]

Convinced that MacDonald was 'ready to go the whole hog' on tariffs, Chamberlain pressed home his advantage in the confident expectation that Simon, Runciman and Reading would remain from the Liberal contingent along with Thomas, Sankey and possibly even Snowden from MacDonald's National Labour following. After an inconclusive Cabinet meeting on 28 September, Chamberlain was determined to see MacDonald in the hope of 'influencing him to a firmer stand' on the basis of his draft election statement calling for a free hand to control imports. When he met MacDonald next day, the Prime Minister had just learned of his expulsion from the Labour Party and he appeared 'very low and depressed', but he read Chamberlain's draft attentively and seemed 'very pleased with it saying he agreed to every word but was doubtful whether the Libs wd. accept it'. In reality, MacDonald's apprehension outlined Chamberlain's precise intention. Keenly aware that Samuel was 'working like a beaver to gain time to find some bridge', Chamberlain was utterly determined that the free trade Liberals 'shall swallow the whole programme or go out'.[118]

At a series of crisis Cabinet meetings between 29 September and 2 October, Chamberlain continued 'searching for a breaking point' but to no avail in face of Samuel's greater determination to evade being manoeuvred into resignation.[119] Even more frustrating was that after Lloyd George told MacDonald that 'he was being made a fool of by those wicked Tories', the Prime Minister's 'nerve went all to pieces' and he drafted a new manifesto which would have 'simply horrified' the Conservative rank and file. Determined to settle the matter once and for all, at a crucial meeting with MacDonald shortly before the Cabinet on the afternoon of 5 October, Chamberlain and Baldwin insisted upon the inclusion of the contentious prior commitment to control imports and threatened to resign if MacDonald refused.[120] In 'the last stage of exasperation and almost in despair', Chamberlain had already resolved that if MacDonald could not find a solution he would force the issue to a crisis himself.[121]

The Cabinet meeting fully justified his expectations. MacDonald's initial attempts at evasion provoked considerable Conservative consternation and, according to MacDonald, prompted Chamberlain to scribble a note to Thomas threatening resignation.[122] Recognising that it was impossible to resist, MacDonald then abruptly announced that an election was inevitable and that only the platform remained to be agreed. Sensing a rupture, at this point Baldwin began his valedictory speech only to find it cut short when Samuel suddenly produced a typed statement accepting that the Prime Minister should issue his own statement for the government, agreed by the party leaders, with a separate appeal by each party.[123] It was a bizarre formula, but the crisis was over. 'I was never so surprised in my life', Lord Sankey recalled in his diary, 'in less than 90 seconds we decided to stick together when it appeared hopeless.'[124] On the following morning MacDonald obtained a dissolution. Fighting on a uniquely advantageous battleground, astonished Conservatives carried all before them. In Edgbaston, Chamberlain faced little real opposition and his West Midland fiefdom proved fiercely loyal to its Chamberlainite heritage as the Conservatives swept every Labour candidate (and all but two Liberals) from the entire area. Nationally, it was a Conservative landslide which gave them 470 of the 615 Members in the new House. In total, the National Government commanded 554 seats.

VII

Chamberlain had always predicted 'a peck of troubles as soon as the election is over, first in the formation of the Government and then in the formulation of policy'. As all recognised, the future tenor of the government would be determined by the political and fiscal complexion of the Chancellor of the Exchequer. Before the election, Chamberlain shared a widespread Conservative fear that MacDonald might attempt to demonstrate his independence by putting a Samuelite or one of his own supporters at the Exchequer with Baldwin's acquiescence.[125] Such fears were well founded. Determined to ensure that the Treasury and Board of Trade were not both held by tariff reformers, MacDonald had initially hoped to persuade Baldwin that Chamberlain should remain at the Ministry of Health, so 'that someone with leanings on the whole to the other side should take the Exchequer, as Cunliffe-Lister is so good at the Board of Trade'. On the day after the election, MacDonald declared 'Runciman was his man' for the Treasury.[126] By this stage, however, the Conservatives were in a position to veto any such proposal because, as Bridgeman warned Baldwin, unless the Chancellor was a Conservative and known 'to be friendly to scientific protection a large section of our side will revolt'.[127] Moreover, this time, Chamberlain experienced none of the personal reluctance or administrative distaste for the idea of the Treasury that had inhibited him in the past. By 5 November, therefore, MacDonald was forced to concede and Chamberlain became Chancellor while Walter Runciman accepted the Board of Trade.

Despite the necessary concession to non-Conservative sensibilities, Chamberlain remained 'very optimistic' because while there were 'some suspicious elements in [the Cabinet] ... they will not really have much chance of obstructing, even if they ... wish to do so'.[128] Above all, he was sanguine about his partner at the Board of Trade, telling his sisters that he 'like[d] Runciman personally and I fancy he likes me so that at least we ought to start fair'.[129] This optimism was not misplaced. Although a lifelong Liberal free trader, during the 1931 crisis Runciman's interpretation of the priorities of his Gladstonian heritage lent greater emphasis to retrenchment than to free trade on the grounds that it was 'an outworn political stunt' and that 'during this present emergency we may have to take many emergency steps as we did in time of war'. By September 1931, therefore, while anxious about food taxes and still proudly proclaiming himself 'the most bigoted Free Trader in the House', Runciman had come as far as any of Simon's Liberal followers on industrial protectionism and the need to redress the adverse balance of trade.[130] On this basis, harmony rather than dissension characterised Chamberlain's relationship with Runciman during the following year as they consummated his father's vision of a protectionist edifice with imperial preferences.

Chapter 8

The Treasury, Tariffs and Economic Diplomacy, 1931–1934

'That you should be C[hancellor] ... at this moment of all others gives me the deepest satisfaction. I was the first Chancellor to introduce in a very humble way Imperial Preference into the Budget. You will be the Chancellor to complete the building for which I laid the first brick in 1919. Father's great work will be completed in his children ... Don't think me absurd or pretentious if I say that I feel something of your success of what Father thought of mine. It is something more than a brotherly interest, it is an immense love and a possessive pride.'

Austen to Neville Chamberlain, 5 November 1931

It suggests much about the divergent aspirations within the National Government that while MacDonald regarded the onset of 1932 with 'many forebodings', Chamberlain eagerly heralded it as 'the year of opportunity'.

Although 1931 was a year of unhappiness, and then a wonderful exhibition of determination and courage on the part of the Nation, 1932 will be the year of opportunity, and, if we do not make good use of it, we shall deserve the condemnation which posterity will certainly mete out to us. In my present office I feel I have perhaps a greater share of the responsibility for the use that is to be made of our wonderful majority than anyone else ... Frankly, although the burden is heavy, I rejoice at it. To be given the chance of directing such great forces where I am convinced they should be applied, is such a privilege as one had no right to hope for; and I intend to make the most of it.[1]

Above all, Chamberlain expected to use his position as Chancellor to impart substance to the incorporeal vision of a 'scientific' tariff and imperial preference invoked by his father some 30 years before. As he rightly forecast, 1932 would be a 'very momentous year ... the turning point, or perhaps ... rather the critical point in my political career'.[2] As a touching signal of this historic significance, he was 'much gratified' to be offered the Freedom of the City of Birmingham in January. As the Lord Mayor who had initiated the practice of erecting tablets bearing the names of Freeman in the Council House, he was particularly satisfied to note that the presence of three names from the same family was a unique achievement.[3]

During the first National Government, Chamberlain had been prepared to subordinate tariffs to the far more urgent task of balancing the budget and saving sterling in the belief that it was becoming 'more and more evident that [they could] not put the situation right without a tariff'.[4] After prolonging the life of the National Government specifically to redress the adverse balance of trade, however, the question of tariff policy immediately emerged at the top of the political agenda. Having persuaded Runciman to accept the idea of an unspecified maximum rate of duty against abnormal imports being 'dumped' on the British market (rather than Runciman's inclination to specify a 10–20 per cent tariff), when they put the proposal to the Cabinet on 12 November Chamberlain was delighted when Snowden then responded to his questions about the maximum rate of duty by suggesting 100 per cent; a proposal the Cabinet duly accepted. Chamberlain's amusement at the success of his strategy was evident: 'Comic isn't it', he wrote to his sisters, 'to think of the Free Traders giving power to two Ministers to put a 100% duty on any mortal manufactured article they like.'[5] A fortnight later, the Cabinet agreed to an emergency duty on non-essential foodstuffs.[6] Almost unobserved, the principle of taxes on food, albeit of a 'luxury' class, had passed into law. Little wonder that in late December Chamberlain seemed 'fairly happy with the progress the Government is making'. As he told his sisters, 'We have witnessed a political revolution in three months and although bloodless it is none the less effective.'[7]

As in the previous September, Chamberlain regarded MacDonald as 'the key to the situation' in his advance towards a 'scientific' tariff structure. Believing his views on tariffs were still largely uncrystallised, Chamberlain assumed the Prime Minister would accept any reasonable solution if it did not involve 'embarrassing political complications' with the free traders and avoided his appearance as 'a mere figurehead, obliged to accept holus-bolus any policy which might be imposed upon him by his Tory colleagues'. Protectionist advance, therefore, depended upon Chamberlain's ability to win the support of a 'sufficiently influential non-Tory section of the Cabinet' to ensure that MacDonald remained 'fairly comfortable'. In particular, if Runciman's assent could be secured for the proposals emanating from the Balance of Trade Committee, Chamberlain felt he 'could have no greater certainty of winning ... the support of the Prime Minister'.[8] Despite Runciman's unexpected flexibility over the emergency tariffs, however, his support was far from guaranteed. Indeed, in a number of private conversations during December Chamberlain found him intractable over tariffs on fundamentals like meat, wheat and steel. Nevertheless, despite Chamberlain's overestimate of his progress in these preparatory talks, Runciman still played a pivotal role in designing and passing the Import Duties Bill. To this extent at least, Chamberlain was successful in creating an understanding which left MacDonald 'very glad' that they were 'getting together and hammering out agreements on some of the big subjects' before them.[9]

The Committee on the Balance of Trade, established in early December to advise upon remedies, was crucial to Chamberlain's strategy of legitimating protectionist aspirations in such a way as to reassure MacDonald and the electorate of a 'National' consensus in favour of tariffs. Having skilfully out-manoeuvred MacDonald over the committee's composition and organisation, Chamberlain intended 'to bring on the battle at an early stage' so the 'fight will come in Committee' which he intended to dominate.[10] His manipulation of the committee's proceedings was characteristically adroit. After a discursive first session, debate was almost entirely confined to memoranda prepared by Chamberlain and Runciman, thereby compelling the free traders to argue their case within the parameters defined by protectionist initiative. Moreover, by the penultimate session, all the committee's members except Samuel and Thomas (who 'could be relied upon to support') had been persuaded to accept Chamberlain's proposals for a flat rate tariff with selective surtaxes to be imposed by an independent Import Duties Advisory Committee. At this meeting, however, Chamberlain's strategy virtually collapsed when Snowden suddenly launched into an 'old time Free Trade disquisition' against a general tariff and then adamantly refused to listen to the pleas from Runciman and Chamberlain designed to change his mind. Worse still, Snowden's resistance encouraged Samuel's refusal to support the proposals and neither Chamberlain or Runciman could budge them.[11]

In a final attempt to obtain Snowden's acquiescence Chamberlain wrote him a long and friendly letter before the Committee's final session, mobilising all the policy and personal arguments for reconsideration. In an equally warm and effusive reply, Snowden adamantly refused to consider them.[12] Although Snowden's determination was predictable, Chamberlain had been obliged to seek an accommodation for two reasons. First, while he despised Herbert Samuel's Liberal free trade following, he had always genuinely held Snowden in high esteem as 'a man of courage'.[13] As such, he did 'not want to see the realist element in the Cabinet weakened' by Snowden's departure because this would deprive him of a powerful ally in the 'large field in which [their] ideas [we]re very nearly identical'.[14] Secondly, Snowden was important to Chamberlain because his support mattered to MacDonald. Neither MacDonald nor Chamberlain took Samuelite threats of resignation seriously, but there was no such lack of confidence about Snowden's sincerity. By alarming MacDonald, therefore, Snowden's intransigence compelled Chamberlain to attempt a reconciliation.

In view of Snowden's increasing belligerence since the election and his letter two days earlier, it is astonishing that Chamberlain should have interpreted Snowden's 'almost complete silence' at the committee's final meeting on 18 January as a sign that his pleas had achieved their purpose.[15] In fact Snowden's silence signified patient fatalism. Shortly before the meeting he had informed Samuel that he was 'definitely opposed to the proposals ... and that he would resign rather than concur'. Samuel's assurance that he and his followers were in the same position, however disingenuous, perceptibly encouraged Snowden into believing that he would not be alone. In order to reconcile the committee's divergent opinions, at their final meeting on 18 January Samuel and Snowden were permitted to submit separate memoranda of dissent.[16]

Although Chamberlain had initially hoped to carry the whole committee with him, once the split occurred he found it relatively easy to portray the majority as moderate pragmatic realists and the dissenters as inflexibly doctrinaire free traders. The magnitude of his success in isolating his opponents became fully apparent during two Cabinet meetings to discuss the Committee's reports on 21 January. Chamberlain stressed the urgency of the problem and argued that the Committee had tried honestly and sincerely to face the problems but that the sacrifices had not been all on one side. Significantly, while the Conservatives all supported the majority report, so did Runciman, Thomas, Sankey and Simon. Despite Baldwin's pointed reference to Conservative parliamentary strength and other warnings that if the Cabinet did not act 'the House of Commons would take matters into its own hands', the studied moderation and pragmatism of the majority served to illuminate the implacability of the free traders who, between the two Cabinet meetings, had finally agreed to concert their threats of resignation. Thus, when MacDonald concluded by aligning himself with the majority, Samuel declared that the free traders could not accept the full protectionist policy which was neither necessary nor a compromise. Deadlocked, the Cabinet adjourned after MacDonald warned that 'all present would have to face what would be the result of the break-up of the National Government'.[17]

Although this rift plunged the Prime Minister into despair, this was precisely the situation Chamberlain had striven to achieve. As a result, when the Cabinet reassembled next day, Samuel's offer 'to sit down again and try to find some other way of agreement' was vetoed by Chamberlain, who blandly reassured MacDonald of the Cabinet's personal confidence in his leadership and the continuation of the 'National' element in the government after the Samuelite departure.[18] Yet at this point, 'when there seemed nothing to do except say "goodbye"', Hailsham suddenly proposed an 'agreement to differ', suspending collective responsibility to permit the dissentients to 'go "as they pleased" on the tariff question'; a suggestion which met with immediate approval except from Chamberlain who appeared manifestly 'not enthusiastic about their remaining'.[19] The supreme irony of this particular outcome was that Chamberlain had initially proposed this very expedient to MacDonald on the previous afternoon in order to retain Snowden in the Lords, without apparently having considered the possibility of its application to Samuelite ministers in the Commons. Despite the retention of the Liberal free traders, however, even Chamberlain professed himself 'well satisfied'. Not only had he prevailed on the tariff, but the public formalisation of free trade dissent actually served to insulate him from intra-party criticism that he had 'sold the pass' by being insufficiently assertive in imposing Conservative tariffs on the rest of the Cabinet.[20]

Introducing the Import Duties Bill on 4 February, Chamberlain carried the House with emotion and a sense of historical fulfilment on 'the great day of [his] life'. Although he would have preferred to have kept his feelings to himself for fear of losing control of his voice, he relented when he 'realised that this would have been misunderstood when everyone else was full of the historic completeness of it all'. In a moving 'personal note' he thus concluded with a tribute to his father's frustrated exertions, declaring that 'he would have found consolation for the bitterness of his disappointment if he could have foreseen that these proposals, which are the direct and legitimate descendants of his own conception, would be laid before the House of Commons … in the presence of one and by the lips of the other of the two immediate successors to his name and blood'.[21] It was a sentiment which found echoes within the entire family and among many old tariff reformers beyond it. 'I can hardly yet believe in the reality', Chamberlain wrote to his step-mother on 6 February: 'success has come so rapidly after all these years of delay and disappointment.'[22] Next day, he revealingly confessed to a stalwart of the pre-war tariff campaign that 'like Hamlet, I have been haunted by my Father's Ghost. Now the Ghost can rest in peace.'[23] The protectionist edifice so long awaited was almost complete; only the Empire remained to be integrated into British tariff arrangements. As it transpired, however, imperial economic unity was to be achieved not through the hearts and emotions of the Dominions, but through their pockets.

II

Despite the hypnotic appeal of Joseph Chamberlain's crusade for imperial federation and commercial union to consolidate the 'great partnership of Empire', his younger son was anything but a dewy-eyed sentimentalist about Anglo-Dominion relations. Neville Chamberlain had never shared the obsessive imperial vision of Leo Amery, who more than once declared that he 'never felt that either of the Chamberlain brothers really regard their father's policy as anything more than a somewhat tiresome legacy'.[24] Although characteristically blinkered, Amery was at least correct in the view that Neville Chamberlain had now jettisoned some of his father's facile optimism about the prospects for imperial economic unity. But the case should not be overstated. Chamberlain looked forward to the forthcoming Imperial Economic Conference at Ottawa as 'the most important event since the War' and the needs of the Empire had been a significant factor in formulating the general tariff.[25] As he told Lord Lloyd soon after introducing the Import Duties Bill, 'I am convinced that this policy and this alone could have saved the Empire. It may not have saved all of it yet. But without it the Empire, as we have known it, was bound to go and to carry with it the greatness of this country.'[26]

This combination of imperial idealism and hard-headed commercial reality was essential to sustain revived Dominion hopes that something may at last be achieved. As past Imperial Conferences had been burdened with an economic conflict of interest almost beyond resolution without the possibility of Britain offering tariff preferences to the Empire in its domestic market, the established pattern of imperial economic relations since the war had become one of 'Dominion importunity, and UK intransigence'.[27] The Import Duties Act ended this deadlock by furnishing the British with a bargaining position from which to negotiate reciprocal arrangements – and they intended to use it to drive a hard bargain. Moreover, contrary to the assertions of some influential historians,[28] this hard-headed commercial spirit owed far more to Chamberlain than it did to Thomas, the Dominion Secretary. Both men were equally convinced that failure to reach agreement at Ottawa would be 'a fatal blow to Imperial interests'.[29] But from the outset, the Cabinet's Preparatory Committee for Ottawa canalised a fundamental conflict of perspectives about the future nature of imperial economic relations into a personal confrontation between these two ministers.

Thomas continued to adhere to the established orthodoxy that imperial tariff preferences should retain the traditional form of unilateral non-discriminatory concessions within the Empire rather than become the subject of bilateral negotiations which might produce 'political and economic dangers of the very gravest character'. Although he intended to press for the maximum concessions at Ottawa, therefore, the maintenance of imperial unity would remain his first priority. In contrast to Thomas' calculated altruism, Chamberlain preferred to place his faith in bilateral bargaining in the belief that 'the policy of the generous gesture' had failed to produce any striking results in the past and that in the prevailing climate of slump and economic nationalism, Dominion politicians would find negotiated agreements with a specific *quid pro quo* far easier to defend to their own electorate.[30] Believing 'the point fundamental and the only way to tie Thomas down to his instructions', in early December this strategic conflict was resolved by the Cabinet in Chamberlain's favour when the Dominions were informed that without adequate reciprocation at Ottawa provisional British preferences would be withdrawn when they lapsed in November. Chamberlain was equally successful in forcing a reluctant and fiscally divided Cabinet 'to face realities' over the crucial necessity for food taxes upon which complete or partial preference could be granted at Ottawa in return for adequate concessions from the Dominions.[31]

Despite this policy success, however, by the end of January Chamberlain recognised that the future shape of imperial economic relations also depended upon personal capabilities and this raised the question of Thomas' leadership of the British delegation – particularly as his retention of the Dominion Office after 1931 had provoked considerable disquiet among Dominion leaders.[32] The true extent of this danger only became fully apparent in February 1932. In drafting the Import Duties Bill, Chamberlain had intended to grant a $33\frac{1}{3}$ per cent preference to the Empire, retaining the remainder for bargaining at Ottawa. Having been 'begged' by Thomas to offer no preference as 'he wanted all he could get to bargain with', Chamberlain acquiesced on the assumption that Thomas 'knew his business well enough to be sure that no mischief would be done'. Four days later, however, Chamberlain learned from Howard Ferguson, the Canadian High Commissioner, that Thomas had been warned of hostile Canadian reactions to such an idea three weeks earlier. Although Chamberlain then revised the Bill accordingly to give the Dominions free entry to British markets until 15 November 1932, after this it was perhaps scarcely surprising that he had 'cold shivers to think how near we were to a colossal blunder' or that he feared Thomas might well destroy all hope of success at Ottawa.[33]

Chamberlain responded to these apprehensions by persuading Baldwin that he should lead the British delegation to Ottawa in the expectation that he would perform the purely ceremonial functions of leader while Chamberlain conducted the negotiations.[34] Although Baldwin was gratified by this proposal, both men were initially reluctant to make the suggestion for fear it would fuel MacDonald's suspicions of a Conservative conspiracy. Two days later, however, Thomas solved this problem by engaging in a drunken quarrel with Ferguson at a large public dinner during which only Austen's intervention to 'knock ... their heads together' averted a diplomatic disaster.[35] After this incident, Chamberlain persuaded Baldwin to join him in writing to MacDonald proposing the plan – with the predictably successful outcome. Thomas' ruffled dignity was appeased with the promise that he should be second in order of precedence and in return he agreed to Chamberlain's inclusion in the delegation to 'complete [his] father's work'. Yet as Chamberlain observed with justifiable cynicism, 'I fear that he will find that his precedence doesn't really depend on his place in a list.'[36]

As one chronicler has observed, the British delegates departing for Ottawa on 13 July 1932 hoped to 'save the Empire by their energy and save the world by their example'.[37] After almost 30 years of struggle, for Joseph Chamberlain's sons and his many other followers, Ottawa was a dream come true; the culmination and consummation of a lifetime's endeavour. Yet even before departure, Chamberlain confessed to being 'very anxious about Ottawa since so much has been said or written about what it should accomplish that I fear disappointment is inevitable'. In part, this was because he expected the Dominions to be 'very hard bargainers' and 'likely to be very exacting, and to claim what will be very difficult for us to give while withholding much of what we should like to have'.[38] But more disturbing was the realisation that Dominion concessions would not immediately translate into anything substantial with regard to enhanced British trade or employment.[39] The effective choice, therefore, was between either adopting a longer-term basis upon which to assess British benefits, or doggedly bargaining for greater immediate concessions with the near certainty of failure for both the conference and possibly the Empire.

Confronted by such a dilemma, Chamberlain opted for the former course, not through 'an almost pathological need to finally achieve his father's dream' as some claim,[40] but rather because he and his colleagues simply refused to contemplate failure for strictly pragmatic reasons. Over a month before sailing for Ottawa, Chamberlain was already emphasising that success should not be measured purely on the basis of short-term commercial reciprocity: 'its real importance', he told his sisters, 'lies in starting the Empire on the new path of mutual preference and provided it does that any initial failures are of minor importance ... [because] the future possibilities of Empire trade ... must be infinitely greater than anything we can hope for from foreigners.' After the opening skirmishes at Ottawa, it was thus soon apparent that Chamberlain was not 'at all in the balance sheet mood'.[41] As he told R.B. Bennett, the mercurial Canadian Premier, they 'were not so much looking to what it might be possible for the United Kingdom to obtain in the immediate future from any settlement at Ottawa, but rather to setting inter-Imperial trade relations on a new road which would give great benefits to future generations in the United Kingdom and other parts of the Empire'. Moreover, this was a pragmatism easily translated into a visionary language which transcended efforts to assess Dominion concessions simply in monetary values. As he told Baldwin in early August, 'if we were to carry our people with us we must show them something that would touch their imagination. We must open up the vision of a great Imperial policy having within itself the mainspring which would continually move us on to closer unity.'[42]

From their first meeting on board ship, Chamberlain dominated the work of the British delegation and he set the tone for its negotiating strategy. He knew Baldwin too well to allow him to draft his keynote opening declaration without close supervision and when Baldwin read 'some very rough notes' to colleagues on 15 July they were 'received with blank dismay by the whole party'. Convinced that 'the speech would have killed the conference almost before it had begun', Chamberlain then not only drafted a new version but also insisted that it should be 'typed and read so as to have no possibility of mistake!' He also drafted 'a series of general propositions for the approval of the Conference both in order to give the lead to the Dominions and the outside public and to form a test to which every proposition afterwards put forward could be submitted'.[43]

This general resolution reflected Chamberlain's curiously optimistic hope of combining high moral purpose and an appeal to a shared sense of 'Britishness' with unambiguous national self-interest. In tones reminiscent of his father, it affirmed that the 'existing measure of Imperial unity in sentiment and purpose would be greatly strengthened by a more complete community of material interests'. On this basis, the resolution contained six propositions designed to provide 'the most hopeful means of reviving trade and of stimulating demand throughout the world'; a policy prescription conveniently defined largely in terms of the British desire to extend tariff preferences only 'by lowering existing duties within the Imperial circle rather than by raising them against other nations'.[44] In the event, tactful Canadian manoeuvring in defence of conflicting Dominion interests ensured the resolution never saw the light of day, but Chamberlain's hope that it could ever have succeeded reflected a high degree of naivety about the ability of Anglo-Saxon sentiment to influence established Dominion tariff structures – particularly when dealing with Dominions like Canada and Australia which sought to maintain a high wage regime behind stiff protective tariffs.[45]

Despite the rejection of his opening resolution, Chamberlain attempted to salvage something of its spirit by promoting two new principles which he hoped would set the Empire on its new path of closer commercial union and progressive tariff reduction. The first was the 'domestic competitor' principle, by which the level of Dominion tariff protection should be no more than to enable domestic producers to compete fairly with British importers. Chamberlain's second idea involved the regulation of output and supply. Although he had been thinking along these lines for domestic agriculture since March 1930, he only considered its application to Dominion and foreign producers on the Atlantic, as a solution to the British delegation's own unresolved differences over meat duties and quotas. As he explained to the Monetary Policy Committee at Ottawa, falling prices had increased (rather than decreased) the volume of production as farmers sought to maintain revenues; a fact which suggested that the real problem was less one of world price levels than over-production. Dominion output should thus be regulated to keep pace with Britain's capacity to absorb it in order to raise wholesale prices within the UK market. Over a period of five or ten years, this market would then be progressively turned over to a larger share of Dominion imports at the expense of foreign suppliers. Although initially to be applied to sheepmeat, with an eye on the World Economic Conference scheduled for June 1933, Chamberlain argued that 'if it could be put into operation with success by the Empire, [it] would give to the world the lead which was so greatly needed and might well result in a similar world scheme for dealing with world price commodities'.[46]

Despite the language of principle and the faint air of moral superiority, Chamberlain's beloved twin principles reflected a high level of British self-interest. They also appear remarkably insensitive to the harsh economic and political realities which confronted Dominion delegates in the depths of a world depression. Above all, for Dominion food exporters, more than ever dependent upon British markets, a far-sighted scheme for the regulation of supply (which might eventually raise wholesale prices) scarcely represented an attractive alternative to an immediate increase in their share of their principal market at the expense of foreign competitors – particularly when it required delegates to explain to domestic electors that this actually meant a short-term contraction of export levels and revenues. Equally important, the removal of often prohibitive protective duties to enable Britain to operate as a 'domestic competitor' in Dominion markets, was not only based on an outmoded economic fallacy, but also flew in the face of a far more fundamental political reality. As the Australian Trade Minister bluntly informed the British at Ottawa, 'unemployment in Australia might not be created in order to give employment in the United Kingdom'.[47]

Against this background, Chamberlain was deeply dismayed to find little evidence of Imperial warmth in the conference bargaining – particularly when negotiating with the two largest Dominions. Australia represented a major problem throughout because its demands were substantial, while the amount of foreign trade likely to be diverted to Britain was considered to be so inconsequential that it was doubtful whether it would even justify the retention of existing preferences.[48] Despite much haggling, brinksmanship and blackmail over a meat duty, Chamberlain skilfully overcame their resistance and an agreement was eventually signed which broadly accepted both of his central principles – although not before a despairing Chamberlain made it clear to Baldwin that if the conference broke down over the refusal of Runciman and Thomas to accept the necessary duty on meat he 'should have to fade out'.[49]

From the outset, however, it was Bennett who gave Chamberlain his 'greatest anxiety'. Although Bennett was known to attach great importance to the conference's success, his attitude towards Britain had hardened so substantially since the abortive Imperial Conference in 1930 that in November 1931 he intimated that failure at Ottawa would result in a US-Canadian trade agreement.[50] Chamberlain was also rightly alarmed by Bennett's insistence upon chairing the conference while representing Canada single-handed.[51] Moreover, when Bennett belatedly produced his 'Mickey Mouse' list of 8000 items for free entry to Canada, analysis soon revealed both a grotesque exaggeration as to its value and an incredible degree of duplication with 'celluloid frogs, fish and rabbits' appearing under no fewer than eight separate entries while crossword puzzle books were recorded under 'books', 'cross' and 'puzzles'.[52]

Far more dispiriting was Bennett's personal conduct. Chamberlain initially imagined fondly that Bennett 'has great confidence and a great regard for me' and would 'take from me what he wouldn't take from anyone else'.[53] Unfortunately, the 'somewhat electrical' atmosphere of the first negotiating session with the Canadians on 4 August swiftly disabused him of this illusion.[54] Moreover, in response to Chamberlain's 'polite but rather stiff reply' to Canada's niggardly list of concessions, at another stormy meeting on 12 August, a 'clearly very angry' Bennett 'flared up with the remark that [the British] proposal was worse than no offer of any kind'. Accusing them of 'leading him up the garden', Bennett declared that 'he had never been so mad in his life: that Americans would not have treated him so, that he had been let down at the last moment & made to look foolish for maintaining … that Englishmen could be trusted to play straight'.[55]

After this outburst, Chamberlain's personal relations with Bennett became 'extremely unpleasant'. 'You can imagine how mortifying all this has been and I am feeling as sore as possible', he confided to his sisters. 'But I can't let personal slight interfere with the attainment of my objects and I am reserving what I shall have to say to Bennett till everything is safely signed & sealed.' But despite this pragmatism, Chamberlain found the experience profoundly unedifying. 'Another black day', he recorded on 15 August after a long meeting with Bennett during which he 'indulged in his usual alternations of sob-stuff and hard business'. Two days later he again found 'Bennett exceedingly offensive and untruthful', but by now he claimed his 'personal annoyance and vexation over B's suspicions of my good faith have evaporated. One can't care what a crook thinks of one.'[56] After further heated exchanges, the Ottawa Conference concluded at 1.30am on 20 August, when the Canadians finally initialled their agreement. Exhausted and frustrated almost to breaking point, Chamberlain wrote angrily to his wife, 'it will take me a week or two to recover from this last week. I never want to see Canada again!'[57]

At Ottawa the work was interminable and Chamberlain undoubtedly carried the greatest burden. In spite of his physical and mental exhaustion, however, he initially believed 'the excitement of pushing through a great enterprise keeps me from feeling fatigue', while he rejoiced that the unity and loyalty of the British delegation meant that it was a 'pleasure to work with such a team ... in which there are no difficulties and no jealousies'.[58] Indeed, it was indicative of the delegation's harmony, that they should have remained united for so long while conceding so much, but in view of their difficulties Chamberlain inevitably commended the delegation upon their 'wonderful achievement' in obtaining such 'excellent' agreements; self-congratulation less perhaps at the terms of the agreements, than at the existence of any agreements at all. For Chamberlain in particular, it was 'a great addition to [his] satisfaction that ... there are still so many of the family left to rejoice in the fulfilment of Father's policy'.[59]

Yet for the British delegation, relief was tainted with a bitter and enduring resentment. Chamberlain and his colleagues returned home believing they had made selfless sacrifices to save the Empire from the rapacious myopia of their Dominion brethren. 'It was a d—d close run thing', he confessed to his sisters from the ship home. 'It was only by the exercise of almost incredible patience, self restraint in face of outrageous provocation, ingenuity in finding new ways round unexpected obstacles and complete confidence in one another that we achieved success.' In the short-term, it was easy to focus these frustrations on the attitude and behaviour of the Canadian Premier. In a phrase much beloved by the British delegates, Bennett had 'the manners of a Chicago policeman and the temperament of a Hollywood film star'. When a *News Chronicle* correspondent declared that Bennett was as 'passionate as a spoilt child, as slippery as an eel, as stubborn as a mule and as hysterical as a woman who had lost her lover', Chamberlain added warmly that he also 'lied like a trooper and ... alternatively blustered, bullied, sobbed, prevaricated, delayed and obstructed to the very last moment'.[60] Despite his attempts at cautious realism before leaving England, therefore, it was apparent to all observers that Chamberlain found this kind of negotiation a 'sad disillusionment'.[61]

For Chamberlain, this personal injury only highlighted a more profound political frustration. 'He looked forward to the prospect of the culmination of his work with sympathetic and willing partners; and Bennett had treated him like a trickster.' In particular, his 'real disappointment' lay in his failure to secure agreement on the general resolutions he had drafted on the outward voyage for acceptance when the Conference opened.[62] In a final effort to enunciate some general principles for imperial economic unity and to give a lead to world recovery, Chamberlain and Hailsham drafted a modified low tariff resolution in the final days of the conference but this 'broad & statesmanlike policy' was also 'roughly swept aside by the most narrow minded of the Dominion delegates'. Instead, on its final day, the conference adopted a series of innocuous declarations which all recognised were nothing but pious platitudes without binding force or enduring significance.[63]

Like his father before him in equally frustrating circumstances, Chamberlain consoled himself with the belief that 'the time was not ripe' for such a visionary imperial policy. 'The countries of the Empire have been drifting apart pretty rapidly' he concluded, but Ottawa had 'been in time to stop the rot' within the fabric of the Empire and time would heal the rest.[64] As he informed the Cabinet after his return to London, he had been forcefully impressed by 'how thin the bonds of Empire had worn, and the growth of nationalism in the Dominions. He did not think that the bonds could have survived but for this Conference, which had strengthened the sense of belonging to a great Commonwealth and the advantages to be derived therefrom.'[65] Such reflections about what Joseph Chamberlain would have called the 'potentialities' of Empire, thus helped to salvage a victory of sorts from the jaws of demoralising defeat.

Consolation of a different sort was provided by the domestic repercussions of Ottawa as the Cabinet free traders finally resolved to exploit the agreements as an advantageous pretext for resignation. Chamberlain had long sought this outcome and on returning from Ottawa he was determined that 'the internal situation of the Nat. Govt. must be reconsidered and cleared up'.[66] Yet while he declared he would 'rejoice' if Samuel resigned, he was also aware that MacDonald was 'not altogether happy about Ottawa ... [and] afraid we are to have resignations'. When MacDonald turned to Chamberlain as a 'comforter' Chamberlain thus assured him the Cabinet 'looked to him not as the leader of the Tory Party but as the symbol of [their] faith that until prosperity returned country must come before party'. He was equally sincere in the view that Samuel was 'emphatically not a man to go tiger hunting with and with his disappearance ... we should be far more homogeneous and we should ... move towards the fused party under a National name which I regard as certain to come'.[67] To achieve this end, Chamberlain actively wooed Simon's Liberal Nationals while simultaneously making himself 'as disagreeable as possible' to Samuel and Archibald Sinclair over their devious conduct in failing to cut police pay in the hope this might force them into resignation. Despite MacDonald's efforts to postpone the crisis, therefore, at Cabinet on 28 September Chamberlain adamantly excluded any prospect of further compromise and the free traders finally departed to provide him with another crucial, if belated, victory.[68]

III

During 1932 Chamberlain's first forays into the realms of economic diplomacy extended beyond the thorny question of imperial economic relations to encompass the bitter political and financial legacy left by the Great War and the Treaty of Versailles. Above all, British policy-makers recognised the critical importance of finding an acceptable solution to the vexed inter-related problems of German reparation payments to the victorious Allies and their own war debts to the United States; issues which forced themselves to the top of the political agenda in November 1932 when the German announcement that they could not continue their reparation payments prompted the Bank of International Settlements to propose an international conference at Lausanne in January 1932 to consider the problem and its ramifications.

The underlying idea of a conference to resolve the broader question of inter-governmental debts conformed well with Chamberlain's existing thinking about the complex web of problems he now confronted. Moreover, although such negotiations were officially a matter for the Foreign Office, Chamberlain's determination to be closely consulted before any action was taken meant that he swiftly came to dictate the substantive policy actually pursued – despite a general recognition that the issue was more political than economic and in face of repeated Foreign Office warnings about the Treasury's negotiating strategy and its insensitive reading of the American situation.[69] These were by no means unreasonable concerns and they precisely foreshadow the far greater tensions between Chamberlain and the Foreign Office when he became Prime Minister. Yet from Chamberlain's perspective, the problem was simple. The myopic intransigence, political cynicism and self-interested greed of France and the United States over inter-governmental debts threatened to undermine world economic recovery and drastic action was necessary to break out of this vicious spiral. 'Any reparations settlement or adjustment must be accompanied by a corresponding settlement or adjustment of war debts', Chamberlain explained to his sisters in December 1931. 'Hoover knows it but darent say so. Unless he says so France darent move and so we are all locked in a suicidal embrace which will probably drown the lot of us!'[70]

In order to escape from this hopeless impasse, Chamberlain intended to proceed in two quite distinct negotiating phases. First, the European Powers needed to settle the problem of German reparations at Lausanne; only then should they make overtures about a corresponding settlement of Allied war debts to the United States. While these were to be tackled as separate phases, however, Chamberlain was always determined to ensure that they remained inextricably bound together in the minds of America's European debtors – both as a means of encouraging them to accept a practicable settlement of their own claims on Germany and to increase their collective leverage over the recalcitrant Americans when the time for a settlement finally arrived after the US presidential elections in November.[71] This 'stage-by-stage' approach remained central to Chamberlain's bargaining strategy throughout the rest of 1932.

With regard to America, the early signs appeared relatively propitious. Since the announcement of President Hoover's moratorium on all inter-governmental payments on 20 June 1931, London and Paris had always vaguely assumed that war debt obligations would not be resumed when the moratorium came to an end in July 1932. Moreover, this expectation was reinforced by American assurances to the visiting French Premier in October 1931, to the effect that the European powers should settle the reparation question and 'then, and only then' would America consider debt revision; an alleged understanding apparently repeated privately by Secretary of State Stimson to the British Ambassador on

28 December.[72] Certainly this expectation underpinned all Chamberlain's thinking about a reparations settlement and in preparing for Lausanne he deprecated any idea of tentative soundings of Stimson's attitude towards British strategy on the grounds that if the world hailed Lausanne 'with a sigh of relief' this 'might have a great effect in the United States'.[73]

By the time the Reparations Conference convened on 16 June 1932 reports of political developments in France and Germany convinced Chamberlain that 'the outlook for Lausanne is improving' and he looked forward to the prospect of a comprehensive settlement. Central to his planning for Lausanne was the hope that at an early stage in the proceedings the five Creditor Powers would pass a resolution declaring that world recovery depended on a comprehensive cancellation of all war debts and reparations.[74] In the event, after a 'very strenuous time' wrestling with the other delegations, Chamberlain and Simon eventually managed to get the declaration adopted by the Conference on 17 June – but only after Chamberlain made himself distinctly 'disagreeable' to Edouard Herriot, the new French Premier. As Sir John Simon, the Foreign Secretary, reported to London, this 'big stroke' helped 'to produce a firm impression that we mean business and will not be content with a mere short moratorium and nothing done'.[75]

Advised that progress depended on taking 'a fairly stiff line', Chamberlain's opening speech also caused 'great delight' at Lausanne by giving an equally unequivocal lead in declaring for cancellation all-round.[76] Warning that the payment of these vast inter-governmental obligations threatened consequences 'disastrous to the whole economic fabric of civilisation', he reminded the conference of Britain's well-established generosity regarding the collection of its own war debts from the Allies. 'To sacrifice our claim for this vast sum which we are entitled to receive is no light undertaking', he told the delegates, but as Britain was fully convinced that only radical measures could restore world confidence and trade, they were 'prepared to take [their] share in a general wiping of the slate, provided that all other Governments concerned would do the same'. Although he diplomatically avoided any reference to 'cancellation', the message was crystal clear to both the French delegates at Lausanne and to the Hoover Administration in Washington.[77] According to Runciman, 'Neville spoke clearly, and was more down-right than either the P.M. (I guess) or the French (certainly) quite liked.' Convinced that 'plain speech' was the only hope of progress, however, Runciman was far from alone in feeling that 'we have reason to be grateful to him for this direct style of doing business'.[78]

Unfortunately, already complaining that it was 'desperately hard work and exhausting to patience and temper', next day Chamberlain was stricken with a severe recurrence of the gout which had flared up immediately after the Budget two months earlier as 'a sign of overwork on the machine'.[79] Chamberlain had inherited gout from his father and he had periodically suffered with it since his youth. Yet in April 1932 it had been the most acute attack for many years and so debilitating that he was forced to discard the usual gout boot for crutches, while the condition and its medication had such a depressing effect on his constitution that he confessed 'life seems insupportable at times'. After suffering a 'pretty rotten time' for a month, he seriously expected it would prevent his attendance at the Lausanne and Ottawa conferences and in late May he even considered the possibility that its persistence might force his reluctant retirement from politics altogether.[80] As he was generally recognised to be the effective leader of the British delegation at Lausanne given MacDonald's burden as chairman of the conference, his own ill-health and his vagueness about the financial detail, it was extremely unfortunate when Chamberlain was compelled to retreat to his room almost immediately, only to re-emerge in a gout boot six days later, a deeply frustrated man humiliated by his inability to pull his weight.[81]

For a man of Chamberlain's direct and businesslike habits of mind, the defensive posturing of conference diplomacy was immensely frustrating. 'This has been an education in the ways of the foreigner', he complained on 26 June. 'He simply can't contemplate getting down to business without long preliminary sparring and skirmishing.'[82] In the event, the principal initial obstacle to the fulfilment of Chamberlain's plans came not from the Germans, who proved 'more helpful and conciliatory than might have been expected from a German Government of the Right', but rather from the French. Indeed, Chamberlain had 'rather a painful surprise' to find the French much less reasonable and supportive of the British policy than hopeful reports from the Paris Embassy had previously suggested. Above all, while he found Herriot 'very attractive, a great talker ... & a capital raconteur', he regularly lamented that 'when it comes to business he always takes refuge in the plea that he doesn't pretend to understand these technical matters only he knows what his people will stand and that they will never agree to total cancellation'.[83]

As he recognised that the French were now so definitely committed to this position that they could never go back, Chamberlain swiftly adjusted to the new reality and concluded they would 'have to look for second best' – although he remained determined to oppose French demands for long-term marketable German railway bonds (or any variant of them) as compensation for a settlement because this 'would only prolong uncertainty and perhaps precipitate disaster'.[84] Thus, on 28 June, while MacDonald met Herriot, Chamberlain sternly informed the German Foreign Minister that 'while we had come to the Conference with ideas which were more agreeable to German than to French aims we now thought the Germans were not making their contribution' and that they 'would miss the boat as this was the critical day'.[85] Next day, a six-man commission representing each of the Inviting Powers agreed within an hour to a British scheme involving the total cancellation of all European reparations and war debts subject to a German lump sum payment into a fund for European reconstruction; a plan which satisfied both the French need to demonstrate that Germany had not been allowed to escape all further burdens while German opinion could be pacified with the thought that the payment would not go directly to France.[86] As Chamberlain rightly assured the British delegation, from their perspective 'the figure was quite unimportant. What was required was a settlement which would create confidence.'[87] Moreover, while

Chamberlain clearly underestimated the degree to which the figure did matter to his French and German counterparts, as he never tired of warning them, 'no one could contemplate the failure of the Conference'.[88]

Throughout these difficult negotiations with intransigent French and German delegations, Chamberlain presented himself 'in the position of the honest broker. He had nothing to gain from the transaction', he assured the Germans on 3 July. 'He only wanted a settlement.'[89] Yet by now his officials were advising that the time had come to exert 'ruthless pressure' to force the Germans into 'the necessary counter-concessions to enable the French to accept the agreement'.[90] This became the central thrust of Chamberlain's efforts for the remainder of the conference as he patiently coaxed and cajoled the Germans into acceptance of the three billion Reichmark payment which was the minimum the French could accept. Despite tense and frustratingly protracted negotiations which regularly lurched towards complete deadlock, an agreement was reached on 8 July when Herriot and Chamberlain negotiated late into the night to produce a final settlement sketched out on the latter's napkin.[91]

Despite his relief at having achieved a European settlement, Chamberlain always recognised that this was only the first step towards his broader objective. As he repeatedly assured sceptical Franco-German negotiators, 'the first thing was to settle the question of Reparations ... then it might be found that the position vis-a-vis America settled itself' because 'the situation would improve so rapidly that the Americans could not take the responsibility of upsetting it' and because they 'would feel ashamed if they did not make some contribution when every other country was doing so'.[92] Furthermore, Chamberlain's conviction that what President Hoover said for domestic consumption before the presidential elections may not be the same as their policy afterwards was apparently confirmed soon after the conference commenced by American hints that if the European Powers ensured the issue remained off the public agenda during the election campaign it might be possible for Hoover to defer the next war debt payment (due on 15 December) until a negotiated settlement had been reached.[93] On this basis, Chamberlain repeatedly emphasised to Germany's creditors at Lausanne that 'it would be understood among ourselves that ratification must depend on the attitude of America'.[94] The conference thus ended with the Creditor Powers signing a secret 'Gentleman's Agreement' postponing ratification until a 'satisfactory settlement' had been reached between the European powers and the United States over their own war debts.

Throughout the final crisis at Lausanne, Chamberlain had demonstrated considerable persuasive power and ingenuity in narrowing the gulf between initial French demands for seven billion Reichmark (soon reduced to four billion) and the German offer of two billion. As a result, although Lausanne was hailed as 'a triumph of British policy and statesmanship', few doubted that Chamberlain had been 'the chief factor in the consummation'. Since the opening session, it had been Chamberlain's 'direct and firm' attitude and formidable reputation which had been crucial to progress – even when stricken with gout. Indeed, as Runciman reported home, 'Neville's illness ... enabled us, while telling him everything that passed & never using a paper or proposal without his previous knowledge, to use him as the dark horse, who *must* be satisfied.'[95] For his own part, Chamberlain later conceded that 'Lausanne ... was an education for me and I have learnt a lot about Europe in those three weeks.' Above all, he claimed that there was 'the satisfaction of finding that I could make a substantial contribution to the work of our team and in particular I established such terms of mutual liking and confidence with Herriot as eased the final passage into port materially'.[96] Since his term as Lord Mayor of Birmingham, Chamberlain had always been convinced of the persuasive power of his 'personal touch' in resolving domestic policy differences. The Lausanne conference convinced him that he could exercise precisely the same magic on the international stage. It was, perhaps, the first step on the road to the Munich conference six years later.

IV

The principal problem confronting Chamberlain's 'stage-by-stage' strategy was that both the American President and Congress were adamantly and publicly opposed to any remission or cancellation of European war debts. Undaunted, Chamberlain admitted that their idiocy and cynicism 'simply infuriates me', but he remained hopeful that 'we shall last out long enough to enable even the Americans to learn a little sense'. To help them to do so, Chamberlain intended to offer a lesson in elementary bookkeeping. 'If we could get no payments from Europe it would be necessary to go to the United States and explain that this made it impossible at the moment to pay', he told the Cabinet's Lausanne preparatory committee shortly before departure.[97] After their return, the Treasury prepared a detailed and compelling case for war debt revision demonstrating that Britain could not pay the £27 million due to America on 15 December without a significant increase in income tax and that neither Parliament nor the electorate would tolerate such an imposition at a time when the British tax burden was already four times greater than that of America's. On this basis, it was agreed that Washington should be informed that their agreement to voluntary suspension was the only method of avoiding default because Britain was '*not* for the future prepared to pay anything in excess of what [they] receive' from their own war debtors.[98]

In accordance with Chamberlain's strategy, within days of Hoover's defeat in the presidential election in November 1932, the British Ambassador at Washington dropped this 'bombshell' in the form of a Note during Secretary of State Stimson's 'Diplomatic Hour' set aside for ambassadorial visits. While accepting that the twelve month Hoover moratorium had been a useful first step, the Note argued that it had not realised its objective. It also pointed to the final settlement of the reparations problem at Lausanne as a major step 'towards the early restoration of world prosperity' and called upon America to enter into a corresponding review of European war debts. As a final settlement was impossible before the next payment was due on 15 December, the specific purpose of the Note was to urge suspension of this payment to enable negotiations to take place unencumbered by such a burden in an atmosphere similar to that employed at Lausanne. Unfortunately, Stimson's reply on 23 November offered little hope of compromise. Reiterating the established American position that reparations were a European issue which did not directly involve the United States, Stimson acknowledged the sacrifice involved in cancelling reparations, but argued that the Administration could not disregard the effects of the British proposal on the American taxpayer in the depths of the slump. On the contrary, he asserted that they attached such importance to the original debt agreements that the arguments for a full payment in December 'far outweigh any reasons now apparent for its suspension'.[99]

After reading Stimson's 'hopelessly unresponsive' reply, Chamberlain found it 'very hard to control [his] feelings about the Americans' who 'haven't a scrap of moral courage' – but he still 'clung obstinately' to the hope that they would suspend the December payment, even though he recognised he was 'almost alone in this view'. His problem, however, was that Stimson had confronted the British with a stark dilemma. As Chamberlain noted with more than a touch of Shakespearean drama for the first (but by no means the last) time in November 1932: 'To pay or not to pay, that is the question.' On one hand, default would encourage every other small debtor nation to do the same and thus gravely undermine confidence in Britain's moral leadership as well as its financial credit. On the other hand, payment would only vindicate American obduracy towards its European debtors to the detriment of world recovery, while encouraging them to expect further instalments at a time when the nominal balance owed by the British amounted to $4700 million – larger than the original advance of $4300 million after nearly half of the original sum had already been paid! Against this background, Chamberlain concluded that 'it really requires more courage to refuse to pay than to pay', but after Stimson's note in late November he was strongly inclined towards non-payment. 'I should not repudiate; I should expressly admit the obligation but at the last moment I should inform the Yanks that my conscience would not allow me to take such a step which I was convinced would upset the world & throw back all chance of recovery for an indefinite period.' At this juncture, he believed Britain should simply insist upon a moratorium pending a final settlement on the grounds that 'the longer they go without payment the more easy will it be for them to accept the prospect that there never will be payment'.[100]

The crucial turning point in the development of Chamberlain's thinking occurred on the afternoon of Sunday 27 November, at a meeting with Montagu Norman, the Governor of the Bank of England. Here Chamberlain was informed that Ogden Mills, the US Treasury Secretary, agreed privately with the British stance and was 'anxious to help'. To this end, Mills had expounded a secret plan in which Britain should propose to a sympathetic American Administration that it wished to separate payments towards the principal and interest on the war debt. This would enable Britain to invoke its right to suspend payments on the former for two years. As only Congress could remit the interest, Britain should offer to pay this in the form of bonds maturing over a three year period to be held by the US government until maturity. From Chamberlain's perspective, the obvious objection to the plan was the American refusal to extend the offer to the French to whom they were violently hostile; a condition he regarded as 'very serious, for it would involve the default of France and the non-ratification of Lausanne'. On the other hand, the Governor warned that the proposed British default would set a dangerous precedent for a creditor nation and would almost certainly prompt Australia, Argentina, Germany and many other countries to default on their payments to Britain. After this stark warning, Chamberlain concluded that while default may eventually be unavoidable, 'the consequences of non payment were so serious that ... we ought to avoid them as long as there remained even a remote chance of a happy ending'.

Against a background of 'great nervousness' in the City created by American intransigence, an informal meeting of ministers assembled on 28 November to avoid the public speculation and alarm likely to attend an emergency session of Cabinet. Outlining Ogden Mills' scheme to his colleagues, Chamberlain enunciated his own new thinking in favour of payment. He emphasised the danger of antagonising France, as this would react on the Disarmament Conference 'and the peace of Europe'. He also highlighted the damaging precedent that British default would create for smaller debtor nations and the 'terrific shock' which such an action would administer 'to a very large number of the best of our people who would feel that England's name had been dragged in the mud and would suffer humiliation accordingly'.[101] On these grounds, Chamberlain informed his colleagues that 'he had at last come to the conclusion that we ought ... to pay' – but only while simultaneously impressing upon Congress the adverse consequences of a resumption of payments for American recovery and the hope that before the next payment in June they would have entered into negotiations for a final settlement. In opposition, Runciman, Hailsham and Cunliffe-Lister emerged as the advocates of default, but Baldwin then decisively stated his support for Chamberlain's arguments, noting that repudiation was 'an ugly word' and that it 'might bring the world within sight of the end of Capitalism. Our word is unique in the world.'[102]

Next day, Chamberlain's initial doubts about the US Treasury Secretary's offer were confirmed. First, his anxiety about abandoning the French was reinforced by the British Ambassador in Paris who warned of the vulnerability of Herriot's position. Then a further interview with Montagu Norman convinced Sir Warren Fisher and Sir Robert Vansittart, the Permanent Secretaries to the Treasury and Foreign Office respectively, that while the Mills plan would never be acceptable to the President or Congress, it would undoubtedly create a rift in the Anglo-French 'united front'.[103] When Norman again pressed the Chancellor to accept the Mills plan later that afternoon, therefore, Chamberlain retorted firmly that it would place everyone in an impossible position. Above all, the exclusion of France would lead to their default on war debt payments and the non-ratification of Lausanne with the result that 'all our work for the establishment of confidence in Europe would be undone'. It would also open Britain to the French allegation that it had betrayed its ally and their 'Gentleman's Agreement' in pursuit of its own selfish interests.[104]

When the Cabinet met that evening, the battle lines of the previous day re-emerged more clearly. Chamberlain again urged the Cabinet to make the December payment in full if the Americans refused a final request to extend the Mills plan to other European debtors. Much to Chamberlain's consternation, however, 'a strong section' led by Cunliffe-Lister and Hailsham were in favour of unilaterally accepting the Mills plan and to 'let the French go hang'. At this juncture, things 'got a bit warm' because Chamberlain was determined to resign rather than accept 'a betrayal of our Ally and a fatal blow to Lausanne'. In the event, however, after Chamberlain read the Cabinet his proposed Note expounding the complete British case for suspension of the December payment it was agreed that this should be despatched to Washington with a vigorous request to extend the offer to France.[105]

Chamberlain's Note represented a powerful and comprehensive exposition of the British case for debt revision, but its appeal to American fairness and enlightened self-interest received 'a good reception [in Britain] but a bad reception in the United States' where Congress 'closed their eyes to it'.[106] When informal consultations on the unofficial American offer also indicated a much less attractive proposal than that originally communicated by Mills, it was decided to make the full British payment of $95 million in gold on 10 December because Chamberlain and most of his Treasury advisers wished to avoid 'demeaning ourselves by begging favours' – with the equally distasteful risk of rebuff or 'contemptuous and condescending acquiescence, probably accompanied by conditions'.[107] To educate American opinion to the realities as he saw them, however, Chamberlain decided that 'the time had come to be a little more outspoken'. Another Note accompanying the payment thus explained unambiguously that the December payment should not be regarded as a resumption of annual payments, but as an 'exceptional and abnormal' capital advance against a final settlement in the near future; a form of words designed to indicate unequivocally that there were 'limits to our squeezability'.[108] Chamberlain followed this on 14 December with the first of several robust speeches outlining British policy towards the American debt which received widespread domestic acclaim but which greatly inflamed the situation in America.[109]

V

Despite his bitter disappointments over American intransigence and the ensuing French default on the December payment, looking back Chamberlain concluded characteristically that he had nothing to regret. Although unable to see how they were to arrive at a satisfactory settlement, he boldly declared that 'I don't despair of getting home with patience and good temper.'[110] Underlying this wishful thinking was the confident belief that the incoming President-Elect would be far more amenable to British pleas than his predecessor;[111] hopes reinforced at the end of January 1933 when Roosevelt responded to tentative British overtures by sending a secret intermediary to meet MacDonald and Chamberlain to discuss war debts. Although of 'an exploratory character', this meeting radiated goodwill and encouraged Chamberlain's expectations of an early settlement on extremely favourable terms. The Cabinet were also reassured by news that Roosevelt was prepared to make a similar offer to the other European debtors and that he was considering a moratorium which (according to MacDonald's account) 'might last so long that the American public could forget what was to be paid'.[112]

On the basis of these indications, Chamberlain reassured the Cabinet in late January that their strategy was apparently bearing fruit.

> It was obvious that American public opinion had a long way to go, as had Mr Roosevelt himself, before their ideas approached to our own. For this a certain amount of time was necessary. So long as we could obtain a moratorium during the conversations it was unnecessary to agitate ourselves about delay. Time must work in our favour, for the facts of the situation would tend to bring the Americans to see the ill effects on the United States of a continuation of payments. Although it was impossible as yet to see our way through the jungle, nevertheless he felt fairly confident in his own mind.

In the belief that any new President was in his strongest position with Congress at the start of his term, the Cabinet responded positively to Roosevelt's eagerness for a private and secret understanding before his inauguration on 4 March. To make this possible, at Chamberlain's suggestion, it was decided to use the British Ambassador in Washington as an intermediary. Sir Ronald Lindsay was thus recalled to London with the effect that Roosevelt immediately invited him to an interview before his departure. 'That's the best news for a long time', Chamberlain noted cheerfully, adding that so long as talks could be kept in unofficial private channels there was some real hope of progress.[113]

Lindsay's meeting with Roosevelt took place at Warm Springs in Georgia on 29 January 1933. According to the Ambassador's report to London, Roosevelt 'spoke throughout with remarkable frankness' about his desire for 'a comprehensive programme in which debts and other questions will automatically fall into their proper places'. But he also stressed his refusal to contemplate piecemeal action because 'only by presenting Congress with the prospect of curing the world as well as the domestic situation can he hope to ensure its support'. To this end, Roosevelt talked optimistically about negotiations with the 'British "number 2 man"' to begin immediately after his inauguration and to be completed by 20 April when he planned 'to present to Congress without delay 5 or 6 great and important measures, to force it to confine itself to these, and to use pressure to make it adjourn within 60 days'. On the substance of the debt issue, however, Roosevelt was far less encouraging. Offering essentially a modification of the existing terms, rather than the immediate final settlement envisaged by Britain and France, Roosevelt asserted that the 'really terrible' condition of his country meant that 'if he and Hoover and an archangel from Heaven were all to be united in asking it for more it would not avail'.[114]

Lindsay's account of Roosevelt's position to the newly-established Cabinet Committee on the American Debt prompted Chamberlain's admission that 'he could not understand what Mr Roosevelt's real intentions were' and he 'doubted whether Mr Roosevelt had formed any clear conception himself'. Nevertheless, the Ambassador's warnings about American opposition to any settlement on terms satisfactory to Britain only reaffirmed Chamberlain's faith in his established strategy. 'Time was on our side', he assured the Committee, 'It should be remembered that we had had to educate Europe on the subject of reparations, and we should now have to educate America on the subject of debts. For this time was necessary, and the question was how to get time; in other words a Moratorium.'[115] To pave the way for such a step, Chamberlain proposed that Lindsay should persuade the President to send a message to Congress declaring that war debts could not be settled until the questions of tariffs, world prices and currency were discussed at the forthcoming World Economic Conference in June 1933 and that to assist these separate but concurrent talks on war debts, a moratorium should be offered until a final settlement was announced. Confident of eventual success, even when Lindsay reported 'most gloomily' on Roosevelt's response in late February, Chamberlain refused to be despondent. 'The picture could hardly look blacker than it does', he confessed to Lord Lothian, 'but, nevertheless, I am not unhopeful of the future since the facts and time are on our side.'[116] Ironically, what he consistently failed to recognise was that his own increasingly robust speeches on the subject made the prospect of a settlement progressively less likely.[117]

In reality, Roosevelt departed little from Hoover's policy on war debts. As Chamberlain's officials feared, the President recognised that full payment was increasingly unlikely, but Congress had forbidden him to reduce or cancel these debts and Roosevelt was far too shrewd as a player of presidential transactional politics to squander his personal capital and leverage in hopeless and peripheral skirmishes when he had far more fundamental battles to fight over the New Deal at home.[118] As a result, British hopes of a moratorium proved to be tantalisingly short-lived. As the President informed Lindsay on 8 June, 'a very serious deterioration ... in the Congressional situation' now made it 'absolutely impossible' to obtain the necessary powers and might even provoke them 'to pass every kind of legislation, mischievous not only to the United States but even to the world in general'. The President thus revived his earlier proposal for an interim British part-payment of $10,000,000 with the assurance that he would accept it as a contribution towards the final settlement – although 'he knew perfectly well that that meant nothing at all'.[119]

When the Cabinet considered Roosevelt's offer on 9 June, Chamberlain's position was significantly less conciliatory than before. Reminding the Cabinet that the December instalment had been paid to avoid default and to pave the way for settlement, he declaimed bitterly 'that payment had not done us much good, as Congress appeared more obdurate than ever. If we paid 10,000,000 Dollars now there was no reason why we should not be asked to pay the same again next December, and two payments of 10,000,000 Dollars would amount to a big figure in one year.' As it would also threaten Lausanne, by compelling Britain to demand increased payments from her own debtors, he announced a part-payment in June 'would … be a mistake, but a token payment as a recognition of the legal position, might be regarded in a different light'. As a result, he proposed to offer 10,000,000 ounces of silver, both to emphasise the token nature of the payment and because it was worth only $5,000,000 and thus much closer to Britain's receipts from Lausanne – but only on condition that the President gave prior assurances that this would not be regarded as default.[120] As in the previous November, Runciman, Hailsham and Cunliffe-Lister emerged as the principal challengers to Chamberlain's authority, arguing forcefully that while default and deferment were 'ugly words', 'to make payment at the expense of our equilibrium and of our recuperative strength is still more dangerous'. However, when challenged directly by the Chancellor on whether 'if the worst came to the worst, we should not pay', there was a general consensus that they should.[121]

Over the next three days, Chamberlain's counter-offer became the subject of intense negotiation in Washington, but while prepared to accept silver, the Roosevelt Administration remained adamant on the amount. After 'a last and urgent appeal' from the White House for $10,000,000 on the grounds that it would make a far more favourable psychological impression on American opinion, on 13 June the Cabinet reluctantly accepted Chamberlain's advice and agreed to the American terms.[122] As he later confessed, it was 'a great relief to my mind' because this outcome represented 'the best of both worlds' on the grounds that 'it is not a nice thing to default and yet payment again really was not possible'. Equally important, he regarded the arrangement as 'a substantial advance in the education of the American people: God knows they want it.'[123] Despite this sanguine optimism, however, within only two weeks the collapse of the World Economic Conference destroyed any hope of a satisfactory debt settlement and confirmed all of Chamberlain's prejudices against Roosevelt and the United States; a mistrust he would carry with him to the grave.

VI

American support for a British proposal to stage a World Economic Conference took 'everyone by surprise', but after his experience at the Danubian and Lausanne conferences, Chamberlain was always anxious about the prospects for tangible progress without detailed prior negotiations among the Powers that mattered – particularly as Britain, France and America were 'very wide apart' on key questions.[124] To bridge this gulf, he approached Pierre Flandin, the

French Finance Minister, unofficially on the subject in mid-November 1932.[125] Three months later, a week before Roosevelt's inauguration, Chamberlain also despatched a comprehensive statement regarding 'Policy on Economic Problems' to the incoming President in the hope of achieving some agreement before the conference convened; a statement which concluded with the warning that war debts represented 'an insuperable barrier to economic and financial reconstruction, and there is no prospect of the World Economic Conference making progress if this barrier cannot be removed'.[126] Despite repeated Treasury insistence that a moratorium was 'absolutely essential', however, the Americans were even more insistent that their attendance was conditional on the complete exclusion of war debts from the agenda.[127]

The central issues before the 65 countries assembled at the Geological Museum in London during June–July 1933 ranged widely across financial questions such as monetary, exchange and credit policy and economic problems, particularly those concerning the need to increase world production and trade through the reduction of tariffs and quotas. For the Chancellor, this was also a crucial opportunity to plead for international cooperation to raise wholesale commodity prices through his scheme for the regulation of output and he was encouraged by the enthusiastic response to his opening speech as leader of the British delegation. 'It really gave the lead and put Britain in its rightful position', Simon congratulated him; 'the contrast with Cordell Hull's performance is the contrast between brains and slush!'[128] Yet from the outset, Chamberlain was deeply apprehensive. 'There is only one possible chance for the success of the Conference', he told his cousin, 'and that is, that it will get into such a mess that someone will have to do something.' He then left for a short fishing trip 'to build up strength enough to face the sixty-five Dagos!'[129]

At the heart of Chamberlain's anxiety was the crucial question of currency stabilisation, at a time when central bank officials from Britain, France and America were working desperately behind the scenes to secure a temporary agreement for the duration of the conference to enable delegates to consider the road to recovery in an atmosphere free from anxieties about speculative exchange fluctuations. The Americans had favoured such an agreement during the early months of 1933. Against a background of domestic banking crisis, however, Roosevelt had withdrawn the United States from the gold standard and floated the dollar on 19 April as a prelude to a dramatic *volte face* on the question. Convinced that dollar depreciation was an essential prerequisite for the increased purchasing power needed for domestic economic recovery, on 22 June the US delegation announced to the World Economic Conference 'that measures of temporary stabilisation now would be untimely'.[130]

Despite this setback, at a private meeting of the British and American delegations on 27 June, Chamberlain launched an impassioned plea for American support for stabilisation to prevent speculation against a depreciating dollar escalating into a general movement against the remaining currencies still tied to gold – with the consequent danger that the collapse of the gold standard would end in 'complete chaos, stagnation of trade and possible grave political and social unrest'.[131] This appeal elicited a negative response, but after two secret meetings at the US Embassy in London with Raymond Moley, one of Roosevelt's closest economic advisers, Chamberlain 'hammered out' a statement on the subject which Moley 'felt pretty sure the President wd sanction'. After rejecting impossible Franco-Italian amendments, a formula for temporary stabilisation was finally agreed on 30 June between Moley, Chamberlain and representatives of the five 'gold bloc' states. Throughout these discussions, Chamberlain had been agreeably surprised to find that Moley was 'prepared to go considerably further than had been expected', but even at this stage he suspected that Moley did not enjoy the President's full confidence.[132] These apprehensions were almost immediately confirmed when Secretary of State Cordell Hull communicated Roosevelt's 'most offensive' message to the conference on 3 July, declaring that it would be 'a catastrophe amounting to a world tragedy' if the conference was diverted from its main business in order to consider 'a purely artificial and temporary experiment' in exchange stabilisation relevant to only a few nations.[133]

Roosevelt may have been correct in the view that 'European statesmen are a bunch of bastards', but this devastating declaration in favour of economic nationalism fatally undermined all hope for the conference.[134] To Chamberlain (and everyone else), it came as a 'bombshell' and he was furious. After quoting 'certain of the more offensive phrases' to the British delegation, he angrily declared 'the message was couched in language which could not fail to give deep offence to almost every other Delegation … Its tone was arrogant and it lectured the Conference in a manner and in circumstances which were hardly believable.' After this statement, however, he also conceded it was 'difficult to see how the problem could be surmounted without some catastrophe'.[135] After 'another bombshell' from Washington three days later, effectively declaring 'it was useless to discuss anything but silver', Chamberlain denounced the Americans for having 'effectively torpedoed the Conference at every point'. On 27 July the World Economic Conference adjourned never to meet again.[136]

To add to Chamberlain's woes, the final stages of the World Economic Conference witnessed a further challenge to his authority and economic strategy – this time from the Dominions. At Ottawa, monetary policy had attracted remarkably little attention compared with trade and tariff negotiations, despite the unofficial efforts of Leo Amery to persuade delegates that the imperial sterling bloc should lead the world to recovery through a policy of monetary expansion.[137] In large part, this was because the Chancellor regarded Amery's prescriptions on monetary policy – like everything else – as 'impractical and dangerous'.[138] Indeed, the priority for Chamberlain and the Treasury was precisely to avoid an inflationary monetary policy or any scheme which gave the Dominions a role in the management of sterling. These concerns explain Chamberlain's trepidation when Bennett first expressed the desire to discuss monetary policy at Ottawa and his prevarications when Thomas sought information about Britain's posture on the question early in 1932.[139] They also explain his successful efforts at stonewalling when addressing the Monetary

Policy Committee at Ottawa. Having adamantly refused to bow to Dominion pressure for a more definite statement, the Committee's final report was thus confined to a few deliberately 'innocuous observations' regarding the need to raise price levels and maintain exchange stability.[140]

Chamberlain was no more receptive to Dominion pressure to provide an international lead on monetary policy at the World Economic Conference ten months later. Yet on the afternoon that Roosevelt's 'bombshell' effectively torpedoed the entire conference, General Jan Smuts, the South African Deputy Premier, suddenly announced at a meeting of Commonwealth delegates that there was 'nothing outrageous in the President's statement'. He then pressed for a 'British group' statement 'declaring in favour of (1) ultimate gold standard (2) raising of price levels (3) expansion of credit & liberal expenditure by loan on public works & reduction of taxation.' Chamberlain was thoroughly alarmed by this far-reaching and wholly unacceptable proposal which he considered 'a thinly disguised attempt to dictate the United Kingdom policy of the Conference' with proposals 'so extravagant that they might almost have emerged from conversations with Mr Lloyd George or Mr Keynes'. Next morning, Chamberlain met Smuts and 'succeeded in quieting him to some extent', but when the Commonwealth delegations reconvened later that afternoon, Stanley Bruce of Australia made himself 'particularly tiresome in trying to insist on public works exp[en]d[iture]'.[141] With the World Conference now drifting aimlessly, Smuts returned to the issue in a forceful paper on 13 July, arguing that 'a merely negative outcome of this Conference will be disastrous so far as the countries off Gold are concerned'. Among the issues raised by Smuts was whether the desired and vital rise in primary commodity prices necessitated an expanded programme of public works in order to stimulate demand.[142]

This line of expansionist thinking was utterly anathema to Chamberlain as a Chancellor of the Exchequer wholeheartedly convinced that recovery depended on the critical importance of 'confidence' based on the appearance of balanced budget orthodoxy. Yet Dominion pressure confronted him with a grave dilemma. On one hand, he did not want the collapse of the conference to be accompanied by a Commonwealth failure to produce some sort of public declaration, but on the other hand he could never tolerate a commitment to the sort of fiscal and monetary expansion favoured by Smuts and the Dominions. Despite an instinctive desire to parry these 'troublesome' proposals with innocuous acceptance, on second thoughts Chamberlain detected the opportunity for 'a sort of sequel to Ottawa'. As a result, he resolved to hijack Smuts' proposal for a Commonwealth declaration by offering to draft a sterling bloc statement of his own – but 'on very different lines from those Smuts ... had in mind' and intended 'to show that something of value to the Empire had resulted from the present Conference'.

It all revolves around Ottawa, recites the conclusions arrived at there and reaffirms them. Thus it is designed to secure the multiple purpose of (1) diverting the Dominions from the dangerous paths of currency depreciation & public works (2) putting out a joint Brit. declaration which may to some extent distract attention from the failure of the Conference and (3) furbish up the Ottawa agreements which have got a little tarnished by reason of the rather equivocal behaviour of some of the Dominions.[143]

When the heads of the Commonwealth delegations met to consider his draft on 25 July, Chamberlain expected it would be received with 'considerable disfavour' as it largely ignored Smuts' case. In the event, however, it 'went much better than [he] had expected' and after Chamberlain's stirring appeal for support as 'the whole spirit of Ottawa was being attacked & we must vindicate it if we were to save it', an amended version was signed by all the Dominions (except the Irish Free State) on 27 July. The statement represented a complete triumph for Chamberlain and everything he had hoped to achieve in salvaging something from the wreckage of the conference.[144] But, when considered as a whole, this was scant consolation for his dashed hopes of a broader international agreement on trade, tariffs, raising wholesale prices and the regulation of supply.

The American retreat into economic nationalism also left the war debt question effectively unresolvable on terms satisfactory to the British. In September 1933, Chamberlain complained they were 'all in the dark as to what is in [Roosevelt's] mind, if there is anything in his mind'. Three days later, Sir Frederick Leith-Ross, the government's Chief Economic Adviser, sailed for New York to begin the long-awaited preliminary discussions, but all the indications were 'distinctly discouraging'.[145] 'As time went on', Chamberlain reported to the Cabinet on 26 October, 'it became clear that the American President was being influenced by the difficulties of his political situation and that in order to escape rebuff, he would have to avoid any controversial settlement.' Advised by Lindsay and Leith-Ross that a permanent settlement was beyond their reach, Chamberlain abandoned hope of anything but a temporary settlement to help further reduce American expectations.[146]

Yet this time, when confronted by the option of default or token payments, Cabinet opposition to the Chancellor's policy was considerably stiffer from the 'good many who wished to sit back & refuse further payments'.[147] Again, the leading critics were Runciman, Cunliffe-Lister and Hailsham supported by Sir William Ormsby-Gore, the First Commissioner of Works. As the usually opaque Cabinet record ominously noted, 'The general tenor of the discussion revealed some hardening of opinion on the subject of payments.' Despite this influential and increasingly determined opposition, however, Chamberlain remained convinced that it was still 'worth our while to pay something though not too much to avoid being denounced however unjustly as defaulters'. After Roosevelt rejected both the proposed British permanent and temporary settlements in favour of another token payment, Chamberlain persuaded the Cabinet to agree in the belief that default would 'wreck all hope' of eventual cancellation.[148]

In January 1934, Chamberlain noted that the announcement of this action had been received 'with quiet satisfaction' in Britain, while in America he thought the 'surprising absence of comment & even of interest ... seemed ... a very good omen for the ultimate settlement'. In the event, however, this further token payment of $7,500,000 in December 1933 prompted a full-scale row with the United States which culminated in the Johnson Act in June 1934, prohibiting all loans to governments defaulting or behind with their payments to the United States. The Johnson Act effectively resolved the British dilemma by precluding the use of further token payments as a means of avoiding default. Confronted by a choice between repudiation or paying the full outstanding balance of $265 million to the detriment of its own economic recovery, and in the certain knowledge that it would receive no further repayments from its own debtors, Britain finally suspended all war debt payments. It was a painful blow to national pride and an even worse defeat for all Chamberlain's hopes of a satisfactory settlement.[149]

VII

The battle over war debts left an indelible mark upon Neville Chamberlain's political consciousness. In reality, he had never nurtured much respect for what he regarded as the self-righteous cant and selfish myopia behind American foreign and commercial policy but these negotiations convinced him that he had 'the misfortune to be dealing with a nation of cads'.[150] After this, his loathing and contempt knew few bounds and these emotions proved a significant factor in shaping his attitude and policy towards Roosevelt and the United States throughout his Premiership – often with good reason. Yet he was also a pragmatist. As a result, such feelings did not prevent his desire for the 'closest and most friendly contact' with the US Treasury regarding cooperation over exchange rate stabilisation after the Belgian devaluation in 1935 or the French devaluation eighteen months later.[151] Nor did distaste for American policy blind him to the need to enter into negotiations for an Anglo-American Trade Agreement at the end of 1936. Chamberlain recognised that in his crusade for trade liberalisation Cordell Hull was determined to dismantle the system of imperial preference as the epitome of everything he most detested. But for a British government confronting the nightmare scenario of war on three fronts without the resources to defend an over-stretched global empire, Chamberlain also understood that the appearance of Anglo-American cooperation had vast political significance as a potential deterrent to the dictators and he was prepared to pay the necessary price – even if this could only be achieved at the expense of Anglo-Dominion relations and the structure of preferences erected at Ottawa.[152]

On the other hand, Ottawa inflicted far more damage upon Chamberlain's psychology of Empire at a moment when its political value was perceived to be on the wane. Although he later described Ottawa as 'an attempt to bring the

Empire together again and to supplement and support the common sentiment by bringing more material interests into line with it', he left Canada with the hope of 'never having to go through such an experience again'.[153] Worse still, he was soon tormented by the recognition that not only had Ottawa failed to inaugurate a new era of imperial economic unity, but that the Dominions were not even honouring their side of the bargain. Chamberlain's hopes for the regulation of supply and the international cartelisation of primary production soon collapsed amidst constant wrangling and ill-will between the Dominions and the mother country. Similarly, 'domestic competition' was a dead letter from the outset, accepted by Canadian and Australian leaders at Ottawa only because the agreements were sufficiently vague as to be unenforceable without their active support.[154] Moreover, within a year Chamberlain's suspicions about Bennett's trustworthiness were confirmed by reports of his unsuccessful efforts to 'pull off a deal in the U.S.A. (not in accordance with the spirit of Ottawa at all!)'.[155] Similarly, the 'unsatisfactory' attitude of Australia soon created a 'very dangerous position' which outraged the Federation of British Industry and prompted the Treasury to prepare a formal protest on the grounds that they had 'every right to expect and demand that Australia shall carry out her side of the bargain both in the letter and in the spirit'.[156]

At a more fundamental level, Chamberlain's attitudes confirm the view that Ottawa 'brutalised Anglo-Dominion relations in the sense that future negotiations showed few signs of that genteel enthusiasm for compromise so obvious before 1929'.[157] Certainly, British policy makers had long memories regarding Ottawa and throughout the rest of the 1930s they demonstrated a stern determination 'to avoid a repetition … of the Ottawa position of a multilateral discussion of our trade relations with the Dominions at which the United Kingdom would find most, if not all, the Dominions ranged against her'.[158] Moreover, contrary to some assertions that negotiations on the Anglo-American trade treaty in 1937–38 demonstrated that the 'position of the Dominions was one which those making foreign policy could not ignore',[159] in reality the complete opposite was the case. Despite the pleas of the Dominions, under Chamberlain's leadership, British policy was guided largely by British perceptions of British interests. Far from being deflected from the pursuit of this strategy by the Dominions, their attitude was considered, noted and (where possible) it was reconciled to British needs – but that was the limit of their influence. Yet in many ways this had been the increasingly central theme of Chamberlain's attitude towards the Dominions since Ottawa. On the one hand, he recognised that to speak as leader of the British Commonwealth of Nations and the Sterling Area enhanced British influence and authority. But on the other hand, this was only acceptable if he could 'direct the Dominions from subjects they don't understand and on which they can be embarrassing to us'.[160]

Precisely the same could be said of Chamberlain's attitude towards the Dominions with regard to his pursuit of European appeasement. Although the memoirs of those directly involved during the late 1930s frequently mention Dominion opposition to British entanglements in Europe as a crucial factor in his decision to pursue the policy of appeasement, there is no evidence to support such a claim. As Dominion Secretary, Malcolm MacDonald was undoubtedly correct in March 1938 when he warned that the Dominions 'feared that a British guarantee to Czechoslovakia might lead to the disintegration of the Empire',[161] but while Dominion preferences conveniently coincided with Chamberlain's views on policy towards the Sudeten problem, they were not a major influence in shaping them. Dominion fears were certainly mentioned regularly in Cabinet, in negotiations with the French and even in Parliament, but rather than redirecting Chamberlain's foreign policy or limiting his freedom of manoeuvre, these were exploited (when needed) as one of several convenient battering rams with which to overcome opposition, in much the same way as he later used them in his fight against the Cabinet's desire for negotiations with the Soviet Union during May 1939, and in his resistance to widespread public clamour for Churchill's admission to the government.[162] Conversely, the Dominions were not consulted over issues where their known positions conflicted with Chamberlain's own, as over Roosevelt's conference proposal in January 1938 and the Polish guarantee in March 1939. By the same token, Dominion reservations about the content and tone of the British reply to Hitler's 'peace offensive' in October 1939 were swiftly brushed aside when they came into conflict with Chamberlain's adamantine determination to avoid any such statement of Allied war aims.[163] It is far too much to claim that all this can be attributed to the brutal disillusionment which Ottawa and its aftermath inflicted upon Chamberlain – but it certainly played its part.

Chapter 9

Depression and Recovery, 1931–1935

'There is nobody more anxious to reduce taxation than I am both on personal grounds and out of sympathy with the taxpayer. But I should conceive I was failing in my duty if I were to undermine the feelings of confidence that have been inspired throughout the world in the stability of this country's finances by any methods unsound in themselves and perhaps not altogether to be defended on the grounds of being an honest Budget. If I were deliberately to unbalance the Budget in order to reduce the income tax ... – well the consequence would very soon be felt in a way far more disagreeable to the taxpayer than even the continuance for a little longer of the burdens which press upon us so badly.'

Neville Chamberlain speaking at Birmingham, 28 January 1933

Neville Chamberlain's second term as Chancellor of the Exchequer between November 1931 and May 1937 is the fourth longest of any of the 40 men who have held that post since 1902. Of all the various phases in his ministerial career, however, this period, during which he presided over Britain's recovery from economic depression, remains unquestionably the most neglected and the most in need of reassessment. Indeed, for at least 30 years after his death in 1940, Chamberlain's reputation was doubly damned. Not only was he the most culpable of the 'Guilty Men' of Munich, but the post-war triumph of Keynesian economics (with its promise of prosperity and full employment) appeared to be an equally devastating condemnation of his supposedly complacent and unimaginative economic response to the challenge of the Great Depression. In this intellectual climate, in which Churchillians and Keynesians reigned supreme, the avenging march of his victorious opponents thus ensured that Chamberlain was robustly denounced for merely 'tinkering with the cancer of massive unemployment' with policies which were 'all small, haphazard, essentially palliative, and unrelated to any long-term constructive economic policy'.[1] Yet in reality, the underlying indictment of Chamberlain's Chancellorship always went much further. As Robert Skidelsky later put it, the failure to tackle unemployment in the early 1930s 'helped to create and confirm a mood of national self-doubt, of pessimism regarding the future, in which appeasement could flourish. The refusal to stand up to the dictators was part of the refusal to stand up to unemployment; the mood of resignation, of fatalism almost, which supported it was the same in one case as the other.'[2]

The breakdown of the Keynesian consensus in the 1970s opened the way for a more sympathetic and open-minded reappraisal of economic policy in the 1930s. Yet notwithstanding the recent publication of much outstanding scholarship effectively challenging the established mythology about Treasury thinking, this process of sustained revisionism has not been paralleled by any corresponding effort to reassess Neville Chamberlain's reputation as Chancellor – far less, has there been any real attempt to consider the aspirations, motives and economic rationality which shaped his approach to these matters. As a result, therefore, Chamberlain is still too often dismissed as the narrow-minded, dead hand of Treasury resistance to new ideas, doggedly adhering to the canons of nineteenth-century financial orthodoxy without the will, imaginative vision or courage to do more than sit back impotently to await rescue from depression and mass unemployment by the 'natural forces of recovery'.[3]

This picture of Chamberlain as a Chancellor hopelessly out of his depth in dealing with complex economic and financial problems was common among his critics even at the time. Leo Amery was typical in arguing that 'the Treasury and City influences were too strong for a Chancellor ... who ... never really understood monetary problems'. After the World Economic Conference in July 1933, Bennett, the Canadian Premier, more sympathetically declared that 'he thought Neville really understood the situation but felt it impossible for the time being to shake himself free of Norman and of the influences of the Treasury'.[4] Rather more remarkably, such a view appears to have been expressed in the privacy of some ministerial households. 'He really isn't good enough', Hilda Runciman noted after hearing Chamberlain's Budget in 1933. 'The great complaint is that he is in the hands of his Treasury officials, having himself no special financial gifts – the level of the Chairman of Birmingham City Council finance committee exactly describes his position – and the officials are not as good as they used to be.'[5] This is a view echoed in a variety of otherwise impressively scholarly studies of economic policy which also seek to portray Chamberlain as a Chancellor capable only of 'slavishly reproducing ... extremely cautious and unimaginative Treasury memoranda'.[6]

It is certainly true that Chamberlain consciously avoided anything 'flashy' during his Chancellorship. Towards the Commons he appeared to approach his task 'from the standpoint of the plain businessman', addressing the House 'in the tone and manner of a company chairman speaking to a meeting of shareholders' without dramatics or imaginative flights.[7] But as George Peden rightly argues, beneath the carefully contrived facade, Chamberlain was an exceptionally strong Chancellor who enjoyed an extremely good relationship with senior officials who regarded him as the most competent Chancellor since Gladstone.[8] In the case of Sir Warren Fisher, the Permanent Secretary to the Treasury, this rapport had been particularly close since Chamberlain's first term at the Treasury in 1923 and after 1931 it developed into something approaching adoration until Fisher became disillusioned with his 'Darling Neville' after the Munich settlement in September 1938.[9]

In practice, this warm relationship between the Chancellor and Treasury was based on a combination of factors. Chamberlain was always the ideal minister and his self-assured, hard-working and methodical manner represented everything the Whitehall community most valued. After 1931 his status as the heir-apparent to the Premiership also increased his leverage across a wide range of policy areas in which he did not hesitate to intervene where he had strong views. In particular, at a time when Fisher hoped to expand the Treasury's role into foreign affairs, Chamberlain was ahead of him in asserting the department's right to displace the Foreign Office in the control of economic diplomacy – as he demonstrated forcefully over war debt policy. Above all, a genuine congruence of policy perspectives was conducive to harmony and mutual respect between the Chancellor and his officials.

But for all that, it is important to recognise that Chamberlain was a policy activist at the Treasury rather than a passive supporter of official positions. As a result, when his opinions did not coincide with the departmental view, he was always sufficiently forceful as a minister to impose his own thinking and priorities upon officials who were either profoundly sceptical as to policy logic and likely outcomes (as with regard to tariffs and their impact upon industrial reorganisation) or who were at worst positively hostile to expenditure on such initiatives (as with the development of regional policy). Moreover, even in that more complex area where the policy preferences of minister and officials did directly overlap – as with regard to budgetary policy – it is clear from closer examination of Chamberlain's own papers (and even more from his annotations on official briefs and memoranda) that not only did he wholly endorse their thinking for reasons of his own but that he also regularly led the way in promoting real policy initiatives.

Chamberlain's characteristic habit of leading from the front within the Treasury was paralleled by an equally conspicuous tendency within the Cabinet to assert his own supreme authority over economic policy as an exclusive political domain. Above all, he was utterly determined to ensure that there should be no repetition of the persistent Prime Ministerial interference with Treasury business under which Snowden had suffered resentfully for so long.[10] As a result, Chamberlain soon resolved that 'if he continues to act as though he were Dictator & not P.M. I shall watch for a suitable opportunity & then show my teeth'. In less than a month a suitable pretext presented itself, when Chamberlain learned that MacDonald had resumed his old habit of convening private meetings of economists and bankers to discuss sensitive matters of economic policy. Speculating with his sisters as to whether there was 'any velvet glove thick enough to overcome the disagreeable impression of the metallic substance inside', MacDonald was sternly warned to curtail this interference and he took the rebuff 'extremely well'. After this, it is scarcely surprising that Chamberlain soon became keenly aware that he occupied 'a very different position in this Cabinet from any other that I have sat in. It seems to me that I carry more weight' he told his sisters in December. 'I certainly speak more; the P.M. shows much deference to what I say and as

S.B. remains silent our people look to me for the lead and I see that they get it.'[11]

II

Alongside his tariff triumph, during the early months of 1932 Chamberlain laid the foundations of the monetary policy which prevailed throughout the rest of the decade. Having been forced off the gold standard in September 1931 by financial panic, monetary expansion through a 'cheap money' policy became a feasible option and interest rates fell sharply from a crisis peak of 6 per cent in September 1931 to 5 per cent on 18 February, before continuing in a series of cuts to a thirty-five year low of 2 per cent on 30 June – where it remained (except for a brief period in August-September 1939) until November 1951. While considerable controversy still surrounds the initial objectives behind 'cheap money', in practice, these appear to have expanded rapidly as policy-makers became increasingly aware of the evolving opportunities. Certainly by October 1932 the Treasury already believed that it was 'highly desirable' that 'the present low rate of interest should gradually permeate the economic structure and quicken industrial enterprise', particularly in house construction.[12] Moreover, while retrospective analysis suggests this policy did not achieve the desired goal in the simple causal manner anticipated by the Chancellor, the fact remains that whatever the *outcome* of the policy, the explicit *objective* was to forge a positive policy to combat depression and in October 1933 the independent Committee on Economic Information confirmed that cheap money had played a key role in recovery.[13] Against this background, it was scarcely surprising that Chamberlain took every opportunity to proclaim that the remarkable economic upturn since his first budget in 1932 should be attributed directly to tariffs and cheap money as the 'two main pillars' of his policy to restore economic prosperity.[14]

One other immediate benefit of this shift to cheap money was that it made possible the conversion of the 5 per cent War Loan 1929/47 to a lower rate of interest following the precedent set by Goschen's conversion operation in 1888. This was certainly not a new policy objective. Debt conversion had been under active discussion since 1927, but at that stage Treasury officials never believed a complete conversion of all £2000 million in one operation was ever a practicable proposition. By the time Chamberlain became Chancellor, however, Britain's departure from the gold standard had opened the way for lower interest rates while the necessary legal powers had been obtained in Snowden's September 1931 Finance Bill.[15] Having bided his time until conditions were favourable, Chamberlain returned secretly from the Lausanne conference on 30 June to inform the Cabinet that later that evening he intended to announce the conversion of the entire 5 per cent War Loan to a 3½ per cent basis. Explaining his reasons for prompt action to a delighted House of Commons, Chamberlain highlighted the benefits of balancing the budget at a lower level by reducing the interest charges on some 27 per cent of the total National Debt at a saving of

£30 million in a full year. By removing this great mass of high interest-bearing debt which had been 'hanging like a cloud over the capital market' and preventing a fall in general interest rates, he also hoped the measure would assist industry to obtain capital at a lower cost and thus stimulate investment and recovery. The strongest argument, however, related to 'the spirit in the country'. Having reduced interest rates to 2 per cent earlier in the day, Chamberlain declared that he was 'convinced that the country is in the mood for great enterprises, and is both able and determined to carry them through to a successful conclusion'.[16]

The conversion operation represented a major triumph for Chamberlain. He entered an expectant House of Commons to a 'great cheer' from both sides of the chamber and although still wearing his gout boot, he appeared 'in excellent spirits and his voice was particularly strong'. According to all present, the Commons adjourned with 'a sense of quiet excitement', convinced that they had 'come to grips with the realities in the most satisfactory manner'.[17] Chamberlain's hope that the country was 'in the mood for a bold policy' and that it would respond generously to a patriotic appeal were more than fulfilled.[18] Of the £2,084,994,086 in 5 per cent War Loan outstanding on 31 March 1932, no less than £1,920,804,243 was converted to 3½ per cent basis, some 92 per cent of the total.

Although careful Treasury wooing of the press and bankers combined with a variety of market factors explain the success of the operation, this positive public response was easily interpreted by supporters as a vindication of the Chancellor's emphasis upon the crucial importance of restoring confidence in the government's financial policy through balanced budgets and a managed currency.[19] Against a background of 'tremendous optimism' in the City after Chamberlain announced the repayment in early March of over half of the £80 million credits obtained from New York and Paris during the struggle to defend the gold standard, this further reduction of interest rates combined with the unexpectedly massive loan conversion soon stimulated 'a little gilt edged boom'. As *The Times* declared, it was a 'demonstration of social and fiscal strength such as has not been rivalled since the great conversion of 1888 or since the loan itself ... was raised'.[20] For a government apparently 'flagging' in public esteem, the 'widest enthusiasm' for this 'sterling act of Courage' was thus generally believed to have restored some of its popularity.[21] It was the prelude to five further conversion operations at even lower rates during 1932 and more followed in 1934–35 which altogether cut over £100 million from the cost of debt servicing. In conjunction with the apparent success of the Lausanne and Ottawa conferences, within a year of becoming Chancellor, Chamberlain cheerfully declared that 'the cumulative effect has been very favourable and confidence is beginning to raise its head in a much shaken world'.[22]

In parallel with the adoption of 'cheap money', Chamberlain's Treasury also moved towards a managed currency to insulate business confidence still further from external speculative pressures. After the suspension of the gold standard in September 1931, the Prime Minister's Committee on Financial Questions urged that 'for the time being we should pursue a waiting policy and allow sterling to settle at whatever level circumstances suggest is most appropriate'.[23] On this basis, the value of sterling fell sharply from its $4.86 parity on the gold standard to $3.23 in early December before a revival of confidence produced a period of stability at around $3.40. Despite some apocalyptic foreboding, however, this dramatic fall did not produce financial panic or hyper-inflation. On the contrary, the authorities soon recognised the very considerable advantages to be derived from a lower exchange value – not least, the hope that (together with cheap money) this would assist the Treasury to achieve its primary objectives of raising wholesale prices, reducing the burden of debt and increasing export competitiveness through currency depreciation.[24] 'The City is buzzing with activity, the Government stocks are booming, the foreigners are buying sterling and we are sitting with all our weight on its head lest it should soar to undesirable heights', Chamberlain noted with satisfaction in late February 1932. In mid-March speculative pressure once more increased the value of sterling, but not as much as feared and Chamberlain hoped to give it 'a bump downwards' in the near future in order to avoid any disadvantageous currency appreciation. Little wonder that Treasury officials felt happier than at any time since 1927 or that the Chancellor rejoiced that 'it is indeed wonderful that the National Government should have so quickly restored confidence when we seemed about to plunge to disaster only a few months ago'.[25]

Yet few beyond the Chancellor and his senior officials knew that the early repayment of French and American credits and the foreign rush to buy sterling was only made possible by the completely unexpected shipment of £2 million worth of gold from India each week as Indians redeemed their traditional savings in gold sovereigns (nominally worth £1) for silver and rupees worth 27/6d (137p). 'The astonishing gold mine we have discovered in India's hordes has put us in clover', Chamberlain noted gleefully on 20 February. 'The French can take their balances away without our flinching. We can accumulate credits for the repayment of our £80M loan and we can safely lower the Bank rate. So there is great rejoicing in the City and sterling remains steady while stocks are beginning to mount again.' On this basis, Chamberlain contemplated the abolition of restrictions on the export of capital and a further reduction in the bank rate.[26] But as he also recognised, this 'very gratifying' financial position contained political dangers – not least by stimulating ill-informed public expectations that the crisis was over and that large cuts in taxation would soon follow. Chamberlain was equally concerned that 'the rush for sterling is getting embarrassing' and he watched speculative pressure 'with a view to action soon' because 'it would be a bad thing to have sterling soaring too high'.[27]

The action which Chamberlain had in mind involved another novel departure in British economic policy designed to manage the exchange value of sterling. Having recognised both the potential dangers of speculative pressures and the benefits of a managed currency, the Treasury swiftly took steps to arm itself with the necessary powers to achieve its broader objectives. In a 'very secret' memorandum prepared by the Treasury and circulated exclusively to Chamberlain and his three colleagues on the Financial Situation Committee on

5 October 1931, an 'especially secret' paragraph warned of the very real danger of panic selling of sterling and the need for 'a cushion with which to support the pound'. To this end, the Treasury enquired whether dollars and francs should be acquired 'as an insurance against the possibility of some temporary collapse'.[28] By early December Chamberlain admitted privately 'the position of the £ does give me a good deal of anxiety. What I fear is a wholesale withdrawal of foreign holdings of sterling which still amount to a very large sum.'[29] Out of these concerns grew the impetus to establish the Exchange Equalisation Account which Chamberlain announced in his first Budget in April 1932. With up to £150 million in gold and reserves set aside to buy and sell foreign exchange, the aim of the EEA was to counter the undue speculative fluctuations in the value of sterling which were so damaging to domestic investment and output, while at the same time helping to maintain 'cheap money' as an aid to economic recovery; an instrument operated with 'consummate skill' during the American financial crisis in March 1933.[30]

III

In contrast with the effectiveness and innovatory nature of British monetary policy after 1931, Chamberlain's contemporary critics invariably contended that his unbending commitment to nineteenth century balanced budget orthodoxy condemned the nation to the persistence of high levels of unemployment which could have been eradicated through the acceptance of bolder, proto-Keynesian policies designed to stimulate economic activity and growth by increasing public expenditure. This criticism of Chamberlain's adherence to the so-called 'Treasury view' appears to have been largely impervious to the recent recognition that Keynesian theories did not offer the ultimate panacea for the economic ills of the 1930s. Thus, just as A.J.P. Taylor could portray Chamberlain in 1965 (when confidence in the Keynesian consensus remained strong) as 'a pure Cobdenite in his reliance on "natural" forces and individual enterprise', much more recently a highly respected authority still summed up a widely held view when contending that the National Government's failure on unemployment placed Chamberlain 'closer to the older orthodoxies of *laissez faire*, essentially pursuing a "good housekeeping" policy while waiting for the natural self-righting forces of the free market to bring back prosperity. His keen but narrow business mind made him an appropriate executor of his strategy.'[31]

Certainly during Chamberlain's Chancellorship public expenditure as a share of national output fell between 1931 and 1934 before stabilising and then rising sharply from 1937 as the effect of rearmament became apparent. In this respect, Britain was far more orthodox than almost any other European state in its policy of balanced budgets,[32] although even modern econometric analysis has not yet resolved the question of whether the real effects of Chamberlain's budgetary stance was broadly neutral in its impact (as Broadberry argues) or more deflationary than it appears from conventional budgetary analysis (as Middleton contends on the basis of the constant employment budget).[33] Yet what is absolutely certain is that, at the time, Chamberlain and his policy advisers perceived the achievement of a budgetary balance to be a crucial cornerstone for any broader policy designed to sustain low interest rates and cheap money, while preventing inflation and maintaining confidence in the economy. Moreover, these domestic forces for fiscal conservatism were reinforced still further by London's emergence at the centre of a sterling area of nations (both within the Empire and beyond it) who pegged their exchange rates to the pound and who held considerable sterling balances in London.[34]

While Keynesian historians have traditionally been dismissive of Chamberlain's repeated emphasis on unprovable psychological arguments about the importance of 'confidence',[35] such scepticism often underestimates the traumatic impact of the 1931 crisis upon perceptions of what was politically and economically possible. 'Hot money' had catastrophically flowed out of London then, and the Chancellor had every reason to fear that it would do so again if the budget was not balanced or if the canons of 'responsible' finance were flagrantly disregarded. Given the circumstances which had brought the National Government to office in the first place, therefore, Chamberlain was determined that there should be nothing in his economic strategy to jeopardise business or investment confidence; a central conviction which effectively precluded the adoption of destabilising or 'flashy' short-term expedients. When Keynes criticised the 1932 Budget on the grounds that '"Sound" finance may be right psychologically, but economically it is a depressing influence', he did so as an expansionist economist anticipating an employment 'multiplier' effect generated by government expenditure on public works – but even he conceded privately that there were 'enormous psychological advantages in the appearance of economy' in order to prepare the ground for debt conversion and lower long-term interest rates.[36] Certainly, for many of Chamberlain's more orthodox contemporaries, the rapid restoration of 'a spirit of imperturbable self-confidence' at home and abroad after the panic of 1931 represented a major policy triumph.[37]

Ultimately, in order to foster and sustain this crucial psychological sense of economic confidence, Chamberlain was prepared to play the long game. 'After such a long period of unsound management, especially in finance, it would be foolish to expect a very rapid recovery' the Chancellor confided to a close friend in January 1932. 'There are serried ranks of apparently insoluble problems in front of us; but given a few years, we shall work through them.'[38] Confronted by a depressing trade and financial position six months later, he consoled himself with the thought that 'one must take a longer view and there are some more hopeful signs'. One such indication was a report from the Committee on Economic Information in May 1932 that 'Psychologically, there is a greater steadiness and confidence in business and industrial circles in Great Britain than in most other countries.' But as Chamberlain always recognised, playing the long game had significant adverse implications for his own reputation in the short-term. After his extremely cautious 1933 Budget, he thus gloomily reflected that 'there will be no praise for the Chancellor till one of my successors is fortunate enough to come in on the upward turn of trade. For myself I must be content to do my duty as I see it and trust to recognition in the future.'[39]

These core values, priorities and expectations were grimly reflected in Chamberlain's budgetary policy throughout the first half of his Chancellorship. Although encouraged by early signs of apparent recovery during the spring of 1932, he was soon concerned that the buoyant position of sterling 'excites the public who don't understand and makes them think that all is well'. Prudent expectations of reduced revenue for the coming year thus inevitably reinforced an already strong instinctive inclination towards fiscal conservatism. Alarmed by press speculation about a substantial reduction in taxation in the forthcoming Budget after an overly optimistic speech by Baldwin at Ilford in early March 1932, three days later Chamberlain promptly attempted to 'damp down these fantastic ideas' in a counterblast at Birmingham in the belief that 'it is certainly too soon to begin dividing up the skin of the bear'. In order to maintain Snowden's small surplus in the previous Budget, he then resolved that there should be neither a reduction in taxation nor a rise in expenditure, despite increased revenues from the tariff. As he told the Commons in characteristically austere terms, he was not prepared to seek 'a little popularity by gambling on the future'.[40]

Response to Chamberlain's first Budget on 19 April 1932 varied considerably. The King was gratified to find that 'at this very critical time in the history of the world' he had 'a government of all the Talents and a Chancellor of the Exchequer in whom everyone has the fullest confidence'.[41] Cabinet colleagues also communicated their customary congratulations, but *The Times* characteristically described the Budget as one of 'puritanical severity' for its lack of concessions and unnecessary orthodoxy. In private, the Prime Minister was equally critical of a Budget speech with 'too many small and wearisome details'. 'Chancellor not in form and showed his weakness', MacDonald noted in his diary, 'lack of imagination and especially of coordinating vision'. Resentful of his exclusion from office, Amery also thought it 'a timid unimaginative performance' and echoed the view that it reflected Chamberlain's 'curiously narrow gauge mind'. His conclusion that opinion in the Commons lobby and tea rooms was 'all very depressed as to the substance of the Budget and as to Neville's delivery' was also probably a fairly accurate assessment. Indeed, for many government supporters it was simply an unimaginative 'flop'.[42]

From Chamberlain's own perspective, the 1932 Budget achieved his limited objectives and, despite sustained backbench criticism of the failure to reduce beer duty to assist the brewing industry, he concluded that he had 'got off very cheaply with such an unpopular Budget'. Above all, he consoled himself with the many 'very gratifying comments showing the wisdom as well as the courage of refusing to make concessions' from those who understood the problems. He was particularly pleased by those from the City and the Governor of the Bank of England which noted that it was 'almost the first honest Budget since the War'.[43] Besides bolstering confidence that there would be none of the irresponsible finance and unbalanced budgets which had created the 1931 financial crisis, Chamberlain was also motivated by the conviction that Britain still needed to make 'further great economies'. As such, he was 'determined to give the grumblers a run for their money and make them face up to realities'. By deliberately being 'very cautious and guarded in [his] language', his explicit intention was to create an atmosphere 'in which the disagreeable things become possible'.[44] As he warned the Prime Minister five months later, declining revenues already suggested the need for 'some very unpleasant forms of economy' which any appearance of weakness would make 'almost impossible'.[45] Unfortunately, Chamberlain's problem in creating a climate of opinion in which 'disagreeable things' became possible was that it demanded enormous parliamentary forbearance at a time when desperate economic conditions inclined opinion towards a more radical and spectacular panacea. As a result, Chamberlain soon found himself assailed both by 'economisers' advocating far greater budgetary severity and 'unbalancers' who believed that salvation depended on controlled inflation and deficit finance to fund large-scale public works.

Predictably, the 'economisers' were largely to be found on the government's own benches. Cuthbert Headlam spoke for many mainstream Tories when he lamented after the 1932 Budget that 'the Cabinet has not gone nearly far enough in economies … The truth of the matter is this Government like any ordinary government, funks taking a really strong line.'[46] When Chamberlain warned these critics during the debate on the Finance Bill that 'before embarking on serious changes of national policy, … some hard thinking should be done', the Conservative backbench 1922 Committee responded two days later by establishing a sub-committee to achieve 'drastic public economy on a scale not yet contemplated'. To Chamberlain's great relief, however, when the report of 'The Economy Bunglers' appeared on 16 November, its proposals for nearly 140 economies amounting to £100 million in a full year were immediately brushed aside by both the press and many Conservative MPs alarmed by the political implications of such draconian measures.[47]

By this stage, however, many government backbenchers had also lost their enthusiasm for Chamberlain's own repeated message about the need for continued financial stringency and 'sacrifice'. After one such gloomy exposition of government policy on 16 February 1933, during which he predicted that they could expect no substantial reduction of abnormal unemployment within the next ten years, even Chamberlain confessed to being 'a little depressed when after all my work … on [the speech] I didn't succeed in carrying the sentiment of the House with me'.[48] In reality, the underlying objective of Chamberlain's 'indiscretion' was to alert the country to the need to find some method of shortening working hours and redistributing work as a prelude to constructive proposals. But this was not how it sounded to shocked and disappointed MPs. 'It is a pity to be too honest in the expression of your opinions', Amery smirked, 'especially if you are wrong as well as unpopular.'[49] Despite the conspicuously chilly response, however, Chamberlain was undeterred, content that he had 'deliberately said unpleasant things because … it was necessary that people should be told the truth'. As he told his sisters with that characteristic note of self-righteous obstinacy so often evident when challenged, 'they will presently see that I was right and respect me all the more for saying what others are afraid to say'. Indeed, so inspired was he by the need to 'tell the truth' that he repeated the same message in speeches at Edinburgh and Derby in early March.[50] Even within the Cabinet, however, the Chancellor's dismal litany about the obstacles to recovery was conceded to be 'unfortunate, and really unfair to himself'. As Runciman put it, it was a habit which reflected 'a fault more of manner than of argument'.[51]

Chamberlain's second Budget on 25 April 1933 followed in 'an orderly and unexciting way' in the logical series from 1932 to 1935.[52] Confronted by what he believed to be an unparalleled level of 'barracking' for 'imaginative finance' and loan-funded public works to remedy unemployment from Keynes, *The Times* and Harold Macmillan's 'Northern Group' of Conservative MPs,[53] Chamberlain recognised that he would 'soon be the most unpopular man in the country' but he adamantly refused to yield. As he confided to his sisters, 'few Chancellors have had a more difficult task than I ... [and] few men in my position would resist the temptation to bid for popularity', but there would be no concessions on expenditure at the bottom of the slump. Nor were there any further hasty economies to reduce taxation, for as he told his wife, 'Imagine cutting off the Widows Pension to chip sixpence off the Income Tax or 1d off beer!'[54]

The key features of the 1933 Budget were a long-awaited reduction in beer duty and the taxation of Cooperative Societies. Chamberlain had planned the latter for 1932 but had been forced to postpone it in deference to MacDonald's desire for an inquiry on a subject he found deeply embarrassing – not least because he had pledged during the 1931 election to resign from the government if it taxed Cooperative Societies. In the event, the Raeburn Committee concluded that 'the Co-op' was no longer a truly mutual organisation and thus it was unfair to other retailers to continue its traditional exemption from income tax on trading profits on these grounds.[55] In response, MacDonald repeatedly pleaded to drop the matter for fear of provoking widespread political opposition within the country and his own National Labour contingent in Parliament, but Chamberlain refused to be swayed. Arguing that he would be placed in an 'impossible position' if he ignored the conclusions of his own inquiry, he characteristically advised 'that if we have sufficient firmness to stand up to the agitation for a month or two it will die down and little more will be heard of it'.[56] Despite MacDonald's gracious acknowledgement in Cabinet that Chamberlain had made every possible effort to secure compromise with the Cooperative Societies, however, in private the conflict reinforced his burgeoning antipathy towards a Chancellor he condemned as hopelessly 'short-sighted' and inflexible and he blamed himself for not forcing Chamberlain's resignation on the issue. 'His attitude has been disappointing: willing to sacrifice us all', he complained in his diary after the matter was settled.[57]

Despite MacDonald's grumbling and apprehensions, Chamberlain rejoiced that the 1933 Finance Bill proceeded smoothly on its 'calm and tranquil course'.

Indeed, when replying to the opening debate, the Chancellor confessed himself embarrassed by the paucity of Opposition criticism to which to reply. This set the tone for the remainder of the Finance Bill's passage through Parliament and the Budget resolution passed without even a division; a proceeding for which no one could recall a precedent.[58] As a result, after it was all over, Chamberlain noted that although it was 'fashionable to say that no one likes the Budget', he believed it had been received 'with general approval' and was 'gradually gaining more appreciation'.[59] Beneath the surface, however, an increasingly critical group of government backbenchers regarded it as 'a cheerless performance' which 'very distinctly depressed the House. Nor did the customary vindication of financial soundness, though acquiesced in by the House, evoke any applause at all. It was a pure Treasury Budget with no glimmering of any constructive solution for the economic problem.'[60]

Of all the aspects of Chamberlain's stewardship of the economy, this failure to depart from an ostensibly severe balanced budget orthodoxy into the realms of large-scale, loan-financed public works to stimulate recovery has undoubtedly aroused most condemnation. For Chamberlain's critics, the maintenance of such a policy long after the crisis had passed suggests that the balanced budget had become 'a fetish to be worshipped in its own right regardless of circumstance'.[61] Even at the time, Chamberlain rapidly came under strong pressure to relax his iron grip on public expenditure as soon as the worst of the depression had passed. In February 1933, the Economic Advisory Council's Committee on Economic Information wrote to the Prime Minister with a vigorous plea for a radical change of policy. While conceding that the restoration of confidence had been the 'paramount consideration' in 1931, the Committee argued that the 'complete transformation' in the economic situation now indicated the need for substantial public expenditure stimulus 'to enable the forces of recuperation to gain the upper hand' at a time when the Chancellor's stringent budgetary policy was acting as 'a definite adverse influence' upon recovery.[62] A month later, the already critical *Times* published four articles by Keynes also arguing that depressed business expectations required the Chancellor to pump £110 million worth of additional purchasing power into the economy through tax cuts and loan-financed public works to stimulate demand and assist in domestic and world reflation; a lead subsequently endorsed by 37 academic economists and even taken up by the *Daily Express* and *Mail*.[63]

The compelling potency of these arguments for deficit finance and contra-cyclical public works gained considerably from the triumph of Keynesian economic ideas after the Second World War. In some respects too, the critics were correct to contend that Treasury arguments against public works in the 1930s appeared to have advanced very little since the Edwardian era while Chamberlain's strong temperamental adherence to 'a hairshirt philosophy of economic policy' was undeniably based partly on a view of budgetary policy as a 'quasi-moral issue'. From this perspective, Chamberlain unequivocally believed that policy-makers confronted a stark choice between either the difficult path of fiscal rectitude with all its attendant odium or the deceptively easy path along which lesser men might succumb to the appeal of popular solutions rather than face 'disagreeable' facts.[64] 'Courage', he told the Commons in his 1933 Budget statement, 'does not always lie in taking the easiest and most popular course.' But while an excess of puritanical zeal may account for the undeviating clarity of Chamberlain's tone, it does not entirely explain his devotion to the appearance of balanced budgets. In this respect, indictments of Chamberlain's profound instinctive scepticism about public works and the economics of budgetary expansion often fail to understand his policy preferences and prejudices within the context of the fears, uncertainties and theories of his own time.[65]

First, there was the problem of deciding whose alternative theory to embrace. It was a good joke to claim that 'where five economists are gathered together there will be six conflicting opinions and two of them will be held by Keynes!', but its pungency was derived from its underlying grain of truth at a time when his ideas were still evolving.[66] As a senior Treasury official warned the Chancellor in October 1932, 'there is no criterion for determining the proper economists to follow, and whoever one chooses, one is apt to find oneself led into actions which are either repugnant to commonsense or incapable of practical achievement'.[67] From Chamberlain's perspective, both objections applied powerfully to Keynesian prescriptions in 1932–33. As John Ramsden shrewdly observes, the adoption of an expansionist policy may have led to financial crisis, 'not because it is wrong, but because it was *believed* to be wrong' at a time when 'the canons of financial rectitude were so deeply engrained within society that any attempt to resort to unusual financial practices would create renewed worries about British financial integrity, the strength of the currency, fear of inflation and the prospects of a flight of capital, which would have brought back "the nightmare of recession"'.[68] As Warren Fisher inscribed on a Treasury note regarding Keynes' call for loan-financed public works in 1933, 'Borrowing for the dole was the principal cause of foreigners finally losing confidence in us in 1931.' It was a sentiment which Chamberlain wholeheartedly endorsed.[69]

Secondly, the problems of theory became even greater when applied to their practical translation into policy. In retrospect, it is clear that public works on the scale advocated by Lloyd George during the 1929 election would have been far too small to have dealt with the subsequent increase in unemployment. They would also have encountered major balance of payments problems and near insuperable practical and administrative constraints beyond the power and authority of a democratic State to overcome.[70] Furthermore, calculations of the likely employment 'multiplier' effect suggests that to deal effectively with three million unemployed the government needed to expend anything between £537 million and £752 million – sums equivalent to at least half of the total budgetary outlay in 1932 and between 14 and 19.3 per cent of GNP.[71] Even excluding the question of where such funds would come from in a bond market where interest rates were at rock bottom, a deficit of this level must have represented a major threat to confidence given the fact that a projected deficit of £120 million in 1931 had brought the entire financial system to the edge of the abyss.

It is also important to note that while modern econometric analysis suggests that there was probably no 'Keynesian solution' to Britain's unemployment problem between the wars, the far more crucial historical point is that the Chancellor and his officials resisted demands for 'imaginative finance' precisely because they understood these practical objections. Indeed, Chamberlain's gloomy and much criticised warning that they should expect ten more years of high unemployment in February 1933 had been accompanied by an analysis of exactly this sort.[72] Similarly, in response to both Smuts' call for a Commonwealth commitment to large scale public works at the World Economic Conference in 1933 and Lloyd George's plans for a British 'New Deal' in January 1935, the Treasury remained convinced that 'public works as a remedy for unemployment are quite futile' given the limited scope for such projects, the time delays involved in execution and the fact that 'the *scale* on which public works can be carried out is out of all proportion to the problem which faces us'; a proposition further substantiated by regular references to the modest scale of Roosevelt's New Deal in relation to the catastrophic collapse in American national income between 1929 and 1932.[73]

A third problem was that the international experience proved no more attractive for the Chancellor's view of proposals to unbalance the budget to finance public works. Even if it is accepted that unorthodox budgetary policies in Sweden and the United States did not automatically lead to financial disaster, at the time Chamberlain was convinced that they would be far more likely to precipitate another crisis of confidence than lead Britain on to the road to recovery.[74] Drawing on a powerful brief prepared by Sir Richard Hopkins, the Chancellor's principal financial adviser, Chamberlain's 1933 Budget statement devoted four columns of Hansard to his reasons for adamantly resisting pressure for 'imaginative finance'; a case based largely on the fact that budget deficits were 'the rule rather than the exception', but that such countries were not enjoying the benefits which the expansionists had predicted. On the contrary, the Chancellor declared, they were suffering from deepening depression, falling price levels and 'the fear that things are going to get worse'. On the other hand, he claimed that Britain had 'stood the test with the greatest measure of success' and was free from such fears largely because it had balanced the budget and pursued a sound financial policy.[75]

In drawing this international comparison, Chamberlain had been accused of 'crude empiricism'.[76] But whether fair or not, his profoundly contemptuous view of Roosevelt and the New Deal was widely echoed by Cabinet colleagues and key Treasury advisers. He also received regular assurances that 'many Americans are of the opinion that if they had foregone their "ballyhoo" & followed our example they would have done all that R[oosevelt] has effected in employment & price raising without any of the present excursions & alarums'.[77] Indeed, only the hope of a war debt settlement during 1933 and Treasury awareness of Washington's sensitivity towards unfavourable references to their budget deficit prevented Chamberlain from declaring publicly that the American experience was an object lesson in everything that should be avoided in economic policy.[78] Nevertheless, in his private assessment of the New Deal for the Cabinet in October 1933, Chamberlain employed a supremely dismissive analogy which represented 'the Yanks as a barbarous tribe and Roosevelt as a medicine man whose superiority over other medicine men consisted in the astonishing agility with which when one kind of Mumbo Jumbo failed, he produced another'.[79] In February 1935, his Chief Economic Adviser provided an equally damning assessment:

> in the United States ... gambling holds much the same place in national life as cricket does in ours. Nothing, therefore, is more natural than that the American government should indulge in a gamble while a British government has to keep a straight bat and sometimes to stone wall. Such tactics may not appeal to those spectators who have more enthusiasm than knowledge of the pitch, but it is to be hoped that the barracking will not affect the batsmen. For the state of England is not such that they can afford to take great risks.[80]

Although it is tempting to sneer at the sporting metaphors and the unabashed tone of effortless superiority, as Chamberlain never tired of saying both in public and in private, it was easy for others without direct responsibility to demand 'imaginative finance', but as Chancellor he had to be 'very sure that the old principles have really failed before we abandon them, and that new experiments are really likely to succeed before we venture to embark upon them'.[81] Convinced that balanced budgets paved the way for cheap money and that this (in conjunction with tariffs) was already producing recovery, the instinct for fiscal conservatism and cautious national self-preservation became almost irresistible. It is thus scarcely surprising that in March 1937 Chamberlain should have underlined with evident approval a Treasury note which declared the Americans 'have secured an appreciable improvement in employment, it is true; and in the process have increased their national debt by 17,000 million dollars. We have secured a greater improvement, without adding to the debt at all.'[82]

A fourth constraint upon the Chancellor was the fact that the Treasury was less convinced that the economy had turned the corner to sustained recovery in 1933 than the Committee on Economic Information and his other critics.[83] Moreover, even if Britain was through the worst, Chamberlain feared the unsettled state of the world economy offered little certainty that it would not be plunged into another crisis as suddenly as in August 1931. Contemplating a decline in revenue in September 1932, he thus warned that it was 'most important not to do anything which would give the impression that the bad times are over and we can begin to slack off our efforts'.[84] Six months later, Hopkins advised the Chancellor that the only time 'for taking risks about an unbalanced Budget is the time when ... the recovery has really begun' but that in present conditions the only certainty was that 'it would be impossible once we had abandoned the principle of paying our way to stop a rising tide of expenditure' – with the consequent danger of a repetition of 1931.[85] By sustaining the impression that the budgetary crisis had not completely subsided, therefore, Chamberlain found both a justification for the rigour of his orthodoxy and a longer-term opportunity to build the national finances into such an unassailable position that a progressive relaxation of the fiscal stance would eventually become possible as the crowning culmination of his Chancellorship.[86] Finally, on top of all these economic factors, during the worst of the slump in 1932 and 1933 Chamberlain was also increasingly mindful of the adverse effects of a reflationary cut in income tax on war debt negotiations, and specifically 'on the mind of the Middle Western Farmer!'[87]

IV

When assailed by this formidable array of factors during the worst of the depression, Chamberlain remained resolutely determined to resist pressure from reflationists urging an unbalanced budget. On 17 March 1933, the day after the last of his expansionist articles in *The Times*, Keynes spent an hour with Chamberlain during which he warned that 'the more pessimistic the Chancellor's policy, the more likely it is that pessimistic anticipations will be realised and vice versa. Whatever the Chancellor dreams, will come true.' Keynes left the meeting ingenuously believing that Chamberlain listened 'with an open mind and an apparently sympathetic spirit'. In reality, however, Chamberlain found Keynes' ideas 'even worse than [he] had supposed', but he also noted shrewdly that 'the trouble is that he is so plausible and confident that people like the ordinary back bencher who have not much knowledge are very likely to be attracted especially when he is backed so strenuously by the Times'.[88] Chamberlain was equally concerned by the launch of Roosevelt's New Deal, on the grounds that if it succeeded it 'will be embarrassing because people will want to know why I haven't done the same'. From the outset, however, he anticipated that Roosevelt's efforts would fail to produce the desired recovery and the slump on the New York Stock Exchange in July 1933 provided Chamberlain with some savage amusement when it 'absolutely silenced the critics who were asking why our Chancellor could not be brave as well as wise like the American President'. As the passage of time exposed further dangers inherent in the New Deal, he thus believed 'our people may gradually come to realise that our slower and less sensational methods are more satisfactory in the long run'.[89]

In fairness, notwithstanding his profound personal antipathy towards Lloyd George and his contempt for Roosevelt's economic understanding, Chamberlain's opposition to expansionist adventures should not be taken to imply a dogged adherence to the canons of nineteenth century financial orthodoxy. On the contrary, recent scholarship demonstrates that the years after 1932 witnessed a number of major departures from orthodoxy at the Treasury. With regard to debt management policy, alongside the conversion operation and the suspension of US war debt payments, the Treasury further relieved the burden on the Budget by abandoning any provision for debt redemption in 1933 and it continued the practice throughout the decade. In 1932 a completely new and radical departure was also made with regard to forward budgetary planning when the Treasury compiled its so-called 'Old Moore's Almanack' to provide a view on future policy options. Equally important was the fact that from 1933 onwards Chamberlain actively engaged in 'fiscal window dressing' in order to shroud deficits with the appearance of balanced budgeting in order to bolster 'confidence' without the full deflationary reality. Similarly, recognising that a further tightening of the fiscal stance was impracticable given the prevailing mood of pessimism in 1932, the Treasury had adopted a 'very negative reaction' to the Ray Committee's proposed cuts of £35–40 million in local expenditure on the grounds that they were made without any reference to their likely adverse economic consequences. On this basis, as Roger Middleton argues persuasively, the Chamberlainite exaltation of orthodoxy which infuriated so many contemporaries (and subsequent historians) actually provided 'an excellent shield for his less orthodox actions' which were simultaneously radical but 'subtle [and] largely invisible to those outside the Treasury and Cabinet'.[90]

While each of these measures represented a substantial departure from the supposed orthodoxy, the far more important point in this context is that Chamberlain played a direct and leading role in initiating many of these policy innovations. For example, although Sir Richard Hopkins is credited with drafting the Treasury's 'Old Moore's Almanack', he did so in response to Chamberlain's specific request for a means by which 'we could without much trouble calculate roughly the Budget outturn for 1935 on the existing basis'; an assessment intended to help form a view about the scope for tax cuts and expenditure increases over a three to four year period.[91] Moreover, contrary to George Peden's dismissal of the view that Chamberlain was seeking to establish medium-term goals for policy, when Hopkins warned about the highly speculative nature of the forecasts which he offered for the Chancellor's 'private information (or perhaps I ought to write "*mis*information")', Chamberlain noted in the margin, 'I recognise all the limitations of this method. But I still think it would be helpful to have the imaginary Budget as some indication of what might possibly be aimed at.'[92] Far from being a passive observer of Treasury innovations or an uncomprehending prisoner of his officials, therefore, at the Treasury (as at every other department) Chamberlain's natural instinct was to lead from the front with an innovative approach to policy problems.

Although much debate still exists as to the relative impact of government action as opposed to non-policy factors in bringing about British economic recovery, Chamberlain's own confidence in the efficacy of his 'hair-shirt' policy soon appeared to be vindicated. As early as May 1932 the Committee on Economic Information reported that without 'the threatening international outlook, there would be ... substantial grounds for confidence in the position of Great Britain' given improved competitive power and an almost unique level of domestic stability and financial confidence.[93] Against a background of impressive and accelerating recovery after September 1932, Chamberlain finally felt able to relax his vice-like grip over the nation's finances. But in Chamberlain's mind this was the direct outcome of a preconceived plan which stretched back to the very start of his Chancellorship. As he explained revealingly to the Cabinet in December 1933:

> when he took office he had made it his definite aim, in dealing with national finance, to build up the resources of the nation until they were in an unassailable condition. He had wanted to demonstrate the strengthening of the national resources by progressive remissions in successive Budgets. So far he had been successful in carrying out that policy. It had been almost an essential of that policy that his first Budget should be an unpopular one. His second Budget had been a little better, and he hoped his third would be better still. To complete the policy it was important to avoid an anti-climax in his fourth Budget ...[94]

Such claims owed nothing to *ex post facto* rationalisation. After all, this was precisely why he instructed the Treasury in March 1932 to prepare its 'Old Moore's Almanack' to plan for a reduction of taxation and an increase in expenditure over a three to four year period. Having reconciled himself to harsh measures and personal unpopularity in the early years, as the economy recovered Chamberlain's posture as the courageous and incorruptible saviour of the nation's finances only further reinforced his status as the driving force behind the National Government and as a future Prime Minister. Paradoxically, however, Chamberlain also recognised that the upturn in economic activity would increase his problems as Chancellor. In preparation for his 1934 Budget he lamented that 'events are justifying my prophesy that my difficulties would begin when there was any sign of anything to distribute. The uproar from the would be recipients is terrific and the papers keep whipping them on by new and more fantastic estimates of what the surplus will be.' As a result, he feared there would be 'a good deal of disappointment' with his Budget and that he would 'once more come in for a good deal of abuse'.[95]

In the event, Chamberlain's third Budget on 17 April 1934 had more leeway for concessions to popular expectations than the Chancellor had initially anticipated. As his old fishing friend Arthur Wood noted, 'almost all of your press photographs in the papers have succeeded in getting a smile on your face, that is a rare thing before the Budget'.[96] The central feature of Chamberlain's financial statement was its note of cheerful optimism. Reporting a rise in wholesale prices, record low levels in short-term interest rates, rising industrial production and the achievement of equilibrium in the balance of payments, the Chancellor declared with a Dickensian flourish that 'we have now finished the story of *Bleak House* and are sitting down this afternoon to enjoy the first chapter of *Great Expectations*'. He then announced the restoration of half of the public sector pay cuts imposed in 1931 along with the full restoration of unemployment benefit and the remission of 6d (2.5p) on the standard rate of income tax on the grounds that this was the relief 'which would confer most direct benefits upon the country, which would have the greatest psychological effect and which would impart the most immediate and vigorous stimulus to the expansion of trade and employment'.[97]

Response to the Budget was generally enthusiastic and conformed well with the mood of economic recovery. MacDonald was characteristically grudging in noting the 'Budget will be acceptable', but even he was compelled to concede that it was 'only [the] first instalment & the second may be the General Election Budget when the policy of the Government may well be taken to the country'. More sympathetic observers believed it had 'a very good reception & has given the Govt. a much needed "reviver"', while even Amery's faint praise for a 'good conventional Budget still pursuing a policy of deflation' did not prevent him acknowledging that 'it went down very well and the restoration of unemployment benefit has rather taken the wind out of the Socialist sails'.[98] At a personal level, Chamberlain was deeply gratified by the fact that 'no Budget in recollection had so good a reception both in the House and in the country'.[99]

The only complication emerged on 9 May, when the published text of the Finance Bill was found to contain a significant provision not mentioned in the Chancellor's Budget speech – the repeal of the land valuation tax which had been the main feature of Snowden's Budget in April 1931. Although always a dead letter, it had been a constant provocation to Conservative MPs who had twice before sought to abolish it, but on both occasions it had been dropped out of deference to National Labour sentiment. In May 1934 MacDonald again attempted to resist abolition, claiming it reflected a Conservative intention to dominate the government, but this time his appeals were to no avail and the unusually short Finance Bill enjoyed an astonishingly easy passage. Indeed, such was Chamberlain's economic ascendancy by this stage that when the Liberals launched an attack on his monetary policy on 5 July, the outcome was a 'very half-hearted' debate among MPs who clearly shared the Chancellor's view that 'when things are going so well it would be a pity to change the course'.[100]

Although not everyone on the government benches shared this sentiment, the strong recovery of the economy appeared to vindicate the Chancellor's confidence. A Labour censure motion on the government's 'gross incompetence' in dealing with unemployment on 13 February 1935 thus enabled Chamberlain to proclaim the benefits of 'cheap money and sound finance' in a manner capable of recitation in the constituencies and he enjoyed a 'tremendous reception' which even he did not fully comprehend.[101] Two months later, Chamberlain's fourth Budget on 15 April 1935 created an equally positive effect. Having for some time contemplated the prospect of a substantial deficit, a succession of fortunate departmental discoveries and improved trade provided a surplus which enabled him to increase tax allowances to enable the small taxpayer 'to have his turn', while the remaining public sector salary cuts of 1931 were finally restored. Against this background, the Chancellor's tone was even more optimistic and confident. Pointing to 'a substantial advance towards recovery', Chamberlain announced that 'this year the people of this country sweetened their lives with 80,000 tons of sugar more. They smoked 6,500,000 lbs more tobacco. They spent £2,750,000 more on entertainments and they washed away their troubles with 270,000,000 more pints of beer and 700,000,000 more cups of that beverage which cheers but not inebriates.' Inevitably, he seized the opportunity to repeat that this 'solid, continuous and steady improvement' since 1931 was to be attributed to tariffs, cheap money and, above all, to balanced budgets. Little wonder that Chamberlain expected it to be 'much the most popular of my Budgets' or that the government were 'very cock-a-hoop'. As all agreed, such palpable evidence of economic success was 'very helpful to the Government's prestige' as it continued on its steady recovery from the electoral doldrums of 1933–34.[102]

For Chamberlain, the successful outcome of the 1935 Budget was the carefully calculated culmination of his three and a half years of prudent stewardship of the nation's finances. As he explained in his radio 'talkie' on the evening of the Budget, 'There is no magic in it. The application of the principles of sound finance has established confidence in industry. Confidence has begotten enterprise and enterprise has increased employment and profits, so that revenue has increased faster than expenditure.' Having reduced taxation by nearly £60 million a year over the last three and a half years, the Chancellor declared that 'if we have no break in the continuity of our policy here I anticipate that 1935 will be as good a year as 1934 and that we may count on making still further progress towards full prosperity'.[103] In the event, such hopes were to be bitterly frustrated. Far from paving the way for full prosperity and an extensive programme of social reforms as Chamberlain had planned, this was the last Budget of the decade to remit taxes. Indeed, in practical terms, it was the last peacetime budget before financial policy became dominated by the needs of rearmament.

1. Neville Chamberlain, April 1938. He regarded this series of photographs by Fayer as 'the best ever taken'.

2. The family at Highbury. (left to right) Neville, Austen and Joseph Chamberlain. Beatrice is seated in front of Neville and Mary is in front of her husband.

3. The dominant patriarch surrounded by his wife and children. Front row (left to right) Mary, Ethel, Joseph, Ida and Hilda: in the back row are Beatrice and Austen. Probably taken in the 1890s during Neville's absence in the Bahamas.

4. Histed portrait of Neville Chamberlain, May 1905. Taken shortly after his return from a five month tour of India, Ceylon and Burma with his cousin Byng Kenrick.

5. Lord Mayor of Birmingham – possibly addressing one of the City Battalions, November 1915.

6. Chamberlain opening the ninth branch of the Birmingham Municipal Bank on Dudley Road, Rotten Park, 16 June 1923. Always intensely proud of the Bank, he later declared 'its foundation was the most important development in the Corporation since Father's day'.

7. Doting parents. Neville and Anne Chamberlain with Frank and Dorothy at Westbourne, circa 1920.

8. The orchid house, Westbourne, 1926: always a source of particular fascination and dedication until the shortage of time (and money) forced its reluctant disposal in November 1936.

9. Westbourne, next to the Botanical Gardens in Edgbaston: Chamberlain's home after his marriage in 1911 but sold shortly after his death.

10. The Minister of Health inspecting new houses on the Roehampton Estate in the mid-1920s.

11. Aboard the *Empress of Britain* on the way to the Imperial Economic Conference at Ottawa, July 1932. (Back row left to right) Sir Philip Cunliffe-Lister, Lord Hailsham, Walter Runciman, Sir John Gilmour; (front row) J.H. Thomas, Stanley Baldwin and Neville Chamberlain.

12. Budget Day, 17 April 1934. The Chancellor had much to smile about. As he told the Commons, 'we have now finished the story of *Bleak House* and are sitting down this afternoon to enjoy the first chapter of *Great Expectations*'.

13. Fishing for trout, 1939.

14. Shooting was Chamberlain's other great weekend pursuit.

15. Boarding the Lockheed Electra for his first flight to meet Hitler at Berchtesgarden, 15 September 1938.

16. After a stormy meeting with Hitler at Bad Godesberg, 22–23 September 1938.

17. Broadcasting over the Imperial radio chain, after his triumphant
     return from the Munich conference, 30 September 1938.
     The Anglo-Germany agreement signed by Chamberlain and Hitler
     earlier that morning is in his right hand.

18. Downing Street, 30 September 1938: 'This is the second time in our history that there has come back from Germany to Downing Street peace with honour. I believe it is peace for our time'.

19. Visit to Rome in January 1939 with Halifax to meet Mussolini (right) and his Foreign Minister and son-in-law Count Ciano (left).

20. The War Cabinet, September 1939. (Back row left to right) Sir Kingsley Wood, Winston Churchill, Leslie Hore-Belisha, Lord Hankey. (Front row) Lord Halifax, Sir John Simon, Neville Chamberlain, Sir Samuel Hoare, Lord Chatfield.

21. An apprehensive wave on the way to the Commons for the final day
    of the fateful Norway debate, 8 May 1940.

Chapter 10

Unemployment, Special Areas and Lloyd George's 'New Deal', 1932–1937

'I know there are some who think I am over cautious – timid, Amery calls it – humdrum, commonplace and unenterprising. But I know that charge is groundless, or I should not have been the one to produce the Unemployment Assistance Board, the policy of regulation of production now generally adopted, the slum and over-crowding policy now accepted by the Ministry of Health, the sending of Commissioners to the derelict areas accepted by the P.M. and the Minister of Labour or the creation of an International Force to maintain the peace and security of Europe, and the making of a commercial and political pact with Japan and China which last two items are at present rejected by our Foreign Office and not accepted by a majority of our colleagues but which they will have to come to some day. I maintain that the fact that I have initiated every one of these things shows that I can be both bold & original when I believe that those qualities are called for'.

Neville to Hilda Chamberlain, 21 April 1934

By international standards, Britain's experience of the Great Depression was relatively mild and its subsequent recovery was strong, sustained and impressive as rising real wages stimulated dramatic improvements in living standards during an era of remarkable economic growth and prosperity. But alongside this increasing affluence in the booming new industries in the Midlands and South, there existed the grim reality of another face of Britain during the 1930s – one characterised by the dole queue, hopelessness and poverty in the north of England, South Wales and industrial Scotland where mass unemployment and industrial collapse appeared endemic and intractable. Although only part of the picture, this was the vision of Britain in the 1930s immortalised in George Orwell's *The Road to Wigan Pier* (1937) and Walter Greenwood's *Love on the Dole* (1933) and for many people even today it remains their abiding image of the so-called 'devil's decade'. As a result, both for his own generation and for many who followed them, the persistent spectre of mass unemployment in such areas has cast the greatest shadow over Chamberlain's reputation as Chancellor.

In recent years, the traditional picture of governments during the 1930s being hopelessly wedded to a failing version of *laissez-faire* has been replaced by what has accurately been described as 'the "crumbling-adherence-to-laissez-faire-and-not-quite-a-managed-economy" school' of thought, which seeks to combine an acceptance of the National Government's tentative promotion of interventionist policies with an underlying proposition about its fundamental desire to preserve untouched the market framework.[1] In this context, economic historians have been particularly dismissive of the National Government's 'piecemeal and opportunist' efforts with regard to industrial and regional policy. As Derek Aldcroft encapsulates the indictment: 'If regional policy failed to create many new jobs, the government's industrial policy produced even less. Not that there was a consistent and coherent industrial policy worthy of the name, more a hotch-potch of *ad hoc* measures to meet particular circumstances.'[2] As Chancellor, Chamberlain is thus accused of remaining so 'resolutely committed to the free market economy' that he had little sympathy or understanding for the burgeoning 'middle opinion' of the decade moving towards new notions of planning and more interventionist forms of capitalism.[3]

When considered from the perspective of measurable success in promoting economic recovery and employment, it is unquestionably true that industrial and regional policy during this period was small-scale in terms of investment and impact. It is also true that these policies evolved gradually as the decade progressed without any broader theoretically coherent blueprint of the sort later provided by Keynesian economics. The fundamental objection to such criticisms, however, is that their focus upon policy *outcomes* obscures any proper consideration of the underlying *intent* and the economic rationality of policy-makers attempting to forge new policy instruments to combat unprecedented problems in uniquely difficult circumstances. Ultimately, when viewed from this alternative perspective, Chamberlain's Chancellorship emerges in a far more favourable light as the period in which Britain took its first significant steps towards 'supportive' management of the economy – albeit, admittedly, a 'managed economy' of a distinctly non-Keynesian variety.[4] Certainly this was how Chamberlain regarded his own ambitions. As he told his sisters in 1934, 'how false is the suggestion that this is a safety first Govt destitute of new ideas, & how in fact it is continually introducing changes of a really revolutionary character'.[5]

Nowhere was this interventionist spirit more evident during the 1930s than in Chamberlain's promotion of recognisably post-war forms of industrial and regional policy against the scepticism, hostility and parsimony of his Treasury officials. In 1926 Keynes had argued that Conservatives ought to be 'evolving a version of individualist capitalism adapted to the progressive change of circumstances', but that 'capitalist leaders in the City and in Parliament are incapable of distinguishing novel measures for safeguarding capitalism from what they call Bolshevism'.[6] Yet in many ways this was precisely what Chamberlain aspired to achieve throughout his political career. As he once told Philip Snowden, 'he was not deterred from extending municipal and public enterprise because some people call it Socialism'. Indeed, he regularly boasted that he and Sam Hoare were 'the only Socialists in the [Baldwin] Government' and it amused him greatly when 'a real old hard shelled crusted Tory' described him as a 'rank Socialist'.[7] In reality, what Chamberlain meant by 'socialism' in this context, was that he supported a variety of collectivism. But whatever one calls it, his faith in the benefits bestowed on the people by the intervention of the State was as substantial as it was far-reaching.

Chamberlain's pragmatic belief in the obligation upon government to resolve the defects of the market mechanism in the interests of social and economic efficiency led him to support international cartelisation, state subsidy and control of ailing industries and even the nationalisation of canals, coal and railways in the immediate aftermath of the Great War.[8] A few months before his death, he still claimed that he had 'no prejudice against land nationalisation'. 'With me it is merely a matter of expediency', he told Lord Bledisloe. 'In the public interest I would have no hesitation in handing over to public ownership any particular piece of land if that would give better results.'[9] In this sense, as in so many others, Neville Chamberlain was (far more than his half-brother) the true political heir of 'Radical Joe'. Certainly his predilection for collectivist and statist solutions to the failings of the market refute allegations of an unreconstructed faith in *laissez-faire*.

The importance of a proper understanding of Chamberlain's motivations and economic rationality can be demonstrated by reference to his most famous economic innovation – the introduction of the full 'scientific' tariff in February 1932. Although a profoundly emotional moment for the many old tariff reformers who had rallied to Joseph Chamberlain's banner almost thirty years before, it is simply nonsense to claim (as many historians do) that 'Protection was advocated for its own sake' and that 'when Neville Chamberlain introduced the Import Duties Bill he was fulfilling the dreams of his father as much as prescribing for the depression'.[10] Far from being the final backward-looking symbolic act in a drama dating back to 1903, Chamberlain had devised the general tariff as part of the government's 'flexible and many-sided policy' designed to overcome economic depression and he commended the Import Duties Bill to Parliament as a panacea for virtually all Britain's industrial and economic ills.[11]

With the benefit of hindsight, it is clear that the general tariff was far less successful than policy-makers hoped and believed at the time. But without the benefit of complex (and still contested) retrospective econometric analysis, the perceived reality for Chamberlain and his colleagues during the 1930s was that by protecting domestic industry from foreign competitors 'the tariff proved on balance of significant and essential value in aiding British recovery, not only by giving an initial stimulus to rise from the slough, but in the longer-term also'.[12] Moreover, as with the evaluation of 'cheap money', the fundamental point is that whatever the retrospective *outcome* of tariff policy during the 1930s, the contemporary *intent* was consciously and explicitly to arm the government with a flexible tool with which to manage the economy and restore industrial prosperity. In this respect, the Import Duties Act represented a victory for the pragmatic protectionists like Chamberlain over the vague but grandiose aspirations of sentimental imperial visionaries like Amery. Ultimately, for

Chamberlain, tariff reform was to be sought less as an end in itself than as an instrumental step towards a far broader and more ambitious economic objective. Indeed, on this basis some have argued that between 1931 and 1935 the National Government 'laid the foundations of the Managed Economy'.[13]

Nowhere was this link more apparent for Chamberlain than in the perceived relationship between the Import Duties Act and the reorganisation of industry, at a time when it was already clear that 'industry ... has neither the will nor the power to reorganise itself'.[14] This had certainly been the Conservative experience with ailing staple trades like iron and steel during the 1924–29 Government, while Baldwin's electoral pledges and Churchill's free trade obstructionism made rationalisation appear to be an alternative rather than an adjunct to tariff protection.[15] In June 1930, however, the Conservative Research Department's report on iron and steel convinced Chamberlain that he now possessed the opportunity to make the latter conditional upon the former because 'in return for a measure of protection the industry is in a mood to pledge itself to almost anything'. A month later, the CRD came to a similar conclusion with regard to cotton.[16] As Chamberlain explained to Snowden in January 1932:

> the coupling with this flat rate tariff of additional powers [to impose selective surtaxes] provides us with such a lever as has never been possessed before by any Government, for inducing or, if you like, forcing industry to set its house in order. I have in mind particularly iron and steel and cotton: and my belief in the advantages of Protection is not so fanatical as to close my eyes to the vital importance of a thorough reorganisation of such industries as these, if they were even to keep their heads above water in the future.

As Chamberlain emphasised repeatedly in the Balance of Trade Committee and later in Cabinet, the basis of his long-term industrial strategy was to create an independent Import Duties Advisory Committee armed with the power to inform ailing industries that if 'you want help ... you must first put your house in order'.[17]

By pursuing these goals through a notionally independent body like IDAC, Chamberlain hoped to depoliticise a highly contentious issue by removing it from the parliamentary and party arena while cloaking its recommendations in an objective authority which made them difficult to challenge. For Chamberlain, however, independence was never synonymous with impartiality or fiscal neutrality. On the contrary, recognising that 'its success will depend a good deal on the Committee', he actively sought a like-minded chairman to employ these new powers in a suitably compliant and interventionist manner; a search which concluded with the appointment of Sir George May, author of the Economy Report in 1931, who he regarded as 'eminently the right man'.[18] Within the Treasury it was well known that Chamberlain was deeply involved with IDAC's deliberations and in view of his explicit objectives it is perhaps not surprising that econometric analysis suggests that it recommended selective duties in accordance with governmental priorities rather than the 'objective' merits of the case or the level of import penetration.[19] Indeed, as one IDAC member later recalled with remarkable candour, their instructions were 'of a vague and general character' but 'everybody understood it was given more of a lead by implication, in the pronouncements of Ministers. The Committee was set up to erect an edifice on the Government's broadly defined plan, … and … it would have been unconstitutional to have a committee acting on a policy, say, of reducing protection when the Government was committed to increasing it.'[20]

In the short-term, Chamberlain was not disappointed by either Sir George May or IDAC. By mid-April 1932, its first report contained a long list of articles to be subjected to new or increased duties at a much higher level than ever anticipated by the Balance of Trade Committee, whose notional maximum of 20 per cent now appeared to be regarded 'as a sort of minimum for fully manufactured articles' without any reference to the efficiency of the industries. More important, these proposals revealed the full implications of passing effective control over tariff levels from the Cabinet and Parliament to an independent body removed from direct political influence but whose personnel were carefully selected by a protectionist Chancellor. MacDonald might angrily protest that May had 'produced as big a piece of shoddy work as was his Economy Report', but Chamberlain was delighted. Despite the alarm of Runciman and MacDonald at the length of the schedule and the speed of protectionist advance, and despite the latter's belated efforts to restore Cabinet control, both were swept aside by Chamberlain's view that it would be improper for the government to interfere with IDAC's recommendations having established an independent body precisely for this purpose.[21]

In this respect at least, Chamberlain enjoyed considerable success and he was optimistic of rapid progress towards the implementation of his industrial policy. Assured by Sir George May in June 1932 that IDAC had 'got the steel industry well under weigh', Chamberlain was confident that 'if he can persuade them actually to carry through the reorganisation plans which they have in hand it will be a great achievement & may have far reaching effects on other industries like cotton which have hitherto resisted all efforts to set them on their feet'.[22] Unfortunately, Chamberlain's hopes that the tariff would provide the necessary lever to force industry to reorganise and restore its own competitiveness proved a sad illusion. Indeed, it soon became apparent that the newly-created British Iron and Steel Federation was 'rather ineffective' in promoting reorganisation, while the industry remained as individualistic, fragmented and uncooperative as ever. As a result, progress towards an agreed scheme of comprehensive reorganisation was so dilatory as to represent an effective breach of faith with IDAC and the government. Worse still, Donald Fergusson, the Chancellor's private secretary, soon warned that the brunt of the criticism for these failures would fall on the Chancellor because 'a great deal of ammunition will be given to those who said that you must make protection conditional on reorganisation and that if you gave protection first you would never see reorganisation'.[23]

Ultimately, this unresolved problem obstructed all progress towards Chamberlain's goal. The spirit and intent were radical and innovative in attempting to provide a mechanism to overcome past entrenched obstacles to reorganisation. The policy was also unequivocally conceived not as a temporary palliative but as a fundamental solution to Britain's key industrial problem and as a basis for the long-term recovery of employment in the most severely depressed regions of Britain. But unwilling to dictate to private enterprise or to become directly entangled in the imposition of State-directed reform from above, Chamberlain persisted in placing far too much faith in the enlightened self-interest of individual firms prepared to cooperate in pursuit of the rational collective good of their industry as a whole, long after both Runciman and his own Treasury officials recognised that the strategy and its central assumptions were fatally flawed.[24] Moreover, even when this fact became impossible to ignore, Chamberlain made it clear that there were limits beyond which he was not prepared to go in engaging the State in industrial affairs. Therefore, when the Treasury representative on IDAC warned in October 1933 that 'in the last resort the Government might be driven to the drastic step of placing the whole control of the industry in the hands of a public body', Chamberlain immediately retorted that 'this alternative must be definitely ruled out' because the government 'could not command the services of men who would be capable of running this complicated industry if those now responsible for its conduct had been first completely antagonised'.[25]

As a result, the iron and steel industry sheltered behind its relatively high tariff and reaped all of the benefits of protection without ever honouring its side of the bargain – for the simple reason that it knew that it was 'politically impossible' for the government to use its ultimate sanction and withdraw the tariff.[26] Chamberlain's bluff had been called. Like his father before him, Neville Chamberlain was a radical prepared to use the State to reform and renovate the system of private enterprise as a means to defend and buttress it, but he was not willing to undermine it. Yet while he can be criticised for a lack of political will in never deviating from his initial indirect approach even when confronted by the continued evasions of the industry, this failure needs to be seen in its broader historical context. Against this background, one of the most striking long-term features of British industrial policy in the years after 1945, under both parties, was the reliance upon the private sector to rationalise itself on a voluntary consensual basis encouraged by the State, in marked contrast to the *dirigiste* approach pursued in Japan and France where the State drew up sectoral plans and employed public sanctions to enforce their implementation.[27]

In other sectors of the economy, Chamberlain employed precisely the same basic approach but with rather more positive effects. This was certainly true of Chamberlain's battle against Runciman over the merger of the White Star and Cunard shipping lines in 1933–34. Contrary to the allegations of his Cabinet opponents, for Chamberlain the objective was never defined principally in terms of national prestige or misplaced sentimentality about the completion of what would become the *Queen Mary*. On the contrary, he always claimed that he was 'after a much larger game' regarding the rationalisation of the North Atlantic shipping trade in order to put 'an end to the cut throat competition which has been ruining both companies'.

> Nominally, the subsidy proposal is to enable [Hull No.] 534 to be completed, British prestige in the N[orth] A[tlantic] to be restored, unemployment reduced and a satisfying impression imprinted on the public mind of broadmindedness, vigour and fearless imagination on the part of Government. Personally I care for none of these things. But I believe this to be a case where the powers of a Government can be properly and usefully employed to assist private enterprise to overcome obstacles which might otherwise prove insurmountable or only surmountable after a longer period than we can afford to wait.[28]

To achieve this objective, Chamberlain was prepared to provide government finance, support and some coercion to overcome corporate jealousies. Equally important, he proved ruthless in deliberately thwarting the development of the rival Red Star Line, on the grounds that it would undermine the government's strategy of creating a monopoly operator in the North Atlantic.[29]

During the early years of his Chancellorship, Chamberlain's attitudes towards industrial policy and the broader issues it raised about the proper relationship between private industry and the State had gradually evolved as a practical response to changing political and economic circumstances. During the summer of 1934, however, he instructed the Conservative Research Department to formulate a general policy on the future relations of industry and the State. When it reported in October 1934, a CRD sub-committee under Chamberlain swiftly rejected the radical proposal of the Industrial Reorganisation League for a general Enabling Bill to force the pace on rationalisation on a far larger scale where the majority of the industry supported reorganisation. There were a variety of sound economic and political reasons for this decision, but as Chamberlain soon made clear, his own preference was piecemeal, incremental and conceived over an unrealistically long time-frame.

> There are undoubtedly cases where it is difficult, if not impossible, for private enterprise to make itself truly efficient without some aid from the Government. Progress, however, must be by steps, one at a time; and our conclusion is that legislation should be *ad hoc* and designed to deal only with particular circumstances in a particular industry. We have already had one example in the Cotton Industry, and we may possibly have another in the Steel Industry in future. By degrees, a body of experimental evidence will be accumulated, and in another generation it may be possible to generalise and lay down the limits of what should be the State interference with industry.[30]

Having disposed of this radical option, Chamberlain assured the sub-committee that 'it should be possible now to set out the arguments in favour of a middle course between *laissez-faire* and state control'; a quest which ended four months later with agreement that government should intervene in an industry only where the necessary reorganisation could not be achieved by natural forces within a reasonable time – and even then it should only act in conjunction with a representative body drawn from the industry. Moreover, once reorganisation had been achieved, the State should withdraw completely after ensuring that there would be no monopoly control and minimal barriers to entry. In reality, this was simply a reaffirmation of the strategy Chamberlain had evolved in practice with regard to iron and steel in 1932–33 and which he would later apply to the coal and cotton industries in 1938. As John Ramsden notes, it also came remarkably close to the policy espoused in Butler's *Industrial Charter* in 1947.[31]

II

In spite of his disappointments with iron and steel, by 1934 Chamberlain interpreted evidence of burgeoning domestic recovery as a complete vindication of the financial and economic strategy he had pursued since becoming Chancellor in the depths of the depression. Unfortunately, his problem was that unmistakable signs of prosperity in many sectors of the economy served poignantly to highlight the embarrassing persistence of unemployment in the chronically depressed 'derelict' and 'distressed' areas like Jarrow and Merthyr where over 60 per cent of insured workers were without jobs. 'The existence of 2 million unemployed is more eloquent than the reduction from 3 million', Sir John Simon noted in his diary in November 1934, 'the plight of utterly depressed areas throws into shadow the enormous improvement elsewhere.'[32]

Like its contemporary critics, historians have often been particularly dismissive of the National Government's efforts to tackle this problem of regional and structural unemployment. In Frederic Miller's much quoted words, the Special Areas Act of 1934 was 'considered more as a public relations exercise than as a break in the policy of non-intervention', while others repeatedly condemn the 'multiplicity of measures which were small in scale and uncoordinated' because of 'the government's reluctance to abandon the base-line of liberal economic orthodoxy'.[33] But as one historian of British regional policy notes, Chamberlain's later critics often 'underestimate the ideological and political significance of *ad hoc* pragmatic policy innovation'.[34] Certainly, in this case, what started from hesitant origins as a form of welfare policy, designed to solve a political problem, gradually evolved during the 1930s into something far bolder, more innovative and far more interventionist than invariably conceded by critics – particularly when the primary focus for evaluation is shifted from policy outcomes (as defined by the number of jobs created) to the underlying intent of its principal architect. Indeed, on this basis, it is reasonable to contend that Chamberlain's initiative ensured that Britain emerged during this period as an international pioneer in the development of a regional policy which laid the foundations for an important feature of post-war policy and economic management.

A proper understanding of Chamberlain's motivations is crucially important in this particular case because one of the most persistent and universal myths about the development of regional policy in the 1930s is the 'generally accepted', but entirely erroneous, view that Chamberlain was literally shamed into action by the public outrage created by a harrowing series of articles on the plight of 'Places without a Future' in *The Times* in March 1934. As a result, Chamberlain is accused of 'calculated expediency' in responding to public clamour for action by simply coordinating existing palliatives with minimal investment and much window-dressing, 'rather than ... breach the declared policy of non-intervention'.[35] While explanations of this sort conform well with the classically negative image of Chamberlain as the soulless and cynical upholder of non-intervention, it is also based on a fundamental misapprehension. Above all, what such criticism fails to recognise is that these articles were actually written for *The Times* at Chamberlain's express instruction by Henry Brooke, whom he seconded from the CRD specifically for the purpose.[36] When this crucial fact is understood, the impetus for the development of Britain's first attempt at regional policy fits perfectly with Chamberlain's long-established practice of planting stories in the press in order to force the pace of reform upon reluctant colleagues. This was a tactic Chamberlain had consistently refined since his mayoralty twenty years before. He had employed it over rural housing in 1926, he was concurrently using it to press the need for House of Lords reform and he would most famously exploit it to bounce the Cabinet into the abandonment of sanctions against Italy in June 1936.[37]

Chamberlain didn't know exactly what Brooke was going to write, but he thought the articles were 'brilliantly written and stuffed full of ideas'. More important, he rejoiced when the published proposals 'put the cat among the pigeons' in the Cabinet – particularly as they made the Minister of Labour 'very nervous'. Moreover, to maximise the effect, on the day *The Times* published the last of its reports (22 March), Chamberlain made a speech in Newcastle advocating a visit to the area by the newly created Unemployment Assistance Board 'to see for themselves what the conditions were', while assuring his audience that they were 'not forgotten in London'. Four days later, when the Minister of Labour proposed immediate action to this effect to the Cabinet, he specifically linked his decision to the lead given by Chamberlain at Newcastle. As a direct result of Chamberlain's covert manoeuvre, therefore, the Cabinet despatched four Special Investigators to the Distressed Areas to propose possible solutions. To highlight the underlying connection further, Brooke was in attendance at Chamberlain's meeting with the Special Investigators at which he 'outlined ideas' before they began their preliminary studies.[38] The much-repeated allegation that Chamberlain was shamed into action as 'a public relations exercise' thus fundamentally fails to grasp the underlying purpose of a strategy designed to railroad the Cabinet into direct engagement with a problem he already wished to tackle.

In the event, although the Special Investigators drew together a large number of minor palliatives they failed to propose any spectacular solutions to the problem. In part, this was predictable, given the Chancellor's clear instruction that they should work on the assumption that there would be no substantial Treasury assistance.[39] Nevertheless, Chamberlain confessed he found their reports 'a little disappointing' as he had hoped for 'something rather bigger in conception'. More important, he was convinced they 'could never strike popular imagination by confining themselves to these small details' – far less would it be possible to satisfy the expectations already generated in Parliament or the country by the high-profile appointment of such investigators.[40]

At a fundamental level, Chamberlain always believed that measures specifically designed to assist the depressed areas were principally intended to be palliatives. Indeed, since the late 1920s he had been convinced that 'the only certain solution of the problem of the workless areas' was the assisted transference of unemployed workers to areas with work. His proposals for a commissioner to achieve this end in December 1927 thus laid the foundations for what became the Industrial Transference Board. But as he also recognised, this would be 'a lengthy process' and would only ever assist the younger and more mobile members of the unemployed. As a result, he conceded that special palliatives were needed to relieve the condition of those incapable of transference; an approach which placed the primary focus upon local welfare efforts to ameliorate the *social* problems of the unemployed in the depressed areas rather than upon a national strategy designed to overcome the fundamental *economic* problem of long-term regional unemployment.[41]

As chairman of the Cabinet committee appointed to consider the Special Investigators' reports in October 1934, Chamberlain was prepared to implement some of their proposed palliatives 'both because they are valuable in themselves, and, because, the fact of their being tried would have an important psychological effect in persuading the persons in the Depressed Areas that the Government had their plight very much at heart'.[42] Recognising the need for something larger in conception and more innovative in approach, however, he also developed an idea proposed by his private secretary and within a week Chamberlain had formulated his own alternative scheme. As he told the Cabinet, they should depart from ordinary rules and practices to enable the four Depressed Areas to be treated 'as special fields for experiment and research, with a view to the initiation, organisation and prosecution of schemes designed to facilitate the economic development and social improvement of the areas'. To this end, commissioners were to be appointed with funds to use at their discretion on projects not ordinarily performed by existing local authorities – including the improvement of local amenities, occupational centres for the unemployed, experimental land settlements and the clearing of slagheaps and derelict sites to help attract business in the future. As he assured the committee: 'It was not a question of spending a great deal of money, but of showing that the matter had not been pigeon-holed, and that the Government was doing its best to help matters.' By the end of November, the Cabinet had agreed to the immediate introduction of the Depressed Areas (Development and Improvement) Bill.[43]

Chamberlain was extremely satisfied with the scheme which he had anonymously authored and then commended as chairman of the Cabinet Committee. 'It might be said that it was a revolutionary step', he told the Committee with exaggerated optimism, 'but one might have to be revolutionary sometimes.' Certainly he believed his 'brilliant idea' would turn the investigator's reports 'into a new feather in the Government's cap instead of a thorn in their side'. He also expected it would be guaranteed a warm reception given the 'great enthusiasm' of some ministers and the fact that two of the Special Investigators 'had almost got tears in their eyes & said it seemed too good to be true'.[44] Unfortunately for Chamberlain, when the Bill was introduced in the Commons on 14 November 1934, the announcement that only £2 million had initially been set aside to begin the work in the renamed 'Special Areas' was greeted with a palpable groan of disappointment on all sides of both Houses given the manifest inadequacy of the figure for the task in hand.[45] Indeed, Chamberlain was fortunate that his initial proposal to allocate only £1 million to the scheme had been amended at the behest of anxious colleagues on the committee.[46] Undaunted, however, he consoled himself with the thought that press leaks had encouraged people 'to expect that large sums would be promptly spent, measuring the quality of the scheme solely by the money to be spent on it'. With time, he told himself, the critics would soon adjust their standards and come to welcome the measure.[47] In this expectation, he was gravely mistaken.

III

Whatever the longer-term potentialities of Chamberlain's strategy towards industry and regional unemployment, by 1934 his problems over Special Areas were symptomatic of a far more fundamental discontent about the Chancellor's stern refusal to countenance any concessions to budgetary expansion. In January 1934, Robert Boothby gave voice to the despair of several other Conservative MPs when he warned Baldwin that the National Government was 'moving towards a very considerable electoral debacle' because of the 'absence of any political philosophy, or theme, or policy adequate to the needs of the time; and ... the lack of any constructive measures'. Central to this indictment was the 'continued and unwarranted retardation of public works'.[48] By December increasingly vocal backbench demands for the Chancellor to be 'more spectacular' with his projected budget surplus forced Chamberlain into a textbook defence of his financial policy. Two weeks later, when Roosevelt's budget message asked Congress for $4000 million for relief works out of a total appropriation of $8520 million, Chamberlain rightly feared the critics of his financial orthodoxy would be encouraged to new and more vigorous denunciations. 'I shall do my best to hold the fort', he assured his sisters, 'but there are many faint hearts among the brethren in the Cabinet and it is rather a thankless task.'[49]

Chamberlain was right to be apprehensive about signs of increasing restiveness within the Cabinet. MacDonald disliked his Chancellor personally and resented both his manner and his increasing efforts to interfere 'not only with the finance of another department but its policy'. He also complained that even when the Chancellor's defence of his financial policy was 'solid in substance', it was 'delivered in that hard unsympathetic manner which is responsible for much of the Government's loss of favour'. But for MacDonald, the real fear was that Roosevelt's New Deal would have 'a very awkward reaction on us here' because 'people will demand demonstrations of our activity and will not be content with solid, unassuming work'. By January 1935, therefore, the Prime Minister was convinced that Chamberlain's brand of 'super careful finance' would 'have to change' and he suspected correctly that within the Cabinet a 'division had been forming for some time and the cause was a conflict with the Treasury on loans for public works'.[50]

One such critic was Walter Runciman, whose outspoken conflict with Chamberlain over American war debts and the Cunard-White Star merger, was paralleled by private concerns about his financial inflexibility.[51] In January 1935, Chamberlain also learned that Sir Philip Cunliffe-Lister, one of his oldest political friends and allies, 'had been the leader in insisting that the financial policy of the Government was all wrong'.[52] In the same month, even Simon protested to Chamberlain that the Treasury's contribution to the League of Nations symposium on public works was 'so dogmatic, not only as to past experience, but as to our future intentions', that he feared it would provide valuable ammunition to the government's expansionist critics.[53] Among the other Cabinet critics, Oliver Stanley, the Minister of Labour, Walter Elliot, the Agriculture Minister, and the younger 'Boy's Brigade' also palpably 'yearned for a smiling Conservatism to replace Chamberlain's monetary rigours' while David Margesson, the Chief Whip, was suspected of wanting 'a more dramatic and Rooseveltian lead'.[54] On 30 January, at Chamberlain's instigation, MacDonald announced the formalisation of the 'Big Six' meetings of party leaders into a new General Purposes Committee of the Cabinet designed to 'discuss matters which did not belong only to one Government Department'. Significantly, the first subject under consideration was financial policy in relation to public works.[55]

This Cabinet challenge to Chamberlain's authority was rendered far more ominous by the sudden re-emergence of Lloyd George on the political stage at precisely the moment when many Conservatives detected 'a psychological need in the nation for national reconstruction' given the government's failure to capture the public imagination.[56] After his poor showing in the 1931 election, Lloyd George had so effectively withdrawn from public life that Chamberlain soon declared that he was 'finished as a force in the country, though no doubt he can still do a certain amount of mischief'.[57] By the end of 1934, however, he had completed his *War Memoirs* and was looking around for an issue with which to restore his political influence. Having resolved that an outright challenge to the National Government over unemployment offered the most effective method of achieving this end, at Bangor on 17 January, his seventy-second birthday, Lloyd George publicly launched his campaign for a British version of Roosevelt's 'New Deal'.

Leading members of the government were as suspicious of Lloyd George's motives as they were contemptuous of his new platform. MacDonald thought the Bangor speech 'just the old stuff of the showman & bounder, demagogue & driver', but he gloomily recognised that it had 'revived the murmur that the Govt should have more "go"'. Sir John Simon was equally dismissive: 'It may be a New Deal, but it appears to be largely a shuffling of the old pack', including public works, tariffs, land settlement and a 'War Cabinet of 4 or 5 super-men'.[58] Chamberlain was even more suspicious. At a policy level, his Treasury advisers all agreed that the clamour for public works to solve regional unemployment simply did not stand up to serious scrutiny.[59] But for Chamberlain, the personal and political case against Lloyd George was always far more compelling. When rumours of his desire to return to office emerged in mid-December, therefore, Chamberlain told Baldwin 'plainly' that he 'would not serve in any Govt of which Ll.G. was a member'; a threat repeated in early January along with some 'very definite statements' about the 'demonstrably self-contradictory & unworkable' nature of Lloyd George's proposals and his inability to work with the National Government except on his own terms. As Chamberlain told Warren Fisher, he was prepared to sacrifice his own career because 'I could not sit with him without selling my principles & becoming party to the destruction of all I had worked for as Chancellor.' A few days later he also informed MacDonald that 'quite definitely he would not serve with Ll.G'.[60]

Given the coincidence of bold policy pronouncements from Roosevelt and Lloyd George and press interest in a good story, Chamberlain was right to feel vulnerable – particularly as some government MPs went out of their way to pay fulsome compliments to Lloyd George in the Commons in January, while Cabinet critics like Cunliffe-Lister were reported to be 'extremely anxious to bring in Ll.G.' By early February, Chamberlain told his sisters with evident alarm that there was 'a good deal of intrigue going on with L.G. who has been privately meeting members of the House and even of the Cabinet and to whom some of our people look as a possible saviour at the election, not because they really believe in his policy ... but because they think he is such a good showman'. For his own part, however, he claimed he had 'not budged from [his] determination to have nothing to do with him'.[61]

Despite the apparent vulnerability of his position, Chamberlain's efforts to exclude his old enemy were actually assisted by Lloyd George's own implicit terms for entry to the government. As Frances Stevenson, Lloyd George's mistress, shrewdly recorded in her diary a week before the Bangor speech: 'One thing is certain: D[avid] will not go into a Government with Ramsay MacDonald, nor will he take office with Neville Chamberlain as Chancellor or Simon as Foreign Minister. It is equally clear that Baldwin cannot get rid of Ramsay MacDonald or Chamberlain.'[62] In reality, Baldwin initially appears to have been surprisingly receptive to the idea of Lloyd George's return, but he also recognised he would 'have the resignation of half the Cabinet on my hands' if he offered him office.[63] In late January he admitted to Runciman that he was still personally prepared to consider an offer to Lloyd George, but by this stage he conceded that Chamberlain's fierce opposition represented an effective veto. On 5 February, Baldwin thus assured Chamberlain that 'he had come to the conclusion that he could not serve with L.G. since that would inevitably split the party'. Two days later, the 'Big Six' agreed that there should be no offer of office to Lloyd George.[64] It was indicative of Chamberlain's insecurity and alarm, however, that he repeatedly exercised his veto with Baldwin and MacDonald throughout the spring of 1934.[65]

Having stymied Lloyd George's hopes of returning to the Cabinet, Chamberlain turned his attention to destroying his policy proposals. Unsurprisingly, the Chancellor regarded the substance of Lloyd George's Bangor declaration as 'the poorest stuff imaginable, vague, rhetorical and containing not a single new idea'. Yet he believed it safest to move cautiously and 'let the little man develop his ideas in more detail before one begins to attack in earnest'. On this basis, he resolved to kill Lloyd George's New Deal with the illusion of kindness after a suitable period of careful consideration. This strategy had two advantages. First, Chamberlain understood that as an old man in a hurry Lloyd George would be prone to displays of public impatience which could only damage his statesmanlike appeal for cross-party cooperation in the national interest.[66] The second advantage of the strategy was that Chamberlain knew from bitter past experience that Lloyd George was a man of big ideas and compelling slogans rather than detailed or carefully costed policy proposals. Having lured Lloyd George into the position where he was obliged to claim that all the plans and estimates were fully worked out, Chamberlain recognised that it would be electorally damaging to be seen to ignore them altogether. On the other hand, however, he anticipated that detailed scrutiny would reveal these plans to be 'sketchy ... full of padding and without details or estimates'.[67]

This was a danger of which Lloyd George's allies were all too acutely conscious. As Sir Edward Grigg confided to Baldwin soon after the government invited Lloyd George to submit his plans for consideration, they were probably 'vague and indefinite – the sort of thing that permanent officials make mincemeat of' but 'it is the man that matters, not the plans'.[68] In reality, Grigg's apprehensions precisely outlined Chamberlain's intentions. As he gloated to a friend, they had 'called Lloyd George's bluff. I fancy that he is under the illusion that this means a defeat for the Chancellor of the Exchequer. If so he has made a bad miscalculation.'[69] The resulting document fully substantiated Chamberlain's expectations. During late March and early April, the committee's ten meetings devoted to Lloyd George's proposals revealed them to be 'all picturesque exaggeration, false perspectives and alluring promise, but no definite or practical help'. Yet although Chamberlain lamented that it was 'a sad waste of time when we have so many things of real importance to attend to', he was determined to be 'very cautious in dealing with him'. After all, Lloyd George was 'a skilful player at the game of politics' and this implied the need to 'keep L.G. guessing until we are ready to come out with a counter memorandum'. Having completed their examination of Lloyd George's proposals by 10 April, the next step was to 'have the little beast in to discuss them'. In preparation for their first meeting on 18 April, Chamberlain took the precaution of writing out in block capital letters the key questions for the Prime Minister to ask.[70]

Perceptions and accounts of this first meeting differed substantially. At this juncture, Lloyd George's friends still appeared to believe that he would be invited to join the government and that Chamberlain was reconciled to the idea. As a result, he arrived 'in excellent form and spirits, not in the least nervous' and in accordance with Chamberlain's plan of campaign, the committee (except Runciman) were 'all friendly in manner towards him'.[71] From the other side of the negotiating table, however, Lloyd George appeared 'very general' and unimpressive, but the meeting ended with both parties feeling content with the first engagement. Chamberlain was satisfied that Lloyd George had been forced into some definite statements about the number of men he expected to put back to work while 'L.G. was kept guessing as to what our real attitude is.'[72] For his own part, Lloyd George concluded that 'they want to make terms ... but of course they want to get as cheap terms as possible'; an assessment which seems astonishing given Chamberlain's comprehensive rejection of a British version of Roosevelt's New Deal in his Budget statement only three days before, but a misapprehension which suggests that Chamberlain's devious strategy had succeeded.[73]

It was not until mid-May that Lloyd George suspected that he had been duped. Through a mutually trusted intermediary, he communicated to Baldwin his fear that the government would postpone its decision on his programme until after a general election designed to capitalise on the patriotic fervour of the Silver Jubilee celebrated that month. If these suspicions were correct, Lloyd George warned that he had ample funds to support 300 Liberal candidates 'to reduce the Conservative majority to so narrow a margin as to make the life of the next Parliament very arduous and uncertain'. Despite repeated assurances that his 'primary concern was for the adoption of his programme, and not for office', he brazenly suggested that if Chamberlain rejected his proposals he might be prepared to become Foreign Secretary to repair relations with Germany.[74]

Lloyd George had every reason to be anxious and despondent. The Cabinet Committee had always been hostile to his proposals and his own dismal performance in defending them often created a deplorable impression when he appeared not to understand his own plans under cross-questioning. The government's deception in order to buy time to prepare their counterblast was finally revealed on 7 June when Baldwin succeeded the ailing MacDonald as Prime Minister. In the ensuing Cabinet reshuffle there was no place for Lloyd George, but Chamberlain was one of the few senior ministers who conspicuously remained in place. Aware that this signalled the defeat of all his hopes, Lloyd George published *A Call to Action* on 12 June; a comprehensive attack upon the government's policy on international peace and unemployment which presaged the formation of a non-party Council of Action for Peace and Reconstruction.

The modest public response to this manifesto confirmed Chamberlain's view that 'there is really no reason why we should be frightened of him'. In the meantime, he set about stealing Lloyd George's thunder by announcing an improvement loan of £35 million for the London Transport Board, as a refutation of the allegation that the government opposed all public works projects. In the belief that Lloyd George's 'evident bad temper' towards the government was damaging his support, however, Chamberlain explained to his sisters that he was 'playing a waiting game over his proposals in the hope of forcing him to publish first for I fear lest he should again revise his document when he sees ours'.[75]

In the event, Chamberlain did not have to wait long. After Baldwin's dismissive words about public works in the censure debate on 9 July, it was clear the government were about to reject Lloyd George's plans. A week later, his much vaunted programme for national salvation appeared under the title, *Organising Prosperity*. 'This is just what we wanted' Chamberlain rejoiced in his diary, but as he also conceded the government's reply 'has given me a lot of trouble'.[76] At a special meeting of the Cabinet on 15 July, by Chamberlain's own admission, his draft reply was subjected to 'a good deal of criticism' and then amended to leave a 'less negative impression'. In private, Chamberlain regretted the need 'to omit some of the sharpness', but he 'absolutely refused to admit any compliments' and 'tore up' Baldwin's over-conciliatory draft covering letter and replaced it with one of his own composition.[77] The government's reply, entitled *A Better Way to Better Times*, appeared on 22 July. Inevitably, it defended the government's record of lasting successes where public works were practical and productive while comprehensively dismissing both Lloyd George's programme and the underlying 'misconception that a vast quantity of hitherto undiscovered work capable of giving employment to a large number of peoples lies waiting to be put in hand'.[78]

Despite the time devoted to the subject, Chamberlain had scored a complete and total victory – Lloyd George would not be offered office in any reconstructed National Government and his proto-Keynesian budgetary expansionism would not be forced upon the Chancellor by his previously anxious and critical colleagues. Furthermore, Chamberlain also rejoiced that Lloyd George's public campaign had apparently 'fallen absolutely flat' and that his old enemy had 'completely missed the bus'.[79] But for all these consolations, the fact remains that the internal and external challenge to his authority on economic management had been a deeply unsettling experience and Chamberlain was not prepared to take any further chances. Treasury officials continued to monitor the activities of Lloyd George's Council of Action and his demands for economic reconstruction until Chamberlain left the Treasury to become Prime Minister in May 1937.[80]

IV

The defeat of Lloyd George and the rejection of his plans for a British New Deal did not end party discontent either with Chamberlain's financial policy or with his failure to resolve the problem of mass unemployment in the Special Areas. Indeed, in the very month of his victory over Lloyd George the issue forced its way to the top of the political agenda once again. To Chamberlain's despair, during the Labour censure debate on the subject on 9 July, Baldwin reiterated his earlier admission that the National Government had no considered 'plan' for dealing with unemployment; an astonishing admission which inevitably prompted backbench critics like Harold Macmillan to demand a more 'inspired' response from the government before it was too late. 'It isn't that he tells truths which had better be concealed', Chamberlain complained wearily, 'but that he doesn't know what the truth is & gives a false picture of the situation.'[81] To make matters worse, eight days later, the pessimistic first report of the Special Areas Commissioner for England and Wales infuriated Chamberlain with its strong suggestion that his efficiency had been handicapped by limitations imposed by the Government – a damaging implication coming only a day after the publication of Lloyd George's *Organising Prosperity*. In order to reveal 'the absurdity of the allegation', Chamberlain publicly reasserted the experimental and evolutionary nature of the policy and declared that it was proving 'most valuable in showing the best ways for future advance and also those that should be avoided'.[82]

There was some truth in this retort, but it also concealed a very large measure of political cynicism. Indeed, as Chamberlain had frankly explained when first unveiling his plans in October 1934, by emphasising the experimental nature of the scheme it would be easy to limit the scale, speed and cost of policy advance by declaring that 'it was necessary first to wait and see whether such experiments would succeed in the four selected Areas before they could be extended to other parts of the country'.[83] Two years later, the Treasury was still repeating this convenient mantra to the intense frustration of the increasingly vocal group of progressive Tories and radical expansionists who sat on the government benches. After a threatened rebellion by forty younger Conservatives in July 1936 over the government's reluctance to act on the Commissioner's Third Report, however, Chamberlain finally recognised that he needed to be seen to do something positive – particularly as Percy Stewart's parting shot before retiring from the post was to declare that most of the major measures possible under the existing legislation had already been adopted and that radical new methods were required to attract industry to the Special Areas.[84]

In private, Chamberlain was utterly contemptuous of his critics. Indeed, he doubted whether 'there is a single one of Stewart's piffling recommendations which would really relieve the situation' and he continued to argue that 'when all is said and done there must remain a large number of people for whom we can find no work in S. Wales & who must either move or stagnate there for the rest of their lives'.[85] Confronted by rising backbench discontent, however, he was again forced to tread the path of political expediency. As he explained in an annotated response to Hopkins' devastating critique of the Commissioner's proposals in mid-November 1936:

> I think it is possible to destroy very effectively *any* proposal for attracting new industries into the S[pecial] Areas. But politically speaking this is not a wholly satisfactory method as it leaves things as before. On the other hand the Comr. has made certain proposals & politically it might be helpful to say 'These are frankly unorthodox & uneconomic but we are ready to try them in these areas'. If they failed, as I think they would, we should have done little harm, but we should have met the reproach that we neither accept others [sic] suggestions nor produce any of our own.[86]

Next day, under further pressure from the backbench rebels, Chamberlain promised to introduce an Amending Act embodying those of Stewart's proposals the Treasury considered practicable. Although this averted the threatened revolt, the debate continued throughout the night and on 8 December Chamberlain was forced to accept an amendment limiting the continuation of the 1934 Act until the end of May, by which time it should be replaced by the promised new Bill. Significantly, many of those prominent in the 'cabals' attacking Chamberlain over the Special Areas, like Lord Wolmer, Ronald Cartland, Harold Macmillan and Bob Boothby, were precisely the same men who would later challenge him over appeasement.[87]

Although Chamberlain was unquestionably forced into action against his better judgement and wishes, the outcome was a radical new approach to regional policy. Since the first meeting of his Depressed Areas Committee in October 1934 Chamberlain had consistently emphasised that he did 'not believe that the introduction of new industries into the depressed areas is going to play any very large part ... in solving the problems' because he 'strongly disliked any idea of Government planning of the location of industry' and he thought it 'useless' to attempt to try to induce businesses to move to such areas.[88] By January 1937, however, Chamberlain was apparently encouraged by a greater responsiveness of industry to such efforts at a time when he urgently needed to do something substantial to defuse simmering backbench rebellion. The resulting Special Areas (Amendment) Act of 1937 radically extended the fundamental objectives of Chamberlain's evolving regional policy. The simple improvement of the social infrastructure (to reduce disincentives for investment), had now developed into the far more ambitious goal of using financial incentives to attract private industry into the depressed areas in the hope of diversifying their industrial structure.[89] In terms of finance, the measure was scarcely a revolutionary departure, but in fairness to Chamberlain he was partly constrained by the flood of complaints from trade organisations 'very nervous lest their interests may be adversely effected by competing units in the Special Areas which enjoy financial assistance from the Government'. Nevertheless, the 1937 Act extended the powers of the Commissioner to enable him to let factories, encourage trading estates and assist with income tax and rates in Special Areas for up to five years, while in 'certified' areas of high unemployment the Treasury could make loans to assist new enterprises.[90] Equally important in the longer-term, on 7 July Chamberlain sought to appease backbench discontent further by announcing the creation of a Royal Commission to consider Stewart's concerns about the geographical imbalances in industrial location. Under the chairmanship of Chamberlain's old Cabinet colleague and fishing friend, Sir Anderson Montague Barlow, the resulting report had a profound influence in shaping all post-war thinking on the subject.

Although Chamberlain defended the policy as the culmination of several other steps and 'when they are put together they make rather an impressive total', by his own admission the new Bill looked 'pretty thin'.[91] Yet the general principles and methods it established remained central to British regional policy until the late 1970s. As such, Chamberlain's Special Areas Acts can be regarded as the direct lineal descendants of post-war regional policy, whether in the form of the Town & Country Planning Act of 1947, the Regional Employment Premium of 1968 or the Industry Acts of 1972 and 1975. Similarly, the idea of appointing a figure responsible for special areas of unemployment set an important precedent for later policy-makers, such as Macmillan's Minister for the North East (Lord Hailsham) and Thatcher's Minister for Merseyside (Michael Heseltine).

If there is a more general case to be made for Neville Chamberlain's record as Chancellor during the 1930s, it is not that he enjoyed a remarkable degree of success when measured in terms of policy outcomes. On the contrary, it is undeniable that many of his policy innovations made little measurable impact upon employment, were often extremely small-scale, tentative and constructed with at least one eye on political and electoral pressures. They were also conceived over far too long an evolutionary time-frame. Yet notwithstanding the many criticisms which can be levelled against his record, given cheap money, tariffs, the encouragement of rationalisation and price-fixing and an evolving regional policy, it is simply not acceptable to continue repeating the claim that the National Government had no unemployment policy at all and that Chamberlain's policy of 'unsympathetic rigidity' made him the worst of the lot in 'waiting out the slump' with a 'policy of passivity'.[92] 'After all', as Derek Aldcroft concludes, 'most of the policy measures adopted in his period pointed in the right direction, albeit not always very strongly, and it may be argued that in each case a policy-on situation was better for employment than the alternative of no policy change at all.'[93] Moreover, at a more fundamental level, when the term is divested of its value-laden post-war Keynesian overtones, Chamberlain arguably deserves to be considered among the founders of a species of 'managed economy' in Britain, in the sense that he prompted state intervention with the explicit intention of guiding the economy away from an outcome where market forces would take it and towards the government's chosen goals.[94]

V

As the economy began to emerge from depression, Chamberlain's rising confidence and restless energy increasingly drove him to extend the scope of his policy authority beyond his own department. 'In my office the amount of work you have to do largely depends on what you make for yourself', he told his sisters in May 1934. 'Unhappily it is part of my nature that I cannot contemplate any problem without trying to find a solution to it.'[95] At times, Cabinet colleagues were still more than capable of mounting stiff resistance to such pretensions, both over crucial collective issues like the payment of the American debt and where the primary interests of their own departments were directly threatened – as demonstrated by Simon's rejection of Chamberlain's suggestions about disarmament and Hore-Belisha's determined resistance as Transport Minister to the Chancellor's efforts to raid the Road Fund in 1935.

An even more important challenge to Chamberlain's imperial aspirations emerged over his radical plans for the restructuring of unemployment assistance. 'It rather takes people's breath away at first', he told his sisters in October 1932. 'It is nothing less than taking the whole relief of the able bodied [unemployed] away from local authorities and ministers & putting it outside party politics by entrusting it to a Statutory Commission.'[96] Above all, however, 'the intention was to bring the treatment of the able-bodied unemployed into line with modern conditions' at a time when 'many … were unemployed through no fault of their own, because there was not enough work to go round'. Besides establishing firm central control over a national uniform standard of relief, Chamberlain also saw this measure as an opportunity for the new Unemployment Assistance Board to provide education, training and voluntary recreation for those he believed would always be surplus to labour market requirements, even after the return of full prosperity.[97]

In the event, Chamberlain was soon 'disconcerted' when Sir Henry Betterton, the Minister of Labour, came out with a strong case against the measure in January 1933.[98] He was still more frustrated when Sir Edward Hilton Young, the Minister of Health, joined in warning that his plan was 'wrongly conceived' and that its adoption would be 'a political blunder'. At the heart of such concerns was the proposed creation of an artificial, unfair and dangerous distinction between those still covered by unemployment insurance and those to be relieved by Chamberlain's new Unemployment Assistance Board, who would be exposed to the indignity of the needs test and other 'Poor Law methods' previously reserved only for vagrants.[99] Unaccustomed to such a direct challenge over an area of established expertise, Chamberlain clearly found the experience an uncongenial affront to his status and authority. Worse still, despite a 'very determined and persistent' struggle, he was eventually obliged to compromise on the structure of the final plan and although he considered the Unemployment Bill was 'a statesmanlike attempt to deal fairly with a very difficult question', it was substantially less than his original proposal to transfer all relief to the new machinery.[100]

The battle over the Unemployment Bill was unquestionably a rebuff to Chamberlain's authority on domestic policy – but it was also an exceptional case. While this policy dominance should not be exaggerated, the fact remains that as Chancellor he ranged widely over the government's activities, involving himself in everything from the formulation of Hilton Young's housing legislation in 1933–34, to the retention of subsidy support for sugar beet in defiance of an expert committee condemning its wasteful and unhealthy effects upon British agriculture. As he boasted in 1932, 'It amuses me to find a new policy for each of my colleagues in turn and though I can't imagine that all my ideas are the best that can be found, most of them seem to be adopted *faute de mieux*!' Indeed, so convinced was he that he was the driving force behind the government, that in June 1934 he declared that it was 'impossible … to get any decision taken unless I see that it is done myself and sometimes I wonder what would happen to this Government if I were to be smashed up in a taxi collision'. By this stage, Chamberlain was already accustomed to speaking privately in a tone which suggested that he exercised quasi-Prime-ministerial powers. 'I am more & more carrying this Govt on my back', he noted in his diary in March 1935. 'The P.M. is ill & tired, S.B. is tired & won't apply his mind to problems.'[101]

Despite occasional localised conflicts with Cabinet colleagues over specific policy issues, therefore, Herbert Samuel was not so far wide of the mark in July 1935 when he reported that the National Government 'was run by Neville Chamberlain. What he says goes. When he puts his foot down and says that something must be done, that decision settles it … It should not be forgotten that Neville Chamberlain was a great power in the Tory Party.' It was a reflection of the underlying truth of this proposition that two months earlier Baldwin had advised the Transport Minister 'not to quarrel with Neville' because he was 'the strong man' of government.[102] In these circumstances, it was inevitable that Chamberlain would soon seek to extend his influence beyond the domestic sphere into the new and very different realms of foreign and defence policy.

Chapter 11

Foreign and Defence Policy, 1934–1937

'Our greatest interest was peace in the sense of general pacification. If tomorrow complete security reigned throughout Europe, that would be the greatest possible boon to us, with our wide trading and financial ramifications ... Either we must play our part in pacification or we must resign ourselves to the staggering prospect of spending £85 million on rearmament in 5 years ... It might be that we could limit our liabilities. Let us explore for if we refused we must give up all hope of a peace based on security.'

Neville Chamberlain Diary, 25 March 1934

During the spring of 1936 Anthony Eden recorded Austen Chamberlain declaring over dinner, 'Neville, you must remember that you don't know anything about foreign affairs.' It was a classical example of the sort of instinctive condescension that had always characterised their relationship and it confirmed Chamberlain's private complaint that his half-brother 'always finds it difficult to realise that I am no longer his little brother'.[1] The words rankled all the more, because by this stage in Neville Chamberlain's career they were far from true. With MacDonald a rapidly fading force, Baldwin completely uninterested in foreign affairs and Simon universally dismissed as an ineffectual failure as Foreign Secretary, since the end of 1933 Chamberlain had taken an increasing interest in the form and direction of British foreign policy. Moreover, while such interventions were generally far less successful than in the domestic sphere, he was still seriously canvassed as Simon's successor in December 1933 and again a year later, but on each occasion Chamberlain rebuffed the suggestion with the protest that he could not afford the additional cost of the office, would 'hate the journeys to Geneva and above all ... should loathe & detest the social ceremonies'. More important, early in 1936 Baldwin suggested that Chamberlain should leave the Treasury to direct the rapidly expanding rearmament programme. Although he again shrugged off the offer as 'very distasteful', the fact remains that Chamberlain was the greatest single force in shaping British defence policy between 1934 and 1939.[2]

Chamberlain's increasing involvement in these policy spheres was scarcely surprising. By the early 1930s, Britain's defences were in a chronic state of disrepair. Soon after Japan invaded Manchuria in September 1931, the Chiefs of Staff had warned that Britain was 'defenceless' in the Far East, incapable of defending its trade routes and without sufficient military resources to meet its treaty obligations. By the time they produced their Annual Review for 1933, Hitler was in power and Germany had withdrawn from the League of Nations; ominous developments which prompted the Service Chiefs to note gloomily that Britain confronted the terrifying prospect of war on two widely separated fronts with a military capacity which would enable it 'to do little more than hold the frontiers and outposts of the Empire'. In direct response to these concerns, in November 1933 the Cabinet established a Defence Requirements Committee (DRC) composed of leading officials and the Service Chiefs in order to consider the most effective means of repairing these glaring deficiencies in Britain's national defences.[3]

Chamberlain was determined to stamp his own priorities upon this exercise from the outset. Central to all his thinking on defence and rearmament in 1934 (and throughout the rest of the decade) was an acute awareness of the yawning gulf which existed between Britain's vast imperial commitments and its limited military capabilities. By the mid-1930s, a small island nation of 47 million was seeking to defend an empire encompassing a quarter of the world's territory and population, with the dismally depleted military resources of a third-rate Power. Worse still, anxiety about the aggressive threat to that Empire posed by Japan in the Far East, Germany in Europe and (from 1935) Italy in the Mediterranean was compounded by the widely shared fear that war with any one of these individual challengers in widely separated theatres might encourage the others to opportunistic acts of 'mad dog' aggression on their own behalf.

Confronted by this fundamental problem, Chamberlain was relatively swiftly converted to the need for rearmament. Admittedly, at the lowest point of the economic slump in March 1932, he had argued forcefully that the Cabinet needed to consider 'one set of risks balanced against the other, and … that at the present time financial risks are greater than any other that we can estimate'. By October 1933, however, he had come round to the view that 'common prudence would seem to indicate some strengthening of our defences' at a time when the Treasury no longer anticipated a budget deficit.[4] Yet notwithstanding this acceptance, Chamberlain was always a pragmatic and reluctant rearmer. For him, the trick was to strike an appropriate balance, to achieve the maximum of effective deterrence for the minimum outlay of non-productive (and possibly unnecessary) expenditure. Ultimately, in Chamberlain's mind, this always demanded compromise and calculated risk in trading off the strategic 'ideal' with the economically and electorally practicable.

From this assessment of Britain's strategic dilemma, Chamberlain arrived at two key conclusions which shaped much of his later policy. The first was that it was essential to establish clear priorities for rearmament, in order to focus resources and expenditure upon the most cost-effective form of security – and in the mid-1930s this was equated with the development of deterrent air power capable of delivering a devastating retaliatory blow against any enemy. As Baldwin had so memorably encapsulated the conventional wisdom in November 1932, 'the bomber will always get through'. As a result, 'the only defence is offence, which means that you have to kill more women and children more rapidly than the enemy if you want to save yourselves'. It was a theory of deterrence future Cold War strategists would label 'mutually assured destruction', but it reflected such a pervasive and apocalyptic vision of the danger that Harold Macmillan was not exaggerating when he later recalled that 'we thought of air warfare in 1938 rather as people think of nuclear warfare today'.[5]

In parallel with these enduring views about rearmament, Chamberlain's second guiding principle was that the intractable nature of Britain's strategic dilemma would always place an extremely heavy burden upon active diplomacy. Even if a massive rearmament effort was desirable and affordable (and he doubted both propositions), it would be impossible to repair Britain's defences immediately to such a level that it could simultaneously fend off all three potential challengers to a far-flung empire. Security at a cost the country could afford, therefore, depended upon focusing on Germany as the principal threat, while reducing the number of Britain's enemies through patient diplomacy to conciliate and appease secondary challengers like Japan and Italy. Equally important, diplomacy was essential to pursue a 'general settlement' of Germany's legitimate grievances left over from the Treaty of Versailles because the removal of this threat to peace would simultaneously reduce the danger from Japan and Italy, who were unlikely to attack the empire unilaterally. And even if Germany could not be appeased, Chamberlain took comfort from the belief that the process would buy sufficient time to repair Britain's defences to meet the threat of war at the predicted moment of maximum danger between 1939 and 1942.

The DRC's first report in February 1934 only partially conformed with Chamberlain's hopes and expectations. He certainly endorsed the identification of Germany as 'the ultimate potential enemy against whom our "long range" defence policy must be directed'. He was much less satisfied, however, with the DRC's proposed spending priorities. In particular, he was alarmed to find that the bulk of the £76.8 million it considered to be the minimum necessary to repair Britain's worst defence deficiencies was assigned to the creation of an expeditionary force to defend the Low Countries and France while the RAF timidly sought only to complete the 52 squadrons approved in their original programme of 1923 – despite the recognition that this made no allowance for defence of the Midlands and North. Convinced this was fundamentally misguided, from the outset Chamberlain was determined to dominate the procedure and conclusions of the Cabinet's Disarmament Committee when it considered the DRC report.

After working until the early hours of the morning in preparation, Chamberlain's opening statement at the Committee's first meeting on 3 May established the key themes as they would eventually develop.[6] Since Britain could not fight a war on two fronts, he proposed 'we should get on friendly terms with Japan so as to be free to use all our resources to meet Germany'; while five years was 'the shortest possible time [in which] deficiencies could be made good', there should be no absolute commitment to completion within that period; above all, 'if it was found we could not afford to do it altogether, then an order of priority must be decided'. Chamberlain was equally emphatic about the nature of these priorities. Indeed, despite his claim that 'he was not trying to set himself up as a military authority in any way', he went on to do just this by suggesting that experience in the last war 'indicated we ought to put our major resources into our Navy and our Air Force'. Conversely, he confessed to being 'a little startled' by the DRC's proposals for an expeditionary force, given both 'impregnable' French defences and his doubts as to whether such a force could be deployed in time to defend the Low Countries.[7] It was a *tour de force* in amateur armchair strategy, but it effectively established the defence agenda for the next five years.

With characteristic and calculated thoroughness, Chamberlain's preparatory deliberations also crucially enabled him to control the committee's procedure. Again, at their first meeting on 3 May, he declared that because the DRC report was 'long, technical and complicated' ministers should consider its proposals initially only on their merits, leaving aside all financial and political aspects. After the completion of this phase, Chamberlain would then revise the DRC's report in the light of both these discussions and the broader financial and electoral considerations.[8] The admittedly 'personal conclusions' contained in Chamberlain's revised paper on 20 June fundamentally redefined the defence priorities enunciated by the DRC – particularly with regard to the allocation of resources. As Chamberlain's paper stridently declared: 'Our best defence would be the existence of a deterrent force so powerful as to render success in attack too doubtful to be worth while. I submit that this is most likely to be attained by the establishment of an Air Force *based in this country* of a size and efficiency calculated to inspire respect in the mind of a possible enemy.'[9]

In stark contrast, despite the perceived primacy of the German threat, Chamberlain swept aside thoughts of an expensive continental commitment. Although he anticipated that Britain would be allied to France in the event of war, he also suggested that this support would be confined to the 'indirect assistance' of air power rather than an expeditionary force – despite the fact that this was scarcely likely to stiffen French resistance or prevent the Germans occupying airfields in the Low Countries from which to bomb London in the event that deterrence failed. But crucially, in Chamberlain's mind, the need to balance risks against resources demanded a compromise between the ideal and the practicable and in this context he regarded the Army as an insurance if deterrence failed rather than the primary deterrent in itself.[10] Given the strength and consistency of Chamberlain's view on this subject until compelled to abandon it in January 1939, it is difficult to accept George Peden's judgement that in expressing this low priority 'he was acting as the "devil's advocate" rather than voicing his own fixed opinions'.[11] As the Royal Navy's programme was also both extremely expensive and directed primarily against Japan, Chamberlain talked in equally dismissive fashion of the need to 'face the facts courageously and realise the impossibility of simultaneous preparation against war with Germany and war with Japan'.[12]

In drafting his revised report, Chamberlain had deliberately 'pitched the note … a little high' and he was not surprised when it provoked a howl of protest not only from the Service Chiefs and the defence departments, but also from the ministerial Disarmament Committee.[13] Even those like MacDonald and Baldwin, who shared his general views about the primacy of finance and the RAF, protested that his paper 'really meant that we should surrender our power on the Sea' while allowing Japan to 'mop up the whole of our possessions in the East'. According to the committee's minutes, the hostile barrage continued for nineteen foolscap pages before Chamberlain intervened to remind his colleagues that it was 'necessary to cut our coat according to the cloth' – and as he effectively dismissed all talk of a defence loan as 'the broad road which led to destruction' he possessed all the leverage. He also stressed that public opinion 'could not be ignored'. Voters might be 'ignorant' about defence, he warned, but they 'were not to be regarded as stupid' and to attempt to persuade them that the Far East was as important as home defence would be 'an extremely difficult task' which risked an electoral backlash capable of jeopardising the entire programme. Anyway, Chamberlain argued, 'his proposals were not really so revolutionary' – particularly as the increased RAF allocation was extremely modest, while the Army's had not been cut but merely delayed beyond the DRC's five year time-frame.[14] Despite the protests, therefore, by the end of July he had carried the bulk of his proposals on a total 'deficiencies' allocation now reduced from £76.8 million to £50.3 million.[15] In such circumstances, it was scarcely surprising that he declared himself 'on the whole well satisfied with our discussion' as he had 'really won all along the line'.[16]

Chamberlain's victory over fierce resistance from a powerful imperial defence lobby concerned with the immediate threat in the Far East represented a pivotal moment in the formulation of British foreign and defence policy. At the time, General Pownall, the Military Assistant Secretary to the Committee of Imperial Defence, considered his ideas on strategy 'would disgrace a board school' and many historians have echoed the criticism that Chamberlain was an arrogant meddler, wholly devoid of clear strategical understanding and excessively concerned about public opinion, political expediency and even the cynical promotion of his own career.[17] In retrospect, it can be rightly objected that the theory of deterrence which underpinned Chamberlain's focus upon offensive air rearmament was ill-conceived, but as one Air Marshal later conceded, at the time belief in the bomber was 'intuitive' and a 'matter of faith'.[18] Chamberlain would be proved even less correct in his assumption that British security was separable from that of France and it is arguable that this error of judgement only encouraged French defeatism for the rest of the decade.

Yet in Chamberlain's defence, others have argued that he displayed decisive leadership and clear-minded foresight at a time when there was little else to be had and that the resulting policy was a 'realistic response' to international threats and ineluctable financial and electoral constraints. After over a decade of financial stringency and economic stagnation, defence deficiencies would always have represented a formidable problem and, as Peter Bell argues, it would have been 'almost miraculous' if a perfect solution had been found. In these circumstances, it is difficult to accept the alternative view that defending the Empire would have served British interests better than protection of the mother country – and the need for a choice was absolutely unavoidable. Moreover, despite the Chancellor's iron grip on the purse strings, within two years the DRC's planned total quinquennial defence expenditure of £620 million had risen to £1000 million. Two years later it stood at £1650 million.[19]

II

The debate over the DRC's first report reflected not just Chamberlain's faith in the critical role of deterrent air power, but also his views about the urgent need to employ diplomacy to avert those secondary threats which could not be contained by military means. One manifestation of this concern was Chamberlain's ill-fated 'limited liability' scheme for Western Europe. During the 'many very tiresome discussions' in Cabinet about responses to Germany's withdrawal from the Disarmament Conference in the last quarter of 1933, Chamberlain had played 'a very active part' in arguing that the real problem was principally one of security rather than disarmament. The former, he argued, would always govern the degree to which it was possible to achieve the latter. As a first step towards breaking the impasse, he thus proposed that Britain should explore the potentialities of Hitler's proposed ten year non-aggression pacts with his neighbours.[20] With this in mind, Chamberlain immediately outlined for Simon a 'limited liability plan' consisting of mutual guarantees from Britain, France, Poland and Czechoslovakia, under which all would contribute to a joint international police force to be deployed in defence of any signatory if subjected to unprovoked aggression. In this way, collective security could be achieved without the danger of Britain being dragged reluctantly into a European war. In the corner of the document which Simon carried away with him, Chamberlain inscribed proudly, 'This is not a paper to be read by the orthodox.'

The plan certainly provoked vigorous opposition from both ministers and the Service Chiefs. Indeed, at Cabinet on 22 March, Cunliffe-Lister became 'very prolix' and vehement in arguing that Britain should avoid all further entanglements in European affairs. In reply, Chamberlain repeated that Britain's 'greatest interest was peace in the sense of general pacification' and that it must either play its part in this quest or resign itself to 'the staggering prospect' of spending £85 million on rearmament over five years while abandoning all hope of peace based on security. In Chamberlain's view it was 'the best thing I have ever done in Cabinet' as its 'overwhelming effect' silenced even Walter Elliot, Ormsby-Gore and other members of the 'Boy's Brigade'.[21] At the ministerial Disarmament Committee next day, however, only Thomas gave the plan full support, despite Chamberlain's private efforts to convince Hailsham, the War

Minister, of its merits earlier in the day. The plan was then referred to the Chiefs of Staff but, as he reported wistfully to his sisters, 'by the time they had done with it you could hardly find a piece of it as big as a halfpenny'.[22] After further unsuccessful efforts to dispel what he believed to be the misunderstandings of the Services and his ministerial colleagues, Chamberlain resigned himself to defeat, consoled only by the conviction 'that sooner or later we shall have to come back to my idea' because it offered 'the only chance of progress towards security ... For the old aphorism "Force is no remedy" I could substitute "The Fear of Force is the only remedy"'.[23]

While Chamberlain hoped to contain the German threat with a combination of air deterrence and mutual guarantees, during 1934 he also laboured hard to achieve a diplomatic rapprochement with Japan to remove the fear of war on at least one front. By this juncture, the scale of the Japanese challenge was already substantial and menacing. As the Chiefs of Staff had warned in 1933, 'the whole of our territory in the Far East as well as the coast-line of India and the Dominions and our vast trade and shipping is open to attack', while the weakness of British defences in the region represented a constant temptation to aggressive elements within Japan. In response to this assessment, Chamberlain declared repeatedly after October 1933 that he 'greatly regretted the weakening of Anglo-Japanese relations' since the end of their formal alliance in 1922, because if Britain 'could be free from all apprehension as to a conflict with Japan the situation would be greatly eased'.[24] Conversely, after his embittering recent experience over war debts and the failure of the World Economic Conference, this enthusiasm for Japan was reinforced by an almost visceral contempt for pious declarations of American goodwill when unsupported by any practical action. 'We ought to know by this time that U.S.A. will give us no undertaking to resist by force any action by Japan short of an attack on Hawaii or Honolulu', Chamberlain angrily declared in July 1934. 'She will give us plenty of assurances of goodwill especially if we will promise to do all the fighting but the moment she is asked to contribute something she invariably takes refuge behind Congress.'[25]

This preference for some sort of accommodation with Japan – if necessary at the expense of relations with the United States – became a central theme of Chamberlain's thinking throughout 1934. During the Cabinet debate on the DRC report in mid-March, he portrayed the Japanese as 'a sensitive people' to whom the termination of the alliance with Britain had been 'a great blow to their *amour propre*', but – in tones foreshadowing his approach to the Sudetenland in 1938 – he 'did not believe that there were any difficulties which frank discussion might not resolve'. In contrast, while he acknowledged the risk of antagonising America, he was profoundly sceptical of the practical value of their friendship and anxious about its effect upon Tokyo. He certainly had no intention of cooperation to 'pull the chestnuts out of the fire for them' at the forthcoming naval disarmament conference if this meant alienating the Japanese;[26] a priority he vigorously reiterated at the Cabinet Committee on Naval Disarmament in April. Moreover, while conceding that Japanese military and economic penetration in China was a problem, both in this committee and that on Japanese trade competition Chamberlain argued there was 'room for both Japan and ourselves' and he even talked of dividing China into spheres of economic influence – to the intense alarm of the Foreign Office which warned of American opposition to any encroachment on their position in China.[27] Little wonder that by early May, the US Ambassador in London warned Washington that Chamberlain led an 'important section of British opinion' opposed to cooperation with America at the forthcoming naval conference.[28]

During the summer recess Chamberlain resumed his pressure in the belief that they had 'a wonderful opportunity to do a great stroke and I am very anxious not to miss it'. Although he recognised that only Thomas supported him wholeheartedly, as so often in his career, he expected that in the absence of any other definite proposal he would gradually gather support within the Cabinet.[29] During two days of unsettled weather while fishing at Dalchosnie, he drafted a Cabinet paper repeating the now familiar advantages of an Anglo-Japanese agreement and urging his colleagues not to be 'frightened out of it by any fears of American objection, unless that objection be founded on really solid and reasonable grounds'.[30] The draft was then sent to Simon with a 'cunning letter' warning that if they failed to explore the possibility, 'what might not be said of us by future historians if we drifted into unfriendly relations with Japan, lost our Far Eastern trade to them, had to look on helplessly while she marched from one aggression to another'.[31]

Despite Foreign Office scepticism, Chamberlain was encouraged in this crusade by increasing indications that the Japanese were thinking on parallel lines. As a result, he was overjoyed when Simon's meeting with the Japanese Ambassador in late September went 'far beyond my anticipations' – not least given Japanese assurances that there was no obstacle to the necessary undertakings about China and the definite intimation that instructions were already on the way from Tokyo regarding a pact.[32] By the end of October, therefore, Chamberlain confessed that he was 'really beginning to entertain hopes at last of a successful issue on this vastly important bit of foreign policy'.[33] In order to consolidate this advance, he instructed Warren Fisher to be 'very indiscreet' in expressing the Chancellor's views to the Japanese Ambassador at their meeting on 24 October, and the response was equally encouraging, although Chamberlain conceded privately he could not yet see how to overcome 'the American obstacle'.[34]

In the event, when the preparatory naval conversations resumed on 23 October 1934, Chamberlain's optimism was swiftly dispelled. The British decision to conduct separate negotiations with America and Japan appeared to be a ploy simply to play off one rival against the other, while the irreconcilable goals of Japan and America at the conference precluded all prospect of agreement. Moreover, as Chamberlain was not a member of the British delegation he lamented from the sidelines that he could 'only pull the strings & hope the puppets will make the gestures I want' – a forlorn hope given his contemptuous view of Simon as 'the weak point of the Government'.[35] By this stage, however, Washington had received supposedly authoritative reports to the effect that the

Cabinet's pro-Japanese group was weakening because Chamberlain 'was now convinced that Japan could not be trusted, that she was perhaps bluffing and that England and the United States must at the proper time take a common stand and call the bluff'.[36] Although this was an exaggeration, the Japanese announcement in December that they would not renew the Washington or London naval treaties when they expired at the end of 1936 torpedoed another of Chamberlain's grand schemes designed to maintain Britain's Great Power status on the cheap. Even as late as the Imperial Conference in June 1937, however, he continued to talk wistfully of a rapprochement with Japan to 'leave us free to prepare for dangers nearer home'.[37]

III

On 7 June 1935, MacDonald belatedly withdrew as Prime Minister and exchanged offices with Baldwin. It was a development which Chamberlain (in common with most Cabinet colleagues) had sought for some time on the grounds that MacDonald was 'getting more & more woolly and more & more out of touch with the House & the Country' while within the Cabinet he tended to 'brake the machine from sheer inability to face up to any decision'.[38] Contrary to some versions, however, Chamberlain entertained no immediate expectation of the Premiership. After all, everyone expected that under the increasingly lethargic Baldwin he would be 'virtually PM' and he appeared to all the world 'like a man who sees things coming and knows that he need do nothing to help or hasten them'.[39] He certainly had little to fear from any rivals for the succession. Although aware that Baldwin was still 'hankering after the idea' of Lloyd George's return to Cabinet in early May, he also knew that his own repeated veto meant there would be no place for him in the Cabinet reconstruction. Similarly, despite Simon's hope that Baldwin might make him Deputy Leader in the Commons to 'soften his fall' from the Foreign Office, Chamberlain was equally sanguine in assuring his sisters that 'I need never be jealous of him because I know now that he lacks certain qualities essential to a leader.'[40]

Beyond all of these reasons for patience, Chamberlain also entertained considerable doubts about Baldwin's own sticking power once he became Prime Minister. While he served as Lord President without any departmental responsibility, Baldwin had found a perfect niche. As Chamberlain noted in December 1934, 'his present position which calls upon him to supply advice and not action exactly suits his temperament and so long as he is permitted to be the 1st lieutenant and not the commander I don't see why he should not go on increasing his hold over the party'. Despite Baldwin's professed desire to continue until his seventieth birthday in August 1937, however, Chamberlain speculated as to whether he would 'be able to stick it when he is exposed once again to the shafts which will be levelled at him as leader? Many doubt it.'[41] Indeed, in February 1935 Baldwin confidentially expressed his own doubts as to how long he would continue to both Chamberlain and MacDonald – although it appears that while he told the former that 'he was the only man' to replace him, MacDonald recorded Baldwin saying that 'he could see no one to succeed'.[42] Nevertheless, with all of this in his favour and still feeling at the peak of his mental powers, Chamberlain had no need for clumsy manoeuvres to hasten his succession in 1935. Anyway, for some time he had been aware that the 'apparently ... influential & growing opinion' within the party which wanted Baldwin to replace MacDonald also expected 'to get rid of him as soon as possible' after the forthcoming general election.[43]

With the transition to a Baldwin Premiership completed, the road was open for a general election. Chamberlain never doubted that they should fight it as a National Government, although he now recognised that it would be 'useless' to propose the formation of a National Party as there were 'too many vested interests in the present party names and no Conservative would give up their name for the pleasure of being in the same boat as MacDonald & Simon'.[44] Yet while convinced that the severe mid-term electoral crisis of confidence was behind them, Chamberlain was determined to ensure that they should enter the election well prepared and vigorous in order to banish the damaging impression of drift which had hung over the government for so long.[45] As early as February 1934, he had thus pressed Baldwin on the need 'to set to work at once to think out (a) what we are going to do during the rest of our administration (b) what we are going to the country on.' When he failed to respond to repeated pleas, Chamberlain seized the initiative by outlining a provisional programme which he presented to surprised and enthusiastic ministers at the newly assembled Cabinet Conservative Committee on 2 March. As he noted with characteristic satisfaction, it made 'a profound impression' and 'in the end they all came through the hole I made for them' and dispersed feeling 'quite stirred up'.[46]

In most respects, Chamberlain's programme outlined predictable themes. Beside sections on empire, parliamentary reform, coordination of defence and foreign policy, Chamberlain clearly envisaged a further extension of his earlier restrictionist and corporatist ideas to revive British and imperial trade and competitiveness.[47] In particular, closer relations between industry and the State were intended to enhance efficiency through rationalisation by tailoring productive capacity much more closely to potential market demand; aspirations which achieved legislative expression in the Cotton Spinning Act of 1936 which established a Spindles Board to purchase and scrap excess capacity funded by a levy on the industry as a whole and developed further in the price-fixing and production quotas introduced under the Cotton Industry (Reorganisation) Act of 1939.

Undoubtedly the most novel aspect of the entire programme related to 'Social Services'. Alongside a voluntary pension scheme for shopkeepers and black-coated workers which came to fruition in March 1937, Chamberlain's key theme dwelt on 'the improvement of national physique' through the State promotion of physical drill, suitable diets, voluntary camps in national parks and periodic inspections of the population to measure the effects. Besides its obvious social benefit, Chamberlain was convinced that this concept had considerable political appeal and genuine novelty by transcending the traditional party auction over the question of 'how far to go & how much money to spend'. It also had the advantage of unifying into a single flagship scheme a variety of hitherto disconnected subjects such as maternal mortality, nursery schools and health insurance for children. 'Taken together these would be merely a series of electoral bribes of rather petty character', he assured his sisters. 'But as parts of a scheme for raising the level of national health they present an idea which is both right in itself and attractive to the public.'[48] After relaunching his 'big idea' at the party conference in October 1936, a Cabinet Committee under Chamberlain's leadership eventually produced a White Paper in January 1937 and the Physical Training and Recreation Act soon implemented his plans.[49] It was the culmination of both his own long-established interest in open spaces and playing fields and a fitting tribute to his cousin, whose unfinished work Chamberlain had taken up after Norman's tragic death on the Western Front in 1917.

Despite his frustration at the need to supply most of the constructive ideas and planning for the election because of Baldwin's reluctance to face 'earthly decisions', Chamberlain undoubtedly shared Baldwin's view that 'you and I are complementary: each puts into the pool his own contribution and we make a jolly effective unit!'[50] As Chamberlain revealingly conceded shortly before the election:

> I am bound to recognise that if I supply the policy and the drive S.B does also supply something that is even more valuable in retaining the floating vote. I suppose we may never get back to the old days when every little boy and girl was either a little liberal or a little conservative. And if that is so it will be the non-party men & women who will decide the nature of the Governments and the S.B.'s, if there are any, will capture them.

This was a shrewd assessment of the strength of Baldwin's appeal and an equally telling acknowledgement of his own weakness when he became Prime Minister, but it did not prevent intense irritation at the indolence and ingratitude of a leader who 'showed no interest in anything that concerned anybody except himself'. As Chamberlain angrily complained in November, Baldwin 'supplied to this election neither policy, nor drive, nor fight, and he doesn't see why he should or why he shouldn't accept the result as a purely personal triumph'.[51] Whatever their respective contributions, however, the result of the November 1935 election was always a foregone conclusion. At a national level the government suffered a net loss of only 90 seats and returned with a parliamentary majority of 255. Despite Chamberlain's fear that they might lose one or two seats in Birmingham, the Conservatives held all twelve seats for the second successive election.

IV

From Chamberlain's perspective one of the most beneficial consequences of Baldwin's Cabinet reshuffle in June 1935 was the replacement of Simon at the Foreign Office by Sir Samuel Hoare. Hoare was one of Chamberlain's closest political friends and allies with whom he shared a high level of mutual confidence and respect. Having played a decisive role in securing this promotion for Hoare, Chamberlain clearly regarded the appointment, at least in part, as a means of extending his own personal influence over foreign policy and he thought it 'a very good thing that he and I almost always seem to have the same sort of outlook on our problems'. After the constant equivocation and opposition encountered under Simon, he particularly rejoiced that it was 'satisfactory to find one's ideas anticipated instead of always having to convince the Foreign Secretary first and then hope that he might be able to convince others'.[52] This perceived empathy was even more important given the rapid deterioration of the international situation. With Japan increasing its stranglehold over China and Hitler's announcement of an air force, the reintroduction of conscription and an extended naval programme in March 1935, it was little wonder that the DRC concluded 'we are living in a world more dangerous than it has ever been before' and that Britain could 'count on no-one but ourselves unless we are strong'.[53]

Always convinced that British military weakness made it imperative to avoid any action likely to antagonise Italy, Chamberlain increasingly came to regard Anglo-Italian cooperation as the most effective counterweight to the rapidly emerging German threat.[54] In May 1935, therefore, he was scarcely exaggerating when he declared that 'nothing could be worse' than reports from Rome that Mussolini 'was going to finish with Abyssinia once & for all' and that 'if the League attempted to stop him he would walk out & never return, and if that destroyed our friendship so much the worse for those who preferred the League to Italy'. Afraid that such an invasion would alienate public opinion at home and render Italy useless as an ally against Germany, the following month Chamberlain favoured a 'secret and most ingenious' plan for territorial exchange in the region.[55] When Mussolini rejected the scheme, Chamberlain then persuaded fellow members of the ministerial group dealing with the problem that the 'ideal way out' was a combination of carrot and stick: Mussolini needed to be convinced that aggression would provoke Anglo-French retaliation, but at the same time they should assure him of their 'desire to save his face and get him some compensation from the Abyssinians'.[56]

When recalled from his holiday in Switzerland to a ministerial conference to consider the possible imposition of League trade sanctions on Italy on 21 August, Chamberlain's main concern was that even if America and Japan agreed to support them, if Germany continued to trade with Italy 'we should have to be very careful if we were not to land ourselves in war with both Germany and Italy'. Convinced that 'the main pivot of our policy' should be concerted action with France, next day the full Cabinet endorsed the Hoare-Chamberlain view that Britain should 'keep in step' with French policy because sanctions should be a collective measure.[57] In reality, however, Chamberlain's enthusiasm for this strategy did not reflect a new faith in the League or collective security. On the contrary, if the threat of sanctions coerced Mussolini into second thoughts over Abyssinia so much the better, but as Chamberlain made clear to Lord Lloyd next day, his real reason for tying British policy so closely to that of France stemmed from his conviction that the French would almost certainly reject sanctions. French refusal to act would then deflect criticism from 'the Left and Middle wing of public opinion in this country' who might otherwise argue that the government was trying to evade its responsibility to the League. Lloyd was appalled by the 'manifest dishonesty of the whole policy', but from Chamberlain's perspective it was a prudent *Realpolitik* response to a variety of worrying diplomatic, military and electoral dangers.[58] Above all, he was particularly mindful of the outcome of the Peace Ballot, published by the League of Nations Union in late June, which suggested that the public would not take kindly to any effort to flout the League or Britain's obligations under its Covenant.

On this basis, Hoare impressed upon the French Foreign Minister at Geneva on 10 September the importance of cooperation in supporting the League over Abyssinia in order to preserve it as a weapon of collective security against a future German threat; a posture of support for 'collective resistance to all acts of unprovoked aggression' proclaimed publicly in Hoare's speech to the League Assembly next day. As there was no longer any danger of Britain being isolated, Chamberlain now concluded that 'the more strength that we show in the Mediterranean the better' because with 'the whole world against him ... [Mussolini] will be much more ready than he was to call a halt or open discussions if he can achieve something which he can describe as a great victory'.[59] Even when Mussolini attacked Abyssinia on 3 October, Chamberlain continued to 'live in hopes that [Mussolini] may be frightened presently into negotiations' by the prospect of 'sanctions at an early date'. As he noted in early December: 'By putting his great army on the other side [of] the Suez Canal Mussolini has tied a noose round his own neck and left the end hanging out for anyone with a navy to pull.' Yet in his heart, Chamberlain recognised the fundamental hollowness of British posturing, because as everyone knew, 'the French are determined not to fight and we are not going to act without them'.[60]

In the event, Mussolini acted contrary to most of Chamberlain's expectations. Indeed, not only did he press on with his imperial adventure, but he also warned that the imposition of oil sanctions would be regarded as an 'unfriendly act'; a threat supported by covert hints of some sort of 'mad dog' response which created 'a very anxious time for those behind the scenes' in London.[61] Chamberlain found this unexpected persistence particularly worrying because he had always been aware that 'if in the end the League were demonstrated to be incapable of effective intervention to stop this war, it would be practically impossible to maintain the fiction that its existence was justified at all'.[62] By late November, therefore, he rightly suspected they faced 'really a critical point in the League's history' and that if the trade embargo failed, the League would be mortally damaged and 'our whole policy would be destroyed'. On these grounds, he favoured bolstering League authority with oil sanctions, arguing that 'if anyone else could give the lead well and good but in the last resort … we ought to give the lead ourselves rather than let the question go by default'. Despite some 'growls & grumbles' about the danger of war, on 4 December the Cabinet provisionally agreed to support oil sanctions if the League proposed them, although Hoare persuaded his colleagues to postpone such action until after his conversations with Pierre Laval, the French Foreign Minister, intended 'to test out the possibility of a general settlement'. At this juncture, Chamberlain wholeheartedly supported Hoare's efforts on the grounds that 'it would obviously be absurd to proceed with [sanctions] if thereby one were to prejudice an opportunity of ending the war by the quickest & most satisfactory method'.[63]

Everything began to unravel when Hoare (accompanied by Vansittart) met Laval in Paris on 7–8 December and agreed secretly that the war should end with Abyssinia ceding some two-thirds of its territory to Italy while the remainder would become a virtual protectorate. Hoare then commended these terms to London on the grounds that it was 'impossible to do better'.[64] According to Chamberlain's recollection, when Hoare left for Paris the Cabinet had no idea that he would consider detailed peace proposals, believing he was simply stopping off for a few hours consultation on his way to a much-needed skating holiday in Switzerland.[65] In reality, this was neither entirely fair nor accurate. On the contrary, the Cabinet had urged Hoare on 2 December 'to take a generous view of the Italian attitude' in order to secure French cooperation and to avoid any danger of Britain's involvement in a war. At this stage, it was envisaged that the Cabinet would be consulted only if there was no 'reasonable prospect of a settlement' or if France refused to cooperate. Furthermore, when the Cabinet discussed the Hoare-Laval terms on 9 December, inevitably misgivings about the 'reward for aggression' and its effect on the League, did not prevent general agreement that they represented 'the best, from the Abyssinian point of view, that could be obtained from Italy'.[66]

Unfortunately for Hoare, the premature leak of these terms in the French press on 9 December provoked an almost immediate Cabinet 'stampede' in response to widespread outrage in the press, Parliament and Geneva.[67] Aware of Conservative backbench calls for Hoare's resignation, Chamberlain complained that 'nothing could be worse than our position. Our whole position in foreign affairs at home and abroad has tumbled to pieces like a house of cards.'[68] Despite his close friendship and genuine sympathy for Hoare as a sick and exhausted man after the prolonged strain of passing the India Act, there was little Chamberlain could do to save him from the ensuing outburst of public indignation. At Cabinet on 10 December, ministers reneged on their earlier collective decision to back the proposals and resolved to make Hoare a scapegoat. Throughout the discussion Chamberlain appeared to be 'cautious', but in private he shared the general view that the Foreign Secretary could 'never recover his position among foreign nations and therefore he had better go and so help the Govt back to its feet'.[69]

Despite this recognition, in his capacity as intermediary between the Cabinet and the unfortunate Hoare, who was confined to his London home in much pain after breaking his nose while skating, Chamberlain did what he could to buy time in the vague hope that a sacrificial resignation might still be averted. Indeed, when Duff Cooper, the War Minister, told him on 17 December that 'there was a strong & growing feeling in the Cabinet that Sam shd be asked to resign', Chamberlain sternly reminded him that it was 'unprecedented & improper' to demand a colleague's resignation in his absence and warned that if Hoare refused to go he hoped those demanding his withdrawal would be prepared to resign themselves. He also declared that as the Cabinet had earlier accepted collective responsibility for the proposals, the Commons would condemn them for making Hoare into a 'scapegoat'.[70] Chamberlain was equally loyal at Cabinet next day when he outlined the content of Hoare's speech for the forthcoming parliamentary debate, informing his colleagues that 'it was not going too far to say that the Foreign Secretary had come to the conclusion that war must be avoided at the cost of a negotiated peace'. In mitigation he also declared that Hoare had been 'greatly misled by his staff' who hailed the meeting with Laval as 'a great day for him' and that Hoare's exhaustion lay at the root of his 'error of judgement'.

It was a good effort to present Hoare's case in the best possible light but the Cabinet mood was strongly against him. Alarmed by a mutinous meeting of the backbench Foreign Affairs Committee on the previous day at which Chamberlain's half-brother had played a prominent role, the Cabinet declared Hoare's proposed defence 'very disconcerting'. They then almost unanimously repudiated him, although not before Chamberlain made a last abortive effort to defer a definite announcement of his resignation pending the outcome of the debate.[71] Hoare resigned later that day. Within weeks, however, Chamberlain began manoeuvring to bring him back into the Cabinet, partly through friendship and partly because the embittered Hoare was evidently determined to force his way back with the implicit threat of joining the government's critics if he was refused.[72] Indeed, in March, Chamberlain's strenuous efforts almost succeeded until Hoare's excessively fawning tribute to Baldwin 'thoroughly shocked the House' as an 'obvious & clumsy bid for favour'.[73] He eventually returned to the Admiralty in June 1936.

The Cabinet's repudiation of Hoare and his proposed pact did not resolve their dilemma over Abyssinia or how to salvage what they could from the wreckage of the Anglo-French relationship with Italy. In overcoming this *impasse* Chamberlain played a substantially more pivotal role. Although alarmed and annoyed at the 'utterly unreasonable' behaviour of the French who wanted to lift sanctions and 'let byegones be byegones' in the hope of recapturing Mussolini's friendship, Chamberlain nurtured even more profound doubts about the League's policy.[74] While dutifully informing the Commons that the League remained the 'keystone' of British policy in late March, therefore, he accompanied this declaration with the expression of concerns about the practical problems of collective security and the future of the League; a candour which received 'considerable applause' from the backbenches.[75] In private, Chamberlain went still further. Convinced that Abyssinia 'demonstrated the failure of collective security as now understood', he concluded that they should work to retain the League 'as a moral force and focus', but should abandon support for its coercive role. In its place, he considered reviving his earlier idea of regional pacts to maintain peace and in the hope of luring Germany back to a reconstituted League.[76] Despite these musings, however, Chamberlain also recognised that 'public opinion here would be greatly shocked if we showed ourselves in too great a hurry to throw up the sponge' regarding sanctions. As a result, in early May he still believed that 'all we need do is to avoid any announcement of policy and adopt a waiting attitude'.[77]

Yet within three weeks Chamberlain's patience was exhausted. His plea to abandon sanctions at Cabinet in late May 'met with a good deal of support' but the decision was deferred.[78] After another unsuccessful effort to precipitate a Cabinet decision on 10 June, Chamberlain decided to force the issue with a 'blazing indiscretion' designed to express in public what many already thought in private. In a speech to the 1900 Club that evening, he declared that collective security had been employed in almost perfect conditions but it had 'failed to prevent war, failed to stop war, failed to save the victims of aggression'. As such, the continuation of sanctions against Italy was (in a favoured Shakespearean phrase) 'the very mid-summer of madness'. Having consulted only Hoare, who strongly approved of the line, Chamberlain deliberately violated the doctrine of collective Cabinet responsibility in the belief that Anthony Eden would have vetoed the idea as Foreign Secretary but that 'the party and country needed a lead and an indication that the government was not wavering and drifting without a policy'. In these circumstances, Chamberlain justified his action on the grounds that 'if those who should give a lead won't, some one else must occasionally do so and it seemed … that this was one of those opportunities which should not be missed'. It was a judgement vindicated by 'irresistible' backbench support at the 1922 Committee, as well as that expressed privately by many individual MPs and ministers.[79] After Eden announced the end of sanctions on 18 June, Chamberlain declared himself 'rather more cheerful about the outlook' regarding Italy, but he prudently concluded that 'we ought not to make any proposals for League Reform until we know where we stand with Germany'.[80]

V

Although Germany's military and territorial ambitions dominated much of the last six years of Chamberlain's life, its financial delinquency created most immediate difficulty during 1934. In late January Chamberlain complained of 'much trouble' when the German government reduced their payments due on long-term debts to Britain at a time when they were meeting their full interest obligations to Swiss and Dutch creditors in return for their acceptance of an increased share of German imports. To add insult to injury, the Treasury were well aware that Germany was buying up its own bonds at a price depreciated by their own partial default upon these payments. When Foreign Office protests proved counter-productive, Chamberlain immediately prepared retaliatory measures in the form of a payments clearing system. Under this rather draconian arrangement, importers of German goods would pay their debts in sterling to a clearing office which would then use part of the proceeds to settle the claims of British bondholders. At the same time, Chamberlain rejected out of hand Montagu Norman's over-generous proposed compromise on the grounds that it represented a 'loss of face and influence'.[81] Chamberlain's brinkmanship in threatening retaliation represented a remarkably bold strategy – particularly as the Bank of England and the City were 'in a blue funk' about the proposed clearing office for fear it would provoke Germany to end the 'Standstill Agreement' on short-term debts agreed in September 1931, with the consequent danger that this would bring down some London discount houses and cause heavy losses for the commercial banks. Nevertheless, within three days, the affair ended with a 'brilliant triumph' for Chamberlain when Germany promised to abandon its discriminatory practices after 30 June. As he noted with justifiable satisfaction in his diary, 'It takes some courage to stand up to these excursions & alarums!'[82] Despite the note of self-congratulation, however, this outcome represented more of an uneasy truce than a settlement and sceptics soon began to speculate as to how long it would survive.

They did not have to wait long to find out. In June the German government announced the suspension of interest payments on its medium and long-term foreign debts; a measure allegedly required to obtain a 'breathing space' in which to re-establish the balance of exchange which had turned against it through the reluctance of foreign states to open their markets to German goods. Again, however, Chamberlain knew 'the Germans were not playing straight' and on 13 June he persuaded the Cabinet to retaliate with legislation creating a debt clearing house in order 'to bring the position home to the Germans' and to protect British bondholders.[83] Despite these sweeping new powers, almost until the last moment Chamberlain feared the Germans would not settle because they 'bluff so persistently and as a rule so successfully that it was hard for them to believe that we really mean business'. On the day before the measure came into operation, however, some 'very difficult' negotiations concluded with the signature of an Anglo-German Transfer Agreement on 4 July 1934.[84] Although there were renewed tensions over German trade debts in October, the introduction of the Anglo-German Payments Agreement on 1 November enabled receipts from German imports to be used to pay UK exporters, to liquidate frozen debts and to meet German interest obligations on its other loans. This arrangement for regulating economic relations on terms favourable to Britain remained in operation until the outbreak of war and it represented a triumph for Chamberlain's determination. As Neil Forbes concludes, the 'shrewd and successful tactics which [Chamberlain] had employed in the first half of the 1930s were a powerful demonstration of the negotiating skills of the businessman-politician'.[85]

Underlying Chamberlain's concern at these dubious financial practices was the recognition that they were all part of a broader plan to finance covert German rearmament. The abortive Nazi *putsch* in Austria and the 'callous brutality' leading to the murder of Chancellor Dollfuss in July 1934 convinced him that Germany was 'once more behind instigating, suggesting, encouraging bloodshed and assassination for her own selfish aggrandisement and pride'. The entire episode, he told his sisters, 'makes me hate Nazi-ism and all its works with a greater loathing than ever'. His only scant consolation was that such outrages reinforced public support for rearmament at home. 'Hitler's Germany is the bully of Europe', Chamberlain told his sisters eight months later. 'Yet I don't despair.' One reason for this confidence was that two weeks earlier the first British 'Statement Relating to Defence' had declared that additional defence expenditure could 'no longer be safely postponed' given accelerating rearmament abroad. As Chamberlain noted, such a declaration was a 'necessary and timely' measure if conversations with Germany planned for later in the month were to 'begin on a basis of reality'.[86]

Chamberlain later encapsulated his attitude and strategy towards Germany in the maxim that 'while hoping for the best it is also necessary to prepare for the worst'.[87] Yet while convinced of the need to spend large sums on a deterrent air programme, he was equally determined that 'we shall do nothing rash' – particularly as he feared there was no one else he 'would trust to hold the balance between rigid orthodoxy and a fatal disregard of sound principles and the rights of prosperity'.[88] Furthermore, as a passionate domestic reformer, he repeatedly lamented that it was 'a sad mad world' in which Britain needed to keep 'spending the tax payers money on more and more planes merely for the purpose of frightening the Germans into keeping the peace'.[89] Indeed, even as late as January 1939, he made a 'great point' of stressing to Mussolini that he had been 'obliged to suffer the disappointment of seeing the result of his careful finance over many years dissipated in building up armaments instead of making improvements in public health and in the conditions of the people and ... he earnestly desired to see the time come when this form of spending money could be exchanged for something more reasonable'.[90]

In 1935 and 1936 the hope of achieving such a balance between external security and domestic progress was less naïve than it now appears and Chamberlain was far from gullible. Pacific utterances and signs of 'definite détente' from Germany were to be warmly welcomed – but partly in the explicit belief that this would permit more time to roll out an economically sustainable rearmament programme.[91] Certainly, Chamberlain's regret at the need to divert resources away from social improvement did not blind him to the ominous nature of the threat. On the contrary, with Germany rapidly rearming, he recognised only too clearly that 'the temptation in a few years time to demand territory etc might be too great for Goering, Goebbels and their like to resist.

Therefore we must hurry our own rearmament'; a lesson forcefully brought home in March 1936 when Germany remilitarised the Rhineland, in flagrant defiance of the Versailles and Locarno treaties, while the Western Powers stood by passively for fear that resistance would lead to war.[92]

To rearm successfully, however, Chamberlain always recognised the crucial importance of educating a pacific public opinion as to its necessity. To this end, his speeches had increasingly advocated the need to repair Britain's defence since his involvement with the DRC in mid-1934. Confronted by Labour condemnation of Tory 'warmongers', in early August 1935 he even proposed 'the bold course of actually appealing to the country on a defence programme' at the forthcoming general election – partly to turn 'the Labour Party's dishonest weapon into a boomerang', partly because attention would be 'diverted from our weakest point, unemployment and the distressed areas' and partly because the creation of new jobs building warships in the distressed areas would enable the government to 'make all our play with the two "bogeys": Stafford Cripps at home and Hitler abroad'.[93] In a speech intended as 'the preliminary to the election campaign' at Kelso in September, Chamberlain thus emphasised defence without consulting any of his colleagues in order to give a lead to the forthcoming party conference and the press; an appeal for an electoral mandate for rearmament he repeated at the Mansion House a week later and at the Scottish party conference on 14 October. In the event, however, Baldwin's pledge that 'there will be no great armaments' set the tone of the election. Even Chamberlain conceded it was 'one of the finest things he has ever done', but it also represented a disastrous retreat into a fantasy world which made the government's subsequent task all the more difficult.[94]

Despite the failure of these efforts to obtain a mandate for rearmament, after the 1935 general election Chamberlain played an increasingly prominent role in the formulation of defence policy. Concerned by the seemingly chaotic development of the rearmament programme, Chamberlain's ideas about the need for greater central control came to fruition with Sir Thomas Inskip's appointment to the newly-created post of Minister for the Coordination of Defence in February 1936, although his efforts to secure the job for the recently disgraced Hoare were unsuccessful.[95] He also continued to lead calls for the construction of a deterrent bomber force, while equally consistently opposing a continental expeditionary force on the grounds that it represented a means of preparing for the next war 'from the point of view of the last'.[96] As a result, when the new Defence Policy and Requirements Committee considered the DRC's proposal for a 'Field Force' of five Divisions capable of being deployed on the Continent within two weeks in November 1935, Chamberlain dug his heels in. Although 'afraid that it would be thought [he] was merely advocating the *cheapest* way of defence instead of the best', he privately encouraged his old friend Lord Weir to use his position as an unofficial adviser to make the running in opposition to the proposal before persuading Baldwin to tell the War Office that it must accept 'a much reduced programme for the Army'.[97] As Chamberlain did 'most of the work' on the DPRC's recommendations to

Cabinet in February 1936, the DRC's initial proposals were 'materially modified as a result' – particularly by rejecting its recommendation to spend £45 million equipping twelve Territorial Divisions.[98] After this, the Army representatives not unnaturally despaired of the Chancellor's 'cold hard calculating semi-detached attitude' and his 'most dangerous heresy … of "limited liability" in a war'. Nevertheless, Chamberlain declared himself 'pretty satisfied now that if we can keep out of war for a few years we shall have an air force of such striking power that no one will care to run risks with it. I cannot believe that the next war, if it ever comes, will be like the last one and I believe our resources will be more profitably employed in the air & on the sea than in building up great armies.'[99]

Chamberlain's battle with the War Office rumbled on into 1937 but he remained adamant that Britain's maximum contribution to a European war should be five Regular Divisions and by February 1937 he rejoiced that the Cabinet's decision on the role of the Army 'practically gives me all I want'.[100] Although Duff Cooper and the War Office persisted, the Chancellor remained utterly unyielding. As the Cabinet minutes reported his view in May 1937:

He did not believe that we could, or might, or, … would be allowed by the country to enter a Continental war with the intention of fighting on the same lines as in the last war. We ought to make up our minds to something different. Our contribution on land should be on a limited scale. It was wrong to assume that the next war would be fought by ourselves alone against Germany. If we had to fight we should have allies, who must in any event maintain large armies. He did not accept that we must send a large army.[101]

By the end of the year, the idea of an expeditionary force had been almost completely abandoned at Chamberlain's insistence and it was not until January 1939 that the Cabinet belatedly decided to reverse its neglect of the Army when confronted by a deteriorating international situation and French suspicions that their British allies were prepared to fight only to the last drop of French blood.[102]

Chamberlain was equally determined to maintain an appropriate balance between short-term Service demands for more resources and the long-term capacity of the economy to sustain those needs – but this proved far harder to achieve. Although he played a crucial role in preparing the substantially enlarged rearmament programme published in March 1936, he had insisted that it should be accompanied by the explicit warning that it 'must be carried out without restrictions on the programme of social services and that the … general industry and trade of the country must be maintained'.[103] Confronted by escalating financial demands from the services, however, in February 1937 Chamberlain was compelled to announce a Defence Loans Bill to enable the government to borrow a maximum of £400 million over five years to help fund rearmament; a cautious but definite departure from budgetary orthodoxy designed to reassure financial markets that this represented an item of exceptional borrowing in unprecedented circumstances.[104] Five days later, the third Statement Relating to Defence declared that it would be 'imprudent' to contemplate a total defence expenditure of much less than £1500 million over the next five years. The total sum 'would come as a surprise to the public, and perhaps as a shock to financial circles', Chamberlain told the Cabinet, but he was now convinced that 'this would do no harm. It was time that the country realised that they could not get armaments without paying. It might also be a good thing for Europe to see how determined we were to re-condition our armaments.'[105]

Yet whatever the compensating political and diplomatic benefits, Chamberlain also lamented that the removal of any pretence at a balanced budget by borrowing would make it increasingly difficult to curb the financial demands of the defence departments. Within only a few months he thus found himself engaged in a 'constant & harassing rearguard action ... against the Services all the time' over the subject. 'No-one is more convinced than I am of the necessity for rearmament & for speed in making ourselves safe', he complained in April 1937. 'But the Services, very naturally, seeing how good the going is now and reflecting that the reaction is sure to follow, want to be 100% or 200% safe on everything.' This was a trend he was determined to control. If nothing else, he feared that the increasing inflationary pressures generated by rearmament 'might easily run, in no time, into a series of crippling strikes, ruining our programme, a sharp steepening of costs due to wage increases, leading to the loss of our export trade, a feverish and partly artificial boom followed by a disastrous slump and finally the defeat of the Government and the advent of an ignorant unprepared & heavily pledged Opposition to handle a crisis as severe as that of 1931'.[106] In order to regain control and avert this apocalyptic vision, in his final weeks at the Treasury, Chamberlain instigated a comprehensive review of the defence programme. The report conveniently endorsed all his worst fears about the dangers of chaotic inter-Service competition.[107] By this juncture, however, Chamberlain was Prime Minister and determined to pursue with far greater vigour the dual policy of rearmament and appeasement which had guided his actions since the end of 1933.

VI

By common consent, 1936 was a difficult year for the National Government. By the summer recess, the Chief Whip condoled with Chamberlain that they had suffered 'a beastly Session; one damned thing after another and the weight of responsibility on your shoulders has been colossal'.[108] Their only consolation was that 'an unpleasant and difficult session had ended well with Government Stock once more on the ungrade' due to the relatively tranquil state of foreign affairs after the crises in Abyssinia and the Rhineland and with 'trade expanding marvellously'.[109] Despite this optimism, however, the fundamental problem of ministerial incapacity and weak leadership remained painfully evident. Since the general election in November 1935, even Baldwin had expressed his concern that MacDonald was a major liability while the Cabinet lacked experience and there were few younger men coming through. Chamberlain wholeheartedly shared all of these apprehensions, but during 1936 his principal source of concern related to Baldwin's own health and constitution. Depressed, obviously deafer, unable to sleep and in a 'strained nervous condition', over the summer Baldwin suffered such a complete breakdown that his physician declared three months complete rest was the minimum necessary for him to recover his strength.[110]

Chamberlain undoubtedly found this final period of transition intensely frustrating. It was also exhausting given the heavy burden imposed by Baldwin's complete withdrawal from active leadership. At times, he confessed, 'as I slave over my papers into the small hours I think a little bitterly of him snoozing comfortably away next door' – particularly given the fact that 'as he does less and less ... he finds it necessary to represent himself as the motive force of the Govt more & more'. Yet notwithstanding the annoyance and additional strain, Chamberlain was candid enough to admit 'I should not like anyone else to act as deputy.'[111] Despite a 'baddish bout' of gout brought on by overwork in late July and a far worse one in October–November, Chamberlain remained in robust health, slept soundly and kept 'marvellously fresh & well'.[112] His political authority and autonomy were also now effectively unchallenged, to the irritation of MacDonald who complained repeatedly that Chamberlain was 'encouraged to take too much upon himself & holds the P.M. in his pocket'.[113] Most important, despite occasional rumours that Inskip was being groomed by Baldwin for the succession, there was absolutely no doubt that Chamberlain would succeed unopposed to the Premiership when the time came, or that while only 'acting P.M.' he had the authority 'to conduct business as if [he] were in fact P.M.'.[114]

Against this background, news that Mrs Wallis Simpson had commenced divorce proceedings in October 1936 prompted Chamberlain to speculate about its likely effect on Baldwin's health and determination to remain in office until the Coronation. Although Chamberlain had liked King George V and found him 'very kind & easy to talk to', it was a respect he never extended to his vain and self-indulgent elder son whose face (even a decade before) had 'the look of a debauchee'.[115] At the Accession Council for Edward VIII in January 1936, the Chancellor already anticipated trouble. As he presciently confessed to his sisters: 'I do hope he "pulls up his socks" and behaves himself now he has such heavy responsibilities for unless he does he will soon pull down the throne.' Even when the new King gave suitable assurances to Baldwin, however, Chamberlain clearly doubted whether the attitude would last long.[116]

Looking back on the Abdication crisis, Chamberlain claimed that he was 'in the middle of things all through and responsible nearly always for the initiative as well as the drafting of all the papers'. This is unquestionably an exaggeration, but it is certainly true that he played a significant role in shaping events as one of the Cabinet's leading hard-liners. Indeed, contrary to Feiling's account, Chamberlain recognised almost immediately that Edward must be forced to depart because 'we should never be free from anxiety while he was King'.[117] With this in mind, he 'prodded' Baldwin to warn the King about the increasing public outrage at his relationship with Mrs Simpson in late October and when nothing happened Chamberlain concluded the best strategy was to issue the King with an ultimatum. With the aid of Warren Fisher and Sir Horace Wilson he thus drafted a formal letter effectively informing him 'that Mrs S. should disappear', while an accompanying informal note was designed to warn that if this advice was rejected the government would resign. When Chamberlain put this proposal to a small group of ministers on 13 November, however, its heavy-handed approach and hectoring tone aroused considerable alarm about the likely adverse public response. As a result, the plan was soon buried, but the meeting still ended with agreement that 'the scandal should be ended and HM brought right up against it'.[118]

To this end, Chamberlain vigorously opposed the King's proposal for a morganatic marriage for fear that it was merely a prelude to making Mrs Simpson the Queen. He also pressed for immediate action to make the necessary legislative and procedural arrangements for a swift abdication to prevent the King changing his mind once he gave way. When the crisis erupted in early December, therefore, Chamberlain immediately demanded a tough line by insisting the King should make a definite and immediate decision to either 'give up his proposed marriage or marry the lady and abdicate'. He was equally determined in leading the ministerial opposition to Baldwin's proposed compromise solution that the Abdication Bill should be accompanied by legislation offering an accelerated decree absolute on the entirely justified grounds that it smacked of 'an unholy bargain to get the K[ing] to abdicate'.[119]

When Edward VIII relinquished the throne two days later, Chamberlain heaved 'a big sigh of relief' on behalf of Britain and its Empire. In part, this was because he already nurtured a deep personal regard for Edward's successors, King George VI and Queen Elizabeth; a sentiment which soon blossomed into something approaching mutual affection. But far more important, Chamberlain's relief reflected a suspicion that Wallis Simpson was 'a thoroughly selfish and heartless adventuress' exploiting the King for her own cynical purposes and that their marriage 'must end speedily in disillusionment and disgust'.[120] Indeed, such was his antipathy to the couple, that he made it clear to the former King's lawyers that if he consorted with Mrs Simpson before the new Civil List was finalised he would 'not get a penny' in the financial settlement because 'Parliament would refuse to pass it.'[121] He also vigorously opposed any Royal presence at Edward's wedding or the conferment of the title HRH on his new wife and in April 1937 he effectively blackmailed the Duke of Windsor into ordering Churchill and Lloyd George to 'cease firing' over the details of the Civil List on the grounds that it jeopardised the Duke's financial interests as well as those of the new King.[122] Eight months later, as Prime Minister, he played an even more prominent role in ensuring that the Duke did not return to England against the wishes of his brother.[123]

VII

Although Chamberlain's political star was in the ascendant by the start of 1937, his personal affairs were in a rather less satisfactory state. Like his half-brother, although with rather less reason, during 1936 Chamberlain complained that his personal finances went 'from bad to worse as the country gets back to prosperity!' Indeed, he confessed to his uncle that for some time there had 'always been an anxiety about the future which has made me uncomfortable over every item of expenditure and has hung over me like a shadow'. In particular, he was deeply worried about the heavy and continuing losses at Hoskins due to 'lax' management. Even when his cousin Arthur intervened to resolve these problems while offering some finance 'to keep the Bank quiet', Chamberlain's 'immense relief ... to be freed from worry' was accompanied by the gloomy recognition that this meant a further worrying loss of income from his £400 salary and share dividends.[124]

To compensate for these losses Chamberlain leased his house in Eaton Square to none other than Joachim von Ribbentrop, the German Ambassador; a situation he declared to be 'very amusing considering my affection for Germans in general and R. in particular'. A less satisfactory consequence of these financial concerns was the decision finally to abandon the vast orchid collection at Westbourne which he now rarely saw. 'It hurts to part with them and I shall miss them in the winter especially' he lamented, but it removed a heavy financial burden and he was content to know that most would find a good home at Kew.[125] Fortunately, shortly before becoming Prime Minister Chamberlain received another generous gift from his favourite uncle, George Kenrick. He also completed the government's review of ministerial salaries and pensions. The resulting Ministers of the Crown Act of 1937 provided for an annual salary of £10,000 for the Prime Minister and a pension of £2000, although even then he anticipated this fairly princely salary 'won't do much more than enable me to make both ends meet if it goes as far as that'.[126]

These financial worries were overshadowed by the devastating and sudden death of his half-brother on 16 March 1937. Although never genuinely close as siblings and despite a distinct coolness between their wives, Chamberlain had rejoiced at Austen's emergence as a respected Elder Statesman on the backbenches after 1931 and the news of his unexpected death came as 'a shattering blow'.[127] Deeply touched by Baldwin's 'beautiful tribute' in the Commons, Chamberlain found much consolation in the 'universal homage' paid to Austen's character and his unswerving sense of personal honour and public duty. He also took comfort from the knowledge that Austen had gone to his grave confident that within ten weeks a Chamberlain would finally become Prime Minister.[128]

Depressed by his loss and one of the worst colds he could ever remember, Chamberlain felt 'thoroughly good for nothing and shaken up'. In such a mood he easily succumbed to gloomy thoughts. 'I am not a superstitious man and indeed I should not greatly care if I were never to be P.M.' he confided to his sisters. 'But when I think of Father & Austen and reflect that less than 3 months of time and no individual stands between me and that office I wonder whether Fate has some dark secret in store to carry out her ironies to the end.'[129] In the event, these pessimistic forebodings about fate's 'dark secret' came much closer to being fulfilled than anyone could ever have imagined – but not because of sudden death, incapacitating illness or misplaced loyalty, but rather from the effect of Chamberlain's sixth and final budget.

Oppressed by the need for exceptional budgetary measures to fund a rapidly expanding rearmament programme, the 1937 Budget caused Chamberlain 'more anxiety than ever before'.[130] The central innovation in his financial statement on 20 April was the introduction of a National Defence Contribution – a graduated tax on the growth in business profits during the period of rearmament, which he expected to yield between £20–25 million in a full year. Having announced the measure, Chamberlain declared it 'the bravest thing I have ever done ... for I have risked the Premiership just when it was about to fall into my hands, although I could easily have left the hornet's nest alone'. When the new tax immediately provoked widespread and violent abuse, Chamberlain inevitably felt 'a bit low and depressed', but he remained confident that it was the right thing to do and that its wisdom would eventually be recognised; an optimism based on the assumption that a single flexible levy was superior to either a succession of new taxes or further additions to Income Tax. Moreover, he initially nurtured high hopes that it would dispel working class resentment about profiteering from the rearmament programme and help educate the electorate to 'the inevitability of sacrifice' while 'teaching [the Services] that there are limits to the amount of money at their disposal'.[131] Given the opposition of the trade unions to the conscription of labour, some even suspected that this first tentative step towards the conscription of wealth represented an effort to appease organised labour by giving 'the impression of liberal mindedness and disregard for vested interests'.[132]

As a policy panacea designed to combat a formidable range of dangers, the logic behind the NDC had much to commend it and Chamberlain undoubtedly regarded it as 'the keystone of the Budget'.[133] Moreover, if the testimony of one party worker during the Stalybridge by-election was anything to go by, the Budget and the NDC had helped to hold this predominantly working class seat for the Conservatives because 'a Conservative Chancellor ... had the courage to recognise that the people who should pay for expenditure on armaments are the people ... whose dividends on ordinary shares will inevitably increase'.[134] But such encouragement was extremely rare. Indeed, a 'hostile buzz' soon emerged within the parliamentary party, while the City and business community furiously besieged the Chancellor with angry deputations warning of apocalyptic consequences.[135] Even Cabinet colleagues with memories of the Excess Profits Tax after the Great War thought it 'a bad tax' unlikely to succeed, while Joseph Ball, Chamberlain's close personal friend and loyal ally at the CRD, for once appeared to be working secretly behind the scenes to defeat him.[136]

Unaccustomed to such opposition, Chamberlain's initial reaction was to defend the NDC in the belief that good sense would prevail once the critics came to recognise its merits. By early May, however, it was clear even to those who supported the NDC that the revolt was 'really very serious' – particularly as it threatened 'the impoverishment of many bright Conservatives who are in stockbroking firms in the City or are in small businesses whose assets have depreciated'.[137] After calculated hostility in the City prompted a dramatic fall on the Stock Market which adversely affected government borrowing for National Defence Bonds, even Chamberlain recognised this was a threat he could not ignore. When further detailed concessions on 31 May failed to appease his critics, Chamberlain agreed to accept 'a simpler tax with a larger yield' next day.[138] Three weeks later, the NDC was replaced by a flat-rate 5 per cent tax on all business profits. Although this dramatic *volte face* inflicted no lasting damage on Chamberlain's reputation, it was an inauspicious end to five and a half hectic years at the Treasury. Writing his last letter to his sisters as Chancellor on 22 May, Chamberlain declared with characteristic defiance that he was 'rather unhappy at leaving, but I regret nothing I have done while I have been at the Treasury'.[139]

Chapter 12

A New Style of Prime Minister, May 1937–February 1938

'It is very pleasant to receive congratulations from old friends ... and to know they feel pleasure in my "promotion" ... As a matter of fact I had for a long time done so much of the work that generally falls to a P.M. that I have slid into my new position without any sense of strangeness and indeed with some relief at being able to carry out my own ideas without having to convert someone else first.'

Chamberlain to Alfred Greenwood, 30 July 1937

For Neville Chamberlain, his succession to the Premiership on 28 May 1937 represented a supreme triumph for the entire Chamberlain 'Click'. As such, it was a moment for becoming modesty. As he told his sisters, the post 'ought to have come to the two senior members of the family & only failed to do so because the luck was against them in forcing them to choose between their natural ambition and their principles'. Instead, he declared it had 'come to me without my raising my finger to obtain it, because there was no one else and perhaps because I have not made enemies by looking after myself rather than the common cause'. Yet having achieved the supreme prize, Chamberlain freely admitted his determination to 'leave my mark behind me as P.M.'.[1] Moreover, the strength of his position in 1937 was prodigious. He commanded a massive majority in the Commons, the electoral position was stable and the economy was still relatively strong. Although at 68 he was the second oldest newcomer to the post in the twentieth century, he also enjoyed exceptionally good health and fitness and he brought to the leadership a vigour, confidence and decisive style wholly beyond Baldwin even at his best.

While these qualities confirmed Chamberlain's reputation within the political community as 'the strong man on whom it was safe to lean', his personality was still far from well known to the general public.[2] In fairness, the electorate had slowly come to know something of Chamberlain's ability and character during his Chancellorship from annual budget broadcasts which still appear relaxed and modern in their ability to talk directly to the camera. Nevertheless, after 14 years of almost continuous ministerial prominence, the life-long aversion to doing 'anything "out of character"' still shrouded Baldwin's successor in an air of remoteness and unfamiliarity.[3] Moreover, what the public did know of him was not always entirely flattering. 'There is a widespread feeling among people that Mr Chamberlain is an autocrat at heart, and that if he were to take

Mr Baldwin's place as P.M. we should be taking a step away from democracy', a senior party official warned during the late summer of 1936. With this in mind, the CRD took particular care in preparing and disseminating his speech for the party conference at Margate, in the belief that anything he did 'to diminish the popular impression that he is an authoritarian at heart ... would be striking a shrewd blow in his own cause'.[4]

Even those who knew Chamberlain rather better expressed some doubts and concerns about the new Premier's character. As the parliamentary correspondent of the *Manchester Guardian* noted in a remarkably perceptive sketch, 'Clarity of mind – and he has it in unusual degree – is not enough if the mind ... sees the field with searching clearness but not the field as part of the landscape, and that kind of limited vision is not necessarily compensated by courage such as Mr Chamberlain has. The two together could be a positive danger.'[5] The *Manchester Guardian* was no friend of Chamberlain's, but such comments had been made before by those who were – and they would be heard far more frequently now that he was Prime Minister. In retrospect, it is tempting to suggest that the qualities which made Neville Chamberlain such an effective ministerial policy-maker and Cabinet politician were precisely those which would serve him least well when in supreme command. Above all, perhaps, the problem stemmed from Chamberlain's approach to decision-making and his faith in the power of 'hard thinking' and 'homework'. Having gathered all the necessary facts and methodically reasoned through the best line to adopt, he was as remorseless in pursuing his chosen path as he was ruthless in sweeping aside all objections.[6] Such methods had generally served him well in the past and they conferred a sense of mastery when dealing with lesser mortals who did not share his unshakeable conviction in their own total correctitude. Unfortunately, what Chamberlain chose to forget, was that such an approach had brought humiliation at the hands of Lloyd George in 1917. More tragically, it would do so again when the train of logic driving his foreign policy hit the buffers of Hitlerian duplicity in March 1939.

Yet in May 1937 all this lay in the future. After six years of increasing personal ascendancy, Chamberlain felt not the slightest hint of self-doubt. On the contrary, political supremacy only reinforced an innate confidence which now bordered on arrogance. Undaunted by the carping of opponents, Chamberlain took up his new post with a sober appreciation of the problems, but still feeling at the peak of his powers he believed himself more than capable of facing its challenges. 'It is a bit late in the day to become Prime Minister at 68 and I can't expect a very long run', he wrote to an old friend, 'But I am glad to have the opportunity of getting some things done that ought to be done.'[7] Beneath these placid observations there lurked an iron determination to inject a new dynamism into the government and the conduct of its business. As he soon made clear to his party, 'I can't do all the things that S.B. did as well as the things he didn't do and I consider that at present at any rate the latter are more important.'[8]

One intended sign of this new style of leadership was a more ruthless attitude to ministerial appointments. Chamberlain had always despaired of the dilatory and sentimental approach to the subject demonstrated by his two predecessors and he was initially resolved not to repeat the mistake[9] – although ironically his failure to dispense with political 'duds' became one of the most consistently damaging criticisms of his entire Premiership. Before succeeding Baldwin, Chamberlain endorsed Sam Hoare's view that 'you must make your new government as unlike the old as you can' because 'the country will be bored from the start if it looks as if you are merely continuing the Baldwin regime'.[10] Yet contrary to Hoare's advice, he refused to strengthen the Conservative right-wing at the expense of non-Conservative allies and he went out of his way to assuage Simonite fears that his succession would signal 'a return to strictly party government'.[11] In the event, therefore, Walter Runciman became the only major victim of Cabinet reconstruction.

Chamberlain had been under pressure to replace Runciman at the Board of Trade for some time, both to infuse new life into the department and to appease agricultural suspicions that Runciman had 'sold the pass'.[12] More important, while he claimed to be 'very fond' of Runciman, over a year before his succession Chamberlain was already convinced that he was not 'a very valuable colleague in Cabinet as he seldom opened his mouth' and tended to be 'lazy'; a criticism given substance by their recent strained relations over Runciman's failure to act on Chamberlain's scheme for the rationalisation of the cotton industry.[13] Runciman also fell victim to the need to maintain a proper party balance. As Simon was keen to go to the Treasury, Chamberlain was determined that a National Liberal should not hold the other key economic portfolio, while Runciman's imminent succession to the Lords precluded the Admiralty at a time when the Air Ministry was already represented in the upper House. For a variety of reasons, therefore, Chamberlain 'did not attach any particular importance to his retention in the Cabinet', but as an act of friendship, he was prepared to offer him the Privy Seal.[14]

This lack of sentimentality and 'extreme frigidity' in dealing with an old friend and colleague caused a bitter rift. Indeed, as Runciman had actually expected to be offered the Treasury, it was a 'painful surprise' when he realised that his services were 'valued ... so low that the only office ... offered to me was the poorest in the Cabinet, with no departmental responsibilities'; an offence aggravated when Chamberlain expressed 'no word of appreciation or regret' at the termination of their association. Outraged at this entirely unintended snub, Runciman made it plain that he would prefer to withdraw altogether if he could render no 'suitable services' and despite the efforts of friends and family to soothe the injury to his pride, he remained implacable.[15] For his own part, Chamberlain felt 'rather indignant' at Runciman's perceived distortion of their conversation, coolly concluding that the incident 'illustrates very clearly what Baldwin has often said to me, namely that no more painful or disagreeable duty falls upon a Prime Minister than that of forming his Cabinet'. Beyond these difficulties, however, the new Prime Minister rejoiced that 'the changeover has gone like clockwork', but this was scarcely surprising given his curious reluctance to execute the sort of wholesale reconstruction that both Baldwin and Hoare believed would be far easier to achieve at this moment than later.[16]

II

Chamberlain's new style of leadership manifested itself most immediately in the more purposeful direction of policy and the use of methods very different from those of his two predecessors. As Chancellor, he had increasingly complained that he shouldered all the responsibilities of the Prime Minister but without the unique authority exercised by that office. As he told his sisters in March 1935, 'I have become a sort of Acting P.M. – only without the actual power of the P.M. I have to say "Have you thought" or "What would you say" when it would be quicker to say "This is what you must do".'[17] In May 1937, all of this changed. Possessed of an almost boundless confidence in his own judgement and impatient to make his mark, Chamberlain intended to exploit the opportunities of his office to demonstrate that he could 'get more done in a month than he could in six when SB was on top'. 'As Ch. of Ex. I could hardly move a pebble', he declared in August 1937; 'now I have only to raise a finger & the whole face of Europe is changed!'[18]

Despite MacDonald's complaint that the coalition nature of the National Government forced its head 'to be a shepherd & not a leader',[19] from the outset, Chamberlain was determined to lead from the front by example and inspiration – and, where necessary, by direct command. A few days before becoming Prime Minister, he told Leslie Hore-Belisha and Nancy Astor that he intended to 'take a new line' and 'wished all his ministers to be in the closest touch with him' because he would adopt a more active role in the coordination of ministerial policy.[20] Within a month he had thus instructed ministers to prepare a two-year policy programme to be collated into a provisional timetable to ensure a properly balanced legislative programme for that Parliament and the next. Besides talking vaguely about 'a sort of inner Cabinet on policy', after an early success in maintaining a proper balance between the Treasury and spending departments in a Cabinet committee on agricultural policy, Chamberlain also decided to extend his direct control by chairing all such major deliberations in the future. Similarly, Simon's frank admission that he knew nothing whatsoever about finance when appointed to the Treasury, and Chamberlain's assurance that he had been selected largely because they 'worked so happily & effectively together', also perhaps suggests that he hoped to retain indirect control over economic and defence policy through a compliant minister in a key department.[21]

This striking preference for 'hands-on' management soon became the basis for frequent (but misleading) allegations of authoritarianism and 'dictatorship' within a 'one-man Cabinet'.[22] But at the time, the party responded well to the decisive smack of firm leadership – and particularly the promise of a more personal interest in foreign affairs. As Simon assured him, the Commons 'liked your manner of standing up at that box and telling them what they ought to think, very different from S.B. fumbling with his papers'. Even Baldwin wrote to congratulate his successor on his good start, his 'A1' speeches and 'admirable' intervention in foreign affairs which left the parliamentary position 'as good as it can be'.[23] Constituency activists were equally well disposed to Chamberlain's fierce brand of partisanship and strong leadership after the consensual tone and frustrating sense of 'drift' during the Baldwin era. 'Greater confidence is inspired by the knowledge that the present P.M. is exercising more *personal* interest and *control* over our foreign policy and its method of conveyance', a Central Office report on the London area noted. 'In other words people feel assured he will *lead* and by so doing he will strengthen and *reclaim* a great deal of Party loyalty and support which had become submerged by apathy or even worse.'[24] Given his rather austere public persona it is also somewhat ironic that Chamberlain won much approval from constituency loyalists through his habit of mingling with the assembled faithful at party rallies, in marked contrast to Baldwin's aloof refusal to engage in such social niceties, while Annie won many hearts with her 'engaging manners', her 'charming' little speeches and her willingness to shake hands with everyone.[25]

The corollary of this decisive lead from the front was an iron determination that the discordant voices of doubters should do nothing to jeopardise his policy or undermine his authority. Confronted by formidable external policy constraints over which he had no control, Chamberlain demanded that his personal will should at least prevail within Whitehall and Westminster. An early victim of this tendency was Sir Robert Vansittart, the vehemently anti-German Permanent Under-Secretary at the Foreign Office, who later freely admitted that Chamberlain was right to dismiss him given his profound contempt for the 'dreamland of Appeasement'.[26] After Vansittart's strenuous efforts to prevent Lord Halifax's unofficial visit to Berlin in November 1937, Chamberlain was furious with the Foreign Office and declared that he was 'only waiting for my opportunity to stir it up with a long pole'. The following month Vansittart was 'kicked upstairs' to become Chief Diplomatic Adviser while Chamberlain rejoiced this would 'make a great difference in the F.O.' because 'when Anthony [Eden] can work out his ideas with a sane slow man like Alick Cadogan he will be much steadier'.[27]

Chamberlain was equally determined to maintain discipline within the Cabinet and parliamentary party and in this endeavour he was ably and enthusiastically supported by Captain David Margesson. As Chief Whip since 1931, Margesson soon earned a well-deserved reputation as a tyrannical martinet with such a long and vindictive memory for backbench disloyalty that Chamberlain's critics had every reason to despair that 'the Conservative party machine is even stronger than the Nazi party machine. It may have a different aim, but it is similarly callous and ruthless.'[28] Yet Chamberlain's demand for obedience and control was not solely the product of an instinctive authoritarianism. On the contrary, it often stemmed from an equally passionate desire to prevent ill-advised attacks on the dictators prejudicing his own delicate diplomatic overtures. Angry at two 'blazing indiscretions' by Duff Cooper in December 1937, Chamberlain thus fired off a ferocious missive which caused its contrite recipient to take his chastisement 'very much to heart'.[29] Similar concerns led directly to Chamberlain's efforts to curb the independence of the backbench Foreign Affairs Committee and the Foreign Office's Press Department.[30] More important, after Goebbels told Halifax during his visit to Germany in November 1937 that 'nothing would do more for better relations than if our Press could be induced to stop attacking Hitler personally', considerable influence was brought to bear to 'tame' Fleet Street and the newsreels by encouraging proprietors and editors to avoid material offensive to Germany.[31] Ultimately, these efforts led Chamberlain to embrace some distinctly underhand methods of media manipulation which showed his personality in an unattractively autocratic light. But given the stakes for which he believed he was playing, he never doubted that the worthy ends justified the somewhat dubious means.

III

Nowhere was Chamberlain's new style of leadership more evident than in his handling of foreign affairs. Having increasingly lamented that Britain was 'drifting without a policy' under Baldwin, from the outset he declared that he 'meant to be his own Foreign Minister' because he was 'very opposed to the continuance of our policy of retreat'.[32] This was a bold ambition given the extremely barren international legacy which he inherited. Confronted by a sudden deterioration in Anglo-Italian relations and fresh Japanese outrages against British interests, in October 1937 Chamberlain warned the Cabinet that he 'could not imagine anything more suicidal than to pick a quarrel with Japan at the present moment when the European situation had become so serious. If this country were to become involved in the Far East the temptation to the dictator states to take action, whether in Eastern Europe or in Spain, might be irresistible.' To make matters worse, it was generally recognised that it was 'beyond the resources of this country to make proper provision in peace for defence of the British Empire against three major Powers in three different theatres of war'.[33] Furthermore, of Britain's potential allies, France was perceived to be weak in the air and dogged by persistent political crisis while the US Congress passed a third and still more stringent Neutrality Act only four weeks before Chamberlain's succession.

Without a proper recognition of this overwhelming preoccupation with what the Chiefs of Staff called the 'three-cornered bogey', there can be little hope of any balanced understanding of Chamberlain's agonising dilemma or the dogged determination with which he pursued his distinctive brand of diplomacy. Whatever his personal feelings of repugnance towards Hitler and Mussolini, as the leader of a militarily weak and globally over-stretched empire, Chamberlain believed that he needed to address himself to the distasteful realities of his actual position – rather than the one about which his critics fantasised and in which Britain possessed the resources to 'stand up to Hitler' and could hope to emerge triumphant from the inevitable conflict. As he noted stoically in January 1938, 'in the absence of any powerful ally, and until our armaments are completed, we must adjust our foreign policy to our circumstances, and even bear with patience and good humour actions which we should like to treat in a very different fashion'.[34]

Any British government in the late 1930s would have been compelled to confront these challenges to imperial security within the relatively narrow parameters defined by a complex and inter-related web of strategic, military, economic, industrial and electoral constraints. The debate at the time (and ever since) has focused on the precise degree of choice exercised by British policy-makers in the face of such threats and constraints. Broadly speaking, Chamberlain's contemporary supporters and a latter-day 'revisionist' school of historians argue that the constraints were compelling, overwhelming and ineluctable. In such circumstances, the question asked at the time and repeated by his defenders ever since was 'what could Chamberlain do other than what Chamberlain did?'[35] Conversely, his contemporary critics and a later 'post-revisionist' school contend that Chamberlain was not the helpless victim of forces and factors beyond his control; rather he made choices and these were consistently in favour of appeasement and negotiation rather than resistance and rearmament.[36] Despite an astonishing amount of scholarly debate on this issue over the past half century, no consensus has emerged on the subject – and all the evidence suggests that it never will. But what is absolutely beyond question, is that Chamberlain *perceived* himself to be trapped in a reactive position as the prisoner of forces largely beyond his control. Moreover, insofar as he did enjoy any freedom of manoeuvre, at no point did he or his principal advisers believe that this included the option of threatening armed resistance as a means of checking the aggression of the dictators – and those who claimed it did he despised as ignorant fools, irresponsible warmongers or worse.

As a self-proclaimed 'realist', Chamberlain's response to Britain's problems was to pursue with renewed intensity what he called 'the double policy of rearmament & better relations with Germany & Italy'.[37] With regard to the former, Chamberlain remained a reluctant but pragmatic proponent, determined to balance the maximum of defensive insurance and security with the minimum of expenditure diverted from social services and with the least disruption to the domestic economy. Yet in practice, it is clear that Chamberlain's assessment of what needed to be spent on defence combined a high level of optimism about the ability to avoid war through diplomatic means, with a wholly justified alarm at the economic consequences of expanding rearmament too rapidly. 'By careful diplomacy I believe we can stave [war] off, perhaps indefinitely', he explained to his sisters in November 1936, 'but if we were now to follow Winston's advice and sacrifice our commerce to the manufacture of arms we should inflict a certain injury upon our trade from which it would take generations to recover, we should destroy the confidence which now happily exists and we should cripple our revenue.'[38]

This was certainly the key message to emerge from a review of the rearmament programme which Chamberlain had set in motion shortly before becoming Prime Minister. Indeed, Inskip's interim report in December 1937 specifically emphasised that expenditure should not be allowed to rise above the agreed ceiling of £1500 million for fear that it would 'impair our stability, and our staying power in peace and war'. On this basis, Chamberlain strongly endorsed the views of Inskip and the Treasury that when 'seen in its true perspective the maintenance of our economic stability would ... accurately be described as an essential element in our defensive strength: one which can properly be regarded as a fourth arm of defence, alongside the three Defence Services without which purely military effort would be of no avail'. As Chamberlain told the Commons when unveiling Inskip's defence priorities in March 1938, 'wars are not only won with arms and men: they are won with reserves of resources and credit'. He was equally receptive to warnings from the Chiefs of Staff that, as there was no hope of defeating Germany in a short war, Britain needed to prepare for a long struggle and that ultimately this meant garnering its financial and economic resources rather than launching headlong into a crash programme of expenditure.[39]

This concept of economic and financial stability as the 'fourth arm of defence' reinforced all that Chamberlain already believed about the urgent need to strike a proper balance between short-term military power and the sort of long-term economic resilience needed to prosecute a protracted war. Yet this was always far easier said than done. As the Chancellor told the Cabinet in March 1938, 'we are in the position of a runner in a race who wants to reserve his spurt for the right time but did not know where the finishing tape was. The danger was that we might knock our finances to pieces prematurely.' As a result, the Treasury argued consistently that 'bringing on an economic crisis by increasing expenditure was unlikely to add weight to British diplomacy'. On the contrary, it feared that a crash programme would lead to a financial crisis comparable with 1931 before any war broke out and 'thus presenting Hitler with precisely that kind of peaceful victory which would be most gratifying to him'.[40]

As a former Chancellor, these economic considerations played an absolutely fundamental role in shaping Chamberlain's perceptions of the international situation, while there is no evidence whatsoever to support the view that they served merely as a convenient rationalisation for a policy he wished to pursue on other grounds. It also needs to be emphasised that there was far more validity in these warnings than Chamberlain's critics were prepared to concede. Britain's heavy dependence on imports for the rearmament programme foreshadowed a serious balance of payments and sterling crisis from the end of 1936 onwards. Equally important, the crucial shortage of industrial capacity, machine tools and skilled manpower inevitably generated inflationary pressures at a time of rapidly spiralling expenditure.[41] During his final months as Chancellor, Chamberlain had drawn particular attention to these bottlenecks when warning that 'even the present Programmes were placing a heavy strain on our resources. Any additional strain might put our present Programme in jeopardy.' 'Admittedly, national safety comes before finance', he declared in February 1937, 'but the bill for armament was running up very heavily … and the danger of overloading the programme beyond the material capacity of the country had to be considered.'[42] In these circumstances, it is reasonable to contend that what Britain needed in the late 1930s was not a greater level of expenditure but rather more time to expand rearmament capacity in order to optimise the use of available resources without jeopardising confidence or overheating the economy: a priority which indicated the urgent need for a carefully-staged expansion and an active role for the Treasury in 'rationing' finance and resources within a global defence budget. Indeed, as defence deliveries actually lagged behind orders and finance, it is highly probable that a more rapid growth in the rearmament programme, as demanded by Chamberlain's critics, would have resulted in fewer modern fighters and anti-aircraft guns, with a consequently far narrower margin of victory in the Battle of Britain.[43]

This is not simply a question of speculation. Chamberlain's warning to the Chancellor in July 1938 that 'we must not let the principle of rationing drop out of sight or we shall pay for it dearly hereafter', was fully vindicated six months later when Simon warned the Cabinet that, 'recent conditions have been painfully reminiscent of those which obtained in this country immediately prior to the financial crisis of September 1931'.[44] Despite efforts by Chamberlain and Simon to curb rearmament expenditure during the spring and summer of 1939, these proved ineffective against Cabinet ministers determined that defence should prevail over any economic considerations. As a direct result, by July these dramatic increases in defence spending had provoked precisely the sort of economic crisis the Treasury had always predicted, as the balance of payments deficit soared, gold reserves plummeted, sterling depreciated and capital flowed out of London.[45] Although Cabinet critics like Hore-Belisha and Kingsley Wood dismissed such warnings as 'a gloomy half-baked effort by the Treasury to slow down rearmament', the reality was very different.[46] Indeed, there is ample evidence to suggest that if war had not come within months, there is every possibility that Britain would have exhausted itself financially even before the conflict began, leaving it unable to withstand the expected first onslaught or to wage the sort of long war which offered Britain's only hope of victory – particularly as Roosevelt's failure to amend US neutrality legislation in June 1939 meant that Britain could expect no immediate aid from that quarter.

This need to strike a delicate balance between economic, strategic and foreign policy considerations involved a high level of risk and was always open to misinterpretation. For Chamberlain's critics, the slow progress of rearmament was easily attributed solely to a naïve belief that war could be averted by appeasing the dictators and his reluctance to do anything to jeopardise domestic prosperity.[47] Within the Cabinet there was a constant battle between those who supported Chamberlain's view that economic strength was Britain's first line of defence and those who placed the over-riding priority

upon short-term military preparedness; a position variously espoused by
Duff Cooper and Swinton (representing the Air Ministry and Admiralty) and
Anthony Eden, the Foreign Secretary. Convinced that 1938 would be a critical
year, in November 1937 Eden argued that Chamberlain's excessive restraint
towards rearmament reflected a misguided set of priorities because a 'good
financial position would be small consolation to us if London were laid flat
because our Air Force had been insufficient'. Deeply frustrated by this attitude,
Eden blamed it on the fact that Chamberlain 'clearly had the financial situation
much in mind' – although typical of many critics he also perversely conceded
that industry was already fully stretched and that he was personally ignorant
of the financial position. Conversely, Chamberlain believed Eden was 'too
alarmist' in his view because 'he did not think anybody was going to attack
us for the next two years' – but this confidence was always predicated on the
assumption that it was 'necessary to follow a very cautious foreign policy'
until the defence programme had been completed.[48] Despite the retrospective
triumph of Churchill, Eden and their version of events, it is sometimes too easily
forgotten that in making this balanced calculation, Chamberlain's assessment
was correct and Eden's was wrong.

For all of these reasons, Chamberlain believed he had every incentive to prefer
a policy of negotiated accommodation, designed to achieve the 'appeasement
of Europe' through the redress of legitimate German grievances, rather than
an expensive and potentially disastrous arms race. Economic constraints
upon the progress of rearmament were by no means the only factors driving
Chamberlain's foreign policy. Yet contrary to some post-revisionist claims, the
need to employ diplomacy to 'buy time' for a carefully-staged expansion of
rearmament at an economically sustainable pace was undoubtedly an important
and explicit factor in reinforcing Chamberlain's personal policy preferences.
News of the Austro-German agreement in July 1936 was thus greeted with the
observation that he did 'not take Hitler's peace professions at their face value',
but any agreement in this volatile area meant that 'danger is removed and once
more we are given a little longer space in which to rearm'. Similarly, a few
months after his succession, Chamberlain confided to Lord Weir that 'the Air
Force must go on and build itself up as rapidly as possible. I hope my efforts
with Germany and Italy will give us the necessary time.'[49]

Unfortunately, the problem for any analysis of Chamberlain's motivation
is that the relative balance between diplomacy and rearmament was never
fixed or immutable in his mind. It is unquestionably true that for most of his
Premiership, Chamberlain believed that better relations with the dictators
represented a viable long-term substitute for complete rearmament. In October
1937, he thus talked privately of his 'far reaching plans ... for the appeasement
of Europe & Asia and for the ultimate check to the mad rearmaments race, which
if allowed to continue must involve us all in ruin'.[50] Above all, immediately after
the Munich conference in September 1938, Chamberlain continued to proclaim
his dual policy but he appears remarkably naïve and credulous in declaring
stiffly to the Cabinet that 'a great deal of false emphasis had been placed on

rearmament, as though one result of the Munich Agreement had been that it would be necessary for us to add to our rearmament programme'.[51] But after Hitler's seizure of the remaining non-German area of Czechoslovakia in March 1939, the emphasis returned to the need for diplomacy to buy a breathing space for the completion of the rearmament programme – although even then, his hopes of an eventual settlement always remained strong. Against this background, while the relative significance attached to the need to 'buy time' varied throughout his Premiership, the post-revisionist allegations that it was merely a cynical retrospective excuse only invented by Chamberlain after his fall in May 1940 is completely without foundation and ignores the fact that it had been a (but not the) central and explicit objective of his policy since 1934.[52]

Ultimately, however, the far more important point is that the presentation of rearmament and appeasement as policy alternatives obscures the far more complex reality that Chamberlain always regarded them as two sides of the same coin at a time when he confronted vast circumstantial constraints which could not swiftly – or possibly ever – be completely overcome. 'The ideal ... was to be prepared to fight Germany or Italy or Japan, either separately or in combination', he told the Committee of Imperial Defence in July 1937, but this was 'a counsel of perfection which was impossible to follow' because there were 'limits to our resources, both physical and financial'. Such an understanding led to a recognition that it was 'impossible to exaggerate the importance of any political or international action that could be taken to reduce the number of our potential enemies or gain the support of potential allies'.[53] Chamberlain would always have been a reluctant rearmer and he undoubtedly employed a high level of political skill to manipulate the argument in order to get his own way. But given the existence of both very real and immediate threats and equally formidable constraints upon a rapid expansion of the defence programme in 1937–38, he never doubted that there were few real alternatives to a strategy of hoping for the best while preparing for the worst.

IV

In a paper for the Foreign Policy Committee shortly before he became Prime Minister, Chamberlain declared that 'the general situation in Europe is such that we cannot afford to miss any opportunity of reducing the international tension' because 'a slight improvement in the international atmosphere may lead gradually to a general *détente*, whereas a policy of drift may lead to general war'. The note of urgency was typical. Until rearmament was completed, the dictators needed to be actively mollified and accommodated in the hope of leading them back to the path of peaceful diplomacy in pursuit of reasonable goals and as part of a broader process of 'European appeasement'.[54] To achieve this objective, Chamberlain believed it essential to play a direct and personal role in the conduct of foreign policy – not least because he wholeheartedly endorsed Sam Hoare's view that 'the F.O. is so much biassed against Germany (and

Italy and Japan) that unconsciously and almost continuously they are making impossible any European reconciliation'.[55] Despite Halifax's assurances in early August that 'the F.O. is coming along very nicely', therefore, Chamberlain remained convinced that 'if left to themselves there would be a danger of their letting pass the critical moment'. A month later, he again complained that he was 'not too happy about the F.O. who seem to me to have no imagination & no courage'.[56]

These were crucial defects given Chamberlain's plan of approach and the perceived urgency of the problems. Neville Chamberlain did not invent the policy of 'appeasement' with which his name is inextricably associated. As Paul Kennedy puts it, the policy had its origins in the mid-nineteenth century and was 'the "natural" policy for a small island state gradually losing its place in world affairs, shouldering military and economic burdens which were increasingly too great for it'.[57] Yet if Chamberlain's policy was 'the continuation in a heightened form' of this tradition, one of its most distinctive themes under his management was a tactical flexibility in seizing opportunities to achieve his broader objectives whenever and wherever they presented themselves. When Amery questioned his strategy and focus in November 1937, Chamberlain retorted that he had to deal with conditions as they actually were, but that speed and flexibility were essential because 'in face of a rising market … the longer we delay, the higher will be the terms asked'.[58] Throughout, therefore, Chamberlain was prepared to alternate his attention between the European dictators as circumstances dictated – not least because he believed that while Italy and Germany had differences, they could be played off against each other in order to increase the diplomatic momentum. As he told Lord Halifax in August 1937, 'these dictators are men of moods. Catch them in the right mood and they will give you anything you ask for. But if the mood changes they shut up like an oyster.'[59]

On these grounds, Chamberlain's initial diplomatic thrust was directed towards Italy – partly because the German Foreign Minister declined an invitation to London and partly in response to authoritative warnings about the need to relieve increasing tensions in the Mediterranean until rearmament was completed.[60] Chamberlain's objective was to detach Mussolini from Hitler while restoring Anglo-Italian amity – and in pursuit of this goal he was prepared to pay a high price.[61] At a remarkably successful and 'extremely frank' meeting on 27 July with Count Dino Grandi, the Italian Ambassador, Chamberlain replied to Mussolini's message of goodwill and the 'immense importance' he attached to *de jure* recognition of his Abyssinian conquest that this 'could only be justified as part of a great scheme of reconciliation'. At the suggestion of Sir Horace Wilson, Chamberlain's principal policy adviser and confidant, he then immediately despatched a friendly letter to Mussolini lamenting the deterioration in relations and proposing a conversation 'with a view to clarifying the whole situation and removing all causes of suspicion or misunderstanding'. After a second useful talk with Grandi on 2 August, at which he delivered Mussolini's equally cordial reply, Chamberlain looked back 'with great satisfaction at the extraordinary relaxation of tension in Europe' and clearly endorsed Grandi's verdict that 'it is 90% due to me'.[62] As he confided in his sisters, such results 'gives one a sense of the wonderful power that the Premiership gives you'. They certainly confirmed his view that he both could and should conduct his own foreign policy on a direct and personal basis.[63]

Yet Chamberlain also recognised that to achieve security, goodwill needed to be consolidated with firm pledges and enduring bonds because even broken agreements were better than none at all – if only for the moral which failure would highlight. Contrary to the allegations of critics that he either nurtured a private ideological sympathy with fascism or was devoid of any conception of international morality, Chamberlain's pursuit of such agreements reflected his own pragmatic determination to address himself to distasteful realities as he saw them; a 'realist' perspective which prompted a profound contempt for 'the lighthearted way in which people who think they are pacifists are yet prepared to advocate measures which would almost certainly bring us into war'. While he understood public outrage at Mussolini's conquest of Abyssinia, therefore, Chamberlain was convinced that Britain would eventually need to acknowledge the new reality with *de jure* recognition. As such, he concluded they 'had better give it while we can still get something in return for it' because 'it has now some marketable value which will continually diminish as time goes on'. Encouraged by the apparent success of his letter to Mussolini, Chamberlain thus came to believe that 'if we follow it up we can to a great extent if not entirely restore Anglo-Italian relations to what they were before the Abyssinian adventure'; an outcome he sincerely believed would mark 'a very important step forward towards European appeasement' while providing a crucial ally in the event of renewed tensions with Germany.[64]

From Chamberlain's perspective, the principal obstacle to his Italian policy was the Foreign Office, whose perceived lack of courage and imagination were exceeded only by their scepticism about the possibility of any durable improvement in Anglo-Italian relations. 'The F.O. persist in seeing Musso only as a sort of Machiavelli putting on a false mask of friendship in order to further nefarious ambitions' he told his sisters in mid-September. 'If we treat him like that we shall get nowhere with him and we shall have to pay for our own mistrust by appallingly costly defences in the Mediterranean.'[65] At this juncture, Chamberlain assumed that his main problem lay with Vansittart and his officials, although he was aware that his Foreign Secretary shared their reservations about tactics, the perceived value of Italian cooperation and the price they were prepared to pay for it – particularly after Mussolini's flagrant bad faith in despatching more troops to Spain on the day after signing an Anglo-Italian 'Gentlemen's Agreement' in January 1937. Aware of this sensitivity, Chamberlain decided to circumvent Eden altogether by intervening personally with the first approach to Mussolini.

This decision was comprehensible but disastrous. Before leaving for a much-needed summer holiday in August, Eden had issued specific instructions that they should 'go slow about Anglo-Italian rapprochement'. Instead, at

Chamberlain's instigation, Halifax worked out a programme for talks with the Italians while he stood in for the Foreign Secretary. Moreover, when Eden twice protested that he would be 'very reluctant' to give *de jure* recognition to the Italian conquest, Halifax dutifully reiterated that they must 'face facts'.[66] In retaliation, Eden was so disturbed by officially-inspired press rumours about forthcoming Italian conversations that he instructed Vansittart to prevent any further correspondence between Downing Street and Rome without consulting him as it would be 'the height of folly to concede in fact what the Italians want, in return for mere promises'.[67]

While Eden fumed angrily on Southampton Water, Chamberlain retired to Chequers to recharge his batteries, satisfied and surprised at the way he had come through his first session as Prime Minister without undue physical exhaustion or mental strain. He then departed for Scotland, to the joys of salmon fishing and the grouse moor. As guests of the Duke of Westminster at Lochmore, Annie was in her element: 'There is no doubt she is a child of luxury by nature and to be the guest of a millionaire, to have all her meals cooked by a first rate artist, to be waited on by three butlers and a footman and have cars & ghillies always at her disposal, all this goes a long way towards making her holiday tolerable.' For his part, Chamberlain spent most of his days fishing for salmon, although the ghillie informed him that he had never known the waters so unresponsive.[68] Nevertheless, as Chamberlain had observed after an equally unsuccessful time on the River Test in pursuit of trout with Joseph Ball in June, he had 'got to the stage now when if only I can find something to fish for, I mind very little whether I bring the victim home or not. It's the effort to outwit him that makes the amusement & interest.'[69] From Lochmore, they proceeded to their usual August haunt at Tillypronie, where Chamberlain enjoyed some of the best days he could remember before travelling on to Balmoral where he hoped to consolidate what he believed to be a developing mutual regard with the royal couple. Under a more relaxed regime than that which existed under George V, the King and Queen behaved 'just like other hosts & hostesses in their easy hospitality'. After shooting with the King and raiding the gooseberry bushes with the Queen, Chamberlain was thus gratified to learn that they were 'very pleased with their P.M. as a guest'.[70] By this stage, however, crises in the Mediterranean and the Far East forced his return to London on 6 September.

At the Cabinet two days later, consideration of specific measures to curb Italian submarine attacks on British shipping in the Mediterranean served as a prelude to a lengthy discussion about Anglo-Italian relations and the formal recognition of Italian sovereignty over Abyssinia. During this discussion, Chamberlain repeated forcefully that he 'regarded the lessening of the tension between this country and Italy as a very valuable contribution towards the pacification and appeasement of Europe' – particularly as it would 'undoubtedly weaken the Rome-Berlin axis'. Yet there were clear signs of impatience in his declaration that the 'very deep impression of rejoicing and relief throughout Italy' created by his letter to Mussolini would fade unless further progress was achieved. While acknowledging Eden's reservations, therefore, Chamberlain 'emphasised that the important thing was to strive for a change of heart and attitude on the part of Italy'.[71] The fact that this discussion followed a debate about further Japanese aggression against British interests in the Far East only highlighted in Chamberlain's mind the need to restore Anglo-Italian relations as a means of exorcising the fearful spectre of war on three fronts.

Unfortunately, Chamberlain's hopes of rapprochement were to be short-lived as the roller-coaster of Anglo-Italian relations lurched in another direction. Despite the progress made in early August, Mussolini's decision to assist Franco with a submarine offensive against all vessels bound for Spanish Republican ports soon led to the sinking of a British-registered tanker – and with it Chamberlain's hopes of an early agreement. Indeed, when an international conference at Nyon in mid-September agreed to retaliate by sinking all 'pirate' submarines on sight, Mussolini became 'aggressive and anti-British' when denouncing potential suitors with 'their minds in the seats of their trousers'.[72] Confronted by this new crisis, Chamberlain inevitably lamented that 'Spain remains a constant source of anxiety' given British demands for the withdrawal of Italian 'volunteers'. As he told the Cabinet in mid-October, 'it did not matter to us which side won so long as it was a Spanish and not a German or an Italian victory. If we could secure the removal of the volunteers it would become a Spanish civil war and not a foreign war.' By this stage, Chamberlain was so anxious for an agreement with Italy that he privately conceded that he 'attach[ed] still more importance to not sending any more in' than to the actual withdrawal of 'volunteers'.[73] For Mussolini, however, Chamberlain's anxious search for rapprochement was increasingly interpreted as a sign of weakness; a perception which both confirmed his contempt for British decadence and served further to stimulate the unruly behaviour these overtures were designed to curb.[74]

V

The other problem which interrupted Chamberlain's summer holiday concerned ominous new developments in the Far East. A skirmish between Japanese and Chinese troops near Peking on 7 July soon spread to Shanghai, threatening not just the large quasi-colonial British presence in the city, but all British interests in China north of the Yangtse valley. Chamberlain initially hoped that it might be possible to avoid any action which required the diversion of over-stretched military resources to the Far East. Unfortunately, this optimism was dashed when Japanese aircraft attacked two British Embassy cars between Nanjing and Shanghai in late August, seriously injuring the Ambassador. This confronted Chamberlain with a particularly thorny dilemma because while he recognised the Japanese government were unable to issue a more apologetic official statement for fear of a violent backlash from its militaristic elements, Britain could not simply acquiesce in such an outrage. As a result, Chamberlain argued the best response would be to express disappointment at the unsatisfactory Japanese reply to British protests, but to declare 'we did not consider that it was consonant with our own dignity to press them further in the matter, as apparently in matters of this kind Japan was unable to attain to the normal standards observed among civilised people'. Although the matter was then adjourned pending the final Japanese reply, in the next item dealing with Japanese interference with British-flagged ships, Chamberlain rightly predicted that 'if nothing was said … the tendency would be for the Japanese to proceed from one improper kind of interference to other and more improper things'.[75]

In opting for a posture which was symbolically firm but unprovocative in military terms, Chamberlain was again guided by his perpetual fear of war on three fronts – particularly given both the sudden deterioration of Anglo-Italian relations after the Nyon resolutions and his enduring contempt for what he regarded as the myopic and self-interested nature of US foreign policy. Since 1932, Chamberlain had considered it his personal mission to 'educate' the Americans to their own best interests in world affairs. Two months before becoming Prime Minister he thus acquainted Treasury Secretary Morgenthau with his views on the German and Japanese threats, urging close Anglo-American collaboration because 'almost any action common to them both would go far to restore confidence to the world and avert the menace which now threatens it'. Yet while Roosevelt was prepared to respond only with 'completely pious' words of endorsement, his trusted advisers in Europe were 'somewhat disturbed about the manner in which Anglo-American relations might develop under Chamberlain as Prime Minister "since if it could be said that any Englishman was anti-American, Chamberlain was that anti-American Englishman".'[76] Soon after he became Prime Minister, however, the US Ambassador optimistically reported home that Chamberlain's formerly 'not … hostile … but uninformed and indifferent' attitude to America had been 'completely reversed'.[77] In order to foster 'an enlightened policy of Anglo-American cooperation', Roosevelt then invited Chamberlain to Washington within a fortnight of his succession; a courtesy Chamberlain gently declined on the grounds that 'the time is not yet ripe', although this did not prevent him hinting that cooperation in the Far East would ease the way to a later visit.[78] Yet notwithstanding all the diplomatic niceties, British hopes that American support would permit a more effective response to Japanese aggression were soon dashed, prompting Chamberlain to conclude wearily that 'the Americans have a long way to go yet before they become helpful partners in world affairs'.[79]

Frustrations of this sort shaped Chamberlain's coolness towards Roosevelt's famous 'quarantine' speech at Chicago on 5 October 1937, in which he declared 'the epidemic of world lawlessness is spreading' and needed 'a quarantine of the patients … to protect the health of the community against the spread of disease'. Despite the President's resolute tone and indirect assurances from Secretary of State Hull that 'the old stubborn isolationism is fast breaking down',[80] Chamberlain concluded the speech was 'contradictory in parts & very vague in essentials'; suspicions confirmed by sources in Washington who correctly reported that it was 'intended to sound out the ground & see how far

[Roosevelt's] public opinion was prepared to go but that he ... had no present intention of doing anything that wasn't perfectly safe'. As a result, Chamberlain welcomed 'the psychological effect of this sudden abandonment of America's attitude of complete detachment' as a sign to 'the totalitarians ... that they can't entirely count on her remaining outside while they eat up the democracies'. Nevertheless, he still rightly feared that 'after a lot of ballyhoo the Americans will somehow fade out & leave us to carry all the blame & the odium' in the Far East; an apprehension confirmed when British warnings about the likely consequences of economic sanctions indicated that 'they hadn't the remotest intention of touching them with the end of the longest imaginable barge pole, and that "quarantine" only referred to a possible ultimate ideal!'[81]

The near certainty that there would be no joint action with America in the Far East condemned Chamberlain to a state of impotence in the face of Japanese aggression in China. As he explained to the Cabinet in mid-October, effective economic sanctions against Japan were impossible without the risk of a retaliatory attack on the East Indies, the Philippines or Hong Kong and the situation in the Mediterranean precluded the despatch of a British naval force to the Far East. As a result, Chamberlain declared they should 'present the object of the [forthcoming Brussels] Conference as appeasement' and that while Britain should attempt to coax the Japanese into concessions to China, 'nothing should be done to suggest the imposition of sanctions'.[82] As if to highlight the vulnerability of the British position, on the day after the conference adjourned in ignominious failure, Cabinet fears about the danger of escalating insults in China were vindicated by reports that the Japanese had seized all Customs vessels at Tientsin and Shanghai. Despite the blatant threat to British interests, the Prime Minister repeated that 'it was clear that we could not put forceful pressure on the Japanese without cooperation of the United States'. In the absence of anything better, therefore, he resolved to ensure the success of forthcoming negotiations on an Anglo-American trade agreement because 'it would help to educate American opinion to act more & more with us'.[83]

Chamberlain's hopes of joint action were briefly revived when Japanese aircraft destroyed the USS *Panay* and attacked three Standard Oil tankers on the Yangtse on 12 December. 'It seems to me just a Heaven sent opportunity and you can bet your bottom dollar I am making the most of it', he wrote to his sisters a few days later. 'It is always best and safest to count on *nothing* from the American except words but at this moment they are nearer to "doing something" than I have ever known them and I can't altogether repress hope.' Despite renewed proposals for naval action 'at least along synchronised parallel lines', however, the White House declined to participate. Obviously disappointed by this response, for Chamberlain the lesson was clear – 'the isolationists are so strong and so vocal that [America] cannot be depended on for help if we should get into trouble' and without the hope of US support in curbing an increasingly insolent Japan, nothing should be permitted to obstruct or distract attention away from the appeasement of European tensions.[84]

VI

Although the fear of war on three fronts compelled Chamberlain to pursue a lasting rapprochement with Mussolini, he always recognised that 'Germany was the real key to the situation.'[85] As he declared in July 1937, if Britain 'could get on terms with the Germans I would not care a rap for Musso' because 'the best way of countering the disquieting attitude of the Italian Government was to cultivate better relations with the German Government'.[86] Ultimately, this meant direct negotiations with Germany 'to find out what she wants', while 'deciding ourselves the direction in which we can best afford to let her expand at the expense of others if we are willing to let her expand at all'.[87] Chamberlain's problem, however, was that the extent of Hitler's true ambitions could not be established definitively until all the legitimate German grievances arising from the Treaty of Versailles had been redressed. Only then could it be ascertained with complete confidence whether Hitler was simply an aggressive patriotic revisionist capable of being appeased or a madman bent upon world domination who needed to be stopped by force. With the wisdom of hindsight, critics accuse Chamberlain of blindness to the 'simple and obvious truth about German intentions' on the grounds that revisionist grievances were merely a 'tactical gambit in the struggle for Europe'.[88] But the contemporary reality was far less clear cut and the final clarification of these intentions did not occur until March 1939. In the interim, Chamberlain believed he had little choice but to seek a negotiated settlement of existing German grievances. Again, it was a case of hoping for the best while preparing for the worst.

In the immediate aftermath of Chamberlain's succession, his real problem stemmed less from the ambiguity of Hitler's underlying ambitions than from the lack of any occasion to discuss them at all. In October 1937, however, Lord Halifax received an invitation (as the Master of the Middleton Fox Hounds) to attend an international sporting exhibition in Berlin. This was the golden opportunity to begin an unofficial dialogue with the German leadership for which Chamberlain had been yearning. Moreover, although 'really horrified' when he had 'to fight every inch of the way' against Vansittart's opposition to the plan, he was fortunate that Halifax wholeheartedly shared his feeling that 'if we could once convince them that we wanted to be friends we might find many questions less intractable than they now appear'.[89] During his four day visit to Germany, Halifax met senior figures in Berlin before going on to Berchtesgaden for a three hour meeting with Hitler himself on 19 November. At this meeting, Hitler appeared 'very sincere' about his desire for friendly relations with Britain. But he was also in a relatively truculent mood and demonstrated little interest in disarmament, objected to the 'Versailles mentality' and declared that it was 'impossible to imagine peaceful revision with the consent of all'. In reply, Halifax emphasised that with regard to Germany's territorial claims, Britain was 'not necessarily concerned to stand for the status quo as today, but we were concerned to avoid such treatment of them as would be likely to cause trouble'. In other words, 'any alteration should come through ... peaceful evolution' rather than by force because the Chamberlain government would acquiesce in treaty revision only as long as the method 'avoided ... far-reaching disturbances'.[90]

Halifax did not rate the value of the talks very highly. Indeed, he privately doubted 'that Hitler understood what he was talking about' when he spoke of a 'general settlement'.[91] Nevertheless, he consoled himself with the thought that they had finally made contact and that this provided some direct insight into Hitler's thinking. On this basis, Halifax reported to the Cabinet on 24 November that while 'the Germans had no policy of immediate adventure', he anticipated 'a beaver-like persistence in pressing their claims in Central Europe, but not in a form to give others cause – or probably occasion – to interfere'. He also concluded 'an understanding might not be too difficult as regards Central and Eastern Europe' and that Britain should pursue the idea of offering Hitler 'a colonial settlement as the price of being a good European', in the hope of limiting German ambitions to those objectives which could be achieved by peaceful means.

Chamberlain hailed Halifax's visit as 'a great success'. Above all, enthusiastic reports from Sir Nevile Henderson, the British Ambassador in Berlin, confirmed that it had achieved the prime objective of 'creating an atmosphere in which it was possible to discuss with Germany the practical questions involved in a European settlement'.

> It was no part of my plan that we should make or receive any offer. What I wanted H[alifax] to do was to convince Hitler of our sincerity & to ascertain what objectives he had in mind and I think both of these objects have been achieved. Both Hitler & Goering said repeatedly & emphatically that they had no desire or intention of making war and I think we may take this as correct at any rate for the present.

Although Chamberlain acknowledged Hitler's ambitions to dominate Eastern Europe and to achieve closer union with Austria and the Sudeten German minority in Czechoslovakia, he also declared that if Germany gave satisfactory assurances that it intended to achieve these goals by peaceful means, Britain would not use force to prevent it.[92] On this basis, Chamberlain concluded from Halifax's report that the obstacles to a comprehensive settlement of German grievances were by no means insuperable – particularly as the commencement of negotiations on an Anglo-American trade agreement on 18 November was believed to have 'frighten[ed] the totalitarians' at a time when internal economic stresses within Germany suggested 'that Hitler might be prepared to go a long way to reach a complete settlement'.[93]

Chamberlain was equally optimistic about the long-term potentiality of colonial appeasement. In response to Hitler's 'peace plan' during the Rhineland crisis in March 1936, he had argued that 'Germany's real object was not raw materials but the return of colonies' and that 'if we were in sight of an all-round settlement the British Government ought to consider the question'. As he explained to his sisters, 'I don't believe myself that we could purchase peace and a lasting settlement by handing over Tanganyika to the Germans, but if I did I would not hesitate for a moment to do so.'[94] Halifax's report thus confirmed Chamberlain's view that Hitler would not fight for colonies, but that an offer in the colonial field might form part of 'a general settlement' which included Central Europe, the League, disarmament and the qualitative restriction of bomber aircraft. After warning the 1937 Imperial Conference in June not to 'close their minds to the possibility' of colonial restitution, in classic nineteenth-century style, Chamberlain began work on a scheme for territorial readjustment in Africa to satisfy Germany while compensating those like Portugal who would be forced to sacrifice existing colonies.[95]

Determined to maintain the diplomatic momentum now that the ice was broken, Chamberlain recognised that the next logical step in his plan was to consult the French Prime Minister. As Camille Chautemps sympathised with Chamberlain's policy, their Downing Street meeting on 29 November proved 'not only successful but most valuable' and all agreed that Chamberlain played a special part in this outcome as he 'won their confidence and respect by [his] handling of the proceedings'.[96] In fact, everyone gained from the meeting. The French were gratified by the promise of future consultations on German developments and the absence of the expected demand for unilateral colonial concessions, while Chamberlain was pleased to find the French remarkably cooperative in accepting British leadership regarding any future approach to Germany. He was even more relieved when the French did not press for a definite commitment to Central Europe. This was a significant triumph for the British Prime Minister and, arguably, it represents the moment at which 'Chamberlain took over the reins of the Franco-British team.'[97] 'That has taken me over the French hurdle and over the first British hurdle without losing a stirrup' Chamberlain confided in his sisters, but he knew there were worse obstacles ahead. At this stage, he planned a 'series of quiet talks' with individual ministers to explain his policy as a prelude to a Cabinet committee to ratify the policy once he had engineered sufficient support. Even then, however, he recognised that it would be a long while before he could put definite proposals before the Germans and that as 'their mentality is so different from ours ... they may easily upset the applecart by some folly before then'.[98]

VII

During the winter recess Chamberlain enjoyed a good rest. Surrounded by his family and sisters at Chequers, all agreed 'it was the best Christmas ... for a long while', and in the New Year he surprised even himself with his shooting prowess in bringing down some remarkably high birds. His physical well-being and high spirits undoubtedly reflected a profound sense of optimism that his personal diplomacy was beginning to show early signs of progress. After he returned to London, however, he almost immediately found himself in 'the thick of a tangle of problems' of which the most pressing concerned Roosevelt's secret overtures regarding a world conference to obtain arms limitation from the dictators, in return for equal access to raw materials and some agreement on the 'norms of international conduct'.[99]

Chamberlain was gravely alarmed when this 'bombshell ... suddenly landed in [his] lap'. After recent difficulties with Washington over the Far East, he regarded it as a 'preposterous effusion' but the fear that it would jeopardise his own policy compelled him to devote 'the most strenuous and anxious endeavours' to defusing it.[100] Without consulting the exhausted Eden on holiday in the South of France, Chamberlain ignored the pleas of the British Ambassador in Washington and despatched a discouraging reply warning that the initiative risked 'cutting across our efforts' at 'a measure of appeasement' with both Italy and Germany and urging the President to consider 'holding his hand for a short while to see what progress we can make'.[101] In reply to this 'douche of cold water', Roosevelt expressed 'a somewhat sulky acquiescence in postponement', along with some 'strongly worded warnings' about the dangers of shocking world opinion with a premature recognition of the Italian conquest of Abyssinia.[102] Thereafter, however, Roosevelt's equivocation towards his own proposal undermined its threat to Chamberlain's own plans. As a result, within a fortnight Chamberlain noted with some satisfaction that the bombshell had still not exploded and he hoped 'to surround it with blankets sufficient to prevent its doing any harm'.[103]

In the event, Chamberlain's skill in avoiding a trans-Atlantic crisis provoked one nearer home. Chamberlain's blunt rejection of Roosevelt's plan had so horrified Oliver Harvey, Eden's devoted private secretary at the Foreign Office, that he immediately recalled his master from the South of France. At Folkestone on 15 January, Eden was briefed by Cadogan and Harvey and he read Roosevelt's proposal for the first time. After this, he swiftly concluded that while some paragraphs were 'not well-worded from our point of view', Anglo-American cooperation was so important that it demanded a warmly supportive response to the President's appeal. Without consulting Chamberlain, Eden then despatched his own reply to Washington which effectively declared, as Chamberlain later recorded in his diary, 'I had not exactly meant what I said.'[104] Eden then proceeded to Chequers to meet Chamberlain, who clearly 'did not very much like' Eden's telegram to Washington, but who agreed to let the matter rest until they received Roosevelt's written message.

Over lunch at Chequers, the outlines of their ensuing conflict emerged clearly. Eden stressed the crucial importance of Anglo-American cooperation and the need to encourage Roosevelt's initiative. He also deprecated formal recognition of Italy's Abyssinian conquest and expressed his profound mistrust of Mussolini. In reply, Chamberlain reiterated that Roosevelt's initiative would jeopardise his own overtures by offending the dictators and provoking 'blast and counter blast between democracies and dictatorships'. He also made it clear that he 'did not agree ... about Italy and that we had a wonderful chance of coming to terms about the future of the Mediterranean'.[105] Although Eden initially thought this meeting 'fairly satisfactory',[106] by the following day he detected the existence of 'a fundamental divergence' in policy and emphasis which he privately attributed to the fact 'that N. believes that he is a man with a mission to come to terms with the Dictators'.[107] Stiffened by his admiring entourage at the Foreign Office into believing that he was 'the most important person in the Cabinet and that if he went the Government would fall', Eden thus came to believe that if only he was 'firm' then Chamberlain must give way but that 'no compromise is possible'.[108] In this determined mood, Eden wrote to Chamberlain powerfully restating his full case. During the following week he then dug his heels in and successfully defied the Prime Minister over both *de jure* recognition and the rebuff to Roosevelt.[109]

In reality, these differences of policy and approach had been simmering since the summer when Chamberlain and Halifax had gone behind Eden's back to prepare the ground for Anglo-Italian conversations. Equally important, however, Eden now suspected that 'the PM wanted to deal with Foreign Affairs himself and to keep A.E. out of the picture'; a concern which only strengthened his belief that Chamberlain and his key ministerial allies were not just 'dictator-minded' and 'far to the right of the H. of C. and the country' but also 'jealous of him and would trip him up if they had half a chance'.[110] During November and December 1937 these accumulating frustrations marked a watershed in their relations at a time when it was increasingly apparent to outsiders that 'the Foreign Office is more bellicose and is basing its policy more and more upon the rearmament programme than the Defence Minister and his experts, who are in favour of solving our difficulties by negotiations and diplomacy'.[111] Furthermore, when Eden did press Chamberlain strongly about the disappointing progress of rearmament and the Cabinet's unwillingness 'to face realities' in November, Chamberlain briskly dismissed these concerns as 'too alarmist', intimating that Eden was '"feverish" on the subject' and that he should 'go back to bed and take an aspirin!'[112]

Despite the existence of well-known policy disagreements of this sort, Chamberlain and other Cabinet observers were curiously unaware of a more fundamental rift. After the 'aspirin' incident, Sir Horace Wilson assured Eden that Chamberlain was 'devoted' to him and that there was 'no question of any personal hostility or jealousy' – but he still could not resist adding that Chamberlain was convinced he was right and he was thus 'saving A.E. from himself'.[113] Even Eden's loyal private secretary noted in December that 'the P.M. and A.E. are now together again' and were 'in absolute agreement about Germany', while Eden ended the year with effusive thanks to Chamberlain for his 'unvarying kindness and help' and in late January he was still assuring him that 'I entirely agree that we must make every effort to come to terms with Germany.'[114] Even with regard to the far more contentious problem of Italy, the cracks were so far from being evident that in mid-February Chamberlain and Eden both suggested they were 'in complete agreement, more complete perhaps than we have sometimes been in the past'; a view echoed by Simon who dismissed stories of a rift as 'nonsense' because 'Eden seems to be rapidly approaching the P.M.'s point of view.'[115] A week later Anthony Eden resigned as Foreign Secretary.

VIII

At precisely the moment when 'the Japs ... [were] getting more & more insolent & brutal' in the Far East, reports of renewed German pressure on Austria in mid-February 1938 played a crucial role in precipitating the final Cabinet confrontation by dramatically increasing Chamberlain's perception of the critical urgency and manifold benefits of an agreement with Italy.[116] Beyond his constant preoccupation with the need to reduce the number of Britain's enemies, Chamberlain believed that such an agreement would curtail Italian attacks upon British shipping in Spain, while the possible need to send a battlefleet through the Mediterranean on its way to the Far East exposed it to the danger of a 'mad dog' act unless good relations with Italy could be guaranteed. In addition, better relations with Mussolini promised significant benefits in North Africa by ensuring the withdrawal of Italian troops from Libya, ending hostile propaganda in the Middle East and opening the way to a friendly understanding over the Red Sea. As share prices tracked international tensions, there was perhaps even the hope that a successful outcome to the talks might bolster business confidence during the sharp economic recession of 1937–38.[117] To add further weight to these arguments, on 16 February the Cabinet discussed Inskip's final report on rearmament recommending an increase in the expenditure ceiling to £1650 million; a necessity accepted reluctantly, but one which convinced Chamberlain that diplomacy was needed more than ever to relieve the financial and military burden in a hostile world. Given all that was at stake, it was not surprising either that Chamberlain was 'most anxious' to achieve better relations with Italy or that he was alarmed by Foreign Office predictions that 'Italy is on the verge of financial collapse and that we ought not to purchase her friendship by such concessions.'[118]

Already convinced that he stood at one of the great turning points of world history, Chamberlain's determination to press ahead was crucially reinforced by news from his sister-in-law in Rome. Austen and Ivy Chamberlain had enjoyed extremely cordial relations with Mussolini since their meeting at the Locarno conference in October 1925. In early December 1937 Ivy returned to Rome to be lavishly entertained by 'the people who count' in her capacity as an unofficial intermediary. By the end of December, she was reading verbatim to Mussolini and Ciano the contents of Chamberlain's private letters reaffirming his desire for an Anglo-Italian rapprochement. Convinced by a second letter a month later that Britain was prepared to commence talks on the formal recognition of Italy's Abyssinian Empire, Mussolini thus urged her to communicate to Chamberlain that he also was 'working in a very realistic spirit' towards 'a full and complete settlement' of differences as a basis for future Anglo-Italian amity.[119] When Eden protested that these unorthodox overtures weakened the British bargaining position by appearing 'over-eager' for negotiations, Chamberlain promised to keep Ivy quiet, but in his turn he pointedly warned that 'we should not in our over-anxiety not to be over-eager, give the impression that we do not want to have conversations at all'. In private, however, he was delighted by the 'magical' effect of her intervention because Mussolini and Ciano were now finally 'convinced of [his] sincerity'.[120]

Against this background, news that Hitler had browbeaten Chancellor Schuschnigg into a reluctant acceptance of Austrian nazification on 12 February 1938 confirmed Chamberlain's determination to achieve an Italian settlement as a barrier to German expansionism in Central Europe. To highlight the urgency of the situation, Ivy from Rome and Ball's secret source at the Italian Embassy both confirmed that if Anglo-Italian talks had started before the Austrian crisis had erupted Mussolini would 'undoubtedly have taken a very strong line with Hitler and have despatched troops to the Brenner Pass' as he had in 1934. Even at this juncture, however, they counselled that 'all is not lost' if immediate action was taken to open conversations.[121] To drive the point home, Ciano ordered the Italian Ambassador to 'give a touch of the accelerator to the London negotiations' by passing on Mussolini's warning that 'this was the last opportunity' for Italy to choose between Britain and Germany.[122] In these feverish circumstances, Chamberlain let it be known through Ball's secret conduit that he was willing to meet Grandi and begin discussions. Convinced that immediate negotiations were critical to European peace and British security, Chamberlain had finally concluded that Eden should submit to his will or resign.

By now Eden had reached the same conclusion. Since New Year's Day he had been engaged in an exchange of correspondence with Chamberlain which explicitly challenged his commitment to a 'rather sordid and ... dangerous' bargain in which *de jure* recognition would be traded for a general settlement. According to Eden, such an arrangement would damage Britain's moral position while providing Mussolini with a diplomatic victory at a time when 'the Abyssinian wine of triumph is beginning to taste sour on the Italian palate'. Anyway, he argued, Mussolini was a 'secondary' consideration when compared with Hitler, because while 'an agreement with the latter might have a chance of a reasonable life ... Musso is, I fear, the complete gangster and his pledged word means nothing.' In reply, Chamberlain declared that his plan was 'to proceed both with Italy and Germany concurrently', but that they needed to act decisively to 'bring appeasement in the Mediterranean (and *inter alia* cover what is now for us a very exposed flank)'.[123] Eden had never accepted these arguments, but by now he was overwrought and repeatedly complaining of a 'fundamental difference between him and the P.M.' and of his increasing desire to resign in order to extricate himself from a failing position. After his 'great triumph' over Chamberlain regarding the reply to Roosevelt's plan in late January, Eden was also convinced by supporters at the Foreign Office that he could 'afford to be as firm as he likes' because Chamberlain and his allies were 'afraid of him'.[124]

This conflict of values and priorities finally erupted on 17 February. Over lunch Eden and then Cadogan vainly attempted to persuade Chamberlain not to participate in the talks between the Foreign Office and Grandi next day. When this feeble manoeuvre failed, Eden wrote to Chamberlain urging him to resist Grandi's pleas to commence diplomatic conversations because there was evidence of 'some kind of arrangement between Rome and Berlin' and that (in Vansittart's words) Mussolini was 'playing us along'.[125] As Chamberlain read the letter at 11pm, he 'felt more and more depressed' but it also convinced him that the 'issue between [them] must be faced and faced at once' because further delay in opening negotiations jeopardised everything.

> I had no doubt at all that in [Mussolini's] disappointment & exasperation at having been fooled with … so long, Italian public opinion would be raised to a white heat against us. There might indeed be some overt act of hostility and in any case the dictatorships would be driven closer together, the last shreds of Austrian independence would be lost, the Balkan countries would be compelled to turn towards their powerful neighbours, Czecho-Slovakia would be swallowed, France would either have to submit to German domination or fight in which case we should almost certainly be drawn in.

As he 'could not face the responsibility for allowing such a series of catastrophes to happen', next morning Chamberlain told Horace Wilson that he was 'determined to stand firm even if it means losing my Foreign Secretary'; a decision soon reinforced by Grandi's calculated assurances that all of Chamberlain's fears were completely justified.[126] When Chamberlain and Eden commenced their meeting with Grandi they thus appeared like 'two enemies confronting each other, like two cocks in true fighting posture'. As the Italian Ambassador left the meeting, he correctly concluded the contestants were 'preparing to play for the high stakes of their future destiny in the Government and in the Conservative Party'.[127] Left alone together in the meeting room, Eden then angrily dismissed 'the "now or never" attitude', while Chamberlain unleashed the full force of his pent up fury against Eden who 'had missed one opportunity after another of advancing towards peace; he had one more chance, probably the last; and was wanting to throw it away'. They then angrily agreed to put the final decision to the Cabinet before giving Grandi their answer on Monday.[128]

When the Cabinet assembled on the afternoon of Saturday 19 February, even Halifax had no idea what was to occur. Chamberlain opened with 'a detailed and very powerful statement' outlining his 'firm determination' to begin immediate negotiations with Italy – but that as a 'sharp difference' of opinion had emerged with Eden, he effectively invited the Cabinet to decide between them. Eden then followed by reiterating his suspicion of Mussolini's motives, his demand that Italy should withdraw its troops from Spain as 'proof of good faith' and his fears about the damage which surrendering to blackmail would inflict on British prestige around the world. Although 'obviously speaking with deep conviction', however, Eden gave 'an impression of being under much strain'. More important, as his opening sentences presented the disagreement as one about the best method of handling the situation, many ministers soon concluded that this was an exhausted and overwrought man who had mistakenly detected a question of principle in what was really 'a matter of procedure and method; nothing more'.

Having forewarned Simon of the crisis and confident of his wholehearted support, Chamberlain then called upon him to speak next and Simon immediately fastened on Eden's admission that the dispute was confined to a question of method and timing. On the central policy issue, however, Simon emphasised that the public expected urgent and positive action both to reassure the smaller European states and to demonstrate to Hitler that Britain was not without resources or support. After this, Chamberlain insisted that every minister should speak and 'the rest of the Cabinet, one by one, expressed agreement with the P.M.'s view' – or at least 14 did while four others did so with reservations. No one backed Eden. After this, Eden declared that he must resign because he could not adhere to this collective policy and, despite several pleas, he persisted until Chamberlain announced they should sleep on the matter. After four hours the Cabinet 'broke up in great bewilderment and distress', although as Duff Cooper conceded, 'anyone who had not already made up his mind must have been convinced by the Prime Minister'.[129]

When Eden met Chamberlain a little after noon next day, they agreed that he should resign because their differences were 'vital and unbridgeable'. At the Sunday Cabinet which followed, Chamberlain reported that Eden had repeated in more definite terms his determination to go, but that this time Eden had broadened the issue when he 'spoke of "fundamental differences of principle" between himself and the Prime Minister' related to Chamberlain's unilateral intervention with both Mussolini in July and Roosevelt in January. Again, Simon, Halifax and Inskip challenged this interpretation but neither their pleas nor Halifax's 'committee of mediators' could dissuade Eden from resigning early that evening. Despite vague intimations that Oliver Stanley, Malcolm MacDonald and Walter Elliot might follow him, when the Cabinet reconvened at 10pm these threats had evaporated, although as Chamberlain noted contemptuously of the wavering Elliot and Stanley, 'A crisis like this brings out the best and the worst in men's characters.'[130]

IX

The precise combination of policy and personal factors which precipitated Eden's resignation have been much debated. Physical and nervous exhaustion straining an overwrought mentality certainly played a significant part. Eden possessed the looks of a matinee idol, the polished charm of a diplomat's diplomat and the languid insouciance of his class, but beneath the veneer he was a chronic worrier – and he had much to worry about given profound doubts regarding a foreign policy for which he was nominally responsible but over which he exercised little direct control. Worse still, he had little to offer by way of a practicable alternative to Chamberlain's policy except the utterly fatuous conviction that Roosevelt would eventually give practical substance to woolly phrases. Little wonder that the burdens of the Foreign Office rapidly took such a heavy toll on his constitution or that despite his holiday in the South of France over Christmas, he soon appeared to be 'sadly overworked' and 'under much strain'.[131] In this condition, Eden's vanity and touchiness were gravely intensified by the fact that this notoriously 'impressionable' man was known to be 'very much under the influence of his admiring entourage at the FO'; a coterie of advisers and junior ministerial supporters like Lord Cranborne and J.P.L. Thomas whose contempt for Chamberlain was matched only by their lack of any political sense or acumen.[132] Yet for all of that, Eden's health and overwrought condition were not quite as significant a factor in his departure as the whips and unofficial government press briefings hoped to suggest.

Simon, Halifax and many others believed the roots of the crisis did 'not lie in any fundamental difference of policy, but largely in the contrast between the temperament and methods of Stanley Baldwin and Neville Chamberlain'. While the former left foreign affairs to Eden, it was obvious to everyone that Chamberlain tended to be 'much more clear-cut' in the manner in which he 'exercises the privilege of supervision and direction'.[133] It is certainly true that rumours that they were 'at cross-purposes' began to circulate as early as October 1937 and the circle around Eden were 'very fussed at intrigues ... against Anthony' regarding Halifax's visit to Berlin in November.[134] Yet such an explanation is not altogether convincing given the Prime Minister's repeated assertions that Eden was 'awfully good in accepting my suggestions without grumbling' and Eden's apparent acceptance of Chamberlain's ultimate authority to assume this role.[135] Indeed, in December Eden twice gave the Runcimans the strong impression that 'he found cooperation with [the] PM agreeable as well as useful to him' while in early January he was positively effusive about their 'partnership' when assuring Chamberlain that 'I do hope that you will never for an instant feel that any interest you take in Foreign Affairs, however close, could ever be resented by me.'[136]

Against this background, it appears that Eden resigned because both men understood more clearly than most that they really were separated by fundamental principle rather than method or *amour propre*. At the Saturday Cabinet, Chamberlain emphasised that 'the main issue was not one of principle ... but rather of method, timing and whether the present moment was opportune or not'. But given his absolutely unshakeable conviction that it was 'now or never ... if we were to avoid another Great War', both men recognised only too clearly that Eden's quibbles about timing and method did represent a fundamental challenge to everything Chamberlain hoped to achieve. Despite encouraging indications from Rome since July, Chamberlain felt that Eden had been given his chance to act and he had squandered it, at a time when he believed it was 'criminal' not to exploit 'one of those opportunities which came at rare intervals and did not recur'. Belatedly convinced that Eden's constant objections effectively precluded any negotiations with the dictators, on the evening before the Saturday Cabinet he told Simon that he was 'determined to tolerate no obstacle now' and that 'Anthony must yield or go.'[137]

Chamberlain knew that Eden's withdrawal would be 'a blow'.[138] But while he expected 'plenty of trouble ahead', he confessed to feeling 'as if a great load was off my mind'. He was also encouraged by the expressions of support received from the 'more serious quarters' of the diplomatic world and the 'general impression' at the Carlton Club that he was correct to pursue a 'realist' foreign policy because under Eden 'the right moment for beginning conversations would never have been reached'.[139] Some sympathisers even proposed that he should take the Foreign Office himself to 'put our foreign policy on right lines'.[140] In the Commons on the day after Eden and Cranborne (his Under-Secretary) resigned, 'the excitement was immense, and the lobbies buzzing', but Chamberlain soundly defeated his critics. The resignation statements were 'eloquent but too bitter' and many MPs shared Amery's view that Eden 'left the impression that there was really no issue to resign upon'. In contrast, Chamberlain was generally considered to have made a 'magnificent speech', which completely destroyed Eden's case and which some deemed to have been 'worthy of [his] father at his very best'.[141] During the censure debate next day, Chamberlain again defeated the 'fierce onslaught' from Churchill and Lloyd George with what Simon (and many others) regarded as 'the best speech I have ever heard from him – perfect in manner and disarming in frankness, but so powerful in argument that our case was completely established'; a personal satisfaction for Chamberlain maliciously intensified by his success in inflicting upon Lloyd George the 'worst humiliation of his life'.[142] Despite the troublesome conscience of Harry Crookshank and Robert Bernays who concluded they 'could not go on' as junior ministers, their anxieties were soon allayed at a private meeting with Chamberlain next day while Oliver Stanley and the other wavering 'lightweights' in the Cabinet almost immediately forgot their talk of resignation.[143]

After this, the crisis effectively subsided. Despite some recent suggestions that 'Eden's departure weakened the Chamberlain government's claim to speak for the nation', the short-term effects of the drama were relatively modest.[144] In early March, the opinion polls showed that 72–73 per cent of voters thought Eden was right to resign and almost the same proportion agreed with him, while only 25 per cent supported Chamberlain's policy. Cuthbert Headlam was thus probably correct in the view that Chamberlain was 'a bit too confident about having public opinion in this country on his side' because 'the floating Liberal vote, on which the National Govt depends, is heartily against the Italian agreement and that if we had a general election tomorrow we might be in the soup'.[145] But the reality was that Chamberlain had no need for a general election until November 1940 and he always recognised that his harsher partisan style alienated such voters.

At Westminster, far from harming Chamberlain, Eden's resignation probably consolidated his support in the parliamentary party. Despite one Conservative voting against the government and thirty abstaining in the censure debates following Eden's resignation, as Simon noted there had been 'an immense scaring over to the Prime Minister's side in all quarters where the vaguest idealism does not obscure realities. Above all, there is a feeling of relief that we have announced a *positive* policy.'[146] Even some supposedly committed Edenites, were reported to have 'completely altered their opinion' after Chamberlain's 'great victory' in the parliamentary debates, while the troublesome backbench Foreign Affairs Committee was soon reported to be 'enthusiastically pro-Neville' – particularly after the discreet withdrawal of the committee's pro-Edenite officials.[147] To consolidate party, press and electoral support, Ball ominously assured Chamberlain from the shadows that he had successfully 'taken certain steps privately, with a view to getting [his] point of view over to the whole country'.[148] It appeared that the Prime Minister had won the first round of the struggle. 'As long as Neville Chamberlain's strength lasts', Butler noted three weeks later, 'things will be alright.'[149]

Chapter 13

The Road to Munich, March–September 1938

'These dictators, so it seemed to him, must ... be reasonable men. They wanted certain concessions and there were certain concessions which Great Britain could afford to make. Therefore, the sooner he could get to grips with them the better. The motive was not dishonourable, the method was not unreasonable. His mistake was only that of the little boy who played with a wolf under the impression that it was a sheep – a pardonable zoological error, but apt to prove fatal to the player who makes it.'
Duff Cooper, 'Chamberlain: A Candid Portrait', n.d. [November 1939],
MRGN 1/5

Chamberlain's relief at the withdrawal of Eden was greatly enhanced by the obvious benefits to be obtained by installing Lord Halifax as his successor. In the shadowy world of diplomatic dealings with erratic dictators, Halifax possessed an unimpeachable reputation for integrity which commanded the highest esteem across the entire political spectrum. The archetypal aristocrat, who less typically of his class combined historic title and rolling acres with high intellectual capacity, Halifax's unblemished Christian conscience made him appear a 'saintly type' and 'a sort of Jesus in long boots'.[1] With Halifax at the Foreign Office, British policy thus seemed to be cloaked in an aura of respectability and unswerving moral purpose. There was also a deep personal sympathy between the two men. Since their first meeting in the early 1920s, Chamberlain had always felt 'more at home' with Halifax than any of his other colleagues. 'I miss you, my dear Edward, a great deal', Chamberlain wrote soon after Halifax became Viceroy of India in 1926. 'Somehow or another ... you are apt to leave a hole behind you which no one-else can quite fill, and ... I do wish very often that you were about to discuss things with.'[2] After his return to England in 1931, this friendship soon blossomed into a mutual respect and admiration of a sort which was never possible between Chamberlain and Eden. As Foreign Secretary, Halifax also started with the inestimable advantage that he fully endorsed all the main lines of Chamberlain's foreign policy. Little wonder that in the wake of the German Anschluss with Austria in March 1938, Chamberlain came to believe this tragedy might have been averted if Halifax had been Foreign Secretary earlier, or that when he wrestled with the Sudeten problem a few months later, he should have rejoiced at 'what a comfort he is to me & how thankful I am that I have not to deal with Anthony in these troubled times'.[3]

This remarkable harmony of policy, thinking and objective between Chamberlain and Halifax was partially assisted by a fortunate 'lack of "heresy hunting" in the Foreign Secretary' which made it easy for him to see 'eye to eye with the P.M.'.[4] It is also true that with Halifax confined to the House of Lords, Chamberlain relished the opportunity to be his own foreign policy spokesman in the Commons. But for all that, the lack of friction between the two men was founded principally upon a genuine convergence of view rather than sycophantic deference or Halifax's thick-skinned indifference to Prime Ministerial interference. Until Munich, this consensus over foreign policy was almost total – but even after it, Halifax's Under-Secretary, 'Rab' Butler, still argued (rather too optimistically) that 'any difference of opinion between the Foreign Office and No. 10 has been so considerably reduced as to be almost imperceptible. There remain the differences of character between the two principal personalities concerned, but barely any difference in design.'[5] Although the lesson of Chamberlain's recent clash with Eden was that he expected loyalty and ultimately subservience now that he was Prime Minister, Chamberlain valued genuine agreement even more highly and in this respect he regarded Halifax as an ideal appointment.

Halifax was equally valuable because he filled a yawning gap in the circle of support around Chamberlain. Since coming to the Premiership, Chamberlain had assembled around him a group of trusted advisers who all passionately shared his vision and priorities. Sir Horace Wilson was nominally the government's chief industrial adviser but everyone recognised that he was 'the Burleigh of the present age'; the *eminence grise* of the Chamberlain regime who operated from a small office immediately outside the Prime Minister's room at Downing Street and who served as gatekeeper, fixer and trusted sounding board because Chamberlain believed he was 'one of that very rare company of Civil Servants who have also a political sense'. He was equally rare in becoming one of his few personal friends. 'He is the most remarkable man in England', Chamberlain told the art historian Kenneth Clark. 'I couldn't live a day without him.'[6] Lord Dunglass, the future Alec Douglas Home and Chamberlain's PPS since 1935, was also a trusted aide and adviser whose devotion and influence were believed by insiders to be second only to that of Horace Wilson.[7] Similarly, the 35-year-old pro-appeasement 'Rab' Butler worked closely with Chamberlain in the Commons where his blandly emollient parliamentary style when handling routine Foreign Office business proved a perfect complement to Chamberlain's naturally more abrasive manner. In his turn, Butler also gradually acquired Chamberlain's confidence – and with it the status of being 'the P.M.s "blue eyed boy"'.[8] Yet, with the exception of Horace Wilson, it was clear even to outside observers that what Chamberlain lacked as Prime Minister was 'a confidential friend to talk things over with'.[9] Despite substantial differences in background and personality, in an important sense Halifax filled this gap. The arrival of a genuine ally and equal, capable of championing his policy and sharing the burden, represented a welcome relief at a time when it was already widely acknowledged that the 'Government's weakness is in putting too much onto the Prime Minister.'[10]

Chamberlain was undoubtedly in need of support and encouragement in the early months of 1938. Although 'most anxious' to build on Halifax's visit to Germany, he had few opportunities until he had 'a "scintillation" on the subject of German negotiations' towards the end of January. In the view of its author, this plan represented 'the opening of an entirely new chapter in the history of African colonial development'. Germany would obtain colonial concessions in central Africa on a 'broad and liberal basis' as part of an international consortium, in return for a 'substantial measure' of air disarmament and a satisfactory resolution of the Czech problem.[11] Before Sir Nevile Henderson could present the plan to Hitler, however, it was thwarted by the sudden dismissal of the German Foreign Minister, the professional diplomat, Konstantin von Neurath. Appointed in his place was the pompous and spitefully overbearing Nazi extremist, Joachim von Ribbentrop; a figure widely despised in London as 'a lightweight, impulsive, not dependable, and anything but favourably inclined towards Great Britain'.[12] As Chamberlain had formed 'a most unfavourable opinion' of Ribbentrop when Ambassador to London, after the shock of his promotion Chamberlain confessed he felt 'all at sea again' about the best method of approach towards the German problem.[13]

Henderson had been in Berlin for a month before he eventually got the opportunity to put Chamberlain's proposed settlement to Hitler on 3 March. When he did so, the German Chancellor maintained 'the most ferocious scowl on his face' as he cursorily dismissed all of Chamberlain's ideas. He then went on to warn that 'Germany would not allow third parties to interfere in the settlement of her relationship with countries of the same nationality or countries with large German populations' and that 'if in Austria or in Czechoslovakia internal explosions took place, Germany would ... act like lightning'.[14] Given increasing indications of German ambitions to absorb Austria, Chamberlain gloomily acknowledged that Britain could do nothing except hope that this would be accomplished without violence, because the ensuing public outcry would jeopardise progress towards any lasting Anglo-German agreement. In the event, when the Austrian Chancellor announced a plebiscite to resist German pressure for an Anschluss on 9 March, Hitler was compelled to launch a pre-emptive invasion to preserve his own prestige. Despite British pleas to Ribbentrop (ironically at a farewell lunch at Downing Street when the news came through), Chamberlain lamented that he was 'always overcome by a feeling of helplessness' when talking to the new German Foreign Minister because he was 'so stupid, so shallow, so self centred and self satisfied, so totally devoid of intellectual capacity that he never seems to take in what is said to him'.[15] Two days later Germany occupied Austria.

It has been argued that the Anschluss with Austria was 'a defining moment for the Third Reich', not least as the first step towards the realisation of Hitler's dream for 'the merger of all Germans ... in a Greater Germany'.[16] Yet for Chamberlain, Austria was not a defining moment. As the overwhelming majority of Austrians provided a rousing welcome to invading German troops, he laid part of the blame on Chancellor Schuschnigg for his provocative action in calling a plebiscite without ever apparently reflecting on his defensive reasons for doing so. More important, while Chamberlain deplored the Anschluss as a 'typical illustration of power politics', the underlying objective fitted comfortably within what he regarded as the tolerable limits of German revisionism. But for all that, Hitler's distasteful methods apparently reinforced his burgeoning conviction that rearmament and defensive alliances were an essential concomitant to effective appeasement:

> It is perfectly evident surely now that force is the only argument Germany understands and that 'collective security' cannot offer any prospect of preventing such events until it can show a visible force of overwhelming strength backed by the determination to use it. And if that is so is it now obvious that such force and determination are most effectively mobilised by alliances which don't require meetings at Geneva and resolutions by dozens of small nations who have no responsibilities? Heaven knows I don't want to get back to alliances but if Germany continues to behave as she has done lately she may drive us to it.

In the hope of avoiding a similar violent coup against Czechoslovakia, Chamberlain resolved that they needed to 'show our determination not to be bullied by announcing some increase or acceleration in rearmament' while 'quietly & steadily pursu[ing] our conversations with Italy'.[17]

Yet despite the resort to bluster and stiff language, Chamberlain was simply whistling in the dark in order to sustain his spirits. Above all, his proposition that force was the only argument Hitler understood was more a knee-jerk reaction borne of frustration than an indication of a new hardening in his attitude. Angry words and actions were thus not intended as a prelude to a termination of negotiations. On the contrary, they were designed to serve as a warning to force Hitler to come to his senses. As a result, the 'severest condemnation' of German aggression and the promise to accelerate air rearmament formed the central themes of the Prime Minister's 'very restrained matter of fact' Commons statement on 14 March.[18] A week later he met the TUC for the first time to appeal for their goodwill and the concessions necessary to accelerate the defence programme.[19]

Inevitably there were times when the concatenation of troubles confronting the Prime Minister temporarily dashed his spirits. In mid-March he briefly experienced such a crisis after a 'grim week' in which intense criticism and internecine plots compounded his anxieties over the troubled state of Europe. 'In face of such problems', he complained angrily, 'to be badgered and pressed to come out and give a clear, decided, bold, unmistakable lead, show "ordinary courage" and all the rest of the twaddle is calculated to vex the man who has to take the responsibility for the consequences.'[20] In part, this outburst was provoked by rumours of an anti-Chamberlain intrigue involving Churchill,

Boothby and Hore-Belisha, but this soon evaporated amidst vigorous denials from all those implicated.[21] But he was already nettled by Churchill's triumphant speech in the Austria debate on 14 March, in which he had glibly advocated a 'Grand Alliance' of states assembled by Britain and France into a mutual defence pact based on the Covenant of the League of Nations. Chamberlain unquestionably had no time for this idea, but the criticism from Churchill and later historians that he was so blinkered in his opposition that he refused to take proper advice on its merits is unfounded.[22] Indeed, Chamberlain had already considered Churchill's notion of a 'Grand Alliance' on the previous weekend and consulted Halifax, the Foreign Office and the Chiefs of Staff and only then did he conclude that it was devoid of either substance or value as a guarantee of future security.

> It is a very attractive idea; indeed there is almost everything to be said for it until you come to examine its practicability. From that moment its attraction vanishes. You have only to look at the map to see that nothing that France or we could do could possibly save Czecho-Slovakia from being over-run by the Germans if they wanted to do it. ... Therefore we could not help Czecho-Slovakia – she would be simply a pretext for going to war with Germany. That we could not think of unless we had a reasonable prospect of being able to beat her to her knees in a reasonable time and of that I see no sign. I have therefore abandoned any idea of giving guarantees to Czecho-Slovakia or to France in connection with her obligations to that country.[23]

This succinct *Realpolitik* exposition of the European situation explains much about Chamberlain's diplomacy in the months leading up to Munich – particularly given his conviction that France was in a 'hopeless position' and the Americans would never intervene in Europe.[24] It also stands as a persuasive rebuttal to 'counter-revisionist' arguments that 'Chamberlain consciously chose "appeasement" ... because he thought it correct and ... was not the mere puppet of circumstantial constraints.'[25] For Chamberlain, as for the British Minister in Prague, the head of the Foreign Office's Central Department and the Chiefs of Staff, the abiding reality was brutally simple. Was Britain prepared to threaten Germany with force on behalf of a state to which it had no formal treaty obligations, which it certainly could not save and which would probably never be resurrected in its existing form – but with the absolute certainty that any attempt to do so would provoke a ruinous and probably unwinnable war which would soon bring in Japan and Italy, destroy the British Empire, squander its wealth and undermine its position as a Great Power. In this context, notwithstanding retrospective wisdom about the insatiable nature of Hitler's ambitions, it should not be forgotten that Chamberlain's dismal prediction about the cost and dangers of war for Britain proved only too accurate.

Against this background, it is not difficult to understand why the Austrian Anschluss did nothing to shake Chamberlain's confidence in his chosen strategy. As he told the Cabinet's Foreign Policy Committee on 15 March, he 'did not think anything that had happened should cause the government to alter their present policy, on the contrary, recent events had confirmed him in the opinion that the policy was the right one and he only regretted that it had not been adopted earlier'. In the absence of any practicable alternative, Britain should ascertain the precise extent of Hitler's demands on the Sudetenland and if these proved reasonable it should urge the Czechs to make concessions in return for German guarantees that it had no further territorial demands. In the interim, Chamberlain and Halifax concluded the best method of exerting British influence and maintaining peace was to revive 'the "guessing Position" ... under which Germany could never be sure that H.M.G. would not intervene in Central Europe and the French could never be sure we *would* – thereby discouraging both from forward policies'. When they expounded this position to the Foreign Policy Committee on 18 March only Hoare and Stanley expressed any support for a new commitment to France.[26] Four days later, the Cabinet also agreed to the Prime Minister's policy, but this time Chamberlain's case was crucially strengthened by the pessimistic conclusion of Chiefs of Staff that 'no pressure which this country and its possible allies could exercise would suffice to prevent the defeat of Czechoslovakia'. Powerfully supported by this expert assessment, Chamberlain thus told the Cabinet that 'he was not in a position to recommend a policy involving the risk of war' over the Sudetenland.[27]

The counter-revisionist claim that the Chiefs of Staff report 'provided a justification, not an explanation, for their actions',[28] gravely understates the degree to which such fears were *the* constant implicit factor narrowing the parameters within which any practicable policy was formulated. Similarly, the more general criticism that 'many of the "constraints" [under which Chamberlain believed he was acting] seemed to have been the product of flawed perceptions of the objective situation',[29] conveniently ignores the fact that (without the wisdom of hindsight) what now appear to be 'flawed perceptions' were at the time Neville Chamberlain's hideous 'objective reality'. Such views may well have been a reflection of an endemic and excessive pessimism within Whitehall since 1935 about the military balance between the Powers, but there is no doubt that Chamberlain's apprehensions were genuine or that they were widely shared. As Halifax noted of the Chiefs of Staff report, it was 'an extremely melancholy document, but no government could afford to overlook it'. Certainly when briefing Churchill next day on his forthcoming policy declaration, Chamberlain emphasised the military aspect of the problem as the 'considerations which had weighed most heavily with me'.[30] They had an equally dramatic effect on Cabinet ministers. As Malcolm MacDonald, the Dominion Secretary, impressed upon Harold Nicolson a week after this Cabinet discussion:

> We are really not strong enough to risk a war. It would mean the massacre of women and children in the streets of London. No Government could possibly risk a war when our anti-aircraft defences are in so farcical a condition. Even if the Germans exploit our present weakness in order to achieve an even

stronger position against us, we must take the risk ... All we can do is by wise retreat and good diplomacy to diminish the dangers being arrayed against us. The Cabinet knows full well that we are shirking great responsibility. But they cannot undertake such responsibility.

As Chamberlain later told the Cabinet, it 'made his blood boil to see Germany getting away with it time after time', but 'sentimental considerations were dangerous' given the relative military weakness of the Western Powers.[31]

Chamberlain's Commons statement on the basis of British foreign policy on 24 March reaffirmed the obligation to defend France and Belgium against 'unprovoked aggression' but did not list Czechoslovakia among British commitments. Nevertheless, he did warn that 'where peace and war are concerned, legal obligations are not alone involved, and, if war broke out, it would be unlikely to be confined to those who have assumed such obligations'. Beneath the firmer tone, this was the apotheosis of the 'guessing position'. Given the recognition of 'an underlying [public] resentment at the idea of constantly having to knuckle under to the dictators for lack of sufficient strength', an acceleration in aircraft production was announced along with a new commitment to 'full priority for rearmament work' to reinforce the central theme of Chamberlain's speech; 'By reason if possible – by force if not.'[32] For Chamberlain and his circle, the speech was 'an éclatant success' which did much to bolster the government's prestige after the blows inflicted by Eden's resignation and the Anschluss. He was particularly gratified by Henderson's report from Berlin that its message was 'taken to heart everywhere, here no less than in France or Czecho-Sl[ovakia]'. Despite prior warnings from 'weak kneed colleagues' like Oliver Stanley and Earl De La Warr, the National Labour Lord Privy Seal, that this policy would provoke a revolt of 50 or 60 government backbenchers, the debate ended without even a vote and with the party solidly behind its leader.[33] Constituency activists were equally supportive, while the polls showed only a third of voters in favour of a commitment to Czechoslovakia.[34]

II

As in the past, signs of intractability and belligerence from one dictator merely reinforced the perceived desirability of improving relations with the other one – particularly as it was suspected that 'Signor Mussolini was annoyed with the Germans' over Austria.[35] Given both Chamberlain's belief that it would be 'most unfortunate if conversations with the Italians were unduly prolonged' and Mussolini's own desire for progress before Chamberlain was overwhelmed by his opponents, the long-planned Anglo-Italian agreement was finally signed on 16 April – but on condition that it would only come into force once a substantial number of Italian 'volunteers' had been withdrawn from Spain.[36] For those close to Chamberlain, the Anglo-Italian Agreement was a very personal triumph and a significant step towards 'a very definite appeasement of international tension'.[37]

Even the ancient problem of Anglo-Irish relations appeared to be amenable to the Prime Minister's personal touch during the spring of 1938 – and here too the central theme of his policy was 'appeasement' over details in pursuit of a general settlement and enduring goodwill. Anglo-Irish relations had deteriorated rapidly after 1932 as the new government of Eamon de Valera sought to overthrow the remaining links with Britain. These efforts almost immediately provoked a full-scale 'economic war' and tensions soon extended to political, constitutional and defence questions. Despite this increasing estrangement, however, by 1936 both sides were ready for a settlement. After tentative talks with de Valera in May, the Dominion Secretary urged an early agreement in view of the harm the dispute was causing to imperial unity in a dangerous international situation; an argument which soon persuaded Chamberlain to abandon his initially uncompromising stance towards Ireland and to throw his weight decisively behind a settlement.

By the time that de Valera revived the idea of negotiations in November 1937, the combination of increasing fears about the state of Europe and American pressure had substantially reinforced Chamberlain's determination to settle the issue once and for all. As he told the Irish Situation Committee in mid-December 1937: 'Even an agreement which fell short of being completely satisfactory would be better than the insecurity of the present situation.'[38] When negotiations began a month later, Chamberlain anticipated 'a toughish job to bring off any satisfactory sort of agreement', but the first round of talks progressed remarkably amicably and Chamberlain was confident that they would eventually obtain a settlement on everything except partition – although significantly even here he did 'not despair of ultimate agreement'. 'It *would* be another strange chapter in our family history', he confided in his sisters in January 1938, 'if it fell to me to "settle the Irish Question" after the long & repeated efforts made by Father and Austen.'[39]

As Chamberlain anticipated, de Valera and his colleagues proved 'extremely hard bargainers' with regard to all the outstanding disputes over trade, finance and defence.[40] Indeed, by late February he was obliged to protest to de Valera that he had 'presented United Kingdom ministers with a three-leafed shamrock, none of the leaves of which had any advantages for the UK'. Without some concessions he pleaded, it would be 'extremely difficult' to justify any agreement to already disgruntled supporters in Parliament and the constituencies. In the event, however, when negotiations appeared deadlocked in mid-March, Chamberlain intervened with a generous final offer to de Valera. Despite concerns on both sides that their respective supporters would not accept the final agreements, Chamberlain was satisfied that he had 'only given up the small things ... for the big things – the ending of a long quarrel, the beginning of better relations between North & South Ireland, and the cooperation of the South with us in trade and defence'.[41] The three agreements signed on 25 April 1938 marked a historic conclusion to the seemingly intractable conflict between the United Kingdom and its Irish neighbour.

In his search for a successful outcome of these Anglo-Irish discussions, Chamberlain always hoped to convey a far broader lesson to Germany about Britain's willingness to negotiate and to accept promises on trust in order to achieve a general settlement of fundamental disputes. As a depressing foretaste of his personal negotiations with Hitler over the Sudetenland six months later, Chamberlain thus assured the Irish Situation Committee on 1 March that 'the best way with Mr de Valera would be to put him on his honour. He would be not only as good but better than his word.' Chamberlain's spirit of enlightened self-interest was most evident with regard to the contentious decision finally to relinquish control over Britain's naval bases at the three 'reserved ports' in Eire to which access was guaranteed by the 1921 Irish Treaty. While Chamberlain had stressed the 'very great importance' he attached to British access to these ports in wartime, he was also prepared to waive insistence upon formal guarantees on the grounds that 'the most valuable part of our agreements with Eire would not be found in black and white. It would consist in what was written between the lines. The great gain would be that the attitude and atmosphere in Eire would be altered. Our trust would be justified by results.'[42]

To relinquish full control over these vital treaty ports at a time when war with Germany seemed imminent was, at best, a calculated gamble and Churchill was not alone in denouncing the threat to Britain's security posed by the loss of these 'sentinel towers of the western approaches'. Yet Chamberlain was confident that his faith would be rewarded. As he told his sisters after the agreements were signed: 'The really important thing is to have a friendly Ireland which we should not have got if we had retained our treaty rights. And in that case they would have been of little use to us for in order to assure them in time of war we should have had to send two divisions over to Ireland to protect them from the hinterland and we haven't got two divisions to spare.' Equally important, he hoped the same magnanimous gesture would drive home the broader lesson to Hitler that even the most acrimonious disputes were capable of resolution given 'a spirit of accommodation and goodwill on both sides'. As he told the Commons on 5 May, a 'general settlement' justified generous concessions to Eire in a manner in which more limited agreements did not.[43]

Unfortunately, Chamberlain's confidence in de Valera's word and goodwill was as misplaced as that which he later bestowed in Hitler. When the war broke out in September 1939, de Valera immediately upheld Irish neutrality and Britain was denied access to the treaty ports to its very considerable detriment during the Battle of the Atlantic. In retrospect, it is perhaps equally tragic that the apparent success of the Irish negotiations reinforced Chamberlain's faith in the critical value of personal summitry and his own persuasive power as a negotiator. As de Valera regularly assured him, agreement had only been possible because of the personal relationship of trust and confidence which Chamberlain had established between them. There was much truth in this view, but by renewing his confidence in 'the Chamberlain touch' such an experience fuelled the overweening sense of hubris which led directly to the Munich conference five months later.

III

Apparently flushed with success, Chamberlain reached the Easter recess in confident and cheerful mood. Despite the reservations of a few ministerial colleagues, he remained firmly in control of the Cabinet and any differences which did exist were attributed to an over-sensitivity to parliamentary and constituency opinion. As for the House of Commons, even Chamberlain's enemies conceded that vocal displays of loyalty from backbenchers suggested he had 'got the confidence of our people as S.B. never had it'. Moreover, despite Central Office concern about waning electoral support after the loss of the West Fulham by-election in April, Chamberlain was equally convinced by a flood of enthusiastic reports that if there was an election 'we should romp in'. Indeed, Chamberlain flattered himself into believing that there was general approval across Europe and all of the Americas for his 'realistic and courageous policy' and his dominating influence upon international affairs.[44]

On the domestic front, during the spring of 1938, Chamberlain also began to enjoy the full fruits of his position as Prime Minister. After eleven months of extensive reconstruction and refurbishment, the Chamberlains finally moved into a modernised and more comfortable No. 10 Downing Street in late April.[45] Yet it was at Chequers that Chamberlain found his true spiritual home and it became one of the most enduring delights of his Premiership. Although on his first visit he concluded that they would spend less time there than Baldwin, it soon became the invariable weekend retreat from the burdens of office. 'I can't tell you what a joy & relief it is to get down here', he wrote in March 1938, 'even 24 hours just makes all the difference.'[46] But, as his father's son, Chamberlain was never content simply to enjoy Chequers in a purely passive sense. He also wanted positively to improve it for future generations as well as for his own edification. New trees and shrubs were ordered at his personal expense and when the trustees refused permission to plant a grand new avenue of trees, Chamberlain revenged himself by planting two groups of elms and a thicket of thorns and gorse before proceeding to set back the railings along the drive to make 'an enormous improvement in the dignity of the approach'. As his wife noted after his death, 'he seemed to gain fresh strength of spirit and purpose from Chequers and the long walks over the Downs and through the bluebell woods. He often said he did not know what he would have done without Chequers.'[47]

Unfortunately, while the sun always appeared to shine on the Prime Minister at Chequers, during the late spring of 1938 the storm clouds were gathering at Westminster. Chamberlain loyalists believed the problem was 'encouraged by a desire on the part of the Opposition to make us all out as Fascists', but even they recognised the unfortunate effects of Chamberlain's abrasive manner. 'He does not like vague and polite phrases but wishes to go straight at the Opposition', Butler noted in March. 'The tradition of soothing Members by such phrases as "the honourable and gallant member will be aware" are usually erased.'[48] As his Commons understudy, Butler inevitably tended to be charitable in his interpretation, but Chamberlain's critics preferred to talk of 'a return to class warfare in its bitterest form' and even Baldwin began venting his 'fury at what Neville C. had done' by prejudicing all his work 'in keeping politics national instead of party'.[49] Above all, what worried Baldwin was the 'growth of the impression that the govt is swinging to the right' in tone and composition. 'In the House the P.M. is supreme', Baldwin conceded in a shrewd assessment of Chamberlain's strengths and weaknesses. 'He is a far better debater than I: he hits his opponents hard and our backbenches are enthusiastic. All good as far as it goes. But the Labour fellows say "We are back to the Party Dog fight ... And there never can be a national foreign policy as long as he is there".'[50]

Chamberlain would have regarded such complaints as a tribute to his own effectiveness, but many close to him shared Baldwin's concerns. Aware of the 'harm which the PM is doing by hitting up the opposition', Halifax appealed for parliamentary cooperation in a speech in mid-May, while the party chairman was forced to acknowledge that Chamberlain's 'outspokenness and precision had probably frightened the rather weak-kneed Liberals who felt safe with S.B.'. Yet Chamberlain remained unrepentant and unperturbed, declaring characteristically that 'I can't change my nature and I must hope to make up for Liberal defection by greater enthusiasm in our own party.'[51] In such circumstances, it was only natural that some yearned for the less confrontational days of Baldwin and a 'broader Government with more idealism and less brutal clarity'.[52]

To make matters worse, during this temporary wobble in confidence, Chamberlain found himself embroiled in a Cabinet reconstruction he had not planned and which briefly threatened to do him some harm. Despite his lavish defence of Lord Swinton's achievements at the Air Ministry in December 1937 and again in March 1938, the press and parliamentary campaign against the slow progress of air rearmament and the overbearing attitude of the Ministry reached a climax on 12 May. In the Lords, Swinton competently defended his department, but in the Commons Winterton performed so poorly during a stormy debate that Chamberlain conceded it was his 'worst day in the House' since becoming Prime Minister and the fact that only 229 government supporters bothered to vote suggests a major abstention in protest.[53]

Chamberlain was already acutely aware of party discontents about air defence after his own difficult meeting with the 1922 Committee a few days earlier. Confronted now by Labour demands for another debate on the subject, he acted decisively to distance himself from the problem – despite the fact that during March and April he had vigorously opposed Swinton's plans to expand the aircraft production programme. While conceding that Swinton had 'done wonders for the Air Force', therefore, Chamberlain conveniently concluded he was 'fighting a losing battle in trying to retain him'. For a department 'under such continuous bombardment', he told the King somewhat disingenuously, it was 'impossible to maintain its position with the head in another place' because the Commons 'simply would not have it'. As he was 'already in trouble with an excess of peers' in the Cabinet after the recent succession of Hartington and Ormsby-Gore to the peerage, he thus resolved to drop both Ormsby-Gore and Swinton.[54] In the former case, this created no obvious difficulty as Chamberlain had little respect for his judgement but Swinton's position was rather different. Swinton, the ennobled Philip Cunliffe-Lister, was one of Chamberlain's oldest and closest political friends and despite serious differences over policy in the past, he still so clearly belonged to Chamberlain's 'inner clique' that many felt that friendship alone would save him.[55] On the day after the disastrous air debate, however, Swinton was summoned to Downing Street and effectively told he must resign. Although offered the choice of several alternative positions, he declined and the replacement of the department's entire ministerial team was announced on 16 May along with news of Ormsby-Gore's unceremonious departure.[56]

At a personal level, Chamberlain knew that Swinton would accept the decision relatively stoically after his past assurances that 'if at any time you think my work is done, or my usefulness accomplished, or if for any reason your task wd be easier without me, I would go at once'.[57] As a result, when the reshuffle was announced, Halifax reported that Swinton had been 'as nice as could be about it all & about you'.[58] After this, the matter blew over so swiftly that the Chief Whip reported that he could not recall a reshuffle of such magnitude which had received such a good reception. In consequence, Chamberlain expected 'a steady improvement of our position', not least because the reshuffle would insulate him from demands for more radical reforms and because Kingsley Wood's appointment soon appeared to have 'greatly improved the atmosphere' at the Air Ministry.[59]

IV

The Czech problem represented a far more formidable challenge. The Treaty of Versailles had transferred three million German-speaking citizens of the Sudetenland from the defunct Austro-Hungarian Empire to the newly-created polyglot Czech State. To complicate the problem further, while this border area was vital to the Czech economy and defences, its German inhabitants inevitably looked to Berlin for protection against Czech rule and as the largest German minority outside the Reich their destiny represented an obvious focus for Nazi propaganda. After the Austrian Anschluss in March 1938, Chamberlain recognised the Czech problem would not go away and that given Hitler's declarations regarding racial unity, this impediment to a general European settlement needed to be neutralised. Although never an easy objective, in retrospect, it is clear that from the spring of 1938 it was all but impossible. As Ian Kershaw notes, this 'marked the phase in which Hitler's obsession with accomplishing his "mission" in his own lifetime started to overtake cold political calculation'. In late May, Hitler thus told his generals that he was 'utterly determined that Czechoslovakia should disappear from the map' and that the time was now ripe for action before the Western Powers were either rearmed or prepared to fight.[60]

At this time, however, Chamberlain was in no position to know (or even guess at) the degree to which Hitler's recklessness would lead him positively to welcome the prospect of war. On the contrary, he told the American Ambassador in early April that he foresaw no immediate difficulties over Czechoslovakia because after the Anschluss 'he likened Germany to a boa constrictor that had eaten a good deal and was trying to digest the meal before taking on anything else'.[61] In these circumstances, Chamberlain's plan remained unchanged. Britain must establish precisely what Hitler wanted and, if reasonable, would endeavour 'to get the Czechs to face up to realities & settle their minority problem'. Yet what this actually meant in practice was that the Western Powers should apply concerted pressure on the Czech government to force it to satisfy the Sudeten Germans at almost any cost – with the threat that they could expect no protection from Britain or France if they refused.[62]

In order to maximise the effectiveness of this strategy, Chamberlain needed to persuade the French that they should withhold support from Czechoslovakia rather than encourage resistance with promises to honour the Franco-Czech mutual assistance treaty of 1925. To this end, the new French Premier was invited to London for talks on 28–29 April. Although Chamberlain did not find Edouard Daladier as 'sympathetic' as Chautemps, he concluded shrewdly that he 'seems simple and straightforward, though not perhaps as strong as his reputation'.[63] He also respected Foreign Minister Bonnet as 'a typical Frenchman' with 'the logical precise mind that I find most congenial'.[64] What Chamberlain did not realise, however, was that the French completely shared his views on the need to put pressure on the Czechs to evade their treaty obligations – but that national honour demanded that they should blame perfidious Albion for the initiative. As a result, Daladier began the meeting by deviously presenting himself as an advocate of a 'determined policy' of resistance towards German demands until Chamberlain mobilised his schoolboy French over lunch and Daladier 'mellowed considerably'. When the meeting resumed, the French then swiftly agreed to Chamberlain's proposal that Britain should obtain a clear statement of German demands on Czechoslovakia, if necessary accompanied by a reminder of his declaration on 24 March that in the event of war Britain might well be drawn in to support France. Although this was precisely what the French wanted, Chamberlain regarded the outcome as a significant triumph for the strategy of restraining hostilities by keeping everyone 'guessing'. The French went away believing they had obtained a far larger commitment than the British intended to deliver, Berlin was 'highly suspicious' that the talks involved new military undertakings and Britain had avoided any new commitment to Czechoslovakia. Above all, Chamberlain rejoiced that as 'it is left to us alone to ask the Germans what they want in Czecho-Slovakia I am not without hope that we may get through without a fresh demonstration of force'.[65]

Such hopes proved depressingly short-lived. 'Those d—d Germans have spoiled another weekend for me' Chamberlain complained bitterly after reports of German troop concentrations on the Czech frontier forced his recall from a trout fishing expedition. On Saturday 21 May, in 'the now familiar atmosphere of a weekend crisis', Berlin was warned that they could not rely on Britain standing aside if France intervened, while the French were reminded that Britain's commitment to defend France from unprovoked attack did not imply joint action to preserve Czechoslovakia from German aggression.[66] In reality, the 'May crisis' was a chimera. There was no German plan for an invasion of Czechoslovakia and thus no retreat before British firmness. But this is not how it was perceived at the time. On the contrary, Chamberlain now appeared 'really ... a strong man' whose 'masterly' handling of the crisis was proclaimed as a success 'in doing the very thing Grey failed to do in 1914, namely make Germany realise the dangers of precipitate action'.[67] This was certainly how Chamberlain saw it. Convinced that only the threat of British intervention had deterred Hitler from his planned coup, he concluded 'the incident shows how utterly untrustworthy and dishonest the German Government is and it illuminates the difficulties in the way of the peacemaker'.[68]

Such an object lesson depressed Chamberlain and it eroded his faith in Hitler's goodwill, but it did nothing to shake his fundamental faith in his own unique ability to overcome the obstacles to a general settlement with Germany. 'These are the sort of days that make you feel inclined to say why should I go on in the face of criticism and discouragement' he complained to his sisters. 'But although I know the danger of thinking that one is indispensable, I do not see anyone to hand over to without undermining confidence ... and of course I know really that I must carry on and do my best till the end comes in some form or other.' Hitler was thus clearly not alone in allowing his sense of 'mission' to cloud his judgement during the spring of 1938. In a significant exposition of his own strengths and weaknesses as Prime Minister, Chamberlain confessed after a furious Labour attack on his policy in July that 'what enables me to come through such an ordeal successfully is the fact that I am completely convinced that the course I am taking is right and therefore cannot be influenced by the attacks of my critics'.[69] Depressed by a recent outbreak of gout and the stress of the Swinton resignation, however, he admitted the Czech crisis had been 'a plateful', but he supposed that everyone in his position had periods of depression 'when the orb of one's fate seems too vast ... But fortunately such moods don't last long and presently one shakes it all off & goes ahead again.'[70]

While Chamberlain continued to live in hope, the May crisis did at least prompt a marginal shift in the balance of his 'double policy', away from conciliation and towards rearmament and effective deterrence. As he noted on 22 May, 'the Germans who are bullies by nature are too conscious of their strength and our weakness and until we are as strong as they are we shall be kept in this state of chronic anxiety'.[71] To redress this balance of power, Chamberlain renewed his efforts to obtain trade union agreement to the de-skilling of production processes necessary to accelerate the rearmament programme. Despite the 'reserved and suspicious' appearance of the TUC at their first meeting in March, Chamberlain proclaimed their second meeting on 26 May 'a complete success', predicting confidently that 'We shall get their help all right.'[72] Unfortunately, this was a further demonstration of his confidence in the value of the 'personal touch' which was wholly unsubstantiated by subsequent events as the employers refused to discuss anything except the suspension of traditional labour practices, while union mistrust of both the employers and Chamberlain stiffened their determination to resist sectional sacrifices. Yet what is also clear from this episode is that Chamberlain lacked the political will to overcome these obstacles in order to win the vital support of organised labour. Within a month he had thus bowed to pressure from the employers for the government to withdraw from the industrial arena completely.[73] Indeed, such was his change of heart that press reports in February 1939 that he was engaged in 'a series of heart to heart talks' with the unions to understand their problems prompted the contemptuous retort that 'the humbug of such an idea sickens me'.[74]

A second and more successful demonstration of Britain's stiffening resolve was the announcement on 27 May of an Anglo-Turkish Guarantee accompanied by industrial and arms credits to prevent Turkey falling under German influence. The idea had originated in early May, when Halifax expounded his variant of the 'domino theory' of German expansion in South-Eastern Europe and the need to create a 'Balkan bloc' around Turkey to check German economic and political penetration in the area. Although he recognised that this 'involved a grave departure from precedent', Chamberlain was initially 'greatly impressed' by the argument. Indeed, while doubtful whether the Turkish credits would ever be repaid, he rated the strategic and diplomatic value of the deal so highly that he rebuffed Treasury opposition with the argument that 'once we had pushed financial orthodoxy away for political reasons we had better go the whole hog and make sure that we get all we were after'. Encouraged by reports from the British Ambassador in Turkey that the effect 'was "electric" and has practically put them in our pockets', Chamberlain even briefly supported Halifax in his desire to extend the policy to Greece.[75]

Despite these tentative steps towards an active strengthening of the British position in the wake of the 'May crisis', their significance for Chamberlain was strictly limited. No progress was made with the trade unions until after the outbreak of war in September 1939. Similarly, while Chamberlain's initial burst of enthusiasm for the Anglo-Turkish agreements signalled a modest shift towards containment and resistance in South East Europe, his consistent opposition to Halifax's efforts to extend the policy further ensured that it was operated on such a depressingly small scale as to be virtually worthless – although in fairness to Chamberlain, he was far from alone in believing that there was neither spare finance nor weapons to devote to such a venture.[76] But more important, these tentative steps were not accompanied by any fundamental sea-change in the general direction of Chamberlain's policy towards either Germany or Italy. In the latter case, he was convinced that the Anglo-Italian agreement in April had given the Rome-Berlin Axis 'a nasty jar', with the result that 'in our future Central and Eastern European policy we may hope for a good deal of quiet help from Italy'. Despite pessimistic reports from the Rome embassy, he was equally optimistic about Italian support in organising a truce in Spain, until Mussolini's disappointment that relations with Britain had not developed as he hoped turned him almost immediately towards Germany. After this, Chamberlain was in despair, partly because 'Musso [wa]s behaving like a spoiled child' and partly because there was nothing he could do to retaliate against renewed attacks on British shipping unless prepared for war with Franco – with the attendant risk of conflict with Italy and Germany which would 'cut right across [his] policy of general appeasement'.[77]

Chamberlain was less pessimistic about Czechoslovakia after his ostensibly successful intervention in the 'May crisis'. In a favourite phrase which would come back to haunt him in April 1940, he was 'disposed to think that [the Germans] have missed the bus and may never again have such a favourable chance of asserting their domination over Central & Eastern Europe'.[78] This assessment was reinforced by further evidence that internal economic stresses were curbing Hitler's policy of aggression and by 'the most binding assurance' of Germany's peaceful intentions and desire for British friendship delivered unofficially by Hitler's personal adjutant on 18 July. In reality, Fritz Wiedemann's visit to London was instigated by Goering, while Hitler was completely uninterested in both the mission and its outcome, but Chamberlain (like Cadogan) proclaimed the prospect of future negotiations with Goering in London as 'the most encouraging move from Berlin that I have heard of yet'.[79] Nevertheless, he also recognised that something needed to be done to alleviate tensions in central Europe. After taking the precaution of warning the German Ambassador in late July that no amount of provocation would justify the use of force to settle the Sudeten problem,[79] he also set aside his earlier reservations and announced that at Czech request Lord Runciman would head a mission to seek a solution to the Sudeten problem.[80]

V

'I am astonished ... at the way I stand the strain, for I don't get much let up', Chamberlain noted on the eve of the summer recess. Despite his relatively advanced age and the occasional recurrence of gout, he enjoyed remarkably good health, slept well and recovered swiftly from his daily strain after a weekend at Chequers. He was equally satisfied that the government's position was 'as strong and solid as ever' with both the economy and rearmament progressing satisfactorily. When he left for his holiday, therefore, he did so 'with a greater feeling of confidence in the future than ... for some time'. Unfortunately, after a day on the river at Lochmore, Chamberlain's sinuses became so inflamed that he spent most of the next day indoors, unable either to taste, smell or smoke his pipe.[81] When his sinusitis got no better and in much pain, he returned to London for expert treatment at precisely the moment when reports of a German test mobilisation apparently confirmed Vansittart's secret intelligence that Hitler was planning to attack Czechoslovakia between the end of September and mid-October. After much discussion, Hitler was eventually issued with a diplomatic note asking 'whether it is really necessary to run such grave and incalculable risks' when they jeopardised the peace of Europe. To reinforce the point, Simon's speech at Lanark on 27 August was carefully crafted 'to warn Hitler that if he uses force it may be impossible to localise the war'.[82]

This new threat of imminent German military action raised in an acute form the perennial policy dilemma – what did Hitler really want and how should Britain respond to these demands. On one hand, Vansittart reported a conversation on 18 August with Ewald von Kleist-Schmenzin, representing the anti-Hitler moderates in the Wehrmacht. Kleist warned that Hitler was 'an extremist' bent on war and he pressed for a definitive public declaration of British policy to dispel Hitler's misapprehension that the Western Powers would not fight. On the other hand, on the basis of his own well-placed sources, General Lord Hutchinson simultaneously confirmed Kleist's account of an imminent invasion of Czechoslovakia but counselled the need to approach Hitler 'and come to some understanding with him forthwith'. Confronted by 'a perfect barrage' of conflicting reports, the bulk of which supported the Kleist view, Chamberlain conveniently inclined towards 'the better and more optimistic forecast', while discounting 'a good deal' of Kleist's advice because he was 'violently anti-Hitler and ... extremely anxious to stir up his friends in Germany to make an attempt at [Hitler's] overthrow'; a decision based largely on the fact that it conformed with his own established preference for negotiation. Nevertheless, confessing to 'some feeling of uneasiness', Chamberlain was 'sufficiently impressed to be inclined to make some warning gesture' to Hitler before his speech to the Nazi Party rally at Nuremberg on 12 September.[83]

An emergency meeting of ministers debated their options on 30 August. Halifax began by conceding that if Hitler had decided on the use of force then the only effective deterrent would be the threat of retaliation, but he opposed this line on the grounds that it would be difficult to implement in practice, would divide public opinion and the Empire and might encourage further Czech prevarication. On the assumption that Hitler had not yet definitely decided on war, Halifax urged a continuation of the existing policy: 'first to keep Germany guessing as to our intentions, and secondly to do all we could to forward the success of the Runciman Mission'. If the policy failed, Halifax recognised they would be told that 'if only they had the courage of their convictions, they could have stopped the trouble', but he defiantly declared that such criticisms 'left him unmoved'. Chamberlain enthusiastically endorsed this 'full and masterly' statement, arguing (as he had so often in the past) that no democratic State 'ought to make a threat of war unless it was both ready to carry it out and prepared to do so'. Moreover, even if such declarations did deter aggression now, he warned that they might leave Hitler feeling 'thwarted' and thus only increase the future danger; an assessment reinforced by Henderson's contention that British threats only strengthened the extremists around Hitler. Contrary to the mythology of Prime Ministerial dictatorship, Chamberlain then asked all 18 ministers to express an opinion. It was a measure of the prevailing policy consensus that only Duff Cooper, De La Warr, Elliot and Winterton expressed any reservations – largely to the effect that Britain should intimate that it was considering force, in the mistaken belief that Hitler was bluffing; a potentially dangerous gamble of precisely the sort that Chamberlain was determined to avoid because of the disastrous consequences if their own bluff was itself called.[84] The meeting thus ended with 'unanimous' support for the Chamberlain and Halifax strategy of adhering to the policy outlined on 24 March and repeated by Simon at Lanark to the effect that they 'should try to keep Germany guessing as to our ultimate attitude'.[85]

After this meeting, Chamberlain was 'clearly very disturbed' and did 'not look at all well'. This was scarcely surprising. As he told the US Ambassador, Joseph Kennedy, 'he was very much afraid that they might be forced into [war] but he definitely would not go until he was absolutely forced to'. Although Chamberlain still appeared hopeful that conflict could be averted, according to Kennedy's assessment 'he regards war as about a fifty-fifty chance'.[86] Thereafter, Chamberlain felt 'the crisis atmosphere was unmistakably present' and it remained with him during his visit to Balmoral over the August Bank Holiday weekend. Despite one 'perfect day' on the moors, neither fishing, shooting nor the kindness of the Royal couple could dispel the cloud of anxiety which, he told Annie, 'hangs over me like a nightmare all the time'.[87] At the root of his anxieties was the recognition that everything hinged on Hitler's speech at Nuremberg on 12 September. 'Is it not positively horrible to think that the fate of hundreds of millions depends on one man and he is half mad', he confided to his sisters, 'I keep racking my brains to try & devise some means of averting a catastrophe if it should seem to be upon us. I thought of one so unconventional and daring that it rather took Halifax's breath away. But since Henderson thought it might save the situation at the 11th hour I haven't abandoned it though I hope all the time that it won't be necessary to try it.'[88]

The idea which had taken Halifax's breath away had been devised late one night in conversation with Horace Wilson in the study at No. 10. This involved Chamberlain flying to Germany to negotiate directly with Hitler if war seemed imminent. Code-named 'Plan Z' to signify that it would only come into operation at 'Zero hour', the idea was to be kept absolutely secret to obtain 'the full benefit of complete surprise and novelty'.[89] Contrary to the sneers of his critics that this represented either a humiliating obeisance by an ignorant amateur at the feet of a dictator, or that it was an arrogant attempt to seize the political limelight, John Charmley comes far closer to the truth when arguing that 'it was the conception of a brave man' acting from 'a deep and humane desire to leave no stone unturned to avoid war' and prepared to risk his personal reputation in order to do so.[90]

In the interim, uncertainty about the content of Hitler's Nuremberg speech inevitably reopened the debate as to whether to warn Hitler in advance of the possibility of war if Germany invaded Czechoslovakia. Despite increasing external pressure to 'stand up to Hitler', three fundamental considerations reinforced Chamberlain's instinctive opposition to explicit threats. First, as he argued on 30 August, threats may provoke a more extreme reaction which would only exacerbate the position. Despite Kleist's contrary appraisal, Chamberlain mistakenly continued to believe either that Hitler was himself a 'moderate' within the Nazi leadership or that 'moderates' were battling for this support. Either way, Britain should avoid doing anything which played into the hands of 'extremists' demanding a violent resolution of German grievances; a policy logic similar to that applied to the Japanese situation. Secondly, Chamberlain opposed public threats because his strategy of restraining both sides by keeping them 'guessing' as to British intentions depended upon enigmatic inscrutability. Once this had been surrendered, however, Chamberlain recognised that it would 'allow the most vital decision that my country could take, the decision as to peace or war, to pass out of our own hands into those of the ruler of another country and a lunatic at that'. Finally, he resisted pressure to 'stand up to Hitler' because of profound doubts about Britain's military capacity to do so decisively; a strategic assessment based on the expert view of the Chiefs of Staff, but fortified by direct comparisons with Canning's foreign policy 115 years earlier. 'Again and again Canning lays it down that you should never menace unless you are in a position to carry out your threats', he wrote to his sisters on the eve of Hitler's speech, 'and ... we are certainly not in a position in which our military advisers would feel happy in undertaking to begin hostilities if we were not forced to do so.'[91]

Chamberlain's preference for an unprovocative posture won majority support within his inner circle of foreign policy advisers. Halifax was 'very depressed and ... very much afraid HMG may yet run away and let the Czechs down', but on 10 September Chamberlain overruled his insistence on further warnings after Henderson advised that it would 'drive ... Hitler straight off the deep end' and provoke him to opt for war rather than diplomatic humiliation: a decision endorsed by the full Cabinet two days later.[92] That same afternoon, Chamberlain established an informal 'Inner Executive' to advise him during the crisis consisting of Simon, Hoare and Halifax (and assisted by Vansittart, Cadogan and Wilson).[93] Even at this juncture, Plan Z remained a closely guarded secret within the circle around Chamberlain, but all broadly approved with the exception of an overwrought Vansittart who 'fought the idea tooth and nail'. While Chamberlain was prepared to await developments, however, he was also increasingly anxious. Above all, he lamented that far from Britain keeping Hitler 'guessing', it now appeared to be the other way around.[94]

Chamberlain's apprehensions were well-founded. Throughout 1938, British policy had been based upon the erroneous assumption that the Sudeten Germans were not operating under German orders and that their demands could be resolved within the existing Czech state through a federal cantonal arrangement. Chamberlain also believed that Hitler was telling the truth when claiming this was essentially a racial issue about the defence of Sudeten Germans against Czech oppression and that if Germany could achieve her goals by peaceful methods 'there was no reason to suppose that she would reject such a procedure in favour of one based on violence'.[95] What he did not know, was that after the May crisis Hitler had declared his 'unalterable decision to smash Czechoslovakia by military action' by 1 October at the latest. Nor did he know that two months earlier Hitler had instructed Konrad Henlein, the leader of the Sudeten German Party, to make demands calculated to be unacceptable to the Czechs.[96] Indeed, it was not until 13 September that Runciman finally decided to withdraw because the now obvious connection between Henlein and Berlin had become 'the dominant factor in the situation' and it was 'not part of [his] function to attempt mediation between Czechoslovakia and Germany'.[97]

In the interim, Chamberlain believed the rising tension and anxiety in London was 'enough to send most people off their heads, if their heads were not as firmly screwed on as mine'. As Halifax told the American Ambassador, 'if they were doing business with a normal man they would have some idea of what might happen but they are doing business with a mad man'. Yet until the last minute, Chamberlain remained fairly confident that Hitler 'won't burn his boats' at Nuremberg. Indeed, even on the day after Hitler denounced the Czechs in terms which clearly foreshadowed armed intervention, Chamberlain optimistically informed the King that Plan Z was 'a last resort, only to be embarked upon if the situation is thought to be otherwise desperate'. In a postscript written later that evening, however, he announced that he would be meeting Hitler next day.[98]

What changed Chamberlain's mind on 13 September was less the gravity of the situation in Czechoslovakia than his fears about the consequences of French panic at having to honour their treaty obligations to the Czechs. It had been painfully obvious since their conference in April that 'the French didn't want to fight, were not fit to fight, and wouldn't fight'. But there were now reports that Bonnet was 'in a state of collapse', saying that 'France would accept any solution of the Czechoslovakian question that would avoid war.'[99] Aware the French were talking of a Three Power Conference to discuss the Sudeten problem, Chamberlain had refused to speak to Daladier when he telephoned earlier that day for fear this proposal would eclipse his own planned initiative. Later that evening, however, Chamberlain and his 'inner executive' agreed that the time had finally arrived to launch Plan Z – without consulting either the Cabinet or the French. Shortly before midnight, Chamberlain's message to Hitler proposed that he should 'come over at once to see you with a view to try and find a peaceful solution'.[100] Despite an anxious wait for the reply, Chamberlain remained confident that Hitler could not refuse to see him 'for fear of the psychological reaction throughout the world'. He also hoped his own action would 'demonstrate to the world that all efforts of his were bent upon preventing war'.[101] The circumstances were precisely as Chamberlain had envisaged to maximise the dramatic effect of his initiative. 'Two things were essential', he explained to his sisters, 'first that the plan should be tried just when things looked blackest, and second that it should be a complete surprise.' The impact was suitably electrifying.[102]

When Chamberlain unveiled the plan to the Cabinet on the morning of 14 September, it certainly did come as a 'complete surprise' to most but 'approval was unanimous and enthusiastic'. Although Lord Zetland spoke for many when he declared that it 'appealed to everyone as a stroke of genius', in private Cooper, Inskip, Stanley, Winterton and De La Warr were all somewhat apprehensive but they had been caught completely off-guard by this 'bombshell'.[103] 'We were neither pro-Czech nor pro-Sudeten German', Chamberlain declared. 'Our business was to keep the peace and find a just and equitable settlement.' What this meant in practice he explained during a lengthy opening statement. Although he feared Hitler might insist on a plebiscite, Chamberlain declared he would accept one if unavoidable. In return for lost defensive security, he was also prepared to countenance British involvement in an international guarantee to the remaining Czech state. At this stage, several ministers expressed concern at the idea of a plebiscite. Oliver Stanley urged delay before accepting this device because it 'would give Herr Hitler everything which he was demanding by force and would be a complete surrender'. While he agreed that the Prime Minister's plan was 'the only possibility', he also warned that 'we must be careful that it did not lead us further along the road to complete surrender': a view endorsed by De La Warr and 'Shakes' Morrison while Winterton and Hailsham opposed a plebiscite altogether and Duff Cooper insisted 'the choice is not between war and a plebiscite, but between war now and war later'. Although the Cabinet approved Chamberlain's visit, therefore, there was a clear consensus that great caution needed to be exercised over the terms of any transfer and that, ideally, the plebiscite should be delayed for five years. The meeting ended with Simon asking his colleagues 'to express their confidence and trust in the Prime Minister'. In reply, while 'much touched by the confidence placed in him', Chamberlain pledged 'he would do his very best in the light of the discussion'.[104]

Notwithstanding these concluding pleasantries, to all present it was clear that Chamberlain 'was going to have a difficult task in deciding how far he could go without committing the Cabinet too deeply in his anxiety to reach an agreement with Hitler'.[105] Yet Chamberlain remained undaunted. He believed he understood the risks and was prepared to accept them in a grimly pragmatic spirit. As he told Ambassador Kennedy immediately after the Cabinet, 'the trouble ... is that Hitler will be winning a victory without bloodshed and make the next crisis ... much easier for him to win out', but he pinned his hopes on persuading Hitler that they needed 'to formulate a settlement for world policy and that after all Czechoslovakia is a small incident in that big cause'. If this failed, Chamberlain reasoned, Britain could legitimately claim that it had tried everything to avert war and he could inform Hitler that Britain would fight alongside France.[106] That same evening as he prepared for his departure, Chamberlain read another depressing report from the Chiefs of Staff categorically reaffirming their view that no military pressure from the Western Powers could ever prevent Germany from over-running Czechoslovakia; that to try to do so would lead to an 'unlimited war' and that sooner or later Britain must suffer 500–600 tons of bombs a day for two months.[107] Chamberlain does not record whether he slept well after digesting this information.

VI

Early next morning, the British Prime Minister flew to Berlin accompanied only by Sir Horace Wilson and William Strang, head of the Foreign Office Central Department. Contrary to the universal myth that this was Chamberlain's first time aboard an aeroplane, he had taken a brief flight (complete with top hat) when escorting the Duke of York around an industrial fair at Birmingham in February 1923.[108] Yet such an experience scarcely compared with the dramatic spectacle of a 69-year-old Premier flying half way across Europe to salvage peace, in the world's first example of 'shuttle diplomacy'. Despite some 'slight sinkings' over London, Chamberlain enjoyed the flight, until forced to fly through storm clouds over Munich when the plane 'rocked and bumped like a ship in a sea' and there were more 'nervous moments' before a German plane guided them in to land. Greeted by Ribbentrop and a Nazi guard of honour on the runway, Chamberlain was delighted by the enthusiastic response of the crowds waiting in the rain as he drove to the station and at every level crossing on the way to Berchtesgaden, Hitler's mountain top retreat in the Bavarian Alps.

At the Brown House he met Hitler for the first time. Dressed in the familiar black trousers, khaki jacket with red swastika armband and Iron Cross, first impressions were less than favourable. As Chamberlain reported to his sisters, he found 'his expression rather disagreeable, especially in repose and altogether he looks entirely undistinguished. You would never notice him in a crowd & would take him for the house painter he once was.' In more forthright language he told the Cabinet on his return, that he was 'the commonest little dog he had ever seen', but he also confessed 'it was impossible not to be impressed with the power of the man'. During tea in the celebrated chamber with its vast picture window overlooking Salzburg, Hitler appeared shy and unrelaxed as his guest laboured at what passed for small talk. Hitler then abruptly turned to business. After ascertaining how Chamberlain wished to proceed, they went upstairs to Hitler's private room accompanied only by an interpreter for three hours of discussions.

> For the most part H. spoke quietly and in low tones. I did not see any trace of insanity but occasionally he became very excited and poured out his indignation against the Czechs in a torrent of words so that several times I had to stop him and ask that I might have a chance to hear what he was talking about. I soon saw that the situation was much more critical than I

had anticipated. I knew that his troops & tanks & guns & planes were ready to pounce and only awaiting his word and it was clear that rapid decisions must be taken if the situation was to be saved. At one point he seemed to be saying that he was going in at once so I became indignant saying that I did not see why he had allowed me to come all this way and that I was wasting my time. He quieted down then [and] said if I could assure him that the British Government accepted the principle of self determination (which he had not invented) he was prepared to discuss ways & means. I said I could give no such assurance without consultation. My personal opinion was that on principle I didn't care two hoots whether the Sudetens were in the Reich or out of it, according to their own wishes but I saw immense practical difficulties in a plebiscite. I could however break off our talk now, go back & hold my consultations & meet him again. That is a possible procedure, he said, ... Then I asked him how the situation was to be held in the meantime & he promised not to give the order to march unless some outrageous incident forced his hand.[109]

Chamberlain's critics feared this visit to Hitler meant 'the policy of appeasement had now become a policy of supplication' which 'in the end ... may boil down to one more surrender we shall be asked to call "peace"'.[110] Yet contrary to the mythology of an easily duped innocent out of his depth, Chamberlain had pondered deeply about this discussion over the preceding fortnight. As a result, from the two official accounts, it is clear that he acquitted himself more than competently in skilfully pinning Hitler down with forensic demands for precise exposition when the German leader resorted to calculated histrionics and threats. Hitler's claim that 'Germans were one' thus forced the admission that this did not apply to the Germans in Memel. When challenged on the argument that it was 'impossible that Czechoslovakia should remain like a spearhead in the side of Germany', he was also obliged to concede that he did not wish to 'dismember' the entire Czech State and that 'he was out for a racial unity and ... did not want a lot of Czechs'; a claim Chamberlain carefully repeated for confirmation. When Hitler attempted to deflect further 'academic' enquiries about the transfer of territory and populations by declaring he was 'prepared to risk a world war rather than allow this to drag on', Chamberlain angrily called his bluff. Similarly, when Hitler refused to issue a joint appeal for restraint on both sides during these negotiations, Chamberlain's calculated move to end the discussion forced Hitler to state his terms in a form which could be brought back for consultation with the British and French governments. Ultimately, it was a measure of Chamberlain's effectiveness that after it was all over, Hitler's boasting to his staff could not obscure the fact that he had evidently been unsettled by the experience and that for the first time he displayed signs of wavering.[111]

Although the meeting had scarcely gone exactly as Chamberlain planned or wished, he still returned to London relatively content with this first personal contact. He was particularly gratified by reports that Hitler had 'obviously been impressed by the Prime Minister', their mutual understanding, 'the directness with which he had talked and the rapidity with which he had grasped the essentials of the situation'. As Ribbentrop's personal secretary archly confided to Horace Wilson, 'Hitler told me he felt he was speaking to a *man*.'[112] Such flattery was cynically calculated to exploit Chamberlain's vanity and it more than succeeded. He thus came away from the meeting feeling that he had 'established a certain confidence which was my own and on my side in spite of the hardness & ruthlessness I thought I saw in his face I got the impression that here was a man who could be relied upon when he had given his word'.[113] Ultimately, this tragic misapprehension stemmed directly from Chamberlain's faith in the value of the 'personal touch' and it remained with him throughout the September crisis.

Yet for all that, in the short-term, Chamberlain believed his visit had purchased a valuable 'breathing space' in which to find a negotiated solution.[114] Back in London late on the afternoon of 16 September, Chamberlain told the 'inner executive' that it was 'impossible' to go to war to prevent immediate self-determination for Sudeten Germans because it was the only realistic outcome.[115] The following morning he and Runciman stressed the same points at an emergency Saturday Cabinet, at which ministers listened with 'breathless interest' as Chamberlain declared that Hitler was telling the truth and that his objectives were 'strictly limited'. When the Cabinet reassembled at 3pm for further discussion, Chamberlain's intentions were accepted in principle regarding both the fate of the Sudeten areas and the British guarantee for the revised Czech frontiers, although Inskip was not alone in the 'painful' impression that Chamberlain had been 'blackmailed' and browbeaten and that 'none of the elaborate schemes … which the Prime Minister had intended to put forward, had ever been mentioned'.[116]

Despite earlier rumours of 'many rumblings' among ministers about the dismemberment of Czechoslovakia and the role of the 'inner cabinet', there was little sign of determined, far less organised, Cabinet resistance. Only Duff Cooper, Stanley, Elliot, De La Warr and Winterton talked of 'complete surrender' or advised that 'if the choice … was between surrender and fighting, we ought to fight'. Nevertheless, while Chamberlain retorted sharply that the acceptance of self-determination was not synonymous with 'abject surrender', there was an emerging consensus that 'a settlement which looks like a surrender to force' would be unlikely to be acceptable to Parliament or the country.[117] But for all that, as Zetland concluded, 'while there was an intense dislike of our being driven to giving Hitler all that he was demanding, few if any would be willing to risk a general conflagration … to prevent the Sudeten Germans from exercising the right … to self-determination'.[118]

The French provided equally few obstacles to Chamberlain's plans. Belatedly summoned to London for consultations, Daladier and Bonnet met Chamberlain on Sunday 18 September. Even before their arrival it was clear that Chamberlain's 'confidence in the French becomes less and less', given their 'appalling' air defence and the wholly justified suspicion that 'the French do not want to fight and they will probably blame [the] whole thing on the British'.

In the event, these talks followed exactly the pattern established in April. During the morning session, an evidently strained Daladier postured with 'sad words' about Czechoslovakia and resistance, but it was painfully obvious that the French had 'their tongues out looking for some way to save themselves from war'.[119] After the usual coaxing over lunch, Chamberlain and the 'inner executive' withdrew to compose a bullying message to the Czech government proposing the transfer of areas with a majority of German inhabitants, in return for an international guarantee for the new frontiers. When the conference reassembled after dinner, Daladier then duly accepted the British draft with what Simon described as 'the greatest show of gratitude that I have ever seen in a spokesman of France'. This was scarcely surprising as it had rescued the French from a dishonourable position when they appeared 'at their wit's end' regarding their treaty obligations to the Czechs. After an 'exhausting day', when the meeting concluded after midnight in unanimity, Chamberlain inevitably felt more than satisfied with a crucial day's work.[120] As Hoare later congratulated him, Britain had got the decisions it wanted, but it 'could not be saddled with the major share of the responsibility'.[121]

On Monday 19 September, the full Cabinet were informed of the Anglo-French plan. In response to widespread alarm about the need for an international guarantee, Chamberlain confessed his own 'considerable misgivings'. But as he also pointed out, it was essential for French agreement, it related only to unprovoked aggression rather than the maintenance of existing frontiers and its main value would be in its deterrent effect. Of the earlier dissenters, Oliver Stanley's vague preference for 'a different policy' was demolished by Chamberlain's pointed query as to 'what policy was that?'; Walter Elliot was 'depressed and bewildered' (for by no means the last time), but he had no 'very clear view about what is to happen next', while Winterton talked feebly about 'fundamental differences' and even Duff Cooper supported self-determination because he found 'the prospect of war so appalling that ... postponement of the evil day was the right course'. As Hore-Belisha noted, 'Most of us disliked the idea, but in the end there didn't seem to be any alternative because of the time factor and we and the French have to be in agreement.'[122]

Having obtained Cabinet assent to the Anglo-French formula, which (unknown to ministers) had already been despatched to Prague, Chamberlain anticipated 'that with many bitter reproaches they will accept'. At this juncture he was full of quiet confidence. He recognised he would 'be charged with the rape of Czechoslovakia', but he also believed the only alternative was a probably unwinnable war and as he pragmatically informed the US Ambassador, he could 'see no rhyme nor reason in fighting for a cause which ... I would have to settle after it was over in about the same way I suggest settling it now'. Although there were still many anxious days ahead, he thus consoled himself with the thought that 'the most gnawing anxiety is gone' and that 'I have nothing to reproach myself with & that on the contrary up to now things are going the way I want'; a satisfaction bolstered by reports that he was now 'the most popular man in Germany'.[123]

Like all the best laid plans, this one soon began to unravel before the eyes of its architect. First, the Czechs did not meekly acquiesce in the proposed dismemberment of their country. Instead, it took two days of unrelentingly 'strong pressure' from British and French ministers to force them to accept. Secondly, at Cabinet on 21 September, anxious ministers succeeded in limiting Chamberlain's freedom of manoeuvre at the next stage of talks by obliging him to refer back to them if Hitler insisted on a parallel settlement for Polish and Hungarian minorities or if he refused to make concessions on either the inclusion of Russia as a joint guarantor or the need for the international boundary commission to report before the German occupation began.[124] Finally, what he did not realise was that the alacrity with which the Western Powers forced the Czechs to comply with German demands served only to convince Hitler that they had absolutely no intention of resistance; an assumption which encouraged him to become more intractable and bellicose in his determination to seize by force what he could have obtained by peaceful means.

On the morning of 22 September, Chamberlain departed in pessimistic mood for his second meeting with Hitler at Bad Godesberg. As one otherwise supportive minister noted, 'He must have been very conscious of the difficulty of the task which lay before him; for the impression left on his mind by the Cabinet discussion must have been that there was grave anxiety lest he commit himself and the country to too great an acquiescence in Hitler's demands.'[125] The Air Ministry's weather report promised 'generally good' conditions for the crossing.[126] Unfortunately, his meeting with Hitler was far less placid. Having coerced the Czechs into acceptance, Chamberlain expected Hitler to be prepared to negotiate an orderly transfer of territory – and even to be grateful to him. Instead, Chamberlain's proposals were brusquely swept aside with the reply 'that won't do any more'. Having reneged on the spirit of their previous agreement, Hitler's angry denunciation of the Czechs was followed by demands for a complete and final settlement by 1 October, 'one way or another, either by agreement or by force'. The occupation should begin on 28 September before a plebiscite and Polish and Hungarian territorial claims also needed to be met – both conditions which the Cabinet had specifically refused to accept.

From the official record it is clear that Chamberlain was devastated by Hitler's attitude and he protested vigorously:

> He had induced his colleagues, the French and Czechs, to agree to the principle of self-determination, in fact he had got exactly what the Fuhrer wanted and without the expenditure of a drop of German blood. In doing so, he had been obliged to take his political life into his hands … Today he was accused of selling the Czechs, yielding to dictators, capitulating, and so on. He had actually been booed on his departure today.

Chamberlain also candidly explained that while unmoved by criticism from the political left, 'his serious difficulties came from the people in his own Party' and public opinion, and he appealed to Hitler to 'help him to prove to his critics that they were wrong'. Fending off demands for a plebiscite, he also retorted that 'it was difficult to see why, if ... Hitler could obtain all that he wanted by peaceful means with complete certainty, he should elect to adopt a course which involved the loss of German lives and a certain element of risk.' Effectively deadlocked, after further desultory discussion Chamberlain adjourned to his hotel on the other side of the Rhine.[127]

As the quintessential rationalist, Chamberlain could barely even comprehend Hitler's logic in issuing his barely disguised ultimatum. Telephoning Halifax that evening he made it clear that Hitler's demand 'would not do', while Halifax replied that the 'great mass of public opinion seems to be hardening in [the] sense of feeling that we have gone to [the] limit of concession and that it is up to the Chancellor to make some contribution'. In the event, Chamberlain did not return for the arranged meeting next morning. Instead, 'to safeguard their own position', he wrote to Hitler stating that it was impossible to approve a plan which world opinion would denounce as 'an unnecessary display of force'. Hitler's lengthy reply did not go beyond what he said on the previous day, but two hours later Chamberlain offered to take Hitler's new demands to the Czechs if formulated into a memorandum.[128]

At their second meeting at 11pm, Hitler was in a much less truculent mood, but his memorandum contained precisely the same terms as those proposed previously. Moreover, when going through the document with Chamberlain, Hitler refused to moderate his demands, agreeing only to soften the language so that 'demands' became 'proposals' and to delay the date of occupation to 1 October. Despite the absurdly flattering assurance that he would only have made such concessions to Chamberlain, this was the limit of Hitler's compromise. The meeting ended somewhat astonishingly with Chamberlain expressing the view that 'a relationship of confidence had grown between himself and the Fuhrer' and that once the Czech crisis was resolved he hoped he would be able to discuss 'other problems still outstanding with the Fuhrer in a similar spirit'; an aspiration Hitler tantalisingly endorsed with the assurance that 'the Czech problem was the last territorial demand which he had to make in Europe'.[129]

Much fortified by these final words, on the morning of 24 September Chamberlain returned to London to confront his increasingly anxious and belligerent colleagues with 'the most agonising of all problems to solve'. As Simon encapsulated their dilemma: 'Was this only a difference of method, in which we must give way, or was it not a difference so fundamental as to merit resistance even to the point of war?' For his own part, Chamberlain had few doubts. As he told the inner executive and then the Cabinet later that day, as his plane flew up the Thames towards London, 'he had imagined a German bomber flying the same course. He had asked himself what degree of protection we could afford to the thousands of homes which he had seen stretched out below him, and he felt that we were in no position to justify waging a war today in order to prevent a war hereafter.'[130] After lunch with Halifax, Chamberlain assured the inner executive of Hitler's honesty and limited objectives, before contending there was 'not much difference' between Hitler's proposals and their own; an account which left Cadogan 'completely horrified' at his 'total surrender'. Yet for Chamberlain it was ultimately still a matter of priorities in pursuit of a supposedly greater good. As he told the inner executive, 'if we got this question out of the way without conflict it would be a turning point in Anglo-German relations' and for him 'that was the big thing of the present issue'; a view which at this stage was still warmly endorsed by Halifax.[131]

At Cabinet later that afternoon Chamberlain again outlined the situation in terms which reflected his undoubted sincerity, but his even greater weakness as a judge of Hitler and his motives. 'Herr Hitler had a narrow mind and was violently prejudiced on certain subjects', he told his colleagues 'but he would not deliberately deceive a man whom he respected and with whom he had been in negotiation.' On this basis, Chamberlain declared 'it would be a great tragedy' if they failed to obtain an understanding with Germany because it offered the hope of a peaceful settlement and 'a wonderful opportunity to put an end to the horrible nightmare of the present arms race'. Warning of the certainty of war and the destruction of the existing Czech state if they refused Hitler's terms, he also reminded ministers of British military inferiority. 'We must not lose sight of the fact that war today was a direct threat to every home in the country', he told them in terms which made it clear that Britain's anti-aircraft defences would provide greater security the longer that war was delayed. When he finished, an astonished Duff Cooper immediately leapt in to protest that the previous choice between war and dishonour was now joined by 'a third possibility, namely war with dishonour' – by which he meant 'being kicked into war by the boot of public opinion'. After this, Hore-Belisha, supported by Elliot, Stanley, De La Warr and Winterton, called for immediate mobilisation as the only method of showing Hitler that Britain really meant business. In this embattled state, at 7.30pm Chamberlain adjourned the Cabinet until next morning.[132]

When the Cabinet reassembled on the morning of Sunday 25 September, Chamberlain's defence of the German demand for immediate military occupation encountered resistance from a far more influential source. Until this point Halifax had wholeheartedly supported Chamberlain's view that 'a strong case' could be made for a transfer of territory and 'against which ... it would certainly have been impossible to justify a European war'.[133] At Cabinet on 25 September, however, Halifax crucially indicated that he was not sure whether 'their minds were still altogether at one'. The Godesberg terms, he tentatively suggested, required 'a new acceptance of principle' because 'it might be held that there was a distinction between orderly and disorderly transfer'. This dramatic *volte face* in Halifax's position had been prompted by Cadogan's stiff words on the previous evening which caused him a 'sleepless night' during which he concluded that resistance was the correct course.[134] Such a 'complete change of view' came as 'a horrible blow' to Chamberlain and he told Halifax as much in a note passed across the Cabinet table. While respecting Halifax's right to his own opinions, his warning that 'night conclusions' were seldom good ones was combined with a veiled threat to resign rather than allow Britain to be dragged into a war on French or Czech coat-tails.[135]

Unfortunately for Chamberlain, such arguments no longer appeared to convince Halifax or his other ministerial sceptics. When the Cabinet resumed after lunch, Chamberlain was evidently losing the initiative in a body which had always been far more collegial in its decision-making than Chamberlain's autocratic reputation ever suggested. Although he had varying degrees of support from Simon, Maugham, Stanhope, Zetland, Inskip, Brown, Morrison, MacDonald and Burgin, it was clear that Hoare and several others wanted immediate military conversations with France (and perhaps Russia) with assurances that if France intervened to defend Czechoslovakia the British would march with them. More important, it was now widely known that five or six ministers, led by Stanley, had declared that 'there must be no giving way again'.[136] Within this group of rebels, Walter Elliot was still depressed and bewildered but his backbone stiffened when De La Warr told him (and almost anyone else who would listen) that he would resign if Elliot did.[137] Winterton was 'truculent' but he was someone 'who nobody takes seriously'.[138] Above all, the tormented conscience of Duff Cooper could stand no more retreat now that the issue had become one of British honour rather than simply Sudeten self-determination – although his declaration that 'when great moral issues were at stake, there was no time to weigh one's strength too carefully' represented an emotional surrender to precisely the sort of quixotic sentimentality that Chamberlain was determined to prevent. Nevertheless, believing public opinion was moving in their direction, Duff Cooper persuaded Stanley that they should both resist. Even Hailsham supported Cooper's line because his son's by-election campaign at Oxford had impressed him with the scale of public opposition to 'surrender'.[139]

For Chamberlain, everything now hinged upon the French. To regain the policy initiative and restore his authority in Cabinet, he needed to cajole Daladier and Bonnet into an admission of military hopelessness to justify acquiescence in the Godesberg terms. He had grounds for optimism in this hope after a misleading telegram from the British Ambassador in Paris suggested that '[u]nless German aggression were so brutal, bloody and prolonged … as to infuriate French public opinion to the extent of making it lose its reason, war would be most unpopular in France'. Yet according to William Strang, the British inner executive meeting with Daladier and Bonnet at 9.15pm that evening was 'among the most painful which it has ever been my misfortune to attend'. Chamberlain began by aggressively demanding to know what the French intended to do in the event of a German invasion of Czechoslovakia. Daladier's evasive reply that they 'would do their duty', then provoked a detailed cross-examination as to their precise intentions, before Simon's forensic skills were deployed to put some brutally 'direct questions' to Daladier along the same lines. Clearly nettled by this interrogation, Daladier repeated that 'each of us would have to do his duty' but that he could not return to France 'having agreed to the strangulation of a people'.[140] Unfortunately for

Chamberlain, the French had finally reached their sticking point. It would no longer be sufficient to blame perfidious Albion for unacceptable concessions because national honour was at stake and French public opinion would not accept a betrayal of the Czechs.

Deeply frustrated by Daladier's resistance, Chamberlain now faced the very real prospect of a ministerial rebellion. When he returned to his third Cabinet meeting of the day shortly before midnight he so misleadingly talked of French indecision that Halifax came close to openly contradicting his account. Even without this veiled dissent, however, Chamberlain found himself in a minority within his own Cabinet as Cooper made himself 'pretty offensive', Hore-Belisha was 'very stiff and bellicose', while Elliot, De La Warr, Winterton, Hailsham and Stanley all expressed open disagreement. Confronted finally by the prospect of outright revolt and repudiation, Chamberlain suddenly declared that as he was 'unwilling to leave unexplored any possible chance of avoiding war', Sir Horace Wilson should fly to Berlin with a conciliatory personal letter to Hitler appealing for concessions regarding the orderly transfer of territory. Although he insisted that this should not contain the threat of war, he was forced to agree that if this approach failed Wilson should warn Hitler verbally that Britain would support France if it came to conflict. Although the announcement was made 'almost casually', Duff Cooper 'could hardly believe [his] ears' at this 'complete reversal' of position, while Stanley observed acidly that the Germans were to be told the French would fight despite Chamberlain's earlier report that they refused to do so. Nevertheless, the government's crisis had been temporarily averted.[141] The Cabinet agreed to Wilson's mission and Daladier did so next morning. In accordance with Cabinet wishes, at his meeting with the French next day, Chamberlain also reiterated that Britain would go 'to her assistance if France were in danger'.[142]

During these tense meetings on the evening of 25 September, Chamberlain looked so 'absolutely worn out' that even Duff Cooper felt sorry for him.[143] Yet looks were deceptive and Chamberlain was far from being either beaten or repentant. In order to retain direct personal control over the presentation of policy, Henderson was secretly instructed to inform Berlin to ignore all statements except those coming from the Prime Minister; a precaution soon justified by Halifax's sharply worded press communiqué stating explicitly that if France was attacked while defending Czechoslovakia, Britain and Russia 'will certainly stand by France'.[144] Similarly, despite apparently explicit assurances to the French, Simon's precise legalistic formula drew a crucial distinction between the French assisting the Czechs by defensive action along the Maginot Line and active hostilities against Germany which the British were not prepared to support. As Simon noted cynically, 'with the limitation introduced into the formula it is really nothing more than the expression of what would have to be our position should the conditions there mentioned arise'.[145] Nevertheless, the deception achieved its purpose. On the morning of 26 September, Stanley and Cooper agreed privately that unless the French were given definite and immediate assurances of British support they would resign. As the Cabinet assembled at noon, both the departing French ministers and then Chamberlain informed them of his pledge to support France in the event of war. After this, Cooper withdrew his threat of resignation and apologised for having expressed his opinions 'too frequently and too forcibly ... thereby add[ing] to the Prime Minister's heavy burden'. At the same time, several other ministers found themselves 'prey to unreasoning optimism' about the prospects for peace based on deterrence.[146]

These hopes reflected a fundamental misapprehension about Chamberlain's underlying objective in proposing the Wilson mission, which was not to threaten Hitler but rather to encourage a friendly gesture in order to strengthen his own ability to resist the Cabinet 'War Party'. In the event, however, Wilson's mission achieved nothing. During a 'very violent hour' of 'insane interruptions' from Hitler on the afternoon of 26 September, Wilson presented Chamberlain's conciliatory letter, but he prudently decided against issuing the accompanying verbal warning and only did so on the following afternoon at Chamberlain's direct insistence because he had given assurances to the French that it would be delivered – although even then Wilson was instructed that it 'should be given more in sorrow than in anger'. The outcome was another frenzied tirade about smashing the Czechs unless they accepted his terms, while the threat of British support for France prompted Hitler's angry retort that they would 'all be at war in six days'.[147]

For Chamberlain these were 'agonising hours when even hope seemed almost extinguished'. Yet he never for one moment wavered in the conviction that safety was best achieved by efforts to conciliate rather than coerce Germany. On the morning of 27 September, Chamberlain issued a press statement calling upon Germany to abandon the threat of force in return for British help in implementing Czech concessions 'fairly and fully and ... with all reasonable promptitude'.[148] His 'rather depressing broadcast' that evening also combined a similar warning of resistance to world domination with an unprovocative appeal for reasonable conduct as he lamented 'how horrible, fantastic, incredible it is that we should be digging trenches and trying on gas masks because of a quarrel in a faraway country between people of whom we know nothing'. While explaining that the British mobilisation was merely a 'precautionary measure', he also declared his willingness to visit Germany for a third time 'if I thought it would do any good'.[149] While this offer prompted the sneering Foreign Office parody that 'if at first you can't concede, Fly, Fly, Fly again', what depressed the ministerial 'War Party' about this broadcast was Chamberlain's expressions of sympathy for Hitler's feelings towards the Sudeten Germans, without any corresponding reference to France, the Czechs or the mobilisation of the fleet; an emphasis and tone which immediately signalled the prospect of further 'scuttle'.[150]

As soon as Wilson returned on the afternoon of 27 September, Chamberlain met Halifax alone for an unminuted conversation before he convened the inner executive for a rehearsal of the gloomy assessment to be put before Cabinet five hours later.[151] At Cabinet, Chamberlain began with a defeatist account of Czech military weakness and Dominion reluctance to fight in order to engineer support for the acceptance of Hitler's demands which he presented as 'perhaps the last opportunity for avoiding war'. Wilson then followed with details of his unsuccessful mission, repeating the view that their only option was to advise the Czechs to evacuate the disputed territory. This was too much for many within the Cabinet. Duff Cooper immediately threatened to resign rather than accept such defeatist views, arguing erroneously that there was 'a much firmer spirit in France' and that Dominion opinion was 'much more favourable than it had been in 1914'. Stanley also emphasised that Chamberlain was asking for assent to a proposal rejected three days earlier. More important, Halifax characterised the plan as a 'capitulation' and declared it wrong to force the Czechs into acceptance. He also argued the Commons would take a similar view and now even Simon agreed. In summing up, Chamberlain was thus forced to acknowledge the 'powerful and perhaps convincing' case against pressing the terms upon Prague, before wearily concluding that 'if that was the general view of his colleagues he was prepared to leave it at that'.[152]

At this point, war appeared inevitable. Hitler's ultimatum expired at 2pm next day. In preparation for the expected 'knock out blow' from massed German bombers, Air Raid Precautions were put on a war footing, gas masks issued, deep cellars were commandeered for shelters, the Fleet and the Auxiliary Air Force were mobilised and the first anti-aircraft batteries appeared on Horse Guards Parade and Westminster Bridge. As Chamberlain wrote to his sisters, 'I only knew that as the hours went by events seemed to be closing in and driving us to the edge of the abyss with a horrifying certainty and rapidity.' While his wife found comfort in prayer, Chamberlain reflected bitterly that 'it seemed only too possible that all the prayers of the peoples of the world including Germany herself might break against the fanatical obstinacy of one man'. Walking in the garden at Downing Street early on 28 September, Chamberlain even told his wife that 'I would gladly stand up against that wall and be shot if only I could prevent war.' It was an absolutely sincere expression of the price he was prepared to pay to avoid the nightmare of war and an indication of his intense despair at the failure of more rational means to reach a settlement.[153]

Whatever else he was, Chamberlain was not a man to wait upon events in such perilous circumstances. In 'the last desperate snatch at the last tuft of grass on the very verge of the precipice', earlier that same morning he drafted personal appeals to both of the dictators. His message to Hitler reiterated his willingness to implement a settlement 'fairly and fully' and to go to Berlin to discuss a peaceful transfer. He did so without consulting the Cabinet or the French – far less the Czechs. 'I cannot believe', he wrote to Hitler, 'that you will take [the] responsibility of starting a world war which may end civilization for the sake of a few days delay in settling this long standing problem.' At the same time, he attempted to enlist Mussolini's support for an international conference to conclude an agreement within a week. At around 11.40 am Hitler agreed to Mussolini's proposal for a postponement of the planned mobilisation to permit a Four Power conference to resolve the Sudeten problem; an invitation communicated to the British Ambassador as he called upon Hitler to deliver

Chamberlain's message. In Berlin, Hitler had taken his opportunity to climb down without losing face.[154]

Meanwhile, in London, Chamberlain opened the Commons debate on the Czech situation with a speech he had been preparing until 2 o'clock that morning. The Commons chamber and galleries were packed to overflowing when the House assembled for what many expected to be the last day of peace. Despite the sombre gravity of the occasion, Chamberlain received a hearty cheer from all sides when he entered the chamber and he was in good voice as he recounted his depressing story while the House listened in 'dead silence'. Towards the end of this long narrative, however, Hitler's invitation to a conference at Munich next morning was passed to Lord Halifax in the Peer's Gallery and then sent via the official box to Dunglass and finally to Simon sitting next to Chamberlain on the front bench. By this stage, Chamberlain had been speaking for over an hour and he was approaching the end of his account. 'The problem', Simon later recorded in his diary, 'was how and when to let the speaker know this encouraging and indeed vital fact without disturbing the flow of his discourse. I waited for some time with the necessary sentences on a piece of paper in my hand ... At last, during a burst of cheering I managed to whisper to him that Hitler's answer had come and gave him the passage to be inserted later on.' With just a suggestion of a smile, Chamberlain briefly resumed his speech before the master showman played his trump card by reading the contents of the note to the Commons. Amid unprecedented scenes of rejoicing, the chamber became 'a forest of waving hands and papers' as MPs stood on their benches bellowing, while Ambassadors in the Diplomatic Gallery broke all the rules and applauded vigorously. As Alec Dunglass later recalled with justifiable irony: 'There were a lot of "appeasers" in Parliament that day.'[155]

Accounts of Chamberlain's reaction differ. According to Harry Crookshank, the Prime Minister was 'nearly overcome ... with emotion' and Harold Nicolson also thought his entire face was transformed as the lines of anxiety and weariness were suddenly removed and 'he appeared ten years younger and triumphant'. Conversely, Simon recalled that Chamberlain exercised an 'amazing' degree of self-control. Either way, he then abandoned his gloomy peroration and sought leave to prepare for his journey, while Attlee wished him God speed and business was adjourned until Monday. 'It was incomparably the greatest piece of real drama that the House of Commons had ever witnessed', a still astonished Simon recorded next day.[156] Contrary to unfounded allegations that it was 'a pre-arranged drama' in which Chamberlain cynically cast himself as 'director, producer and leading actor',[157] this climax was all the more remarkable because Chamberlain had no idea that his speech would end in this manner. As he noted four days later, that 'news of the deliverance should come to me in the very act of closing my speech in the House was a piece of drama that no work of fiction ever surpassed'.[158] It was his finest hour and the supreme vindication of all his hopes of both the dictators. 'I will always remember little Neville today', the besotted 'Chips' Channon recorded later that night, 'with his too long hair, greying at the sides, his smile, his amazing spirits and seeming lack of fatigue, as he stood there, alone, fighting the gods of war single-handed and triumphant – he seemed the incarnation of St George – so simple and so unspoilt ... I don't know what this country has done to deserve him.'[159]

VII

Chamberlain was deeply touched when he found next morning that, at Simon's suggestion, the Cabinet – all except 'that absurd dissenting nanny-goat Eddie Winterton' – had gone to Heston to see him off and to cheer his plane as it left the ground.[160] Although Hitler's manner initially suggested that 'the storm signals were up', he gave Chamberlain the double hand-shake reserved for specially friendly greetings and his opening sentences to the conference were 'so moderate and reasonable' that Chamberlain felt 'instant relief'. After opening statements and then lunch, the meeting soon turned to consideration of the Italian written proposals which, unbeknown to Chamberlain, had been drafted by the Germans on the previous day and later formed the basis for the Munich Agreement. These proposals were skilfully contrived to represent a sufficient softening of Hitler's Godesberg terms to enable Chamberlain to claim that he had obtained real concessions, while giving Hitler all that he demanded regarding the occupation of the Sudetenland.[161] But while critics would soon accuse Chamberlain of betraying Czechoslovakia by accepting terms barely altered since Godesberg, Cadogan and most of Chamberlain's supporters declared them 'far better than ... expected' in the circumstances. Indeed, upon his return to London, Chamberlain justified his claim that 'he had done his best for Czechoslovakia' at Munich, by explaining to the Cabinet the 'main differences' between the Godesberg terms and the final agreement under no fewer than ten separate headings.[162]

Beyond the immediate objectives of the conference, Chamberlain seized the opportunity to address the issues he always considered to be of more fundamental significance. Despite an initial snub from Mussolini, Chamberlain persisted in discussing the possibility of a Four Power appeal for a truce in Spain. Far more important, at one o'clock in the morning while waiting for the draftsmen to complete the agreement and without consulting Daladier, Chamberlain proposed another talk with Hitler to clear away all other outstanding difficulties. Hitler apparently 'jumped at the idea', proposing they should meet at his private flat in the city later that morning. The result was 'a very friendly & pleasant talk' on Spain, South East Europe and disarmament, before Chamberlain suddenly produced a three paragraph declaration which he and Strang had drafted earlier and which he asked Hitler to sign. As Chamberlain later recounted to his sisters, as the interpreter translated the request, 'Hitler frequently ejaculated Ja! Ja! And at the end he said Yes I will certainly sign it. When shall we do it. I said "now", & we went at once to the writing table & put our signatures to the two copies which I had brought with me.' This three paragraph 'Anglo-German Agreement' declared itself 'symbolic of the desire of our two peoples never to go to war again' and their joint determination 'to continue … efforts to remove possible sources of difference and thus to contribute to assure the peace of Europe'.[163]

In reality, the perfunctory manner in which Hitler signed the document suggests just how little significance he actually attached to its content. But for Chamberlain, this famous 'piece of paper', which he read triumphantly to the jubilant crowds at Heston and waved from the window of Downing Street was the ultimate goal and vindication of all his efforts. Having obtained Hitler's signature to the document Chamberlain was so delighted that when he returned to his hotel for lunch, Strang records he 'complacently patted his breast-pocket and said "I've got it!"' Czechoslovakia had been dismembered, but as Chamberlain told Lord Dunglass, this personal agreement represented far more than the temporary avoidance of a war. At best, it meant permanent peace with a sated Germany. At worst, any future threat to peace would expose Hitler to the entire world as an evil monster bent upon global domination.[164] This, ultimately, was what Chamberlain had hoped to achieve at Munich and it was what Horace Wilson meant when he later declared that 'our policy was never designed just to postpone war, or enable us to enter war united. The aim of appeasement was to avoid war altogether, for all time.'[165]

In the short-term, Chamberlain basked in his role as the saviour of European peace. In Munich, his car was surrounded by ecstatic rejoicing as he drove to the airport and on his return to England there was more of the same. After a brief speech to the waiting newsreels at Heston at which he waved his famous document, Chamberlain began his slow journey to Westminster. 'Even the descriptions of the papers gives no idea of the scenes in the streets as I drove from Heston to the Palace', he wrote to his sisters. 'They were lined from one end to the other with people of every class, shouting themselves hoarse, leaping on the running board, banging on the windows & thrusting their hands in to the car to be shaken.'[166] At Buckingham Palace, Chamberlain enjoyed the exceptional honour of joining the King and Queen on the balcony to wave to an excited crowd standing in the rain, while in Downing Street these jubilant scenes culminated in his appearance at the same first floor window from which Disraeli had announced 'Peace with Honour' after the Congress of Berlin in 1878. Overwhelmed by the rejoicing all around him and intensely proud of his own achievement, even this supremely unemotional man became sufficiently infected by the mood to allow his guard to drop. Accounts differ as to who suggested that he should adopt Disraeli's phrase and when first proposed as he ascended the stairs he apparently snapped back, 'No, I don't do that sort of thing.' But by the time he reached the window to address the cheering crowds he had relented, declaring that it was 'the second time in our history that there has come back from Germany to Downing Street peace with honour'. Thanking the nation 'from the bottom of a proud heart' he then urged the crowds to 'Go home to your beds; it is peace for our time.'[167]

Although Chamberlain's triumphant homecoming had been carefully staged for the newsreels and press, these phrases were not the premeditated product of mature reflection and almost immediately Chamberlain regretted his surrender to emotion. As almost hysterical relief at national salvation became tainted with the shame that it had been achieved at such a high cost to the Czechs, the phrase suggested a complacent insensitivity which troubled even the least delicate of consciences. When winding up the Munich debate on 6 October, Chamberlain took the opportunity to explain that the words had been used 'in a moment of some emotion, after a long and exhausting day, after I had driven through miles of excited, enthusiastic cheering people' and that they should 'not read into those words more than they were intended to convey'.[168] It was a prudent and completely truthful explanation – but it was also far too late. For later generations and for many of his own, Neville Chamberlain's name would always be synonymous with that hollow promise of 'peace for our time'.

Chapter 14

Betrayal,
October 1938–March 1939

'It is difficult to judge how the country will react to Chamberlain's sell out of Czechoslovakia. I think Blum has expressed the public feeling well when he said his own feelings were a mixture of cowardly relief and shame. If this is so, it is to be expected that many people – to hide their cowardice from themselves – will vent their shame on Chamberlain … People who would not want a stand to be made, had it actually been made, may now damn Chamberlain for not making a stand.'

Patrick Gordon Walker Diary, 21 September 1938

Chamberlain's supporters advanced a variety of seemingly impressive arguments in defence of the Munich settlement. As his sister later recalled in a classical exposition of the case, Munich upheld the principle that territorial adjustments should come through negotiation rather than force while providing Hitler with proof that legitimate grievances could be settled without war. It also bought the Western Powers a crucial 'breathing space' to rearm, while Chamberlain's unflinching efforts to preserve peace shrouded British policy in a cloak of moral superiority which served to educate Dominion, American and neutral opinion into support for Britain when war came in September 1939, in a manner in which they would not have supported it a year earlier.[1] As Chamberlain's Principal Private Secretary put it in April 1940, 'it is to the P.M. we owe our excellent case in the present war: if it had not been for Munich and the policy of appeasement our case would have lost half its strength, our desperate anxiety to maintain peace might have been questioned and, … we should in 1938 have been in a hopeless position of inferiority as regards armaments.'[2] From the perspective of 1940, or even September 1939, there was much to be said for such arguments. Unfortunately for Chamberlain, this was not the case he declared publicly in September 1938. On the contrary, while he unquestionably strove for these very substantial secondary benefits, he also believed that Munich really did herald 'peace for our time'. Ultimately, it is the supreme tragedy of Neville Chamberlain's reputation that this short-term illusion has tended to obscure and negate much of the credit he certainly deserves for achieving these longer-term but wholly planned strategic objectives.

In the immediate aftermath of Munich, however, such calculations of long-term costs, benefits and motivations were largely irrelevant to most of Chamberlain's fellow countrymen. What mattered was that a catastrophic war had been averted and that while there were often 'mixed feelings', many privately conceded that these were 'dominated by a craven reluctance to see the end of the world'. Only later, after the initial euphoria had passed, did Munich become the 'peace of which everyone was glad and nobody proud'.[3] Yet, ultimately, it was precisely this intense ambivalence of feeling which ensured that Munich became such an indelible stain upon the reputation of its principal architect. For a people unwilling to fight themselves, but ashamed of the consequences of not doing so, Neville Chamberlain became the scapegoat for a truly collective sense of guilt. 'Why blame the democratic statesmen for the policy of appeasement', the American Carlton Hayes asked in *The Inevitable Conflict*. 'They were simply trying to do what their peace-loving peoples wanted done.' In retrospect, it is evident that opinion was not quite as solidly behind Munich as it appeared at the time. Even within local Conservative associations there was rather more unease than the flood of loyal constituency resolutions and the cheers of Tory backbenchers necessarily indicated.[4] Similarly, it is now clear that Chamberlain and Ball were engaged in such a spectacular and highly professional campaign of news management that by the autumn of 1938 large sections of the press and newsreels had 'clearly abandoned their role of articulating public opinion in favour of a religiously partisan support for Chamberlain'; an enthusiasm reflected in the overwhelmingly positive tone of media coverage of the Munich Agreement.[5]

Yet evidence of cynical party and press manipulation to convey the impression of national consensus should not blind us to the perceived reality of the time. Contemporary critics inevitably interpreted public opinion to suit their purposes and prejudices. Lloyd George's associates predictably claimed they had 'never known a more complete revulsion of feeling'.[6] Similarly, many Edenites preferred to believe that opinion was 'conscience-stricken & humiliated by our treatment of the Czech nation & especially by the way that we have acted as messenger boy to the dictators', even if other anti-appeasers were more realistic in acknowledging that public opinion was 'delirious with enthusiasm and gratitude to Neville' and unwilling to hear contrary views.[7] Most observers, however, would simply have agreed with one veteran lobby correspondent who reported a sense of public relief 'unequalled since the Armistice of 1918'.[8] Indeed, from the King and Queen downwards, Chamberlain was showered with compliments and praise for his courage and persistence in the quest to avert war. 'Neville was a hero' Runciman declared, while Margot Asquith proclaimed him 'the greatest Englishman that ever lived'.[9] 'Good man' was Roosevelt's brief but heart-felt congratulations, while the former Kaiser wrote to Queen Mary for the first time since 1914 declaring that 'Chamberlain was inspired by Heaven and guided by God.'[10] It was probably a verdict echoed by a large mass of public opinion.

In the days after Munich, Chamberlain received more than 20,000 letters and telegrams containing touching expressions of thanks for having averted a great war just 20 years after the 'war to end all wars'. A popular song was entitled 'God Bless you Mr Chamberlain', newsreel audiences wildly applauded his return from Germany and he was inundated with an 'embarrassing profusion' of gifts of every description, including countless fishing flies, salmon rods, Scottish tweed for sporting suits, socks, innumerable umbrellas, pheasants and grouse, fine Rhine wines, lucky horseshoes, flowers from Hungary, 6000 assorted bulbs from grateful Dutch admirers and a cross from the Pope.[11] Such was the national mood, that when the *Daily Sketch* offered an art plate of Chamberlain and his wife in Downing Street after Munich for 3d (1p.) in stamps, they immediately received 91,802 applications. Even in December, Chamberlain reported the 'tide of letters, flowers, testimonials and gifts continues to flow in without much abatement' and the deluge resumed again for his seventieth birthday in March.[12]

It should also be remembered that this eruption of intense relief was not confined exclusively to Chamberlain's political supporters, although in less sympathetic circles it was often mixed with an uneasy feeling of troubled conscience. The veteran socialist Beatrice Webb had always despised Chamberlain, but when she heard the news of the Munich agreement she asked herself the crucial question: 'A sense of personal relief, or a consciousness of disgust for one's own outlook on life – which was the greatest? I think the sense of relief … The wild enthusiasm of the reception of the two Prime Ministers in London and Paris proved that it was so with the man and woman in the street.'[13] Similarly, the economist John Maynard Keynes regarded Chamberlain as 'the lowest … flattest-footed creature that creeps', but he also confessed that his reaction to Munich was 'painful in the way in which only a mixed state can be. Intense relief and satisfied cowardice join with rage and indignation, *plus* that special emotion … of having been *swindled* … as never before in [our] history.'[14] This intense ambivalence throughout much of the nation engendered what Collin Brooks described as a 'Hosanna today: crucify him tomorrow mentality' in which adulation in the immediate wake of salvation gradually gave way to revulsion and condemnation as shame and regret asserted themselves. As Halifax lamented on the day after the Munich conference, Chamberlain deserved all the credit and 'his admiration for him surpassed all bounds', but he foresaw 'political trouble ahead, both in Parliament and in the country'.[15]

II

According to close observers, 'the most remarkable personal aspect of this whole business has been the quite amazing patience and self-control which Chamberlain has shown'.[16] Yet beneath the surface the crisis exacted such a heavy emotional toll on the Prime Minister's resources that when he reached Chequers on 1 October he was in a state of complete physical and mental collapse. Walking up through Crow's Close towards the church, he later confessed to his sisters, 'I came nearer there to a nervous breakdown than I have ever been in my life.' He then 'pulled [him]self together' in readiness for the four day debate on Munich, but declared that he must soon 'get away & recover my soul'.[17] Chamberlain's mental anguish was not calmed by the knowledge that he had to face a Cabinet and Parliament that did not altogether share the public rejoicing at the outcome of Munich. Although information from secret sources suggested that Churchill was carrying on 'a regular conspiracy' with the Czech Minister in London, this was dismissed as characteristic duplicity. Rather more worrying and certainly more frustrating was the threatened 'defection of the weaker brethren' within his own government.[18]

In reality, the fear was always more of government embarrassment than of real crisis. Duff Cooper was the only minister prepared to resign over Munich, but he did not really count for much except among convinced anti-appeasers. Conversely the other waverers were the same despised 'lightweights' who had supported Eden's challenge to Chamberlain in February but then remained in office to demonstrate they 'hadn't the courage of their innermost convictions'. The most senior of these was Oliver Stanley whose hollow talk of resignation in February had deservedly prompted Lady Cranborne's contemptuous observation that 'the Stanleys have been trimmers ever since Bosworth'.[19] True to form, Stanley had been conspicuous in organising resistance to the Prime Minister's policy during the Czech crisis and he denounced Munich 'not as "peace in our time" but as an uneasy truce'.[20] Yet despite his 'constant qualms', Chamberlain always believed Stanley 'had no courage' and he was probably correct in suspecting he never really meant to resign either.[21]

Walter Elliot was another prominent 'Boy's Brigade' ditherer, but he was an acknowledged 'windbag' and while conscious of the risk of conceding too much in negotiations with Hitler, he soon reconciled himself to the dangers of the 'slippery slopes' because 'they're better than a vertical drop'. As a result, he was probably relieved to be talked out of his pledge to resign with Duff Cooper, although he still claimed the terms stuck in his throat 'as much as they ever stuck in Duff's'.[22] After a final challenge over the need to accelerate rearmament from Elliot and De La Warr at Cabinet on 3 October, the danger of ministerial revolt collapsed, while Winterton actually went so far as to declare that his personal admiration for Chamberlain had increased.[23]

After Cabinet on 3 October, Chamberlain went to the Commons for the debate on Munich where his spirits were further dampened. Duff Cooper began the proceedings with a well-crafted resignation statement which impressed some MPs with its indictment of the agreement and the naivety of the Prime Minister's 'sweet reasonableness', but Chamberlain's supporters thought his speech 'not very impressive' and 'very rude'. Opinions differ on whether Chamberlain was 'good and respectfully listened to' or 'not very good', but even the besotted Channon thought he appeared tired and that the 'glow had gone' as he talked optimistically of 'further progress along the road to sanity' now that the Sudeten problem was behind them.[24] The rest of the first and most of the second day of the debate proved no more encouraging. The 'ceaseless stream of vituperation being poured upon me' had 'a somewhat depressing effect on my spirits' Chamberlain later told his sisters, but he still found 'an antidote to the poison gas by reading a few of the countless letters and telegrams which continued to pour in expressing in most moving accents the writers heartfelt relief and gratitude. All the world seemed to be full of my praises except the House of Commons.'[25]

At this juncture, Chamberlain was once again troubled by the conscience of Harry Crookshank. Although only a junior minister, Crookshank displayed the pretensions of a ministerial grandee, combining frustrated and overweening ambition with a comically inflated view of his own importance. Convinced that the Munich agreement was 'a complete concession to Hitler' and that Chamberlain was 'crazy & hypnotized by a loony', he soon concluded that he and Bernays should resign immediately. When an 'agitated' Chief Whip telephoned to say that this was 'not the way to treat one's boss', however, Crookshank was summoned to an 'extraordinary conversation' with the Prime Minister. According to Crookshank's account, Chamberlain declared 'it was a frightful shock to him & ... was obviously trying hard to keep me', while Crookshank was 'very frank' in his criticisms, but he agreed to leave the matter until he had heard Chamberlain's final statement on 6 October. What was most extraordinary about this interview was that it ended with Crookshank specifying three conditions for his support 'rather like an ultimatum'; that Chamberlain should retract his words about 'peace with honour', press on with rearmament and work towards collective arrangements which would include Russia 'if not for material, for moral reasons'. He also extracted a pledge that there would be no immediate general election. 'Pure comic opera' Crookshank noted later: 'I gave notice (like a cook) & it has not been accepted so I am left in suspended animation.'[26]

Despite these difficulties, by the third day of the Munich debate 'things began to mend'. While Baldwin steadied Tory wobblers in the Lords, Simon opened with a 'masterpiece of close knit argument and persuasive reasoning' which silenced the Opposition and, by all account, had a 'most marked effect in rallying the doubters and in encouraging our friends'. Chamberlain's own speech on the final day of the debate also reflected his more buoyant mood and drew compliments from across the entire political spectrum as he announced another review of the rearmament programme. Indeed, Amery and Eden were so impressed by the statement that they 'very, very nearly' voted with the government and only abstained out of loyalty to stronger-willed backbench followers.[27] Chamberlain's speech also did enough to reassure the sceptics within the government. After repeated coaxing, Stanley 'declared all his doubts resolved', although the agonies of indecision soon returned as he lurched towards 'the edge of a breakdown'. As Chamberlain's speech satisfied Crookshank's conditions, he also decided that he 'must gulp hard & stay', while in the lobby after the vote Bernays assured a surprised Chamberlain that his final speech 'had put everything right'.[28] More important, despite an often disproportionate historical emphasis upon the activities of a disparate and tiny minority of dissident anti-appeasers during this period, no Conservatives voted against the government and only between 22 and 25 abstained, while the overwhelming majority suppressed any private doubts and dutifully voted for Chamberlain out of loyalty to a leader they 'regarded … rather like an Old Testament patriarch who had returned with God's blessing to preserve peace in our time'.[29] Little wonder that Chamberlain was 'positively jubilant' as he left the chamber to another ovation. With this 'pretty trying ordeal' behind him, he then departed for ten days complete rest at The Hirsel, the Scottish residence of the Earl of Home and his son, Alec Dunglass.[30]

III

Shortly before departing for Scotland, Chamberlain told Halifax that in dealing with the dictators, their approach was best summed up by the maxim 'that while hoping for the best it is also necessary to prepare for the worst'.[31] At best, he told himself, Munich was the first step on the road to the 'general settlement of Europe' for which he had striven for so long. At worst, it provided time to complete the costly rearmament programme already underway. Either way, however, he recognised that Munich was only the first step on the path to security and national salvation. Unfortunately, over the next eleven months Chamberlain gave mixed signals as to the appropriate balance to be struck between these two positions as circumstances and audiences varied. Although acutely conscious of the cost of rearmament, he assured a peace campaigner that it was necessary because 'the stakes are so big, the existence of the British Empire as we have known it, that I dare not gamble them on trust in the pacific intentions of the dictators'.[32] In private, however, Chamberlain's willingness to 'prepare for the worst' had always been significantly outweighed his capacity to 'hope for the best' and his faith in the Anglo-German Declaration still further tilted the balance of Chamberlain's priorities. 'We have avoided the catastrophe', he told his step-mother. 'But that … is not enough. What I want is a restoration of confidence that would allow us all to stop rearming and get back to the work of making our world a better place to live in.' Beneath the tone of sober realism about the obstacles ahead, these sentiments came from the heart of an indefatigable optimist. As he admitted to his sisters next day, 'my policy is summed up in the old trinity of Faith Hope and Charity'.[33]

Unfortunately, while Munich reinforced Chamberlain's policy priorities, it also substantially reinforced his hallucination of personal indispensability in the pursuit of lasting peace. 'The only thing I care about is to be able to carry out the policy I believe, indeed *know* to be right, and the only distress that criticism or obstruction can cause me is if it prevents my purpose. There indeed I do suffer from the foolish things that people & papers say in this country. Nevertheless though the dogs bark the caravan does move on.'[34] This evangelical sense of almost spiritual mission served only to further intensify Chamberlain's covert efforts to manipulate party, press and public opinion in support of his policy while undermining and coercing those who opposed him.

In retrospect, Chamberlain's optimism about Hitler's good intentions in the wake of Munich appears to be facile and naïve. But in fairness, it is important to emphasise that this never precluded support for what he considered to be necessary defensive rearmament. Although he persisted for far longer than most of his colleagues with the illusion that appeasement might still achieve its ultimate objective, Chamberlain always knew that it was never an 'all-or-nothing' gamble. If diplomacy failed, he took comfort from the knowledge that Anglo-French defensive weaknesses were being addressed while these negotiations took place. That, after all, was the principal purpose of a 'double policy' designed to deliver 'peace if possible, and arms for certain'.[35] Soon after Munich he thus told the Conservative backbencher, Sir Henry Page Croft, that while Hitler's emphatic assurances about peace 'rang absolutely sincerely', Britain must still rearm because 'if in a year or two he changed his mind he would be so ruthless that he would stop at nothing'. Anyway, experience had shown 'only too clearly that weakness in armed strength means weakness in diplomacy'.[36] Notwithstanding such declarations, however, Chamberlain also drew a sharp distinction between a prudent acceleration of the agreed deficiencies programme and any talk of allowing it to expand substantially in scale; a course he deprecated on the grounds that it both threatened domestic economic stability and jeopardised hopes of any negotiated settlement by acting as a standing provocation to the dictators. While a new Committee on Defence Preparations and Accelerations was appointed on 27 October, therefore, the Prime Minister stoutly resisted pressure for the mobilisation of industry on a quasi-war footing for fear that Hitler would regard it as 'a signal that we had decided at once to sabotage the Munich Declaration'. In early November, he reaffirmed his support for the priority upon defensive fighter aircraft over the Air Ministry's preference for heavy bombers on similar grounds.[37]

To maintain the momentum behind his own preferred policy, Chamberlain needed to stifle those for whom the principal lesson of Munich was that Britain needed a crash programme of rearmament. When challenged on precisely this point by Elliot in early October, Chamberlain retorted with a classic exposition of his 'double policy'. As the Cabinet minutes recorded:

> He had been oppressed with the sense that the burden of armaments might break our backs. This had been one of the factors which had led him to the view that it was necessary to try and resolve the causes which were responsible for the armament race.
>
> He thought that we were now in a more hopeful position, and that the contacts which had been established with the Dictator Powers opened up the possibility that we might be able to reach some agreement with them which would stop the armaments race. It was clear, however, that it would be madness for the country to stop rearming until we were convinced that other countries would act in the same way. For the time being, therefore, we should relax no particle of effort until our deficiencies had been made good. That, however, was not the same thing as to say that as a thanks offering for the present *détente*, we should at once embark on a great increase in our armaments programme.

All such calls for increased defence expenditure in Cabinet and Parliament were parried with the same view. 'Our Foreign Policy is one of appeasement', he sternly reminded the Cabinet four weeks later. In this context, he made it abundantly clear that he believed 'a great deal of false emphasis had been placed on rearmament, as though one result of the Munich agreement had been that it would be necessary for us to add to our rearmament programme. Acceleration of existing programmes was one thing but increases in the scope of our programme which would lead to a new arms race were a different proposition.'[38] Although this posture increasingly depressed his critics, even they were forced to concede that many government backbenchers agreed with Chamberlain.[39]

Yet, ironically, Chamberlain's ability to uphold this position became progressively more difficult simply *because* of Munich and the successful manner in which he had shaped the debate about options. Certainly in the weeks surrounding Munich, authoritative rumours about the parlous state of Britain's air defences convinced many observers that Chamberlain had saved Britain from an unwinnable war with unimaginable casualties. 'We had not the means of defending ourselves and he knows it', General Ironside noted in his diary during the crisis. '*We cannot expose ourselves to a German attack. We simply commit suicide if we do.*'[40] The problem, however, was that while such terrifying calculations helped justify Chamberlain's actions at Munich, they also perversely made it extremely difficult for him to restrain burgeoning demands for a rapid acceleration of the rearmament programme to ensure that Britain should never again find itself in the same position of vulnerability. To make matters worse, the growing hostility of the dictators after Munich substantially undermined Chamberlain's authority in attempting to lead foreign and defence policy in the desired direction. The more insolent and threatening the behaviour of the dictators, the stronger became the demands for accelerated rearmament and an end to Chamberlain's policy of negotiated accommodation.

One possible method of reasserting his personal authority and control was to obtain an electoral mandate for his chosen policy. During the spring of 1938, Chamberlain had ordered Joseph Ball to prepare an autumn propaganda campaign to culminate in a general election by the end of the year.[41] After Munich, this possibility appeared far more alluring, particularly as many now felt that 'it would be 1931' all over again at a time when Chamberlain still basked in the approving afterglow of public admiration.[42] Although Halifax warned Chamberlain against such temptations as they drove back from Heston, many other associates took a different view. Sam Hoare soon advised that 'with Parliament nearing its end you will not get a fair run for a policy of peace'. Kingsley Wood was also reported to want 'a khaki election like L.G.'s in 1918' and he persisted with the idea of an election to 'clear out the wobblers' for some time.[43]

Chamberlain clearly considered this option – despite his assurances to Crookshank on 4 October that he had no intention of a dissolution. In the event, however, a variety of factors eventually persuaded him that it was 'bad tactics'.

Certainly the party chairman feared 'it would be fatal if the Party seemed to be trying to capitalise Neville's peace making work' – although such delicacy did not preclude the possibility of an election within a few months, 'before people have forgotten the gas masks'. Another problem was that the constituency soundings provided no definite indication of which way electoral opinion had swung in response to Munich. As a result, therefore, Chamberlain publicly repudiated the idea of a dissolution on 6 October.[44] Nevertheless, he also recognised that he would not be able to 'settle down comfortably here or succeed in establishing confidence abroad ... till I have got a mandate on that policy from the country' and he intended to 'watch eagerly for an opportunity to seek it'.[45] This need for delay was undoubtedly disappointing but it is important not to overstate the magnitude of Chamberlain's problem at a time when Parliament still had over two years left to run. Moreover, while the Chief Whip had 'never looked forward less to the opening of a session [with] everyone with a complaint about guns or sheep or Czechs or something',[46] murmurs of backbench unrest could be largely ignored given a parliamentary majority of well over 200 – particularly given both the dismal failure of Churchill's efforts to organise a mass parliamentary revolt in mid-November and the assiduous efforts of Central Office to ensure that loyal 'Blimps' in the constituency parties brought the full force of their displeasure to bear upon Chamberlain's backbench critics.[47]

On the other hand, Eden's siren calls for a more 'national' approach to policy represented a potentially more dangerous challenge to Chamberlain's support within the electorate, the parliamentary party and the Cabinet – particularly as he posed as a principled, constructive and loyal supporter urging much needed reform from outside. Since his resignation in February, Eden had carefully restored cordial relations with Chamberlain, while heeding Baldwin's advice to avoid the sort of captious opposition which so undermined Churchill's credibility as a critic. Instead he made it clear that he stood for 'postwar England' and Baldwin's consensual brand of inclusive Tory liberalism against 'the old men' and Chamberlain's harsher style of partisanship.[48] While 'very wrought up and anxious' during the Sudeten crisis, Eden's deliberately moderate contribution to the Munich debate had thus called for 'a united effort by a united nation' to assist the defence effort by putting Britain on a proper war footing. As a direct corollary, he proposed a radical reconstruction of the government with places for both Liberals and Labour to win trade union support for rearmament.[49] Among those approached with such ideas, Eden attempted to persuade Halifax of the need for a broader base for government support. Reporting this conversation to Chamberlain on 11 October, Halifax added ominously that he 'felt there was force in this' and that they should attempt 'something of the kind' because 'this is the psychological moment for endeavouring to get national unity and that ... it may be a long time before another recurs'.[50]

Chamberlain could safely ignore Eden's public campaign because he was widely perceived to be far too anxious to avoid allegations of disloyalty to strike a decisive blow against the Prime Minister.[51] When Eden was supported by Halifax, however, Chamberlain faced a far more formidable challenge

-- even when expressed in such courteous and deferential language as this. To make matters worse, he could scarcely plead lack of opportunity because Duff Cooper's resignation and the sudden death of Edward Stanley left him with two government places to fill. Nevertheless, Chamberlain was determined to resist. In private, he dismissed Eden's coalition ideas as 'perfectly futile' on the grounds that such an arrangement might work in wartime, but 'in peace we could never agree and we should soon break up'. Above all, despite Eden's ingratiating efforts to assure him of his personal support, Chamberlain remained convinced that 'the difference between Anthony & me is more fundamental than he realises'.

> At bottom he is really dead against making terms with dictators and what makes him think it possible to get unity is my insistence on the necessity for rearmament and the news that I didn't like Hitler personally. He leaves out or chooses not to see for the moment that the conciliation part of the policy is just as important as the rearming, and I fear that if he were again a member of the Cabinet, he would do what he did before, always agreeing in theory but always disagreeing in practice. And if we had Labour men in I see them forming a group with him which would keep up a constant running fight over every move in the international game. That would soon make my position intolerable. I have had trouble enough with my present Cabinet and I feel that what I want is more support for my policy and not more strengthening of those who dont believe in it, or at any rate are harassed by constant doubts.[52]

This was a remarkable admission of Chamberlain's private sense of vulnerability only a fortnight after his triumphant return from Munich, but he was absolutely correct in his suspicion that Eden expected to return to government on his own terms.[53] Always most formidable when in a tight corner and in absolutely no mood to make concessions to his critics, Chamberlain thus politely informed Halifax that there would be no invitation to either Labour or Eden.[54] After this, he rejoiced that with every one of Eden's 'daily' speeches, he 'did himself no good with our party' by making it 'plain beyond a peradventure that the difference between him and me is fundamental' and that he was actually engaged in 'all-round criticism of the Government and a bid for support for himself in opposition to it'.[55] Furthermore, Chamberlain's delight was intensified by his awareness of the peculiar difficulty of Eden's position. As he noted with malicious satisfaction, 'our Anthony is in a dilemma from which he would like me to extract him', because while his eagerness for office made him reluctant to do anything to alienate Chamberlain, he also needed to maintain the enthusiasm of backbench followers who expected him to lead a crusade against the Prime Minister. Little wonder that when Halifax revived the possibility of Eden's return in January 1939, Chamberlain firmly rejected the idea and he did so again in the following month in response to reports that Eden was privately angling to rejoin the government.[56]

Yet despite his hostility to Eden's rehabilitation, Chamberlain was reluctantly forced to make some concessions to mounting electoral, parliamentary and Cabinet pressures during the autumn and winter of 1938. First, he grudgingly accepted the need to broaden the base of the government with non-Conservatives – but only those upon whom he could rely for support. The impetus for this reform came from Hoare, who only a week after Munich had proposed that Chamberlain should appoint Runciman as Lord President while Sir John Anderson, the distinguished former civil servant turned Independent MP, should head a new Ministry of Supply and Lord Chatfield, a former First Sea Lord, should become Minister for the Coordination of Defence. Such appointments, Hoare advised, would 'impress the public, and the men themselves would add much intellectual strength to the Cabinet'.[57] As Runciman was a Liberal National and the other two were politically independent technocrats, Chamberlain also hoped their inclusion would demonstrate a commitment to tackle problems with the best men available.[58] Having discarded Runciman so ruthlessly in May 1937, however, his refusal to join except as Lord President now involved Chamberlain in the 'very painful proceeding' of hustling the ailing Lord Hailsham out of the post in October 1938 with a stirring appeal to 'do a last service to an old friend'.[59] On the same day, the troublesome Earl De La Warr was moved to make way for Anderson as Lord Privy Seal, while Chatfield eventually became Minister for the Coordination of Defence in January 1939. The only Conservative promotion in the reshuffle was Lord Stanhope, whose principal qualification for the Admiralty was Chamberlain's personal affection for him and his wife who regularly acted as weekend hosts at Chevening.

Beyond these personnel changes, Chamberlain responded to growing political discontent by making prudent concessions on those demands of which he approved, in order to frustrate those he did not. Above all, he recognised that something urgently needed to be done to improve ARP and anti-aircraft defences in order to bolster public confidence – particularly given the chaotic deficiencies exposed by national mobilisation during the Czech crisis. After briefly pondering the idea of a new Ministry of Civilian Defence, Anderson was eventually given special responsibility for handling this sensitive issue and he soon succeeded in silencing the critics.[60] Similarly, contemplation of voluntary National Service provided the right signals about the government's determination to resist Nazi aggression while satisfying a defensive need. In December 1938, the TUC thus agreed to join local National Service Committees to stimulate voluntary recruitment for all forms of civil and military defence, and this was accompanied by tentative discussions about the wartime regulation of wages, strikes and the supply of labour. On the other hand, Chamberlain vigorously resisted the growing clamour for a new Ministry of Supply with powers to direct industry and labour on the grounds that it was 'unnecessary at the present time' and raised 'very difficult questions of political expediency at home and implications & repercussions abroad.'[61] He was equally unenamoured by Hoare's suggestion that 'for peace purposes' they should consider a 'small war Cabinet' and he was completely deaf to Warren Fisher's pleas for steep rises in taxation 'to introduce a new and more realistic psychology'.[62]

In conjunction with these limited and cosmetic reforms, in the aftermath of discouraging post-Munich by-elections, Chamberlain again turned his mind to active news management and propaganda in order to consolidate public support behind his own policy while undermining his opponents. At the same time, he regarded the adverse impact of hostile British press reporting upon the attitudes of the dictators to be an 'exceptionally depressing' factor in a difficult international situation. As a direct result of these twin concerns, by early December 1938 he was 'beginning to wonder whether we shan't presently have to follow the example of the Dictators in starting a Ministry of Propaganda, though I would hope on far better lines than theirs'.[63] He was assisted in these black arts by the shadowy figure of Sir Joseph Ball. As Director of the CRD, Ball had worked extremely closely with Chamberlain since 1930 and he rapidly acquired the status of trusted adviser and political fixer. He was also a close personal friend with whom Chamberlain spent many weekends fishing for trout on the River Test. Although always to be found operating at the murkier edges of British politics, during Chamberlain's Premiership Ball's special skills and contacts as a former intelligence officer were put to regular service – whether operating his 'secret channel' to Mussolini within the Italian Embassy, or clandestinely organising British propaganda into German homes through the Radio Luxembourg transmitter or in his role as the secret controller of the right-wing journal *Truth*, promoting Chamberlain's policy while slandering opponents like Eden, Churchill and later Hore-Belisha.[64]

Soon after Munich, Chamberlain instructed Ball to devise a scheme to establish a national organisation 'to provide accurate and unbiassed information about foreign affairs, and, at the same time to promote friendly intercourse with other countries'. This benignly labelled 'British Association for International Understanding' was designed to cooperate with a range of non-political organisations like Chatham House, the Film Institute and the British Council as well as grassroots bodies like the Women's Institute and British Legion. The explicit purpose of this new body was to cultivate support for the government's policy as a direct counterblast to the hostile propaganda of the League of Nations Union – a body Chamberlain had always believed was 'past praying for' as a haven for the 'kind of person who … is almost invariably a crank and a Liberal'.[65] In order to boost the prestige of this new association, Chamberlain persuaded Baldwin to become president. It was launched on 29 March 1939 and continued to operate into the war under Butler's leadership.[66]

IV

Despite these concessions, Chamberlain reached the Christmas recess in an embattled and harassed state at the head of a government evidently going through 'a very difficult period'. Arab terrorism in Palestine gave much cause for concern, the burden of rearmament was having an alarming effect upon financial confidence, rural areas were 'in the depth of despair' at poor agricultural prices and the forced withdrawal of the Milk Bill was a humiliating reverse for the government. Worse still, as appeasement was 'not yielding any fruits ... it [wa]s difficult to make constructive speeches about it'. Little wonder that Chamberlain complained about growing scepticism within the government, 'a very odd mood' in the House of Commons and the instability of a Conservative party which seemed to be 'all over the place'.[67]

Yet to outward appearances, Chamberlain still appeared at the peak of his powers and in complete command of himself and the political situation. During the censure debate on the eve of the parliamentary recess in December he seemed 'at his best – tolerant, easy, smiling but important', employing all the old rhetorical tricks with masterly effect to thrill the House – he even roared with genuine laughter when Lloyd George twitted him in a speech which convulsed the chamber.[68] Yet beneath the carefully contrived persona, Chamberlain was increasingly prey to intense feelings of melancholy and political loneliness. Indeed, in the months after Munich he appeared to reflect more than ever before the ultimate isolation of supreme leadership. News of Simon's illness in December 1938 thus prompted an uncharacteristically effusive declaration of personal sentiment: 'I confess that in these difficult times I do occasionally feel rather lonely and if you were to become *hors de combat* I should miss terribly your counsel and support.'[69] Such feelings were probably intensified by a rift with Warren Fisher over Munich which severed a close official relationship of almost 15 years and ended in Fisher's complete exclusion from Chamberlain's confidence.[70] Sam Hoare had accepted Munich as an unpalatable necessity rather than as a prelude to a permanent settlement and he now also began to display a new independence which manifested itself in an impatience towards Chamberlain's negativity and lack of urgency about rearmament.[71] Far more troubling, however, was the growing gulf over policy with Halifax since his polite but profoundly damaging revolt during the Czech crisis.

Shorn of past illusions, Halifax was now convinced that Hitler was 'a criminal lunatic' and that Munich had been 'a horrid business and humiliating'. Although 'better than a European war', he 'obviously wasn't very proud of the result' and was known to have said there would be 'no more Munichs for me'.[72] As a result, while still 'very loyal' to Chamberlain, genuinely sympathetic to his burden and convinced he was 'right to grasp every opportunity for peace as long as he can', Halifax adopted a far more robustly independent line over the next year as he insistently pressed the need for rearmament, conscription, a Ministry of Supply, a continental commitment to France, economic aid to South East Europe and an all-party government.[73] Little wonder that Chamberlain complained to his sisters shortly before Christmas, 'While S.B. was Prime Minister he had me to help him, but I have no one who stands to me in the same relation and consequently I have to bear my troubles alone.' Exhausted, depressed by the political situation and frustrated by a disappointing day's shooting, he wearily declared with more than a little self-pity that 'Sometimes ...

I wish democracy at the devil and I often wonder what P.M. ever had to go through such an ordeal as I.'[74]

In these circumstances, Chamberlain was his own worst enemy. Resentful at Halifax's perceived desertion, his 'very odd behaviour' towards him in early October was a prelude to efforts designed to circumvent the Foreign Secretary's opposition to appeasement.[75] But in practice, these manoeuvres only made Cabinet management more difficult and intensified Chamberlain's sense of estrangement from a once close and kindred spirit. Another direct consequence of his isolation was that he increasingly came to rely upon an inner circle of trusted advisers like Simon, Hoare and Sir Horace Wilson who were widely mistrusted and lacked weight in '"putting it across" to the country'.[76] As Chamberlain's friends warned in December, his own stock was 'higher than that of any P.M. within memory', but the Commons regarded the government as 'a one man show' because 'Some of the seniors lack drive & push and some of the juniors are not loyal.'[77]

This was certainly the lesson to emerge from the so-called 'Under-Secretary's revolt' in mid-December during which Robert Hudson, the Overseas Trade Secretary, intimated to Chamberlain that he and his friends wholeheartedly supported appeasement but they 'and many people in the country thought that certain members of his Government were not contributing as fast as we should like to see to the essential corollary of appeasement, namely rearmament'. This junior minister then coolly informed Chamberlain that unless Inskip and Hore-Belisha (and preferably Winterton and Runciman) were dismissed, he and at least four other junior ministers would have 'to consider their position'.[78] Although Chamberlain had been 'surprisingly patient' with this impertinent threat, Hoare immediately aggravated the crisis by telling Beaverbrook, with the result that the story appeared in the *Evening Standard* on 19 December. By this stage, however, the affair had 'pretty well fizzled out', leaving Hudson 'a rather solitary figure' after Lord Feversham dissociated himself from the action and Lords Dufferin and Strathcona both communicated to Chamberlain that Hudson had 'gone beyond his brief' by attempting 'to put a pistol at [his] head'. Nevertheless, they still reiterated their desire 'to get rid of L.H[ore] B[elisha] and ginger up production' and 'thought it absolutely right that [he] should be aware of their feeling', while Hudson's complaints were simultaneously confirmed by private warnings from other sources. To make matters worse, Chamberlain was soon confronted by further press demands for the removal of 'Shakes' Morrison, the beleaguered Agriculture Minister and Malcolm MacDonald, now the Colonial Secretary.[79] As a result, Chamberlain complained that much of Christmas and January were devoted to 'frantic efforts to find how to put the jigsaw puzzle of the Cabinet together'; a quest which ended with Chatfield's appointment as Minister for the Coordination of Defence on 29 January, along with Sir Reginald Dorman-Smith, the former NFU chairman, who became Minister of Agriculture in the hope both of 'satisfy[ing] the farmers without undue strain on the exchequer'. In order to maximise the impact of these appointments, press attention was drawn to the fact that they were both acknowledged experts in their fields.[80]

Unfortunately for Chamberlain, the only course he believed likely to improve the political situation radically was 'to get rid of this uneasy and disgruntled House of Commons by a General Election'. This, however, he considered to be 'suicidal' in view of electoral concerns about foreign policy, rearmament and agriculture; a view reinforced by a pessimistic CRD analysis of by-election trends in late November which suggested that the outlook was 'far less promising than it was a few months ago'. Chamberlain thus concluded he had no choice but to 'grin and bear it', although at the back of his mind he found it 'hard to believe that if the country were really made to face up to the question whether they wanted a change of policy … they would not draw back & prefer the devil they know to the devil they don't know'. But this was a dangerous gamble without careful preparation and it was indicative of his doubts that at Chequers in mid-December he gloomily speculated as to how much longer he would enjoy such visits.[81] Despite all the setbacks and disappointments, however, Chamberlain remained as convinced by the wisdom of his chosen 'double policy' as he was of his own indispensability in carrying it out. 'Fortunately my nature is as Ll.G. says extremely "obstinate" and I refuse to change', he noted defiantly on 8 January, 'but if anything happened to me I can see plainly that my successor would soon be off the rails and we should once more be charged with that vacillation which in the past has made other diplomats despair.'[82]

V

At the heart of Chamberlain's depression was the increasing recognition that Munich did not signal a new era of progress towards peace and negotiated settlement. Despite his assurances to the Cabinet that Hitler wanted to take 'active steps to follow up the Munich agreement by other measures aimed at securing better relations', with every day that passed the dictators became more insolent in their undisguised contempt for the democracies – with the effect that his own 'double policy' became progressively more difficult to pursue.[83] If Chamberlain was ever to vindicate his strategy and silence the critics, therefore, he needed to make some demonstrable and enduring progress with the dictators now that Hitler's last territorial demand had been granted. With this in mind, in late October he told Geoffrey Dawson, the editor of *The Times*, that he planned 'to get on with Italy first, & more or less leave Germany alone until early next year, & then bring up the question of colonies in a bold & comprehensive manner'.[84]

Unfortunately, such hopes and plans were repeatedly shattered during the six months after Munich. On 3 October, Count Ciano, the Italian Foreign Minister, peremptorily demanded that the Anglo-Italian Agreement should come into effect within three days or they would 'have to take "certain decisions which they would prefer not to take"'; a threat interpreted to mean a tripartite military alliance with Germany and Japan. Yet while Halifax was 'very anxious' to give the necessary assurances and Chamberlain agreed 'on merits', they dared not make such an announcement given the excitable state of Parliament and the fear of ministerial resignations. As a result, Chamberlain resolved 'to reject Musso's "ultimatum" & hope for the best'; a gamble which paid off when his request for 'a short breathing space' was granted in order to ease Chamberlain's 'shaken' position and to preserve hopes of a rapprochement with Britain at a time when Mussolini recognised that closer ties with Germany and Japan would be 'most unpopular in Italy'.[85] Despite these early difficulties, however, Chamberlain remained convinced that Rome was 'the end of the axis on which it is easiest to make an impression'. To this end, in late October the Cabinet were asked to approve the implementation of the Anglo-Italian Agreement with the explicit objective of separating Rome from Berlin.[86] After this, Chamberlain hoped to arrange a visit to Italy in January for a 'heart to heart' with Mussolini to inspire confidence in British friendship, to 'help him … escape from the German toils', to persuade him once more to encourage Germany along the path of peace and 'to prevent Herr Hitler from carrying out some "mad dog" act'.[87]

An essential diplomatic preliminary to these Italian overtures was a public demonstration of Anglo-French solidarity. Chamberlain and Halifax accompanied by their wives visited Paris in late November with the intention of allowing the French people 'an opportunity of pouring out their pent up feelings of gratitude and affection'. More important at a diplomatic level, Chamberlain hoped to strengthen Daladier's political position and encourage him to improve French defences while demonstrating that British overtures to the dictators did not imply any abandonment of established allies.[88] The visit lived up to all these expectations. The British ministers received a 'wonderful reception' from cheering crowds in Paris, while Chamberlain was 'well satisfied' with the ministerial conversations which ended in 'complete harmony' – despite unsuccessful covert efforts by the British General Staff to encourage Daladier to embarrass Chamberlain into a continental commitment. Moreover, as the British Ambassador reported to London, the visit successfully persuaded the French that the forthcoming Italian talks were to be 'accepted … as a matter of course'.[89]

No sooner had this thread been successfully woven into Chamberlain's strategy than it all began to unravel. On 30 November, in a speech to the Italian Chamber of Deputies, Ciano launched a well-orchestrated anti-French campaign which included territorial demands for Tunis, Djibouti, Corsica, Nice and Savoy. Besides infuriating French opinion and reigniting their alarm at the British visit to Rome, this outburst also inflamed British opposition to such a visit and even raised doubts in Chamberlain's mind as to whether it could now produce the desired results; a warning communicated to Mussolini in the hope of inducing more reasonable behaviour.[90] In order to reconcile his policy towards both existing and potential allies, Chamberlain thus assured the French that the Anglo-Italian Agreement provided for the maintenance of the *status quo* in the Mediterranean, while simultaneously displaying some guarded sympathy for Mussolini's more moderate claims.[91] Despite 'a good deal of trepidation and doubt as to the possibility of bringing off any tangible result', however, Chamberlain had 'no shadow of doubt' that he was right to go because the 'true test' of his mission would be his ability 'to establish a relation of confidence in Musso'.[92]

In the event, Chamberlain returned from his exhausting four day mission to Italy on 14 January claiming that he had 'achieved all I expected to get and more' and that he was 'satisfied that the journey has definitely strengthened the chances of peace'; an optimism endorsed by the previously sceptical Halifax. By all accounts, the 'most striking feature of the visit' was the astonishingly enthusiastic response of the Italian people everywhere they went – in direct defiance of Mussolini's orders.[93] Although Chamberlain spent less than three hours in conversation with Mussolini, this was sufficient to warn him of the 'terrible tragedy' if aggression took place under the misapprehension that Britain and France would not fight. Moreover, Chamberlain had been impressed by Mussolini's attractive sense of humour and considered the talks 'a much pleasanter affair than with Hitler' because he felt he was 'dealing with a reasonable man, not a fanatic, and he struck us ... as straightforward and sincere in what he said'.[94] In this context, Chamberlain would undoubtedly have been devastated to learn that Mussolini thought his visitors were 'not made of the same stuff as Francis Drake and the other magnificent adventurers who created the Empire' but rather were 'the tired sons of a long line of rich men, ... [who] will lose their Empire'. Worse still, Mussolini regarded Chamberlain's characteristic umbrella with utter contempt; a sign of bourgeois decadence which convinced him that Italy could ignore Britain in its preparations for war with France.[95]

The apparent success of Chamberlain's Italian visit did much to dispel his brooding melancholy of the previous month and when he returned home he was lauded by *The Times* as 'an architect of peace'.[96] Indeed, by mid-February his optimism had soared to such a point that he predicted that they were 'getting near to a critical point where the whole future direction of European politics will be decided'. Although Mussolini would need 'to be handled with the utmost care and tact', Chamberlain was confident that he could 'carry him along without causing him humiliation'. Indeed, as he told Ambassador Kennedy, he considered him 'a practical operator ... who likes to see the whole picture, very much like himself, as against Hitler, who looks out of the window at Berchtesgaden, dreamingly considering the future prospects of Germany without being very practical'.[97]

In adopting this more optimistic posture, Chamberlain did not conceal from himself the obstacles in his path. Eden's increasingly obvious efforts to return to office might create difficulties, but Chamberlain felt neither the need nor inclination to respond to his overtures. Anyway, he feared such an appointment 'might even tempt [the Dictators] to break out now before the democracies had further strengthened their position'. Spain represented another potentially dangerous complication as the civil war moved rapidly towards a close – particularly as Chamberlain could never be certain that the Foreign Office would not revive the 'old Eden lines' of hostility to the dictators. 'I simply cannot keep their minds fixed on our real purpose', he complained in mid-February, 'the dislike they have of the totalitarian states is so strong that it will keep bursting out.'[98] Even here, however, he remained confident that Britain would not only be able to establish good relations with Franco but could use the end of the civil war as an opportunity to reduce Franco-Italian tensions. On this basis, he continued to nurture hopes of commencing disarmament talks with Mussolini as a prelude to renewed overtures towards Germany. 'At any rate that's how I see things working round and if I am given three or four more years I believe I really might retire with a quiet mind.'[99]

VI

Laying the foundations for a rapprochement with Hitler represented a more formidable challenge to the Prime Minister's patience and ingenuity. In the aftermath of Munich, Chamberlain believed that he was more popular in Germany than Hitler and that his enormous prestige abroad derived from the fact that his name was 'almost a synonym for peace'.[100] There was a faint glimmer of truth in this view, but Hitler had been infuriated by the jubilant cheers of '*Heil* Chamberlain' from the Munich crowds and he rapidly came to hate 'that silly old man ... with his umbrella'. Worse still, he soon came to regard Munich less as a bloodless victory than a defeat which had deprived him of the opportunity to appear as a conquering hero at the head of a victorious army, wreaking vengeance on the Czechs for their past defiance. As a result, in early October when the Downing Street press secretary requested some expression of German friendship from Berlin to strengthen Chamberlain's domestic position in time for a general election, all he received in return was a series of extravagantly abusive speeches denouncing Chamberlain's 'governessy interference'. As these attacks were deeply resented by British opinion, they still further reduced the scope for Chamberlain to pursue a policy of negotiation.[101]

The infamous Nazi pogrom unleashed against the Jews during the night of 9–10 November 1938 outraged British public opinion and made Chamberlain's task almost impossible. Named *Kristallnacht*, after the millions of fragments of broken glass on German pavements outside looted Jewish property, this wave of anti-Semitic terror effectively precluded further approaches to Hitler. Chamberlain was genuinely 'horrified' by *Kristallnacht* and he intervened personally to ease the entry restrictions on alien refugees into Britain, despite backbench and grassroots disquiet at the influx.[102] But at the same time, he inevitably lamented that there seemed 'to be some fatality about Anglo-German relations which invariably blocks every effort to improve them'. Confronted by public outrage, Chamberlain thus attempted to tread a delicate tightrope – 'to avoid condonation on the one side or on the other such criticism as may bring down even worse things on the heads of these unhappy victims' given his entirely accurate assessment that 'Nazi hatred will stick at nothing to find a pretext for their barbarities.' On this basis, he told the Foreign Policy Committee that 'disagreeable' though it was, as Britain could 'do nothing except pin-prick' he proposed to confine action to the relief of Jewish suffering, in order (as he put it), to 'ease the public conscience'. The unemotional pragmatism of this proposition was more than Halifax could stomach. Declaring angrily that he saw 'no useful purpose' in further conversations with Germany, the Foreign Secretary openly defied the Prime Minister by arguing forcefully that they should correct 'the false impression that we are decadent, spineless and could with impunity be kicked about'.[103]

Confronted by this upsurge of public and Cabinet disgust, Butler concluded 'our policy of appeasement must for the time being be put on the shelf'.[104] Certainly for Chamberlain, *Kristallnacht* implied only a necessary tactical withdrawal to appease inflamed sensibilities at home, rather than any fundamental reversal of strategy abroad. While he talked of 'the disappointing way in which the situation had developed in Germany since the Munich settlement', therefore, he pointedly dismissed Halifax's reports of Hitler's increasing hostility to Britain as vague 'generalisations'.[105] At the same time, the Foreign Office was horrified to learn from intelligence intercepts that the Downing Street chief press officer was still in contact with Berlin through his counterpart at the German Embassy. Halifax was equally appalled by the optimistic tone of Chamberlain's speech to the Foreign Press Association on 13 December which 'laid too much stress on appeasement & was not stiff enough to the dictators'; a difference of strategy which ended in a 'slight tiff' when Chamberlain refused to amend the speech at Halifax's request.[106] Indeed, it was indicative of their changed relationship since September that even admirers noted that Chamberlain was now 'extremely bad at not showing such speeches in time to Halifax. He does not mean to treat anyone badly, but this is the [same] sort of occurrence as that which lay behind his parting with Anthony.' In the New Year, Chamberlain's encouragement for Montagu Norman's private visit to Berlin only further confirmed suspicions about 'the PM's policy of working behind his Foreign Secretary's back and keeping a side line out to the dictators'. Little wonder that even the sympathetic Butler thought 'the P.M. sometimes reminds me of the Stuart Kings – he is clear and upright but inelastic'.[107]

Despite revulsion at home and alarming indications that Hitler was 'more and more under the influence of Ribbentrop and Goebbels and less accessible to his more moderate advisers', Chamberlain attempted to reopen communications with Berlin in late January 1939, fortified by reports of Nazi fears that the Anglo-American trade agreement contained secret military clauses.[108] In a major speech at Birmingham on 28 January, Chamberlain resisted all Halifax's efforts 'to put some stiffening into it', by proclaiming his desire for international peace. Significantly, in a direct personal appeal to Hitler he declared that 'the time has now come when others should make their contribution'. In order to assist this process of reciprocation, Wilson sent an advance copy of the text to

Berchtesgaden for Hitler to consider as he prepared his own Reichstag speech for 30 January; overtures which appeared to bear fruit when it was reported that Hitler's conciliatory reference to a 'long peace' in his own speech was included as a direct response to Chamberlain's invitation.[109]

After hearing Hitler's Reichstag speech, Chamberlain cheerfully concluded that 'at last ... we are getting on top of the dictators'. In that much-favoured phrase which contributed so much to his downfall in 1940, Chamberlain confided in his sisters: 'They missed (or rather Hitler missed) the bus last September and once you have done that in international affairs it is very difficult to reproduce the situation.' Above all, he was now confident that weaknesses in Anglo-French defences had been addressed since Munich, 'so that they could not make nearly such a mess of us now as they could have done then, while we could make more of a mess of them'. Moreover, confident that German public opinion had been so alarmed by the prospect of war in the previous September that they were unlikely passively to accept it again, he rejoiced in the fact that it was increasingly evident that 'in case of trouble it would not take much to bring U.S. in on the side of the democracies'. While all these factors 'add to the weight on the peace side of the balance', Chamberlain thus recognised (for the first time), that together they were now 'sufficiently heavy to enable me to take that firmer line in public which some of my critics have applauded without apparently understanding the connection between diplomacy and strategic strength which ... has been always stressed by the wisest diplomats & statesmen in the past'.[110]

This 'stiffening attitude' which Chamberlain believed had 'done much to make Hitler believe that the English would not take a fight lying down', reflected a new mood of resolution in British foreign policy every bit as significant as the far more famous guarantee to Poland seven weeks later.[111] Over the winter of 1938–39 a steady flow of secret intelligence from the German conservative 'resistance' to Hitler suggested that he was 'barely sane, consumed by an insensate hatred of this country, and capable of ordering an immediate aerial attack on any European country and of having his command instantly obeyed'.[112] In late January, reports of an imminent attack on Holland and France plunged Halifax into such a state of anxious despondency that he demanded the removal of all financial restrictions on rearmament. For his own part, Chamberlain dismissed such rumours as untrustworthy efforts by the anti-Nazi resistance within Germany designed to further their own ends by frightening the British into a firm line. But while this assessment was essentially correct, the Cabinet were no longer able to ignore either these threats to the West or French suspicions that Britain 'want[ed] to fight her wars on the Continent with French Soldiers'. Having secretly agreed that a German attack on Holland would constitute a *casus belli*, on 6 February Chamberlain reluctantly announced that any threat to 'the vital interests of France ... must evoke the immediate cooperation of Great Britain';[113] an acceptance of the long avoided continental commitment which served as a prelude to the first Anglo-French staff talks since the Great War and the announcement of plans to equip an expeditionary force a month later. By the end of March, Chamberlain and Hore-Belisha agreed almost casually to double the size of the Territorial Army to 26 Divisions in order to provide unobtrusively for the permanent manning of anti-aircraft defences.[114]

The salutary effects of this new continental commitment were reinforced by information about German economic weakness and increasing tensions within the Nazi regime as inflation, working hours and taxation all rose sharply. Although Halifax thought differently, one of the recurring themes underpinning Chamberlain's optimistic appraisal of Hitler's future intentions was the belief that rearmament had imposed such an enormous strain upon Germany's financial position that Hitler's only option was peaceful trade to restore the balance of payments and the standard of living. As a result, he told Ambassador Kennedy in mid-February that he saw 'a very definite chance of arriving at some solution through economics', while Hitler's public acknowledgement of these problems in his Reichstag speech convinced him that Germany was 'not in a position ... to start a deathly struggle'.[115] Contrary to Vansittart's gloomy prognostications of impending aggression, therefore, Chamberlain's information from Germany – largely from the over-conciliatory Henderson – suggested that 'Hitler and Ribbentrop so far from hatching schemes against us are searching round for some means of approaching us without the danger of a snub';[116] an impression strikingly confirmed by a *Deutsche-Englische Gesellschaft* dinner in honour of the returning Henderson on 15 February, at which the Duke of Saxe-Coburg's speech was reported to have been 'rewritten "under higher authority"' during the banquet itself to create a more conciliatory tone.[117]

Greatly encouraged by this gesture, Chamberlain regarded it as the first step towards the final settlement which had so long eluded him – although he recognised it would 'take some time before the atmosphere is right' because 'people have got so frightened and "het up" about [Germany] that we should have to approach the subject with the greatest care'.[118] While Hoare launched a 'counter-campaign' against press and public pessimism at home, therefore, Chamberlain's own speech to a packed audience at Blackburn on 22 February signalled his hope that Hitler would seek a solution to his economic problems through trade and a reduction in armaments rather than through a war of conquest; a hint gratifyingly reported by the German press.[119] In order to give substance to such aspirations, an Anglo-German coal agreement was signed on 3 February and plans were made for Stanley to lead an industrial mission to Berlin.[120] Convinced that these industrial contracts were 'steps in the right direction', Chamberlain and Halifax were thus both reported to be 'keeping their fingers crossed'. Yet as Ambassador Kennedy shrewdly reported to Washington after long talks separately with both men in mid-February, 'I think that the point of difference on the whole question of England's relationship with Germany is that the Foreign Office believe that Hitler is not to be trusted at all and that he will do something that will provoke trouble any day. Chamberlain's idea is that he is going to go along, preparing and arming all the time, but assuming that he can do business with Hitler.'[121]

VII

More convinced than ever that everything 'point[ed] in the direction of peace', by mid-February Chamberlain was 'going about with a lighter heart than ... for many a long day'. By early March he appeared to have every reason for confidence. Abroad, he expected a 'period of gradually increasing peacefulness' leading ineluctably to disarmament and prosperity. Hitler was privately denounced as 'impractical and fanatical', but Chamberlain assured the American Ambassador that 'the only hope of doing business with Hitler is to take him at his word', on the grounds that 'it was by no means certain that the word will be kept, but up to date he had no reason personally to disbelieve it'.[122] At home, the government remained firmly in control, while reports from the constituencies left Chamberlain supremely confident that they would 'romp in' at an autumn election – particularly following the outbreak of internecine strife within the Labour Party over Sir Stafford Cripps' campaign for a Popular Front against fascism.

Even the problems with his parliamentary party, which had so depressed him over the Christmas recess, were now dispelled by two months of decreasing international tension. Indeed, by mid-March, Chamberlain was amused to find that 'all the prodigal sons are fairly besieging the parental door' as committed opponents like Churchill, Eden, Duff Cooper, Wolmer, Vernon Bartlett and Harold Nicolson publicly professed their support, while Jim Thomas (who resigned with Eden) wanted to become a whip, Duncan Sandys was 'a reformed character' and even 'poor Leo Amery' was reported to be 'eating humble pie'. Little wonder that at a dinner with the 1936 Club on 7 March, Chamberlain appeared 'jolly, enjoying himself and amazingly open and confiding' as he assured the 40 MPs present that 'the dangers of a German War [were] less every day, as our rearmament expands'. After this 'phenomenal success' he even concluded that such occasions 'go a long way to break down the isolation in which the P.M. necessarily lives'. Despite Labour insinuations about his alleged fascist sympathies and the 'hypocritical cant' of Sinclair and self-proclaimed moralists like Gilbert Murray which made him 'hate & despise the Liberals in a way I don't feel about Labour', Chamberlain demonstrated an unshakeable conviction that events were finally vindicating his policy and that this made him more than ever indispensable. 'Like Chatham "I know that I can save this country and I do not believe that anyone else can"', he wrote six days before his seventieth birthday. 'But I want a few more years for it, and if I can put any credence in the reports that reach me I shall get there.'[123]

Chamberlain's sense of personal well-being rose with his political fortunes. Despite the exertions of his Rome visit, Geoffrey Dawson was 'struck by how fit he looked – bronzed & very vigorous' and concluded that 'one thing that keeps Chamb. fresh is his absolute immunity from worrying or brooding. He makes up his mind what is the best *immediate* thing to do, & does it with all his might, to the exclusion of doubts & alternatives.'[124] Lavish flattery from the Italian and German embassies undoubtedly helped, as did assurances from Ambassador

Kennedy that America was slowly coming over to his side and that Eden's recent visit to Washington had failed to impress Roosevelt. As always, the first signs of spring in the garden also roused Chamberlain's spirits, while his mission to restore the woodlands at Chequers provided an engrossing source of distraction from the burdens of office. Despite his robust health, on the eve of his own seventieth birthday, Chamberlain had briefly pondered the fact that only two days after Birmingham's spectacular celebrations to mark his father's seventieth birthday he had suffered the devastating stroke which ended his political career. Yet when he compared himself with his father at the same age, he never doubted that he was in better condition and talked of being 'good for at least one more Parliament' – if only to infuriate his critics. As all agreed, Chamberlain 'seemed to be adding years to [his] life instead of taking them off!'[125]

In this buoyant mood, Chamberlain suddenly gave way to another act of hubris comparable with his unfortunate promise of 'peace for our time'. In an unofficial briefing to lobby correspondents on 9 March 1939, Chamberlain predicted that Europe was settling down to a period of tranquillity and that a disarmament conference would meet before the end of the year. Unfortunately for Chamberlain, their rather 'clumsy' verbatim reporting of what he intended to be a background briefing brought a stern rebuke from Halifax on the grounds that he did not share Chamberlain's confidence and feared that Hitler would be 'encouraged to think that we are feeling the strain ... and the good effect that the balance you have up to now maintained between rearmament and peace efforts is tilted to our disadvantage'. Despite a suitably contrite apology, however, Chamberlain remained unrepentant. As he told his sisters, it was 'a good thing that the dictators should be made to feel our confidence'.[126] To drive the point home, next day Sir Samuel Hoare dutifully obeyed Chamberlain's instructions and informed his Chelsea constituency association that if European leaders worked with singleness of purpose 'in an incredibly short space of time' the world could 'look forward to a golden age of prosperity'.[127] Five days later, German troops marched into what was left of Czechoslovakia.

Chapter 15

The Coming of War,
March–September 1939

'Hitler let me down shamefully, but by his own action he has created a new and far less reasonable situation for himself. He has shown the world beyond question that his word is not to be trusted and has enabled me therefore to unite this country and the Empire in resistance to further aggression. It remains to be seen what steps he will take to get his own back, for he seems to be a revengeful little thing. But my impression is that there are those about him who will not let him plunge the world into war on a hopeless quest.'

Chamberlain to Lord Weir, 3 April 1939, Weir MSS

By extinguishing the last vestiges of Czech independence and absorbing eight million non-Germans into the Reich on 15 March 1939, Hitler brazenly discarded the pretence that the Sudetenland was his 'last territorial claim' and 'appeared under his true colours as an unprincipled menace to European peace and liberty'.[1] After this devastating blow, Chamberlain was scarcely exaggerating when he declared it had been a 'black week'. 'No balder, bolder departure from the written bond had ever been committed in history', Channon recorded in his diary. 'The manner of it surpassed comprehension and his callous desertion of the Prime Minister is stupefying.'[2] Despite words of sympathy from the King and the assurances of friends that there was 'nothing on your side that you need regret', nothing could obscure the fact that it appeared 'his whole policy of appeasement is in ruins'.[3] Moreover, coming only a few days after his public declaration that European tensions were decreasing, the Prague invasion raised the most fundamental questions about Chamberlain's judgement and credibility.[4]

Yet if Hitler's treachery gravely damaged Chamberlain's prestige, the Prime Minister was solely responsible for turning this crisis into a potential disaster. Despite intelligence warnings for over a week before, Chamberlain was evidently stunned by Hitler's coup. He told the Cabinet on the day of the invasion that 'Czechoslovakia had spontaneously fallen apart' and at one point even declared that 'the German military occupation was symbolic, more than perhaps appeared on the surface'. His only comfort was the thought that 'our guarantee was not a guarantee against the exercise of moral pressure'; a logic which conveniently evaded the need to act on the transitional Franco-British undertaking regarding Czech frontiers given at Munich. After this, the Cabinet

351

agreed that action should be confined to the cancellation of the Hudson-Stanley visit to Berlin and the recall of the Ambassador to report. Unfortunately, at this rather disorientated stage of proceedings, Chamberlain reluctantly gave way to pressure for an immediate statement. That afternoon he thus informed the Commons that he 'bitterly regretted' German action, but that despite 'checks and disappointments from time to time, the object that we have in mind is of too great significance to the happiness of mankind for us lightly to give it up or to set it on one side'.[5] Although Chamberlain looked miserable, his tone and emphasis disastrously suggested that he was unmoved either by the Czech tragedy or the Nazi betrayal.

It was Chamberlain's personal decision to add this final point to the agreed text and according to Cadogan it was 'Fatal!' Supporters thought it a 'restrained but well received statement', but to critics already convinced that only force would halt Nazi aggression it represented an outrage. 'Your hero Chamberlain took a pluperfect pearler yesterday', Brendan Bracken sneered to Beaverbrook next day. 'Instead of telling Parliament that Hitler had broken the promises he made at Munich, he entered into a protracted legalistic argument worthy of Uriah Heep or Simon, or both.'[6] As a result, exultant critics rejoiced 'that Chamberlain will either have to go or completely reverse his policy'. Some even fantasised briefly about a government under Halifax with Eden leading in the Commons, while the mass of the parliamentary party privately voiced its alarm at the backbench Foreign Affairs Committee.[7] By then, however, Chamberlain had recognised his fundamental tactical error. As one Foreign Office sceptic put it, throughout Whitehall it was possible to detect 'a strange sound as if of the Turning of Worms'. British policy had apparently 'reached the crossroads'.[8]

By his own later admission, Chamberlain's initial statement was made in response to Opposition demands 'before we knew all that had happened and when we had had no time to consider our attitudes'. As a result, he felt 'obliged to be cool and so was accused of being unmoved by events'. As soon as he had time to consider the implications of Hitler's actions and to recover from the shock, however, he 'saw that it was impossible to deal with Hitler, after he had thrown all his own assurances to the winds'. Having repeated this conviction to Halifax and Butler next day, Chamberlain's planned speech to the Birmingham Unionist Association's annual dinner on 17 March provided him with 'a great opportunity to speak to the world' and he seized it with both hands.[9] Now fully conscious of widespread discontent, the original text on economic recovery and social services was discarded. The Prime Minister who addressed the world from Birmingham was a very different man from the one who had urged further appeasement and conciliation only two days before. As Butler recalled, it was 'more like an oration by the younger Pitt'.[10]

After explaining away the misapprehensions created by his earlier 'somewhat cool and objective statement', Chamberlain devoted half the speech to defending Munich as a means of enabling Hitler to prove his desire for peace and cooperation. He then unequivocally condemned German aggression as a wanton betrayal of the Munich agreement and speculated about his future policy: 'Is this the last attack upon a small State, or is it to be followed by others? Is this, in fact, a step in the direction of an attempt to dominate the world by force?' Although Chamberlain made no effort to answer this question, his peroration hinted at a new policy. While he was not prepared to enter into 'new unspecified commitments operating under conditions which cannot now be foreseen', he warned that 'no greater mistake could be made than to suppose that, because it believes war to be a senseless and cruel thing, the nation has so lost its fibre that it will not take part to the utmost of its power in resisting such a challenge if it were ever made'.[11]

When put in these robust terms, the Birmingham speech achieved all of its objectives. Despite the diplomatic language, Chamberlain had drawn the first proverbial line in the sand as a warning to Hitler. In so doing, he reassured his supporters and even temporarily silenced his critics. As most agreed, the speech helped to 'put him right after his restraint in the House of Commons'.[12] At the War Office, Hore-Belisha privately despaired that 'Neville has no intention of doing anything' because he 'still believes he can control Hitler and Mussolini' and other colleagues complained that Chamberlain was 'still not quite tough enough on the question of getting ready for war'. But notwithstanding such complaints, Malcolm MacDonald encapsulated the general Cabinet view when declaring that 'whereas the Prime Minister was once a strong advocate of peace, he has now definitely swung around to the war point of view'.[13] Listening to Chamberlain's speech at a constituency meeting in Southend, 'Chips' Channon certainly thought it 'was strong meat', while Margesson assured Chamberlain that 'all is well with the Party they are solid behind you; the few croakers cut no ice at all'. Even supporters of Lloyd George conceded that while there was 'a general acceptance that Chamberlain is incompetent, gullible and totally unfitted for the role he is called upon to play', it was also true that 'nobody can suggest an alternative that would command general confidence'.[14] For the time being, Chamberlain had regained control. Whether he could retain it, however, depended upon the ability to match his words with actions.

II

The destabilising effects of the German occupation of Prague set in train a process which embroiled Britain in precisely the sort of commitments Chamberlain had fought to resist since becoming Prime Minister – but ironically, the resulting guarantees were almost exclusively conceived and carried through the Cabinet by Chamberlain and Halifax before disorientated ministers had time to consider the implications. On the day of Chamberlain's Birmingham speech, Virgil Tilea, the Romanian minister in London, misleadingly told the Foreign Office that his government had received a German ultimatum demanding privileged rights to key exports and enquired as to the likely British response to a German attack if they resisted. In response to this request, Halifax took soundings in various European capitals and then informed the Cabinet that if another act of naked aggression took place 'it would be very difficult for this country not to take all action in her power to rally resistance ... and to take part in that resistance herself'. Chamberlain then made it abundantly clear that he shared this view and that he stood solidly behind his Birmingham declaration:

> The Prime Minister said that up till a week ago we had proceeded on the assumption that we should be able to continue with our policy of getting on to better terms with the Dictator Powers, and that although those Powers had aims, those aims were limited. We had all along had at the back of our minds the reservation that this might not prove to be the case but we had felt that it was right to try out the possibilities of this course ... he had now come definitely to the conclusion that Herr Hitler's attitude made it impossible to continue to negotiate on the old basis with the Nazi regime.

As he told the Cabinet, 'he regarded his speech [at Birmingham] as a challenge to Germany on the issue of whether or not Germany intended to dominate Europe by force. It followed that if Germany took another step in the direction of dominating Europe, she would be accepting the challenge.' It was a view the rest of the Cabinet willingly endorsed.

Although Chamberlain remained convinced that Britain was not yet strong enough to overwhelm Germany by force, by now he had concluded that they needed 'to go on rearming & collecting what help we could get from outside in the hope that something would happen to break the spell, either Hitler's death or a realisation that the defence was too strong to make attack feasible'. His policy had thus apparently shifted from trying to coax Hitler with kind words and concessions into an attempt to deter him with the threat of collective resistance and the fear of war on two fronts. As he told the Cabinet, this implied action 'to ascertain what friends we have who will join us in resisting aggression'. But given his belief that 'Poland was very likely the key to the situation', he argued that Britain should particularly enquire how far Warsaw was prepared to go in joining a structure of interlocking alliances. Ministers also agreed to establish another committee to consider the acceleration of the defence programme.[15]

It soon became apparent what this more assertive language meant in practice. After his Birmingham speech, Chamberlain curtailed his seventieth birthday celebrations in order to return to London where he began 'working flat out' on a 'pretty bold and startling' plan for a Four Power declaration by Britain, France, Russia and Poland to consult when the security or independence of a European State was threatened; a commitment stiffened to include 'joint resistance' at the insistence of Charles Corbin, the Counsellor at the French Embassy. Yet from the outset, Chamberlain stressed that this did not necessarily mean a guarantee of existing frontiers, nor would aggression against Memel or Danzig automatically trigger action if it did not undermine the independence of Poland. This plan was approved by the Cabinet on 20 March and despatched to the potential signatories the same day.[16] At the same time, Chamberlain and Wilson drafted another direct appeal to Mussolini designed to encourage his restraining influence over Hitler and 'to ascertain if it is possible to start driving in the wedge between Germany and Italy'; an objective for which Chamberlain was prepared to 'pay a big price' if Mussolini could deliver the goods. As he explained to his sisters, 'As always I want to gain time for I never accept the view that war is inevitable.'[17]

Next day, Tuesday 21 March, Chamberlain endured the tense climax of a 'grim week'. After two meetings with Service Chiefs and their ministers to consider immediate defensive measures against a surprise 'knock out blow' from the air, Chamberlain arrived at a State banquet in honour of the French President in time for Hore-Belisha to whisper the news that 20 German Divisions had been mobilised on their western frontier; alarming information which only compounded the depressing effect of reports earlier in the day that Ribbentrop had demanded the surrender of the largely German port of Memel 'by peaceful agreement' or Lithuania would be invaded at once. Little wonder that Chamberlain found it 'more than usually difficult to keep a smiling face' during the banquet or that he resorted to the unusual precaution of a sleeping pill to guarantee him some rest before his negotiations with the French next day.[18]

In the event, rumours of German troop movements were unfounded and Hitler did not launch a 'mad-dog' bombing raid on London. On the contrary, as the week progressed a temporary lull palpably relieved the rising tension. But Chamberlain's diplomatic overtures on 20 March brought him little comfort either. Mussolini did not bother to reply to Chamberlain's appeal for eleven days. And when he did, it was only to refuse to intercede unless France made territorial concessions, although the reply was 'wrapped in such a cloud of meaningless words' that Chamberlain did not discount the possibility that he had communicated with Hitler 'in a moderating sense'. The failure of Chamberlain's proposed Four Power declaration became evident rather sooner given Polish mistrust of Soviet involvement and their fear that any commitment to the containment of German ambitions would be likely to provoke the very attack the declaration was designed to prevent. As Chamberlain already sympathised with this mistrust of Stalin, when Poland rejected the Four Power Declaration on 24 March, he announced immediately that 'the Declaration is dead' and began exploring other means to achieve the same end.[19]

The alternative took the form of an interlocking structure of mutual defence agreements in which Poland would defend Romania from attack to preserve its own future security, while Britain and France would intervene to assist Polish resistance. In Chamberlain's mind this represented 'a more practicable scheme' than the Four Power Declaration and one which the Poles might well accept; a preference substantially reinforced on 22 March when the French insisted upon Polish participation in order to coerce Hitler with the threat of a war on two fronts. Moreover, as the principal focus of the plan was on Poland and Romania, and as they both profoundly mistrusted the Soviets, it was agreed that Russia should be invited to participate as a guarantor only after the primary agreement had been signed. Assured of French support, Chamberlain then brushed aside some strong objections to the exclusion of the Soviets at the Foreign Policy Committee on 27 March and the Cabinet two days later. Poland was of 'vital' significance, he told the sceptics, because 'Germany's weak point was her inability to conduct a war on two fronts.' On this basis, ministers found themselves being hustled into accepting 'the necessity for urgent and immediate action' to forge a bilateral agreement with Poland by a Prime Minister and Foreign Secretary who both knew precisely what they wanted and who were absolutely determined to prevail over non-specialist colleagues in order to achieve it.[20]

The perceived need for urgency was increased still further at 6pm on 29 March when Halifax and Cadogan pressed the Prime Minister to meet Ian Colvin, a young *News Chronicle* journalist who had just been expelled from Germany, but whose excellent contacts in Berlin made him one of Vansittart's intelligence sources. According to Colvin's 'hair-raising' account, Hitler 'had everything ready for a swoop on Poland' as a prelude to the absorption of Lithuania and other States. After this, Colvin warned, Hitler considered the possibility of a Russo-German alliance and 'finally the British Empire, the ultimate goal, would fall helplessly into the German maw'.[21] Chamberlain was initially sceptical of these warnings – but not because of an alleged 'cognitive dissonance' which encouraged him blindly to suppress all information which conflicted with his own prejudiced views[22] but rather because parts of Colvin's account seemed 'so fantastic as to make [Chamberlain] doubt his reliability' and because he had heard it all before. Indeed, after a steady flow of similar reports throughout the winter of 1938–39, Chamberlain had arrived at the essentially correct conclusion that these were 'absolutely planted' either by the Nazis to keep the Western Powers 'in a state of jitters' or by anti-Nazis 'hoping to start a war and then have a chance to rise against Hitler'. For this reason, after hearing Colvin's tale, Cadogan also noted that he was 'not entirely convinced. I am getting used to these stories.'[23]

Yet while Chamberlain and Cadogan were sceptical, Halifax 'seemed impressed' by Colvin and he was now determined to force the pace. In the event, the convenient arrival of simultaneous confirmation of Colvin's story from the Military Attaché in Berlin finally persuaded Chamberlain to set aside his doubts in the belief that unless action was taken they 'might wake up on Sunday or Monday morning to find Poland surrendering to an ultimatum'. As a result, after Colvin left the room, Chamberlain and Halifax 'then & there decided that we should have to make some such declaration' to the effect that Britain would go to Poland's assistance if its independence was threatened.[24] Next day, a British Military Intelligence assessment also warned that 'Germany proposes to "force the pace" over Danzig' and this was likely to occur 'in the first week of April either by force or by agreement'.[25] Seizing their moment, Chamberlain and Halifax then skilfully exploited these reports in order to stampede the Cabinet into an immediate guarantee of Polish independence to deter Hitler long enough to construct a 'peace front' in Eastern Europe.

According to Chamberlain's account, 'The rest of the week was a nightmare succession of Cabinets, Cabinet Committees, interviews with the opposition … drafting of telegrams and constant discussions with Halifax & Cadogan.' At an emergency Cabinet meeting on Thursday 30 March, Halifax advocated a British guarantee to Poland on the grounds that 'the best means of stopping German aggression was almost certainly to make clear that we should resist it by force', while Chamberlain emphasised that this represented the 'actual crossing of the stream' to a British commitment to war over Eastern Europe. Convinced that time was of the essence, Chamberlain then took the leading role in drafting a statement intended to be 'unprovocative in tone but firm' in stressing the important point 'that what we are concerned with is not the boundaries of states but attacks on their independence. And it is we who will judge whether their independence is threatened.'[26] In this manner, Germany would be left in no doubt that a still clearer line had been drawn in the sand, while Britain retained control over the interpretation of any future *casus belli*. Next day, the Cabinet agreed to the terms of the Polish guarantee without any detailed consideration of military capabilities or the means by which it would ever be implemented.

Once the decision had been made, there was a collective feeling 'almost of relief' among ministers who now recognised that nothing would deter Hitler 'short of a definite warning that force would be met by force'.[27] Properly oppressed by his unique responsibilities as Prime Minister, during that week of 'nightmares and momentous decisions', Chamberlain recalled that he could 'never forget that the ultimate decision, the Yes or No which may decide the fate not only of all this generation, but of the British Empire itself, rests with me'. But having resolved to act, he also confessed that he felt a 'load off [his] mind'.[28] At 2.52pm on the afternoon of Friday 31 March, Chamberlain informed the Commons of the British (and French) guarantee to lend Poland 'all support in their power' in the event of 'any action which clearly threatened Polish independence'; an undertaking designed to be the prelude to 'an agreement of a permanent and reciprocal character'. By all accounts this 'great and historic statement … went extremely well' and the House cheered the news.[29] Convinced that 'Hitler has received a definite check which will enormously affect his prestige', Chamberlain then retired to the peace of Chequers to survey the new tree planting and to revive abandoned dreams that he might still get away for his usual Easter fishing holiday after all.[30]

Although Chamberlain fully comprehended the momentous significance of the Polish guarantee, it is important to recognise that he did not regard it as a decisive step along the road to an inevitable war. On the contrary, its primary purpose was to bring Hitler to his senses to avert precisely this eventuality. In this context, he accepted the need for a Polish guarantee, like the decision to double the size of the Territorial Army two days before, largely as an exercise in gesture politics and diplomatic bluff designed to demonstrate to the world that 'we meant business in resisting aggression'.[31] The old strategy of keeping everyone 'guessing' had now been replaced by an explicit desire to remove any shadow of doubt about Britain's response to future Nazi expansionism. If this succeeded in restraining Hitler, well and good, but even if Hitler could not be restrained by such means, Chamberlain and Halifax agreed 'it was better that the nations under threat should stand and fight together, than that they should await German attack one by one'.[32] In the short term, however, Chamberlain was clearly gratified by the positive response to the Polish guarantee in the weekend press, concluding that it demonstrated 'the immense importance of correct timing, a factor which is frequently left out of account by critics who say Ah! at long last you are doing what I always said you ought to do'.[33] To ensure the limitations of the guarantee were clearly understood, a government-inspired leader in *The Times* next day noted pointedly that it 'does not bind Great Britain to defend every inch of the present frontiers of Poland. The key word in the declaration is not integrity but "independence".'[34]

For the time being, even the critics were silenced. Having briefed Lloyd George on the Polish guarantee at their first private meeting alone for over 20 years, Chamberlain recorded that 'all my bitterness seemed to pass away for I despised him and felt myself the better man'. He was probably equally gratified to hear that Eden's motion calling for national unity after Prague had 'put Anthony back a mile for its disloyalty and its futility'; an assessment confirmed when Eden and his supporters meekly assured Chamberlain of their complete support for the Polish statement.[35] Indeed, such was the breadth of consensus that in the Commons debate on 3 April dissident Tories like Eden and Churchill joined Opposition leaders like Greenwood, Sinclair and Lloyd George in expressing their support, leaving only Cripps to sound a discordant note with his left-wing attack. Having convinced the Commons that 'he will be as determined on the new policy as he was on the old', MPs reported that public opinion was now as solidly behind the Prime Minister as it had been after Munich and 'in many cottages their prayers are for you'. After a large meeting in Newcastle, even Eden informed Chamberlain that he had 'seldom seen such enthusiasm' for the government's policy.[36]

III

No sooner had one crisis been resolved than another one emerged to disturb the peace of Europe. On Good Friday, 7 April 1939, Italian forces invaded Albania. Despite assurances from the Italian Chargé d'Affaires that the invasion would 'take place in such a form as not to provoke a crisis in Anglo-Italian relations, or the international situation in general',[37] Chamberlain was depressed and infuriated by a 'dictator mentality' which prompted Mussolini to seize by force what he could have achieved by more acceptable methods without weakening the front against Hitler. After all, Albania had effectively been under Italian control since 1921 and it had been evident for some time that preparations for annexation were underway. In these circumstances, Chamberlain hoped until the end that 'Musso would so present his coup as to make it look like an agreed arrangement and thus raise as little as possible questions of European significance.' Instead, after Mussolini's resort to naked aggression, Chamberlain could only mourn the betrayal of his hopes of cooperation which his advance notice to Rome regarding the Polish guarantee had been intended to consolidate. As he confessed to his sisters: 'I am afraid that such faith as I ever had in the assurances of the dictators is rapidly being whittled away.' In such a mood, Chamberlain's attitude inevitably hardened towards Mussolini who had 'behaved to me like a sneak and a cad. He has not made the least effort to preserve my friendly feelings – on the contrary he has carried through his smash & grab raid with complete cynicism and lack of consideration.' Despite his refusal to denounce the Anglo-Italian agreement, a 'very distrustful' Chamberlain lamented that 'any chance of further rapprochement with Italy has been blocked by Musso just as Hitler has blocked any German rapprochement'.

At a personal level, Chamberlain also had cause to lament another 'completely wrecked holiday' as the Albanian crisis compelled his immediate return from Castle Forbes after only a few hours fishing. This time, however, it mattered far more to him than his recall during the Czech crisis seven months earlier because, as he told his sisters, 'though my physical condition is luckily wonderfully good I must admit that the mental strain is very great when it is so prolonged and I am disappointed at having to come back before I could get any benefit at all from the change'. A week later, he was still complaining that the interruption of his holiday 'made it much worse than if [he] had never gone away'. Moreover, Chamberlain's frustration and anger at the duplicity of the dictators was intensified by a painful awareness that events in Prague and Albania 'enable my enemies to mock me publicly and to weaken my authority in this country'.[38] As a result, in Parliament and even within his own Cabinet, he soon gave every indication of 'being on the run'; an impression reinforced when his opposition to any extension of British guarantees to cover Italian aggression was swept aside by Halifax's insistence upon further commitments to Greece and Romania.[39] After this defeat in mid-April, Chamberlain confided in his sisters that he had been 'at the nadir all this week' and felt 'very dispirited & very lonely'.

This gloom was further compounded by his reluctant decision to recall Parliament from its Easter recess to debate the Italian invasion. Having briefed the Labour leadership on several occasions during the week leading up to the debate on 13 April, Chamberlain expected their full support for the new guarantees to Greece and Romania – the latter specifically requested by Attlee and Dalton. Instead a 'dumbfounded' Chamberlain protested that 'Attlee behaved like the cowardly cur he is' by attacking and misrepresenting the policy; a betrayal of confidence which provoked a furious backlash. 'I have done with confidences to the Labour Party', he wrote after the debate. 'They have shown themselves implacably partisan and this game in which they have all the advantages of a truce & none of the disadvantages is too one-sided for me to go on with.' He had also hoped for better from Churchill after a personal briefing, but Churchill's bitterness that Chamberlain's summons did not herald his appointment to a new Ministry of Supply produced an 'acid undertone' which drew approving cheers from the Labour benches. As a result, it was scarcely surprising that the whole thing cast Chamberlain still deeper into depression after 'a rotten debate unworthy of the House'. Moreover, while he recognised that he was paying too much attention to personal abuse because of his 'rather "edgy" condition', he also complained that 'it is hard when one is fighting against such odds abroad to be continually having to ward off attacks at home'.[40]

It was symptomatic of Chamberlain's feeling of depressed isolation that for the first time he did not dismiss out of hand Churchill's crude attempts to return to office communicated via Margesson immediately after the Albania debate. As Chamberlain freely admitted, he 'was certainly feeling the need of help', but the dilemma was always the same: 'The question is whether Winston, who would certainly help on the Treasury bench in the Commons, would help or hinder in Cabinet or in council ... Would he wear me out resisting rash suggestions ...?' In part such doubts were a matter of temperament. As Chamberlain had noted during the Rhineland crisis in March 1936, Churchill was 'in the usual excited condition that comes on him when he smells war, and if he were in the Cabinet we should be spending all our time in holding him down instead of getting on with our business'; concerns amply reinforced during the recent Albanian crisis when Churchill had been 'the worst of the lot, telephoning almost every hour of the day' with various dangerous and inflammatory suggestions. Beyond these doubts about judgement, there was also the question of loyalty – or rather, Churchill's complete lack of it. After hearing one of Churchill's apparently sincere protestations renouncing intrigue and ambition a year earlier, Chamberlain noted shrewdly that 'he doesn't want office as long as he knows he can't have it, & though he won't intrigue himself he doesn't mind others doing it provided they are successful'. Despite this justifiable mistrust, however, Chamberlain also confessed, 'I can't help liking Winston although I think him nearly always wrong and impossible as a colleague.'[41] In the event, the Prime Minister's personal crisis soon passed and with it went Churchill's last hope of rehabilitation to office in peacetime. After a brief visit to Chequers to inspect his new trees and a magnificent display of daffodils in mid-April, Chamberlain felt '*ever* so much better for the change'. Having finally persuaded the Chequers Trustees to permit the Forestry Commission to manage the woodlands, he told his sisters that this took 'quite a load off my mind', but he added poignantly, 'I *must* remain P.M. a little longer to see the scheme well under way.'[42]

IV

This improvement in Chamberlain's spirits during the second half of April can be attributed largely to a general relaxation of international tension and the apparent success of the measures already taken to curb future aggression.

British guarantees to Greece and Romania on 13 April and an Anglo-Turkish agreement on joint action against aggression in the eastern Mediterranean a month later convinced him that they had 'gone a long way towards security in the Balkans'.[43] There were also more hopeful indications from Rome. Encouraged by Mussolini's 'most friendly and cordial' response over a petty diplomatic wrangle, just three weeks after the invasion of Albania Chamberlain decided to renew his overtures to Mussolini in the belief that since Prague he was 'getting more and more irritated with Hitler'. As in the past, he did so in the belief that if judiciously handled 'it might be possible to give the axis another twist and that this might be the best way of keeping Master Hitler quiet'.[44] In this mood, even the announcement of the so-called 'Pact of Steel', formalising the military alliance between Germany and Italy on 7 May, did nothing to shake Chamberlain's conviction that the Italians did not want Hitler to drag them into a war. Equally convinced that 'Mussolini would welcome in his heart an agreement with the French', in mid-July Chamberlain appealed to Daladier to consider possible concessions in order to encourage Mussolini to exercise 'a restraining influence' over Danzig, to buy time for further rearmament and to refute the allegation that the Western Powers only talked of negotiated settlements without ever giving them any substance; a request strengthened by the British Ambassador's reminder of the three important recent concessions Chamberlain had made to assist Daladier. 'As always', he wrote to his sisters, 'I regard Rome as the weak end of the axis and we should always be trying to bend it.'[45]

If continuity characterised Chamberlain's policy towards Italy after the invasion of Albania, much the same could still be said of his attitude towards Germany after Prague. Chamberlain declared the Polish guarantee to be an epoch-making step in Britain's foreign commitments and it was widely regarded at the time as a complete reversal of the policy of appeasement. Yet Lord Halifax overstated the case when he later recalled that the Prague invasion 'marked a turning point in Chamberlain's thought'.[46] Or rather, if Prague signified a watershed for Chamberlain, it was much more one of method and approach than of broader strategic conception. Indeed, for those in his circle, it was evident soon after the Polish guarantee that 'his heart is not really in this new policy which has been forced upon him by Hitler' and after similar guarantees to Greece and Romania, he again appeared 'unhappy in his new role of the protagonist of diluted collective security'.[47] Moreover, this was a demeanour which did not go undetected for long among Chamberlain's critics. 'There is a very widespread belief that he is running a dual policy', one anti-appeaser noted in late April; 'one the overt policy of arming, and the other the *secret de l'Empereur*, namely appeasement plus Horace Wilson.'[48]

There was much truth in these suspicions. At times during the spring and summer of 1939, Chamberlain appears utterly credulous in his pursuit of the receding mirage of permanent peace and with the benefit of hindsight it is easy to sneer at his lack of perspicacity. But until it was absolutely certain that Hitler could not be appeased or deterred, Chamberlain was driven by an overwhelming compulsion to pursue the possibility of peace to the end – because to accept the inevitability of war was an impotent refutation of statesmanship. As he assured one doubting supporter in January 1939, 'I am not a "peace at any price" man; but I must in any given situation be sure in my own mind that the cost of war is not greater than the price of peace.'[49] This was a conviction substantially reinforced by Chamberlain's sincere belief that since Munich 'the world had gained time, and time might also be useful in bringing Germany to reason'. Every extra month of peace, he reasoned, narrowed the military gap to such an extent that even a 'fanatic' like Hitler must eventually come to his senses and recognise that this was a war he could not win against rapidly rearming democracies and the force of world opinion.[50]

Although 'very leery of what Hitler has in the back of his mind', Chamberlain's self-appointed role was to ensure that Hitler arrived at precisely the same conclusion.[51] But as Sam Hoare warned, this required an exquisitely delicate balancing act. On one hand, while rearmament and defensive alliances were necessary, 'we shall force the mad dog to bite and he will have behind him the whole German people if they are made to believe that we are determined to put our feet on their heads'. On the other hand, however, in making friendly noises to Hitler there was 'the opposite risk that any word of caution that you say will excite the suspicions of all those who do not believe that you mean business'.[52] It was an extremely shrewd assessment, but for all the dangers and problems, Chamberlain was convinced that everything hinged upon Germany and that he was playing for the highest imaginable stakes. After all, if the German threat could be neutralised, the Italian challenge in North Africa and the Mediterranean would also be defused, leaving Britain free to respond to a far less plausible Japanese menace in the Far East. But the problem was that a carefully balanced policy on this scale demanded a subtlety and forbearance which Chamberlain's critics tended to mistake for a cynical retreat towards another 'Munich' at the expense of Poland.[53]

Despite encouraging news brought back from Hitler's fiftieth birthday celebrations in April by the Duke of Buccleuch and Lord Brocket, their well-known Nazi connections ensured that Chamberlain greeted such reports with some scepticism. Yet there was always hope. 'Perhaps Hitler has realised that he has now touched the limit and has decided to put the best face on it', Chamberlain speculated on 15 April. 'But we won't take any chances.'[54] After a protracted battle and an 'unpleasant interview' with Hore-Belisha, Chamberlain consulted Wilson and Weir on conscription, supply and the taxation of profits, before finally giving way to the increasing clamour to place Britain on an overt war footing. On 20 April Chamberlain belatedly announced the creation of a new Ministry of Supply.[55] Despite his previously adamant opposition to compulsory military service for fear of alienating the TUC and inflicting a serious check on the rearmament programme, on the same day he also gave way to increasing domestic and international demands for conscription. Six days later a Military Training Bill introduced six months national service for men aged 20–21 for the first time in British peace-time history 'as an earnest of our intention to resist aggression and ... to provide the solution for certain urgent problems of defence preparedness during prolonged periods of tension'.[56] Deaf to complaints that he should have gone further and taken power to direct labour and industrial production, Chamberlain congratulated himself on his unerring fisherman's instinct for the correct timing having 'hit on the right moment when public opinion was ripe for the move and when the foreigners would not have been satisfied to wait for it much longer'. One further crumb of comfort was that medical examination of the conscripts rejected only 27 of the first 17,000 as unfit for military service; a stark contrast with the appalling results in the Great War and one which apparently vindicated his social reform record and refuted Labour allegations of widespread malnutrition. Three months later, 'shocking' revelations regarding the deprivation of the urban poor exposed by evacuation came as a bitter blow to this confidence, but even then Chamberlain consoled himself with the thought that 'however bad conditions are I am still convinced that they are infinitely better than they were 20 years ago'.[57]

It was indicative of Chamberlain's continued faith in his established 'double policy' that even these modest measures of deterrence were still accompanied by a tactful absence of provocation. On the day before Chamberlain's announcement of conscription, the dictators were privately reassured of its defensive rather than aggressive intent. More important, the choice of a complete non-entity like Leslie Burgin to head the new Ministry of Supply instead of Churchill, was dictated entirely by Chamberlain's belief that so long as there was 'any possibility of easing the tension and getting back to normal relations with the Dictators I wouldn't risk it by what would certainly be regarded by them as a challenge'.[58] As a result, 'long and prolonged cheers' at this announcement of decisive action were turned immediately into a 'gasp of horror' and 'real dismay' by his 'refusal to include any but yes-men in his Cabinet'.[59] Moreover, any positive goodwill created by these concessions to the rising mood of national resistance was almost completely dissipated by a series of letters in *The Times* during the first week of May urging the need to settle international disputes through negotiation; opinions expressed in terms which suggested to Chamberlain's critics that they were inspired (or even drafted) by Horace Wilson with the intention of surreptitiously preparing the ground for a resumption of overtures to Germany.[60]

Despite these damaging suspicions and the setbacks over Czechoslovakia and Albania, Chamberlain clearly still felt he was in a sufficiently strong position to be able to ignore his critics and to 'snap [his] fingers at Winston and Attlee & Sinclair'.[61] How far Chamberlain was correct in this belief was widely debated at the time. The Chief Whip (and others) regularly assured the Prime Minister that he enjoyed unprecedented levels of popularity within the parliamentary party and there was also no shortage of constituency resolutions reaffirming support for both him and his foreign policy.[62] On the other hand, however, after a visit to the Commons Smoking Room, Lord Davidson had been so 'extremely disturbed' at 'the state of discontent, and the way in which Winston and his friends, Anthony and his friends, and in the background

Ll.G., are making hay' that he immediately warned Ball. The criticism was 'not against Neville as a man, but as a statesman' – particularly given the weakness of his government, the 'laughable' appointment of Burgin and Chamberlain's isolation from the Commons and the Labour Party. 'In my long experience of intrigue and turbulence', Davidson concluded, 'I do not think I have ever known a situation in the House so fraught with danger to the Government, and especially to the P.M. himself ... to put it frankly, the situation could not be worse.' As part of a more general retaliatory campaign to mobilise active support for the Prime Minister, in May 'sound Chamberlain chaps' packed the Foreign Affairs Committee to ensure the election of Sir John Wardlaw-Milne as chairman in the belief that he would 'be fair and ... tolerate no nonsense from the Glamour group' led by Eden.[63]

The Prime Minister's standing with the broader public is more difficult to assess accurately. Chamberlain often remarked on the sharp contrast between the 'continuous marks of respect & affection from the general public' and the 'unending stream of abuse' in the Commons. After Munich, London 'society' appeared to drift away from Chamberlain to the uncomprehending despair of the still adoring 'Chips' Channon, but his hold over the ordinary voter was probably more assured.[64] Indeed, since becoming Prime Minister, Chamberlain had developed his own distinctly understated brand of charisma rooted in an almost messianic self-belief in his historic mission to save the nation. Although 'charisma' is a term which few within Whitehall, Westminster or Clubland would necessarily have employed, it is appropriate because, in an almost Gladstonian fashion, Chamberlain sought to mobilise the 'virtuous passion' of the people by appealing over the heads of the Cabinet, Commons, editors and press barons to enter into a direct personal dialogue with an inarticulate public desire for peace. As Duff Cooper later concluded about precisely this phenomenon, Chamberlain's hold over his fellow citizens stemmed from the fact that 'the ordinary Englishman sees in him an ordinary Englishman like himself' – decent, honest, but, above all, supremely anxious for peace.[65] Whatever the reason, the cheering crowds encountered everywhere from Glyndebourne to an 'enemy stronghold' like South Wales, convinced Chamberlain that he retained widespread public support and reports from both his own supporters and the purloined minutes of a recent Labour NEC meeting (presumably obtained covertly by Ball) all apparently confirmed this view.[66] 'In spite of the recent attacks upon Neville', Sam Hoare recorded in mid-July 1939, 'his position is very strong. Ninety per cent of the Party are solidly behind him in the House of Commons, and I believe that if there were an election tomorrow we should be returned with a thoroughly effective majority.'[67]

V

In mid-June 1939 Chamberlain once more asked himself 'whether any Prime Minister ever had to contend with such a series of critical events'.[68] This time the Japanese were the cause of his despair. The Tientsin incident was merely the culmination of a succession of increasingly aggressive acts, but it could not have come at a worse time or have threatened more alarming ramifications given escalating tensions in Europe. The British concession at Tientsin in northern China was protected by a single infantry battalion, in a region otherwise completely controlled by a Japanese military force which bitterly resented the perpetuation of privileged western enclaves within its emerging empire. When four Chinese suspected of murdering the manager of the Japanese-controlled Federal Reserve Bank took refuge within the concession, the British authorities initially cooperated with Japanese demands until an ill-judged and belated Foreign Office intervention decided that the men should not be returned to their custody. As a reprisal, Japanese troops blockaded the concession on 13 June, restricting the passage of vital supplies and subjecting British subjects to a campaign of bullying, strip searches and other calculated indignities.

Chamberlain's attitude towards Japan had hardened considerably since 1934 and for some time it had been clear to insiders that 'the PM does not like the Japs!'[69] Nevertheless, he rightly blamed the Foreign Office for misjudging the situation and was even more alarmed when it began talking vaguely about 'retaliation' on the grounds that this was 'only another name for sanctions and Abyssinia has shown us that sanctions are no good unless you are prepared to use force'; a possibility which the crisis in Europe and the Mediterranean definitely precluded. Assured there was no possibility of American naval support, Chamberlain thus concluded he had no option but to open negotiations with Tokyo – despite the deplorable effects this might have on Britain's friends and enemies alike.[70] For Chamberlain's Conservative critics, however, it was just one further example of his policy of craven retreat before outrageous insults, even if their moral indictment blithely ignored the fact that at no point after 1935 was a unilateral show of force a viable option in the Far East.[71]

On the other hand, tensions with Japan inevitably raised the question of Britain's strategic relationship with the United States – and this did appear to be improving. During the Czech crisis, two American cruisers had been stationed conspicuously in British waters and the transfer of the US fleet back to the Pacific in April 1939 was designed to be equally helpful as a check upon Japanese ambitions at a time when Britain needed to focus on the Mediterranean in the aftermath of the Albanian coup. These hopeful signs of better relations were reinforced over the winter of 1938–39 by messages from Roosevelt privately assuring Chamberlain of his 'real friendship' for Britain and his desire to do all in his power to ensure that if war came it would have the industrial resources of the United States behind it.[72] For his own part, during the spring and summer of 1939 Chamberlain regularly repeated to Washington 'how psychologically important it was in the drive for peace that Hitler believed the United States was definitely on the side of the democracies', although in deference to the difficulties of Roosevelt's position he always heeded Ambassador Kennedy's advice 'to be most careful not to ask for anything or speak as though we could count on them'.[73] These efforts were eventually rewarded a week after the declaration of war when Roosevelt sent a friendly personal letter assuring Chamberlain that it was 'definitely a part of the Administration policy' to revise the US Neutrality Act by repealing its arms embargo. In reply, Chamberlain thanked the President for both the promise of material assistance and the 'profound moral encouragement' as these were likely to have 'a devastating effect on German morale'.[74]

Chamberlain's willingness to set aside past prejudices towards the United States in the interests of national security was not matched by any parallel degree of softening in his attitude towards the Soviet Union. While capable of blowing hot or cold towards Hitler and Mussolini as circumstances dictated, Chamberlain's profound antipathy towards the Soviet Union was one of the most consistent features of his personal diplomacy. According to Ivan Maisky, the Soviet Ambassador in London, Chamberlain once referred to the Russian government as 'our enemies'; an alleged slip of the tongue which confirmed suspicions on the left that he would 'sooner see Hitler overrun Europe than find himself fighting Fascism as an ally of the Soviet Union'.[75] He was equally contemptuous towards 'the absurd hysterical passion of the Opposition egged on by Ll.G. who have a pathetic belief that Russia is the key to our salvation'. In late March 1939 he gave his sisters a classical exposition of these feelings and he repeated them regularly throughout the summer:

> I must confess to the most profound mistrust of Russia. I have no belief whatever in her ability to maintain an effective offensive even if she wanted to. And I distrust her motives which seem to me to have little connection with our idea of liberty and to be concerned only with getting every one else by the ears. Moreover she is both hated and suspected by many of the smaller states notably by Poland, Rumania and Finland so that our close association with her might easily cost us the sympathy of those who would much more effectively help us if we can get them on our side.[76]

Convinced that Soviet military weakness would encourage them to do everything possible to 'see the "capitalist" Powers tear each other to pieces while they stay out themselves', Chamberlain also feared that a Soviet alliance 'would definitely be a lining up of opposing blocs and an association which would make any negotiation or discussion with the totalitarians difficult if not impossible'.[77]

Chamberlain's historical reputation has paid a high price for resisting the clamour for a Soviet alliance, but his opposition arose from more than simple prejudice and it was shared even by some of his most vehement Conservative critics. Stalin's military purges between June 1937 and July 1938 destroyed almost the entire Soviet High Command along with half the Red Army officer corps, with such catastrophic effects that the British Embassy in Moscow repeatedly warned that it was 'not capable of carrying the war into the enemy's territory with any hope of ultimate success'.[78] Similarly, Chamberlain's contention that Russia was 'a very unreliable friend with very little capacity for active assistance but with an enormous irritative power on others' was amply confirmed by the very real hostility of Poland and its neighbours in response to British soundings about a Four Power Declaration in late March. When forced to choose, therefore, Chamberlain concluded 'our first task must be to erect a barrier against aggression in Eastern Europe on behalf of States directly menaced by Germany. Until that barrier had been erected it was clear that we ought to do nothing to impair the confidence of those States.'[79] Furthermore, as he told Labour's Hugh Dalton, 'the key to the position is not Russia, who has no common frontier with Germany, but Poland, which has common frontiers with both Germany and Romania'.[80]

Unfortunately for Chamberlain, the Polish guarantee increased rather than decreased the pressure to clarify Anglo-Soviet relations – but, this time, he faced far more concerted ministerial opposition to his preferred policy. Having been stampeded into the Polish guarantee by Chamberlain and Halifax in late March, the full Cabinet now had both the time and the inclination to make its own decision about a Soviet alliance. In doing so, it inflicted a substantial policy defeat upon Chamberlain, who had hitherto blithely imagined that his main problem was simply how 'to keep Russia in the background without antagonising her'.[81] Chamberlain's initial response to these pressures was to evade any bilateral commitment to the Soviets by persuading the Cabinet that Russia should follow Britain's lead with a unilateral declaration to assist any of its neighbours if they became the victim of aggression.[82] When the Soviets refused to discuss anything except a mutual defence pact, however, Chamberlain rapidly found himself the isolated voice of resistance as the Foreign Office, the Chiefs of Staff and most of the Cabinet reluctantly gave way when they realised they were 'coming up against [a] choice between Soviet alliance ... and breakdown – with all consequences'.[83] Worse still, the harder he fought against this gradual drift towards commitment during April and early May 1939, the more obvious it became that he bitterly resented 'being pushed all the time into a policy ... he does not like and that he hated abandoning the last bridge which might still enable him to renew his former policy'.[84]

This conflict of priorities came to a head at the Foreign Policy Committee on 19 May when Chamberlain found that Halifax – and even Simon – had now deserted him in favour of the dominant view that an alliance was preferable to nothing at all. Moreover, worse disappointments were soon to follow. When Chamberlain told Cadogan next day that he would rather resign than accept such a policy, he did so in the absolutely confident expectation that Poland and Romania would decisively repeat their implacable opposition to a Soviet alliance. As a result, it came as a devastating blow when Halifax reported from Geneva that while the Soviets still adamantly demanded a tripartite alliance, Poland raised no objection and the Dominions were divided. In these circumstances, Chamberlain seemed 'depressed' but 'apparently resigned' to defeat on the grounds that his only supporter was Butler ('and he was not a very influential ally') while further resistance would create 'immense difficulties in the House' – even if he could persuade the Cabinet.[85] Despite all his efforts, therefore, on 24 May the Cabinet finally agreed to negotiate a tripartite mutual defence pact with the Soviets. Later that afternoon, Chamberlain rashly informed the Commons that an alliance was as good as made.[86]

This marked a significant defeat for Chamberlain, but he characteristically believed he had lost a battle rather than the war. Indeed, after a talk with Horace Wilson, he rejoiced at his new and 'most ingenious idea' in which the tripartite alliance would be linked to the fulfilment of obligations under Article XVI of the League Covenant relating to collective resistance to aggression. From Chamberlain's perspective, this plan had the substantial advantage that it gave the Russians and the Cabinet what they wanted 'in form and presentation' and would 'catch all the mugwumps' at home while avoiding anything as definite as an actual alliance. Moreover, by tying it to Article XVI, the arrangement assumed a 'temporary character' because Chamberlain assumed this provision would soon be repealed or amended. Confident that the Soviets would find it difficult to refuse such a condition, Chamberlain thus recovered his equanimity and took on a 'happier mood'. In the event, however, this satisfaction was extremely short-lived because while his deception apparently fooled the Foreign Office and the French, Molotov, the new Soviet Foreign Minister, immediately saw it for what it was and contemptuously rejected any reference to the League – on the not unreasonable grounds that an uninvolved state like Bolivia could delay action at Geneva while Moscow was being bombed.[87]

These exchanges set the tone for the interminable and ultimately unsuccessful Anglo-French talks with the Soviets during the summer of 1939. While Western negotiators proved dilatory and evasive on the points to which Molotov attached most importance, he was offensive, overbearing, utterly impervious to argument and incurably suspicious of both the good faith and military value of the Western Powers. Yet from Chamberlain's still resentful perspective, Molotov's tactics played directly into his hands. Although initially uncertain 'whether the Bolshies are double crossing us … or whether they are only showing the cunning & suspicion of the peasant', it soon ceased to matter when it became evident that they were 'the most impossible people to do business with'.[88] With every further act of Soviet intransigence, Chamberlain rejoiced that 'we can't go on much longer on our present course' and he exploited every opportunity in the Foreign Policy Committee to raise the stakes in the hope of provoking a rift. In particular, evidence of Halifax's growing frustration with the 'maddening' Molotov during July, encouraged him to manoeuvre towards a breach by despatching a 'rather stiffer note' to Moscow warning that British patience was 'pretty well exhausted'. 'I would like to have taken a much stronger line with them all through', he confessed despondently to his sisters in mid-July, 'but I could not have carried my colleagues with me.'[89]

In the event, Chamberlain was denied his expected triumph by Molotov's sudden insistence that negotiations on a military alliance should begin at once. By the time these talks began on 12 August, however, it was already too late and on the third day they came to a complete halt when confronted by obdurate Polish and Romanian resistance to the idea of allowing Soviet troops on their territory. After this sobering demonstration of Anglo-French inability to deliver even the most basic of Soviet requirements, Molotov renewed his secret contacts with Germany. The resulting Nazi-Soviet Pact on 21 August, came as a bitter blow to both sides of the debate in Britain – but Chamberlain was by far the greater loser. Despite repeated warnings of a possible German-Soviet rapprochement, he had consistently declared such rumours were 'a pretty sinister commentary on Russian reliability' but, as he told the Cabinet in mid-July, he 'could not bring himself to believe that a real alliance between Germany and the Soviet Union was possible'.[90] When it became a reality, Chamberlain stoically shrugged off the news as having no bearing on the British obligation to Poland and to frustrate the Nazi hope that 'this bombshell would destroy the peace front' embassies abroad were instructed to adopt the same dismissive posture.[91]

Despite Chamberlain's studied insouciance, historians often argue that if the British had pursued these negotiations more vigorously during the summer of 1939 a Soviet alliance would have been the best, even the only hope, of curbing Germany without a war.[92] Yet it is extremely doubtful whether this was ever a realistic possibility given both Soviet suspicions that the West really wanted to turn German aggression against Russia and the meagre military assistance the Western Powers were prepared to offer. This was certainly the view of Lord Halifax, who soon concluded that Soviet thinking had turned towards an opportunistic marriage of convenience with the greater immediate threat from Germany simply as a means of 'buying time' to complete the Five Year Plan and restore the Red Army 'against the evil day which was probably bound to come'.[93] Moreover, given what is now known of Hitler's ambitions and his craving for war, the suggestion that an Anglo-French pact with the Soviets – or anything else except an assassin's bullet – would have provided a durable deterrent to Hitler's war must be even more questionable.

Yet while this is all conjecture, two things are absolutely certain. The first is that Chamberlain bears a substantial burden of personal responsibility for ensuring that this option was consistently obstructed and prejudiced, despite a growing body of Cabinet and parliamentary opinion which thought it should be pursued. In so doing, his grudging spirit may well have finally convinced the Kremlin's pragmatists that the Western Powers lacked both commitment and value to Soviet defence. Secondly, and even more crucially, although a tripartite pact would probably never have permanently deterred Hitler from aggression, by removing the fear of war on two fronts, the Nazi-Soviet pact made a conflagration an absolute and almost immediate certainty. On the day the Nazi-Soviet pact became public, Hitler informed his generals that the attack on Poland would take place without delay and that the Western Powers would not fight. 'Our enemies are small worms' he told his now fatalistic generals. 'I saw them at Munich.'[94]

VI

After the absorption of the vestigial Czech State and Memel into the Reich in March 1939, it was obvious to everyone that Danzig would be next. Danzig, modern day Gdansk, was a League of Nations 'free city' overwhelmingly German in population and politics, but located at the head of a 'Polish Corridor' to the sea. Since November 1938 Hitler had been planning the seizure of Danzig at 'a politically opportune moment' and tensions had steadily increased. Although Marcel Déat, a former French minister, had asked incredulously in May 1939, 'Who will die for Danzig?', in Britain there was a growing awareness that there might be no alternative. As one mainstream Conservative MP put it, 'in his heart of hearts every sane Englishman must realise that it would be grotesque and wicked to start a European war over the matter of Danzig and the Polish Corridor. But I don't see the country standing for another Hitler coup.'[95]

In May 1939, Chamberlain was not entirely joking when he remarked privately that he was at a loss to see how any Anglo-German *détente* could come about 'as long as the Jews obstinately go on refusing to shoot Hitler!' Nevertheless, he still believed German assurances that they had no plans to attack Danzig and was even hopeful that 'they realise that this time they can't get what they want without fighting for it'. But to take no chances, he devoted 'an unusual amount of trouble and worry' to a speech for the Women's Unionist Association at the Albert Hall on 11 May in which he declared that any effort to use force over Danzig 'would inevitably start a general conflagration in which this country would be involved'. It was an apparently unambiguous warning, but as Horace Wilson assured Henderson in Berlin, 'to make it perfectly plain to everybody that our policy is a balanced one ... he made it equally plain that we are very open-minded on everything else'.[96] Chamberlain's problem, however, was that this sort of 'balance' was far easier to discuss in theory than to deliver in practice. As he told a Labour delegation on 28 June, it would 'be dangerous to say either too much or too little; too much, so that Hitler should feel he had no alternative but war, and the Poles be unreasonably encouraged; too little, lest Hitler should think there were some steps which he could take with impunity and then find out that he had been wrong'.[97] In practice, it was certainly true that Chamberlain's tone had distinctly stiffened since Prague. Indeed, in July he briskly rejected Mussolini's proposal for another Munich agreement over Danzig at the expense of Poland as 'not good enough'.[98] But on the other hand, during the late spring and summer of 1939, he remained utterly impervious to Halifax's renewed pleas for finance to assist Polish rearmament on the grounds that Britain had neither arms nor money to spare. Anyway, he retorted, Britain's gold reserves were already 'strained to the utmost' supporting sterling and 'if we lose gold unnecessarily we shall not be able to maintain the fight ourselves for so long'.[99]

In many respects, Chamberlain was undoubtedly correct in claiming that it all came down to a question of priorities about 'how best to distribute our financial resources' – and given his past emphasis on economic strength as the 'fourth arm of defence' it was scarcely surprising that he opposed such aid to Poland.[100] Moreover, given the narrow margin of survival in the Battle of Britain, it was perhaps fortunate that Chamberlain did place immediate British needs above those of its allies. But the price of that decision was to turn his earlier brave talk of a European 'peace front' into a hollow sham. What had been conceived as a system of alliances capable of restraining Germany with the threat of war on two fronts, had been reduced to a few unilateral guarantees to isolated allies without any semblance of military credibility.[101] Always convinced that national salvation lay along the path of negotiation, in the end this became Britain's only option in the absence of any credible means of issuing an effective threat of deterrence. Yet if Chamberlain ever recognised these policy implications, he was apparently unconcerned by them. He always knew that it would be 'very difficult' to solve the Danzig problem, but he never despaired of a peaceful resolution; an unquenchable optimism which stemmed from his tragic misapprehension that Hitler was 'not such a fool as some hysterical people make out and that he would not be sorry to compromise if he could do so without what he would feel to be humiliation'. His own destiny, Chamberlain doggedly maintained, was to make this dignified retreat possible, difficult as it was 'when there are so many ready to cry "Nous sommes trahis" at any suggestion of a peaceful solution'.[102]

In this respect, Chamberlain's efforts were certainly not assisted by the embarrassing revelation of Robert Hudson's unofficial talks with Helmut Wohltat, Goering's deputy and head of the German Four Year Plan, about economic cooperation, colonies and even a possible British 'peace loan' to Germany in return for disarmament. When this became public knowledge on 22 July, Chamberlain rightly dismissed the incident as an unauthorised blunder by a conceited junior minister with 'a very bad reputation as a disloyal colleague who is always trying to advance his own interests'. But while all of this was true, the ensuing scandal was a disastrous blow, particularly when it emerged that Horace Wilson had also seen Wohltat secretly in June and July – thus giving the 'peace loan' idea 'a demi-semi-official air'. As Chamberlain noted in despair, 'all the busybodies in London, Paris and Burgos have put two & two together and triumphantly made five'.[103]

Despite these repeated setbacks and multiplying anxieties, by July Chamberlain still believed his long-term strategy was about to be vindicated. Indeed, this belief probably helped to stiffen his resistance both to Halifax's pleas for financial aid to Poland and towards the idea of Soviet negotiations. As he explained revealingly to his sisters on 23 July:

> One thing is I think clear, namely that Hitler has concluded that we mean business and that the time is not ripe for the major war. Therein he is fulfilling my expectations. I go further and say the longer the war is put off the less likely it is to come at all as we go on perfecting our defences, and building up the defences of our Allies. That is what Winston & Co never seem to realise.

You don't need offensive forces sufficient to win a smashing victory. What you want are defensive forces sufficiently strong to make it impossible for the other side to win except at such a cost as to make it not worth while. That is what we are doing and though at present the German feeling is, It is not worth while *yet*, they will presently come to realise that it never *will* be worth while. Then we can talk. But the time for talk hasn't come yet because the Germans haven't realised that they cant get what they want by force.[104]

In this mood, rumours of an imminent German coup against Danzig around the third week of August left him unconcerned because 'nearly always it is the predicted crisis that never materialises'. Anyway, as he told his sisters portentously, there were 'more ways of killing a cat than strangling it'. Next day, he told the King in equally vague terms that he was 'considering further means of bringing ... home' to Hitler that 'we mean business this time'.[105]

What Chamberlain meant by these tantalisingly opaque references was that he was engaged in a series of highly secret and unofficial contacts with the Nazi leadership through private individuals. The ultimate purpose of the approaches was to create the conditions in which formal negotiations could be resumed, while at the same time warning privately that Britain was not bluffing about its support for Poland. The possibility of using unofficial conduits for the task had first been considered in April when a constituent of Butler's had offered his services as an intermediary with the Nazi regime 'to promote better understanding'. The individual concerned was Ernest Tennant, the chair of the pro-Nazi Anglo-German Fellowship who for many years had been a close personal friend of Ribbentrop.[106] When conciliatory overtures from Goering were conveyed to Chamberlain via Axel Wenner Gren, a prominent Swedish businessman, in early July he finally decided to act.[107] For Chamberlain, the principal objective behind such contacts was to impress forcefully upon the Nazi leadership that 'the two phases of [British] policy are: – (a) Determination; and (b) Willingness to reason with reasonable people as soon as confidence is restored.' But as Horace Wilson's careful briefings to these unofficial intermediaries made absolutely clear, 'the essential thing was to see whether the German Government were prepared to create the conditions in which international confidence could be restored'.[108]

This message was carried to Ribbentrop by Tennant; to Goering by Wenner Gren and to other prominent Nazis by Arthur Bryant, the popular historian. Moreover, by the end of July such methods appeared to be bearing some fruit when Lord Kemsley, the owner of the *Sunday Times*, reported to Downing Street that during his recent visit to Hitler it had been suggested that each country should put its demands on paper as the basis for discussion. Clearly encouraged by this proposal, Chamberlain and Halifax agreed to despatch a secret reply but their efforts prompted no further German response.[109] When the German Embassy followed up the Wohltat conversations on 3 August, however, Chamberlain took the opportunity to repeat emphatically the crucial importance of adhering to 'the two phases of the Government's policy and that the second phase was dependent entirely upon the pre-restoration of the confidence that had been shattered in March'.[110]

While Chamberlain flew his various secret kites during July, his failure to threaten Germany publicly about Danzig ensured that British politics reached the summer recess in apprehensive and suspicious mood. In the Commons, the tensions were palpable as ill-tempered Opposition parties forced four major speeches – two on foreign affairs – from the Prime Minister in the final week of an exhausting session. During the great debate on the European situation on 31 July, Chamberlain endured Sinclair's prolix attack on his backsliding towards appeasement with 'good humoured dignity', before a 'most brilliant speech' in which he released a 'quiver ... full of arrows ... with deadly aim' against his tormentors. The debate on the adjournment two days later was characterised by even greater asperity on both sides when it became clear that a Labour amendment for Parliament to reassemble on 21 August (rather than 3 October) was intended as an occasion for Eden's 'Glamour Boys' to attack the Prime Minister personally. In retaliation, Chamberlain launched another devastating assault upon his detractors on both sides of the House and he sat down to 'roars of delight and approval, but also some of rage'. The motion was then defeated by 118 votes after Chamberlain made it a vote of confidence, but this did not prevent some 40 government supporters from abstaining and the House dispersed in an angry mood on 4 August.[111]

By now, Chamberlain was in an equally truculent frame of mind. Feeling more resentful than ever towards intra-party dissent and challenges to his authority, particularly where this extended to voting against him in the lobbies, Chamberlain was determined to use the forthcoming election to wreak vengeance upon some of his most bitter Conservative critics like 'Top' Wolmer and Ronald Cartland, a Birmingham MP who he believed had always been 'a disloyal member of the team' and whose stinging personal attack during the Adjournment debate left the lobbies 'humming'. In both cases, Chamberlain recognised that the party might lose the seat as a result but, as he noted angrily, 'I would rather do that (temporarily) than have a traitor in the camp.'[112]

VII

Judging by the brilliance of Chamberlain's attack upon his opponents during the final week of the Session, he had lost none of his vigour or determination to go on. 'The PM walks and talks like a debutante', the infatuated Channon noted after the foreign affairs debate on 31 July. 'What a remarkable old man he is, surely the most miraculous human being alive. He never shows any sign of fatigue, of age, of exhaustion, even of irritation.' Yet beneath the well-contrived appearance of 'a man at peace with himself', Chamberlain complained that 'it hardly represents my real frame of mind, for I confess that I do sometimes feel terribly discouraged'. This admission reflected Chamberlain's anxiety about the looming prospect of war and his bitterness towards unfair personal attacks – but it also now indicated a state of profound mental exhaustion. Despite gloomy forebodings that an international crisis might compel him to abandon his Scottish holiday, as he told his sisters in late July, 'I should give it up with great regret. I do feel that I should be a better instrument if I could get an unbroken fortnight in the solitude of Sutherlandshire.'[113] After a single night at Chequers, however, he soon recovered his spirits and 'worked like a beaver in the garden & woods' for two days before departing for a fortnight's rest in the highlands. At this juncture, he believed Hitler had been persuaded 'he can't grab anything else without a major war and has decided therefore to put Danzig into cold storage'. Given the mobilisation of the British fleet and Territorials and practice flights by RAF bombers over France, Chamberlain accurately anticipated some demonstration of Hitler's military strength 'to show he is not frightened', but he was prepared to accept this as 'part of the war of nerves' and determined not to over-react because this would 'play straight into Hitler's hands' and 'give the world the impression that we are in a panic'.[114]

Events followed the predicted pattern. At Lochmore, Chamberlain soon declared himself 'wonderfully well', walking long distances over steep terrain, catching three salmon in an hour on one day and indulging in the comfort of the Duke of Westminster's lodge where he and Annie enjoyed 'the perfection of luxury'.[115] But while Chamberlain tried unsuccessfully to relax, Hitler manipulated the crisis in Danzig to ensure that tension continued to simmer without boiling over too soon. When convincing secret reports of imminent German action against Poland prompted Chamberlain's recall to London on 19 August, he confessed that it was not too great a disappointment because he had 'never enjoyed a carefree mind' the entire time that he had been away. 'Phew! What a week' was his reaction to the days which followed his return:

> Whether this be a war of nerves only or just the preliminary stages of a real war it takes very strong nerves to stand it and retain one's sanity and courage. I feel like a man driving a clumsy coach over a narrow crooked road along the face of a precipice. You hardly dare look down lest you should turn giddy and there come times when your heart seems to stop still for minutes together until you somehow round the next corner and find yourself still on the track.

Yet even during this final crisis Chamberlain never entirely despaired. 'I count every hour that passes without a catastrophe as adding its mite to the slowly accumulating anti-war forces', he explained on 27 August. Every postponement served 'to enable world opinion to show itself and to isolate the man or the nation that would disturb the peace'.[116] On 21 August British Intelligence reported that Goering wanted to come to London and secret preparations were made for a meeting with Chamberlain at Chequers, but nothing more was heard of the idea.[117] Later that evening, news of the Nazi-Soviet pact came as a 'complete bombshell' to Anglo-French policy-makers, but Chamberlain still vainly entertained the hope that 'this coup which occasioned such joy in Berlin will be found to have been a boomerang'.[118] On 23 August Henderson delivered Chamberlain's forthright letter to Hitler repeating his warning that there could be 'no greater mistake' than to doubt Britain's intention to honour its obligations to Poland. Next day, Chamberlain solemnly informed the Commons that the Nazi-Soviet Pact had been 'a surprise of a very unpleasant character' but that Britain would fight to defend Poland. If his efforts for peace failed, he declared, 'we shall not be fighting for the political future of a far away city in a foreign land; we shall be fighting for the preservation of those principles ... the destruction of which would involve the destruction of all possibility of peace and security for the peoples of the world'.[119] In contrast with his broadcast exactly eleven months earlier, all talk of conflict in 'a faraway country between people of whom we know nothing' had been eclipsed by higher questions of national honour and principle. By all accounts, Chamberlain was 'dignified and calm' but spoke 'with little passion or emotion'. As Harold Nicolson complained, 'He was exactly like a coroner summing up a case of murder.'[120] After passing the Emergency Powers Act, Parliament adjourned until 31 August. Abroad, Polish reservists were mobilised and British subjects were advised to leave Germany, but Chamberlain still resisted Hore-Belisha's pleas for a general mobilisation for fear of Hitler's likely reaction.[121]

The 'worst trial' of the week for Chamberlain and his colleagues came around noon on Friday 25 August when they learned that Hitler had summoned Henderson. There followed 'a most trying period of waiting' during which Chamberlain remained with Annie in their drawing room, 'unable to read, unable to talk, just sitting with folded hands & a gnawing pain in the stomach'. Initially expecting the characteristic ultimatum leading inexorably to war, as the hours passed without news Chamberlain's spirits slowly began to improve. At length, reports arrived that Hitler had given Henderson a message which denied any desire for world domination but denounced Polish provocations as 'intolerable' and warned that Chamberlain's attitude would produce only 'blood and incalculable war'. Yet this was apparently accompanied by the promise of a 'large comprehensive offer' guaranteeing the British Empire in return for limited colonial concessions after the Polish problem had been settled – at which point Hitler declared that he would retire to the contemplative life of an artist. Chamberlain received the first of two telegrams with the full text of Hitler's offer over dinner and found it sufficiently 'unilluminating' that he refused to stay up until after midnight for the second to be decyphered. In a similar defiant spirit, next morning he had his breakfast and read the papers as usual before opening the box with the second telegram which had been on the table throughout.[122]

Sir Nevile Henderson never resolved in his own mind whether Hitler's 'offer' of 25 August represented a genuine last hesitation or merely a final effort at deception, but the latter was far closer to the truth.[123] Having failed with the stick, Hitler dangled the carrot in an attempt to detach Britain from Poland and so prevent a localised campaign escalating into a European war. Indeed, while Henderson was still listening to Hitler's offer in the Reich Chancellery, the final preparations were being made for the Polish invasion scheduled for 4.30am next morning, Saturday 26 August. At the very last moment, however, the invasion order was rescinded – not to allow the British time to consider his 'offer', but because Mussolini had warned that Italy was in no position to offer any military assistance, while the belated signature of the Anglo-Polish military alliance came as a 'bombshell' in Berlin by confirming that Britain really was serious about its obligations.[124] After these shocks, Hitler briefly verged on a breakdown and even in London the general impression was that he had got 'cold feet'.[125]

Chamberlain and his closest associates spent Saturday 26 August, in various attempts to concoct a satisfactory reply to Hitler's new offer – albeit perhaps less in the hope of success than the determination not to squander even the faintest possibility of averting war. The 'almost cringing ... tone' of the Prime Minister's initial draft ensured that it was 'practically torn to pieces' in Cabinet; a rebuff Chamberlain 'did not take ... in any unfriendly spirit' on the grounds that he had been up most of the night on the draft and 'did not see it as objectively as those ... who came to it with a fresh mind'.[126] But despite Halifax's hope that 'something can be made' of Hitler's offer and suspicions that Butler and Wilson were still 'working like Beavers' towards another 'Munich' to sell out the Poles, Chamberlain had finally reached his sticking point. Hitler was to have no free hand for eastward expansion and Britain would acquiesce in no settlement which destroyed Polish independence or the 'peace front'. It had been 'a gruelling day' and, as so often in the past during moments of acute crisis, Annie's calm, cheerful steadiness proved an 'unfailing help and encouragement'. As Chamberlain noted with grim irony, the motto on his calendar for the day proclaimed, 'Remember that the tide turns at the low as well as at the high level.'[127]

The British response to Hitler's 'offer' took almost three days to complete after three drafts and two Cabinets. Only after final approval by the Cabinet on Monday 28 August, did Henderson return to Berlin with a complete rejection of Hitler's attempt to drive a wedge between Britain and Poland. 'Our word was our word, and we had never and would never break it', Henderson declared when he delivered the reply to Hitler at 10.30pm. It was 'now or never' and the choice between Poland and England rested with Hitler. At this stage, Hitler appeared friendly, reasonable and 'not dissatisfied' with the British response, but he still talked incessantly about 'annihilating' Poland. By the time Henderson returned to collect Hitler's reply next evening, however, the German press had reported the murder of six Germans in Poland and the meeting ended in a shouting match. In the German reply, the usual frenzied denunciation of Poland's 'barbaric ... maltreatment' of Germans was accompanied by demands for the return of Danzig and the Polish Corridor. Although 'sceptical' about British proposals for negotiations with Poland, Hitler now agreed – but only if a Polish plenipotentiary arrived within 24 hours; a deliberately unreasonable stipulation designed to attach the blame for the breakdown of negotiations on the Poles in order both to justify German aggression and to give Britain a reason for failing to honour its obligations.[128]

At this juncture, Birger Dahlerus, another secret Swedish intermediary shuttling between Berlin and London, told the British that Goering was 'working very hard for peace and that things were by no means hopeless'. On this basis, the full text of Hitler's note did not initially seem too discouraging when it arrived in London.[129] Indeed, at Cabinet on the morning of 30 August there was still a faint glimmer of optimism that Hitler's note suggested an effort to extricate himself from an 'awful fix', although Chamberlain adamantly insisted there would be no repeat of Munich and he blankly refused to consider demands for the immediate despatch of a Polish negotiator.[130] Yet while events in Danzig were running out of control, Chamberlain still refused to resign himself to the prospect of war. On the contrary, having despatched another conciliatory private message to Hitler during the afternoon, at a meeting with Joseph Kennedy that evening he claimed to be 'more worried about getting the Poles to be reasonable than the Germans' – particularly given the efforts of Churchill and Eden to encourage Polish resistance. In the meantime, he was 'urging Henderson to keep telling Hitler that after all the Danzig situation is a small item and that what really needs to be done is to work at the whole European economic political problem'. 'He is not at all enthusiastic about the prospects', Kennedy noted, 'but he is hopeful.'[131]

In retrospect, the remarkable persistence of such fantasies about a negotiated settlement suggests that Chamberlain had lost all touch with the realities of Hitler's increasingly manifest ambitions. Yet in fairness to Chamberlain, it is only reasonable to question what else he could have done at this juncture, given both his determination to leave no stone unturned in the quest of peace and a collective incredulity that anyone (even Hitler) could seriously contemplate a repetition of the horrors of 1914–18. At no point, however, was Chamberlain prepared to consider Ciano's proposal on 31 August for the Poles to surrender Danzig as a precondition for a Five Power conference.[132] Moreover, if the Prime Minister was guilty of wishful thinking, it was nothing compared with Hitler's fatal delusion that Chamberlain was not prepared to declare war over Poland if it was forced upon him.

Looking back on these exchanges, Chamberlain concluded that they 'looked rather promising at one time' as Hitler 'wavered' in his invasion preparations until 'some brainstorm took possession of him ... and once he had set the machine in motion he couldn't stop it'.[133] This was another illusion. Since April, Hitler had been determined to crush Poland and even warnings from pro-German sources in Britain failed to convince him that the Western Powers really meant what they said about war. Despite his brief hesitation on 25 August, three days later Hitler fixed the Polish invasion for 1 September, even before receiving Dahlerus' report on his unsuccessful mission to London. There had been no 'last chance' of peace and if there was a 'brainstorm' it was not a sudden lapse but the culmination of months of planning. Nor was there any real hope of averting war with the Western Powers unless Chamberlain and Daladier had been prepared to accept total humiliation. Until the last moment, however, Hitler never seriously expected that Britain and France would fight – but if they did, he was prepared to accept the risk and to take them on regardless.[134]

VIII

After a number of staged incidents, at 4.45am on Friday 1 September the attack on Danzig commenced before German troops crossed the Polish frontier and the Luftwaffe bombed Warsaw. The British Cabinet met at 11.30am. 'The events against which we had fought so long and so earnestly had come upon us', Chamberlain declared at the start of the meeting. 'But our consciences were clear and there should be no possible question now where our duty lay.' The Cabinet then ordered full mobilisation and agreed upon a 'stiff' message to Hitler, warning that unless German troops were withdrawn Britain would 'without hesitation fulfil their obligation to Poland'. Despite Chatfield's pleas, no time limit was set on what some mistakenly took to be an ultimatum, while Chamberlain and Halifax were authorised 'to take such action as they thought fit' when working out the procedural details with the French.[135] By now the country was largely united in a grim fatalism about the inevitability of war. Hitler had been given his chance and he had revealed himself to be the untrustworthy gangster that many always suspected.

At 6pm the Commons reassembled in an already darkened chamber. After a special prayer for 'the wisdom and courage to defend the right', Chamberlain and Arthur Greenwood, the acting Labour leader, entered together to a loud cheer. Chamberlain then at once began his sombre statement reminding the Commons with some emotion that he had prayed it would never fall to him to ask the country to accept the 'awful arbitrament of war' and he struck the dispatch box with a clenched fist when he declared that 'we stand at the bar of history knowing that the responsibility for this terrible catastrophe lies on the shoulders of one man, the German Chancellor, who has not hesitated to plunge the world into misery in order to serve his own senseless ambition'. As even his most committed critics noted, he was 'evidently in real moral agony and the general feeling in the House is one of deep sympathy with him and of utter misery for ourselves'. At this moment, Chamberlain clearly did speak for England with his solemn tone, the appearance of decisive action and the declaration that Britain had 'no quarrel with the German people', but that as long as the Nazi regime remained 'there will be no peace in Europe'. In such circumstances, all accepted the absence of a time limit as a necessary means to concert strategy with the French and to enable the completion of evacuation and mobilisation. As a result, Chamberlain and Halifax authorised Henderson to present Germany with 'a warning and not an ultimatum' to the effect that their troops should be withdrawn immediately.[136]

Unfortunately for Chamberlain's reputation, while he urged the nation to prepare itself for the impending struggle, Bonnet telephoned from Paris to say that the constitution prevented France from agreeing to anything until Parliament met the next evening – and even then he urged a 48 hour delay. In reality, Bonnet was conniving to overcome Daladier's resistance in order to explore Ciano's proposal for another Munich conference on 5 September. London had already cold shouldered this idea, but when Ciano pressed it again at 2.30pm on 2 September Halifax agreed to consider the possibility only on condition that German troops were withdrawn from Poland before any negotiations commenced. To allow time to explore this option, Halifax and Harvey then dashed to the Commons to postpone Simon's proposed announcement that Henderson would soon be delivering the British ultimatum in Berlin. Instead MPs were promised a Prime Ministerial statement later that evening.

During all of these developments, Chamberlain and Halifax genuinely wanted only to delay long enough to synchronise action with France and to force a German withdrawal. But ironically, of all Chamberlain's perceived failures and evasions over the past year, this delay was regarded by friends and foes alike as the most damaging. At a hastily summoned meeting at 4.30pm on 2 September, the Cabinet was 'in an extremely difficult mood' when it became clear that Halifax and Chamberlain were still prevaricating. This time, however, they faced a revolt. Led by the once loyal Hoare, the rebels insisted that public opinion would never accept further delay and that Britain should honour its pledge to Poland and declare war at midnight unless the Germans complied with the British ultimatum. The meeting concluded with Chamberlain saying he needed to consult the French along these lines. Yet when Bonnet demanded more time for evacuation and mobilisation, Chamberlain and Halifax recognised the force of these pleas and decided to ignore what the Cabinet had taken to be a definite agreement that their ultimatum should expire at midnight.[137] For Chamberlain and Halifax, these were the crucial considerations. Whatever Bonnet's hopes, there was never a British plan to renege on the obligation to Poland because Chamberlain had made it abundantly clear that complete and immediate German withdrawal was the critical prerequisite for any future conference over Danzig.[138] Unfortunately, that was not how it appeared to MPs – or even to many ministers.

Parliament received the news of delay as badly as the Cabinet. The Commons had assembled at 2.45pm on Saturday 2 September in a mood of intense disquiet at the inexplicable failure to deliver an ultimatum and afraid that Chamberlain was planning 'a new Munich over Poland's prostrate body'.[139] Having swiftly passed the National Service Bill extending conscription to all aged 18–41, at 6.30pm the Speaker suspended the sitting until Chamberlain's statement. In the interim, while the ministerial War Party 'fed the flames of suspicion' within Parliament,[140] nervous and anxious MPs took refuge in the Smoking Room and many returned to the chamber an hour later with flushed faces and 'full of "Dutch Courage"'. Whether it was the alcohol, anxiety or irritation at the long wait, they reassembled in 'an unpleasant silence' as they waited for Chamberlain's expected announcement that Britain would be at war at midnight. Instead he read them a 'clumsy' statement informing them that the Italian proposal was still under consideration and that they were consulting with France as to the time limit; a declaration which struck even some ministers as 'very badly worded and the obvious inference was vacillation and dirty work'. Little wonder that there were 'murmurs of "Appeasement!"' as he proceeded with his non-committal statement or that when Greenwood rose to cheers from his own supporters these were echoed in a second and greater wave from Chamberlain's own benches.[141]

At this point, Chamberlain recalled the Commons became 'out of hand, torn with suspicions, and ready ... to believe the Govt guilty of any cowardice and treachery'. He was particularly nettled when Amery called out 'Speak for England' as Greenwood rose to express collective alarm at the delay. Throughout this angry demonstration, the government frontbench 'looked as if they had been struck in the face'. In reply, Chamberlain anxiously expressed his horror that such suspicions should exist, ascribing the delay to the difficulties of telephonic communication with Paris and suggesting that a more definite statement would be forthcoming by noon next day. In so doing, he unsuccessfully attempted to mislead the Commons into believing that the French were not weakening in their resolve at a time when many knew only too well of Bonnet's deceit and prevarication. 'In those few minutes he flung away his reputation' Nicolson noted as the House adjourned in a bitter and angry mood.[142] Indeed, such was the mood of hostility and suspicion that Chamberlain feared the government would fall next day and Halifax claimed he 'had never seen the Prime Minister so disturbed'. To conceal the full extent of the drama from the wider public, Simon telephoned the BBC to insist on cuts in their reporting of proceedings.[143]

The Cabinet were even less pleased to find that Chamberlain had placed them in a 'false position' by ignoring the views they had articulated with such vehemence earlier that afternoon. When the Commons adjourned, ten 'completely aghast' ministers led by Stanley and Elliot assembled in Simon's room in 'a state of semi revolt' and expressed themselves in such strong language that Simon immediately informed Chamberlain of their anger and the fact that he shared it. The rebels were then ushered into the Prime Minister's room 'looking very sullen', whereupon Simon told him 'very forcibly' that the ultimatum must be issued immediately. While Chamberlain then retreated to Downing Street to consult with his advisers, the rebels returned to Simon's room to draft a letter repeating their view that a midnight deadline was too late unless this had definitely been agreed with the French.[144]

Chamberlain later attempted to minimise the significance and impact of this Cabinet challenge by claiming that 'a certain number of my colleagues in the Govt, who always behave badly when there is any trouble about, took this opportunity to declare that they were being flouted & neglected and tried to get up a sort of mutiny. Even Edward Halifax found their behaviour unbearable and declared that I had the temper of an archangel!'[145] Yet Chamberlain was obviously more than 'a little rattled' by the revolt of the 'War Party' and together with Halifax, Cadogan and Wilson he struggled hard to impress upon the French

Ambassador and Daladier the urgency of their position and the need for an immediate synchronised ultimatum.[146] After further pressure from the rebels, Chamberlain's peacetime Cabinet reassembled for the last time at 11.30pm on 2 September against the fitting background of a violent thunderstorm. Overwhelmed by 'the strength of feeling ... even among the most loyal supporters of the Government', Chamberlain and 'the Overruled Peace Party' were now compelled to acknowledge that Britain must act decisively before Parliament reassembled at noon next day. It was thus agreed that the British ultimatum should be presented in Berlin at 9am next morning and expire two hours later, despite the French inability to act in parallel.[147] The Cabinet then dispersed into the pitch black downpour on the last night of peace.

At the appointed hour next morning, in full ambassadorial uniform, Sir Nevile Henderson handed the British ultimatum to the principal interpreter at the German Foreign Office because Ribbentrop refused to accept it.[148] At 11.15 on the morning of Sunday 3 September, the Prime Minister solemnly informed the nation that the required assurances had not been received 'and that consequently this country is at war with Germany'.

> You can imagine what a bitter blow it is to me that all my long struggle to win peace has failed. Yet I cannot believe that there is anything more, or anything different, that I could have done, and that would have been more successful ... We have a clear conscience, we have done all that any country could do to establish peace. The situation in which no word given by Germany's rulers could be trusted, and no people or country could feel themselves safe has become intolerable ... Now may God bless you all. May He defend the right. It is the evil things that we shall be fighting against – brute force, bad faith, injustice, oppression, and persecution – and against them I am certain that the right will prevail.[149]

Like the assassination of John F. Kennedy, anyone who lived through this crisis can remember where they were on that glorious sunny morning when Chamberlain broadcast from the Cabinet room at 10 Downing Street. Lord Winterton remembered because, unlike the overwhelming majority of his fellow countrymen, he missed the broadcast as he sat sunning himself on the terrace of the House of Commons. At Buckingham Palace, King George VI experienced 'a certain feeling of relief that those ten anxious days of negotiation were finally over', while his mother heard the news over a radio set up in the village church at Sandringham as she took matins.[150] Halifax heard it from the passage outside the Cabinet room and 'had seldom felt more moved'. 'Chips' Channon was at the Foreign Office wireless station depressed that his world, 'or all that remains of it, is committing suicide, whilst Stalin laughs'. John Colville, soon to become one of Chamberlain's private secretaries, listened in an empty lecture theatre at the LSE, where the broadcast 'made with slow, solemn dignity, induced a numbness'. Perhaps inevitably most people listened in their own homes sitting around the wireless with their families. Beatrice Webb, who had once nearly married Joseph Chamberlain to become Neville's step-mother, was struck by the fact that his voice sounded 'strikingly like his father's'. Although a committed critic of the 'tragic absurdity' of appeasement, like many others, she thought that in 'his sorrowful admission of the failure of his policy ... and sombre but self-controlled denunciation of Hitler ... he was at once more appealing and impressive'.[151] Only the inclusion of a highly personal tone shocked some of his less forgiving critics.[152] The broadcast had barely concluded when the sirens in London announced the first air-raid of the war. In fact, it was a false alarm, but at the time it seemed real enough and Colville was far from alone in expecting London to 'be reduced to rubble within minutes of war being declared'.[153]

Parliament met that afternoon – the first Sunday session for nearly 120 years. Depending on the sympathies of the observer, Chamberlain looked either 'smiling and well' as he entered to the cheers of his supporters or 'very ill'. Rising to more cheers, he again spoke movingly of the collapse of his hopes: 'Everything that I have worked for, everything that I have hoped for, everything that I have believed in during my public life, has crashed into ruins. There is only one thing left for me to do: that is devote what strength and power I have to forwarding the victory of the cause for which we have sacrificed so much.' Supporters like Channon listened 'wet-eyed, but indignant with the Opposition for their bad manners' and even his critics felt the statement 'restrained and therefore effective'.[154] Others who recalled the start of the Great War noted 'the House was quiet, unemotional, determined and almost united, which was very different from the wild enthusiasm, emotion bordering on hysteria, and the self-righteous patriotism of August 1914'.[155]

Whatever Chamberlain said about continuing to lead the struggle, many of his now vindicated critics believed that 'he cannot possibly lead us into a great war'.[156] Yet they would be confounded on both counts; there was no 'great war' of any sort in the West until May 1940 and Chamberlain remained Prime Minister until the very day that Hitler launched this offensive. In the interim, Chamberlain derived solace from the 'great number of very wonderful letters' of continued support which assured him that although a tragedy for Europe, it was not a personal defeat. When he saw the King that evening he appeared 'very upset' that all his efforts had failed, but also 'very calm'.[157] 'It was of course a grievous disappointment that peace could not be saved but I know that my persistent efforts *have* convinced the world that no part of the blame can lie here' he told his sisters. 'That consciousness of moral right, which it is impossible for the Germans to feel, *must* be a tremendous force on our side.'[158] In this judgement at least, he was undoubtedly correct.

Chapter 16
'The Bore War',
September 1939–January 1940

'How I do hate and loathe this war. I was never meant to be a War Minister and the thought of all those homes wrecked with the Royal Oak makes me want to hand over my responsibilities to some one else. Even the triumph of U-boats destroyed gives me a very uncomfortable feeling. If they called in at our ports in peace time we should probably say what good fellows the officers & crew were. And we have to kill one another just to satisfy that accursed madman. I wish he could burn in Hell for as many years as he is costing lives.'

Neville to Hilda Chamberlain, 15 October 1939

Long before American journalists coined the term 'Phoney War', that curious interlude between the official end of peace in September 1939 and the launch of the German offensive in the West in May 1940 had become known as 'The Bore War'. At sea, the war began at once when the Cunard liner *Athenia* was sunk by a U-boat on 3 September, with the loss of 120 passengers and crew. Yet on the home front, war came as a curious anticlimax. It was all quiet on the Western Front and the bombers, so long expected to deliver the 'knock-out blow' from the air, did not materialise. Apart from the sandbags and gas masks seen everywhere, the black-out at night and barrage balloons during the day, the war seemed 'very unreal' in the glorious September sunshine. As the Italian Ambassador to Paris told his British counterpart, 'I have seen several wars waged without being declared; but this is the first I have seen declared without being waged.'[1]

The absence of mortal peril had a curiously corrosive impact upon national unity and morale which made the task of government far more difficult than if the declaration of war had been followed swiftly by the long anticipated carnage. Although Chamberlain regularly remarked it was 'better to be bored than bombed', ministers soon became aware that the 'daily irritation of the country looms large in proportion to the scarcity of big news in the war'.[2] The longer this 'war twilight' continued, the more intense became public frustration with the many minor inconveniences and niggling restrictions upon normal life. As 'Chips' Channon put it on 10 December: 'The war is 100 days old, and damned bore it is, though no one seems to talk about it now. It might be somewhere very remote, and I feel that there is a definite danger in such detachment.' With boredom and grumbling, came the fear that 'a defeatist spirit is growing in the country' which might spread to the Commons.[3] Indeed, such was the ministerial concern about morale and public discontents that in November the War Cabinet began to relax many of the controls so recently imposed, while in the following month the Chancellor warned of adverse public reaction to the inevitable fall in the standard of living once the war began in earnest.[4]

One of the most remarkable features of the 'Bore War' was the degree to which it impinged so little upon the daily lives of Chamberlain and his Cabinet colleagues. Every morning he walked around the lake in St James' Park with his wife, discreetly followed by a single detective, just as he had in peacetime. He then returned to meet Margesson in the Cabinet room at eleven and 30 minutes later the War Cabinet assembled. A week after the declaration of war, Chamberlain thus noted with surprise that despite 'some dreadful anxieties, especially during one sleepless night, the tension has actually decreased and I have occasionally times, perhaps an hour or even more, when there has been nothing for me to do'. Indeed, such was the relaxation of tension that he almost immediately introduced a system where only three of the War Cabinet's nine members needed to remain in London on each Sunday, enabling the Chamberlains to retire to the peace of Chequers on two weekends out of every three.[5] At this juncture more than ever before, the tranquillity of Chequers proved an 'immense boon' and in order to insulate himself further from the outside world, Chamberlain continued to make it clear that he disliked being disturbed by telephone at weekends and he rarely took a private secretary with him. Even on those weekends when he was 'on duty' in London, he still found time to read all of Shakespeare's comedies and visit favourite peacetime haunts like Kew Gardens, London Zoo and Richmond Park, where he enjoyed the autumn colour and the birds, despite being 'plagued to death' by waving well-wishers and autograph hunters.[6]

For a man in his seventieth year, Chamberlain initially bore the physical and mental strain of war remarkably well. In late October, however, he suffered a particularly severe recurrence of the gout that had always afflicted him at moments of greatest stress. To make matters worse, it was accompanied by new symptoms in the form of an intensely irritating rash over his legs, palms and wrists which disturbed his sleep well into December. Such was the overall effect of this indisposition that Chamberlain was confined to bed for a week before arrangements were made to transport him downstairs to the morning meetings of the War Cabinet on a chair. He did not resume his daily walks around St James' Park until the end of the month. The severity of this attack inevitably raised in some minds the possibility that he was too old and infirm to remain in office and that he would soon retire. Perhaps with this in mind, in late November his first wartime broadcast began with an assurance that he was speaking 'happily with health and strength unimpaired'.[7]

Critics certainly hoped 'the authors of our present misfortunes (Chamberlain above all) will have to go and a *genuine* National Government will have to be formed'.[8] In the event, however, it was another eight months before Chamberlain lost the Premiership and his survival in office can be explained by reference to two factors. The first was the apparent absence of a credible successor. Despite regular comparisons with Asquith's lack-lustre leadership during the Great War, the critical ingredient was missing. As one of Chamberlain's private secretaries put it, 'I can see no Lloyd George on the horizon at present: Winston is a national figure, but is rather too old and the younger politicians do not seem to include any outstanding personality. Halifax would be respected, but he has not the drive necessary to keep the country united and enthusiastic.'[9] The second factor prolonging the Chamberlain regime was his absolute refusal to retire gracefully at a time when his entire career remained stained indelibly with humiliating defeat and failure. As he regularly acknowledged privately, he would hand over to someone else if a fighting war began in the West, but while this 'war twilight' continued he was able to bear the strain and he had much to offer.[10] Furthermore, Chamberlain was characteristically determined to govern in his own fashion, without pandering to the rising clamour for new and more dramatic responses to the challenge of war. This obstinate refusal to appease the expectations of informed opinion inflicted an ultimately disastrous blow upon his reputation and credibility as a war Prime Minister.

The War Cabinet announced on 3 September was widely interpreted as a damaging reflection of this uncompromising reluctance to adapt to new circumstances. At the outbreak of war, Chamberlain issued formal invitations to join the government to Labour and the Liberals. Both parties refused. Painful memories of the compromising position created by Arthur Henderson's membership of the Asquith and Lloyd George coalitions during the Great War persuaded Labour that no one should join a 'mixed bag government' without authorisation; a decision reinforced by the fear that Chamberlain might attempt to recruit Labour leaders on a selective basis. As Dalton explained, if the Labour Party were given 'one seat in the Inner Cabinet, plus the Postmaster-General and the Secretaryship of State for Latrines, we should not only be uninfluential within, but we should lose most of our power to exercise influence from without … [and] much of our credit amongst our own people, who would be filled with suspicions of our official participation'. There was much validity in these tactical fears, but rejection also undoubtedly reflected the almost visceral loathing and mistrust that Chamberlain evoked within the entire Labour movement.[11] Eight months later this very personal animosity would destroy Chamberlain's Premiership.

In the short-term, Chamberlain's sincerity in extending this invitation to Labour must be open to question. His contempt for the Labour leadership was legendary, but it is possible that he genuinely wanted Greenwood for whom he had far more respect than Attlee. Indeed, his 'very friendly & confidential talks' with Greenwood during the last months of peace might possibly have taken place unknown to the rest of the Labour leadership, while Greenwood's nervous reaction towards the veto on individuals accepting office without collective approval might indicate that he was open to such an idea.[12] But in practice, it is unlikely that Chamberlain wanted any formal Labour participation in the government. On the contrary, given his consistent expectation that the war would soon peter out leaving the way clear for an election, he had absolutely no incentive to share any of the credit for the resumption of peace with his Labour opponents.

It is absolutely certain that Chamberlain was merely going through the motions in making a similar offer to Sir Archibald Sinclair and his Liberal following. Despite pleas from Hoare and Churchill that this would have 'the great advantage of eliminating one of the oppositions and getting their very influential press on our side', Chamberlain's inability to conceal his personal contempt for the Liberal leader resulted in regular irritable exchanges.[13] In these circumstances, it was scarcely surprising that Sinclair declined Chamberlain's modest offer of office in September 1939 on the grounds that the Liberals could 'not accept responsibility for the policy and actions of the Government without being received into its innermost councils and having full opportunities of influencing the big decisions of policy'.[14]

Without the support of the two Opposition parties, Chamberlain was obliged to construct a War Cabinet from the 'National' support he had at his disposal. On 3 September, it was announced that the nine-man War Cabinet consisted of Chamberlain, Halifax, Simon, Hoare, the four service ministers – Kingsley Wood, Chatfield, Hore-Belisha and Churchill – with Lord Hankey as Minister without Portfolio combining a lifetime of experience with the first War Cabinet and the Committee of Imperial Defence with his other role to 'keep an eye on Winston'.[15] In addition, Eden reluctantly recognised that he had been superseded by Churchill when he accepted the Dominion Office outside the Cabinet on the 'humiliating' understanding that he would be 'a constant attender at meetings'; a concession which effectively left him a passive 'spectator' in all discussions outside his departmental remit.[16] There was no place for past opponents like Duff Cooper, nor for Amery who protested that it was 'absurd' that he should not be employed given his experience, but when Eden mentioned Amery's name Chamberlain gave 'a flash of his old vindictiveness' before dismissing the idea with an 'irritated snort'.[17] Despite the offer 'to serve anywhere, at any time, in any capacity', even former stalwarts like Swinton were not recalled in the nation's hour of crisis.[18] Beyond the minimum of prudent concessions to his Conservative critics, therefore, the supposedly 'new' War Cabinet really consisted of the 'old gang' in their old positions; a source of considerable disquiet for those who were concerned by 'the shadow of "appeasement" which still besets the Prime Minister'.[19]

Undoubtedly the most crucial outcome of Labour's refusal to serve under Chamberlain was that it compelled him to guard his own flank by restoring Churchill to office. This was a prospect which Chamberlain had actively striven to avoid since 1931, because as he told Joseph Kennedy in July 1939, Churchill 'has developed into a fine two-handed drinker ... his judgement has never been proven to be good' and if he had been in the Cabinet 'England would have been at war before this.'[20] Equally important, Chamberlain's doubts about Churchill's policy and character were spiced with increasing animosity towards the latter's wholly deserved reputation as a self-seeking, duplicitous renegade whose public smile concealed the conspirator's poisoned dagger. But while Chamberlain believed he could safely exclude Churchill in peacetime, he always recognised that the outbreak of war would fundamentally transform both of their positions. He thus offered Churchill the Admiralty with a seat in his nine-man War Cabinet on the night of 1 September convinced that 'he would have been a most troublesome thorn in our flesh if he had been outside'.[21]

Although Churchill was in his element at the Admiralty, his febrile imagination and restless dynamism made him a 'difficult' Cabinet colleague, a worse departmental minister and the worst of subordinates for a man of Chamberlain's orderly methods. Within days of Churchill's return, rumours abounded 'that Winston is already driving the Admiralty to distraction by his interference and energy'.[22] He had the same effect on Chamberlain who shared the War Cabinet's general frustration at Churchill's tendency to be 'very rhetorical, very emotional and, most of all, very reminiscent'.[23] Contrary to all expectations, however, Chamberlain was also soon gratified to note that the Cabinet was 'getting along quite well' and that 'Winston's conclusions and mine have been the same though we haven't always arrived at them by the same road.' Although Churchill was 'difficult', as Hoare told Inskip in late November, 'the P.M. handles him very well'.[24]

On the other hand, such consolations could not forgive Churchill's habit of deluging the Prime Minister with interminable epistles on all manner of subjects well beyond his own departmental responsibilities. This barrage of advice and suggestions began immediately. On the day after Churchill's appointment he sought to impinge upon the Prime Minister's prerogative over appointments. 'Aren't we a vy old team?' he asked. 'I make out that the six you mentioned yesterday aggregate 386 years or an average of over 64! Only one year short of the old age Pension!' The addition of Sinclair and Eden, he suggested, would reduce the average to just over 57 years while broadening the base of the government to appeal to both the Conservative group around Eden and moderate Liberal opinion. At midnight he despatched a second missive repeating these concerns. These were to be but the first of a torrent of lengthy letters during the early weeks of the war covering everything from the need to avoid taking the initiative in bombing, the equipment deficiencies of the BEF, the supply of the Army and the need for a Ministry of Shipping – all richly elaborated with reference to Churchill's ministerial experiences during the Great War and with the assurance that they were offered 'only in my desire to aid you in your responsibilities, and discharge my own'.[25]

This was more than Chamberlain was prepared to tolerate. He recognised that Churchill was 'enjoying every moment of the war' and that his attempted interference was largely the result of a restless imagination. But he thought these detailed missives a waste of his time when they met every day in the War Cabinet and complained that such ideas should have been 'brought up in Cabinet *when matured* not flung out from hour to hour without being thought out and often abandoned as soon as written'. Worse still, he rightly suspected 'these letters are for the purpose of quotation in the Book that he will write hereafter'. After a letter on 15 September, 'so obviously recording his foresight and … warnings so plainly for the purposes of future allusion', Chamberlain resolved to end the practice once and for all. When these efforts failed, the first minor crisis in their relationship boiled to the surface on 2 October when another letter arrived dealing with subjects as diverse as Indian troops, the formation of new RAF squadrons and the adverse effects of lighting restrictions – all of which had been discussed previously in the War Cabinet. After this Chamberlain had a 'very frank talk' with his over-zealous subordinate during which Churchill promised to write no more letters. He also 'swore vehemently that he had no desire or intention of intrigue' and that 'his sole desire was to help me to win the war'; protestations which Chamberlain concluded were sincere, but that 'Winston is in some respects such a child that he neither knows his own motives or sees where his actions are carrying him.' After this talk, Churchill went off 'in the highest good humour' to demonstrate a personal loyalty to Chamberlain which Tory dissidents felt he did not deserve and of which loyal Chamberlainites had previously suspected he was incapable.[26]

From Chamberlain's perspective, minor difficulties created by Churchill's excessive zeal were as nothing compared with the constant criticism provoked by the composition and structure of the government; an issue which remained a running sore throughout his Premiership. The failure to bring 'new blood' into the War Cabinet immediately aroused unrest and fuelled widespread expectations that it would soon need to be reconstructed. Yet Chamberlain refused to give way, convinced that the War Cabinet was 'working together very harmoniously & successfully' and that 'the real test' of its suitability was its effectiveness as a decision-making body; a view widely endorsed by its members and wholly in accordance with Hankey's authoritative advice that 'he must try and get men whose loyalty he trusted and would make a team with him'.[27] To coordinate the broader work of the government, Chamberlain also soon began meeting his extra-Cabinet ministers to 'prevent their feeling that nobody is interested in their troubles'.[28] By early December the so-called 'children's hour' had become a weekly event which Chamberlain, Halifax and Chatfield took in strict rotation and he rightly considered it a 'well worthwhile' exercise in maintaining government cohesion.[29]

Ultimately, however, the problem was that Chamberlain's profoundly managerial style of leadership blinded him to the crucial distinction between administrative reality and public perception. Certainly his sanguine complacency about Cabinet efficiency was not shared by many outside his immediate circle. Chamberlain's habit of making unfortunate appointments had long been a source of discontent – as demonstrated by the response to his appointment of colourless figures like Chatfield, Anderson and Burgin. Yet his decision to bring Sir John Gilmour out of retirement to head the newly-created Ministry of Shipping on 13 October was heavily criticised even within Downing Street and it made Chamberlain's despairing opponents 'wonder whether he is *trying* to win the War'.[30] To some extent, this insensitivity to the expectations of informed opinion can be attributed to Chamberlain's obstinate refusal to pander to what he regarded as ill-considered pressure for spectacular measures to stir the public imagination.[31] But much of the blame for these appointments can also be laid at the door of Margesson and Horace Wilson, who were both suspected of being determined 'to keep out of the Government any one who was not in their particular swim'.[32] Rather like Margaret Thatcher in her final 'siege mentality' phase, Chamberlain's increasing reliance on a small closed circle of advisers during this period insulated him from a proper sensitivity to the broader political impact of his actions.

Despite concerns about personnel, a far more fundamental criticism of Chamberlain's government concerned the organisational character of the War Cabinet. According to the 'War Book' compiled by the Committee of Imperial Defence in preparation for a future possible conflict, the final decision about the 'Organ of Supreme Control' rested with the Prime Minister of the day. After consulting Hankey, the CID's former Secretary, on 1 September Chamberlain informed ministers that if war came he would establish a small War Cabinet similar to that employed between 1916 and 1919.[33] Given his previous scepticism about the viability and effectiveness of this model,[34] however, when Chamberlain constructed his own War Cabinet he actually ignored Hankey's advice and the general conclusion of the entire inter-war debate about the critical importance of a small executive body consisting of senior ministers unencumbered by specific portfolios. Indeed, of the nine members of Chamberlain's War Cabinet no fewer than five carried heavy departmental burdens; an arrangement which prompted a 'gravely perturbed' Cabinet Secretary to warn on the day it was announced that 'this might expose the Prime Minister to a good deal of criticism'.[35] These concerns were given substance next day in the columns of *The Times* and they remained a major source of criticism throughout Chamberlain's wartime Premiership.[36]

In fairness, Chamberlain's War Cabinet was initially intended to be smaller, but the threatened resignation of the excluded Air and War ministers when they learned that Churchill was to be a member forced their addition to the membership.[37] More important, it could be reasonably objected that the contrast between the models adopted by Chamberlain in 1939 and Lloyd George in December 1916 was rather less striking than it appears – particularly given the rapid proliferation of non-members in attendance at the latter's War Cabinet meetings – and Hankey later recalled, 'Mr Chamberlain's War Cabinet did not suffer in any respect' when compared with Lloyd George's in 1917–19 or with Churchill's after May 1940. Certainly Chamberlain dismissed unfavourable comparisons as absurd, given the existence of both an efficient planning staff and a structure for liaison with the French which was 'far closer, goes deeper and covers a wider field' than anything in the Great War.[38] If there was a problem with efficiency in Chamberlain's War Cabinet, it actually stemmed far less from its composition than from his temperamental inclination to encumber it with too much detail which should have been consigned to the rapidly expanding network of inter-departmental committees. But whatever the organisational reality, the crucial perception at the time was that Chamberlain lacked the necessary dynamism, flexibility of mind and sense of critical urgency required of a successful war leader.[39]

Damaging perceptions of this sort were compounded by widespread condemnation of Chamberlain's failure to achieve any effective control over the economy for war purposes. Simon's severe emergency Budget on 27 September reflected Chamberlain's conviction that 'the only thing that matters is to win the war, even though we may go bankrupt in the process'.[40] But for many critics, it was the continuity with peacetime practice which most strikingly characterised the 'Bore War' period, as Chamberlain sought to preserve as much of the pre-war order as possible with the minimum of disruption. As a result, government expenditure rose slowly from £20 million a week at the outbreak of war to only £33 million six months later and much of this nominal increase was accounted for by price inflation. Similarly, little was done to curb the manufacture of non-essential items.[41] Most alarming was the fact that the number of insured workers registered as unemployed after six months of war had actually risen by 205,000 to a peak of 1,466,000 – despite the recruitment of two million men into the armed forces.[42]

Appalled by this state of affairs, on 3 October William Beveridge launched a campaign for an 'economic general staff' to promote effective State planning and direction of the economy, along with a non-departmental War Cabinet (on Lloyd George lines) to improve policy coordination.[43] This initiative from a widely respected civil servant, academic and social reformer, rapidly set in motion a groundswell of discontent with Chamberlain's fundamental approach and inflexibility at a time when the administrative shortcomings of the ministries of Supply and Economic Warfare were under attack and when responsibility for the war economy was divided between no fewer than seven government departments. In response to this clamour, Chamberlain almost immediately created a new inter-departmental committee under Lord Stamp to review and coordinate the economic effort of the country and to make necessary plans for Anglo-French cooperation on the subject. Unfortunately, the establishment of a Ministerial Committee on Economic Policy two days later almost immediately had the effect of retarding progress by blurring the boundaries of jurisdiction.[44] Worse still, although Stamp was the obvious candidate for the job after his work surveying Britain's financial and economic war planning during the summer of 1939, the fact that he divided his time between this committee and his directorship of a railway company inevitably fuelled public alarm and contempt.[45] Despite further detailed structural reforms, the fragmentation of economic control and the need for a genuinely non-departmental War Cabinet became the regular hobby horse of a wide range of critics over the next seven months. Ultimately, Chamberlain would pay a very high price for this obstinate refusal to bow to such demands in May 1940.

II

Chamberlain's problems during the 'Bore War' were not confined simply to matters of administrative efficiency. Indeed, it is often suggested that Chamberlain's ultimate failure as Prime Minister stemmed more from his inability to don the mantle of a credible and inspirational war leader. Many at the time (and ever since) have gone much further to argue that he was completely out of his depth after September 1939 and that increasing public awareness of this fact opened the way for Churchill's brand of more decisive leadership. The reality, however, was very different – at least, as far as the general public were concerned. During the last quarter of 1939, Chamberlain's approval rating actually rose by an average of ten percentage points over the level recorded during the final year of peace to reach a peak of 68 per cent, before falling back to (but not below) his peacetime standing during the first quarter of 1940. Similarly, in December 1939, some 61 per cent of voters declared themselves satisfied with the conduct of the war compared with only 18 per cent who were dissatisfied and the figures remained virtually the same in March 1940. Despite Churchill's frantic efforts at self-publicity and his fortunate association with a variety of naval successes, it is also important to note that when offered the choice of Prime Minister in December 1939, 52 per cent of the electorate still opted for Chamberlain compared with only 30 per cent who preferred Churchill.[46]

While Chamberlain undoubtedly did suffer from major and damaging problems with his image as a war leader, therefore, these existed mainly within the political community at Westminster, the press and the 'chattering classes' rather than among the general public. In reality, Chamberlain's force of personality and experience still enabled him to remain a respected and dominant voice within the War Cabinet, but within the broader political community many frustrated observers would have endorsed the verdict of the inexperienced Military Assistant Secretary to the War Cabinet that Chamberlain 'was so clearly out of his element in warlike matters that he achieved little except the orderly conduct of Cabinet business. He was a fine chairman of a board of directors. He was not the managing director that is necessary in war.'[47] In fairness, there were occasions when Chamberlain recognised these deficiencies and attempted to overcome them. For example, a week after the declaration of war he decided to fly to France for the first meeting of the Supreme War Council (rather than accept Daladier's offer to come to England), because he sensed that 'the moment for a mildly spectacular move on my part has come'.[48] But Chamberlain's innate personality and natural style possessed little of the dynamic charisma expected of a war leader – not least because of his fundamental hatred for war itself. As he candidly admitted after touring defensive positions in France in mid-December, 'it sickened me to see the barbed wire & pill boxes and guns & anti tank obstacles, remembering what they meant in the last war'.[49] In stark contrast, war was Churchill's natural element and at the Admiralty he exploited every opportunity to project an image of dynamic leadership when directing the only real war in which British forces were engaged until April 1940.

Chamberlain's image problem encompassed words as well as deeds. Chamberlain's restrained weekly surveys of British policy during the 'Bore War' impressed sympathisers with their sound appeal to reason, but they conveyed none of the charismatic unifying fervour of Churchill. During his statement on 20 September, Chamberlain looked 'tired and depressed' and the effect of reading it from a manuscript had a most discouraging and soporific effect on MPs. 'The Prime Minister has no gift for inspiring anyone', Harold Nicolson complained; 'he might have been the Secretary of a firm of undertakers reading the minutes of the last meeting.' A week later, the contrast was highlighted even more as 'the confidence and spirits of the House drop[ped] inch by inch' until Chamberlain sat down in almost complete silence, before Churchill rose to loud cheers to deliver a rollicking account of the naval position during which 'he sounded every note from deep preoccupation to flippancy, from resolution to sheer boyishness' and observers 'felt the spirits of the House rising with every word'. Harold Nicolson was a prejudiced observer, but there was much truth in his verdict and even Chamberlain's admirers were forced to concede as much.[50] Unfortunately, it was a sad reflection on Chamberlain's political instincts that he never comprehended the importance of oratorical tone over substance. To him, Churchill's speeches and broadcasts were too often tactless and embarrassing to the government in their crude appeal to public opinion. As he lamented after one 'sensational' world broadcast which 'deeply affronted' neutral opinion: 'It is a heavy price that we have to pay for our Winston and the groundlings whose ears are so tickled by his broadcasts do not stop to consider whether their satisfaction that the things we all feel & say in private should be said in public, is not too dearly gained if it damages the prospects of achieving the purpose for which we are fighting.'[51]

While Chamberlain's deficiencies as a war leader undoubtedly eroded confidence in his Premiership over the long-term, it is important not to exaggerate their effects upon government supporters in Parliament during the early months of the 'Bore War'. It is true that there were soon reports that the Commons was 'really suffering from a bad attack of nerves ... and is seething with intrigue, with Winston and his friends, and of course Ll.G., in full cry' while 'Neville's little band' was reported to be 'desperate'.[52] Indeed, within ten days of the outbreak of war, the Edenite 'Glamour Boys' met to condemn almost everything the government had done, before Harold Macmillan proposed that 'a rather wider Group might be formed from the Conservative benches with the object of keeping Ministers up to mark in the effective prosecution of the war'. After this, a small group of established malcontents met for weekly dinners in the backroom of the Carlton Hotel restaurant until Chamberlain's fall.[53] Yet, despite these conspiratorial mutterings, the membership of this and related groups like the 'All-Party Parliamentary Action Group', established by the Liberal National MP Clement Davies in September 1939, consisted overwhelmingly of already fully paid-up members of the anti-Chamberlain awkward squad.[54]

In contrast, the majority of the parliamentary party were more bored and depressed by the performance of their leader than positively rebellious. In order to steady his backbench followers, on 22 November Chamberlain dined with the 1922 Committee and devoted much effort to his speech on the grounds that it was 'one of those occasions when a leader if he catches the right mood, raises his followers to fresh enthusiasm and excites them to renewed personal loyalty. Whereas if he puts a foot wrong he sends them all away disheartened and discouraged.' In the event, a record attendance of nearly 200 Conservative MPs gave him 'a wonderful reception' and he went away convinced that 'everyone was delighted' with his speech.[55] Unfortunately, not all those present shared Chamberlain's confidence. As a committed and resentful critic, Amery predictably considered it 'a City Councillor's speech' which appeared to be 'lacking real grip of things as well as platitudinous in diction and wholly without inspiration'. But more worrying was the fact that even 'a good yes-woman' like Nancy Astor confessed that 'what he said depressed me more than anything else since the war began' because 'he meant it to be a fighting speech, but its effect … was to make me wish that Winston were P.M.'.[56] Nevertheless, at this stage, even dedicated anti-Chamberlainites had little reason to doubt the parliamentary party's ultimate loyalty to its leader. As Brendan Bracken complained as late as March 1940, 'the Tory party were tame yes-men of Chamberlain. 170 had their election expenses paid by the Tory Central Office and 100 hoped for jobs; what independence or criticism … could be expected?'[57] Moreover, despite concerns that the whips were 'thoroughly inefficient',[58] Margesson still exercised an iron discipline over potential critics, while the admission of Eden and Churchill to the government effectively bridled their supporters who were now far more likely to abstain from parliamentary criticism for fear of damaging their heroes.[59]

Although Chamberlain continued to command his own backbenchers, relations with the parliamentary Opposition remained as hostile as ever. In reality, little of substance divided Chamberlain from Labour in their shared hope that the war would simply fizzle out with the collapse of the Nazi regime, but Labour hatred for Chamberlain, Hoare and Wilson ran deep and his relations with the trade unions were initially no better at a time when the interests of employers predominated in government departments. This Labour antipathy was all the more damaging because Parliament refused to be relegated to the margins of politics after September 1939 as it had during the Great War. On the contrary, unlike the patriotic unity and deference of 1914, Chamberlain lamented that he was extremely unfortunate in confronting a 'very restless and quarrelsome' Opposition, while 'the fact that nothing much is going on seems to encourage them in nagging and fault finding'. After regular visits to the Commons, Chamberlain's wife was even more forthright in expressing her fury towards Labour backbenchers who behaved 'just like schoolboys … grinning at each other whenever they think that one of their leaders has scored a point – and they try to score points quite irrespective of the truth just in order that publicity should be given to what they say'.[60]

This behaviour outraged Chamberlain's natural sense of fair play – and it showed. While prepared to concede that not all his ministers were instantly successful, he felt they were doing their best in difficult circumstances and in his view 'it does not promote national unity to have every effort sneered at and crabbed and every complaint exploited to the uttermost'.[61] Indeed, such was Chamberlain's annoyance at these tactics that after Prime Minister's Questions on 24 October he harangued Attlee, Greenwood and Sinclair with some vigour 'about the disloyalty of the Opposition', but while they emerged from the meeting 'looking very chastened' the attacks did not abate.[62] Chamberlain's regard for the integrity and spirit of the Labour Opposition was not softened either by reports that they were cynically exploiting the Conservative Party's patriotic suspension of grassroots activity in support of the war effort in order to strengthen their own position in the constituencies. Less than a month after the outbreak of war, warnings on the subject from the National Union and Sam Hoare prompted Chamberlain to call together leading Conservative ministers, the Chief Whip and party chairman with a view to reviving their local party machine.[63] In particular, local associations were advised to retain their agents wherever possible and if they were not required entirely for party work they should be 'lent out for any other work which they may be able to do for the country'.[64] Nine months later, even after Labour had joined the Churchill coalition, Chamberlain was still urging the National Union Executive to preserve the party's fighting efficiency through meetings and continued contact with agents, on the grounds that it was 'all the more necessary because our opposite numbers had not played fair'.[65]

III

In summing up the general tenor of the 'Bore War', Mass-Observation noted that it was 'difficult to over-estimate the importance of wishful-thinking in Britain' because it made 'it all the more difficult to deal with the reality [of] situations and dangers in the future'.[66] It was a remarkably perceptive verdict about the attitudes of Britain's Prime Minister as well as of the people he led. In order to understand Chamberlain's reluctant approach to the challenges of war it is essential to understand his perceptions of how that conflict would develop. 'One thing comforts me', Chamberlain explained revealingly to his sisters a week after the outbreak of war. 'While war was still averted, I felt I was indispensable for no one else could carry out my policy. Today the position has changed. Half a dozen people could take my place while war is in progress and I do not see that I have any particular part to play until it comes to discussing peace terms.' Although he conceded that peace talks might be a long way off, he clearly did not believe they would be. In response to Goering's intimations of future peace, on 9 September the British government announced that it was planning for a three year war as a symbolic act of determination. Beneath the bold public defiance, however, Chamberlain believed that 'it won't be so very long' before the widespread demand for peace across all of Europe would find expression and that he would be called upon once more to assume the mantle of the peacemaker.[67]

Chamberlain's expectations about the limited nature of the war stemmed from two key assumptions which he shared with Halifax, Churchill, his Cabinet military experts and many of his critics, but which reflected how little any of them had learned about the nature of the Nazi regime and the reckless megalomania of its leader. First, although Hitler was now irrevocably damned as an 'accursed madman' bent on world domination, Chamberlain remained convinced that even he would be restrained from aggression in the West by the recognition that 'the attempt whether successful or unsuccessful would entail such frightful losses as to endanger the whole Nazi system'.[68] In part, this view was based on assurances that in military terms 'our hand is a better one to play than that of the enemy'.[69] But at the root of this assumption about Hitler's rationality was Chamberlain's own confident belief that 'a complete and spectacular military victory ... is unlikely under modern conditions'.[70] This fundamental strategic misapprehension was deeply influenced by the thinking of Basil Liddell Hart, the military commentator and historian, who forecast that the defensive positions of the Maginot and Siegfried lines were too strong to be attacked successfully.[71] As a result, he predicted that the war would simply peter out through lack of momentum and after Chamberlain's visit to the Maginot Line in mid-December he felt 'even more strongly than before, that neither side could or should attempt to break through the fortified lines'.[72] If generals can be accused of always fighting the last war, the same can be said of Neville Chamberlain as he planned to re-fight a war of static defence and economic blockade rather than the one which the Polish campaign probably should have told him they would actually confront.

Chamberlain's second and still more crucial assumption was that even if the German people followed their increasingly messianic leader down the path towards collective catastrophe, the German economy would never stand the strain. Just as Chamberlain always hoped that internal economic weakness would ultimately restrain Hitler's ability to launch a war, he now believed that an effective economic blockade would simply starve Germany into submission and instigate the collapse of the Nazi regime, without the need for prolonged military conflict. As he told a like-minded Roosevelt, an Allied victory depended on 'convincing the Germans that they cannot win. Once they have arrived at that conclusion, I do not believe they can stand our relentless pressure, for they have not started this war with the enthusiasm or the confidence of 1914.' As they were 'already half way to this conviction', Chamberlain was particularly grateful for Roosevelt's assistance in repealing the US arms embargo in early November, as this was likely to have a 'devastating effect on German morale'.[73] Given these hopes and assumptions, Chamberlain never ceased to believe that time was on the side of the Allies. On this basis, the 'waiting policy' became a central article of faith within Downing Street on the grounds that 'every day's delay is so much gain to us as far as war production is concerned'.[74]

Critics would later portray Chamberlain as a naïve optimist who ingenuously nurtured the facile illusion that Hitler could be removed as a prelude to a peaceful compromise with a successor regime. But there was rather more substance in his widely-shared assumptions than is sometimes recognised. The Wehrmacht had been less impressive in Poland than expected and despite public rejoicing at their swift victory in the East, the German public mood soon came round to a strong desire to avoid a war in the West at a time when discontent at deteriorating working conditions and living standards was rapidly increasing.[75] It should also be recalled that Chamberlain's confidence about time being on the side of the Western Powers echoed the views of British intelligence, Churchill and Hitler's own constantly repeated obsession. 'Time is working for our adversaries', Hitler warned a meeting of senior officers at the Reich Chancellery on 23 November 1939. 'Now there is a relationship of force which can never be more propitious for us, but which can only deteriorate.'[76]

Despite the apparent coherence of Chamberlain's logic about the likely course of the 'Phoney War', his analysis suffered from at least three fundamental flaws. First, whatever the structural constraints upon the German war machine, he never came close to understanding the mentality he was fighting or the irrationality of the logic which drove Hitler on. 'Germany will either be a world power, or there will be no Germany', Hitler had written in *Mein Kampf*. It was a sincere declaration of his mission to expunge the humiliation inflicted on Germany in 1918 and the price he was ultimately prepared to pay for it, but Chamberlain had never read *Mein Kampf* and (even if he had) he would have dismissed such statements as ridiculous rantings because his rational ordered mind and revulsion against war rendered him incapable of ever truly comprehending Hitler's instinctive recklessness. This miscalculation made Chamberlain easy to manipulate in the months leading up to Munich and ultimately it led directly to his fall from office in May 1940.

The second flaw was that while a 'waiting policy' was a rational response to the situation as Chamberlain saw it, it failed to acknowledge the degree to which the domestic political community was becoming bored with the 'Bore War'. As one Downing Street insider noted barely three weeks into the war, public opinion was 'unable to appreciate the essential merits of a waiting policy' and was already 'showing signs of impatience and ... asking what we are fighting for'.[77] In reality, a significant majority of the general public was not eager to engage British troops in action anywhere, while in December 1939 (and again in February 1940) the polls showed that those 'satisfied' with the government's conduct of the war outnumbered those 'dissatisfied' by a ratio of over three to one.[78] Within the political elite, however, the inevitable frustrations and doubts inseparable from Chamberlain's 'waiting policy', had a corrosive effect upon his reputation and authority – particularly as the failure to drop anything other than leaflets on Germany, while Poland was being 'bombed to pieces', simply fuelled the suspicion that Chamberlain was 'waiting' only for the opportunity to stage another 'Munich'.[79]

The final flaw in Chamberlain's strategy was that a reassuring faith in blockade as a substitute for military action increasingly flew in the face of the available evidence. Despite talk of 'rearmament in depth' as part of a long-term programme of expansion, progress was far from impressive and the conversion of British industry to a full war economy was depressingly slow. On the other side of the equation, it was also soon recognised that even if blockade drastically reduced essential German imports, the Nazi war machine would still be able to run at full strength for up to 18 months. Furthermore, the effectiveness of the blockade was never going to be decisive given German expansion to the East, while the threat to the Scandinavian States gave it access to still greater economic reserves. Despite Chamberlain's continued claim about Hitler having 'missed the bus' in September 1938 and that time was on the side of the Allies, therefore, the reality was rather different. As the Chiefs of Staff warned in March 1940: 'Time is on our side only if we take the fullest possible advantage of it.'[80] Unfortunately, harsh realities of this sort fitted poorly into Chamberlain's fixed preconceptions and so he tended to ignore them. For him, the war could be won simply by sitting it out and doing nothing positively to lose it while Hitler came to his senses, lost them altogether or was overthrown by a German High Command reported to be 'disgusted by his intolerable brutality'.[81] As a result, he continued to think of rearmament within 'sensible' proportions and the need to preserve as much of the peacetime organisation of economy and society as possible.

Worse still, the longer the Phoney War continued, the more assured Chamberlain became that he was correct and that all his military advisers were wrong in their assessment of future risks. Even before the Polish surrender, Hitler had ordered an offensive in the West. Yet while British military chiefs anticipated this development, Chamberlain emphatically refused to accept this view because he saw 'no possibility of his scoring a major success in the West & surely he must have one to keep up the spirits of his people and encourage neutrals to take sides'. Indeed, when considering the options being assessed by British military planners in late September, Chamberlain dismissed any prospect of a frontal attack on the Maginot Line because the 'losses would be too severe to make it worth while'. Conversely, while he deemed a rapid mechanised push through Holland and Belgium 'the most promising alternative' from a military perspective, he regarded it as unlikely because it involved 'a gamble which would entail disastrous results to Germany if anything went wrong'. Similarly, the possibility of an air campaign against Allied aerodromes as a prelude to a land offensive, was rejected in the belief that success was 'extremely doubtful' given the loss of surprise, the remarkable efficiency of the British 'Chain Home' radar stations, the superiority of Spitfire and Hurricane fighters and the danger that such an attack 'would entail retaliation which might have unexpected effects on morale in Germany and ... would be a burning of the boats which Hitler has hitherto shown no sign of caring to undertake'.[82]

Given all of these assumptions about the limited nature of the existing conflict, Chamberlain reasoned that Britain had absolutely nothing to gain and much to lose by escalating the war. In part, this conviction reflected a sensitivity to the opinion of neutral States and the need to preserve Britain's moral advantage. As he told his sisters, 'I do not believe that holocausts are required to gain the victory, while they are certainly liable to lose us the peace.' Despite much criticism at home, this meant dropping nothing but propaganda leaflets over Germany except in retaliation for German bombing action because if 'it must come it would be worth a lot to us to be able to blame them for it'.[83] But beyond such considerations, Chamberlain's strategy of avoiding any intensification of the war was based on a clear understanding of military realities. As the like-minded Hankey advised, Britain should confine itself to 'a war of nerves' because 'at this stage in the war we ought not to take any action which is calculated to endanger ultimate victory by frittering away our resources'.[84] From this perspective, Chamberlain freely conceded that a war confined to the high seas 'suits us very well and I hope it may continue on those lines for some time longer – even into the Spring'. He was equally convinced that the RAF should be kept in reserve while it was expanded in size until the decisive moment arrived, confident that in men and machines – if not in numbers – the RAF was superior to the Luftwaffe.[85] For any of these hopeful strategic assumptions and prophecies to come to fruition, however, Chamberlain recognised that Britain needed still more time.

IV

Since the declaration of war, Chamberlain had repeatedly confessed in private that his greatest fear was not military defeat, but rather 'a skilfully timed carefully planned attack on our home front' in the form of a 'peace offensive'.

> One can see already how this war twilight is trying people's nerves. Without the strong centripetal force of mortal danger all the injustices, inconveniences, hardships & uncertainties of war time are resented more & more because they are felt to be unnecessary. You see in the increasing sharpness of criticism in the H. of C. the same forces at work. Last week 17% of my correspondence was on the theme 'stop the war'. If I were in Hitler's shoes I think that I should let the present menacing lull go on for several weeks and then put out a very reasonable offer.

This possibility confronted Chamberlain with a difficult dilemma. On one hand, he never deviated from the view that Britain should reject a specious peace offer from Hitler based on any acceptance of the new territorial *status quo* in Eastern Europe. On the other hand, however, he greatly feared that such an approach would be difficult to resist because it would encourage both the 'peace-at-any-price people' and the opposing camp urging an immediate war of aggression against Germany. Anxious to restrain both groups, by late September Chamberlain had resolved that the only sensible strategy was 'to throw back the peace offer and continue the blockade' in the belief that in 'a waiting war of that kind ... we could outlast the Germans'.[86]

In reality, Chamberlain did not oppose concessions to Germany in a future negotiated peace, even one which included Nazi leaders like Goering. On the contrary, he was prepared to listen to a variety of secret and often bizarre 'peace feelers' during the first months of the war to 'see what they may produce'. And in the case of those from Prince Max von Hohenlohe he even favoured a 'much more encouraging reply' than the Foreign Office.[87] But this open-mindedness was always accompanied by the utterly implacable conviction that it was 'essential to get rid of Hitler' because he was now 'beyond any conceivable pale' and because his 'brutality was matched by his unreliability'. There was undoubtedly an element of affronted vanity in this fierce determination which mirrored Chamberlain's hatred for Lloyd George after 1917. Having trusted Hitler's word at Munich, the Prague invasion had been the most personal of betrayals and when war was forced upon him by 'the wickedness of one man' there could be no peace until he had been permanently removed.[88]

As Chamberlain predicted, Hitler's 'peace offensive' opened in earnest at the moment when Poland collapsed. On 26 September, the War Cabinet met without officials or a record to discuss reports from Dahlerus that Goering wanted to negotiate a peace. Two days later, the wandering Swede arrived secretly in London for discussions.[89] In response, however, Chamberlain remained convinced that 'though Hitler would certainly like to call off the war he is not prepared to pay the price so that there is no reasonable prospect of a peace such as we could accept'. At this stage, he correctly anticipated that Hitler's terms would be 'the same old story', based on an acceptance of German territorial gains and a free hand in the East in return for negotiations with Britain to settle outstanding issues.[90] On 6 October, exactly as prophesised, Hitler's speech to the Reichstag questioned why a war in the West should be fought at all. Making it abundantly clear that the 'Poland of Versailles will never rise again', he proclaimed that all of the remaining issues could be settled around the conference table because he had no further claims against France and had never 'acted contrary to British interests'. In order to cast himself as the conciliatory peacemaker, he also added, 'Let those who consider war to be the better solution reject my outstretched hand.' It was peace, but on Hitler's terms and with the threat of destruction if the Western Powers rejected his generous 'offer'.

Precisely as Chamberlain feared, Hitler's overtures did encourage 'the peace-at-any-price people'. In the next three days some 1860 of the 2450 letters received by the Prime Minister advocated 'Stop the war in one form or another.'[91] Even the backbench 1922 Committee appeared to be 'pretty well out of hand' after its meeting on 4 October seriously discussed the idea of a negotiated peace.[92] Chamberlain was equally anxious about the response of neutral and American opinion to the ostensibly conciliatory tone of Hitler's 'clever speech', at a time when the increasingly defeatest American Ambassador was reporting to Roosevelt that it was 'by no means a popular war' in Britain as there was a 'very definite undercurrent … for peace' and that this was likely to grow.[93] With these anxieties in mind, Chamberlain recognised that Hitler's offer must be rejected – but in such a way as to '"pass the buck" once again'. As a result, the peripatetic Dahlerus was sent back to Berlin to present an uncompromising British reply on 8 October, demanding the restoration of Polish statehood, the immediate destruction of all aggressive weapons and a plebiscite within Germany on Hitler's foreign policy. According to Chamberlain's account, Hitler raged to Dahlerus that the British response 'must be considered a declaration of war'.[94] What he did not know, was that Hitler had never nurtured much hope of British acceptance and that between his two meetings with Dahlerus he had ordered a German offensive 'at the earliest possible moment and in the greatest possible strength' through the Low Countries and Northern France 'to serve as a base for the successful prosecution of the air and sea war against England'.[95]

While Hitler was planning to extend his war, Chamberlain's War Cabinet devoted four discussions and many hours to drafting and redrafting Britain's public response to Hitler's 'peace offer'. On 9 October, Chamberlain argued that the generally critical reaction to Hitler's proposals abroad justified them in a 'somewhat stiffer tone' in reply. While avoiding any statement of British war aims, they should thus reject Hitler's claim that Poland was beyond redemption as 'an impossible basis for starting peace negotiations' – although the note 'should not definitely shut the door'. Chamberlain, Halifax, Simon and Churchill then laboured long and hard to polish the wording, before the Dominions objected that the draft 'went too far in the direction of "slamming the door" on further discussions' and that it needed an accompanying statement of Allied war aims to appeal to neutral and moderate German opinion.[96]

Concern about the absence of explicit Allied war aims was not confined simply to its effects on opinion overseas. As Lord Davidson had complained a few days earlier: 'The Government have not yet got across to the public that this War is not a war in the ordinary sense: it is a Holy War between the forces of right and the forces of wrong.'[97] Even the government's own Home Policy Committee conceded that 'a very great sense of bewilderment' existed in the country as to war aims; a view confirmed by correspondence in the press and the opinion polls.[98] Yet while Halifax supported an immediate statement of Allied war aims, Chamberlain adamantly opposed the idea on the grounds that he had 'always believed it would be a mistake to enumerate specific objects which must be achieved before the War could be brought to an end'.[99] In particular, there was the problem of what to say about Poland because (as Chamberlain told the War Cabinet a month earlier), 'this might have the effect of tying us down too rigidly and might prejudice an eventual settlement' after the 'destruction of Hitlerism'. As a result, he 'reacted rather irritably' to Dominion pressure and their 'lack of the sense of realism'. After discussing another draft of the British reply to Hitler on 11–12 October, Chamberlain (supported by Churchill) thus dug in his heels against further delay or amendment, declaring that war aims would be dealt with in future statements.[100]

On 12 October the War Cabinet finally agreed the terms of its third revised statement, designed 'to put Herr Hitler in the dilemma of having to decide what steps he would take in order to show that his desire for peace was genuine'. As one minister noted, 'it would be impossible to improve upon it. It bears every evidence of the collective mind of the best brains in the Cabinet.'[101] That afternoon, an 'icy and calm' Chamberlain delivered Britain's reply to Hitler's 'offer' in a crowded and attentive House of Commons. Declaring that Britain was fighting 'simply in defence of freedom' and 'those values ... of life which have ... been at once the mark and the inspiration of human progress', he warned of Hitler's 'repeated disregard of his word' and rejected his peace proposal as 'vague and uncertain'. On these grounds, Chamberlain announced 'the German Government must give convincing proof of the sincerity of their desire for peace by definite acts and ... effective guarantees ... or we must persevere in our duty to the end'. As intended, the buck had effectively been passed. By all accounts the Prime Minister sat down to much cheering from both sides of the chamber and his stock rose accordingly – particularly as the Dominions also expressed approval and public opinion was reported to be 'practically unanimous in support of the Government's war policy'.[102] As expected, Hitler's public riposte angrily declared that Britain had been offered peace but had chosen the path of war.[103]

Despite this satisfactory outcome, Chamberlain always anticipated a further 'peace offensive' on the grounds that it represented 'much the most effective way of achieving his purpose ... to be able to get away with his conquests without a major war'.[104] Despite these fears, however, he was determined to limit any statement of war aims to 'the vaguest of generalisations'. In his world broadcast on 26 November, Chamberlain thus repeated that 'We entered the war to defend freedom and to establish peace.' By distinguishing between the immediate 'war aim' of defeating the enemy and future 'peace aims' to be achieved 'in conditions we cannot at present foresee', he explained that the latter could be defined 'only in the most general terms'; a claim wholly substantiated by references to his admittedly 'utopian' vision of a Europe with a 'new spirit' of 'good will and mutual tolerance', where trade flourished, all had the 'unfettered right' to choose their own form of government and in which 'armaments would gradually be dropped as a useless expense'.[105] By this stage, however, another secret 'peace offensive' had fizzled out. And when more 'unofficial feelers' resumed in mid-December, Chamberlain remained adamant that it was 'too late for that sort of arrangement if it ever could have been discussed'.[106]

In formulating Britain's public response to Hitler's Reichstag proposals, Chamberlain had been guided by the belief that 'it was too early for any hope of a successful peace negotiation, the Germans not yet being sufficiently convinced that they could not win'. The longer the Phoney War continued, the more confident he became that Hitler would eventually come to the same conclusion and the German 'peace offensive' only confirmed him in the wisdom of his existing strategy: 'Hold on tight. Keep up the economic pressure, push on with munitions production & military preparations with the utmost energy, take no offensive unless Hitler begins it.' On this basis, he predicted that 'if we are allowed to carry on this policy we shall have won the war by the Spring'. Unfortunately for Chamberlain, the gulf between his perceptions and Hitler's plans widened rapidly over the next seven months. For Hitler, it was always a matter of time before the great offensive was launched in the West. Conversely,

Chamberlain preferred to believe the 'peace offensive' would continue because 'however much the Nazi's may brag and threaten I don't believe they feel sufficient confidence to venture on the great war unless they are forced into it by action on our part. It is my aim to see that that action is not taken.' While conceding that 'the soldiers are all against me', as the weather deteriorated during October and the Allied defences became stronger, he consoled himself with the thought that it made operations on the Western Front progressively 'more remote and impossible'. Predictions of this sort became the recurrent theme of his correspondence during the late autumn and winter of 1939. Moreover, as he confessed in early November: 'As my general diagnosis of the position seems to be coming out right I naturally grow more confident.'[107]

Central to Chamberlain's confidence was his perception of the situation in the Low Countries. Here he was guided so strongly by wishful thinking and his own intuition that he preferred to 'steadfastly disbelieve' evidence about German troop movements and apparently authoritative reports. As he outlined in early November, in terms depressingly reminiscent of his pre-war views about rearmament, 'my general principle is Rule out nothing as impossible and make what preparations you can to meet it. Only ... the extent and cost of preparations must bear some relation to ... [the] probability that they will be required.' In this context, Chamberlain's instinct and logic told him that the economic and diplomatic disadvantages of an invasion of Holland outweighed the advantages and 'could only be justified as the last desperate gambler's throw in an apparently hopeless situation'.[108] Again, however, his own cautious rationalism prevented him from comprehending the recklessness and determination of a dictator who was prepared to gamble everything on an all-or-nothing struggle for world domination before the military balance swung decisively against him.

In reality, Hitler had resolved to hurl his offensive against the Low Countries on the morning of 12 November. When the German High Command failed to dissuade him from this course, Colonel Hans Oster of the *Abwehr* created panic by secretly warning the Dutch and Belgian legations in Berlin of the plan. When Chamberlain heard these rumours, however, he remained sceptical, while further reports from various 'well informed sources' of a German offensive against Holland on 3 December (as a prelude to a massive attack on Britain), prompted only the weary observation that 'We have been given definite dates for offensives on so many previous occasions that I have ceased to pay any serious attention to them.'[109] In retrospect, this supremely dismissive attitude appears to be at best naïve and at worst arrogantly reckless – particularly given what is now known of Hitler's ambitions. Yet in assessing Chamberlain's behaviour it is important to recall that he had been inundated with such reports for well over a year and that even nine months earlier Colvin's hair-raising stories along similar lines had aroused a good deal of scepticism on the grounds that policy-makers had heard it all before. Moreover, everything that had happened since the outbreak of war appeared to confirm Chamberlain's belief that he alone had been right all along about the essentially limited nature of

German war aims and his expert military advisers were excessively alarmist in their predictions.

As the winter set in, Chamberlain became ever more convinced that 'Hitler will abstain from any action which would entail real bad fighting with heavy losses for fear of alienating German opinion.' Hitler's intention, Chamberlain believed, was to restrict the war to bombing raids on military targets, mine-laying and submarine attacks in the hope that it would 'do enough damage ... to induce us to listen to peace terms such as would allow him to "get away with it"'. As a result, when his military advisers warned that '*the* testing time will be ... in March or in April, & that if we don't do this or that now we shall be overwhelmed', Chamberlain refused to be swayed. He had been correct in the autumn in dismissing such fears, and he had 'a "hunch" that the war will be over before the spring'.

> It won't be by defeat in the field but by German realisation that they *can't* win and that it isn't worth their while to go on getting thinner & poorer when they might have instant relief and perhaps not have to give up anything they really care about. My belief is that a great many Germans are near that position now and that their number, in the absence of any striking military success, will go on growing with increasing rapidity.[110]

Despite fears that the failure of the Russian offensive against valiant Finnish resistance during the winter of 1939–40 would 'have the effect of throwing them into Germany's arms' and encourage dangerous joint adventures in Scandinavia and South East Europe, Chamberlain entered 1940 in a relatively sanguine mood. 'I am no pessimist', he confided in his sisters on 30 December. 'I stick to the view I have always held that Hitler missed the bus in Sept 1938. He could have dealt France and ourselves a terrible, perhaps a mortal, blow then. The opportunity will not recur.' In such a mood he speculated about his chances of ever getting two or three consecutive days trout fishing again. 'I suppose if things went on like this there is no reason why I shouldn't' he wrote to Joseph Ball, 'but it is impossible to believe that the situation will not change radically before the trout season comes round again.'[111] It was one of his few entirely accurate predictions during this period.

V

On the home front the situation was rather less encouraging. Admittedly, the secret session of Parliament on 13 December did something to restore Chamberlain's sense of his own ascendancy after a difficult session during which his parliamentary stock had plummeted. The debate itself was 'very ragged and ill tempered', with the 'Glamour Boys' so vocal that 'at one time things were rather ugly', while Labour were also 'very noisy and aggressive' during Burgin's statement. On the other hand, Chamberlain interpreted their silence during his own largely impromptu winding-up speech as 'obvious marks of approval at the passages in which [he] tried to put the debate on a higher plane' and the Liberal Chief Whip confirmed his own impression that he had been 'very successful'.[112] Other ministers, however, took a far less positive view of Chamberlain's 'poorish speech'. Indeed, on the front bench Burgin at one point even went so far as to urge Hore-Belisha to contradict their own leader's claims about the history of Army rearmament.[113] After a four day tour of Allied defensive positions in France and a meeting of the Supreme War Council in Paris, Chamberlain then obtained the 'heaven sent relief' of a month long parliamentary recess. Unfortunately, while an enjoyable Christmas was spent at Chequers with his wife, children, sisters and niece Valerie, a severe attack of gout on 27 December compelled him to abandon a New Year family party at Chequers. Worse still, the recurrence of gout so soon after the last bout left him 'worried at the prospect of not being able to carry on if these attacks increase in number and violence'.[114]

In this gloomy mood Chamberlain confronted a major political crisis. Shortly before Christmas, the eruption of a 'first-class row' between Hore-Belisha as War Minister and Lord Gort, the BEF's Commander-in-Chief, prompted thoughts of a radical Cabinet reconstruction.[115] Although this dispute arose ostensibly over the minister's tactless handling of a disagreement over pill-box construction in France, the crisis was the culmination of an enduring military animus towards Hore-Belisha which had already become legendary long before the outbreak of war. Chamberlain had appointed the ambitious and abrasive Hore-Belisha because he was convinced the War Office needed 'many and drastic changes' and he soon declared himself 'very well satisfied' that his 'new broom ... [wa]s sweeping with great vigour & determination and ... entirely on lines approved by me'.[116] It was an open secret that these drastic military reforms were 'the result of Neville's pushing' but it did nothing to mitigate Army and departmental loathing: 'It was a swine's job and he did it like a swine.'[117] As a result, Gort and other senior officers had openly endorsed Hudson's indictment of Hore-Belisha during the 'Under-Secretary's Revolt' in December 1938 and denounced him generally as a 'lazy', untrustworthy and egotistical self-publicist.[118] To make matters worse, during his tour of inspection to France in November 1939 he arrived 'arrayed like a Bond Street bum-boy' in spats, only to be exposed to all manner of spiteful indignities by Gort's staff.[119] This combination of personal failings and military contempt ensured the rapid growth of an 'anti-Belisha faction' in Parliament, the War Office and Army, all determined to seize this carefully premeditated opportunity to destroy him. After informing the King and the Prime Minister of the gravity of the problem, Gort's Chief of Staff noted, 'it's no good being Old School Tie with H-B, you have to fight him with his own weapons. One crushes a snake even if it does happen to be on the ground.'[120]

Chamberlain had been well aware that 'for some time past things have been very difficult not to say explosive at the War Office', but during his own tour of inspection in France in mid-December he had hoped a 'frank talk' with Gort would dispel any misunderstandings. Instead, although he attempted to defend Hore-Belisha, Chamberlain was alarmed to find sentiment much worse than he had anticipated, with officers reportedly saying 'We have now two enemies to fight – one out here and one at home.'[121] Chamberlain's personal feelings towards Hore-Belisha had always been somewhat ambivalent, but during the 'Under-Secretary's Revolt' in December 1938, he had loyally defended him from allegations of failure and declared that he considered him 'the best S. of S. for War since Haldane'.[122] When confronted by this renewed outburst of military hostility, however, Chamberlain swiftly decided that the discontent against the minister would inevitably soon break out again – particularly as the King pointedly made it clear that he 'was under no illusions about Hore-Belisha and realize[d] that he must go'.[123]

Chamberlain swiftly arrived at the same conclusion, largely because he knew Hore-Belisha's detractors had a point. He conceded that Hore-Belisha undoubtedly possessed 'very exceptional qualities of courage, imagination and drive' and that his military reforms had been vital and successful, but he also recognised that he had 'always been a stormy petrel and in every office he has held he has without intending it been a recurrent source of trouble to me'. In particular, he believed his poor relations with both civilian and military staff at the War Office arose 'partly from his impatience and eagerness, partly from a self-centredness which makes him careless of other people's feelings and partly from the impression he creates that he is more concerned with publicity and his own personal ambitions than he is with the public interest'.[124] To make matters worse, when Chamberlain frankly outlined the Army's indictment to Hore-Belisha on 20 December immediately after his return from France, he came away convinced that Hore-Belisha did not fully realise what he had done and Hore-Belisha's own diary account of Chamberlain's 'fatherly' rebuke appears to confirm this assessment – particularly as it concluded with the observation that Chamberlain was 'extremely nice throughout and ended by saying that he had complete confidence in me'.[125] As this response indicated an inevitable recurrence of trouble, Chamberlain thus resolved to transfer Hore-Belisha at the first favourable opportunity, because in wartime 'nothing could be worse than perpetual friction & want of confidence between the Secretary of State and the C.in C. in the field'. Having already decided to replace the manifestly failing Lord Macmillan at the Ministry of Information, Chamberlain regarded Hore-Belisha as the obvious successor, replacing him at the War Office with Oliver Stanley 'as the greatest contrast in temperament [he] could find'.[126]

When Chamberlain confided this plan to the Foreign Secretary on 23 December, Halifax expressed grave doubts as to whether 'LHB is quite big enough' for the MOI and that it would be 'rather a pill for that already ailing ministry to digest' if it was made to appear 'the dumping ground for someone who had to be moved from another Dept'.[127] When Horace Wilson also opposed the scheme, Chamberlain sounded Churchill, Kingsley Wood, the proprietor and editor of the *Sunday Times*, and Attlee, but they all agreed upon the wisdom of the proposed transfer, while Hoare and Simon expressed vague reservations. Thinking the way was now clear, shortly before Cabinet on 4 January Chamberlain arranged to see Hore-Belisha at 2.45pm that afternoon. Unfortunately, at this moment the plan began to collapse. After Cabinet, Halifax suddenly declared himself 'unhappy' about the appointment as it would have 'a bad effect on the neutrals both because H.B. was a Jew & because his methods would let down British prestige'. Chamberlain and Wilson had already considered the danger that Nazi propaganda would exploit Hore-Belisha's racial origins, but had been assured such concerns were 'entirely baseless'. Nevertheless, with only an hour before his meeting with Hore-Belisha, Chamberlain decided to defer to Foreign Office objections and to offer him the Board of Trade as Halifax and Hoare proposed.[128]

According to Hore-Belisha's account of 'a most painful interview', Chamberlain declared that 'there was an overwhelming prejudice against him', that he personally disagreed with it and regretted it, but that he could not resist it and so wished him to move to the Board of Trade. The announcement obviously 'came as a complete surprise to H.B. and it was evidently a shattering blow'. But when Hore-Belisha requested time to consider the offer, it was Chamberlain's turn to display his 'utmost surprise' that such an ambitious man was prepared to consider the political 'wilderness' and he pressed repeatedly for an immediate answer. Having finally allowed Hore-Belisha until the following morning to consider the offer, to 'save him a sleepless night', Chamberlain then sent a sympathetic note assuring him the move was 'not as tragic as it seemed at first' but that in wartime 'no one can feel satisfied unless he has made some sacrifice'.[129]

Much to Chamberlain's surprise, later that evening Hore-Belisha wrote to refuse the Board of Trade because of the 'circumstances' in which the transfer was proposed. In particular, he referred to Chamberlain's sudden *volte face* since his assurances of 'complete support' on 20 December and the fear that in future his tenure of office might 'not depend on the merits of my work'.[130] Furthermore, when Hore-Belisha returned to Downing Street next morning, he demanded 'somewhat aggressively' to know the precise nature of the prejudice to which Chamberlain had alluded vaguely on the previous afternoon and accused him of 'delivering [him] to [his] enemies'. Feeling 'a little nettled' at this challenge, Chamberlain then delivered 'a frank & somewhat brutal account of the complaints against him by civilians as well as soldiers', adding for good measure that even the Cabinet found him 'a difficult colleague and a bad team-worker'. Chamberlain believed that Hore-Belisha had accepted this candour in the same friendly spirit as that adopted on similar occasions in the past and he strongly pressed him to take the alternative office, but an evidently shaken Hore-Belisha refused on the grounds that 'the same "prejudice" which had brought about his removal from the W.O. might act in another office'. Later in the day, however, Hore-Belisha communicated indirectly to Chamberlain and the Cabinet through Kingsley Wood that if it was announced that his transfer was designed to coordinate the economic front with the right of attendance at Cabinet like Eden and Anderson, he would accept the offer. This Chamberlain refused to contemplate and after Wood's further intercessions, Chamberlain was relieved to learn that Hore-Belisha had declined to change his mind.[131]

Chamberlain's hopes that Hore-Belisha would do nothing to prevent his own later return to office were soon dashed. During the afternoon, Hore-Belisha secretly visited the proprietors and editors of the principal London newspapers offering what Chamberlain considered 'such a distorted account of the incident' that he drafted a 13-page 'commentary' to contradict the 'entirely false impression' Hore-Belisha had created. According to Hore-Belisha's account to the press, he was an innocent victim of Gort's over-sensitivity and the prejudiced influence of the military brasshats and the Palace – particularly through the malign influence of the Duke of Gloucester and the Earl of Munster, Gort's Military Assistant. To increase the sense of innocent tragedy, Hore-Belisha told the press and others that he would never serve under Chamberlain again as he could no longer be trusted. Ironically, this was a choice he would never have to make, for although Hore-Belisha prudently concealed his secret revenge even from his own diary, the Prime Minister was determined that he would neither forgive nor forget the betrayal.[132]

As Chamberlain predicted, his own enemies were only too eager to exploit this crisis at a time when Hore-Belisha was 'obviously making mischief' by exploiting to the full his gifts for self-publicity and his contacts in the press. Yet within a week, Chamberlain noted with satisfaction that the 'H.B. sensation has died down as quickly as it began.'[133] Although he expected some trouble when Parliament reassembled to hear the resignation statement on 16 January, by then Chamberlain had obtained an undertaking from Hore-Belisha that 'he had nothing to worry about' in the speech and Attlee promised to confine discussion to the strictly public aspects of the affair. Perhaps more important, while Hore-Belisha's unpopularity with government backbenchers ensured that few tears were shed at his departure, Joseph Ball sought to marginalise him further by launching a venomous anti-semitic attack in *Truth*, which was then despatched to MPs and other prominent figures.[134] Despite these precautions, however, Hore-Belisha's resignation speech clearly embarrassed the Government while Chamberlain's reply was poorly delivered and ended amid a storm of interruptions from the Opposition. To make matters worse, his ensuing statement on the war situation 'was too long and ... seemed to bore the House with its dreary details'. As even his most devoted admirers conceded, Chamberlain was 'not ... at his best, and he seemed for the first time aged and colourless'.[135]

Embarrassing complications in his plan to reconstruct the War Cabinet were not confined solely to Hore-Belisha's antics. Indeed, the principal aspect of 'the daring project' he had originally envisaged was nothing less than the removal of Simon from the Treasury; a scheme conceived by Horace Wilson and Montagu Norman, but strongly supported by Margesson who regarded Simon (and Hoare) as 'egocentric intriguers' who had to be 'got rid of'.[136] After considering Reginald McKenna and 'unattractive bureaucrats' like Anderson as replacements, Chamberlain eventually decided on Lord Stamp, the Government's Chief Economic Adviser. Various motives have been proposed for Chamberlain's decision to remove Simon, ranging from 'the simple desire to settle scores' over his part in the revolt on the eve of war, to the 'more intriguing possibility' that Chamberlain was thinking of clearing a path for the appointment of some of Labour's leaders.[137] Yet in reality, as so often, the more prosaic explanation comes far closer to the truth. Simon had found the burden of the Treasury so onerous that on the eve of war Wilson, Hankey and Bridges, the Cabinet Secretary, were gravely concerned about his marked deterioration and by the end of 1939 Norman advised Chamberlain that it was imperative to replace his Chancellor.[138]

While Simon's removal offered political advantages in its own right, his replacement by a non-party 'expert' like Stamp conformed well with both Chamberlain's technocratic preferences and with his need to silence the growing parliamentary clamour for more dynamism and coordination in the direction of the war economy. To this end, Hankey and Wilson took 'very secret soundings' regarding the possibility of allowing Stamp to be 'dis-peered' (as Chamberlain put it) and to become an MP.[139] In the event, however, the plan was abandoned less because Chamberlain could not afford to axe two Liberal National ministers at the same time, than because 'the individual for whom [he] had designed the hero's role ... showed such a very unheroic trepidation at the prospect that [he] saw he would be hissed off the stage'. Simon thus remained at the Treasury 'blissfully unconscious' of the plan, but as an increasing liability to Chamberlain; a fact demonstrated by renewed parliamentary agitation for a Minister for War Economy later in the month.[140]

As a result of these unforeseen complications, the major reconstruction which Chamberlain had initially planned was greatly diminished by the time it was announced on 5 January 1940 and few were impressed by such meagre efforts to reinvigorate the image of the government. Although Sir Andrew Duncan was a widely-respected businessman and 'expert' at the Board of Trade, even within Downing Street it was recognised that Lord Reith's appointment to the MOI 'may not be well received by the outside world' who looked upon Reith as 'the man who failed first at the B.B.C. and then at Imperial Airways'. Worse still, even government supporters regarded Stanley as 'a dry stick', while its critics lamented his move to the War Office on the grounds that he was 'a weak man, and ... that ... has been his chief recommendation in the eyes of the P.M.'.[141] Although *The Times* welcomed the changes, even it noted next day that this could only be regarded as an interim measure until a more radical reform of the size and composition of the War Cabinet was introduced. Unfortunately, when a more extensive reshuffle eventually did take place in early April, it was both too little and far too late to inspire any real confidence in Chamberlain's ability to win the war.

VI

In the immediate aftermath of the Hore-Belisha 'sensation', an already weary and harassed Prime Minister became increasingly irritable and intolerant of all criticism and opposition. Confronted by a tactlessly phrased Foreign Office parliamentary reply in late January, Chamberlain became so angry that his private secretary confessed he had been 'surprised at the violence of his fury which I could never have expected in such a cold man'.[142] Chamberlain was no more favourably disposed towards 'the vile press' whose 'abominable' conduct only made his task more difficult while it did nothing to acknowledge the government's many real successes.[143] Chamberlain's relations with the Labour Party also inevitably deteriorated still further during this period. In fairness, Chamberlain's relationship with Attlee and Greenwood had improved somewhat since the war began, but he retained an abiding and fully reciprocated contempt for Dalton and Morrison whose unabated partisanship he found increasingly 'poisonous' and intolerable. In order to reduce these tensions, in early February Chamberlain's Principal Private Secretary was active behind the scenes in persuading Morrison to 'moderate his tone', but to the frustration of all his staff 'the P.M. failed to respond or to pick up the olive branch'. As another Downing Street private secretary encapsulated the collective despair:

> the P.M. is incapable of being gracious at the right moment. He is a curious mixture of qualities and defects: I have nothing but admiration for his forcefulness, precision and capacity for hard work; and yet at the same time he is obstinate and vain ... In N.C.'s case this vanity takes the form of resenting any kind of criticism or mockery. He feels it acutely when he is attacked personally in the press or in Parliament; ... and there is no surer way of gratifying him than to make some allusion to the exceptional importance of his position. In other words, he likes to be set on a pedestal and adored, with suitable humility, by unquestioning admirers.[144]

This was an astute diagnosis of the malady which afflicted Chamberlain after September 1939. Once the initial mood of national unity ebbed away, Chamberlain received precious little adulation or humble adoration from the press or the parliamentary opposition. 'I confess the House of Commons depresses me' he noted after the debate on Hore-Belisha's resignation. In particular, he deplored the 'fine patriotic spirit' with which the PLP attacked Attlee for his restraint and the fact that his own speech was 'continuously interrupted with shouts, sneers and derisive laughter'. As he complained to his sisters, 'I don't show any sign of disturbance so people naturally think that I am not disturbed but it makes me sick to see such personal prejudice & such partisanship when I am doing my best to avoid any party provocation in the national interest'; a resentment intensified still further by Lloyd George's conspicuous efforts to encourage 'the opposition riff-raff'. Next day, after Dalton's attacks on the Ministry for Economic Warfare, Chamberlain was again 'disgusted … with the eternal carping and intrigue of the Opposition' who were 'saturated with the pettiness of party politics' and who 'only paid lip-service to the universally accepted doctrine that everything must be subordinated to the efficient prosecution of the war'. Perhaps inevitably, Chamberlain's anger towards this torrent of press and parliamentary abuse only sharpened his tendency to be 'a bit acrimonious' in tone and manner. Nevertheless, for the time being, it looked as if he was still secure in his position as Prime Minister and he showed no real desire to give it up or to doubt his own indispensability. On the contrary, as he noted in late January during a bout of depression about such attacks, 'it does make one sometimes feel that there would be compensation if one were forced to hand over to another. Only I don't see that other to whom I could hand over with any confidence … would be better than I.'[145]

Chapter 17

Decline and Fall,
February–May 1940

'We are both numbed by the sudden change to such an extent as to be incapable of any strong emotion; in fact my only desire is to get out of this horrible condition of chronic misery & I frankly envy Austen's peace. But there it is. One just goes on doing what lies in front to the best of one's ability without troubling to think of the future in this world or the next.'

Neville to Hilda Chamberlain, 17 May 1940

During the early months of 1940, the curious tempo of the Phoney War continued much as it had since September 1939. Despite periodic crises, the rota system still allowed Chamberlain to visit his beloved Chequers two weekends out of three where he relaxed, pondered the behaviour of its birds and rejoiced in the simple pleasure of walking the grounds with Spot, the Chequers dog. Similarly, during his morning strolls around the St James' Park lake he had sufficient time to record an unseasonal Common Sandpiper and to seek out a Smew, forced inland by the exceptionally severe winter. Such was the apparent normality of life that even when 'on duty' in London, worries about the deteriorating military situation in Finland did not prevent visits to the Royal Horticultural Society's gardens at Wisley with his son, to London Zoo with his niece and a walk around Kensington Gardens with his wife all in the same weekend.[1] Despite passing his seventy-first birthday in March, Chamberlain also remained extraordinarily fit and vigorous; a robust physical and mental constitution which enabled him to retain all of his old mastery in Cabinet.

> The P.M. is standing the strain wonderfully well and is an assiduous reader of all memoranda; masters them in a way no other member of the Cabinet does and by his thorough knowledge of each item on the agenda dominates his colleagues. Even Winston I hear is impressed with the way in which the P.M. sums up a debate and has been known to be brought round to a view opposed to that with which he started.[2]

Even during the final depressing stages of the Norway campaign in late April, the young men on his staff commented that his 'incredible capacity for hard work, and his apparent immunity from fatigue continue and seem even to increase as the problems become more difficult and the days heavier with work. His seventy-one years lie very easily upon his shoulders.'[3]

Although unable to compete with Churchill's oratorical pyrotechnics, during this period Chamberlain perceptibly grew in confidence about the effectiveness of his broadcasting style. His stirring Mansion House address on 9 January was widely hailed as a personal triumph; a feat all the more impressive when one realises that he dutifully remained at the microphone while agitated officials extinguished the blaze above his head caused by a fused light.[4] After his broadcast speech from Birmingham Town Hall in early March, he believed he had now really acquired the ability to inspire his listeners, because 'I feel confident and my voice sounds as if I were more confident than I am.'[5] Similarly, in the Commons, his devastating argumentative power still remained evident to the dismay of Opposition challengers and to the delight of his friends. During the Finland debate on 19 March, Chamberlain thus celebrated his birthday with 'the speech of his life', which so completely demolished the case against him that even bitter critics were compelled to concede that he was 'a remarkable man ... There is also no doubt that he wants to win the war. He gave the impression of great obstinacy and has enhanced his reputation.' It was a measure of Chamberlain's undiminished grasp over a section of the electorate that his birthday prompted another flood of letters and telegrams from well-wishers.[6]

Abroad, the situation provided grounds for both concern and satisfaction. In the Far East, the Japanese eagerly exploited British entanglements in Europe to obtain further advantage, but direct tensions in January 1940 caused by the British seizure of the Japanese steamer, *Asama Mara*, were soon patched up. Closer home, he found the behaviour of the European neutral states exasperating when they sought to treat the warring sides as if it was 'six of one and half a dozen of the other, hoping thereby to conciliate their terrible neighbour' and he was particularly despondent about the 'natural but sadly inglorious part' played by Norway and Sweden in their willingness to 'put up with any humiliation rather than face the Germans'. On the other hand, Mussolini remained on the sidelines and Chamberlain rightly suspected that for the moment he had no intention of intervening to assist Hitler for fear of provoking a revolution.[7] More immediately alarming was the gradual collapse of Finnish resistance to Soviet aggression given agreement at the Supreme War Council in early February that 'the defeat of Finland would be the defeat of the Allied cause'. Nevertheless, having decided to intervene, Chamberlain rather optimistically claimed that once modern Allied fighter aircraft were deployed 'there won't be a Russian left in Finland'.[8]

With regard to the possibility of a German offensive in the West, Chamberlain remained 'very sceptical' – even when the forced landing of a German plane in Belgium dropped genuine details of Hitler's offensive planned for 17 January into the Allied lap. Moreover, while the old illusion that Germany simply could not fight a long war remained as deeply-rooted as ever, Hitler's speeches also appeared to confirm earlier hopes. 'I think he is certainly getting madder', Chamberlain recorded in late February. 'It can only be a question of time before he goes off his head altogether.' In these circumstances, he confidently dismissed prophesies of a spring offensive in the West and he continued to say so until Hitler invaded Scandinavia six weeks later. Yet from Chamberlain's perspective, nothing had really changed. Despite continued peace 'feelers' from various sources in Germany, everything appeared to confirm the wisdom of his initial conclusion that Hitler had 'missed the bus' in September 1938 and that all Britain needed to do to win was to 'hold on tight', keep up the economic blockade and avoid any intervention which would expose them to the risk of losing the war before it had actually begun. While recognising the need to 'beware of wishful thinking', therefore, Chamberlain concluded in February that 'we have no reason to be dissatisfied with the opening phases of the war'.[9]

This aura of complacency infuriated Chamberlain's Tory critics who were increasingly demanding a more vigorous prosecution of the war. In late December, Richard Law, son of the former Conservative Prime Minister, had raged that 'wars don't win themselves & I think it likely that we shall pay bitterly for believing that they do'. Despite Chamberlain's effective defence of the government's policy after the collapse of Finland in mid-March, therefore, his critics still contended that Britain had lost the diplomatic and military initiative and it was unlikely ever to regain it under his control. Equally frustrating for these backbench dissidents, former leaders like Eden and Churchill appeared to have adopted 'a defeatist attitude not about the war but about the old man'; a state of mind which reconciled them to accept that 'death will provide the only release'. Yet for Chamberlain's most disaffected backbencher opponent, this was not sufficient – particularly in view of the dramatic effect produced by the removal of the *Munichois* in France. 'The more we weaken the govt', Law wrote on 1 April, 'the more, I honestly believe, we strengthen England.' At this stage, he could only console his allies with the thought that 'events ... will take a hand'.[10] Within a week, however, the fulfilment of such hopes left Chamberlain confronting the greatest crisis of his turbulent Premiership.

II

Throughout his political career, Chamberlain had emphasised the critical importance of timing. In April 1940, this factor contributed substantially to his downfall in two key respects. First, Chamberlain's last Cabinet reshuffle on 3 April was too little and far too late to dispel the powerful suspicion that the war could not be won under his leadership. Thwarted in his plans for a more extensive reconstruction in January, he was already considering a radical reorganisation of the entire government when the sudden death of Sir John Gilmour on 30 March provided the perfect pretext to act.[11] At this stage he told the King that he intended both to create a War Cabinet 'whose members will be concerned with coordination rather than departmental duties' and to offer places in it to the Opposition parties.[12] Yet despite widespread rumours that Chamberlain had offered three Cabinet posts to Labour, he appears to have told none of his other confidants of the scheme and (if it ever existed) it was soon abandoned.[13] He also ignored Churchill's advice to appoint Kingsley Wood as an overall 'Economic Minister' to 'satisfy the very large movement towards that plan'.[14] As a result, the ensuing reconstruction was confined to an exercise in ministerial musical chairs as Hoare and Kingsley Wood exchanged jobs within the War Cabinet, while outside it De La Warr, Ramsbotham, Tryon and Morrison did the same. Perhaps the only significant change was the abolition of Chatfield's redundant portfolio as Minister for the Coordination of Defence; a development which enabled Churchill to become chairman of the Military Coordination Committee, presiding over the three Service Chiefs and their ministers, in order to act collectively as a clearing house for new strategic ideas.

Chamberlain always recognised these changes were unlikely to receive a good press but he still obstinately refused to bow to public expectations or to court cheap popularity. The changes, he confided to his sisters, 'are not designed to placate the disgruntled but ... they will make for better working and will justify themselves in time'.[15] Unfortunately, this characteristic emphasis upon private efficiency over public perception received a predictably 'mixed reception' in the country, the press and Parliament. Even within the government, Euan Wallace warned Margesson shortly before the announcement that 'the very worst possible thing' would be simply to exchange offices, while after it Zetland's junior minister almost resigned in protest and Crookshank declared the 'P.M. must be mad.'[16] This was a view shared by Chamberlain's parliamentary critics in the newly-established 'Watching Committee' of influential peers and MPs, created 'to make representations to the Government where they consider there is a risk of mistakes being made or where it seems that the trend of public opinion is not appreciated'. At their first meeting on the day after this disappointing reshuffle, the Committee resolved to inform Chamberlain of the need for a 'real War Cabinet', but Salisbury's efforts to do so were rebuffed by a 'very friendly' but utterly impervious Prime Minister who appeared 'thoroughly pleased with himself and his recent reshuffle and not in the least minded to consider ... that things wanted conducting with greater vigour'.[17]

On the day after this government reshuffle, Chamberlain's second error of timing came in the form of a disastrous speech which soon crystallised all of these burgeoning anxieties about his war leadership. Since Munich, Chamberlain had never deviated from the view that Hitler had 'missed the bus' in September 1938 when the military balance was at its most favourable to Germany. 'After all', he asked his sisters in late March, 'if the Germans can annihilate us so completely, why haven't they done it?' Having attempted to place himself in Hitler's position, Chamberlain's answer was always the same: 'To try the offensive is to gamble all on a single throw. If he succeeds, well & good; he has won the war. But if he doesn't succeed he has lost it, for he will never have another chance as good ... I know which I should choose & therefore can't help believing that he will choose the same.'[18] The methodical strategic assessment and the overriding priority upon the avoidance of slaughter and incalculable risks were absolutely typical of Chamberlain's own mentality, but again they reflected a critical weakness when seeking to understand the mind of a reckless gambler prepared to wager everything in pursuit of world domination.

To express such views in the confessional secrecy of his correspondence with his sisters was one thing, but to voice the same opinions in public was quite another. Yet in a speech to the Conservative Central Council on 4 April, Chamberlain declared that after seven months of war he felt 'ten times as confident of victory as I did at the beginning' given the rapid progress of Allied rearmament – adding with cheery hubris, that whatever the reason for Hitler's failure to launch the much-vaunted offensive, 'one thing is certain: he missed the bus'. At the time, Chamberlain noted this remark was 'very warmly received and the informality and "jauntiness" of "Hitler missed the bus" seems to have given peculiar satisfaction'.[19] He was correct in this assessment, but five days later Hitler had the last laugh by occupying Denmark and launching the invasion of Norway. In the aftermath of this decisive blow, Chamberlain's lacklustre Cabinet reconstruction appeared to be symptomatic of everything that was wrong with the British war effort, while his ill-timed remarks about Hitler having 'missed the bus' made his propensity for facile optimism appear to be a national danger greater even than Hitler himself. Little wonder that on the day after the launch of the Scandinavian offensive, Chamberlain was reported to be 'rather depressed at the situation' because he had 'never expected the war to flare up as it has now'.[20]

One of the ironies of Hitler's Norway campaign was that when speculating about future developments over Christmas, Chamberlain had declared that he 'would like to see the Germans involved in war with Sweden & Norway, but the advantages to us are so obvious that I fear it won't happen'.[21] Scandinavia was critical to Germany's war effort. Sweden supplied Germany with iron ore, but with the Baltic frozen in winter this needed to be transported by rail to the northern Norwegian port of Narvik before shipment through their territorial waters to Germany. To protect these vital supplies and pre-empt an expected Allied landing, on 1 March Hitler ordered that military operations against Scandinavia should precede the already planned offensive against France. The date was set for 9 April.[22]

By another irony, this date coincided exactly with Allied action in Scandinavia designed to disrupt this traffic and with it the entire Nazi war machine. The possibility of mining Norwegian waters had been on the War Cabinet agenda since mid-December when Churchill contended that to stop the iron-ore traffic would be 'a blow ... struck at [Germany's] war-making capacity equal to a first class victory ... and without any serious sacrifice of life'.[23] Despite regular discussion, however, the plan was shelved in early January and again in late February and only revived a month later when the fall of Daladier's government – largely because of its failure to prosecute the war with sufficient vigour – obliged its successor to demonstrate more aggression by proposing that the war should be extended to Norway, the Black Sea and the Caucuses oilfields. Chamberlain initially 'went through the ceiling' when he heard of these 'wild proposals for drastic action'. Convinced the Allies needed more time to maximise war production, at his first meeting with the new French Premier at the Supreme War Council on 28 March, Chamberlain thus demonstrated remarkable political skill in steering the discussion to a 'very successful' conclusion.[24] As General Ironside recorded, Chamberlain 'took all the thunder out of Reynaud's mouth and left him gaping with no electric power left. All the "projects" that Reynaud had to bring forward, Chamberlain took away. It was most masterly and well done.' As a result, the Allies finally agreed to confine action to the mining of Norwegian waters, along with Churchill's soon to be abandoned plan to drop 'fluvial mines' along the Rhine to paralyse river traffic. The date for the commencement of mining operations in Norway was 8 April.[25]

While British warships began mining the waters around Narvik, German forces seized Denmark early on 9 April and began the occupation of Norway. In response, the War Cabinet ordered the recapture of Trondheim and Bergen and the occupation of Narvik.[26] From the outset, this ill-conceived and hastily improvised campaign, proved to be a disaster of amateurish muddle, hesitation and miscalculations. Until 20 April Chamberlain remained optimistic. After news that the military situation had deteriorated next day, however, he endured 'one of the worst, if not *the* worst, week of the war' and he confessed to feeling 'really tired'. Confronted by military disaster, the Allies had little option but to cut their losses. On 26 April the War Cabinet agreed to prepare for a possible withdrawal from Norway south of Narvik.[27] Narvik was evacuated on 8 June and the last Norwegian forces surrendered two days later.

The German victory in Norway proved remarkably costly in men, aircraft and ships – but it was still a victory. In contrast, Chamberlain consoled himself with the thought that the campaign had been a devastating demonstration to Allied strategists of the dangers of unopposed air power and that 'if they have learnt the lesson we have not paid too dearly for it'. There was also the political dimension to weigh in the balance. 'Looking back I do not see how we could have done anything but what we did', he concluded, particularly as Norway and Sweden had both threatened to surrender unless an immediate operation was launched to capture Trondheim. There was also the broader strategic consolation that Allied success in Scandinavia might have created a costly entanglement which would have drained vital air and naval resources away from the defence of a vulnerable Britain. On this basis, Chamberlain had a point when he claimed the Allies had been right to try but that they were equally right to withdraw.[28] Yet while all of this was reasonable enough, none of it was sufficient to obscure either the fact that Chamberlain's government had suffered a humiliating defeat or that someone would have to pay for this failure.

III

The supreme irony of the Norway campaign as the proximate cause of Neville Chamberlain's downfall is that the principal beneficiary of the ensuing political crisis was the man who bore most direct responsibility for the military fiasco which brought it about. In fairness, throughout the Phoney War, Churchill had dutifully played the role of Chamberlain's loyal, if impulsive, lieutenant. Despite repeated rumours of Churchillian intrigues and secret collaboration with old cronies like Lloyd George, Churchill's frustrated supporters complained bitterly that he neglected his friends while carrying loyalty to new colleagues to absurd lengths.[29] Against this background, Chamberlain was broadly correct when he asserted at the end of March 1940 that Churchill remained 'absolutely loyal'.[30] But genuine loyalty did not imply that Churchill was either oblivious to his rising prestige or prepared to forego opportunities to enhance his stature and influence. On the contrary, as the war was confined to the high seas, the Admiralty provided Churchill with an unrivalled platform for the brazen self-promotion of his image as the great war lord when announcing the destruction of U-boats, the sinking of the *Graf Spee* and the capture of the *Altmark*. In the public mind, Churchill gradually became the model for the sort of inspirational spirit and martial qualities which were so desperately needed to defeat Hitler and so conspicuously absent in Chamberlain.

Contrary to Churchill's later account, the Norway campaign revealed the vast gulf between his limited capacity for strategy and the popular mythology of the great war leader so assiduously propagated by the Admiralty's publicity machine. Indeed, for many close observers, Churchill's impatience, impetuosity and lack of consistent purpose over Norway suggested that he had learned nothing from the Dardanelles disaster in 1915 with regard to the dangers of improvised large-scale combined operations. Chamberlain had every right to lament the damaging consequences of Churchill's repeated changes of mind over the Trondheim operation. He was equally critical of his poor judgement regarding the deployment of the Mediterranean fleet, when Churchill again dangerously ignored the air threat and only ordered the Navy's larger ships to Alexandria after Chamberlain forced him to accept direct personal responsibility for an alternative strategy the Cabinet had already denounced as foolhardy. While not blaming Churchill for these 'natural alterations … in … awful times', Chamberlain strongly resented the fact that 'they don't square with the picture the gutter press & W.C.'s "friends" try to paint of the supreme War Lord'.[31]

Alongside reliable warnings that Churchill was drinking too much,[32] his working methods provoked widespread fury and despair at the Admiralty and within Whitehall generally. Only days after the start of the Norway campaign, Chamberlain lamented that 'although Winston only means to be helpful he does give me more trouble than all the rest of my colleagues put together'.

> His methods of work are most wearing to others. He goes to bed after lunch for a couple of hours or so and holds conferences up to one in the morning at which he goes into every detail … that could quite well be settled by subordinates. Officers and officials in his own and other departments are sent for and kept up till they are dropping with fatigue and service Ministers are worn out in arguing with him. I say to myself that this is just the price we

have to pay for the asset we have in his personality and popularity but I do wish we could have the latter without the former.[33]

Similar problems emerged with Churchill's executive capabilities as chairman of the Military Coordination Committee after Chatfield's resignation on 3 April. Although Churchill was 'in his seventh heaven' in this new position, his conduct produced such chaos and friction that the Committee was soon reported to be in 'an almost mutinous condition'.[34] Early on 16 April, General Ismay warned the Cabinet Secretary 'there was every chance of a first-class row' if Churchill chaired the MCC that day because the Chiefs of Staff were complaining that he prevented them meeting to discuss proposed action and the Joint Planning Staffs 'were being squeezed out of the picture'. At around the same time, Simon (representing Hankey and Kingsley Wood) protested to Horace Wilson that the War Cabinet were being denied access to written appreciations from the Service Chiefs on potentially hazardous operations.[35] Chamberlain was scarcely exaggerating, therefore, when he spoke of the MCC 'getting into a sad mess, quarrelling and sulking, with everyone feeling irritable and strained and with a general conviction that Winston had smashed the machine we had so carefully built up to ensure that all projects should be thought out or examined by a planning staff drawn from all services'. In fairness to Churchill, Chamberlain attributed the problem to the fact that 'he does enjoy planning a campaign ... so much and he believes so earnestly in all his own ideas (for the moment) that he puts intenser pressure on his staff than he realises'. Nevertheless, he also recognised that the 'result is that they are bullied into a sulky silence – a most dangerous position in a war'. Confronted by this alarming situation, Chamberlain took the chair on 16 April with the 'magical' result that daily meetings were concluded in little more than half an hour in unanimity and with clear orders agreed.[36]

For those who recalled Churchill's impulsiveness and obsessive lack of judgement during the genesis of the Dardanelles campaign in 1915, the MCC crisis further reinforced doubts about his judgement and leadership capabilities and an anxious Hankey drew this specific parallel to Chamberlain's attention in mid-April.[37] Yet although Churchill thanked Chamberlain for 'having got him out of a hole' on 16 April and asked him to continue to take the chair 'at any rate while the present affair was in progress', he inevitably drew a personally more convenient and very different conclusion from his problems with the MCC. At its meeting on the evening of 23 April, Churchill truculently challenged everything the Chiefs of Staff said and generally behaved 'like a spoiled & sulky child'. Next morning he conducted himself no better at the War Cabinet and dropped hints about withdrawing from the MCC altogether because 'his opinion [was] to be weighed with other opinions'.[38] After privately sounding Labour, Sinclair and Salisbury's Watching Committee, on 24 April Churchill even drafted a letter to Chamberlain proposing his own appointment as Minister for Defence but he eventually decided not to send it.[39] By then, however, Chamberlain had been warned that Churchill was 'complaining bitterly of being "thwarted" and not having sufficient powers'. He thus summoned Churchill for a friendly talk late that evening during which Churchill announced his desire to be Minister of Defence amidst seemingly genuine protestations of loyalty. In reply, Chamberlain asked for time to think it over and to consult the Service Ministers.[40]

According to Professor Addison, the crisis ended with Chamberlain surrendering to a demonstration of *force majeure* wielded by a figure so indispensable to the government's survival that it 'could not last a day if Churchill resigned on the issue of the conduct of the war'.[41] This is something of an overstatement. Jock Colville, one of Chamberlain's assistant private secretaries, did record that Churchill threatened to go to the Commons and disown responsibility for what was happening, with the danger of 'a first-class political crisis' if Chamberlain refused his request, but Chamberlain makes no such record during an otherwise friendly conversation. More important, Churchill was not in a sufficiently strong position to risk such a dangerous gamble in the wake of the MCC fiasco and the Norway campaign. Nor was Chamberlain prepared to surrender very much in order to conciliate his wayward colleague. Obviously 'depressed and at a loss to solve the Winston impasse', Chamberlain may have consulted Baldwin about the problem over lunch on 25 April. Alec Dunglass certainly 'pumped' Channon on his behalf to see whether Churchill could be 'deflected' by removing him from the Admiralty.[42] Convinced that the public mood would probably not tolerate his removal, however, Chamberlain was compelled to seek another solution.

Six weeks earlier Chamberlain had noted that 'Winston would like very much to become Minister for Defence with authority over the War Office and Air Ministry and that just won't do.'[43] After everything that had happened since, he was even more convinced of this view. While he conceded that Churchill very rarely fought for his frequently 'nonsensical proposals' against reasoned argument, as Prime Minister he was simply not prepared to take the risk of making him 'sole director of military policy without safeguards which would ensure the Cabinet getting the independent advice of the Chiefs of Staff before taking decisions'. As a result, Chamberlain characteristically began 'trying to find a way of satisfying him without dangerously weakening the authority of the Cabinet'.[44] The outcome of these deliberations, announced to Churchill on 30 April, was that he would chair the MCC in Chamberlain's absence. On behalf of the Committee, he would also be responsible 'for giving guidance and direction' to the Chiefs of Staff Committee with the power to summon them when necessary. To assist him, General Ismay was appointed as head of a small staff (separate from the Admiralty) with an additional seat on the Chiefs of Staff Committee.[45]

It has been claimed that this represented 'the last despairing tactical manoeuvre' of a Prime Minister who was running out of both time and options, but this verdict only really appears convincing with the benefits of hindsight.[46] Chamberlain's proposal actually fell a long way short of a Prime Ministerial surrender to a stronger subordinate and despite Churchill's initial hope that he would become 'a sort of Supreme Controller', a sceptical Ismay soon educated him to the harsher reality of this 'rather odd' arrangement.[47] Ultimately, all this amounted to in practice was that Chamberlain offered a prudent tactical concession designed to deliver the maximum satisfaction to Churchill at the lowest possible cost to himself. Some concession was unavoidable given Churchill's rising public stature and the unscrupulous manner in which he was 'too apt to look the other way while his friends exalt him as the War Genius & hint that if only he had not been thwarted things would have gone very differently'. To achieve his objective, Chamberlain was also compelled to expend some political capital. In particular, when the other Service ministers threatened to resign rather than accept the new arrangement, Chamberlain was obliged to call their bluff by declaring that he would rather resign himself – with the result that Churchill would then become both Premier and Defence Minister anyway. Yet while prepared to browbeat expendable ministers into compliance, Chamberlain's carefully worded safeguards in the paper outlining Churchill's new position were designed to confer all the responsibility and the title without any real authority. Moreover, if Churchill attempted to go beyond this remit, Chamberlain believed the entire structure would break down, with presumably some of the damage falling upon Churchill himself. In this context, Channon was closest to the mark when he believed that Chamberlain was 'playing a deep game. To gain time he has given Winston more rope, and made him what amounts to Director of Operations.'[48]

Despite the skill with which Chamberlain executed this manoeuvre, it is reasonable to suggest that 'by confining Churchill to an ill-defined role, Chamberlain provided both a rod for his own back and an alibi for Churchill should the [Norway] campaign misfire'.[49] This was certainly the outcome and only the latter man emerged from this military debacle with his public and parliamentary reputation enhanced. In early May, an opinion poll showed only 30 per cent of voters thought the Allies had done everything possible to secure victory in Norway and Chamberlain's approval rating had plummeted to a dismal 33 per cent.[50] At the same time Churchill's acolytes were busily engaged in establishing friendly contacts with the two opposition parties and Salisbury's Watching Committee while cynically attempting 'to represent the Norwegian business as the result of timid colleagues restraining the bold, dashing, courageous Winston'. As Colville noted perceptively at the end of April: 'If Norway goes seriously wrong, then I suppose the popular outcry may force a reconstitution of the Government and Winston, to whom as much blame should attach as any other single individual, will ride triumphantly forward on the wave of undeserving national popularity.'[51]

IV

Against a background of British failure in Norway, the campaign against Chamberlain rapidly developed a momentum of its own in Westminster. On

29 April, Salisbury's Watching Committee bluntly informed Halifax that they were 'not satisfied' with either his confident survey of the war situation or the lack of British initiative and planning.[52] Next day, before the decision to evacuate central Norway became public, Sinclair made a speech in Edinburgh calling upon the government not to 'scuttle away' from its defence; a cynical manoeuvre to embarrass Chamberlain based on leaked information which led to an angry confrontation when reports of Sinclair's tapped telephone conversations from his home in Caithness (within an area of special security) reached Downing Street.[53] By now the Commons was 'buzzing like a swarm of angry bees'. On Thursday 2 May, Clement Davies and his associates in the All-Party Parliamentary Action Group decided to turn the debate on the Whitsun adjournment into a direct challenge to Chamberlain. That weekend Labour leaders like Morrison and Dalton began to call for the resignation of Chamberlain, Hoare and Simon, while telling Tory dissidents they 'should only win this war under a Labour government'.[54] Press clamour also culminated on Sunday 5 May with 'a storm of abuse of the P.M.'. Against this background, it was evident that the government was lurching towards 'a first class political struggle between the Chamberlain men and the "glamour" group'. Moreover, while Margesson talked gravely of 'the greatest political crisis since August 1931', in the corridors and Smoking Room of the House of Commons Chamberlain's critics more damagingly contended that 'it is 1915 over again' and that the dilatory Asquithian spirit must give way to the Lloyd Georgian vigour and popularity of Churchill. In such circumstances, even Chamberlain loyalists were 'beginning reluctantly to realise that Neville's days are, after all, numbered'.[55]

Yet as Paul Addison rightly notes of the crisis in May 1940, with hindsight 'we must remark how uninevitable the "inevitable" seemed to be at the time given widespread expectations that Chamberlain would survive and that Halifax rather than Churchill would succeed Chamberlain when he did resign'.[56] Certainly Chamberlain had absolutely no intention of giving up without a fight and he remained confident of victory until the very end. Repeated warnings that the Opposition parties intended to support a Conservative revolt to instal Churchill left him 'shaken and indignant' on 26 April, but this mood soon hardened as he became 'outraged and full of fight'. During his talk with Reith on 1 May, Chamberlain certainly left absolutely 'no doubt how he feels about Churchill', but he also recognised that 'if there was to be a debunking it would have to be done by someone else'. Yet this did not deter him from private efforts to undermine Churchill with senior figures.[57] Nor did it prevent the Conservative whips 'putting it about that it is all the fault of Winston who has made another forlorn failure' – to the alarm of Churchill's supporters who feared he might be too damaged by the Norway fiasco to succeed to the Premiership.[58]

Chamberlain's mood in the week leading up to the opening of the two-day Norway debate on 7 May fluctuated considerably. Although still sleeping well at the end of April, he admitted to exhaustion and frayed nerves because of 'constant gnawing anxiety' and the Liberal Chief Whip thought him 'thoroughly depressed and grave' at their meeting on 29 April.[59] On the other hand, Chamberlain claimed to be feeling 'light-hearted' when he saw Reith on 3 May. Next day he wrote to his sisters from Chequers: 'It's a vile world, but I don't think my enemies will get me down this time. I should be sorry if they did because I should then have to leave this lovely place. You couldn't imagine anything more perfect than it is today.'[60] When he had digested the Sunday press, he once more became 'very down and depressed', but this was scarcely surprising given the ferocity of the attack upon a government denounced by the *Manchester Guardian* as 'weaker than any … that has made war since Addington faced Napoleon'.[61]

Despite all of this, Chamberlain never expected to be defeated in the debate. He certainly recognised that there were some implacable personal enemies who were determined to destroy him, but he angrily concluded that they were 'really traitors just as much as Quisling'. On the other hand, however, he derived much comfort from the belief that 'there are a lot of other critics, not malevolent at all, but merely not very intelligent, and it should be possible to answer them effectively'. Margesson, Butler and Dunglass also agreed that 'the position is good politically, even though strategically and diplomatically it may be precarious' and Margesson even considered the possibility of a confidence motion to isolate their critics should the debate go well. As Colville summed up the prevailing mood within Downing Street, although many awkward points would be raised, 'obviously the Government will win through'.[62]

Chamberlain received a warm welcome from a crowded House as he took his seat on 7 May, but even many loyal supporters thought his opening statement 'rather a lame performance' as he 'fumbled his words and seemed tired and embarrassed'.[63] Perhaps in order to cool partisan passions and win over his 'unintelligent' but unmalevolent critics, Chamberlain confined his speech largely to events in Norway and he put his case 'quite dispassionately and calmly', refusing to be rattled by the constant mocking taunts from the Opposition benches about Hitler having 'missed the bus'. Whatever Chamberlain's precise intention, Amery maliciously recorded 'the flop could be heard in Birmingham'. The overall effect was to leave an already irritable House 'restive and bored', while in the gallery the Egyptian Ambassador was noticed to be asleep. Nevertheless, when Chamberlain sat down to the applause of 'the Yes-men', his staff believed 'it was generally agreed that the Government was going "to get away with it"'.[64]

This confidence was reinforced by the opening Opposition attack which appeared 'a half-hearted affair, almost a failure'. Attlee declared Norway was 'a culmination of many other discontents' and denounced those responsible, while striving to absolve Churchill from much of the blame which Chamberlain had implicitly attempted to heap upon him. Sinclair then followed with an 'eloquent and venomous speech' which again reflected awareness of confidential information but he was 'badly tripped' in his allegations by both Chamberlain and Churchill.[65] According to Sinclair, however, his tactical intention had been to woo dissident Tories in the belief that 'violent attacks always disconcert them, but if we sing in a low key they are more likely to sing out'.[66] There then followed another anti-climax as Sir Henry Page Croft rose to loud moans from the Labour benches before Josiah Wedgwood's ill-judged speech confirmed the general impression that he was 'a little off his head'.[67]

While all this was going on, Admiral Sir Roger Keyes entered the chamber in full dress uniform bedecked with rows of medals. Keyes was an embittered pro-Churchill reactionary with a private grievance about the recent pusillanimity of the naval staff and a thwarted ambition to be recalled to duty as an 'Extra First Sea Lord'.[68] Claiming 'to speak for some officers and men of the fighting, sea-going Navy who are very unhappy', Keyes launched 'an absolutely devastating attack' upon the conduct of the Norway campaign which also pointedly excluded Churchill from criticism. Renowned as an appalling speaker, Keyes read his speech throughout, but he 'gripped the House with every syllable' before he sat down to thunderous applause – an indictment which was all the more damaging because everyone recognised he was neither a scheming intriguer seeking office nor a captious critic with a record of disloyalty.[69]

Amery was another notoriously boring parliamentary performer. He began his 'terrific attack' in an empty House at 8pm but spurred on by the rising mood of a rapidly filling chamber, he cast caution to the wind and ended with a dramatic quotation from Cromwell's injunction to the Long Parliament: 'You have sat too long here for any good you are doing. Depart, I say, and let us have done with you. In the name of God go!' As Churchill later recalled, 'these were terrible words, coming from a friend and colleague of many years, a fellow Birmingham member, and Privy Councillor of distinction and experience'.[70] Many later regarded this as the critical moment of the entire debate as Amery both articulated widespread backbench dissatisfaction and increased the momentum towards a hostile division. Oliver Stanley then wound up the first day of the debate with 'a shocking performance, luke-warm and ineffectual'. Little wonder that in the lobby afterwards even 'a firm supporter of Chamberlain' like Lord Camrose appeared 'much shaken' when he declared 'the Government is very rocky and anything may happen tomorrow'.[71]

Despite these gloomy predictions, Chamberlain was far from doomed. Indeed, Margesson considered it 'a reasonably good first day'.[72] Criticism was one thing and this would need to be addressed, but much depended on whether the adjournment became a vote of censure. On the first evening of the debate, the Amery group met Clement Davies' followers to concert strategy and they were 'on the whole inclined to deprecate a Division and gathered the Labour leaders themselves were doubtful of its advisability'.[73] Next morning, Salisbury's Watching Committee agreed that it was 'really no alternative to create a strong War Cabinet under Chamberlain, since the efficacy of the Government depended upon the character of the Prime Minister and the Prime Minister's character had not proved sufficient'. But for all that, when they learned that Labour intended to press for a vote, Salisbury 'begged' the Watching Committee not to vote against the government and even a vehement anti-Chamberlainite like Harold Nicolson thought it 'a mistake ... since it will create a bad impression in the country and leave much bitterness behind'.[74]

Unfortunately for Chamberlain, his other opponents soon detected an opportunity and their collective defiance carried all before it. As Cuthbert Headlam noted, '"C[hamberlain] M[ust] G[o] if we are to win the war" is now a battle cry.' Sinclair sensed 'a strong movement' among Tory backbenchers and together with Attlee he explained to Amery and Law that 'if they could undertake to produce twenty votes in the lobby we should divide the House'.[75] On the morning of 8 May, Labour's Parliamentary Executive thus ignored Dalton's fear that a vote would consolidate the Government majority and agreed to press for a division at the end of the debate.[76] By the time the members of Salisbury's Watching Committee got to the Commons, they also had concluded that 'the position had gone too far and that abstention was really impossible', while all but one of the Serving Member's Committee (which represented MPs in the armed forces) thought the same. At 6pm the various rebel groups met together and agreed that the time had come to vote against the government.[77]

By this juncture, Downing Street and the whips were making frantic efforts to halt the slide against the Prime Minister. Chamberlain's staff were soon plunged to 'the nadir of gloom' by developments on the previous evening and they talked of a reconstituted government under Chamberlain, but with places for Labour in return for the sacrifice of the unpopular Hoare, Simon and Kingsley Wood. If Labour refused, there was even fevered speculation about a 'Government of national figures' including Lloyd George.[78] It was a measure of this rising alarm within Chamberlain's personal entourage that on the afternoon of 8 May, Dunglass told Emrys-Evans and Derrick Gunston on the Commons Terrace that if their colleagues in the Watching Committee (and presumably the other rebels) voted for the government they could meet Chamberlain next morning to put their demands before him. In extending this offer, Dunglass made it clear that Chamberlain was now prepared to make a 'drastic reconstruction' which included the expulsion of Simon and Hoare. In reply, Emrys-Evans declared that 'the time had now passed' for abstention and compromise, but he promised to put the proposition to the rebel meeting. When they unanimously reaffirmed their earlier decision, Emrys-Evans duly reported this rebuff to Dunglass. At around the same time, Brendan Bracken informed the rebels that it was unlikely that Churchill would be prepared to serve under Halifax.[79]

While these decisions were being made behind closed doors in the committee rooms of the House of Commons, the debate went from bad to worse for the Prime Minister. Herbert Morrison opened the second day with a vituperative speech in which he declared that Chamberlain, Hoare and Simon must all go and he ended by announcing that Labour would divide the House. Confronted by this news, Dalton noted that an angry and exhausted Chamberlain leapt to his feet and, 'showing his teeth like a rat in a corner', accepted the challenge as a highly personal attack upon his position. With an alleged 'leer of triumph', he then gestured to the government benches and called upon his 'friends – and

I still have some friends in this House – to support the Government tonight in the lobby'.[80] In fairness to Chamberlain, the reference to his 'friends' was a conventional parliamentary expression for party colleagues rather than a cynical call upon personal friendship and many MPs clearly understood it as such.[81] Chamberlain and his entourage also clearly believed (as Dalton feared) that by making it an overtly personal issue, the Labour challenge would consolidate an instinctive Conservative loyalty towards their leader.[82] Yet to phrase his reply in these terms was a substantial error of judgement. At best, it was 'tactless'.[83] At worst, many were 'really horrifi[ed]' by Chamberlain's apparent effort to turn the whole debate into a party issue when the gravity of the war situation demanded national unity. Worse still, as one observer noted from the gallery, the 'unfortunate phrase … became the "leit motif" of his ruin' as it was thrown back into his face by subsequent speakers. 'Anyone else might have said it with impunity – but it was so profoundly, fatally characteristic to make this tremendous issue a matter of who were, & who were not, his friends.'[84]

After this disastrous exchange, all the debating honours went to Chamberlain's enemies. Although previously hesitant to speak for fear of damaging Churchill's position, Lloyd George gave vent to the accumulated hatred of 20 years in a devastating attack which held the Commons 'spellbound as he flung his arms about and denounced the incapacity of the P.M. and the Government' while the Opposition 'shouted themselves hoarse'. In contrast to these oppositional pyrotechnics, the government's supporters were as dismal and uninspired as on the first day and Hoare was 'so bad that he emptied the House'. As time went on, 'the temperature rose, hearts hardened, tempers sharpened' and towards the end, 'it was like bedlam'. Into this highly-charged atmosphere, Churchill produced 'a slashing, vigorous speech' when winding up on behalf of a government he was constitutionally obliged to defend, but in whose cause he did not believe and whose downfall would enable him finally to take his long-awaited walk with destiny. When the division bells sounded the atmosphere was electric with government's supporters shouting 'Quislings' and 'Rats' at the rebels who jeered back at the 'Yes-men'. After the Speaker declared the government's majority had fallen to only 81 pandemonium broke out. To shouts of 'Resign' and 'Go', Josiah Wedgwood began singing 'Rule Britannia' while (to Chamberlain's disgust) Harold Macmillan joined in and even the most respectable Tory dissidents yelled themselves hoarse.[85]

Chamberlain recalled a few days later that the Norway debate had been 'a very painful affair to many besides myself and in particular for its exhibition of personal and party passion'.[86] He was scarcely exaggerating. To outward appearances, Chamberlain seemed to have endured the ordeal well, doubtless oblivious to the fact that Channon was sitting immediately behind him 'hoping to surround him with an aura of affection'. Yet when the result was declared even he 'appeared bowled over by the ominous figures' and amid scenes of ecstatic Opposition jubilation he left the Chamber with what one sympathetic lobby correspondent considered the 'pathetic look of a surprised and sorely stricken man'. 'No crowds tonight to cheer him, as there were before and after

Munich', Channon lamented in his diary, 'only a solitary little man, who had done his best for England.'[87]

V

The scale of the rebellion took everyone by surprise. After Munich, the Commons approved Chamberlain's action with a majority of 222. In May 1940 opponents believed that the maximum possible majority was still over 200.[88] This was certainly an exaggeration given many absences for military service and other duties, but estimates vary as to the precise scale of the rebellion. Jorgen Rasmussen calculated a maximum of 43 MPs who could have been present and abstained, to add to the 40 who voted against the government – a fifth of all government backbenchers.[89] Nick Crowson follows Emrys-Evans in putting the figures at 44 rebels and 60 more abstainers, while Kevin Jeffreys estimates 40 rebels and at least 30 deliberate abstainers.[90] Whatever the precise figure, it has traditionally been accepted that a majority of 81 was 'a technical victory and a crushing moral defeat' and that this outcome directly resulted in the only twentieth-century example of a majority government being forced out of office by a parliamentary vote.[91] More recent analysis, however, suggests that the extent of the rebellion has been inflated and that only 38 government MPs (33 Conservatives) voted with the Opposition and that 'most of them were confirmed members of the "awkward squad"' while only 20–25 deliberately abstained. On this basis, Nick Smart claims that the notion of 'moral defeat' as the cause of Chamberlain's downfall is an 'enduring piece of nonsense' because the reduced figure 'made post-debate speculation much more finely balanced than is often supposed'.[92]

At one level, this critique does appear to possess some substance. It is certainly true that perceptions of the magnitude of the crisis and its likely outcome varied widely – at least in the immediate aftermath of the vote. The loose coalition of anti-Chamberlain forces inevitably interpreted the vote as a clear signal that the Premier should be replaced.[93] Conversely, within Chamberlain's immediate circle the vote was not initially perceived to be catastrophic. Modest consolation was even derived from reports that 'the "Glamour" element' were excited but perhaps 'disappointed too, as they hoped for a greater number of defections' and some within the Premier's entourage believed that 'with a majority of 81, Neville could still make minor changes and remain'.[94] Certainly the chairman of the backbench 1922 committee wrote to Chamberlain at the request of members next day to assure him 'that you, & you alone, have their confidence & are the leader of the great mass of moderate Conservative opinion, in this House, in the Party & in this country'; a body of opinion which included the overwhelming majority of the older backbenchers representing safe seats and thus 'the steadiest element in the population, the least affected to [sic] the ups & downs of war, of rumour, or press campaign, & the most likely to see this war through'. On this basis, Chamberlain was urged to defend his Premiership in any future negotiations with his opponents.[95]

There was also much balm for Chamberlain's wounds in the prevailing diagnosis as to the causes of the revolt. Given the jubilation of his enemies, many inevitably regarded him as the victim of 'the seekers after office & the forty thieves outside & the Quislings inside the Government'. From the official gallery, Sir Horace Wilson remarked that 'the hatred written on their faces astonished him: it was the pent-up bitterness and personal animosity of years'.[96] As for the rebels who were not established members of the 'awkward squad', Chamberlain believed that the 'long period of waiting without any real set back to German prestige, and then the sudden and bitter disappointment over the hopes that had been so recklessly and unjustifiably fostered by the Press, just boiled up with the accumulated mass of grievances to find expression'. This was a widely echoed and largely accurate view of events. Chamberlain was equally correct in the view that the MPs in the armed forces who defected were influenced by their direct personal experience of defence deficiencies, although (contrary to mythology) it should be remembered that 32 MPs serving in the forces voted for Chamberlain compared with 16 who voted against him – and of these rebels at least six were confirmed opponents.[97]

Against this background, Chamberlain rightly concluded that not all the government rebels had cast their votes with the specific intention of destroying his Premiership. On the contrary, he soon received a number of letters declaring 'that they had nothing against me except that I had the wrong people in my team'; an explanation he attributed to the concerted press campaign which blamed all wartime failures on the composition of the Cabinet.[98] One MP thus wrote next day to assure the Prime Minister that he still enjoyed 'the fullest confidence and the greatest affection of almost, without exception, the whole of your party colleagues in the House, including the *large majority* of those who voted in the Opposition lobby last night. We would regard it – and I am not exaggerating or being fulsome when I say so – as a national disaster were you to go.'[99] Similarly, while Quintin Hogg had won the Oxford by-election as a defender of Munich, he had joined the rebels as 'the only means of registering his protest on the eve of embarkation with his battalion at the total failure of the War Office to provide for their equipment or training'. Yet next day he assured Chamberlain 'you *have* your friends even amongst those who did not vote with you'.[100] Roy Wise acted from similar motives and he visited Chamberlain with some fellow rebels on the morning of 10 May to apologise for their actions.[101] As the Secretary of the 1922 Committee soon reported, there was already a 'great reaction' underway and among the rebels there were now 'three quarters who are ready to put Chamberlain back'.[102]

Yet although there was no shortage of good reasons for Chamberlain to fight it out, it does not follow that there is scope for a revisionist interpretation which argues that because the scale of the defection was far smaller than commonly supposed, the threat to Chamberlain was correspondingly reduced. First, the contemporary perception was that the vote represented a grievous blow and even the initial optimism of Downing Street staff rapidly ebbed away as the rebel interpretation gained ground. Secondly, and more important, the actual numbers involved ceased to be of any practical significance once the initial shock created by the vote had instigated a crisis, from which it was universally acknowledged that the only escape was a true all-party National Government with full Labour participation. As Geoffrey Dawson recognised from the public gallery immediately after the vote was declared, 'there was a general conviction that it meant reconstruction at once'.[103] In this context, revisionism is carried to extravagant lengths in claiming either that Chamberlain stood a real chance of saving himself by reconstructing his government or that it is 'open to question' whether it was inevitable that Labour would exercise their veto on his efforts so to do.[104] Indeed, as both Dalton and Morrison told Butler on the evening of the vote, Labour would never serve under Chamberlain even if he 'pruned his team first ... The Labour party had too many grudges against Neville.'[105]

Ultimately, this implacable Labour hatred lay at the heart of all Chamberlain's problems. The Norway vote had released the opposition genie from the bottle and he simply lacked the capacity, resources and political capital to recapture it. As Prime Minister it was certainly within his power to dismiss chronic liabilities like Simon, Hoare, Wood and Elliot, whose unpopularity gravely aggravated general discontents. But Chamberlain shared the now almost universal recognition that the rebellion implied a far more radical reconstruction and that this transferred the political initiative to his Labour enemies who would never serve under him and without whom he could not continue. This conclusion does not require any elaborate speculation about Chamberlain's motives. Indeed, early on 9 May, he told his wife that the vote had been a 'mortal blow' and that he could not continue in face of such opposition at home. As he explained to his sisters in the immediate aftermath of his fall, 'it did not take me long to make up my mind what to do. I saw that the time had come for a National Government in the broadest sense. I knew that I could not get it, but it was necessary to get an official confirmation of the Opposition attitude, if only to justify my resignation to my own party.'[106]

In an atmosphere 'full of rumour and intrigue, plot and counter-plot', the general feeling in Westminster, Fleet Street and the London clubs was that Chamberlain must now go. When the Watching Committee met early on 9 May, Amery made 'it quite clear that the Prime Minister cannot really survive for more than a week or two' and that the 'sooner he goes the better'. Like everyone else, the committee recognised that 'a drastic reconstruction of the Government on a National Basis had become inevitable' because Labour would not serve under Chamberlain.[107] A majority at the National Labour gathering at noon also agreed that Chamberlain had to go, while a joint meeting of government rebels under Amery's chairmanship voted to support any Premier capable of forming a proper National Government but this 'must be a Government of personalities and not of Parties'. In this context, it was simply evasion when they 'particularly refrained from saying who that Prime Minister should be'.[108] Whoever it would be, Labour's ferocious antipathy toward Chamberlain guaranteed that it would not be him – despite the implausible report of Sir Patrick Hannon, a fellow Birmingham MP and loyalist, who tried to persuade his leader that Attlee and Sinclair were prepared to serve under him if Simon and Hoare were 'eliminated'.[109] The views of the Labour leadership and rank-and-file were more accurately encapsulated in the *Daily Mirror* headline, 'I Say Get Out', published the same morning over 'the most bitter indictment' Herbert Morrison had ever written.[110]

VI

Amid widespread rumours of impending resignation, Chamberlain spent much of 9 May discussing the succession with Halifax, Churchill, Hoare, Wood and finally the Labour leaders. Among his apprehensive enemies, rumours flourished that he was still attempting to save himself. According to Dalton, the 'Old Man' was telephoning personally from early morning trying to woo the rebels by abandoning Simon, Hoare and Wood, but he was 'determined himself to stick on – like a dirty old piece of chewing gum on the leg of a chair'. Others reported that the whips were 'putting it about that the whole business was a snap vote cunningly engineered by Duff Cooper and Amery, and that all good Party men must rally round the Prime Minister', while rumours circled that Margesson intended to 'organise an Iron Guard and fight a rearguard action'.[111] Some of this anxiety was undoubtedly prompted by unofficial soundings on Chamberlain's behalf, such as those by Hannon, but Dunglass did instruct Channon to approach Labour's Lord Nathan to ascertain whether they would serve under Chamberlain, while the Prime Minister met some Conservative MPs that afternoon and obtained a pledge of continued support in return for 'drastic changes in the Government'.[112]

When Chamberlain gave his sisters the impression that he was just going through the motions by approaching Labour, he somewhat understated the persuasive power put behind these soundings. At 6.30pm on 9 May Chamberlain asked Attlee and Greenwood whether Labour would join a new government under his leadership and, if not, would they serve under someone else. According to Dalton, 'the Old Man ... had once more begged them to enter the Government' and Channon and Attlee both confirm that he did make a definite effort to persuade them to join 'a real Coalition'.[113] In reply, Attlee bluntly declared his personal view was that 'our party ... won't have you and I think I am right in saying the country won't have you either'. When Chamberlain pressed his questions, however, the Labour leaders promised to consult the National Executive then assembled at the party conference in Bournemouth and to reply on the following afternoon.[114]

In anticipation of Attlee's inevitable response, two hours earlier Chamberlain, Halifax, Churchill and Margesson had effectively decided the succession. Chamberlain's preference for Halifax was well established and there is absolutely no evidence to substantiate the suggestion that he privately preferred Churchill as a means to return after the war but that he did not wish this to be known publicly.[115] Chamberlain also correctly believed that Labour favoured Halifax over Churchill.[116] On both these grounds he attempted to steer the meeting decisively to his preferred outcome.[117] To his intense disappointment, however, these efforts at manipulation failed to achieve their purpose because Churchill proved far more determined in exploiting the crisis for his own ends, while Halifax was reluctant to press his own claims and Attlee had no strong feelings either way – all that mattered to him was to get Chamberlain out.[118]

When Hitler's armies swept into the Low Countries at dawn on 10 May, Chamberlain briefly revived hopes that this providential development might save his Premiership just as it had persuaded Paul Reynaud to withdraw his resignation in France. As he wrote to Beaverbrook, 'we cannot consider changes in the Government while we are in the throes of battle' and he soon began to circulate rumours to this effect.[119] 'Perhaps the darkest day in English history' was Channon's verdict on the German offensive but he also echoed 'the popular view ... that Neville was saved'. It was a measure of this renewed hope that over lunch at the Dorchester, Chamberlain appeared 'calm and charming and showed little effects of the battle that had been waging about him', while Dunglass took malicious pleasure in ruining the lunch of some prominent rebels at the Traveller's Club by announcing that 'the formation of a new Government might be postponed'.[120] But if Chamberlain seriously entertained hopes that Hitler's action would save his Premiership, these were swiftly dispelled by Kingsley Wood who told him bluntly that he must make way and by Attlee's telephone call at 5pm informing him that Labour's NEC had decided to enter a new government – but only under a different Prime Minister.[121] It was 'the last blow which dislodged the old limpet', Dalton recorded with sneering delight. Little wonder that during a 'pathetic interview' with some loyal backbenchers that afternoon Chamberlain appeared so 'terribly shaken' he could scarcely rise from his chair as they entered the room.[122]

An hour after Attlee's call, Chamberlain went to the Palace to resign where he found the King 'as nice as possible' in expressing his 'very genuine regrets' at his fall. While Churchill accepted the Premiership, Chamberlain drafted a resignation broadcast in which he urged the nation to 'rally behind our new leader, and with our united strength, and with unshakeable courage fight and work until this wild beast, that has sprung out of his lair upon us, has been finally disarmed and overthrown'. By all accounts, it was a very dignified performance and the Queen told Chamberlain that Princess Elizabeth cried as she listened to his appeal.[123] Even bitter opponents like Harold Nicolson conceded that it was 'a magnificent statement' and that as he heard the words 'all the hatred that I have felt for Chamberlain subsides as if a piece of bread were dropped into a glass of champagne'. Chamberlain and what many of his critics believed to be the 'unholy and essentially dishonest coalition of 1931' had finally been toppled.[124] But if Neville Chamberlain was down, he certainly was not yet out.

Chapter 18

Epilogue,
May–November 1940

'It has been my fate to see the failure of all my efforts to preserve peace; and the destruction of all the hopes I had entertained that I might be able to steer this country into calmer waters and gradually to raise the standards of life among the people. Yet I do not feel that I have anything to reproach myself for in my attempts to avoid the present war, which might well have succeeded if they had not come up against the insatiable and inhuman ambitions of a fanatic.'

Chamberlain to King George VI, 30 September 1940, NC7/3/48

Churchill later recounted that in May 1940 he felt as if he was 'walking with destiny' and that his entire 'past life had been but a preparation for this hour and this trial'.[1] Yet although he now possessed 'the authority to give directions over the whole scene', it is significant that his first act after accepting the King's commission to form a government was to write to Chamberlain confessing 'how grateful I am to you for promising to stand by me & to aid the country at this extremely grievous and formidable moment ... With yr help & counsel & with the support of the great party of wh you are the leader, I trust that I shall succeed ... To a vy large extent I am in yr hands – & I feel no fear of that.'[2] Chamberlain was evidently touched by this 'most handsome' acknowledgement, but he also understood that it was no more than the truth. Although no longer Prime Minister, in both a formal and a very real sense, Chamberlain still remained the leader of a party which was largely appalled by the idea of a Churchillian regime with its unscrupulous hangers-on and disreputable jackals. Indeed, Chamberlain himself noted with evident distaste the 'very different crowd' around Churchill, while his methods of Government-making he found 'disagreeably reminiscent of Lloyd Georgian ways'.[3]

Such sentiments found even stronger echoes elsewhere within the party.[4] Shortly after hearing the news of Chamberlain's fall, Dunglass, Colville, Butler and Channon met at the Foreign Office. 'We were all sad and angry and felt cheated and out-witted', Jock Colville noted as they 'drank in champagne the health of the "King over the Water" (not King Leopold but Mr Chamberlain)', while Butler declared 'the good clean tradition of English politics, that of Pitt as opposed to Fox, had been sold to the greatest adventurer of modern political history'.[5] Lord Davidson was no admirer of Chamberlain's, but he also conceded that the party did not trust Churchill and lamented that he was 'putting in the

431

jackals' while ousting even the successful members of 'the respectable rump of the Tory Party' who remained faithful to the Baldwin-Chamberlain tradition. Collin Brooks put the contrast more bluntly some months later: 'Poor old Neville. He was a good fellow. He simply didn't know that there are shits in the world ... Now, Winston knows that shits exist – *and likes 'em.*'[6]

Aware of these pervasive suspicions, Churchill carefully refrained from creating a coalition based on anti-Chamberlainite factionalism. As a result, some two-thirds of those ministers who served under Chamberlain continued to hold portfolios, while Churchill's loyalists were rewarded in a relatively modest and discreet fashion. Among the few victims of Chamberlain's fall, only Hoare was expelled from the government altogether, to be consigned to a miserable and isolated war as British Ambassador in Madrid, while Simon was moved to the Woolsack with a Viscountcy. The principal victim of the avenging Churchillians was Sir Horace Wilson, who was returned to his duties as Permanent Secretary to the Treasury with the blunt warning that if he ever visited Downing Street again the new Prime Minister would 'make him Governor of Greenland!'[7] Although Chamberlain claimed privately that he would 'much rather have gone out altogether' had it not been his duty 'to set an example', this probably needs to be taken with a fairly large pinch of salt.[8] Anyway, Churchill always recognised that he needed Chamberlain because his exclusion 'would create such embitterment among his friends as to make the life of the new Government "brutish and short"'. Confronted by fierce Labour opposition to Churchill's plans to offer him the Treasury and then the Leadership of the Commons, Chamberlain recognised immediately that the 'only chance of letting their passions die down is to take a place which does not bring me into conflict with them'. He thus willingly accepted the Lord Presidency with a seat in the five-man non-departmental War Cabinet.[9]

Churchill's assessment of Chamberlain's pivotal significance to the government was entirely accurate. With Chamberlain and Halifax in the Cabinet, Conservatives hoped they would impose 'some restraint on our new War Lord', help 'give some respectability to the firm' and enable the leadership 'to keep the Party together and compact on the back benches'.[10] In a touching personal letter of gratitude for past kindnesses, Butler assured Chamberlain that he remained the guarantor of 'certain virtues and values' essential to the party and that he should 'always realise the strength and number of your friends and how much we count on your presence in the Government'.[11] As if to emphasise the point, on 13 May, as Chamberlain entered the Commons for the first time since his fall, 'MPs lost their heads; they shouted; they cheered; they waved their Order Papers; and his reception was a regular ovation'; an enthusiasm which contrasted sharply with the sullen coolness displayed towards his successor in both Houses.[12]

In these unpropitious circumstances, Churchill prudently urged Chamberlain to retain the Conservative leadership, supposedly on the grounds that 'as Prime Minister of a National Government, formed on the widest basis, ... it would be better for me not to undertake the Leadership of any one political Party'.

Yet as Chamberlain recognised privately, this 'was essential if Winston was to have whole hearted support' from the Conservative party given the intense simmering resentment among Chamberlainite loyalists 'both at my treatment and at the way the "Treachery Bench" has been given office'. By leaving Chamberlain in place, it was hoped that the party would follow his magnanimous example and accept the change.[13] As one loyalist confided to his leader: 'The fact that you are prepared to serve under the new Prime Minister resolves the doubts of a good many of us who had been doubtful of whether we would take the Whip under these circumstances. If he is good enough for you he must be good enough for us.'[14] Unfortunately for Churchill, not all Conservatives were prepared to be so forgiving. To drive this point home, Walter Liddall's 'Loyalty to Leader' group remained in existence within the parliamentary party and pledged itself to support Chamberlain 'not for a day or a month, but always', while even Churchill's greatest oratorical efforts – such as his 'Fight them on the Beaches' speech in early June – were consistently subjected to a 'very half-hearted' response.[15] Little wonder that victorious Churchillians were soon complaining that 'the new Government – or rather the new elements in it – are fighting a war on two fronts, against Hitler and against enemies nearer home'.[16]

In the event, this crisis of allegiance was so profound and so debilitating that Chamberlain was forced personally to intervene in late June, when he learned that hostile Republican isolationists in the United States were seeking to obstruct aid to Britain on the grounds that a 'considerable party in England headed by Chamberlain means to oust [the] Churchill Government and make peace'. When alerted by a *Financial Times* journalist to the fact that 'the conspicuously passive attitude' of Conservative backbenchers towards the new Prime Minister was having a damaging impact upon foreign confidence in the British war effort, Chamberlain acted swiftly to remedy the situation.[17] In press interviews with prominent American correspondents he thus publicly refuted the allegation, while in terms reminiscent of Churchill's 'Finest Hour' speech earlier in the month, Chamberlain's defiant world broadcast on 30 June scotched rumours of defeatism by declaring that Britain 'would rather go down to ruin than admit the domination of the Nazis'.[18] Equally important, in an effort to reconcile the party to the new regime, he assured the National Union Executive that relations with Churchill since his fall had been 'cordial in the extreme' and that there were 'no differences whatever between them on any … point of policy'.[19] Behind the scenes, Chamberlain also crucially ensured that Margesson brought pressure to bear upon the parliamentary party and this soon bore fruit in a well-orchestrated cheer for Churchill on 4 July – the first he had received from his own benches since May.[20] Churchill was evidently 'quite overcome' by this demonstration and later declared it represented a watershed in his relations with Chamberlain's party, but he remained painfully aware of the need to treat it with 'consideration'.[21] As a result, after Chamberlain's final withdrawal from office, Churchill still felt it necessary to display an appropriate deference to Chamberlainite sensibilities in reconstructing the government. Even as late as

1941–42, military disappointments occasionally revived longing whispers that 'if only Mr Chamberlain was alive'.[22]

II

Although Chamberlain's political position still remained extremely strong, during the weeks after his fall from the Premiership he experienced the most painful melancholy of his life. 'All my world has tumbled to bits in a moment', he lamented to his sisters on 17 May. 'We keep well here', he noted a month later, 'but there is no pleasure in life and no prospect of any.' There was certainly some consolation in kind words from loyal followers and during the week after his resignation the Chamberlains received over 2000 letters of continued support.[23] Yet despite the sympathy, Chamberlain was haunted by the realisation that his Premiership had collapsed in disaster, France was on the verge of defeat and Britain confronted the prospect of invasion for the first time since Napoleon – but with the added danger that it was now vulnerable to devastating attack from the air. Little wonder that Sam Hoare soon detected 'none of his old resiliency and obstinacy' or that he concluded 'his life, with its mainspring broken, was certain to run down very quickly'. As Joseph Kennedy noted after meeting Chamberlain on 16 May, his 'ghastly' appearance was symptomatic of the fact that he was 'a heartbroken and physically broken man'.[24]

In a perverse sense, the devastating speed of the German advance in the West helped Chamberlain to put his own personal troubles into proper perspective. Holland surrendered within five days and Belgium followed on 28 May. Almost a month later, France capitulated – a little over five weeks since the commencement of the offensive. Although this left Britain to fight on alone, Chamberlain noted angrily that they were 'at any rate free of our obligations to the French who have been nothing but a liability to us. It would have been better if they had been neutral from the beginning.' Meanwhile, there were further blows as Turkey reneged on its treaty obligations to support the Allies; anti-British feeling erupted in Iraq; Eire was 'a worry' given its obstinate neutrality; the Americans were a long way from giving substantial material assistance; London began to suffer heavy bombing raids and all the talk was of imminent German invasion. When compared with these momentous events, Chamberlain readily conceded that his own plight and 'everything else seems small and petty'. Indeed, despite 'harrowing anxieties' as a member of the War Cabinet, he actually derived some comfort from the fact that the 'national peril has so swamped all personal feelings that no bitterness remains'. Furthermore, now that a real fighting war had finally broken out, he freely confessed to relief at being released from the 'agony of mind it would mean for me to give directions that would bring death & mutilation & misery to so many'.[25]

In these disastrous circumstances, Chamberlain derived no satisfaction from the fact that the rapid Allied collapse in France apparently vindicated his stand in September 1938. But nor did personal and military defeat do anything to prompt a reassessment of his policy or encourage him to recant past errors. On the contrary, as he told Margot Asquith on the day after his resignation: 'The day may come when my much cursed visit to Munich will be understood. Neither we nor the French were prepared for war. I am not responsible for this lack of preparation, I blame no one ... I did what I thought right.'[26] By now he had also convinced himself that appeasement had been designed principally to buy time for rearmament and that the real 'guilty men' sat on the Opposition benches:

> It would be rash to prophesy the verdict of history, but if full access is obtained to all the records it will be seen that I realised from the beginning our military weakness and did my best to postpone if I could not avert the war. But I had to fight every yard against both Labour and Liberal Opposition leaders who denounced me for trying to maintain good relations with Italy and Japan, for refusing to back Republican Spain against Franco and for not 'standing up to Hitler' at each successive act of aggression. It is they who ought to be held responsible for this fight, but they don't admit it naturally & perhaps they will succeed in covering up their tracks.

As the Luftwaffe bombed Allied troops on the beaches at Dunkirk and German armour thrust south towards Paris, Chamberlain also inevitably reflected upon what Munich might have achieved: 'If only we had had another year of preparation we should have been in a far stronger position and so would the French. But anyway and whatever the outcome it is as clear as daylight that if we had had to fight in 1938 the result would have been far worse.'[27]

Yet neither sympathetic words of support nor any sense of vindication could ever remove the bitter feelings of personal humiliation and resentment at shattered hopes and dreams. 'We are both numbed by the sudden change to such an extent as to be incapable of any strong emotion', Chamberlain confided to his sisters a week after his resignation; 'in fact my only desire is to get out of this horrible condition of chronic misery & I frankly envy Austen's peace.'[28] He did not realise it at the time, but within six months his wish would be granted. To ease the transition from the Premiership, Churchill considerately told Chamberlain he need not move into 11 Downing Street for a month and Chamberlain took him at his word. Even when he did move house, the combination of a vitriolic campaign against him and rumours of impending invasion deterred him from hanging his pictures until mid-July. When contemplating the loss of his beloved Chequers and an end to all his plans for its gardens and woodlands, he confessed bitterly that it would be 'a bad wrench to part with that place where I have been so happy'. In the event, Chamberlain and his wife made a short final visit on 19 June to say goodbye to the staff and to take a last walk around the estate. 'I am content now that I have done that, and shall put Chequers out of my mind', he confided to his sisters. 'We have had some happy days there but they are over anyhow and it is difficult to see how there can be much more happiness for any of us.'[29]

III

Despite this inner turmoil and anguish, Chamberlain was not a man to shirk a responsibility or to place personal considerations above public duty. As a result, he immediately mustered his strength and resigned himself to 'just ... doing what lies in front to the best of one's ability without troubling to think of the future in this world or the next'. From his new office in 'quite a nice old room' in the Privy Council Office, Chamberlain assumed vast responsibilities, far greater than those of any past Lord President, and he consoled himself with the thought that his still considerable skills were put to best use by releasing Churchill to concentrate entirely on military affairs.[30] Churchill unquestionably appreciated Chamberlain's loyalty in a personally difficult position and sincerely valued his practical assistance and expertise.[31] In return, he demonstrated a touching and tenacious loyalty in defending Chamberlain from opponents seeking to expel him from the government. Thus, although in the immediate aftermath of his fall there was 'no bit of doubt as to what Chamberlain thinks of Churchill', these feelings (like those towards Attlee and Sinclair) rapidly abated as they developed an 'admirable' working relationship.[32] Indeed, like his National Labour colleagues after 1931, in Churchill's new coalition Chamberlain noted that Labour Ministers rapidly found that he was 'a very different person from what they supposed' and they soon 'considerably revised their ideas of [his] value to the Government'. 'He worked very hard and well', Attlee later recalled; 'a good chairman, a good committee man, always very businesslike' and 'free from any rancour he might well have felt against us'. Even Sinclair, now Air Minister outside the War Cabinet, wrote to Chamberlain after years of mutual contempt, that he had 'learned to appreciate the value of your counsel'.[33]

Chamberlain's brief period as Lord President was anything but a meaningless sinecure, notable only as a means of filling the final months of a dying man. Much insider testimony exists about the dynamic impact of Churchill's emergence as Premier upon the Whitehall machine and the war effort.[34] But such verdicts often misleadingly suggest that this was the direct consequence of a change of leadership, from Chamberlain's supposedly sluggish complacency to Churchill's dynamic demands for 'Action this Day', without any proper acknowledgement of the far more galvanising effects of the transition from the 'Bore War' to a full-scale struggle for national survival. Nor do later Churchillian accounts give adequate (or often, any) credit to Chamberlain for his role in introducing this new vigour into the home front. Yet Churchill freely recognised from the outset that Chamberlain was 'the best man he had – head and shoulders over the average man in the administration' and that he did not know what he would do without him.[35]

As a reflection of this esteem, Chamberlain chaired the War Cabinet in Churchill's regular absences. He was also directly involved in all of the most sensitive diplomatic and strategic decisions taken during this period – and particularly those relating to proposals for an 'indissoluble' Anglo-French Union to forestall French surrender and in making a direct personal appeal to de Valera to abandon Eire's neutrality by granting the Royal Navy access to its Atlantic ports – if necessary at the price of a united Ireland.[36] By far the most important of these contributions, however, was Chamberlain's crucial intervention in the intensely heated War Cabinet clash between Churchill and Halifax over the latter's proposal for an Anglo-French approach to Italy to explore the possibility of mediation and a negotiated peace. When Halifax first urged his colleagues to consider the idea on the morning of 26 May, Churchill immediately retorted that he could 'never accept' such a suggestion. The battle of wills and strategy then rumbled on for a further eight meetings of the War Cabinet over the next two and a half days before reaching a climax on the afternoon of 28 May. During this 'rather strong discussion', Halifax repeated his earlier argument that 'we were prepared to fight to the death for our independence, but that, provided this could be secured, there were certain concessions we were prepared to make'. Anyway, he contended vigorously, 'we must not ignore the fact that we might get better terms before France went out of the war and our aircraft factories were bombed, than we might get in three months time'. In a characteristically impassioned reply, Churchill warned again about the dangers of 'the slippery slope'. If Britain was lured prematurely to the negotiating table, the Prime Minister argued, 'all the forces of resolution which were now at our disposal would have vanished' while Hitler's terms would inevitably 'put us completely at his mercy. We should get no worst terms if we went on fighting even if we were beaten.'

During the opening exchanges in this battle, Chamberlain said relatively little and refrained from any definite commitment. Devastated by the speed and scale of the Allied military collapse, his diary during this period reflects a rapidly growing sense of depression at both Britain's 'desperate' position and the dismal performance of the French Army. In this state of mind, Chamberlain initially appeared tentatively to support Halifax on the grounds that there was 'no harm in trying Musso & seeing what the result was'. In the Cabinet record for the morning of 27 May, his statement that Britain should tell the Dominions that 'even if France went out of the war, there was no prospect of our giving in', is thus accompanied by a parenthetical qualification to the effect that this applied only to the immediate situation and 'would not mean that if at any time terms were offered they would not be considered on their merits'.

Despite this apparent open-mindedness, however, Chamberlain fundamentally endorsed Churchill's doubts about the possibility of buying off the dictators and his fears about the 'most unfortunate results' of attempting to do so at this stage of the struggle. As a result, at the War Cabinet on the afternoon of 27 May Chamberlain declared that the proposed approach to Mussolini 'would serve no useful purpose' but that 'we ought to go a little further with it, in order to keep the French in a good temper' – and to keep them fighting. These observations set the tone for Chamberlain's decisive intervention on the following afternoon as the battle reached its climax. While acknowledging Halifax's proposition that 'if we thought it was possible that we could get terms which, though grievous, would not threaten our independence, we should be right to consider such terms', Chamberlain frankly declared his doubts as to whether any approach to Mussolini would ever produce an acceptable offer. Moreover, to general murmurs of agreement, he observed that 'on a dispassionate survey, it was right to remember that the alternative to fighting on nevertheless involved a considerable gamble'. On this basis, his conclusion that they should not pursue the scheme 'at the present time' decisively helped to turn the War Cabinet in favour of Churchill's determination to fight to the bitter end whatever happened in France.

As John Lukacs argues persuasively, in many ways this was the real 'hinge of fate' in the Second World War. This was the moment at which Hitler came closest to achieving ultimate victory and when Britain stood on the brink of defeat had the Cabinet decision gone the other way. In this context, it is ironic that Neville Chamberlain, the man reviled by so many of his fellow countrymen as the high priest of appeasement, should have played such a pivotal role in the triumph of Churchill's strategy of blind resistance over Halifax's pleas for a negotiated settlement. Had he counselled in favour of Halifax, it is likely that the Prime Minister's case for resistance would have been dangerously compromised, even undermined – with perhaps the most profound consequences for the history of Churchill's wartime government, Britain and the entire free world.[37]

Although these military and foreign entanglements were crucially important, Chamberlain's principal practical contribution to the war effort was on the home front. Almost immediately he was active in preparing an extended Emergency Powers Act designed to introduce sweeping new controls, noting with more than a touch of malicious irony that the measure, so widely hailed as a refreshing demonstration of the new government's vigour, was actually undertaken at his instigation. But as he also noted with a characteristic lack of modesty: 'It is a satisfaction to me to know that I can do things that probably no one else could as it is the justification for my being in the Government.' He then began work on legislation for additional emergency powers, along with an astonishingly wide variety of other problems ranging from financial policy and exports, the supply of labour to agriculture, the position of aliens, the organisation of underground warfare in the event of invasion and the disruptive effects of German air raids on munitions production. At a more melancholy level, he was also kept busy writing letters of condolence to relatives of men killed in action. Thinking back to his days as Lord Mayor of Birmingham, it was another pungent reminder of the failure of his mission. 'It is too awful to have to do that twice in a lifetime' he told his sisters. 'Thrice accursed Hitler.'[38]

A particularly important aspect of Chamberlain's work concerned his chairmanship of the Lord President's Committee. Established on 4 June, this new organ of control was designed to remedy the lack of effective central direction over the economy which had been such a damaging indictment of his own government. In theory, if not in title, Chamberlain thus effectively became the 'Home Front Prime Minister', although in practice the new structure initially proved something of a disappointment as the committee soon became bogged down in too many minor policy details, while subordinate bodies were either deadlocked over priorities or met too infrequently to fulfil their functions.[39] Nevertheless, as one economist who worked closely with the committee later recalled, 'because of the superior administrative capacity of Neville Chamberlain, the one Minister in this field from whom you could get clear and immediate directives, ... by the time he came to go away and die, it had become in effect the main organ of economic coordination in the Government'. Given the gravity and scale of these various responsibilities, it is scarcely surprising that after Chamberlain's death, Churchill asked 'What shall I do without poor Neville? I was relying on him to look after the Home Front for me.'[40]

For all this valuable work as Lord President, however, Chamberlain's position increasingly came under intense attack as the war went from bad to worse. Despite immense collective relief at the miraculous scale of the Dunkirk evacuation, within days the government's Home Intelligence unit detected a burgeoning feeling of 'Anti-Chamberlainism' as the nation became seized by a desire to find scapegoats for the disaster which had so suddenly befallen it. In these circumstances, it was inevitable that the blame fell principally upon pre-war leaders who would soon be immortalised as the 'Guilty Men' – or that chief among these culpable 'Men of Munich' was Neville Chamberlain, whose alleged negligence ensured that the Battle of France was 'the story of an Army doomed *before* they took the field'.[41] Yet notwithstanding the later notoriety of *Guilty Men* as an indictment of the Chamberlain regime, its success at the time was largely derived from the fact that it articulated an existing sense of public outrage. Indeed, some weeks before its publication, the speed of the Allied collapse in France aroused widespread anger at 'the blind, smug inertia of Neville Chamberlain & his followers' and 'their refusal to believe in war, to prepare for it, or even to meet it when it came'; a 'criminal' negligence made all the more infuriating because it was 'not they who are paying the penalty but the innocent young whom they have sacrificed & betrayed'. Moreover, as Bob Boothby noted, this 'savage hatred of Chamberlain and Simon' was dramatically reinforced by 'a wave of deep popular resentment arising out of stories told all over the country by men of the B.E.F.' who had returned from Dunkirk in 'a highly inflamed state of mind'.[42]

Chamberlain dismissed these allegations with anger and contempt. 'The small men – the mean men – rage but the voice of history is not the voice of the present day' he assured his wife. Encouraged by aircraft production figures which now substantially exceeded those of Germany and impressed by the superiority of RAF pilots, in early July he retorted that such evidence seemed 'to be sufficient commentary on the constant accusations by more venomous opponents that I am personally responsible for "bringing the country to this pass". If I am personally responsible for deficiencies of tanks and A.A. guns I must be equally personally responsible for the efficiency of the Air Force & the Navy.' Above all, he took comfort from the fact that the operational strength of Fighter Command as it fought out the Battle of Britain in the skies over southern England was ten times greater than it had been in the summer of 1938 and, as he not unreasonably protested, 'No one can suppose that all our equipment has been turned out in the last six weeks' since his fall from the Premiership.[43]

In this mood, the press clamour was initially dismissed as 'only part of the political and personal campaign against me', but he was more concerned about the antics of established enemies who were now more vocal and vicious than ever. In particular, he directed his anger towards Clement Davies, 'that treacherous Welshman who ratted from the last Government' and who had reconvened his 'sordid gatherings at the Reform Club' with malcontents like Amery, Macmillan and Boothby – but which, Chamberlain noted with some dismay, also occasionally attracted Attlee, Greenwood and Sinclair.[44] Worse still, Chamberlain suspected that Labour intended to exploit the forthcoming secret session of Parliament to launch a direct assault upon his position in the government. Indeed, such was his despondency, that on 5 June he went to Churchill prepared to resign and he fully expected the offer to be accepted. Instead Churchill loyally assured Chamberlain that he was a valuable minister 'and he wasn't going to have the Government which he had only just formed knocked about'. Seizing his opportunity, Chamberlain then pointed out that he could only defend himself against Labour smears by denouncing his new colleagues – but as this was impossible with the enemy at the gates he persuaded Churchill to defend him against the further press and parliamentary attacks by calling for national unity.[45]

By harnessing Churchill's authority as a weapon in his own defence, Chamberlain had apparently achieved a remarkable triumph. But salvation came at a high price. Since coming to power, Churchill had wanted to offer Lloyd George a post in the government, but only on the clear understanding that if Chamberlain vetoed the proposal it would not proceed. Chamberlain, however, was rightly convinced that 'Ll.G. will never rest in his efforts to get me out and that if he comes into the Government in any capacity that would be his first & chief object.' As a result, when Churchill had previously broached the subject on 10 and 28 May, Chamberlain made it painfully clear that he would retire immediately if Churchill considered Lloyd George to be a more useful colleague, but he 'could not work with him. I did not trust him, or believe his word, or feel his motives were the same as mine.' After this unequivocal declaration, Churchill backed down, assuring Chamberlain that he had 'merely toyed with the idea' and that he would carry it no further: 'We had gone in together & would if necessary go down together.' As he also told Lloyd George, he had 'received a very great deal of help from Chamberlain. His kindness and courtesy to me in our new relations have touched me. I have joined hands with him and must act with perfect loyalty.'[46]

When Churchill returned to the matter in his talk with Chamberlain on 5 June, however, he now commanded far more leverage. After all, Chamberlain had arrived at their meeting prepared to resign in face of mounting press and parliamentary hostility and had been deeply gratified by Churchill's touching declaration of loyalty. Churchill thus again reaffirmed that if forced to choose between them he would select Chamberlain over Lloyd George, but this time he shrewdly questioned whether he should be forced to make a choice because 'personal differences ought not to count now & he was quite sure that L.G. would work loyally with [him]'. Having made this persuasive point, they parted 'very amicably' to allow Chamberlain time to consider the request. After a further written appeal from the Prime Minister next day, Chamberlain finally succumbed because 'when men are giving their lives for their country any lesser sacrifice doesn't count'. But this did not stop him from stipulating that Lloyd George should give a personal assurance that he would abandon his feud and that the press campaign against him should be stopped before any announcement about Lloyd George was made in order to prevent the appearance of a bargain. He also requested an opportunity to speak at the War Cabinet to 'clear up the position as between ourselves'.[47]

After the War Cabinet concluded its agenda on 6 June, Chamberlain tackled his colleagues about the virulent campaign against him. While denying any complaint about their personal behaviour, he questioned why they permitted their parties to make these venomous attacks when they were all supposed to be working harmoniously to win the war. After this, Churchill intervened personally with Fleet Street and the campaign 'stopped even more suddenly than it had begun'. As Chamberlain noted: 'It was like turning off a tap & shows how completely artificial the whole thing was.'[48] Despite a so-called 'Under Secretary's' plot' organised by Boothby, Amery, Lloyd and Macmillan to expel Chamberlain from the government in mid-June, this intrigue also collapsed after Churchill issued a ferocious warning that ministers who were not prepared to work within the existing government should resign.[49]

While Chamberlain's bargain with Churchill effectively curbed the parliamentary and press campaign, public criticism of Chamberlain continued throughout the summer, spurred on by the publication of *Guilty Men* on 5 July. This hastily-written and tendentious polemic 'sold like a pornographic classic' at a time when a Gallup poll reported that 77 per cent of voters wanted Chamberlain dismissed from the government.[50] In retaliation, Central Office planned to rebut the indictment with their own version of 'Guilty Men' designed to expose Labour's far more damaging record on rearmament, while Chamberlain's speech to the National Union Executive on 27 June launched a slashing attack on Labour's 'outrageous and monstrous' efforts to shift the burden of responsibility which 'lies on them more than anyone else'.[51] Yet as Beaverbrook noted on the same day, while the 'grumblings against Neville still go on in some of the newspapers ... there is no concerted attack. And things are moving so swiftly that I do not think there can be an effective movement against him.'[52] Moreover, Chamberlain still enjoyed enthusiastic majority support within the parliamentary party; a source of strength paraded by the chairman of the 1922 Committee when he warned publicly on the day before the planned secret session of Parliament in mid-June that if the Opposition launched the predicted attack, the Chamberlainite majority would be forced to retaliate. Similarly, the inept efforts of Clement Davies to organise an all-party meeting at the Commons on 3 July to whip up feeling against the *Munichois* turned into 'a fiasco' when 180 loyal Conservatives packed the meeting and rousingly expressed continued support for their fallen leader.[53] Much to Chamberlain's relief, the prospect of a Lloyd George resurgence receded with the threat from his press and parliamentary critics. Indeed, as Chamberlain (and many others) soon concluded, Lloyd George's well-known defeatism had convinced him to stay out of office ready to negotiate peace in his new role as 'the Marshal Pétain of Britain'.[54]

IV

Through these trials Chamberlain soldiered on with a characteristic display of resilience. By mid-July, friends were all saying that he still looked remarkably fit. 'But I have lost my spring & my spirits', he complained to his sisters. 'All my recreations, flowers, fishing & shooting, country life have been taken from me and there is nothing to look forward to.'[55] The profound gloom hanging over Chamberlain during the weeks after his fall was undoubtedly intensified by a growing awareness of a serious health problem which his sister Hilda always attributed directly to 'the torture of his mind during the previous eighteen months'.[56] His first private reference to 'considerable pain' in his abdomen appears in his diary on 16 June, but he refrained from mentioning it to his sisters until a month later when he finally confessed to 'considerable trouble with my inside which hasn't been working properly for a long time & is getting worse'. Although his physician did not initially take the problem seriously, it was a measure of its significance that Chamberlain admitted that 'it is very tiresome and adds a good deal to the miseries of life'.[57] After an X-ray on 26 July, the verdict was that a partial obstruction of his lower bowel required a colostomy and even then he only had 'even chances' of avoiding a second and more serious operation. As he noted in his diary, 'if the odds go against me, I am doubtful whether I should be the same man, and I think it would be very difficult to come back "on appro[val]".' In order to spare his sisters needless worry, he wrote that it was 'not in itself a serious operation and I should be out again in a fortnight but the consequences will not be altogether pleasant and I shall have to adjust myself to a new condition of things'. As he noted with a fatalistic stoicism, '1940 has not been one of my happiest years, but it has been much worse for many other people than it has for me.' Perhaps he had simply lost the will to go on in a world in which he felt 'there is no pleasure in life and no prospect of any'.[58]

Despite the pain, Chamberlain kept up a heavy burden of work until the end. A few days before entering hospital, he spent ten hours inspecting east coast defences and this took a lot out of him, although he returned home more convinced than ever that the expected invasion could not now succeed. On 29 July Chamberlain entered the Nuffield House nursing home with a 'wonderfully calm mind'. That afternoon he had his operation and the doctors reported that it had been successful and he would not require further surgery;

a deliberate half-truth which concealed the fact that he was actually suffering from a terminal cancer of the bowel.[59] During the next fortnight, he went through 'fair hell', but having passed the worst he told Baldwin that he expected to 'go forward like a two year old now'.[60] On 12 August the 'star patient' left hospital four weeks earlier than predicted and transferred to Highfield Park, near Basingstoke, to convalesce in the quiet comfort of a grand house lent by his aunt Lilian. Having spent all the next day in bed, the following afternoon he got up at 5pm and began work on his papers.[61]

During Chamberlain's convalescence, Churchill displayed great consideration in keeping him abreast of war developments and the recipient was deeply touched by the kindness. Churchill also wrote regularly urging him not to return until he was fully fit because it would be 'the greatest mistake not to build up a proper reserve of strength' and Chamberlain was evidently relieved at his patience.[62] In the immediate aftermath of his operation, Lord Horder, his physician, forecast that Chamberlain would be back at work within a fortnight, but this must always have been an astonishingly optimistic prediction given the severity of the surgery, the age of the patient and the nature of his condition.[63] In the event, he convalesced for six weeks before returning to London on 9 September and even then he warned Churchill that he would not 'attain full efficiency all at once'. At this juncture, Chamberlain still did not fully realise the gravity of his position. As he noted in his diary that day:

> ... I have still to adjust myself to the new life of a partially crippled man, which is what I am. Any ideas which may have been in my mind about possibilities of further political activity and even a possibility of another Premiership after the war, have gone ... At the present, I have come into the very centre of the battle for Britain and the next few weeks may well see the turn of the tide one way or another. If we are still alive and free as I think we have every reason to hope I should like to go on working in my present capacity till the end of the war, and then get out; and try and fill up the remainder of my days without further public responsibilities.

This new effort at realism about his prospects was still far wide of the mark. Pale and tired, Chamberlain chaired the War Cabinet on 12 September while Churchill toured defensive positions in Kent. Five days later, he attended the secret session in the Commons where he received the customary ovation as he took his seat for the first time since his operation. Even to the most sympathetic eye he looked 'fairly well, but lacking his usual colour and animation' and appeared somewhat 'shrunken'.[64] At noon next day, he attended his last Cabinet meeting after over 17 years of almost continuous service. Despite an excellent recovery he was simply not strong enough to continue – particularly as his return to London followed only two days after Hitler ordered a dramatic intensification of the air war against Britain.

After enduring 'rather a nightmarish week' of almost continuous bombing raids, Chamberlain was forced to acknowledge defeat. At night, he had gathered what sleep he could in an air raid shelter, before snatching a couple of hours in bed in order to rise at 8am, but the afternoon rest upon which he still relied was often disturbed by the wail of sirens. To add to his discomfort, he complained that problems with his teeth added 'just another M[inor] M[isery] of which I seem to have rather an accumulation just now'.[65] At his juncture, Churchill intervened decisively to persuade 'Mrs Neville' that he should return to Highfield Park. Worn down by continuous air raids and a condition which demanded constant medical attention, he consented on the verge of collapse.[66] By the time he left London for the last time on 19 September, Chamberlain had the considerable consolation of knowing that the decisive climax of the Battle of Britain had passed four days earlier and that Hitler's invasion threat had been averted. But he was also aware that his condition meant that he would 'never live a normal life again' and that he had 'nothing to look forward to but a progressive deterioration during which ... I shall be an increasing burden & nuisance to those about me.'[67]

On his arrival at Highfield, Chamberlain spent the next three nights and two full days in almost continuous sleep. Having thought deeply over his position, he tendered his resignation on 22 September and although he still hinted at the possibility of a subsequent return, he was now 'a good deal more pessimistic' about the prospects. Confessing that he found it hard to resign when his nerve was unshaken and his mental power unimpaired, he derived some solace from his father's maxim that 'It is of no use to kick against the pricks.'[68] Despite having spoken privately to Eden about his filling Chamberlain's place in the War Cabinet on the day of the operation, however, Churchill initially declined Chamberlain's resignation with a plea to give himself a fair chance to recover so they could 'go on together through the storm'. Chamberlain was deeply touched and grateful for Churchill's 'generous attitude', but as all now recognised, this could only be an interim expression of courtesy.[69] Suffering 'a pretty poor time' with persistent nausea, too lame to walk, tormented by chronic toothache but too weak to have the offending teeth extracted, Chamberlain was clearly never going to return. As he conceded, this 'terrible catalogue of small miseries' were 'nothing to what many others are enduring', but they were proof that he was not shirking and he envied his old friend Eileen Stanhope the peace brought by her recent death.[70]

Churchill had been deeply moved by Chamberlain's distress as well as the loyalty he had shown him since May. Yet it was not personal sympathy for Chamberlain's plight so much as his own political necessity which finally induced the Prime Minister to accept his offer of resignation. On 29 September, in the wake of the humiliating failure of an Anglo-French operation to seize Dakar, Kingsley Wood was despatched to Hampshire to tell Chamberlain that 'Winston was very worried' about the prospect of parliamentary criticism and he 'was thinking of distracting attention from that issue by making a number of changes in the Government'. Recognising what this message meant, Chamberlain repeated that his office was at the disposal of the Prime Minister at any time, although he added that Churchill 'wd be wise to keep me as long as possible, because if I did get well enough I could give him more help personally & ensure him more support politically than anyone else'. Later that evening, however, Churchill wrote thanking him for his 'heroic effort ... to do yr duty & to see this grim business through', but told him that he could no longer delay the reconstruction of his government. When he received this letter, Chamberlain finally confessed that he was 'definitely very relieved' because his physical condition had deteriorated and he was 'perpetually haunted by doubts whether it was [his] duty to go on or give up'. As a mark of respect, Churchill hoped Chamberlain would follow his half-brother in accepting the Order of the Garter, but true to his Radical heritage and his objections in Austen's case, he replied that he would 'prefer to die plain "Mr Chamberlain" like my father before me, unadorned by any title'.[71] Perhaps in deference to Chamberlain's warnings about the adverse Conservative reaction, Churchill did not replace Halifax with Eden at the Foreign Office as he had initially proposed.[72]

On the afternoon of 9 October, a party meeting at Caxton Hall heard Lord Halifax record their high appreciation for Chamberlain's 'singleness of purpose and devotion to duty' before it endorsed Churchill's succession as party leader. According to Halifax, the unanimous goodwill and 'the evident personal feeling of real sorrow and regret and regard' was most touching and he wished Chamberlain had heard the tributes as 'some small recompense for all you have tried to do for them and for us all ... It makes your critics seem very small.'[73] It was a message echoed by many other loyal supporters, as the simmering discontents towards Churchill expressed by the 1922 Committee earlier in the day made all too evident.[74] Two days later, Chamberlain made his final broadcast, defiantly proclaiming that 'it is not conceivable that human civilisation should be permanently overcome by such evil men and evil things, and I feel proud that the British Empire, though left to fight alone, still stands across their path unconquered and unconquerable'.[75] On 31 October, Chamberlain finally relinquished his chairmanship of the Conservative Research Department after ten crucial years.

V

Just as political nemesis followed so swiftly after the zenith of Chamberlain's career as Prime Minister, so the end of his life came with an even more dramatic suddenness. Although 'very sad' to be ending his public work, Chamberlain soon confessed to be 'conscious of a relief, now that I know I have no alternative'. Having tortured himself over every setback in his recovery, he was now reconciled to the end of his career 'without bitterness and with a reasonably clear conscience'.[76] He was wounded by the 'short, cold & for the most part depreciatory' press comments on his retirement, 'without the slightest sign of sympathy for the man or even any comprehension that there may be a human tragedy in the background'.[77] Yet among the hundreds of affecting letters he received, his pain was eased particularly by Simon's assurance that he had 'the priceless consolation that you have spent yourself in the country's service and have done more than any man alive to improve the conditions of life of humble folk, as well as leading a united nation into war when your struggle for peace finally failed'. Deeply touched by this testimonial, Chamberlain inscribed his own unrepentant obituary:

It gave me particular pleasure that ... you remembered my efforts for social improvement ... [I]t was the hope of doing something to improve the conditions of life for the poorer people that brought me at past middle life into politics, and it is some satisfaction to me that I was able to carry out some part of my ambition, even though its permanency may be challenged by the destruction of war. For the rest I regret nothing that I have done & I can see nothing undone that I ought to have done. I am therefore content to accept the fate that has so suddenly overtaken me and only trust that I may not have to bear my disabilities too long.[78]

The fate of which Chamberlain had spoken came upon him far sooner than he ever imagined. Indeed, his first thought was of the eventual purchase of a substantial new residence near Highfield Park and his sisters at Odiham. Yet when he finally insisted upon being given a definite medical prognosis in early October, Chamberlain recorded that Horder told him that 'he would be surprised if I were not here in 3 months time but more surprised if I were here in 12 months'. This news he found 'very helpful and encouraging, for it would be a terrible prospect if I had to wait indefinitely for the end, while going through such daily miseries as I am now enduring. As it is, I know what to do and shall no longer be harassed by doubts and questions.'[79] Indeed, the prospect of impending death was greeted with undisguised relief by a man who had always been tormented by the painful recollection of his father's 'eight years of martyrdom' after his devastating stroke in 1906. 'He dreaded years of invalidism such as his father had known', his sister later recalled, 'and once he had heard the verdict he suffered himself to relax his iron will, and died not in six months, but in six weeks.'[80]

At Chamberlain's request, a few of his closest political friends visited him shortly before he died. On 14 October, the King and Queen drove from Windsor for an affectionate farewell to a loyal and respected servant. Prominent among the others was Sir Horace Wilson, his closest adviser and the one with whom he had enjoyed the sort of unparalleled intimacy only possible among truly kindred spirits. Having suffered most from the spiteful vindictiveness of the avenging Churchillians, Wilson was deeply saddened by his friend and master's retirement, 'both because of his ill fate & because of the consequences to us all of the withdrawal of his guiding hand & orderly mind'. When he heard the news of his death he was 'heart-broken' because, as he also told Baldwin, after three years of working so closely together his 'initial feelings of regard & respect' had become 'enlarged into affection'.[81]

Chamberlain's mind remained alert and active until the end and his physical condition only deteriorated rapidly in his last days as the cancer advanced. On

28 October he sent Joseph Ball a 'rather more intimate account of [his] present condition' than that given to other friends: 'All food is loathsome to me and drink the same. I have given up smoking altogether and port no longer has any attraction for me; for … I am never free from this feeling of sickness except when I am … asleep. In its worst form it is accompanied by a most intense depression and general inability to do anything.' Next day, he went out for a drive with Annie and walked quite a long distance enjoying the autumn colour on the trees. On 30 October, however, he had a 'bad day' and after this he steadily declined.[82]

When Halifax visited for the last time on 7 November he found Chamberlain 'pretty bad' and although in no pain he was still suffering from nausea and 'dreadfully weak'. But for all that, he spoke movingly of their work together and all that it had meant to him. 'Poor old boy!', Halifax noted after he returned to London. 'It was a melancholy visit, but he was very brave and contented. And much touched by the kindness of his friends – & indeed of hundreds more who had written.'[83] Two days later, Arthur Neville Chamberlain died in his sleep early on the morning of 9 November. For his friends and many genuine admirers it was a blessed release from physical illness, mental anguish and political despair. As 'Chips' Channon noted after receiving the news, 'though I loved him, I am glad: the shafts of malice had hurt him, and probably killed him. Now the reaction, already begun, will have added impetus, and his place in history will be more secure. He had nothing more to live for; all his hopes had gone.'[84]

Churchill was equally magnanimous. At the War Cabinet on 11 November he talked of the severe loss to the nation: 'Mr Chamberlain's great grief in leaving life had perhaps been that he had not lived to see the end of the struggle … But maybe he had lived long enough to feel confident as to the outcome.' The same day he sent his condolences to Chamberlain's widow in equally generous terms.

> During these long violent months of war we had come closer together than at any time in our twenty years of friendly relationship amid the ups & downs of politics. I greatly admired his fortitude and firmness of spirit. I felt when I served under him that he wd never give in: & I knew when our positions were reversed that I cd count upon the aid of a loyal and unflinching comrade.[85]

Next day, in their cramped and temporary wartime quarters in Church House, the Commons assembled to hear Churchill speak of Chamberlain 'in measured, stately English'. By all accounts, 'it was well done; dignified and sincere'. 'Whatever else history may or may not say about these terrible, tremendous years', the Prime Minister declared, 'we can be sure that Neville Chamberlain acted with perfect sincerity according to his lights and strove to the utmost of his capacity and authority, which were powerful, to save the world from the awful, devastating struggle in which we are now engaged.'[86] Although many were impressed with Churchill's oratory, to loyal Chamberlainites like

Tufton Beamish the deliberately 'faint praise' revealed 'a clear intention to make the late P.M. shoulder the blame for what has happened and to buttress his own efforts past and present'. For such men, this animus and mistrust towards Churchill would persist well into 1941.[87]

At noon on 14 November, Neville Chamberlain's funeral took place at Westminster Abbey and his ashes were interred next to those of Andrew Bonar Law. Afraid that a judiciously placed bomb might kill the entire government, the time and place were not publicised and accounts vary as to the attendance. Yet all agreed that the mourners froze in arctic conditions as they sat beneath bomb-shattered windows enduring 'that terrible ecclesiastic cold known only to English churches'. Margesson and the War Cabinet followed the pall bearers, while other ministers stood in the choir stalls, during a 'long, dignified and moving' service. Many were evidently distressed and Churchill 'had the decency to cry as he stood by the coffin', but among Chamberlain's still loyal followers there remained an enduring sense of anger to see assembled 'all the little men who had torpedoed poor Neville's heroic efforts to preserve peace and made his life a misery' – particularly as some seemed to be 'gloating'. At the end of the service, Sir Horace Wilson, the once seemingly powerful *eminence grise* of the Chamberlain regime, was seen 'alone, his face contorted with grief, praying for his dead friend'.[88]

VI

Chamberlain's fall and subsequent death marked more than one significant watershed in British history. Arguably, for the nation, 1940 signalled the beginning of a gradual transition from one established order of politics to another as the Attlee consensus replaced Baldwin's.[89] It certainly marked the end of the Unionist ascendancy in a West Midland fiefdom which had been controlled by the Chamberlain dynasty since the 1860s, while in his native Birmingham Labour won ten of the city's 13 seats in 1945 with a devastating swing of 23 per cent against the Conservatives. For Chamberlain's devoted followers, 1940 also represented a crucial turning point for their party in a rather different sense. 'I do not think the Party will ever be the same again', Rab Butler wrote to Chamberlain's widow in December 1940, 'I looked upon him as the last leader of the organisation in the State which I joined very late in its life, but which had the responsibility for so much of England's greatness.'[90] It was a verdict widely echoed by those Conservatives who survived the fall only to be too disorientated to exploit the possible benefits of coalition or to rise to its challenges. With Halifax's reluctant removal to the Washington Embassy in December 1940, it appeared to Chamberlain loyalists that the government had now been 'reduced entirely to Thugs and Under-Secretaries'.[91]

Despite his bitter reversal of fortune, Chamberlain was far from pessimistic in his final days. He acknowledged that the Conservative Party would 'have to go through a period of eclipse', but he prophesied that this would only be temporary because 'the women of this country are by instinct and temperament Conservative in the main'. Above all, he died secure in the knowledge that his successor as Prime Minister would never surrender and that eventually Britain would prevail, even though he knew he would not live to see victory. Most important, he never deviated from the confident expectation that when the history of those tumultuous years was written 'the broad outlines of the story will be plain enough' and that his policy and reputation would be fully vindicated. Warned of a renewed Labour vendetta against him a few days before his death, Chamberlain was sanguine and counselled inaction:

> So far as my personal reputation is concerned, I am not in the least disturbed about it. The letters which I am still receiving in such vast quantities so unanimously dwell on the same point, namely without Munich the war would have been lost and the Empire destroyed in 1938 ... I do not feel the opposite view ... has a chance of survival. Even if nothing further were to be published giving the true inside story of the past two years, I should not fear the historian's verdict.

As he put it in reply to words of sympathy from a loyal National Liberal, 'though peace could not be maintained the three things that were gained – a united Country and Empire, the moral support of the decent part of the world, and time for preparation – contribute a sufficient sum of achievement to satisfy one's mind'. In such a mood, he declared defiantly, 'I regret nothing in the past.'[92]

Chamberlain's many friends and associates also thought about his eventual place in history and they wholeheartedly echoed this belief. Malcolm MacDonald spoke for most of them when he declared that although Munich failed to achieve lasting peace, 'by postponing the present war for a whole year it gave Britain time to make military preparations which will turn what would probably have been defeat into what will now ... certainly be a victory for European civilisation'. It was, he assured Chamberlain, 'a personal achievement without precedent in the history of statesmanship, and long, long after all the scribblers who have attacked you are forgotten your name will be amongst the most honoured in the dynasty of our Prime Ministers'.[93] An old friend since his days at Rugby School was equally certain that the eulogies in Parliament and the press reflected some true appreciation of the man, but that was 'not nearly good enough. As time goes on Britain & the Empire & the World will gradually realise how much praise he deserves.'[94] One minister who had served under Chamberlain in 1939–40 went further in declaring that 'he will some day be regarded as the greatest living Englishman of his times'. Viscount Simon also believed that 'his reputation is quite secured in history. The only thing that made one sick was to hear people who cheered him so lustily when he delivered them from the fear of immediate war, kick him quietly when he couldn't do them any more good.'[95]

Given the circumstances and the character of the man, it was perhaps inevitable that Chamberlain should expect that history would vindicate his policy and rehabilitate his reputation. Yet this was by far the greatest miscalculation of his entire public career. Recollections of Chamberlain's uniquely personal association with the failed efforts to preserve peace during the last three years of his life inexorably tainted perceptions of his entire life and obliterated from public memory his far broader achievement over the preceding quarter century as both a radical social reformer and a successful Chancellor of the Exchequer. At the same time, it also conveniently obscured the shared guilt, the inconsistencies and equally substantial errors of judgement among triumphant Labour and Conservative critics who rose to power by denigrating his efforts. Above all, the generosity and magnanimity which Churchill felt towards Chamberlain during the summer of 1940 soon gave way to renewed memories of hostility and an altogether less charitable verdict. During an outburst against 'the people who had let us in for this most unnecessary of all wars' only seven months after Chamberlain's death, Churchill 'was harsh about Chamberlain whom he called "the narrowest, most ignorant, most ungenerous of men"' and one who 'knew not the first thing about war, Europe or foreign politics'.[96]

This would be the picture which Churchill immortalised in his extremely influential but highly coloured account of the *Gathering Storm* and for more than 30 years this version of events held the field unchallenged and unchallengeable, with its central assumptions and counter-factual scenarios conveniently untested by events. This grotesque caricature of the 1930s painted in the simplistic but compelling monochrome shades of black and white, good and evil, courage in 'standing up to Hitler' versus craven appeasement, still continues to hold sway in popular memory, television dramas and far too often in historical texts even to this day. Indeed, if anything, it has actually enjoyed something of a resurgence in recent years with the emergence of a post-Revisionist school which (in its most extreme expressions) brings the historiography of appeasement back to its point of departure with the *Guilty Men* in 1940.[97]

Yet the reality of the 1930s was neither so simple nor so clear cut for British statesmen struggling to confront an incalculable and evil dictator in uniquely difficult circumstances. Despite the compelling power of hindsight, the failure of Chamberlain's 'double policy' of rearmament and appeasement does not imply the existence of a 'correct' or potentially successful alternative strategy which was capable of avoiding war in the late 1930s. On the contrary, given what we know both of Hitler's insatiable ambitions and the vast and complex web of imperial, strategic, military, intelligence, economic and electoral constraints upon British policy, Paul Kennedy (and many others) are almost certainly correct in arguing that 'the real dilemma facing British decision-makers was not that they had to steer the right course through the storm to the safe harbour beyond, but that there was no such haven: there was no good or "correct" policy. Appeasement had its dangers and disadvantages but so, too, did the opposite course of action.'[98] In these circumstances, Jock Colville's verdict shortly before Chamberlain's death cut directly to the heart of the matter. 'He has been greatly maligned; but I believe historians, if they try to throw themselves back into the conditions in which decisions were taken, and refrain from judging solely by what happened afterwards, will mix their censure with much praise for his honest efforts.' Or as Chamberlain's loyal supporters always maintained, 'it was better to have tried and lost than never to have tried at all'.[99]

Notes and References

Unless otherwise specified, Chamberlain refers to Neville Chamberlain. In the interests of consistency, clarity and brevity, the following family correspondents are referred to in the notes by their forename only:

Beatrice Chamberlain (1862–1918).

Eldest child of Joseph Chamberlain; Neville's step-sister.

Dorothy Chamberlain (1911–92).

Neville Chamberlain's first child; married Stephen Lloyd, July 1935.

Frank Chamberlain (1914–65).

Neville Chamberlain's second child.

(Caroline) Hilda Chamberlain (1871–1962).

Joseph Chamberlain's fifth child and full sister to Neville.

(Florence) Ida Chamberlain (1870–1943).

Fourth child of Joseph Chamberlain and full sister to Neville.

Mary Crownishield Endicott (1863–1957).

Joseph Chamberlain's third wife, 1888–1914; married Canon William Carnegie in August 1916.

Norman Chamberlain (1884–1917).

Cousin and extremely close friend to Neville Chamberlain.

In the bibliographical notes, the place of publication is London unless otherwise stated.

A key to the standard abbreviations employed with regard to collections of private and official papers can be found in the Bibliography. Other abbreviations used are as follows:

BCUA	Birmingham Conservative and Unionist Association
DBFP	*Documents on British Foreign Policy, Series 2–3, 1919–1939*
DGFP	*Documents on German Foreign Policy, Series D, 1936–1941*
FRUS	*Foreign Relations of the United States*
H.C. Debs, 5s	*Parliamentary Debates: House of Commons Debates*, Fifth Series

Preface

1. Keith Feiling, *The Life of Neville Chamberlain* (1946), p.v.
2. David Reynolds, *In Command of History, Churchill's Fighting and Writing of the Second World War* (2004), pp. 32–4, 92–3.
3. Feiling to Lord Swinton, 13 August 1944, SWIN 270/5/4.
4. Iain Macleod, *Neville Chamberlain* (1961), p. 13; Taylor review, *New Statesman*, 1 December 1961.
5. H. Montgomery Hyde, *Neville Chamberlain* (1976), pp. vi–vii.
6. David Dilks, *Neville Chamberlain, Volume One : Pioneering and Reform, 1869–1929* (Cambridge, 1984).
7. David Dutton, *Neville Chamberlain* (2001), p. 1.
8. Feiling to Lord Swinton, 26 August 1944, SWIN 270/5/4.

Chapter 1: The Chamberlain Enigma

1. Chamberlain to Archbishop Cosmo Lang, 14 October 1940, NC13/18/870.
2. Chamberlain to Hilda, 2 October 1938; Lord Zetland to Lord Brabourne, 1 October 1938, Brabourne MSS Eur. D609/71.
3. Lord Halifax, 'A Record of Events before the War, 1939', Annex IV, FO 800/317/89.
4. Viscount Mersey, *A Picture of Life* (1941), p. 432.
5. 'Premier League: How Churchill Fought off History's Rivals', *Guardian*, 27 December 1999.
6. *H.C. Debs*, 5s, 351, col 292, 3 September 1939.
7. Arthur Salter, *Slave of the Lamp: A Public Servant's Notebook* (1967), p. 142.
8. Earl of Swinton, *Sixty Years of Power: Some Memories of the Men who Wielded it* (1966), p. 108.
9. Harold Macmillan, *Winds of Change 1914–1939* (1966), p. 521.
10. Winston S. Churchill, *The Second World War, Vol I: The Gathering Storm* (1948), pp. 173, 199; A.L. Rowse, *The Later Churchills* (1958), pp. 462–6.
11. Both the attribution and phrasing vary considerably. Most credit it to Lloyd George but some attribute it to Churchill including Francis Williams, *A Pattern of Rulers* (1965), p. 140. Oswald Mosley, *My Life* (1968), p. 176, erroneously claims an 'adequate Lord Mayor' for Birkenhead.
12. Dutton, *Neville Chamberlain*, pp. 184–5.
13. Headlam Diary, 15 December 1925 and 8 February 1926; Jones Diary, 20 May 1923 reporting Bonar Law and 30 September 1923 and 5 December 1928 reporting Baldwin.
14. Bridgeman Diary, November 1929 (written mid-1930).
15. Robert Self (ed.), *The Austen Chamberlain Diary Letters: The Correspondence of Sir Austen Chamberlain with his sisters Hilda and Ida, 1916–1937* (Cambridge, 1995), pp. 2–3, 11–21.
16. Swinton, *Sixty Years of Power*, p. 112; Alec Dunglass notes, Kenneth Young, *Sir Alec Douglas-Home* (1970), p. 47.
17. Chamberlain to Hilda, 3 January 1920 and 15 April 1928.
18. 'Recollections of their father's own childhood written for Dorothy & Frank by their Aunt Ida Chamberlain, January 1941', BC5/11/1 (hereafter 'Recollection'), fol. 4, 6–7; 'Portrait of three Chamberlains and my Eldest

sister Beatrice written for their descendants', July–November 1956, BC5/10/1 (hereafter 'Portrait'), fol. 12, 14.

19. Sir Douglas Veale interviews with Professor Brian Harrison, 1969, British Library, National Sound Archive, F4381-3.

20. See Robert Self, *The Neville Chamberlain Diary Letters, Vol. 1: The Making of a Politician, 1915–20* (Aldershot, 2000), pp. 24–31.

21. Mary Carnegie [Chamberlain] to Chamberlain, 31 October 1923, NC1/20/2/17.

22. Ida Chamberlain, 'Recollection', BC5/11/1, fol. 7.

23. Bridgeman Diary, November 1929; Lord Citrine, *Men and Work: An Autobiography* (1964), p. 368.

24. Macmillan, *Winds of Change*, pp. 172–4, 521.

25. Lord Snell, *Men, Movements, and Myself* (1936), p. 248.

26. J.R. Clynes, *Memoirs, 1924–1937* (1937), p. 252; Citrine, *Men and Work*, p. 366; Ronald Tree, *When the Moon was High: Memoirs of Peace and War 1897–1942* (1975), p. 51.

27. A.J. Sylvester Diary, 21 February 1938. Bevan used the same phrase in June 1937, M. Foot, *Aneurin Bevan: A Biography, Vol I: 1897–1945* (1962), p. 257.

28. Salter, *Slave of the Lamp*, p. 144; Macmillan, *Winds of Change*, p. 172; Duff Cooper, 'Chamberlain: A Candid Portrait', n.d. [November 1939], MRGN1/5.

29. Lord Vansittart, *The Mist Procession* (1958), pp. 429–30.

30. Nicolson Diary, 15 June 1954, reporting Lord Halifax. Also Viscount Stuart of Findhorn, *Within the Fringe: An Autobiography* (1967), p. 83.

31. Snell, *Men, Movements, and Myself*, p. 248. Citrine, *Men and Work*, p. 367; Swinton, *Sixty Years of Power*, p. 110; Lord Morrison, *An Autobiography* (1960), p. 75.

32. Brendan Bracken to Beaverbrook, 16 March 1939, R. Cockett (ed.), *My Dear Max: The Letters of Brendan Bracken to Lord Beaverbrook, 1925–1958* (1990), p. 45; Pownall Diary, 28 November 1938, 13 September 1939; Nicolson Diary, 24 August 1939; Richard Law to Paul Emrys-Evans, Emrys-Evans MSS 58239/3; Amery Diary, 11 May 1940.

33. Chamberlain to Hilda, 5 July 1919; to Ida, 26 June 1920.

34. Morrison, *Autobiography*, pp. 175–6.

35. Churchill, *The Gathering Storm*, p. 389.

36. A. Duff Cooper, *Old Men Forget: The Autobiography of Duff Cooper, Viscount Norwich* (1953), p. 188. Young, *Sir Alec Douglas-Home*, p. 46; Lord Home, *The Way the Wind Blows: An Autobiography* (1976), p. 60; John Colville, *The Fringes of Power: Downing Street Diaries 1939–1955* (1985), p. 35.

37. Arthur Salter, *Security: Can We Retrieve It?* (1939), p. 284; Percy Harris, *Forty Years In and Out of Parliament* (n.d.), p. 133.

38. L.S. Amery, *My Political Life* (3 vols, London, 1953–55), III, p. 226.

39. Young, *Sir Alec Douglas-Home*, p. 41. Stuart, *Within the Fringe*, p. 83; Channon Diary, 6 June 1937.

40. Alistair Horne, *Macmillan 1894–1956: Vol I of the Official Biography* (2 vols, 1988), p. 80.

41. Austen Chamberlain to Ida, 2 November 1924, AC5/1/339.

42. See, for example, repeated entries in Channon Diary, R.R. James (ed.), *Chips: The Diaries of Sir Henry Channon* (1967), pp. 117, 146, 150, 159, 162,

172, 192, 260; J.H. Thomas, *My Story* (1937), pp. 235–6; Earl of Onslow, *Sixty-Three Years: Diplomacy, The Great War and Politics* (n.d.), p. 181.

43. Chamberlain to Hilda, 15 November 1924, 2 January, 14 February, 19 July 1925, 10 August 1926, 10 April 1937.

44. Chamberlain to Hilda, 29 May 1927.

45. Harold Macmillan, *The Past Masters: Politics and Politicians, 1906–1939* (1975), p. 134.

46. Colville Diary, 2 February 1940.

47. Chamberlain to Ida, 17 April 1921 and 12 May 1934; to Hilda, 17 May 1922; Hilda Chamberlain, 'Portrait', BC5/10/1, fol. 12–13.

48. David Dilks transcript of an interview with Mr and Mrs Stephen Lloyd, 11 April 1983, NC20/1, fol. 70–71 (hereafter 'Dilks Transcript'); Chamberlain to Hilda, 26 March 1933; to Ida, 27 April 1940.

49. Viscount Simon, *Retrospect* (1952), p. 278; Hilda Chamberlain, 'Portrait', BC5/10/1, fol. 17.

50. Chamberlain to Ida, 7 August 1921; 'The First Baldwin Government', Templewood MSS XX/5; Bridgeman Diary, November 1929; P.J. Grigg, *Prejudice and Judgement* (1948), p. 119.

51. Thomas Jones to A. Flexner, 12 January 1940, Thomas Jones (ed.), *A Diary with Letters, 1931–1950* (1954), p. 445.

52. Foot, *Aneurin Bevan*, I, p. 258.

53. Headlam Diary, 6 March 1933; Thomas Jones interview with W.P. Crozier, 30 April 1940, A.J.P. Taylor (ed.), *W.P. Crozier: Off the Record, Political Interviews, 1933–1943* (1973), pp. 164–5. See also the views of Simon and Morrison in the same volume, pp. 153–4.

54. Rowse, *The Later Churchills*, p. 462.

55. Duff Cooper, *Old Men Forget*, p. 200 and his anonymous 'Chamberlain: A Candid Portrait', n.d. [November 1939], MRGN1/5.

56. Horne, *Macmillan*, I, p. 115.

57. Templewood, *Nine Troubled Years*, pp. 26–7; Viscount Swinton, *I Remember*, (n.d.), p. 265.

58. A.P. Herbert, *Independent Member* (1950), p. 39.

59. D.C. Watt, *How War Came: The Immediate Origins of the Second World War, 1938–1939* (1990), p. 78.

60. David Lloyd George, *The War Memoirs of David Lloyd George* (6 vols, 1934), III, p. 1367.

61. Hilda Chamberlain, 'Portrait', BC5/10/1, fol. 13.

62. Violet Markham, *Return Passage* (1953), p. 152; Lord Samuel, *Memoirs*, (1945), p. 215.

63. Tree, *When the Moon was High*, p. 51; Salter, *Slave of the Lamp*, p. 143.

64. Hugh Dalton, *The Fateful Years: Memoirs, 1931–1945* (1957), p. 162.

65. Citrine, *Men and Work*, pp. 366–7; Granada, *Clement Attlee: The Granada Historical Records Interviews* (1967), p. 17.

66. Lord Butler, *The Art of the Possible* (1971), pp. 78–9; Earl of Avon, *Facing the Dictators* (1962), p. 486.

67. Chamberlain to Ida, 2 June 1929.

68. See D. Smith, 'Englishness and the Liberal Inheritance after 1886' in R. Colls & P. Dodds (eds.), *Englishness: Politics and Culture, 1880–1920* (1986), pp. 254–82.

69. Derek Walker-Smith, *Neville Chamberlain: Man of Peace*, (n.d. 1940), p. 12.
70. Sir Edward Bridges to Viscount Templewood, 6 January 1954, Templewood MSS XIX/12.
71. Chamberlain Diary, 18 March 1928.
72. Jones Diary, 20 March 1924; Grigg, *Prejudice and Judgement*, pp. 119, 262.
73. E.S. Fawcett to Chamberlain, 29 August 1917, NC8/5/3/7. Also Arthur Robinson to Chamberlain, 14 April 1939; Osmund Cleverly to Chamberlain, 5 May 1939, NC7/11/32, 44, 203; Sir Arthur Rucker interviews with Professor Britain Harrison, 19 May 1969, British Library, National Sound Archives, C608/01,F4382 (hereafter 'Rucker interview').
74. Headlam Diary, 1 March 1927, 3 December 1930 and 6 March 1933.
75. 'A Gentleman with a Duster' [H. Begbie], *The Conservative Mind* (1924), p. 73. Also Sir Alexander Mackintosh, *Echoes of Big Ben: A Journalist's Parliamentary Diary, 1881–1940* (1945), p. 97.
76. Watt, *How War Came*, p. 76.

Chapter 2: Formative Influences: From Highbury to Andros

1. Winston S. Churchill, *Great Contemporaries* (1937), p. 73; Austen Chamberlain to Hilda, 7 December 1932 and 24 April 1933, AC5/1/602, 614.
2. Joseph Chamberlain to Jesse Collings, 26 June 1876, J.L. Garvin, *The Life of Joseph Chamberlain, Volume I, 1836–1895* (1932), p. 202.
3. Neville Chamberlain's introduction to the German edition of Austen's books, reprinted in Charles Petrie, *The Chamberlain Tradition*, (1938), p. 280; Hilda Chamberlain, 'Portrait of the Three Chamberlains', BC5/10/1, fol. 1.
4. Chamberlain to Queen Elizabeth, 23 June 1938, NC7/4/7.
5. Chamberlain memoir of his father for 'My dear children, Dorothy and Frank', 6 July 1914 (hereafter 'Neville Chamberlain memoir of his father'), NC1/16/11, p. 4; Peter Marsh, *Joseph Chamberlain: Entrepreneur in Politics*, (New Haven and London, 1994), pp. 140–41.
6. Hilda Chamberlain broadcast on her father, 15 September 1953, NC1/15/6/4.
7. See David Dutton, *Austen Chamberlain: Gentleman in Politics* (Bolton, 1985), Chapter 1.
8. Hilda Chamberlain, 'Portrait', BC5/10/1, fol. 12; Ida Chamberlain, 'Recollections', BC5/11/1, fol. 4, 6, 7.
9. Thomas Turner notes, n.d., NC9/2/81.
10. Joseph Chamberlain to Jesse Collings, 28 October 1890, J.L. Garvin, *The Life of Joseph Chamberlain: Vol. 2, 1885–1895* (1934), p. 499.
11. Austen and Neville Chamberlain to Joseph Chamberlain, 10, 23, 24 November and 25 December 1890, NC1/6/10/1–3, 8–9.
12. Neville Chamberlain memoir of his father, 1914, NC1/16/11, pp. 6–7.
13. Ibid.; Neville Chamberlain to Joseph Chamberlain, 6 June, 23 August and 23 September 1891, NC1/6/10/16, 23, 25.
14. Neville Chamberlain to Mary, 26 November, 17 December 1891, 23 January 1892, NC1/20/1/7–9.
15. Neville Chamberlain to Joseph Chamberlain, 23 September 1891; to Austen Chamberlain, 15 January 1892, NC1/6/10/25, 35.

16. Neville Chamberlain to Joseph Chamberlain, 22 October 1892 and 5 January 1893; to Austen Chamberlain, 20 January 1893, NC1/6/10/47, 52–3.

17. Joseph Chamberlain to Neville Chamberlain, 6 November 1893, NC1/6/9/15.

18. Neville Chamberlain to Joseph Chamberlain, 12 November 1893, 21 October 1894, NC1/6/10/64, 83.

19. Chamberlain to Beatrice, 26 November 1894, NC1/13/3/27; to Ida, 7 December 1894.

20. Neville Chamberlain to Joseph Chamberlain, 27 February 1895, NC1/6/10/93.

21. Neville Chamberlain to Austen Chamberlain, 29 January 1895, AC5/3/131.

22. Neville Chamberlain to Joseph Chamberlain, 8 November 1895, NC1/6/10/102.

23. Neville Chamberlain to Joseph Chamberlain, 1 and 17 January, 27 February, 14 and 27 March 1896, NC1/6/10/106–7, 110–12.

24. Neville Chamberlain to Joseph Chamberlain, 24 and 28 April 1896, 11 January 1897, NC1/6/10/113–14, 117; to Alfred Greenwood, 11 July 1896, NC7/8/3.

25. Lawrence H. Officer, 'What is the Relative Value in UK Pounds?', www.eh.net.

26. Neville Chamberlain to Joseph Chamberlain, 28 April 1896, NC1/6/10/114.

27. Chamberlain to Hilda, 1 July 1917.

28. Dilks transcript, NC20/1, fol. 62–4; Chamberlain to Hilda, 15 April 1928.

29. Ida Chamberlain, 'Recollections', BC5/11/1, fol. 9; Hilda Chamberlain, 'Portrait', BC5/10/1, fol. 13–14; Neville Chamberlain memoir of his father, p. 8.

30. Peter Clarke, *A Question of Leadership: Gladstone to Thatcher* (Penguin ed., 1992), p. 212.

31. Larry W. Fuchser, *Neville Chamberlain and Appeasement: A Study in the Politics of History* (New York, 1982), pp. 9–18.

32. Dilks transcript, NC20/1, fol. 65. Also Austen Chamberlain, *Politics from Inside: An Epistolary Chronicle* (1936), pp. 16–17.

33. Dilks transcript, pp. 48–9; Hilda Chamberlain, 'Portrait', BC5/10/1, fol. 11; Chamberlain to Ida, 27 March 1926; to Hilda, 26 October 1928.

34. Chamberlain to Hilda, 25 May 1931; Chamberlain Diary, 19 February 1936.

35. Home, *The Way the Wind Blows*, p. 60; Richard Lamb, *The Drift to War, 1922–1939* (1989), p. 258.

36. Hilda Chamberlain, 'Portrait', BC5/10/1, fol. 12.

37. Chamberlain to Alfred Greenwood, 27 June and 11 July 1896, NC7/8/2–3.

38. See Chamberlain's four Elliott's notebooks for this period, NC5/7/1–4.

39. Chamberlain to Hilda, 28 June 1914 and 3 November 1917.

40. David Cannadine, *Class in Britain* (New Haven and London, 1998), pp. 129–30.

41. Neville Chamberlain memoir of his father, 1914, p. 5.

42. Chamberlain to Hilda, 31 July and to Ida, 21 August 1921.

43. 'List of Birds Noticed at Highbury, 1890–1910', NC6/2/17; Chamberlain to Hilda, 26 March 1922 and 15 April 1928; to Ida, 24 March 1929; to *The Times*, and other correspondence, NC7/11/26/4–26.

44. 'The Natural History of Downing Street', *The Countryman*, October 1937, pp. 46–7; Home, *The Way the Wind Blows*, p. 14.

45. Chamberlain to Ida, 18 June 1916 and 4 August 1934.

46. Chamberlain to Hilda, 20 June 1931; Fishing Diaries, NC6/3/2–3.

47. Chamberlain to Hilda 12 September 1920 and 3 December 1921; also to Ida, 16 September 1921.

48. Hilda Chamberlain 'Portrait', BC5/10/1, fol. 26.

49. Thelma Cazalet-Keir, *From the Wings* (1967), p. 95; Chamberlain to Hilda, 15 April 1928.

50. J. Dover Wilson to Chamberlain, 12 January 1936 and 20 December 1937, NC7/11/29/57–9; Chamberlain to Ida, 12 February and 11 November 1933.

51. Dilks transcript, NC20/1; Chamberlain to Hilda, 4 June 1922 and 23 November 1935.

52. Chamberlain to Hilda, 15 February 1920; to Ida, 12 May 1934.

53. Chamberlain to Hilda, 4 June 1922.

54. Chamberlain to Alfred Greenwood, 25 April 1909, NC7/5/17.

55. Chamberlain to Alfred Greenwood, 8 April 1899, 26 December 1901, 26 June 1907, 25 April 1909, NC7/5/7,10, 12, 14.

56. General Hospital notebook, 1906, NC5/7/5.

57. Notes by Harold Shrimpton, February 1941, NC5/1/34; 'Proposed Scheme for Reform of Out-Patient Departments', 3 February 1908, NC5/1/4; *The Hospital*, 10 October 1908, pp. 17–18; *Birmingham Daily Post*, 30 September 1908.

58. Chamberlain to T.D. Neal, 16 December 1924; to William Cadbury, 12 December 1924, NC5/8/1/16, 18.

59. Chamberlain to Frank Newman, 12 March 1926, NC5/2/1/49; to Ida, 12 January 1929, 12 April 1930.

60. Chamberlain to Lord Nuffield, 29 May 1938; Neville Moss to Chamberlain, 23 June 1938, NC5/8/1/66–7.

61. Marsh, *Joseph Chamberlain*, pp. 568, 605–6, 627.

62. Neville Chamberlain memoir of his father, 6 July 1914, NC1/16/11, pp. 18–19.

63. Chamberlain to Hilda, 27 February 1908; Chamberlain Diary, 3 July 1914.

64. Hilda Chamberlain 'Portrait' BC5/10/1, p. 12; Chamberlain to Ida, 29 January 1933; to Hilda, 31 October 1936.

65. Chamberlain to Mary, 20, 28 October and 15 November 1903, 1 May 1904, NC1/20/1/37–9, 43.

66. Hilda Chamberlain, untitled memoir, January 1941, NC9/2/9.

67. Ibid.; Chamberlain to Anne Vere Cole, 2 December 1910, NC1/26/2.

68. George Lane-Fox to Lord Irwin, 1 August 1928, Irwin MSS Eur. C152/18/106; Hilda Runciman Diary, n.d. [3 September 1939], Runciman MSS Additional A/14.

69. Chamberlain to Mary, 14 January 1914, NC1/20/1/76.

70. Chamberlain to Hilda, 18 March 1928; Hilda Chamberlain, untitled memoir, January 1941, NC9/22/9.

71. Hilda Chamberlain, 'Portrait', BC5/10/1, fol. 15.
72. Chamberlain to Mary, 7 May 1911, NC1/20/1/80; to Beatrice, 10 May 1911, BC2/2/22.
73. Chamberlain to Alfred Greenwood, 26 December 1911, NC7/5/20; to Mary, 22 March 1914, NC1/20/1/87; Dilks transcript, NC20/1, fol. 65.
74. Chamberlain to Hilda, 21 February 1914, 17 May 1916, 24 April 1920; to Ida, 24 March 1917.
75. Fuchser, *Neville Chamberlain and Appeasement*, pp. xi, 1, 199. Also Correlli Barnett, *The Collapse of British Power* (Gloucester, 1984), p. 456; Williams, *A Pattern of Rulers*, p. 136.
76. Chamberlain to Hilda, 23 January and 1 February; to Ida, 23 March 1926.
77. Chamberlain to Ida, 5 March 1932 and 17 September 1933; to Hilda, 11 March and 29 September 1934; to his wife, 2 May 1933, NC1/26/488.
78. Chamberlain to Ida, 11 September 1938; to Hilda, 2 October 1938, 19 March 1939.
79. Hilda Chamberlain, 'Portrait', BC5/10/1, fol. 15; Crawford Diary, 9 February 1938 and 2 May 1939; Channon Diary, 19 May 1938; Dilks transcript, NC20/1, fol. 67.
80. Sir William Teeling, *Corridors of Frustration* (1970), p. 36.
81. Headlam Diary, 8 February 1926.
82. Sir Douglas Veale interview.
83. Dilks transcript, NC20/1, fol. 67; Chamberlain to Hilda, 19 October 1924.
84. John Lloyd, 'A Memory of Neville Chamberlain', *Friends' Quarterly Examiner*, January 1941, p. 80; Chamberlain to Hilda, 30 May 1937.

Chapter 3: Birmingham and National Service, 1911–August 1917

1. Leslie Scott, 'Obituary', *The Meteor* (Rugby School), 16 December 1940; F.P. Evers to Anne Chamberlain, 6 February 1941, NC11/15/54; Ida Chamberlain, 'Recollections', BC5/11/1, fol. 8.
2. Chamberlain to Alfred Greenwood, 7 October 1900, 5 June 1910, NC7/5/8, 18.
3. Chamberlain to Alfred Greenwood, 26 December 1901 and 25 April 1909, NC7/5/10, 17.
4. Chamberlain to Mary, 26 March 1911, NC1/20/1/78.
5. All Saints Ward, Election Address, October 1911, NC5/12/6.
6. Gordon Cherry, 'The Place of Neville Chamberlain in British Town Planning', in Cherry (ed.), *Shaping an Urban World* (1980), pp. 163–6.
7. Hilda Chamberlain, 'Portrait', BC5/10/1, fol. 7.
8. Jones Diary, 26 February 1937, reporting Stephen Gwynn. See also Channon Diary, 1 April 1939, reporting Lord Queensborough.
9. Chamberlain to Hilda, 3 February 1914.
10. *Birmingham Daily Post*, 28 July 1915.
11. Chamberlain to Beatrice, 21 November 1915, NC1/13/3/37; to Mary, 8 November 1915; to Mrs Endicott, 13 November 1915, NC1/20/1/97–8.
12. Chamberlain to Ida, 5 December 1915; Hilda to Neville Chamberlain, 31 July 1915, NC1/15/3/149.
13. Chamberlain to Ida, 19 December 1915; Chamberlain Diary, 25 December 1915.

14. Chamberlain to Ida, 19 December 1915, 9 January, 19 March, 29 October 1916.
15. R.H. Brazier and E. Sandford, *Birmingham and the Great War, 1914–1919* (Birmingham, 1921), pp. 214, 328–31.
16. Chamberlain interview, *Birmingham Daily Post*, 20 May 1916; George Newman Diary, 23 September and 18 October 1915, MH139/2.
17. Brazier and Sandford, *Birmingham and the Great War*, p. 288; Asa Briggs, *A History of Birmingham, Vol II: Borough and City, 1865–1938* (1952), pp. 202–3.
18. Chamberlain to Ida, 9 January and to Hilda, 29 January 1916.
19. Chamberlain to his wife, 3 March 1916, NC1/20/80.
20. John Rae, *Conscience and Politics: The British Government and the Conscientious Objector to Military Service, 1916–1919* (1970), pp. 242–5.
21. Chamberlain Diary, 16 June 1915; *Birmingham Daily Post*, 5 October 1915; Henry Carter, *The Control of the Drink Trade: A Contribution to National Efficiency, 1915–1917* (1918), pp. 113–14.
22. Richard Cross to Lloyd George, 30 May 1915, Lloyd George MSS D/20/1/6; Chamberlain to his wife, 28 May 1915, NC1/26/64.
23. Chamberlain to Ida, 19 December 1915 and 9 January 1916.
24. A. Shadwell, *Drink in 1914–1922: A Lesson in Control* (1923), pp. 95, 102–3; Chamberlain to Ida, 1 and 15 October 1916.
25. Brazier and Sandford, *Birmingham and the Great War*, pp.303-5.
26. Trevor Wilson, *The Myriad Faces of War: Britain and the Great War, 1914–1918* (Cambridge, 1988), pp. 390–93, 510.
27. Chamberlain to Ida, 5 February 1916; to Hilda, 12 February 1916; *Birmingham Daily Post*, 15 February 1916.
28. See J.P. Hilton, *Britain's First Municipal Savings Bank: The Romance of a Great Achievement* (1927) for the 'official' history of the Bank.
29. Chamberlain to Hilda, 28 November 1915; to Ida, 5 December 1915.
30. Chamberlain to Ida, 23 April 1916.
31. Chamberlain to Hilda, 14 May 1916.
32. Chamberlain to Hilda, 29 April and 25 June 1916; to Ida, 21 May 1916.
33. Chamberlain to Hilda, 22 October 1916.
34. Brazier and Sandford, *Birmingham and the Great War*, pp. 275–6.
35. Chamberlain to Ida, 19 March 1916; to Hilda, 14 June 1924.
36. Chamberlain to Beatrice, 24 March 1916, NC1/13/3/39.
37. Thomas Beecham, *A Mingled Chime: Leaves from an Autobiography* (1944), pp. 67, 110, 152–5; Chamberlain to Hilda, 2 September 1916; to H.M. Stevenson, 20 December 1917, NC5/9/11; Briggs, *History of Birmingham*, II, p. 318.
38. *Sunday Chronicle*, 23 April 1916; *Birmingham Daily Mail*, 19 July 1916.
39. Chamberlain to Hilda, 22 October 1916.
40. Brazier and Sandford, *Birmingham and the Great War*, p. 288; Briggs, *History of Birmingham*, II, pp. 202–3.
41. Chamberlain to Hilda, 26 February 1916.
42. Briggs, *History of Birmingham*, II, p. 224.
43. See the press reports in NC5/9/44-6. Also Chamberlain to J. Hilton (Garton Foundation), 13 and 23 September 1916, NC7/11/9/6, 8.
44. Chamberlain to Beatrice, 24 March 1916, NC1/13/3/39.

45. Chamberlain to Beatrice, 10 September 1916, NC1/13/3/40.
46. Chamberlain to his wife, 3 January 1917, NC1/26/97.
47. Macleod, *Neville Chamberlain*, p.53; Milner to Chamberlain, n.d., NC7/11/9/11.
48. Chamberlain to Ida, 19 December 1915; to Hilda, 3 December 1916.
49. Chamberlain to Ida, 21 May and 2 July 1916.
50. Chamberlain to Hilda, 3 December 1916; Dilks transcript, NC20/1, fol. 65.
51. Chamberlain to his wife, 3 June 1915, NC1/26/66.
52. Chamberlain to Ida, 24 October 1915; to Hilda, 25 March 1916.
53. Chamberlain to Ida, 24 March 1910; to Hilda, 21 February 1914.
54. Chamberlain to Hilda, 25 March, 14 May; to Ida, 16 July and 15 October 1916.
55. Neville Chamberlain to Austen Chamberlain, 13 December 1916, AC15/3/9; to Ida, 24 October 1915; to Hilda, 29 April 1916.
56. Chamberlain to Milner, 15 December 1916, Milner MSS dep. 353/189–90.
57. *Birmingham Daily Post*, 20 December 1916.
58. David French, *British Economic and Strategic Planning, 1905–1915* (1982), Chapter 5.
59. John Turner, *British Politics and the Great War: Coalition and Conflict 1915–1918* (New Haven and London, 1992), Chapter 3.
60. Austen Chamberlain to Hilda, 21 and 24 December 1916, AC5/1/4–5.
61. *H.C. Debs*, 5s, 88, col 1353, 19 December 1916.
62. Chamberlain to Norman, 7 January 1917, NC/7/1/18/2/10.
63. Ida and Hilda to Chamberlain, 20 December 1916, NC18/2/45–6.
64. Chamberlain to Mary, 19 December 1916, NC1/20/1/107; to Norman, 7 January 1917; to Ida, 24 December 1916.
65. Chamberlain to Mary, 19 December 1916, NC1/20/1/107.
66. Sir Almeric Fitzroy Diary, 22 August 1917.
67. Chamberlain speech to the Grand Committee of the Birmingham Liberal Unionist Association, 18 December 1917, NC8/5/5/3.
68. Chamberlain to Hilda, 31 December 1916.
69. Austen Chamberlain to Hilda, 21 December 1916, AC5/1/4.
70. Violet Markham to C.P. Scott, 19 August 1917; Markham to May Tennant, 7 June 1917, Markham MSS 4/5–6.
71. J. Jeffrey to Markham 19 August 1917, Markham MSS 4/9.
72. Chamberlain to Ida, 15 October 1916.
73. Chamberlain to Ida, 25 May 1916; to Hilda, 5 November 1916; to Lloyd George, 27 January 1917, Lloyd George MSS F/7/1/3.
74. Amery Diary, 14 February 1917.
75. Lloyd George, *War Memoirs*, III, p. 1368. Also Sylvester Diary, 18 March and 13 September 1938.
76. Addison Diary, 23, 27, 30 December 1916, Addison MSS, dep. c.2. fol. 244, 247, 253; Chamberlain to Lloyd George, 25 December 1916, Lloyd George MSS F7/1/10; to his wife, 28 December 1916, NC1/26/93.
77. Macleod, *Neville Chamberlain*, pp. 61, 62–3; Walker-Smith, *Neville Chamberlain*, p. 95; John Grigg, *Lloyd George: War Leader 1916–1918* (2003), pp. 211–12.

78. Chamberlain to Hilda, 24 December 1916; to his wife, 9 January 1917, NC1//26/100.
79. Chamberlain to Ida, 24 December and to Hilda, 31 December 1916.
80. Chamberlain to his wife, 14 June 1915, NC1/26/70; 'Neville Chamberlain on the need for Service', *The Times*, 1 June 1915.
81. Chamberlain to his wife, 28 December 1916 and 1 January 1917, NC1/26/94–5.
82. Lloyd George, *War Memoirs*, III, p. 1368.
83. Chamberlain to Norman, 7 January 1917, NC1/18/2/10.
84. Amery, *My Political Life*, II, p. 100; Thomas Jones to Violet Markham, 5 September 1940, Jones (ed.), *Diary with Letters*, p. 470; Amery Diary, 26 October 1932; Sylvester Diary, 27 April 1937 and 3 September 1939.
85. Lord Riddell Diary, 14 January 1917; Hankey Diary, 12, 14, 18 January 1917, HNKY1/1; C.P. Scott Diary, 28 January 1917.
86. Simon, *Retrospect*, p. 278.
87. Riddell Diary, 13 August 1917.
88. *H.C. Debs*, 5s, 88, col 1353, 19 December 1916.
89. French, *British Economic and Strategic Planning*, pp. 153–5.
90. Chamberlain to Ida, 9 January 1916 and 5 April 1925; Hilda Chamberlain 'Portrait', fol. 16.
91. Addison Diary, 28 December 1916 and 6 January 1917, Addison MSS dep. c.2. fol. 248–9 and dep. d.3. fol. 3; Riddell Diary, 13 January 1917.
92. Chamberlain to Amery, 12 August 1917, NC7/2/30.
93. Chamberlain to Norman, 7 January 1917 and to Hilda, 14 January 1917. Also Fitzroy Diary, 20 April 1917; Chamberlain to Amery, 12 August 1917, NC7/2/30.
94. Arthur Collins, 'The History of National Service', n.d., NC8/5/4/1; War Cabinet 31(17)3, 10 January 1917, CAB 23/1.
95. Hankey Diary, 12 and 14 January 1917, HNKY1/1.
96. Chamberlain to his wife, 2 January 1917, NC1/26/96.
97. NSR.1, Report of the Director-General on his Proposed Organisation, 13 January 1917, NATS1/71; Addison Diary, 19 January 1917, fol. 27.
98. Chamberlain to Ida, 21 January 1917.
99. NSR. 2, Second Report of the Director-General to the War Cabinet, 3 February 1917, NATS1/71; CAB 55(17)1 and Appendix 1–2, 19 January 1917, CAB 23/1.
100. *Birmingham Daily Post*, 22 January 1917; Minutes of National Service Meeting, Central Hall, 6 February 1917, NATS 1/1114.
101. 'Proceedings of Conference at St. Ermin's Hotel', 26 January 1917, NATS 1/1114.
102. Chamberlain to Hilda, 10 February 1917.
103. Unsigned memorandum, 5 April 1917, NC8/5/4/11; Keith Grieves, *The Politics of Manpower, 1914–1918* (Manchester, 1988), pp. 109–14.
104. Hankey Diary, 18 February 1917. But see the compliments in Strachey to Chamberlain, 16 March 1917, Strachey MSS 4/7/3.
105. Lloyd George to Chamberlain, 20 and 24 February 1917, NC8/5/2/19–20; *Sunday Times*, 27 May 1917; Lloyd George, *War Memoirs*, III, p. 1369.
106. Chamberlain to Hilda, 22 July 1917.
107. Markham, *Return Passage*, pp. 150–51.

108. Milner Diary 31 March, 7, 8 April, 4 May 1917, Milner MSS dep. 88; Milner to Markham, 8 April 1917, Markham MSS 4/9; Arthur Henderson to Lloyd George, 19 March 1917, Lloyd George MSS F/27/3/11.

109. Milner to Bonar Law, 28 June 1917, Law MSS BL82/1/22; Riddell Diary 14 January 1917.

110. Chamberlain to his wife, 1 January 1917, NC1/26/95.

111. Grieves, *The Politics of Manpower*, pp. 74, 100–101. Markham to Tennant, 7 June and 17 July 1917, Markham MSS 4/5.

112. Addison Diary, 9 and 12 March 1917; Addison to Milner, 6 March 1917, Addison MSS dep. d.3. fol. 109, 112.

113. Addison Diary, 8 March, 5, 12, 18, 19, 24 April 1917 and Addison to Milner, Henderson and Lloyd George, 24 April 1917, Addison MSS dep. d.3. fol. 147, 153, 171, 184, 198–205.

114. Chamberlain memorandum to Milner and Henderson, 31 March 1917, NATS 1/59; Cecil Harmsworth to Lloyd George, 28 June 1917, Lloyd George MSS F/7/29/5.

115. J. Hodge, *Workman's Cottage to Windsor Castle* (1931), pp. 199–200; CAB 55(17)1, 19 January 1917, CAB 23/1; Markham to Tennant, 18 July 1917 reporting Milner, Markham MSS 4/5.

116. Markham to Jeffreys, 10 August; to Lord Derby, 19 August 1917; to Milner, 26 July 1917, Markham MSS 4/6 and 4/9; Chamberlain to Hilda, 31 March and 14 April 1917. See also the cuttings in Rey MSS 1/3/40.

117. Chamberlain to Hilda, 10 February and 17 March 1917; to Ida 21 January and 4 March 1917; Chamberlain Diary, 16 January 1917.

118. Chamberlain to Ida, 8 April 1917; Violet Markham, 'Memo on New Proposals for dealing with National Service Volunteers', 11 April 1917, Markham MSS 4/5; Bridgeman Diary, February 1918; Addison Diary, 18 April 1917.

119. Chamberlain to Hilda, 27 May and 17 June 1917.

120. Markham to Jeffrey, 30 June 1917, Markham MSS 4/5.

121. Hiley to Chamberlain 24 May and reply NC8/5/2/12–15; *Sunday Times*, 27 May 1917, NC8/5/2/15.

122. Markham to Tennant, 7 June 1917, Markham MSS Box 19; Milner Diary, 14 July 1917.

123. Tenth Report of the Director General to the War Cabinet, 22 June 1917, NATS1/71.

124. Chamberlain to Hilda, 1 July 1917.

125. Hankey Diary, 11 and 12 January, 1 and 18 March 1917, HNKY1/1; Markham to Tennant, 18 July 1917; Milner to Markham, 27 July 1917, Markham MSS 4/9.

126. Chamberlain to Hilda, 1 July 1917; to Lloyd George, 29 June and reply, 3 July 1917, NC8/5/2/24–5.

127. Chamberlain to Ida, 9 July 1917; to Lloyd George, 19 July 1917, Lloyd George MSS F/7/1/11.

128. Lloyd George to Chamberlain, 20 July and replies, 21 and 27 July 1917, NC8/5/2/28–30.

129. Milner to Markham, 17 July 1917, Markham MSS 4/9; Derby to Lloyd George, 25 July 1917, Lloyd George MSS F/14/4/59.

130. Chamberlain to Lloyd George, 8 August 1917, Lloyd George MSS F/7/1/13; Chamberlain Diary, 7–9 August 1917, NC8/5/4/17; Chamberlain to Hilda, 12 August 1917.
131. K.O. Morgan, *Lloyd George Family Letters, 1885–1936* (Cardiff and London, 1973), p. 185.
132. Markham to Tennant, 17 August 1917, Markham MSS 4/6.
133. Stephen Walsh to Chamberlain, 10 August 1917. Also letters from Beck, Fawcett, Hewett and Taylor, NC8/5/3/2, 7, 9, 15.
134. Chamberlain to Ida, 19 August 1917.
135. Turner, *British Politics and the Great War*, p. 166.
136. Christopher Addison, *Politics from Within* (2 vols, 1924), II, pp. 119, 170.
137. Almeric Fitzroy Diary, 22 August 1917; Milner to Markham, 6 August 1917, Markham MSS 4/9.
138. Gerard De Groot, *Blighty: British Society in the Era of the Great War* (1996), p. 101.
139. *H.C. Debs*, 5s, 90, col 1890–91, 27 February 1917 (Tyson Wilson).
140. D.R. Woodward, 'Did Lloyd George Starve the British Army of Men Prior to the German Offensive of March 1918?', *Historical Journal*, 27 (1984), pp. 250–51.
141. Chamberlain Diary, 28 January 1935; Chamberlain to Hilda, 13 March 1920; to Amery, 12 August 1918, NC7/2/30.
142. Chamberlain to Hilda, 4 June 1921 and 4 August 1930; to Ida, 7 January 1922.
143. Markham, *Return Passage*, pp. 150, 152; John Grigg, *Lloyd George: War Leader* (2002), p. 212; Amery, *My Political Life*, II, p. 101; Swinton, *Sixty Years of Power*, p. 113.

Chapter 4: The Frustrated Backbencher, August 1917–October 1922

1. Chamberlain to Norman, 7 January 1917, NC1/18/2/10.
2. Chamberlain to Hilda, 1 July 1917.
3. Chamberlain to Charles Vince, 22 August 1917, NC5/10/2.
4. Chamberlain to Mary, 14 August 1917, NC1/20/1/111; to Hilda, 7 October 1917.
5. Chamberlain to Ida, 19 August and 17 October 1917.
6. *H.C. Debs*, 5s, 101, col. 78, 14 January 1918.
7. *Birmingham Liberal Unionist Association: Speeches Addressed to the Grand Committee*, 18 December 1917, NC8/5/5/3; Austen Chamberlain to Hilda, 19 December 1917, AC5/1/51.
8. Chamberlain to Ida, 22 December 1917; Chamberlain Diary, 25 December 1917.
9. Chamberlain to Hilda, 29 December 1917 and 8 June 1918.
10. Chamberlain to Amery, 12 January 1913, NC7/2/14.
11. Chamberlain to Hilda, 27 August and 21 October 1917; to Mary, 14 August 1918, NC1/20/1/111.
12. Chamberlain to Vince, 22 August 1917, NC5/10/2.
13. Hilda to Chamberlain, 24 August and reply, 27 August 1917.
14. *Birmingham Daily Post*, 7 September and *Birmingham Daily Mail*, 17 November 1917.

15. A.H. Stephenson and Vince to Chamberlain, 6–7 September 1917, NC5/10/3–4.
16. Austen Chamberlain to Neville Chamberlain, 30 August, 12 and 24 September, 19 and 23 December 1917, NC1/27/9–10, 12, 17–18.
17. Chamberlain to Hilda, 3 November, 15 December 1917, 17 January 1918; Chamberlain Diary, 17 December 1917.
18. Chamberlain to Bonar Law, 8 September and 14 November 1913, Law MSS 30/2/9 and 30/4/34.
19. Sir Frank Lowe to Chamberlain, 10 December 1917; 'Supplementary Report …', 22 January 1918, NC5/10/5, 11.
20. Chamberlain to Hilda, 3 August 1918. Also Birmingham Conservative and Unionist Association Minutes, 7 August 1918.
21. Harry Pratt to Chamberlain, 8 March 1932, NC7/11/25/28.
22. Neville Chamberlain to Austen Chamberlain, 9 October 1917, AC35/1/28; to Hilda, 17 November 1917.
23. Chamberlain to Sir Arthur Steel-Maitland, 19 June 1918, Steel-Maitland MSS GD193/274.
24. Chamberlain to Ida, 29 June 1918.
25. Midland Union, General Purposes Sub-Committee, 28 June 1918 (Conservative Party Archive); Bayford Diary, 3 March, 9 June, 14 July 1918; Chamberlain to Ida, 16 February 1918.
26. Chamberlain to his wife, 21 July 1918, NC1/26/146; Midland Union, Executive Committee Minutes, 19, 28 June, 25 October 1918 and 28 April 1919.
27. Chamberlain to Ida, 29 June 1918.
28. Chamberlain, 'Introduction' to W. Haywood, *The Development of Birmingham: An Essay with Designs* (Birmingham, 1918), pp. 13–17.
29. Chamberlain to Ida, 2 June 1918.
30. Chamberlain to Hilda, 23 June 1918.
31. William Ashley to Chamberlain, 8 September 1919 and 8 March 1920; T.S. Ashton to Chamberlain, 23 May 1920, NC5/8/1/6–9.
32. Chamberlain to Hilda, 22 September 1923; to Gilbert Barling, 10 May and 12 September 1923, NC5/8/1/12–13.
33. Neville Chamberlain to Austen Chamberlain, 21 September 1918, AC36/1/26.
34. Chamberlain to Ida, 6 May, 24 November 1917 and 18 May 1918.
35. Chamberlain to Ida, 8 December 1917, 9 and 16 February 1918; to Hilda, 23 February 1918; Chamberlain Diary, 10 and 27 February 1918.
36. Chamberlain, *Norman Chamberlain: A Memoir* (1923).
37. Chamberlain Diary, 22 November 1918.
38. Chamberlain to Ida, 1 December 1918.
39. Lloyd George and Bonar Law to Chamberlain, 20 November 1918, NC5/12/7. This is marked 'Not Used'.
40. 'To the Electors of Ladywood Division 1918', NC5/10/79; 'A Word to the Ladies!', NC18/1/38.
41. J.W. Kneeshaw Election Address, 1918, NC5/12/10.
42. John Maynard Keynes, *The Economic Consequence of the Peace* (1920) p. 133.
43. K.W.D. Rolf, 'Tories, Tariffs and Elections. The West Midlands in English

Politics, 1918–1935', (Unpublished D.Phil thesis, Cambridge University, 1974), pp. 277–83.

44. Austen Chamberlain to Neville Chamberlain, 26 August 1917, NC1/27/8.
45. Chamberlain to Ida, 23 February 1919; to Hilda, 15 March 1919; to his wife, 12 March 1919, NC1/26/165.
46. Chamberlain to Hilda, 3 July 1920 and 26 March 1922; to Ida, 30 April 1922 and 26 October 1924.
47. Chamberlain to Hilda, 23 August 1919.
48. 'Mr Chamberlain's Work in Parliament', n.d. [possibly 1921], NC5/10/39.
49. Chamberlain to Hilda, 8 November 1919 and 19 June 1920.
50. Chamberlain to J. Hilton (Garton Foundation), 13, 23 September 1916, NC7/11/9/6, 8.
51. Committee on Inland Waterways; Second Interim Report, paras 8–14, NC8/2/28.
52. Chamberlain to Ida, 16 November 1918.
53. Cherry, 'The Place of Neville Chamberlain in British Town Planning', pp. 168–75; Gerald Rhodes, *The Government of London: The Struggle for Reform* (1970), pp. 5–6.
54. Chamberlain to Ida, 14 December 1917; to Hilda, 13 April 1919; Unhealthy Areas Committee: Second and Final Report, April 1921, NC8/6/2.
55. For details see J.P. Hilton, 'Municipal Banks', *Municipal Journal*, 16 January 1920, NC5/2/30.
56. *Annual Report*, 1943, NC5/2/72; Dilks, *Neville Chamberlain*, p. 488.
57. Sir John Bradbury to Chamberlain, 21 July and reply 23 July 1927, NC7/11/20/12-13.
58. Hilda Chamberlain 'Review of Feiling', 1946, BC5/12/1; Chamberlain to Hilda, 16 June 1923.
59. Ladywood Unionist Association, Annual Report, 1921–22 and 1922–23.
60. Ladywood Women's Unionist Association Minutes, 28 February and 11 April 1919; Ladywood Unionist Association, Annual Report, 1919–20 and 1921–22.
61. Chamberlain to Ida, 7 January and to Hilda, 29 January 1922.
62. BCUA, Minutes for 28 May, 9, 26 July, 15 October 1920, 8 April 1921.
63. Midland Union, General Purposes Committee, 17 June, 16 September 1921 and 9 January 1922, Vol I, pp. 159–60, 182.
64. Chamberlain Diary, Christmas Day, 1919.
65. 'Mr Chamberlain's Work in Parliament', n.d., NC5/10/39; Chamberlain to Hilda, 20 November 1920.
66. Chamberlain Diary, 27 December 1919; to Hilda, 23 August 1919.
67. D.H. Close, 'The Growth of Backbench Organisation in the Conservative Party', *Parliamentary Affairs*, 27.4 (Autumn 1974), pp. 375–9; 'Mr Chamberlain's Work in Parliament', NC5/10/39.
68. Bayford Diary, 31 March 1920; George Terrell to Bonar Law, 16 March 1920, Law MSS 98/8/9.
69. Chamberlain to Hilda, 13 March 1920; to Bonar Law, 13 March 1920, Law MSS 98/8/8.
70. Neville Chamberlain to Austen Chamberlain, 28 June 1917, AC35/1/25;

speech to Birmingham Liberal Unionist Association, 18 December 1917, NC8/5/5/3.

71. Chamberlain to Hilda, 7 December 1918.
72. Chamberlain to Ida, 26 June 1920.
73. Chamberlain to Hilda, 23 November 1919.
74. Chamberlain to Hilda, 29 February and to Ida, 22 May 1920; Chamberlain Diary, Christmas Day, 1919.
75. Lord Robert Cecil to Steel-Maitland, 15 September 1921 and 'List of People to whom Memorandum ... was sent', 28 February 1922, Steel-Maitland MSS GD193/276/3–4, 110–11.
76. Chamberlain Diary, 27 December 1920.
77. Chamberlain to Ida, 19 March 1921; to Hilda, 31 July 1921.
78. Chamberlain to Hilda, 15 January, 12 February 1921; to Ida, 19 March 1921.
79. Chamberlain Diary, 31 December 1921.
80. Neville Chamberlain to Austen Chamberlain (and memorandum), 29 December 1921, AC32/2/13–14. The latter is also in Lloyd George MSS F/7/5/1.
81. Chamberlain to Hilda, 14 January and to Ida, 21 January 1922; Midland Union Executive Minutes, 9 January 1922; BCUA Minutes, 14 July 1922.
82. Chamberlain to Hilda, 14 January 1922; to Ida, 4 and 18 March 1922.
83. Chamberlain to Hilda, 12 February 1922.
84. Chamberlain to Hilda, 4 January 1919; to Ida, 16 November 1918, 23 February 1919 and 23 January 1921.
85. Chamberlain to Ida, 1 April 1922.
86. Chamberlain Diary, 4 September 1922.
87. Chamberlain to Hilda, 24 September 1922.
88. Chamberlain to Hilda, 24 October 1922; Chamberlain Diary, 22 October 1922.
89. Amery to Bonar Law, 31 October 1922, Law MSS 108/1/28.
90. Chamberlain to Hilda, 31 October 1922; Amery Diary, misdated 25 October 1922.
91. Chamberlain Diary, 19 November 1922 and 'The Unionist Government under Bonar Law'.
92. Austen Chamberlain to Hilda, 4 March and 29 August; to Ida, 10 March 1923, AC5/1/267–8, 287; to Neville Chamberlain, 28 and 30 August 1923, NC1/27/73–4A; Chamberlain to Hilda, 9 September 1923.
93. Amery Diary, 19 October 1922; Amery to Bonar Law, 31 October 1922; Edward Goulding to Law, 20 October 1922, Law MSS 108/1/13, 28.
94. Chamberlain to Bonar Law, 31 October 1922, Law MSS 109/2/11a.
95. Maurice Cowling, *The Impact of Labour 1920-1924: The Beginning of Modern British Politics* (Cambridge, 1971), p. 296.
96. Bonar Law to Chamberlain, 1 November 1922, NC7/11/15/10. Also Chamberlain to Ida, 22 November 1930, NC18/1/718.
97. Ladywood Minute Books 2–3, NC5/11/1–2; Chamberlain to Ida, 11 November 1922.
98. Austen Chamberlain to Ida, 18 November 1922, AC5/1/250.
99. BCUA: Central Committee Minutes, 2 December 1921, 17 March 1922 and 13 April 1923; Ladywood Unionist Association: Annual Report, 1921–22, p. 16.

100.   Chamberlain to Ida, 7 January 1922.

Chapter 5: A Rising Star, October 1922–October 1924

1. Cuthbert Headlam Diary, 20 October 1922, Headlam MSS D/He/18/ 297.
2. Chamberlain to Ida, 11 November 1922.
3. Chamberlain to Hilda, 27 January and 11 March 1923.
4. Chamberlain to Bonar Law, n.d., Law MSS 113/3/3; Asa Briggs, *A History of Broadcasting in the United Kingdom, Volume I, The Birth of Broadcasting* (1961), pp. 148–50.
5. Chamberlain to his wife, 23 January 1923, NC1/26/313; Chamberlain Diary, 28 February 1923; CAB 13(23)1, 28 February 1923, CAB 23/45.
6. Thomas Jones, *A Diary with Letters 1931–1950* (1954), p. xxviii.
7. Chamberlain to Ida, 19 March 1921; to Hilda, 13 March 1920; to Bonar Law, 31 October 1922, Law MSS 109/2/11a.
8. Chamberlain Diary, 'The Unionist Government under Bonar Law' and 26 January 1923; Chamberlain to Hilda, 13 and 27 January 1923.
9. Robert Blake, *The Unknown Prime Minister: The Life and Times of Andrew Bonar Law, 1858–1923* (1955), p. 518.
10. Chamberlain Diary, 23 November 1930, reporting Lord Beaverbrook.
11. Chamberlain to Mary, 10 March 1923, NC1/20/1/122.
12. Chamberlain to his wife, 23 January 1923, NC1/26/313; Chamberlain Diary, 26 January 1923.
13. Chamberlain to Hilda, 27 January and 11 March 1923; to his sisters, 8 March 1923.
14. Chamberlain to Mary, 10 March 1923, NC1/20/1/122; to Sir Gilbert Barling, 13 March 1923, NC Letters Additional 2.
15. Onslow, *Sixty-Three Years*, p. 181.
16. Marion Bowley, *Housing and the State, 1919–1944* (1945), pp. 10–13, 24–5.
17. Walker-Smith, *Neville Chamberlain*, p. 138.
18. Chamberlain to Hilda, 11 March 1923.
19. Ibid.; to Ida, 17 March 1923; to Mary, 10 March 1923, NC1/20/1/122.
20. Chamberlain to his wife, 8 January 1923, NC1/26/309.
21. H(23) 1st Conclusions of Cabinet Housing Committee, 8 December 1922, CAB 27/208; CP 8(23), 8 January 1923, CAB 24/158.
22. Chamberlain Diary and CAB 3(23)2, both 26 January 1923, CAB 23/45.
23. *H.C. Debs*, 5s, 163, col. 303–22, 24 April 1923.
24. CP 110(23) and CP 133(23), 19 and 28 February 1923, CAB 24/158–9.
25. *H.C. Debs*, 5s, 163, col 325–32, 24 April 1923 (Wheatley); Chamberlain to his wife, 22 January 1923, NC1/26/312.
26. Chamberlain to Ida, 17 March 1923; CAB 15(23)7, 14 March and CAB 17(23)9, 28 March 1923, CAB 23/45.
27. *Times Housing Supplement*, May 1920; Hilda Chamberlain, 'Review of Feiling 1946', BC5/12/1.
28. Chamberlain to Hilda, 17 October 1925.
29. CAB 12(23)1, 24 February 1923, CAB 23/45.
30. Chamberlain Diary, 9 March 1923.
31. Chamberlain to Ida, 18 February, 17 March 1923.

32. George Newman Diary, 7, 11–12 May 1923, MH139/4; Sir George Newman, *The Building of a Nation's Health* (1939), p. 51.
33. Austen Chamberlain to Hilda, 9 June 1923, AC5/1/272.
34. Chamberlain to Ida, 9 June 1923; Bayford Diary 29 April and 9 June 1923.
35. Chamberlain to his wife, 12 March 1919, NC1/26/165.
36. Chamberlain to Ida, 26 May 1923; to Mary, 8 September 1923, NC1/20/1/125.
37. Baldwin to Chamberlain, 14 August and reply, 16 August 1923, NC7/11/16/3–4.
38. Baldwin to Chamberlain, telegram, n.d., NC7/11/16/5.
39. Chamberlain to Mary, 8 September 1923, NC1/20/1/125; to Hilda, 26 August 1923; Chamberlain Diary, 17 September 1923.
40. E. Sandford Fawcett to Chamberlain, 3 September 1923, NC8/7/22.
41. Chamberlain to Hilda and Diary, both 19 May 1923.
42. Baldwin to Chamberlain, 4 May 1923, NC7/11/16/2; Chamberlain Diary, 6 and 23 May 1923.
43. Lord Curzon to Chamberlain, 27 August 1923, NC8/7/17.
44. Chamberlain to Mary, 8 September 1923, NC1/20/1/125; Sir Arthur Robinson to Chamberlain, 28 August 1923. See also letters from Aubrey Symonds and Douglas Veale, 25 and 27 August 1923, NC8/7/48, 55, 59.
45. Chamberlain to Mary, 8 September 1923, NC1/20/1/125.
46. Baldwin to Lord Derby, 17 August 1923, Baldwin MSS 3/92–6; Chamberlain at Birmingham, 13 October 1923, *Gleanings and Memoranda*, November 1923, p. 453.
47. Curzon to his wife, 18 November 1923, Marchioness Curzon, *Reminiscences* (1955), p. 191; Crawford Diary, 8 December 1923 and 8 January 1924.
48. Herbert Gladstone to Donald Maclean, 12 January 1924, Gladstone MSS 46474/64.
49. Derby Diary, 14 November 1924.
50. David Dilks, *Neville Chamberlain*, p. 339.
51. Amery Diary, and to Chamberlain, both 30 August 1923, NC8/7/3.
52. See Robert Self, *Tories and Tariffs: The Conservative Party and the Politics of Tariff Reform, 1922–1932* (New York and London, 1986), pp. 79–110.
53. Chamberlain to Hilda, 6 October 1923.
54. Chamberlain Diary, 10 October 1923.
55. Baldwin to Chamberlain, 11 August 1923, NC11/16/3; Chamberlain Diary, 24 August 1923.
56. Amery Diary, 14 October and 10 November 1923.
57. Chamberlain to Hilda, 21 October; Chamberlain Diary, 26 October 1923.
58. CAB 50(23)4 and CAB 51(23)3, 23 and 29 October 1923; Derby Diary, 14 November 1923.
59. Chamberlain to Austen Chamberlain, 23 October 1923, AC35/3/10.
60. Austen Chamberlain to Lord Lee, 14 December 1923, AC35/3/18.
61. Chamberlain to Ida and Diary, both 26 October 1923.
62. Dilks, *Neville Chamberlain*, pp. 346–7; Chamberlain Diary, 26 October 1923.
63. Chamberlain Diary, 26 October 1923; *The Times*, 27 October 1923. See also Derby Diary, 14 November 1923, reporting Geddes.

64. Chamberlain Election Address and handbill, December 1923, NC5/12/24–5.
65. BCUA: Report of Management Committee, 15 February 1924, Vol. III, pp. 155–8.
66. Chamberlain to Baldwin, 3 December 1923, Baldwin MSS 159/42; Chamberlain Diary, 9 December 1923.
67. Ibid.; Chamberlain to Hannon, 11 December 1923, Hannon MSS 17/1; BCUA: Special Meeting of Management Committee, 21 December 1923.
68. Chamberlain Diary, 13 and 18 January 1924; Chamberlain to Hilda, 18 May and to Ida, 7 June 1924.
69. Amery to Baldwin, 21 December 1923, Baldwin MSS 42/150; Chamberlain to Ida, 23 December 1923.
70. Lord Midleton to Salisbury, 8 January 1924, Salisbury MSS 108/30.
71. Chamberlain to Ida, 12 January and to Hilda, 24 January 1924.
72. Chamberlain Diary, 8 June 1923.
73. Austen Chamberlain to Hilda, 24 January 1924, AC5/1/304.
74. Chamberlain and Amery Diary 23–24 January and 4 February.
75. Chamberlain Diary, 6 February 1924; to Hilda, 9 February 1924; Austen Chamberlain memorandum, 7 February 1924, AC35/4/5.
76. Austen Chamberlain to Sir Samuel Hoare, 28 January 1924, Templewood MSS V. I; to Hilda, 24 January 1924, AC5/1/304.
77. Chamberlain Diary, 17 March 1924; to Hilda, 23 February and 22 March 1924.
78. Chamberlain Diary, 17 March 1924; Chamberlain to Hilda, 9 March 1924.
79. Amery Diary, 6 March 1924; Chamberlain Diary, 17 March 1924.
80. *H.C. Debs*, 5s, 171, col 2303 and 2207, 2 April and 31 March 1924.
81. *H.C. Debs*, 5s, 174, col 247–9, 27 May 1924; Chamberlain to Hilda, 1 June 1924.
82. Cowling, *The Impact of Labour*, pp. 296–7, 376.
83. *The Times*, 5 June 1924.
84. Chamberlain to Hilda, 1 and 28 June, 12 July 1924.
85. Bowley, *Housing and the State*, pp. 97–9, 129.
86. Chamberlain Diary, 6 February 1924.
87. Commons Standing Committee, Minute 8(24)6.1, 15 April 1924, Worthington-Evans MSS c.895/14.
88. L[eader's] C[onference] 3(24), Chamberlain memorandum, Worthington-Evans MSS c.895/5–8. Chamberlain to Ida, 4 May 1924.
89. *Gleanings and Memoranda*, July 1924, pp. 11–15.
90. Sir Edward Grigg to Sir Abe Bailey, 10 July 1924, Altrincham MSS; Hewins Diary, 20 June and 3 July 1924; Lord Robert Cecil to Lord Salisbury, 17 May 1924, Salisbury MSS 109/50.
91. BCUA: Management Committee Minutes, 29 December 1922.
92. Ladywood Unionist Association Minutes, 23 January 1924; Agent's Report and Annual Report, 1923–24, April 1924.
93. Chamberlain to Ida, 16 February and Hilda, 23 February 1924.
94. Chamberlain to Ida, 1 November 1924; Mosley, *My Life*, pp. 176–7.
95. Chamberlain to Ida, 11 October 1924.
96. Chamberlain to Hilda, 7 September; to Ida, 13, 27 September 1924; to John St Loe Strachey, 20 September 1924, Strachey MSS5/4/7/4.

97. Chamberlain to Hilda, 14 February 1925.
98. Chamberlain to Ida, 26 October 1924, 8 February 1925; Amery Diary, 1–3 November 1924.
99. Chamberlain Diary, 5–6 November and 1 December 1924.
100. Arthur Collins to Chamberlain, 7 November 1924, NC7/11/16/6; Chamberlain to Ida, 1 November 1924.

Chapter 6: The Ministry of Health, November 1924–May 1929

1. Chamberlain to Simon, 5 October 1940, Simon MSS 87/5. See also Chamberlain, *The Struggle for Peace* (1939), p. 210; 'Review of Feiling' by Hilda Chamberlain, 1946, BC5/12/1.
2. Chamberlain to Ida, 28 October and to Hilda, 3 November 1917.
3. Beaverbrook to R.L. Borden, 28 January 1925, Beaverbrook MSS C/51.
4. John Ramsden, *The Age of Balfour and Baldwin, 1902–1940* (1978), p. 187.
5. CP 499(24), 19 November 1924, CAB 24/168.
6. A.J.P. Taylor, *English History, 1914–1945* (1975), p. 303; Bentley B. Gilbert, *British Social Policy 1914–1939* (1970), p. 195; R. Blake, *The Conservative Party from Peel to Thatcher* (1975), p. 228; David Willetts, *Modern Conservatism* (1992), p. 135; M.A. Crowther, *Social Policy in Britain 1914–1939* (1988), p. 8.
7. Sir Douglas Veale interviews, 1969, National Sound Archives, F4381–3.
8. Anderson Committee Report appended to CP 204(25), 18 April 1925, CAB 24/173.
9. Chamberlain to Hilda, 22 March and 12 July 1924.
10. *Gleanings and Memoranda*, November 1924, p. 505; Neville Chamberlain Election Address, October 1924, NC18/1/457a.
11. Martin Gilbert, *Winston S. Churchill, Volume V, 1922–1939* (1976), pp. 77–8.
12. CAB 64(24)6, 26 November and CAB 65(24)5, 3 December 1924, CAB 23/49; Churchill to Baldwin, 28 November 1924, Baldwin MSS 7/289–90; Chamberlain Diary, 26 November 1924.
13. Chamberlain to Ida, 28 March 1925; to Hilda, 5 April 1925; Chamberlain Diary, 26 March 1925.
14. PW(25) 3rd Meeting of the Cabinet Pensions Committee, 4 April 1925, CAB 27/276.
15. CP 204(25), 18 April 1925, CAB 24/173. *H.C. Debs*, 5s, 184, col 92, 18 May 1925.
16. Baldwin to King George V, 19 May 1925, Baldwin MSS 60/451–7; Chamberlain to Hilda, 2 May; to Ida, 23 May 1925.
17. CAB 32(25)14, 1 July 1925, CAB 23/50; Chamberlain to Ida, 5 July 1925.
18. Baldwin to King George V, 2, 15, 16, 23 July, 25 November and 1 December 1925, Baldwin MSS 61/96–100, 144–8, 176–83, 290–91.
19. 'W[idows'] & O[rphans'] Insurance Scheme', Beveridge MSS IIa.
20. P.M. Williams, 'The Development of the Old-Age Pensions Policy in Great Britain, 1875–1925' (Unpublished Ph.D., London, 1970.), pp. 436, 443.
21. Hoare to Chamberlain, 23 July 1925, Templewood MSS V/3/26a.
22. CP 189(25), CP 193(25) and CP 209(25) 31 March, 2 and 22 April 1925, CAB 24/172–3.

23. CAB 23(25)7, 29 April 1925, CAB 23/50.
24. Chamberlain to Baldwin, 30 August 1925, Baldwin MSS 43/51; Chamberlain Diary, 9 August 1925.
25. CAB 50(25)6, 23 October 1925, CAB 23/51; Chamberlain to Ida, 22 November 1925.
26. Chamberlain to Ida, 17 March 1923; *H.C. Debs*, 5s, 163, col 303–22, 24 April 1923.
27. Churchill to Baldwin, 28 November 1924, Baldwin MSS 7/293.
28. See 'Lord Weir notes', n.d. Weir MSS DC96/11/10. Also W.J. Reader, *Architect of Air Power: The Life of the First Viscount Weir of Eastwood 1877–1959* (1968), pp. 117–26, and idem, *The Weir Group: A Centenary History* (1971), pp. 98–102.
29. Reader, *Architect*, p. 120; Paul Addison, 'Churchill and Social Reform' in Robert Blake and Wm. Roger Louis, *Churchill* (Oxford, 1996), p. 67.
30. Chamberlain to Ida, 19 July 1924.
31. WH(25) 1st Conclusions of the Cabinet Committee on Weir Houses, 24 February 1925, CAB 27/266; Reader, *Weir Group*, p. 100.
32. Ibid. Also Weir to Gilmour, 3 November 1925, Weir MSS DC96/11/10.
33. Weir to Chamberlain, 28 February, 1925, CAB 27/266; Chamberlain to Hilda, 21 February 1925; CP 132(25), 3 March 1925, CAB 24/172.
34. Chamberlain to Ida, 23 September 1925; CP 411(25), 28 September 1925, CAB 24/175; CAB 47(25)5, 7 October 1923, CAB 23/51.
35. CAB 52(25)8, 11 November 1925 and CAB 60(25)1, 18 December 1925, CAB 23/51.
36. Chamberlain to Ida, 23 September; to Hilda, 14 November 1925.
37. Weir to Gilmour, 3 November 1925; to Baldwin, 11 February 1926, Weir MSS DC96/11/10.
38. CP 290(26), 27 July and CP 357(26), 21 October 1926; CP 64(28), 28 February 1928, CAB 24/180–81, 193.
39. Chamberlain to Ida, 23 May 1925.
40. Chamberlain Diary, 22 January 1926; CAB 1(26)1, 19 January 1926, CAB 23/53; CP 30(26), February 1926, CAB 24/278.
41. For these activities see MH80/7–9.
42. Chamberlain to Hilda, 18 April, 13, 20 June 1926; Hugh Dalton, *Call Back Yesterday: Memoirs 1887–1931* (1953), pp. 160–61.
43. Chamberlain Diary, 28 March 1926.
44. M.A. Crowther, *The Workhouse System, 1834–1929* (1981), p. 106.
45. Chamberlain Diary, 2 August 1925 and 3 May 1926; Chamberlain to Mrs Endicott, 17 May 1926, NC7/11/19/13.
46. Chamberlain Diary, 16 March and 16 June 1927; Chamberlain to Baldwin, 8 March 1927, NC7/11/20/7.
47. Hilda Chamberlain, 'Review of Feiling', 1946, BC5/12/1; Sir Douglas Veale interview.
48. Baldwin to King George V, 6, 10 July, 3 December 1926, Baldwin MSS 61/385, 423 and 62/79–80; M. Epstein (ed.), *The Annual Register, 1926*, pp. 40–41.
49. Chamberlain to Ida, 13 and 27 March 1926.
50. Baldwin to King George V, 9 and 13 July 1926, Baldwin MSS 61/410, 432. Austen Chamberlain to Neville Chamberlain, 13 July 1926, NC1/27/92.

51. *Clement Attlee: The Granada Historical Records Interviews*, p. 17.
52. Chamberlain to Ida, 19 June 1927; to Hilda, 3 April 1927.
53. Pat Thane, *Foundations of the Welfare State* (1996), pp. 31–7, 66–79.
54. Gilbert, *British Social Policy*, pp. 196, 204, 210–12; Clive Unsworth, *The Politics of Mental Health Legislation* (Oxford, 1987), pp. 236–7; Crowther, *The Workhouse System*, p. 102.
55. Dilks, *Neville Chamberlain*, p. 493.
56. Sir Douglas Veale interview.
57. Jones Diary, 2 December 1927.
58. CP 266(23), 6 June 1923, CAB 24/160.
59. Chamberlain to Ida, 10 October and 22 November 1925.
60. See Home Affairs Committee, HA 20(26) 'Guardians (Default) Bill', 24 June 1926, CAB 26/8. For the issue generally see Alan Deacon and Eric Briggs, 'Local Democracy and Central Policy: The Issue of Pauper Votes in the 1920s', *Policy and Politics*, 2 (1974), pp. 353, 355, 358–64.
61. Sidney and Beatrice Webb, *English Poor Law History: Part II: The Last Hundred Years* (1929), pp. 926–9. See also MH 68/81–5 for West Ham.
62. CP 379(25), 3 August 1925, CAB 24/174 and CAB 43(25)7, 5 August 1925, CAB 23/50.
63. Chamberlain to his wife, 29 September 1925, NC1/26/356.
64. CP 468(25), 11 November 1925; CP 158(26), 19 April 1926, CAB 24/175, 179.
65. Chamberlain to Hilda, 28 November 1925; CP 50(26), 9 February 1926, CAB 24/178.
66. Chamberlain Diary, 28 March 1926; CP 182(26), 30 April 1926 and CP 74(28), 12 March 1928, CAB 24/193, CAB 24/179, 193.
67. CAB 40(26)1, 42(26)7 and 43(26)13 dated 16, 23 and 30 June 1926, CAB 23/53.
68. For Chester-le-Street and Bedwellty see MH 79/264–6.
69. Webb, *English Poor Law*, pp. 929, 934–45; Gilbert, *British Social Policy*, p. 222.
70. Chamberlain to Ida, 4 December 1927; Sir Douglas Veale interview.
71. DAC (28) 1st Meeting of Cabinet Committee on Distressed Areas, 14 December 1928 and Chamberlain's 'Distress in Coalfields', 13 December 1928, CAB 27/381.
72. Chamberlain memorandum, 29 December 1921, AC32/2/14; CP 499(24), 19 November 1924.
73. CP 219(25), 4 April 1925, CAB 24/173.
74. Chamberlain to Ida, 14 March 1925; VPC(25) 6th Conclusions of the Valuation, Rating and Poor Law Reform Committee, 28 April 1925; Paper VPC(25)12, March 1925, CAB 27/263.
75. CAB 25(25)1, 13 May 1925 and CAB 50(25)9, 23 October 1925, CAB 23/50–51.
76. Churchill to Chamberlain, 13 March 1928, NC7/9/22.
77. Chamberlain Diary, 16 June 1927; Chamberlain to Hilda, 24 July, 30 October and 12 November 1927; Chamberlain to Lord Irwin, Christmas Day 1927 and 12 August 1928, Irwin MSS Eur.C.152/17/227A and 152/18/114A.
78. Chamberlain Diary, 26 November and 1 December 1924; P.J. Grigg, *Prejudice and Judgement* (1948), p. 174

79. Chamberlain to Hilda, 17 October 1925.
80. Chamberlain to Hilda, 16 October 1926; CP 389(26), 18 November 1926, CAB 24/182.
81. CP 395(26), November 1926, CAB 24/182.
82. Chamberlain to Hilda, 27 November 1926; CP 392 and 396(26), both 23 November 1926, CAB 24/182; CAB 60(26)7, 24 November 1926, CAB 23/53.
83. CAB 66(26)5 and CAB 67(26)3, 16–17 December 1926, CAB 23/53.
84. Keith Middlemas and John Barnes, *Baldwin: A Biography* (1969), p. 456.
85. CAB 5(27)5, 2 February 1927, CAB 23/54; Chamberlain to Hilda, 5 February and 19 March and to Ida, 26 March 1927; Chamberlain Diary, 12 February and 4 March 1927.
86. Bayford Diary, 13 March and Chamberlain Diary, 10 March 1927.
87. Chamberlain Diary, 4 March 1927.
88. Paper GC(27)4, Block Grants Committee, CAB 27/362; Chamberlain to Churchill, 28 March 1927, CHAR18/62/88.
89. Chamberlain Diary, 16 June 1927.
90. Chamberlain to Ida, 26 March 1927.
91. Chamberlain to Churchill, 28 March and 15 July 1927, CHAR18/62/88–91 and 18/63/1–4.
92. Chamberlain Diary, 10 March and 16 June 1927.
93. Churchill to Baldwin, 6 June 1927, Baldwin MSS 5/125–35.
94. Churchill to Chamberlain, 7 June and reply 10 June 1927, CHAR18/64/38–9.
95. Chamberlain Diary, 16 June 1927; to Hilda, 24 July, 30 October and 12 November 1927.
96. Chamberlain Diary, 16 June 1927.
97. A.W. Hurst and Warren Fisher minutes to Churchill, n.d. and 19 August 1927, CHAR18/63/13–16, 22–6.
98. Chamberlain to Irwin, 12 August 1928, Irwin MSS Eur.C.152/18/114A.
99. Churchill note to Hopkins and Hurst, 27 September 1927, CHAR18/63/27.
100. Chamberlain to Churchill, 14 October and reply, 18 October 1927, NC7/9/12 and CHAR18/63/28–35.
101. Cunliffe-Lister to Churchill, 11 April 1928, CHAR18/89/56.
102. Chamberlain Diary, 9 December and to Hilda, 11 December 1927.
103. Chamberlain Diary, 9 and 17 December 1927.
104. Churchill to Chamberlain, 17 December 1927, NC7/9/14.
105. Chamberlain to Irwin, Christmas Day 1927, Irwin MSS Eur.C.152/17/227A.
106. Churchill to Chamberlain, 21 December 1927, NC7/10/8; Chamberlain Diary, 9, 17 and 22 December 1927.
107. Chamberlain to Irwin, 12 August 1928.
108. Chamberlain to Churchill, 24 December 1927 and 'Memo on the Chancellor's Scheme', CHAR18/65/134–9; Chamberlain to Baldwin, 24 December 1927, Baldwin MSS 162/67.
109. Chamberlain Diary, 22 December 1927; Baldwin to Chamberlain, 27 December 1927, NC7/11/20/c.
110. Churchill to Baldwin, 4, 5 and 7 January 1928, Baldwin MSS 5/148–70; Churchill to Hopkins, 2 January 1928, CHAR18/85/15–22.

111. CP 8(28), 20 January 1928, CAB 24/192; Chamberlain to Hilda, 22 January 1928; CAB 2(28)1, 20 January 1928, CAB 23/57.
112. P(28) 3rd and 4th Meeting of Cabinet Policy Committee, 27 February and 5 March 1928, CAB 27/364.
113. Chamberlain to Hilda, 18 March 1928; P(28) 5th Meeting, 12 March 1928, CAB 27/364 and P(28) Paper 6, 9 March 1928, CAB 27/365.
114. Churchill to Chamberlain, 13 March 1928, NC7/9/22.
115. Chamberlain to Churchill, 14 March 1928, NC7/9/23; to Hilda, 18 March 1928.
116. Dilks, *Neville Chamberlain*, p. 547. For the allegation see P.J. Grigg to Churchill, 6 March 1928, CHAR18/87/72.
117. Chamberlain to Hilda, 18 March 1928; to Churchill, 14 March 1928, CHAR 18/87/95; Chamberlain Diary, 21 March 1928.
118. Chamberlain Diary, 18 April 1928; P(28) 7th Meeting, 26 March 1928, CAB 27/364.
119. Chamberlain Diary, 28 March and 4 April 1928; Amery Diary, 2–3 April; CAB 19(28)4, 3 April 1928, CAB 23/57.
120. Chamberlain Diary, 4 April 1928.
121. Churchill to Chamberlain, 7 April and reply 12 April 1928, CHAR18/89/51–61; Baldwin to Churchill, 14 April 1928, CHAR18/89/62.
122. Chamberlain Diary, 18 April 1928.
123. Chamberlain Diary, 18 and 19 April 1928; Chamberlain to Ida, 21 April and to Hilda 29 April 1928.
124. Chamberlain Diary, 20 April 1928; CAB 23(28)4, 20 April 1928, CAB 23/57.
125. Chamberlain to Hilda, 15 April, 24 June 1928.
126. M. Epstein (ed.), *The Annual Register 1928* (1929), p. 108.
127. A.W. Hurst to Chamberlain, 7 March 1929, NC7/11/22/13.
128. *H.C. Debs*, 5s, 223, col 68, 26 November 1928.
129. Epstein (ed.), *The Annual Register 1928*, pp. 109–10; Baldwin to King George V, 27 November 1928, Baldwin MSS 63/223.
130. Winterton Diary, 26 November 1928.
131. Chamberlain Diary, 1 December 1928 and 24 February 1929.
132. Sir Douglas Veale interview; Baldwin to King George V, 14, 19 December, 29–30 January, 2 and 19 February 1929, Baldwin MSS 63/162–330.
133. Bryan Keith Lucas, *The History of Local Government in England* (2nd ed., 1970), p. 232.
134. Webb, *English Poor Law*, pp. 985, 1019. For the scope of the Act see Cmd. 4664, Fifteenth Annual Report of the Ministry of Health, 1933–34, by Sir Arthur Robinson, pp. 34–96.
135. Ramsden, *The Age of Balfour and Baldwin*, p. 290.
136. Webb, *English Poor Law*, pp. 986–7; Keith-Lucas, *History of Local Government*, p. 231; Gilbert, *British Social Policy*, pp. 229, 232–3; Crowther, *The Workhouse System*, p. 109.
137. VPC (25) 7th Conclusions, 16 June 1925, CAB 27/263.
138. Gilbert, *British Social Policy*, pp. 203–4, 232–3; Pat Thane, *The Foundations of the Welfare State* (1982), p. 176.
139. Chamberlain in *The Times*, 11 April 1929.
140. Crowther, *The Workhouse System*, pp. 110, 112, 153–5; Thane, *Foundations*, p. 176.

141. Chamberlain to Ida, 17 November 1929.

142. CP 108(29) 'Slum Policy', 27 March 1929, CAB 24/202.

143. Chamberlain to Irwin, 12 August 1928, Irwin MSS Eur.C.152/18/114A.

144. Middlemas and Barnes, *Baldwin*, p. 286.

145. Crowther, *The Workhouse System*, pp. 106–7, 260–63.

146. Chamberlain to Kate [?], 12 November 1924, NC Letters Additional 86.

147. Chamberlain at Leeds, 8 May 1928; to Hilda, 16 November 1928.

148. Newman, *The Building of a Nation's Health*, pp. 157–62.

149. Chamberlain to Arthur Collins, 12 October 1940, NC7/6/33.

150. Paul Addison, *The Road to 1945: British Politics and the Second World War* (Quartet ed., 1975), p. 33; Douglas Veale to Chamberlain, 21 and 24 May 1928, NC7/11/21/22–3.

151. Chamberlain to Hilda, 5 May 1929.

152. Jones Diary, 25 February 1929.

153. Chamberlain to Baldwin, 22 August 1927, Baldwin MSS 162/65; to Irwin, 12 August 1928, Irwin MSS Eur.C.152/18/114A.

154. Chamberlain to Hoare, 29 September 1928, Templewood MSS V:3(32); to Ida, 28 September and 4 November 1928.

155. Chamberlain to Hilda, 25 May 1929.

156. Chamberlain Diary, 8 June 1929.

157. Chamberlain to Ida, 2 June 1929. Also Bridgeman Diary, July 1929; Lord Younger to Davidson, 27 December 1926, Baldwin MSS 53/31–3.

158. Chamberlain Diary, 3 May 1926; Irwin to the Earl of Crawford, 25 June and reply 27 July 1927, Irwin MSS Eur.C. 152/17/245, 293.

159. Baldwin to Irwin, 15 September 1927; Chamberlain to Irwin, 12 August 1928, Irwin MSS Eur.C.152/17/253–4 and 152/18/114A.

160. Chamberlain Diary, 1 July 1927; Chamberlain to Irwin, 25 August 1927, Eur.C.152/17/249c.

161. Chamberlain Diary, 5 October and 1 November 1925.

162. Chamberlain Diary, 1 July 1927; Chamberlain to Irwin, 12 August 1928, Irwin MSS Eur.C.152/18/114A.

163. Jones Diary, 19 June 1929.

Chapter 7: Opposition and the Financial Crisis, June 1929–October 1931

1. Chamberlain to Ida, 2 June 1929; to Mary, 1 June 1929, NC1/20/1/147 and Chamberlain Diary, 8 June 1929.

2. Chamberlain to Baldwin, 2 June 1929, Baldwin MSS 36/211; Chamberlain to Hilda, 9 June 1929; to Mary, 1 June 1929, NC1/20/1/147.

3. Chamberlain Diary, 8 June and 26 July 1929.

4. Lord Beaverbrook, 'Who is for the Empire?' and 'The New Project of Empire', *Sunday Express*, 30 June and 7 July 1929.

5. Austen Chamberlain to Hilda, 13 July 1929, AC5/1/478; Chamberlain Diary, 26 July 1929; Churchill to Chamberlain, 5 July 1929, NC7/9/30; Churchill to Linlithgow, 10 July 1929, Hopetoun MSS 1002.

6. Hoare to Chamberlain, 8 October 1929, Templewood MSS VI:I (10).

7. Amery Diary, 11 July 1929; Chamberlain to Ida, 13 July 1929.

8. Chamberlain to Hilda, 29 July 1929; to his wife, 25 October 1929, NC1/26/417.

9.   Ibid.; Chamberlain to Elibank, 9 July 1929, Elibank MSS GD32/25/76.
10. Chamberlain Diary, 4–5 November 1929.
11. Chamberlain Diary, 8 December 1929; Chamberlain to Hilda, 24 November 1929.
12. Press release, 16 November 1929, Ball MSS Eng.c.6652/26.
13. Chamberlain Diary, 8 December 1929.
14. Chamberlain to Hilda, 17 January 1930; East Africa travel diaries, NC2/14–15.
15. Amery Diary, 10 March 1930.
16. Lord Rothermere to Sir Henry Page Croft, 9 August 1925, Croft MSS 1/17/39; *Daily Mail* (editorial), 28 October 1925.
17. H.A Gwynne to Baldwin, 21 February 1930, Gwynne MSS 15.
18. Chamberlain to Ida, 22 March 1930.
19. 'Notes re Empire Free Trade' (hereafter called Elibank Diary), 10 and 11 March 1930, Elibank MSS GD 32/25/69 fol. 29–30; Chamberlain Diary, 12 March 1930; Hannon 'Notes for Diary', 11 March 1930, Hannon MSS 17/1; Davidson memoranda, 12 and 14 March 1930, Davidson MSS 190.
20. Elibank Diary, 20 and 25 March 1930, fol. 41–3.
21. Davidson to Chamberlain, 26 March 1930, Davidson MSS 190.
22. Beaverbrook to Rothermere, 3 July 1929, Beaverbrook MSS C/284.
23. Elibank Diary, 29 March 1930, fol. 43; Chamberlain to Ida, 6 April 1930.
24. Chamberlain to his wife, 4 April 1930, NC1/26/422; Davidson to Chamberlain, 3 April 1930; Topping memorandum to Davidson, 2 May 1930, Davidson MSS 190.
25. Chamberlain to Ida, 17 May 1930.
26. Chamberlain to Ida, 6 April and to Hilda, 12 April 1930, 25 May and 21 June 1930; Chamberlain Diary, 22 June 1930; Hoare to Irwin, 31 May 1930, Irwin MSS Eur.C.152/19/71.
27. Chamberlain to Ida, 21 August 1921; to Hilda, 18 May 1924.
28. Chamberlain to Lord Derby, 27 June 1930, Derby MSS.
29. For these fears see Chamberlain to Hilda, 10 May and 8 June; to Ida 17 May 1930.
30. Chamberlain to Hilda, 25 May and 21 June 1930.
31. Chamberlain to Ida, 12 July 1930; to Beaverbrook, 11 July 1930, Beaverbrook MSS C/80; Chamberlain Diary, 19 and 20 July 1930.
32. Amery Diary, 19 July 1930; Chamberlain Diary, 29 and 30 July 1930.
33. Chamberlain to Hilda and to his wife, both 4 August 1930; Amery Diary, 30 July 1930.
34. Beaverbrook-Bridgeman exchange, 2, 3, 6 September; Bridgeman to Chamberlain, 9 September 1930, NC8/10/1–4.
35. Chamberlain to Bridgeman, 11 September 1930, NC8/10/13a; to Hilda, 21 September 1930.
36. Chamberlain to Ida, 26 July 1930.
37. Chamberlain to Ida, 4 April 1930; to Hilda, 25 May 1930.
38. Chamberlain to Hilda, 16 August and 7 September 1930; to Ida, 22 August 1930; Chamberlain 'Holiday Diary', August 1930, NC 2/16.
39. Chamberlain to Ida, 28 September 1930.
40. Chamberlain to Hilda, 7 September 1930; to his wife, 10 and 16 August 1930, NC1/26/435, 437; Amery Diary, 20, 22 July 1930.

41. Chamberlain to Hilda, 21 September 1930; to his wife, 21 August 1930, NC1/26/441.
42. Bridgeman to Irwin, 15 June 1930, Irwin MSS Eur.C.152/19/79.
43. Sir Henry Page Croft to Chamberlain, 4 October 1930, Croft MSS 1/7/6; Chamberlain Diary, 11 October 1930.
44. Lord Tyrrell to H.A. Gwynne, 1 October 1930, Gwynne MSS 14; Chamberlain to Ida, 28 September 1930.
45. Bridgeman to Chamberlain, 2 October 1930; Chamberlain to Bridgeman, 5 October 1930, NC8/10/6 and 13b; Chamberlain Diary, 11 October 1930.
46. Croft to Chamberlain, 4 October 1930, Croft MSS 1/7/6.
47. Chamberlain Diary, 11 October 1930. For oblique references to the plot see Chamberlain to Austen Chamberlain, 8 and 10 October 1930 and reply, AC39/2/39–40 and AC58/75.
48. Ian M. Drummond, *Imperial Economic Policy 1917–39: Studies in Expansion and Protection* (1974), pp. 154–5.
49. Chamberlain to Austen Chamberlain, 8 and 10 October 1930.
50. *The Times*, 10 October 1930; Chamberlain Diary, 11 October 1930.
51. Chamberlain Diary, 19 October; to Ida, 11 October; to Hilda, 18 October 1930; to Bridgeman, 1 November 1930, NC8/10/16c.
52. Chamberlain to Ida, 11 October; to Hilda, 18 October 1930.
53. Chamberlain Diary, 6 November 1930; Beaverbrook to Croft, 4 November 1930, Croft MSS 1/4/14; Chamberlain to Ida, 8 November 1930.
54. Chamberlain to Bridgeman, 18 November 1930, NC8/10/16d; to Beaverbrook, 19 and 26 November 1930, Beaverbrook MSS C/80.
55. Beaverbrook to Chamberlain, 28 November 1930, Beaverbrook MSS C/80.
56. Chamberlain to Hilda, 14 December 1930; Chamberlain Diary, 1 February 1931.
57. Chamberlain Diary, 23 February 1931; Chamberlain to Hilda, 14 February 1931.
58. Topping memorandum to Chamberlain, 25 February 1931, Baldwin MSS 166/50–53. For an alternative view see Stuart Ball, *Baldwin and the Conservative Party: The Crisis of 1929–1931* (New Haven and London, 1988), pp. 137–42.
59. Chamberlain Diary, 1 March 1931.
60. Chamberlain Diary and to Hilda, both 1 March 1931; Chamberlain to Baldwin, 1 March 1931, Baldwin MSS 166/47–9.
61. Ibid.; Jones Diary and Baldwin to Jones, both 11 March 1931, Baldwin MSS 166/54.
62. Chamberlain Diary, 3 March 1931; Bridgeman Diary, 1 March 1931; Chamberlain to Ida, 7 March 1931; Middlemas and Barnes, *Baldwin*, p. 590.
63. Amery Diary, 5–6 March 1931; Chamberlain Diary, 11 March 1931; Davidson to Irwin, 6 March 1931.
64. Austen Chamberlain to Hilda, 11 October 1930 and 7 March 1931, AC5/1/517, 533.
65. Austen Chamberlain to Ida, 13 March 1931, AC5/1/534; Amery Diary, 6–7, 11 March 1931.

66. Chamberlain Diary, 11 March 1931; Amery Diary, 7 and 11 March 1931.
67. Chamberlain Diary, 14 March 1931; Chamberlain to Baldwin, 13 March 1931, Baldwin MSS 166/58–60.
68. Baldwin letter to Colonel Butchart and speech at the Queen's Hall, *Morning Post*, 8 and 18 March 1931.
69. Chamberlain Diary, 21–31 March 1931.
70. John Ramsden, *The Making of Conservative Party Policy: The Conservative Research Department since 1929* (1980), p. 63; Joseph Ball to Chamberlain, 19 May 1931, NC7/11/24/2.
71. Forrest Capie, *Depression and Protectionism: Britain between the Wars* (1983), pp. 61–76.
72. Cunliffe-Lister to Steel-Maitland, 17 July 1929, Steel-Maitland MSS GD193/120/3(2).
73. Chamberlain to Cunliffe-Lister, 16 July 1931 SWIN174/2/1/9.
74. Chamberlain to Hilda, 3 January and 14 February 1931; Lord Selborne to his wife, 23 April 1931, reporting Chamberlain, Selborne MSS 106/117.
75. Chamberlain Diary, 21 November and 5 December 1930; Simon Diary, 9 December 1930, Simon MSS 249/45–6.
76. Chamberlain to Ida, 8 February, 5 and 18 April 1931; to Sir Edward Grigg, 20 February 1931, Altrincham MSS.
77. Chamberlain Diary, 6 July 1931; Chamberlain to Hilda, 4 July 1931.
78. Amery Diary, 31 July 1931; Chamberlain Diary, 24 July 1931; Middlemas and Barnes, *Baldwin*, pp. 613, 617, 620, 621.
79. 'The First National Government', n.d., Templewood MSS VII/1; Chamberlain to Hilda, 16 August 1931.
80. J.D. Fair, 'The Conservative Basis for the Formation of the National Government of 1931', *Journal of British Studies*, 19 (1980), pp. 143, 164.
81. David Wrench, '"Cashing in": the Parties and the National Government, August 1931–September 1932', *Journal of British Studies*, 23 (1984), pp. 135–53; Stuart Ball, 'The Conservative Party and the Formation of the National Government, August 1931', *Historical Journal*, 29 (1986), pp. 159–82; idem, *Baldwin and the Conservative Party*, pp. 151–97; Andrew Thorpe, *Britain in the 1930s: The Deceptive Decade* (Oxford, 1992), p. 10.
82. Graham Stewart, *Burying Caesar: Churchill, Chamberlain and the Battle for the Tory Party* (1999), p. 112.
83. Macmillan, *Winds of Change*, p. 260; *The Times*, 9 January 1931.
84. Chamberlain Diary, 24 July 1931; Chamberlain to Hilda, 14 February, 18 July 1931.
85. Chamberlain to Ida, 9 May 1931; to Hilda, 6 June 1931; *H.C. Debs*, 5s, 255, col 2497–520, 30 July 1931.
86. Amery Diary, 15, 21, 25 August 1931; Sir Robert Horne to Chamberlain, 15 August 1931, Baldwin MSS 44/25–34.
87. Chamberlain to his wife, 23 August 1931, NC1/26/477.
88. Chamberlain to H.A. Gwynne, 13 August 1931, Gwynne MSS 17.
89. Chamberlain to Hilda, 3 January 1931; to Elibank, 7 January 1931, Elibank MSS GD32/25/75.
90. Chamberlain Diary, 3 September 1931.
91. Chamberlain to Hilda, 16 August 1931.
92. E.R. Peacock to F.S. Oliver, 1 August 1931; Philip Williamson, 'A "Bankers'

Ramp"? Financiers and the Political Crisis of August 1931', *English Historical Review*, 94 (1984), p. 788. Emphasis added.

93. Chamberlain to Ida, 9 August 1931.
94. Chamberlain to Cunliffe-Lister, 15 August 1931; Geoffrey Lloyd to Cunliffe-Lister, 14 August 1931, SWIN174/2/1/11, 27.
95. Ibid.; Chamberlain to Austen Chamberlain, 14 August 1931, AC39/3/26; to Hilda, 16 August 1931.
96. Chamberlain to H.A. Gwynne, 13 August 1931, Gwynne MSS 17.
97. Chamberlain to Austen Chamberlain, 14 August 1931, AC39/3/26; to Cunliffe-Lister, 15 August 1931, SWIN174/2/1/11–12; to his wife, 23 August 1931, NC1/26/447.
98. Chamberlain Diary, 22 August 1931; Chamberlain to Austen Chamberlain, 14 and 23 August 1931, AC35/3/26 and NC1/26/477; to his wife, 21 August 1931, NC1/26/446.
99. Chamberlain and MacDonald Diary, both 22 August 1931; Chamberlain to Ida, and to his wife, both 23 August 1931.
100. Cunliffe-Lister to his wife, n.d. Friday (21 August 1931), SWIN 313/1/5.
101. For example, Middlemas and Barnes, *Baldwin*, p. 621; Roy Jenkins, *The Chancellors* (1998), p. 342.
102. Chamberlain Diary, 6 July 1931.
103. Chamberlain to Hilda, 2 August 1931; Austen Chamberlain to Ida, 2 August 1931, AC5/1/550; Cunliffe-Lister to his wife, 'Friday' (30 July 1931), SWIN270/3/22.
104. Chamberlain to Ida, 23 August 1931; 'The Second Labour Government', Templewood MSS VI:1(57).
105. Chamberlain Diary, 23 August 1931.
106. Chamberlain to his wife, 23–24 August 1931, NC1/26/447–8; Davidson draft memoir, Robert Rhodes James, *Memoirs of a Conservative: J.C.C. Davidson's Memoirs and Papers, 1910-1937* (1969), p. 368.
107. Chamberlain to Ida, 23 August; to Hoare, 24 August 1931, Templewood MSS VII:1(1).
108. Hoare to Chamberlain, n.d. (24–25 August 1931?), NC7/11/24/13; Austen Chamberlain to his wife, 28 August 1931, AC6/1/806; Marjorie Maxse to Chamberlain, 28 October 1931, NC7/11/24/22.
109. CAB 47(31)1, 24 August 1931, CAB 23/68.
110. 'Memorandum written at the Conference at Buckingham Palace, 24 August 1931', Samuel MSS A78/11a.
111. Chamberlain to his wife, 25 August 1931, NC1/26/440; MacDonald Diary, 1 September 1931, MacDonald MSS PRO 30/69/1753 fol. 395.
112. CAB 50, 53, 54 (31), 1–2 and 7 September 1931, CAB 23/68; EN(31) 1st Meeting of Cabinet Economy Committee, 27 August 1931, CAB 27/456.
113. Chamberlain to Ida, 19 September 1931.
114. Chamberlain Diary, 19 September 1931.
115. Hankey Diary, 20, 25 September 1931, HNKY1/7 fol. 28–30.
116. Chamberlain to Sir Edward Grigg, 16 September 1931, Altrincham MSS; 'The First National Government', Templewood MSS VIII/I; Chamberlain Diary, 19 September 1931.
117. Chamberlain to Ida, 19 September 1931; Chamberlain Diary, 19 and 24 September 1931.

118. Chamberlain to Hilda, 12 and 26 September 1931; Chamberlain Diary, 29–30 September 1931.
119. Chamberlain Diary, 29 September to 2 October 1931; Hankey's 'Notes on events during the week ended Saturday 3 October 1931', Magnum Opus MSS (31)7, CAB 63/44.
120. Chamberlain and Amery Diary, both 5 October 1931; Chamberlain to Hilda, 10 October 1931.
121. Austen Chamberlain to his wife, 5 October 1931, AC6/1/324 and to Hilda, 3 October 1931, AC5/1/556.
122. MacDonald Diary, 5 October 1931. Neither the Chamberlain nor Hankey diaries mention this threat.
123. Chamberlain Diary, 5 October 1931.
124. Sankey Diary, 5 October 1931, Sankey MSS c.285 fol. 81.
125. Chamberlain to Hilda, 10 October; to Ida, 8 October 1931.
126. MacDonald Diary, 1 November 1931; MacDonald to Baldwin, 3 November 1931, Baldwin MSS 45/199; Hankey Diary, 28 and 30 October 1931.
127. Bridgeman to Baldwin, 2 November 1931, Baldwin MSS 45/194–5.
128. Amery Diary, 31 October 1931; Chamberlain to Elibank, 10 November 1931, Elibank MSS GD32/25/75.
129. Chamberlain to Hilda, 7 November 1931. For a contrary view emphasising the 'nervous tension' see Victor Cazalet Diary, 7 June 1932, Robert Rhodes James, *Victor Cazalet: A Portrait* (1976), p. 144.
130. Runciman to Lord Forres, 6 October 1931; to E.J. Beavis, 5 November 1931, Runciman MSS 245 and 221; Runciman interview, *Daily Mail*, 17 September 1931; *H.C Debs.* 5s, 256, col 331, 10 September 1931.

Chapter 8: The Treasury, Tariffs and Economic Diplomacy, 1931–1934

1. MacDonald to Lady Londonderry, n.d., David Marquand, *Ramsay MacDonald* (1977), p. 690; Chamberlain to Sir Francis Humphrys, 8 January 1932, NC7/11/24/15.
2. Chamberlain to Hilda, 3 January 1932.
3. Chamberlain to Sir Gilbert Barling, 23 January 1932, NC Letters Additional 5.
4. Cunliffe-Lister to Elibank, 4 September 1931, Elibank MSS GD32/25/75.
5. Chamberlain to Ida, 15 November 1931; CAB 76(31)1, 12 November 1931, CAB 23/69.
6. CAB 81(31)5, 25 November 1931, CAB 23/69.
7. Amery Diary, 20 December 1931; Chamberlain to Ida, 29 December 1931.
8. 'Notes on Proceedings in Cabinet and elsewhere on the formulation of Government Policy on the Balance of Trade, concluded 30 January 1932' (hereafter 'Chamberlain memo'), NC8/18/1, para. 5.
9. Runciman to MacDonald, 21 December and reply 26 December 1931, Runciman MSS 245; Chamberlain memo, para. 7.
10. Chamberlain memo, para. 2–4; Chamberlain to Ida, 12 December 1931.
11. BT(31) 4th Conclusions of the Balance of Trade Committee, 13 January 1932, CAB 27/467; Chamberlain memo, para. 7, 8, 11; Chamberlain to Hilda, 17 January 1932.

12. Chamberlain to Snowden, 15 January and reply 16 January 1932, NC7/11/25/41–2.

13. Chamberlain to Irwin, 25 December 1927, Irwin MSS Eur.C.152/17/227A.

14. Chamberlain to Snowden, 15 January 1932, NC7/11/25/41.

15. Chamberlain memo, para. 12.

16. 'The course of political events, 19–25 January 1932', Samuel MSS A87/7; BT(31) 5th Conclusions, 18 January 1932, CAB 27/467.

17. CAB 6(32)1, 21 January 1932, CAB 23/70.

18. Chamberlain memo, para. 16; Chamberlain Diary, 22 January 1932; Chamberlain to Ida, 23 January 1932.

19. Chamberlain memo, para. 17; Sankey Diary, 22 January 1932, Sankey MSS c. 286 fol. 8.

20. Chamberlain Diary, 22 January 1932; Chamberlain to Ida, 23 January 1932; to Elibank, 5 February 1932, Elibank MSS GD32/25/30.

21. Chamberlain to Ida and to Mary, both 6 February 1932, NC/20/1/156; *H.C Debs*, 5s, 261, col 296, 4 February 1932.

22. Chamberlain to Mary, 6 February 1932, NC1/20/1/156.

23. Chamberlain to Lord Lloyd, 7 February 1932, Lloyd MSS GLLD19/6.

24. Amery Diary, 27 May 1937.

25. Chamberlain to Mary, 19 May 1932, NC1/20/1/157 ; BT(31) 3rd and 5th Conclusions, CAB 27/467; *H.C. Debs*, 5s, 261, col 286–8, 296, 4 February 1932.

26. Chamberlain to Lord Lloyd, 7 February 1932, GLLD19/6.

27. Drummond, *Imperial Economic Policy*, p. 171.

28. Ibid., p. 183; R.F. Holland, *Britain and the Commonwealth Alliance 1918–1939* (1981), pp. 135–9.

29. OC(31) 1st Meeting of the Ottawa Preparatory Committee, 16 November 1931, CAB 27/473.

30. Ibid.

31. Chamberlain to Hilda, 21 November, 6 December 1931; CAB 84(31)2 and CAB 92(31)5, 2 and 16 December 1931, CAB 23/69.

32. Chamberlain to Ida, 29 November 1931.

33. Chamberlain to Ida, 6 February 1932.

34. Chamberlain to Hilda, 27 February 1932.

35. Austen Chamberlain to Hilda, 5 March 1932, AC5/1/577; Amery Diary, 29 February 1932.

36. Chamberlain to Ida, 5 March 1932; to Hilda, 12 March; Baldwin to MacDonald, 5 and 6 March and Chamberlain to MacDonald, 6 March 1932. MacDonald MSS PRO30/69/2/12 II and 30/69/678/1/167–8.

37. W.K. Hancock, *Survey of British Commonwealth Affairs, Volume II: Problems of Economic Policy, 1918–1939* (1940), p. 217.

38. Chamberlain to Mary, 13 July 1932, NC1/20/1/159.

39. O(UK)(32) 9th Meeting of UK Delegation to the Ottawa Conference, 20 July 1932, CAB 32/101; Chamberlain to his wife, 24 July 1932, NC1/26/469.

40. Holland, *Britain and the Commonwealth Alliance*, p. 138.

41. Chamberlain to Hilda, 11 June 1932; Amery Diary, 8 August 1932.

42. O(UK)(32) 30th Meeting, 4 August 1932, CAB 32/101; Chamberlain's Ottawa Diary, 7 August 1932, NC2/17.

43.	O(UK)(32) 3rd, 5th and 6th Meeting, 15, 16 and 18 July 1932, CAB 32/101; Chamberlain to Ida, 17 July 1932; to his wife, 15 July 1932, NC1/26/467; Ottawa Diary, 15 and 18 July 1932.

44.	'Draft Resolution, 1st Revise' attached to O(UK)(32) 3rd and 9th Meeting, 15 and 20 July 1932, CAB 32/101.

45.	O(UK)(32) 13th Meeting, 23 July 1932, CAB 32/101.

46.	Ottawa Diary, 16 July 1932; Chamberlain to Hilda, 27 July 1932; O(UK)(32) 21st and 45th Meeting, 29 July and 11 August 1932, CAB 32/101.

47.	O(UK)(32) 24th Meeting, 2 August 1932, CAB 32/101.

48.	O(UK)(32), 7th, 9th and 24th Meeting, 17, 20 July and 2 August 1932, CAB 32/101.

49.	O(UK)(32) 35th, 37th and 40th Meetings, 5, 7–8 August 1932, CAB 32/101; Chamberlain to his wife, 10 and 16 August 1932, NC1/26/473–4; Ottawa Diary, 12 and 15 August 1932.

50.	Chamberlain to Ida, 29 November 1931; to Hilda, 27 July 1932; CAB 84(32)2, 2 December 1931, CAB 23/69.

51.	Chamberlain to Hilda, 27 July 1932; to his wife, 24 July 1932, NC1/26/469.

52.	W.B.B. to Baldwin, memorandum, 27 July 1932, Baldwin MSS 98/143–4; Richard Kottman, *Reciprocity and the North Atlantic Triangle* (Ithaca, 1968), p. 27; O(UK)(32) 30th and 32nd Meetings, 4 August 1932, CAB 32/101.

53.	Chamberlain to Hilda, 27 July 1932.

54.	O(UK)(32) 30th and 32nd Meeting, 4 August 1932, CAB 32/101.

55.	Chamberlain to his wife, 10 August 1932, NC1/26/473; O(UK)(32) 48th Meeting, 12 August 1932, CAB 32/101.

56.	Chamberlain to Hilda, 11 August 1932; Ottawa Diary, 15 and 17 August 1932.

57.	Chamberlain to his wife, 16 August 1932, NC1/26/474.

58.	Chamberlain to his wife, 10 August 1932, NC1/26/473; to Ida, 21 August 1932; to Hore-Belisha, 29 August 1932, HOBE1/1/86–7.

59.	Ottawa Diary, 20 August 1932; Chamberlain to his sisters, 21 and 30 August 1932.

60.	Chamberlain to Hilda, 11 August; to Ida, 21 August 1932; Ottawa Diary, 15 and 17 August 1932.

61.	Cunliffe-Lister to his wife, 19 August 1932, quoted in Alan Earl, 'The Political Life of Viscount Swinton; 1918–1938' (unpublished M.A., Manchester, 1960), p. 248.

62.	Ibid.; CAB 46(32)1, 27 August 1932, CAB 23/72.

63.	O(UK)(32) Paper 50 and 55, CAB 32/103; Chamberlain to Ida, 21 August 1932; Runciman to MacDonald, 2 September 1932, MacDonald MSS 30/69/1/594; Cmd. 4174, pp. 9–10.

64.	Ottawa Diary, 20 August 1932; Chamberlain to Hilda, 30 August 1932.

65.	CAB 46(32)1, 27 August 1932, CAB 23/72.

66.	Chamberlain to Hore-Belisha, 29 August 1932, HOBE1/1/87.

67.	Ottawa Diary, 20 August 1932; Chamberlain to Hilda, 30 August and 18 September 1932. For his private hope that 'we may presently develop into a National Party, and get rid of the odious title of Conservative, which has kept so many from joining us in the past', see Chamberlain to Hilda, 24 October 1931.

68. Chamberlain to Ida, 12 September and to Hilda, 18 September 1932; CAB 47(32)1, 28 September 1932, CAB 23/72.

69. See correspondence in T172/1506/24-86; also Vansittart to Leith-Ross, 18 November 1932, T188/49/70.

70. Chamberlain to Hilda, 6 December 1931.

71. See LC(B) 1st and 2nd Meetings of Lausanne Conference (British Preparatory Committee), 7 June 1932, CAB 29/139; Chamberlain to Hilda, 11 January 1932.

72. Stimson Diary, 23 October 1931; RWD(31)10, Telegram from Sir Robert Lindsay [British Ambassador to Washington], 28 December 1931, CAB 27/466.

73. RWD(31) 1st and 4th Conclusions of the Reparations and War Debts Committee, 15 December 1931 and 13 January 1932, CAB 27/466; LC(B) 1st Meeting, 7 June 1932, CAB 29/139.

74. Chamberlain's annotations on Leith-Ross note of 24 May 1932, T172/1788 and Leith-Ross note for Chancellor, 27 May 1932, T172/1788; LC(B) 1st Meeting, 7 June 1932, CAB 29/139.

75. Chamberlain to Hilda, 19 June 1932; L(UK) 2nd Meeting of UK Delegation at Lausanne Conference, 16 June 1932, CAB 29/139; Simon to Vansittart, 20 June 1932 appended to CAB 37(32), 22 June 1932, CAB 23/72; Chamberlain's Lausanne Diary, 17 June 1932, NC2/16.

76. Chamberlain to Baldwin, 18 June 1932, Baldwin MSS 119/3; Hore-Belisha to Runciman, 20 June 1932, Runciman MSS 260.

77. Lausanne Diary, 17 June 1932; Lausanne Conference: Second Plenary Session, 17 June 1932, CAB 29/139.

78. Runciman to Hore-Belisha, 17 June 1932, HOBE3/2.

79. Chamberlain to Hilda, 23 April 1932; to his wife, 17 June 1932, NC1/26/460.

80. Chamberlain to Ida, 30 April, 21 May 1932; to Baldwin, 28 April, 20 May 1932, Baldwin MSS 167/31-4; to Lord Reading, 30 May 1932, Reading MSS Eur.F118/22.

81. Chamberlain to Baldwin, 24 June 1932, Baldwin MSS 119/24.

82. Chamberlain to Hilda, 26 June 1932.

83. Chamberlain report to Cabinet, CAB 41(32)2, 30 June 1932, CAB 23/72; to Hilda, 19 June; to his wife, 17 June 1932; to Baldwin, 17 June 1932, Baldwin MSS119/2-3.

84. Lausanne Diary and Chamberlain to Hore-Belisha, both 22 June 1932, HOBE3/3.

85. Lausanne Diary, 28 June 1932.

86. Lausanne Diary and L(B) 1st and 2nd Meetings of the Bureau of the Six Inviting Powers, all 29 June 1932, CAB 29/139.

87. L(UK) 11th Meeting of British Delegation, 4 July 1932, CAB 29/139.

88. L(FGE) 1st and 2nd Meetings of French, German and British Delegations, 28 June 1932, CAB 29/139.

89. L(GBG) 3rd Meeting of British and German Delegations at Lausanne, 3 July 1932, CAB 29/139.

90. E. Rowe Dutton note to Leith-Ross and his annotations for the Chancellor, 29 June 1932, T172/1788.

91. Lausanne Diary, 3–7 July 1932; L(GBF) 11th Meeting of Franco-British Delegations, 8 July 1932, CAB 29/139.

92. L(FGE) 2nd Meeting of French, German and British Delegations, 28 June 1932; L(GBG) 3rd Meeting of British and German Delegations, 3 July 1932, CAB 29/139.

93. Chamberlain to Ida, 20 June 1932; Lausanne Diary, 18 June 1932; Simon to Vansittart, 20 June 1932, appended to CAB 37(32), 22 June 1932.

94. L(AB) 6th Meeting of Inviting Powers other than Germany, 2 July 1932 and Annex, CAB 29/139.

95. Runciman to Chamberlain, 10 July 1932, NC7/11/25/33; to Baldwin, n.d., Baldwin MSS119/30–31; Chamberlain to his wife, 3 July 1932, NC1/26/464.

96. Chamberlain to Mary, 15 July 1932, NC1/26/467.

97. Chamberlain to Hilda, 15 May 1932; to Ida, 5 June 1932; LC(B) 1st Meeting, 7 June 1932, CAB 29/139.

98. Leith-Ross, 'Note on conversation with Vansittart and Lindsay about War Debts', 7 October 1932, T188/49/51–5.

99. Stimson Diary, 10 November 1932, Stimson MSS XIX:76; CP 389(32), 10 November 1932, CAB 24/234, published as Cmd. 4192 (1932). For the US reply see Cmd. 4203, 23 November 1932.

100. Chamberlain to Hilda, 26 November 1932; to Ida, 4 December 1932; Donald Fergusson [Private Secretary to the Chancellor] to Chamberlain, 27 November 1932, T172/1507/154.

101. Chamberlain to Ida, 19 November, 4 December 1932.

102. Meeting of Ministers, 28 November 1932, appended to CAB 63(32), 29 November 1932, CAB 23/73.

103. Vansittart and Fisher memorandum for the Chancellor, 28 November 1932, T172/1507/126–8.

104. Chamberlain to Ida, 4 December 1932.

105. Chamberlain to Ida, 4 December 1932; CAB 63(32)1, 29 November 1932, CAB 23/73.

106. CP 416(32), 1 December 1932, CAB 24/235; CAB 65(31)1, 7 December 1932, CAB 23/73.

107. Fisher memorandum for Chancellor, 6 December 1932, T188/49/163–5.

108. Cmd. 4215, Further Note by His Majesty's Government related to British War Debts, 11 December 1932; Chamberlain to MacDonald, 5 December 1932, T188/49/150–51; to Hilda, 10 December 1932.

109. Chamberlain to Ida, 17 December 1932, 29 January 1933; BDA(33) Committee on the British Debt to America, 1st Meeting, 6 February 1933, CAB 27/548.

110. Chamberlain to Mary, 17 December 1932, NC1/20/1/189.

111. A.J. Cummings to Runciman, 9 September 1932 and his 'Memorandum on conversation with Governor Roosevelt at Albany on 31 August 1932', Runciman MSS 259/30–38.

112. CAB 5(33) Appendix, 30 January 1933, CAB 23/75.

113. Ibid.; BDA(33) 1st Meeting, 6 February 1933, CAB 27/548; Chamberlain to Ida, 29 January 1932.

114. CP 29(33), 30 January 1933, CAB 24/237.

115. BDA(33) 2nd Meeting, 7 February 1933, CAB 27/548.

116. Chamberlain to Ida, 12 and 25 February 1933; to Lord Lothian, 17 February 1933, Lothian MSS GD40/17/200/220–21.

117. Stimson Diary, 3 and 27 January 1933, Stimson MSS XXV: 70–71, 195; Lothian notes, 'Lamont dinner', n.d.; W.Y. Elliott to Lothian, 1 February 1933, Lothian MSS GD40/17/199/138–9, 183.

118. Hopkins and Waley note for Chamberlain, 27 March 1933, T175/79/4/8.

119. Lindsay telegrams 381–2, appended to CAB 39(33)2, 9 June 1933, CAB 23/77.

120. CAB 39(33)2, and Appendix II, 9 June 1933, CAB 23/77; Leith-Ross, 'Note of what I can remember of a telephone conversation with the Chancellor … this afternoon', n.d. [8 June 1933], T188/74/54.

121. CP 134(33) 'War Debts' by Runciman, 24 May 1933, CAB 24/241; CAB 39(33)2, 9 June 1933, CAB 23/77.

122. CAB 41(33)1 and Appendix I–V, 13 June 1933, CAB 23/77.

123. Chamberlain to Amery, 16 June 1933, NC7/2/62; to Reading, 17 June 1933, Reading MSS Eur.F.118/24; to Hilda, 10 June 1933.

124. CAB 30(32)2, 1 June and CAB 68(32)4, 21 December 1932 CAB 23/71, 73.

125. Chamberlain to Lord Tyrrell, 17 November 1932 and 'Notes on conversations with M. Flandin, November 1932', NC7/11/25/47–8.

126. Cordell Hull to Roosevelt, 27 February 1933 and 'British Policy on Economic Problems', Roosevelt MSS OF17.

127. Hopkins and Waley note to Chancellor, 27 March 1933, T175/79/4–8.

128. Simon to Chamberlain, 15 June 1933, NC7/11/26/36.

129. Chamberlain to Arthur Chamberlain, 30 May 1933, NC7/6/22.

130. ME(UK) UK Delegation to Monetary and Economic Conference , 6th and 7th Meetings, 22 June 1933, CAB 29/142.

131. ME(UK) 12th Meeting, 27 June 1933, CAB 29/142.

132. Chamberlain Diary, 29 June and 2 July 1933; ME(UK) 18th Meeting, 2 July 1933, CAB 29/142.

133. Chamberlain Diary, 4 July 1933; Cordell Hull Statement, 3 July 1933, Roosevelt MSS OF17.

134. Henry Morgenthau Diary, 9 May 1933.

135. Chamberlain Diary, 4 July 1933; ME(UK) 19th and 21st Meeting, 3 and 5 July 1933, CAB 29/142.

136. Chamberlain Diary, 6, 13 and 17 July 1933.

137. Amery Diary, 27 June and 5 August 1932.

138. Chamberlain to his wife, 15 July 1932, NC1/26/467.

139. Thomas to Chamberlain, 4 January and 3 March 1932 and reply 4 March 1932, T172/1738.

140. O(UK)(32) 21st and 40th Meeting, 29 July and 8 August 1932, CAB 32/101; Hoare to Lord Willingdon, 29 September 1932 and 'Confidential Report on Discussion of Monetary and Financial Questions at the Imperial Conference' by Strakosch and Schuster, 23 September 1932, Hoare MSS Eur. E.240/2/441–75 especially pp. 249–50.

141. Chamberlain Diary, 4–5 July 1933; ME(UK) 21st Meeting, 5 July 1933, CAB 29/142.

142. ME(BC)(33) Paper 22, 'Monetary Policy' by General Smuts, 13 July 1933, T172/1810C.

143. Chamberlain to Hilda, 23 July 1933, Chamberlain Diary, 24 July 1933; ME(UK) 28th Meeting, 24 July 1933, CAB 29/142.
144. ME(UK) 30th Meeting, 26 July 1933; ME(BC)(33) 11th (A) Meeting of British Commonwealth Delegations, 25 July 1933, T172/1810C; Chamberlain Diary, 27 July 1933.
145. Chamberlain to Hilda, 24 September 1933; Leith-Ross to Runciman, 17 September 1933, Runciman MSS 265/53; CP 222(32), 25 September 1933, CAB 24/243.
146. CAB 58(33)1, 26 October 1933, CAB 23/77.
147. Chamberlain to Ida, 28 October 1933.
148. CAB 58(33)1, 26 October and CAB 59(33)6, 2 November 1933, CAB 23/77; Chamberlain to Ida, 28 October 1933.
149. Chamberlain Diary, January 1934. For these events see Robert Self, *Britain, America and the War Debt Problem 1917–1934* (forthcoming).
150. Chamberlain to Hilda, 8 October 1916, 11 July 1920, 20 March 1926, 4 February 1933.
151. George C. Peden *The Treasury and British Public Policy 1906–1959* (Oxford, 2000), pp. 281–2.
152. CAB 39(37)7, 27 October 1937 and CAB 36(38)3, 28 July 1938, CAB 23/89, 94; Amery Diary, 21 September 1937, reporting Eden.
153. Hancock, *Survey of British Commonwealth Affairs II: Problems of Economic Policy*, p. 233; Chamberlain to Ida, 21 August 1932.
154. Chamberlain to Baldwin, 4 January 1935, Baldwin MSS 170/51; Drummond, *Imperial Economic Policy*, pp. 238, 307–17, 389–412.
155. Hilda Runciman Diary, 12–15 June 1933, Runciman MSS Additional 8.
156. 'Commercial Relations with Australia: Summary', 14 July 1933, T172/1810C/108–21. See also Moir Mackenzie to Lord Weir, 17 July 1934 and other documents in Weir MSS DC96/16/3.
157. Holland, *Britain and the Commonwealth Alliance*, p. 144.
158. EDA (35) 1st and 2nd Meetings of Cabinet Committee on Economic Discussions with Australian Ministers, 25 March and 11 April 1935, CAB 32/124; IC (36) 1st Meeting of Cabinet Preparatory Committee for 1937 Imperial Conference, 10 November 1936 and E(B)(37) 6 'Review of Progress of Empire Trade', April 1937, CAB 32/127.
159. Ritchie Ovendale, *'Appeasement' and the English Speaking World: Britain, the United States, the Dominions, and the Policy of 'Appeasement' 1937–1939* (Cardiff, 1975), p. 20.
160. Chamberlain to Hilda, 23 July 1933.
161. FP(36) 26th Meeting of Cabinet Foreign Policy Committee, 18 March 1938, CAB 27/623.
162. CAB 30(39)1, 24 May 1939, CAB 23/99; Chamberlain to Ida, 8 July 1939.
163. War Cabinet Conclusions, WM 43(39)13, WM 44(39)17, WM 45(39)7, 10–12 October 1939, CAB 65/1.

Chapter 9 : Depression and Recovery, 1931–1935

1. Robert Boothby, *My Yesterday, Your Tomorrow* (1962), p. 125.
2. Robert Skidelsky, *Politicians and the Slump: The Labour Government of 1929-1931* (Pelican ed., 1970), p. 424.

3. Peter Clarke, *The Keynesian Revolution in the Making, 1924–1936* (Oxford, 1988), pp. 294–5.

4. Amery, *My Political Life*, III, p. 81; Amery Diary, 29 July 1933.

5. Hilda Runciman Diary, 25 April 1933.

6. Drummond, *Imperial Economic Policy*, p. 30.

7. F.W. Pethick-Lawrence, *Fate Has Been Kind* (n.d.), p. 190; Gervais Rentoul, *This is My Case: An Autobiography* (n.d.), p. 120; Walker-Smith, *Neville Chamberlain*, p. 177.

8. Peden, *The Treasury and Public Policy*, p. 249.

9. Warren Fisher to Chamberlain, 4 June 1924, NC7/11/17/7, 27 May and 30 June 1932, NC7/11/25/9–10 and 18 January 1933, NC7/11/30/48.

10. Snowden to Chamberlain, 29 December 1931, NC7/11/24/30.

11. Chamberlain to Ida, 15, 29 November and 12 December 1931.

12. Sir Frederick Phillips to Hopkins and Chancellor of Exchequer, 19 October 1932, T175/70.

13. CAB 61(33)10, 8 November 1933, CAB 23/77.

14. B.E.V. Sabine, *British Budgets in Peace and War, 1932–1945* (1970), p. 80; Sir Henry Clay, *Lord Norman* (1957), p. 442.

15. Susan Howson, *Domestic Monetary Management in Britain, 1919–38* (Cambridge, 1975), pp. 71–4, 76, 88.

16. CAB 41(32)3, 30 June 1932, CAB 23/72 and *H.C. Debs.* 5s. 268, col 2121–6, both 30 June 1932.

17. Austen Chamberlain to Hilda, 2 July 1932, AC5/1/588; Rose Rosenberg to MacDonald, 1 July 1932, MacDonald MSS PRO30/69/678/3/503.

18. Chamberlain to Beaverbrook, 30 June 1932, Beaverbrook MSS C/80.

19. Hopkins to Fergusson, two notes, 4 July 1932, T172/1796B/158-61; CAB 50(32)2, 11 October 1932, CAB 23/72.

20. Collin Brooks Journal, 2 March and 1 July 1932; *The Times*, 'A Great Conversion Scheme', 1 July 1932.

21. Hore-Belisha to Runciman, 1 July 1932, Runciman MSS 260; Beaverbrook to Chamberlain, 2 July 1932, Beaverbrook MSS C/80; Rosenberg to MacDonald, 1 July 1932.

22. Chamberlain to Arthur Chamberlain, 24 October 1932, NC7/6/20.

23. 'The problems arising from the suspensions of gold payments', 24–25 September 1931, CAB 58/169.

24. Hopkins memorandum, 15 December 1931, T172/1768; Phillips, 'The Present Position of the Pound', 24 February 1932, T175/57.

25. Chamberlain to Hilda, 27 February and 12 March 1932.

26. Chamberlain to Ida, 20 February and to Hilda, 27 February 1932.

27. Chamberlain to MacDonald, 5 March 1932, MacDonald MSS PRO30/69/678/2/237–8.

28. 'Very secret' memorandum, 30 October 1931, para. 16, NC8/12/1–2.

29. Chamberlain to Hilda, 6 December 1931.

30. Susan Howson, *Sterling's Managed Float: the Operation of the Exchange Equalization Account, 1932–39* (Princeton, 1980), pp. 1, 7–8; CAB 14(33)2, 6 March 1933, CAB 23/75.

31. A.J.P. Taylor, *English History 1914–1945* (Harmondsworth, 1975), p. 375; Clarke, *A Question of Leadership*, p. 119. See also Kevin Jeffreys, *The*

Churchill Coalition and Wartime Politics, 1940–45 (Manchester, 1991), p. 13; Robert Blake, *The Conservative Party from Peel to Thatcher*, pp. 237, 245.

32. Roger Middleton, *Towards the Managed Economy: Keynes, the Treasury and the Fiscal Policy Debate of the 1930s* (1985), pp. 111–12; Jim Tomlinson, *Public Policy and the Economy Since 1900* (Oxford, 1990), pp. 111–12.

33. S.N. Broadberry, 'Fiscal Policy in Britain during the 1930s', *Economic History Review*, 2nd ser. 37 (1984), pp. 95–102; R. Middleton, 'The Constant Employment Budget Balance and British Budgetary Policy 1929–39', *Economic History Review*, 2nd ser. 34 (1981), pp. 266–86.

34. Tomlinson, *Public Policy*, p. 112. I.M. Drummond, *The Floating Pound and the Sterling Area, 1931–39* (Cambridge, 1981), pp. 15, 22, 25–6, 130–32.

35. Donald Winch, *Economics and Policy: A Historical Study* (Fontana ed., 1969), p. 218.

36. Robert Skidelsky, *John Maynard Keynes, Volume Two: The Economist as Saviour, 1920–1937* (1992), p. 436.

37. Ursula Hicks, *The Finance of British Government, 1920–1936* (Oxford, 1938), p. 362.

38. Chamberlain to Sir Francis Humphreys, 8 January 1932, NC7/11/24/15.

39. Chamberlain to Hilda, 11 June 1932 and 29 April 1933; CP 161(32), 25 May 1932, para. 14, CAB 24/230.

40. Chamberlain to Ida, 5, 19 March; to Hilda, 12 March 1932. *H.C. Debs*, 5s, 264, col 1438–9.

41. Sir Clive Wigram to Chamberlain, 16 April 1932, NC7/11/25/49.

42. MacDonald, Amery and Headlam Diary, all 19 April 1932; Geoffrey Lloyd to Davidson, 29 April 1932, Davidson (Indian) MSS Eur.C.557/116–22.

43. Chamberlain to Hilda, 23 April 1932; Montagu Norman to Chamberlain, 22 April 1932, NC8/16/1, 4.

44. Chamberlain to Hilda, 15 and 29 May 1932.

45. Chamberlain to MacDonald, 6 September 1932, MacDonald MSS 30/69/2/12 II.

46. Headlam Diary, 26 April 1932.

47. *H.C Debs*, 5s, 266, col 2338–48, 10 June 1932; Philip Goodhart, *The 1922: The Story of the 1922 Committee* (1973), pp. 52–62; Stuart Ball 'The 1922 Committee: the Formative Years, 1922–1945', *Parliamentary History*, 9 (1990), pp. 141–5.

48. *H.C Debs*, 5s, 274, col 1224–39, 16 February 1933; Chamberlain to Hilda, 18 February 1933.

49. Chamberlain to Weir, 4 March 1933, WEIR 11/13; Amery and Headlam Diary, 16 February 1933.

50. Chamberlain to Hilda, 18 February 1933; to Arthur Chamberlain, 20 February 1933, NC7/6/21; to Weir, 4 March 1933, WEIR 11/13.

51. Runciman to J.F. Simpson, 21 March 1933, Runciman MSS 265/26; MacDonald Diary, 21 December 1934.

52. Jenkins, *The Chancellors*, p. 351.

53. Northern Group deputation and memorandum, 16–17 February 1933 and Hopkins response, 20 March 1933, T171/309/140–69; Conservative Chief Whip's Office, WHIP 2/8.

54. Chamberlain to Hilda, 1 April 1933; to his wife, 18 January 1933, NC1/26/482.

55. CAB 22(32)1, 18 April 1932, CAB 23/71; TCS(33) Cabinet Committee on Taxation of Cooperative Societies, 20–23 February 1933, CAB 27/546.
56. CAB 9 and 23–4(33), 15 February and 5 April 1933 CAB 23/75; MacDonald to Chamberlain, 27 March, 3 and 6 April 1933; Chamberlain to MacDonald, 31 March 1933, MacDonald MSS PRO30/69/679.
57. MacDonald Diary, 19 February, 7 April, 21 May 1933.
58. Chamberlain to Ida, 7 May 1933.
59. Chamberlain to Hilda, 24 June 1933; Chamberlain Diary, 8 May 1933.
60. Amery and Headlam Diary, both 25 April 1933.
61. Winch, *Economics and Policy*, p. 215; Clarke, *Keynesian Revolution in the Making*, p. 33.
62. EAC(SC)6, Letter to the Prime Minister, 9 February 1933, CAB 58/18; CP 34(33), 15 February 1933, CAB 24/238.
63. *The Times*, 13–16 March 1933. Expanded and reprinted as *The Means to Prosperity* (1933); Winch, *Economics and Policy*, p. 217.
64. Middleton, *Towards the Managed Economy*, pp. 114–15. For lesser men and disagreeable facts see Chamberlain to Hilda, 18 February and 1 April 1933 and to Arthur Chamberlain, 20 February 1933, NC7/11/26/9.
65. *H.C. Debs*, 5s, 277, col 58, 25 April 1933.
66. Thomas Jones to his daughter, 20 October 1931, Jones (ed.), *A Diary with Letters*, p. 19.
67. Sir Richard Hopkins to the Chancellor, 20 October 1932, T175/70.
68. Ramsden, *From Balfour to Baldwin*, p. 339; Derek Aldcroft, *The British Economy: Volume I, The Years of Turmoil, 1920–1951* (Brighton, 1986), p. 105.
69. 'Mr Keynes first article: Treasury note', T171/309/107–11.
70. Roger Middleton, 'The Treasury in the 1930s: Political and Administrative Constraints on the Acceptance of the "New" Economics', *Oxford Economic Papers*, 34 (1982), pp. 48–77 and 'The Treasury and Public Investment: a Perspective on Inter-War Economic Management', *Public Administration*, 61 (1983), pp. 351–70.
71. Aldcroft, *The British Economy*, pp. 110–12; Sean Glynn and P. Howells, 'Unemployment in the 1930s: the "Keynesian Solution" Reconsidered', *Australian Economic History Review*, 20.1 (1980), pp. 28–45, but see T.J. Bolton's response, *AEHR*, 25(1985), pp. 1–30.
72. See 'Mr Keynes' Articles', n.d. and other Treasury briefs in T171/309 and T175/17; *H.C. Debs*, 5s, 274, col 1216–31, especially 1218–19, 16 February 1933.
73. ME(UK)28, 'Memorandum by Treasury on General Smuts' Memorandum', 17 July 1933, T172/1810C; Fergusson note for Chancellor, n.d. [26 January 1935], T172/1828/127.
74. Chamberlain to Hilda, 24 June 1933; to Ida, 28 October 1933.
75. 'Arguments against Unbalancing the Budget' and Hopkins to Fergusson, 7 April 1933, T171/309/213–18; *H.C. Debs*, 5s, 277, cols 57–61, 25 April 1933.
76. Middleton, *Towards the Managed Economy*, p. 115.
77. Chamberlain to Hore-Belisha, 26 September 1933, HOBE3/13/30.
78. Fergusson to Herbert Henderson, 16 February, 1933, T171/309/182–7.
79. Chamberlain to Ida, 28 October 1933.

80. Leith-Ross memorandum, 'The New Deal and British Trade', 6 February 1935, T188/117/51.
81. Chamberlain at the Lord Mayor of London's banquet, 1933, Walker-Smith, *Neville Chamberlain*, pp. 181–2.
82. Note to Chancellor, 10 March 1937, T172/1828/76.
83. Hopkins to the Chancellor , 16 February 1933, T175/93.
84. Chamberlain to MacDonald, 6 September 1932, MacDonald MSS 30/69/2/12 II.
85. Hopkins to Fergusson, 7 April 1933 and 'Arguments Against Unbalancing the Budget', T171/309/213–18.
86. CAB 68(33)5, 6 December 1933, CAB 23/77.
87. Chamberlain to Ida, 25 February 1933.
88. Skidelsky, *John Maynard Keynes*, II, p. 474, Clarke, *Keynesian Revolution*, p. 294; Chamberlain to Hilda, 18 March; to Ida, 25 March 1933.
89. Chamberlain to Hilda, 24 June, 23 July 1933; to Ida, 28 October 1933.
90. Middleton, *Towards the Managed Economy*, pp. 104, 114–15, 209. For Treasury recognition of this point see Hopkins to Fraser, 27 November 1936, T177/25.
91. Hopkins note to Chancellor and Warren Fisher, 11 and 21 March 1932 and his 'Speculative Forecast of 1935 on the basis of "Old Moore's Almanack"', T171/296.
92. Chamberlain annotations dated 13 and 22 March 1932 on Hopkins notes to Chancellor and Warren Fisher of 11 and 22 March 1932, T171/296.
93. CP 161(32), 25 May 1932, para. 13, CAB 24/230.
94. CAB 68(33)5, 6 December 1933, CAB 23/77.
95. Chamberlain to Ida, 17 March 1934.
96. Arthur Wood to Chamberlain, 18 April 1934, NC7/8/5.
97. *H.C. Debs*, 5s, 288, col 903, 919–24, 17 April 1934.
98. MacDonald and Amery Diary, 17 April 1934; Austen Chamberlain to Ida, 22 April 1934, AC5/1/660.
99. Chamberlain to Hilda, 21 April 1934.
100. Chamberlain to Hilda, 17 June and to Ida, 22 June and 7 July 1934.
101. Chamberlain to Ida, 16 February 1935.
102. *H.C. Debs*, 5s, 300, col 1615–35, 15 April 1935; Chamberlain to Hilda, 21 April 1935.
103. 'Talkie', 15 April 1935, NC7/11/28/44.

Chapter 10: Unemployment, Special Areas and Lloyd George's 'New Deal', 1932–1937

1. Alan Booth, 'Britain in the 1930s: a Managed Economy? A Reply to Peden and Middleton', *Economic History Review*, 2nd ser. 42 (1989), pp. 550–52.
2. Winch, *Economics and Policy*, p. 224; Aldcroft, *The British Economy*, pp. 110–14, 119, 125, 131; M.W. Kirby, *The Decline of British Industrial Power Since 1870* (1981), pp. 67–8.
3. Jeffreys, *The Churchill Coalition and Wartime Politics*, p. 13.
4. Samuel H. Beer, *Modern British Politics: A Study of Parties and Pressure Groups* (1965), Chapter 10; Alan Booth, 'Britain in the 1930s: a managed economy?', *Economic History Review*, 2nd ser. 40 (1987), pp. 499, 522.

5. Chamberlain to Ida, 10 November 1934.
6. John Maynard Keynes, *Collected Writings of John Maynard Keynes: Volume IX, Essays in Persuasion* (1972), p. 299.
7. Philip Snowden, *Autobiography* (2 volumes, 1934), II, p. 963; Chamberlain to Hilda, 2 March 1919 and 12 July 1924.
8. Chamberlain to Hilda, 15 March and to Ida, 22 March 1919.
9. Chamberlain to Lord Bledisloe, 17 July 1940, NC7/11/33/29.
10. Taylor, *English History*, p. 410; H.W. Richardson, 'The Economic Significance of the Depression in Britain', *Journal of Contemporary History*, 4 (1969), pp. 3–19; Winch, *Economics and Policy*, p. 214; Middlemas & Barnes, *Baldwin*, p. 655.
11. *H.C Debs*, 5s, 261, col 286–8, 4 February 1932.
12. Sir Herbert Hutchinson, *Tariff Making and Industrial Reconstruction: An Account of the Work of the Import Duties Advisory Committee, 1932–1939* (1965), p. 165.
13. Beer, *Modern British Politics*, pp. 278–9.
14. Henry Clay, *The Postwar Unemployment Problem* (1929), pp. 176, 178.
15. Self, *Tories and Tariffs*, Chapter VIII.
16. CRD/2 'The Iron and Steel Industry' and Chamberlain's covering letter, 25 June 1930; CRD/3 'The Cotton Committee', 14 July 1930, AC49/1/2, 4; Chamberlain to Ida, 21 February 1931.
17. Chamberlain to Snowden, 15 January 1932, NC7/11/25/41; BT(31) 2nd and 4th Conclusions, 8, 13 January 1932, CAB 27/467; CP 25(32), para. 22, 19 January 1932; CAB 5–6(32)1 and CAB 10(32)2, 21 and 29 January 1932, CAB 23/70.
18. Chamberlain to Hilda, 13 February and to Ida, 20 February 1932.
19. Fergusson to Chancellor, 14 October 1932, T172/1772/41; Capie, *Depression and Protectionism*, p. 94.
20. Sir Sydney Chapman, Unpublished Autobiography, pp. 298–9; Hutchinson, *Tariff Making*, pp. 155–6.
21. Runciman to Chamberlain, 13 April 1932, Runciman MSS 254; MacDonald Diary, 18 April 1932; CAB 23(32)1, 18 April 1932, CAB 23/71; CP 149(32), 4 May 1932, CAB 24/229.
22. Chamberlain to Hilda, 11 June 1932.
23. Fergusson to the Chancellor, 14 October 1932, T172/1772/41–2 and 8 February 1933, T172/1773.
24. Runciman to Chamberlain, 5, 6 October 1932 and Chamberlain note, 15 October 1932, T172/1772/44, 108-12.
25. A.W. Hurst, 'The Reorganisation of the Iron and Steel Industry: Report on the Present Position', 31 October 1933; 'Record of a conversation between the Chancellor of the Exchequer and Sir George May', 2 November 1933, T172/1773/15–16, 366–7.
26. Ibid.
27. Peter Hall, *Governing the Economy: The Politics of State Intervention in Britain and France* (Oxford, 1986), p. 54.
28. Chamberlain to Runciman, 27 August 1933, Runciman MSS 265/62; Chamberlain Diary, January 1934; CAB 69(33)4, 13 December 1933, CAB 23/73.
29. Sir Thomas White to Baldwin, 8 December and reply 13 December 1934,

Baldwin MSS 169/365–7; *H.C.Debs*, 5s, 295, col 1543–4, 4 December 1934.

30. Chamberlain to Lord Weir, 8 November 1934, Weir MSS DC 96/22/2. See also Sir Horace Hamilton, 'Industrial Reorganisation', 10 May 1936, T188/117/77–8.
31. Ramsden, *The Making of Conservative Party Policy*, pp. 81–2.
32. Simon Diary, 20 November 1934, Simon MSS 7 fol. 2–3.
33. Frederic Miller, 'The Unemployment Policy of the National Government, 1931–1936', *Historical Journal*, 19.2 (1976), p. 467; Peter Dewey, *War and Progress* (1997), p. 251; Aldcroft, *The British Economy*, pp. 119, 125; W. Ashworth, *An Economic History of England, 1870–1939* (1960), p. 405; Scott Newton and Dilwyn Porter, *Modernisation Frustrated: The Politics of Industrial Decline in Britain Since 1900* (1988), p. 85.
34. Wayne Parsons, *The Political Economy of British Regional Policy* (1988), p. 1.
35. W.R. Garside, *British Unemployment 1919–1939: A Study in Public Policy* (Cambridge, 1990), pp. 251–5; Miller, 'The Unemployment Policy of the National Government', pp. 465–6; Macmillan, *Winds of Change*, p. 295.
36. Chamberlain to Hilda, 24 March 1934; Chamberlain Diary, 26 April 1934.
37. Chamberlain Diary, 27 January 1934.
38. *The Times*, 23 March 1934; CAB 13(34)14, 28 March 1934, CAB 23/78; Chamberlain Diary, 26 April 1934.
39. Davidson 'Memorandum on Chancellor's suggestions at meeting this morning', 26 April 1934, Davidson MSS 208.
40. DA(34) 1st Meeting of the Committee on the Reports of Investigators into Depressed Areas, 11 October 1934, CAB 27/578.
41. DAC(28) 1st Meeting of Distress Areas Committee, 14 December 1928; Chamberlain's 'Distressed Areas' paper, 13 December 1928, CAB 27/381; Chamberlain Diary, 4 and 9 December 1928.
42. CP 227(34) Depressed Areas Committee: Interim Report, 22 October 1934, CAB 27/577.
43. Chamberlain Diary, 17 October and to Ida, 27 October 1934; CAB 36(34)11, 24 October 1934 and CAB 43(34)19, 28 November 1934, CAB 23/80.
44. DA(34) 2nd Meeting, 18 October 1934, CAB 27/578; Chamberlain to his wife, 11 October 1934, NC1/26/502; to Ida, 27 October 1934.
45. R.A. Butler to Lord Brabourne, 15 November 1934, Brabourne MSS Eur. F97/20B/114.
46. DA(34) 3rd Meeting, 1 November 1934, CAB 27/578.
47. Chamberlain to Hilda, 17 November 1934.
48. Robert Boothby to Baldwin, 31 January 1934, Baldwin MSS 169/41.
49. Chamberlain to Ida, 24 November 1934 and 6 January 1935; *H.C Debs*, 5s, 296, col 1609–22, 21 December 1934.
50. MacDonald Diary, 21 December 1934, 23, 30 January, 10, 18, 20 February 1935; MacDonald to Sir Henry Betterton, 4 August 1933, MacDonald MSS PRO30/69/679/204.
51. Hilda Runciman Diary, 25 April 1933.
52. Chamberlain and MacDonald Diary, both 30 January 1935.
53. Simon to Chamberlain, 17 January 1935, Simon MSS 81/31–2.
54. MacDonald Diary, 23 January 1935; Butler to Brabourne, 20 December 1934, Brabourne MSS Eur.F97/20B/89.

55. CAB 6(35)1, 30 January 1935, CAB 23/81; Chamberlain Diary, 11 December 1934, 24 and 30 January 1935.
56. Butler to Brabourne, 20 December 1934.
57. Chamberlain to Arthur Chamberlain, 11 February 1932, NC7/8/19.
58. MacDonald Diary, 21 January 1935; Simon Diary, 20 January 1935.
59. Notes to the Chancellor from Fisher, Fergusson and Phillips, 25–26 January 1935, T172/126–37.
60. Chamberlain to Ida, 6 January 1935; to Baldwin, 4 January 1935, Baldwin MSS 170/51; Chamberlain Diary, 14 [?] December 1934, 28 January 1935; MacDonald Diary, 4 February 1935.
61. Chamberlain to Hilda, 26 January 1935; to Ida, 2 February 1935; Chamberlain Diary, 28–30 January, 3 February 1935.
62. Frances Stevenson Diary, 10 January 1935.
63. Jones Diary, 17 November 1934.
64. Chamberlain Diary, 28 January, 5 and 7 February 1935; MacDonald Diary, 12 February 1935.
65. MacDonald Diary, 21 March 1935; Chamberlain to Ida, 4 May 1935.
66. Chamberlain to Ida, 20 January, 16 February 1935; to Hilda, 23 February 1935.
67. Chamberlain Diary, 8 and 18 March 1935; Chamberlain to Ida, 3 March 1935.
68. Sir Edward Grigg to Baldwin, 6 March 1935, Baldwin MSS 47/32.
69. Chamberlain to Lord Weir, 5 March 1935, Weir MSS DC96/22/2.
70. Chamberlain to Ida, 3 and 30 March 1935; to Arthur Chamberlain, 12 April 1935, NC7/6/26; to Hilda, 6 and 21 April 1935.
71. Collin Brooks Journal and Frances Stevenson Diary, both 18 April 1935.
72. MacDonald and Chamberlain Diary, both 18 April 1935; Chamberlain to Hilda, 21 April 1935.
73. Frances Stevenson Diary, 18 April 1935.
74. Thomas Jones to Baldwin, 16 May 1935, Baldwin MSS 47/40–42. A copy to 'My dear Chief' is also in the Lloyd George papers in G/41/24/4.
75. Chamberlain to Ida, 15 June and 6 July 1935.
76. CAB 36(35)1, 10 July 1935, CAB 23/82; Chamberlain Diary, 12 July 1935.
77. Chamberlain to Ida, 20 July 1935; CAB 37(35)1, 15 July 1935, CAB 23/82.
78. 'Statement by HMG on Certain Proposals submitted by Lloyd George', 18 July 1935, T172/1841B; *The Times*, 22 July 1935.
79. Chamberlain to Ida, 20 July and to Hilda, 28 July 1935.
80. 'Council of Action: Public Works', 5 March 1937 and note to the Chancellor, 10 March 1937, T172/1828/74–81.
81. Chamberlain to Hilda, 14 July 1935.
82. DA(34) 6th Meeting, 15 July 1935 and Appendix, CAB 27/578; CP 197(35), 18 October 1935, CAB 27/577.
83. DA(34) 2nd Meeting, 18 October 1934, CAB 27/578.
84. 'The Continuance of the Special Areas Act', 16 November 1936, T172/1828/154.
85. Chamberlain to Ida, 22 November 1936.
86. Hopkins memorandum and Chamberlain's note, both 16 November 1936, T172/1828/181–5.

87. Butler to Brabourne, 18 November 1936 and 2 March 1937, Brabourne MSS Eur.F97/21/126-29, 79.
88. DA(34) 1st Meeting, 11 October 1934 and Document DA(34)4, 27 September 1935, CAB 27/577–8; Chamberlain's annotation on Hopkins note, 16 November 1936, T172/1828/184.
89. DA(34) 10th and 11th Meeting, 26 January and 10 February 1937, CAB 27/578; Cmd. 5386, Statement Relating to Special Areas, March 1937, para. 15, T172/1828.
90. CP 57(37) and CAB 8(37)6, 17 February 1937, CAB 23/87; Browett to Chegwidden, 8 March 1937, T172/1828/120–22.
91. Chamberlain to Ida, 20 February 1937.
92. Miller, 'The Unemployment Policy of the National Government', pp. 453–4, 476.
93. Aldcroft, *The British Economy*, pp. 134–5; Peden, *The Treasury and Public Policy*, p. 248.
94. Booth, 'A Reply to Peden and Middleton', p. 551.
95. Chamberlain to Ida, 12 May 1934.
96. Chamberlain to Hilda, 15 October 1932.
97. CP 10(33), 23 January 1933, CAB 24/237; CAB 25(33)2, 7 April 1933, CAB 23/75.
98. Chamberlain to Ida, 17 December 1932 and 29 January 1933; CP 10(33), 10 January 1933, CAB 24/237; CAB 3(33)1, 25 January 1933, CAB 23/75.
99. CAB 25(33)2, 7 April 1933 and CAB 48(33)12, 26 July 1933, CAB 23/75, 77; CP 190(33) and 195(33), 21–22 July 1933, CAB 24/242.
100. Chamberlain Diary, January 1934; Eric Briggs and Alan Deacon, 'The Creation of the Unemployment Assistance Board', *Policy and Politics*, 2.1 (1974), pp. 43–62; Frederic Miller, 'National Assistance or Unemployment Assistance? The British Cabinet and Relief Policy, 1932–35', *Journal of Contemporary History*, 9.3 (1974), pp. 163–84.
101. Chamberlain Diary, January 1934 and 8 March 1935; Chamberlain to Hilda, 30 October 1932 and 28 July 1935; to Ida, 17 March and 9 June 1934.
102. W.P. Crozier interview with Herbert Samuel, 19 July 1935; Hore-Belisha Diary, 7 May 1935, HOBE1/2.

Chapter 11: Foreign and Defence Policy, 1934–1937

1. Earl of Avon, *Facing the Dictators* (1962), p. 445; Chamberlain Diary, 19 February 1936.
2. Chamberlain Diary, January and 3–5 December 1934, 16 and 19 February 1936; Austen Chamberlain to Hilda, 29 February 1936, AC5/1/727.
3. Michael Howard, *The Continental Commitment: the Dilemma of British Defence Policy in the Era of Two World Wars* (Penguin ed., 1974), p. 105; CAB 62(33)5, 15 November 1933, CAB 23/77.
4. CP 105(32), 17 March 1932, CAB 24/229; Chamberlain to Hilda, 21 October 1933.
5. *H.C. Debs*, 5s, 270, col 632, 10 November 1932; Macmillan, *Winds of Change*, p. 575.
6. Chamberlain Diary, 3 May 1934; Chamberlain to Ida, 12 May 1934.

7. DC(M)(32) 41st Conclusions of the Ministerial Disarmament Committee, 3 May 1934, CAB 16/110.

8. Ibid.; DC(M)(32) 44th Conclusions, 10 May 1934; Chamberlain Diary, 6 June 1934.

9. DC(M)(32) Paper 120, 'Note by the Chancellor ... on the Report of the DRC', 20 June 1934, para. 9, CAB 16/111.

10. DC(M)(32)41, 44–45th and 51st Meeting, 3, 10, 15 May and 22 June 1934, CAB 16/111; Chamberlain Diary, 6 June 1934.

11. G.C. Peden, *British Rearmament and the Treasury, 1932–1939* (Edinburgh, 1979), p. 123.

12. DC(M)(32) Paper 120, para. 5, 14.

13. Chamberlain to Hilda, 1 July 1934.

14. MacDonald Diary and DC(M)(32) 50th Meeting, both 25 June 1934.

15. CP 205(34), CAB 24/250, Chamberlain Diary and CAB 31(34) Appendix, CAB 23/79, all dated 31 July 1934.

16. Chamberlain to Hilda, 28 July 1934.

17. General Sir Henry Pownall Diary, 3 May and 18 June 1934; Keith Neilson, 'The Defence Requirements Sub-Committee, British Strategic Foreign Policy, Neville Chamberlain and the Path to Appeasement', *English Historical Review*, 116 (2003), pp. 678, 680–83; Howard, *Continental Commitment*, pp. 112–13; Brian Bond, *British Military Policy between Two World Wars* (Oxford, 1980), p. 212.

18. Air Marshal, Sir John Slessor, *The Central Blue* (1956), pp. 204–6.

19. Peter Bell, *Chamberlain, Germany and Japan 1933–34* (1996), pp. 22, 118, 130, 145–7; Peden, *British Rearmament*, pp. 77–8.

20. Chamberlain Diary, January 1934; CAB 10(34)2, 19 March 1934, CAB 23/74.

21. Chamberlain Diary, 25 March; to Hilda, 24 March 1934; CAB 12(34)1, 22 March 1934, CAB 23/78.

22. Chamberlain Diary, 27 March 1934; Chamberlain to Ida, 1 April 1934.

23. Chamberlain to Hilda, 5 May and to Ida, 12 May 1934.

24. CAB 57(33)2, 26 October 1933, CAB 23/77. See also Committee of Imperial Defence, (CID), 261st Meeting, 9 November 1933, CAB 2/6.

25. Chamberlain to Hilda, 28 July 1934.

26. CAB 9(34)13, 14 March 1934, CAB 23/78.

27. NCM(35) 1st Meeting of the Committee on the Naval Disarmament Conference, 16 April 1934, CAB 27/147; JTC (34) 1st and 2nd Meetings of the Committee on Japanese Trade Competition, 27 March and 11 April 1934 CAB 27/568; DC(M)(32) 40–41st Meeting, 1 and 3 May 1934, CAB 27/506.

28. Robert Bingham [US Ambassador, London] to Davis (telegram paraphrase), 2 May and to Roosevelt, 8 May 1934, Roosevelt MSS PSF 32/302.

29. Chamberlain to Hilda, 27 August 1934.

30. 'The Naval Conference and our Relations with Japan', September 1934, NC8/19/1.

31. Chamberlain to Hilda, 8 September 1934; to Simon, 1 September 1934, *DBFP*, Series I, XIII, pp. 24–5.

32. Chamberlain to his wife and Diary, both 9 October 1934, NC1/26/501;

Simon to Sir R. Clive [British Ambassador, Tokyo], 8 October 1934, T172/1831/53–4.

33. Chamberlain to Hilda and to his wife, both 21 October 1934, NC1/26/505.

34. Chamberlain to Ida, 27 October 1934; Chamberlain Diary, 25 October 1934.

35. Chamberlain to Hilda, 17 November 1934.

36. Norman Davis to Cordell Hull, 21 November and to Roosevelt, 27 November 1934; Donald Cameron Watt, *Personalities and Policies* (1965), p. 98.

37. E(PD)(37) 11th Meeting of Principal Delegates to Imperial Conference, 2 June 1937, CAB 32/128.

38. Chamberlain to Ida, 9 and 22 June 1934.

39. MacDonald Diary, 15 and 28 May 1935.

40. Chamberlain Diary, 3 May 1935; to Ida and Hilda, 9 December 1934.

41. Ibid.; Chamberlain to Hilda, 22 May 1935.

42. Chamberlain Diary, 11 February 1935; MacDonald Diary, 10 February, 21 March and 30 April 1935.

43. Chamberlain to Hilda, 11 March 1934; to Ida, 17 March 1934; Chamberlain Diary, 10 March 1934.

44. Chamberlain to Ida, 29 April 1934.

45. Chamberlain to Hilda, 18 May 1935; to Ida, 20 July 1935.

46. Chamberlain to Ida, 10 February and 3 March 1934; Chamberlain Diary, 3, 6, 17, 28 February and 3 March 1934.

47. 'Memo of new programme subjects prepared by N.C. and laid before the C[abinet] C[onservative] C[ommittee] on Friday March 2, 1934', NC8/20/1.

48. Chamberlain to Ida, 17 March and 7 July 1934.

49. Chamberlain to Hilda, 4 October 1936; PT(36) Committee on Physical Training, CAB 27/612; Cmd. 5364, January 1937 and other papers in NC8/23/1–25.

50. Chamberlain to Baldwin, 2 November and reply, 5 November 1934, Baldwin MSS 170/52–3 and NC7/11/28/3.

51. Chamberlain to Hilda, 9–10 November and to Ida, 17 November 1935.

52. Chamberlain to Hilda, 22 June, 7 and 22 September 1935.

53. DRC 37: Final Report, 21 November 1935, CAB 16/112.

54. Chamberlain to Ida, 30 March 1935.

55. Chamberlain to Hilda, 12, 18, 26 May and 22 June 1935.

56. Chamberlain Diary, 5 and 18 July; Chamberlain to Ida, 6 and 20 July 1935.

57. Conference of Ministers, 21 August 1935, CAB 23/82; Chamberlain to Ida, 25 August 1935.

58. Lord Lloyd to his wife, 23 August 1935, Lloyd MSS GLLD19/7.

59. Chamberlain to Ida, 16 September and to Hilda, 22 September 1935; to his wife, 15 September 1935, NC1/26/512.

60. Chamberlain to Ida, 5 October and 8 December 1935.

61. Chamberlain to Ida, 8 December 1935.

62. Chamberlain Diary, 5 July 1935.

63. Chamberlain Diary, 29 November and 8 December 1935; CAB 51(35)1, 2 December 1935, CAB 23/82.

64. Hoare to Baldwin, 8 December 1935, Avon MSS AP20/4/12B.
65. Chamberlain to Hilda, 15 December 1935.
66. CAB 51–3(35)1, 2 and 9–10 December 1935, CAB 23/82; Chamberlain Diary, 15 and 17 December 1935.
67. 'December 1935 Crisis', Templewood MSS XIX/6.
68. Chamberlain to Hilda, 15 December 1935.
69. Simon Diary, 11 December 1935; Chamberlain to Hilda, 15 December 1935.
70. Chamberlain Diary, 17 December 1935.
71. Simon and Chamberlain Diary and CAB 56(35)1, all 18 December 1935, 'The Italo-Abyssinian Dispute', CAB 23/90B.
72. Chamberlain to Ida, 16 February 1936; Hoare to Chamberlain, 18 January, 23 February and 19 March 1936, NC7/11/29/27, 29 and Templewood MSS VIII:6(21).
73. Chamberlain Diary, 11 March 1936.
74. Chamberlain to Ida, 13 April; to Hilda, 2 May 1936.
75. *H.C. Debs*, 5s, 310, col 2555, 26 March 1936; Butler to Brabourne, 27 March 1936, Brabourne MSS Eur.F97/21/149.
76. Chamberlain and Eden Diary, both 27 April 1936.
77. Chamberlain to Ida, 10 May 1936.
78. CAB 39–40(36), 27–29 May 1936, CAB 23/83–4.
79. Chamberlain Diary, 17 June 1936; to Hilda, 14 June; to his wife, 11 and 15 June 1936, NC1/26/516–17; Amery Diary, 15 June 1936.
80. Chamberlain to Ida, 20 June 1936; to Baldwin, 21 August 1936, Baldwin MSS 171/45–6.
81. Chamberlain Diary, 22 January 1934; CAB 2(34)5, 24 January and CAB 5(34)21, 14 February 1934, CAB 23/78.
82. Chamberlain Diary and to Hilda, both 3 February 1934; CAB 3(34)24, 31 January and Appendix, CAB 23/78.
83. CAB 24(34)11, 13 June 1934, CAB 23/79.
84. Chamberlain to Ida, 7 July 1934; CAB 27(34)3 and Cmd. 4640, both 4 July 1934.
85. Neil Forbes, *Doing Business with the Nazis: Britain's Economic and Financial Relations with Germany, 1931–1939* (2000), p. 92 and Chapters 3–4.
86. Chamberlain to Hilda, 28 July 1934 and 9 and 18 March 1935.
87. Lord Halifax to Chamberlain, 11 October 1938, NC11/31/124A.
88. Chamberlain to Hilda, 23 May 1935; to Ida, 4 August and 8 December 1935.
89. Chamberlain to Hilda, 9 February 1936.
90. 'Note of conversation [with Mussolini]', n.d. [January 1939], PREM 1/327/57; Lord Zetland to Lord Linlithgow, 24 January 1939, Zetland MSS Eur.D609/11/16.
91. Chamberlain to Hilda, 26 May and 22 June 1935.
92. Chamberlain Diary, 2 August 1935 and 11 March 1936.
93. Chamberlain Diary, 2 August and 19 October 1935.
94. Chamberlain to Hilda, 22 September, 9–10 November 1935; to Baldwin, 2 November 1935, Baldwin MSS 170/52–3.
95. Chamberlain Diary, 11 February to 11 March 1936; to Hilda, 9 February 1936.

96. CAB 75(36)6, 16 December 1936, CAB 23/86.
97. Chamberlain Diary, 19 January 1936.
98. DRC 37: Third Report, 21 November 1935, CAB 16/112.
99. Pownall Diary, 27 January 1936; Chamberlain to Hilda, 9 February 1936; CP 26(36) and CAB 10(36)1, 25 February 1936, CAB 23/83.
100. Chamberlain to Ida, 6 February 1937.
101. CAB 20(37)4, 5 May 1937, CAB 23/88.
102. Inskip Diary, 11 January 1939.
103. CAB 13(36)2, 2 March 1936, CAB 23/83.
104. *H.C. Debs*, 5s, 320, col 1206–17, 17 February 1937; Peden, *British Rearmament*, pp. 71–3.
105. CAB 7(37)13, 10 February 1937, CAB 23/87.
106. Chamberlain to Hilda, 25 April 1937.
107. CP 165(37) 'Defence Expenditure', 27 June 1937, CAB 24/270.
108. Margesson to Chamberlain and reply, 1 and 2 August 1936, NC7/11/29/40 and MRGN1/3/13.
109. Chamberlain Diary and to Ida, both 2 August 1936; Simon Diary, 11 August 1936.
110. Chamberlain to Ida, 28 March, 13 April, 20 June 1936; Chamberlain Diary, 26 July 1936; Baldwin to Chamberlain, 19 August 1936, NC7/11/29/2.
111. Chamberlain to Margesson, 2 August 1936, MRGN1/3/13; to Ida, 13 April and 19 July 1936; to Hilda, 27 June, 11 July, 26 August and 4 October 1936.
112. Chamberlain to Hilda, 27 June and 17 October 1936.
113. MacDonald Diary, 11 March, 7 April, 11 June and 26 June 1936.
114. Chamberlain Diary, 7 October 1936.
115. Chamberlain to Hilda, 28 November 1925 and 17 October 1937; to Ida, 16 September 1935.
116. Chamberlain to Hilda, 25 January 1936; Chamberlain Diary, 20 January 1936.
117. Chamberlain to Alfred Greenwood, 3 January 1937, NC7/5/31; Chamberlain Diary, 7 December 1936.
118. Warren Fisher to Chamberlain, 7 November 1936 and two drafts, all in PREM 1/463; Chamberlain to Hilda, 14 November 1936; Chamberlain and MacDonald Diary, 19 November 1936.
119. Chamberlain Diary, 26 October, 25 November and 4–6 December 1936; Cabinet Record 27 November and 4 December 1936, PREM 1/475.
120. Chamberlain Diary, 7 December and to Hilda, 13 December 1936.
121. Sir Horace Wilson note to Chancellor, 11 December 1936, NC8/22/2; Chamberlain Diary, 7 and 9 December; to Hilda, 13 December 1936; Simon Diary, 9 December 1936.
122. Chamberlain to Alfred Greenwood, 3 January 1937, NC7/5/21; Chamberlain Diary 12 April and 30 May 1937; Sir Clive Wigram to Chamberlain, 11 April 1937, PREM 1/463.
123. Chamberlain to the Duke of Windsor, 7 January and reply 12 January 1938, PREM 1/465.
124. Chamberlain to Hilda, 11 July 1936 and 6 September 1936; to George Kenrick, 14 February 1937, NC1/12/2; to Mary, 10 July 1936, NC1/20/1/172; to his wife, 25 August 1936, NC1/26/519.

125. Chamberlain to Hilda, 23 September and 14 November 1936.
126. Chamberlain to George Kenrick, 14 February 1937, NC1/12/2; to Arthur Chamberlain, 20 October 1937, NC7/6/27.
127. Chamberlain to Churchill, 18 March 1937, NC7/9/34; Chamberlain Diary, 16 March 1937.
128. Chamberlain to Vansittart, 25 March 1937, Vansittart MSS 1/5/18; to Baldwin, 17 March 1937, Baldwin MSS 173/32; to Hilda, 30 May 1937.
129. Chamberlain to Ida, 21 March 1937.
130. Chamberlain to Hilda, 10 April 1937.
131. Chamberlain Diary, 21 and 24 April; to Hilda, 25 April 1937; *H.C. Debs*, 5s, 322, col 1601, 1615–20, 20 April 1937.
132. Butler to Brabourne, 1 May 1937, Brabourne MSS Eur.F97/21/43; Amery Diary, 20 April 1937.
133. Runciman to Lord Lothian [?], 21 June 1937, Runciman MSS 285/28.
134. Charles Grey to Chamberlain, 1 May 1937, NC7/11/30/56.
135. Amery Diary, 20 April and 27 May 1937; Headlam Diary, 22 April 1937; Chamberlain to Hannon, 23 April 1937, Hannon MSS 17/1; Deputations to the Chancellor on NDC, T172/1856.
136. Hilda Runciman Diary, 19–26 April 1937; Ramsden, *The Making of Conservative Party Policy*, pp. 87–8.
137. Butler to Brabourne, 23 April and 5 May 1937, Brabourne MSS Eur. F97/21/30, 46.
138. Chamberlain Diary, 29 April and 17 May; to Hilda, 30 May 1937; *H.C. Debs*, 5s, 324, col 916–17, 1 June 1937.
139. Chamberlain to Ida, 22 May 1937.

Chapter 12: A New Style of Prime Minister, May 1937–February 1938

1. Chamberlain to Hilda, 30 May 1937; to Ida, 16 October 1937.
2. *Morning Post*, 31 May 1937.
3. John Reith, *Into the Wind* (1949), p. 308. For his contempt for popularity-seeking 'humbug' see Horace Wilson's memoir, 'Munich', October 1941, CAB 127/158, pp. 9–10.
4. Ramsden, *The Making of Conservative Party Policy*, p. 66; Chamberlain to Hilda, 4 October 1936.
5. Francis Boyd, *Harry Boardman: The Glory of Parliament* (1960), p. 49.
6. Chamberlain to Hilda, 27 March 1938. See also Anne Chamberlain to R.A. Butler, 7 January [1941], Butler MSS G11/185; Horace Wilson, 'Munich', October 1941, CAB 127/158, pp. 1–2, 13–14.
7. Chamberlain to Leslie Scott, 18 June 1937, NC Letters Additional 56.
8. Chamberlain to Ida, 16 October 1937; Hore-Belisha Diary, 25 May 1937, HOBE1/4.
9. Chamberlain to Ida, 3 March and to Hilda, 11 March 1934.
10. Hoare to Chamberlain, 17 March 1937, NC7/11/30/74.
11. Simon to Chamberlain, 15 September 1936, NC7/11/29/45 and reply, 23 September 1936, Simon MSS 83/193.
12. Margesson to Chamberlain, March 1937, NC8/24/1.
13. Chamberlain to Hilda, 22 June 1935; Chamberlain Diary, 8 and 21 February 1936.

14. MacDonald Diary, 18 May 1937; Chamberlain Diary, 11 February and 13 March 1937; to Hilda, 30 May 1937.
15. Chamberlain to Runciman, 6 May 1937, Runciman MSS 285/37; and reply, 7 May 1937, NC7/11/30/112; Hilda Runciman Diary, 4 May 1937.
16. Chamberlain Diary, 11 May 1937; to Hilda, 30 May 1937; to Runciman, 10 May 1937, NC7/11/30/113.
17. Chamberlain to Hilda, 23 March 1935.
18. Amery Diary, 21 September 1937; Chamberlain to Ida, 8 August 1937.
19. MacDonald Diary, 9 January 1934.
20. Hore-Belisha Diary, 30 May 1937, HOBE 1/4; Thomas Jones to A. Flexner, 30 May 1937, Jones (ed.), *Diary with Letters*, p. 350.
21. Chamberlain to Hilda, 26 June and 1 August 1937; Chamberlain Diary, 19 March, 11 May 1937; Simon Diary, 20 May 1937.
22. Amery Diary, 13 July 1937 and 24 October 1938.
23. Chamberlain to Hilda, 26 June 1937; Baldwin to Chamberlain, 23 July 1937, NC7/11/30/23.
24. N.J. Benson to Lord Rushcliffe, 16 October 1937, NC7/11/30/26.
25. Headlam Diary, 17 July 1937; Crawford Diary, 9 February 1938 and 2 May 1939.
26. Lord Vansittart, *Lessons of my Life* (n.d. [1943]), pp. 33, 106, 169, 187.
27. Chamberlain to Hilda, 24 October; to Ida, 12 December 1937.
28. 'Lunch with Hore-Belisha, 27 March 1939', Liddell Hart MSS LH11/HB1939/3.
29. Chamberlain to Hilda, 17 December 1937; to Duff Cooper, 17 December and reply 19 December 1937, NC7/11/30/39–40.
30. Butler to Brabourne, 2 and 15 March 1937, Brabourne MSS Eur.F97/22B/75, 84; Sir Nevile Henderson, *Failure of a Mission: Berlin 1937–1939* (1940), p. 65.
31. Lord Halifax to Henderson, 24 November, 3 and 9 December 1937; to Lord Southwood, 1 December 1937; 'Memorandum of a Conversation between Lord Halifax and Dr Goebbels on November 21, 1937'; Hickleton MSS, A4.410.3.3; Chamberlain to Ida, 28 May and 6 August 1938; to Hilda, 24 July 1938. Also Richard Cockett, *Twilight of Truth: Chamberlain, Appeasement and the Manipulation of the Press* (1989).
32. Chamberlain Diary, 17 June 1936; Thomas Jones to A. Flexner, 30 May 1937 reporting to Nancy Astor, Jones (ed.), *Diary with Letters*, p. 350; Nicolson Diary, 30 June 1937, reporting 'Shakes' Morrison; Horace Wilson, 'Munich', October 1941, CAB 127/158, p. 2.
33. CAB 36(37)5, 6 October 1937, CAB 23/89; CP 24(38), 8 February 1938, CAB 24/274.
34. CP 199(38), 14 September 1938, CAB 24/275; Chamberlain to Mrs Morton Price, 16 January 1938, Feiling, *Life of Neville Chamberlain*, p. 324; Horace Wilson, 'Munich', October 1941, CAB 127/158, p. 34.
35. Simon, *Retrospect*, pp. 252–3; Viscount Maugham, *At the End of the Day* (1954), p. 381; Sir Horace Wilson to Anne Chamberlain, 18 July 1948, NC11/1/925.
36. For the most sophisticated 'counter-revisionist' case see R.A.C. Parker, *Chamberlain and Appeasement: British Policy and the Coming of the Second World War* (1993), pp. 137, 364–5.

37. Chamberlain to Mrs Morton Price, 16 January 1938; to Hilda, 1 August 1937.
38. Chamberlain to Hilda, 14 November 1936; Horace Wilson, 'Munich', October 1941, CAB 127/158, pp. 16–17.
39. CP 316(37), 15 December 1937, CAB 24/273; CAB 48–9(37), 22 December 1937, CAB 23/90; *H.C.Debs*, 5s, 333, col 1558, 7 March 1938.
40. CAB 13(38)1, 14 March 1938, CAB 23/92; Hopkins to Simon, 29 October 1938, PREM 1/236.
41. Peden, *British Rearmament*, pp. 12–13, 63, 179–84; R.A.C. Parker, 'British Rearmament 1936–39: Treasury, Trade Union and Skilled Labour', *English Historical Review*, 96 (1981), pp. 306–11 and idem 'The Pound Sterling, the American Treasury and British Preparations for War, 1938–39', *EHR*, 98 (1983), pp. 261–79.
42. CAB 5(37)14 and CAB 8(37)4, 3 and 17 February 1937, CAB 23/87.
43. Richard Overy with Andrew Wheatcroft, *The Road to War* (revised ed., 1999), pp. 95–6. Peden, *British Rearmament*, pp. 179–84.
44. Chamberlain to Simon, 31 July 1938, Simon MSS 84/191–2; CAB 1(39)9, 18 January 1939, CAB 23/97.
45. CP 149(39) 'Note on the Financial Situation', CAB 24/287; CAB 36(39)2, 3 July 1939, CAB 23/100.
46. Hore-Belisha Diary, 3 July 1939, HOBE1/5.
47. Paul Emrys-Evans to Lord Salisbury, 21 July 1943, Emrys-Evans MSS 58247/4.
48. Chamberlain to Eden, 3 and 16 November 1937, AP20/5/12–14; Eden Diary, 8 November 1937; Harvey Diary, 16 November 1937.
49. Chamberlain to Ida, 19 July 1936; to Lord Weir, 1 August 1937, Weir MSS DC96/22/2.
50. Chamberlain to Ida, 30 October 1937.
51. CAB 48(38)5 and CAB 51(38)3, 3 and 31 October 1938, CAB 23/95–6.
52. For the allegation see Sidney Aster '"Guilty Men": the Case of Neville Chamberlain' in Robert Boyce and E.M. Robertson (eds.), *Paths to War: New Essays on the Origins of the Second World War* (1989), pp. 250, 267 footnote 52; Peter Clarke, *Hope and Glory: Britain 1900–1990*, (1996), p. 189.
53. Committee of Imperial Defence, 296th Meeting, 5 July 1937, CAB 2/6; CP 296(37), 3 December 1937 and CAB 49(37)1, 22 December 1937, CAB 23/90.
54. Foreign Policy Committee Paper, FP(36)23, 'Anglo-German Relations', 2 April 1937, CAB 27/626; Chamberlain to Hilda, 29 August 1937.
55. Hoare to Chamberlain, 17 March 1937, NC7/11/30/74.
56. Chamberlain to Ida, 8 August; to Hilda, 12 September 1937.
57. Paul Kennedy, 'The Tradition of Appeasement in British Foreign Policy 1865–1939' in his *Strategy and Diplomacy 1870–1945* (Fontana ed., 1985), p. 38.
58. Amery to Chamberlain, 10 November and reply 15 November 1937, NC7/11/30/6–7.
59. Chamberlain to Halifax, 7 August 1937, PREM 1/276/288.
60. Hankey to Chamberlain and memorandum, 19 July 1937, PREM 1/276.
61. Chamberlain to Halifax, 7 August 1937 and 'Notes on Anglo-Italian discussions', n.d., PREM 1/276.

62. Wilson note to Chamberlain, 26 July 1937; Chamberlain to Mussolini, 27 July and reply, 31 July 1937; Chamberlain notes on meetings with Grandi, 27 July and 2 August 1937, PREM 1/276.
63. Chamberlain to Ida, 8 August 1937.
64. Chamberlain to Hilda, 29 August 1937; to Halifax, 7 August 1937; Chamberlain notes, 28 August 1937, PREM 1/276.
65. Chamberlain to Hilda, 12 September 1937; to Weir, 15 August 1937, NC7/11/30/141.
66. Eden to Halifax, 1 August 1937, Hickleton MSS A4.410.21.1; Chamberlain to Halifax, 7 August 1937; 'Record of a Meeting … on 10 August 1937', PREM 1/276; Halifax – Eden exchange, 9, 11, 12, 13 August 1937, AP20/5/25–25A, 26–26A.
67. Avon, *Facing the Dictators*, pp. 454–5.
68. Chamberlain to Ida, 8 August 1937; to Lord Weir, 15 August 1937, NC7/11/30/141.
69. Chamberlain to Lady Ball, 15 June 1937, Ball MSS Eng.c.6656/5.
70. Chamberlain to Ida, 22 August, 7 September 1937.
71. CAB 34(37)6, 8 September 1937, CAB 23/89.
72. Count Ciano Diary, 11 and 14 September 1938.
73. Chamberlain to Ida, 26 September, 16 October 1937; CAB 37(37)1, 13 October 1937, CAB 23/89.
74. Ciano Diary, 14 October 1937, 29 August and 22 September 1938.
75. CAB 34(37)1–2, 8 September 1937, CAB 23/89.
76. Chamberlain memorandum to Morgenthau, 20 March 1937; Roosevelt to Sumner Welles, 28 May 1937; William Bullitt to Roosevelt, 5 May 1937, Roosevelt MSS PSF 32/303, 30, 37.
77. Robert Bingham to Cordell Hull, 6 July 1937, Roosevelt MSS PSF 32/303.
78. Norman Davis to Chamberlain, 10 June and reply, 8 July 1937, Sumner Welles MSS 162/05; Chamberlain to Roosevelt, 28 September 1937, Roosevelt MSS PSF 32/303.
79. Chamberlain to Hilda, 29 August 1937.
80. Lord Tweedsmuir to Chamberlain, 25 October 1937, Simon MSS 84/145–9.
81. Chamberlain to Hilda, 9 October and to Ida, 16 October 1937.
82. CAB 37(37)3 and CAB 38(37)4, 13 and 20 October 1937, CAB 23/89; Chamberlain to Ida, 16 October 1937.
83. CAB 43(37)5, 24 November 1937, CAB 23/90; Chamberlain to Hilda, 21 November 1937.
84. Chamberlain to Hilda, 17 December 1937 and 9 January 1938; Chamberlain Diary, 19 February 1938.
85. CAB 46(37)10, 8 December 1937, CAB 23/90.
86. Chamberlain to Ida, 4 July 1937; CAB 30(37)6, 14 July 1937, CAB 23/89.
87. Amery Diary, 9 November 1937 reporting Chamberlain.
88. Barnett, *The Collapse of British Power*, p. 514.
89. Chamberlain to Hilda, 24 October 1937; to Ida, 14 November 1937; Halifax to Chamberlain, 8 and 9 November 1937, NC7/11/30/67 and PREM 1/330; Halifax to Ormsby-Gore, 12 November 1937, Hickleton MSS A410.3.2.

90. 'Lord Halifax Diary: Visit of the Lord President to Germany, 17 to 21 November 1937'; 'Conversation with Herr Hitler – 19 November 1937', Hickleton MSS A4.410,3.3 (VI) and A4.410.3.6.

91. Butler to Brabourne, 1 January 1938, Brabourne MSS Eur.F97/22B/100.

92. CAB 43(37)3, 24 November 1937, CAB 23/90; Henderson to Halifax, 23 November 1937, Hickleton MSS A4.410.3.2; Chamberlain to Ida, 26 November 1937.

93. Chamberlain to Hilda, 21 September 1937; FP(36) 10ᵗʰ Meeting of Foreign Policy Committee, 10 May 1937, CAB 27/622.

94. CAB 20(36)1, 16 March 1936, CAB 23/83; Chamberlain to Ida, 13 April 1936.

95. E(PD)37, 11ᵗʰ Meeting of Principal Delegates to Imperial Conference, 2 June 1937, CAB 32/128.

96. Chamberlain to Hilda and Harvey Diary, both 5 December 1937.

97. Anthony Adamthwaite, 'Reactions to the Munich Crisis' in Neville Waites (ed.), *Troubled Neighbours: Franco-British Relations in the Twentieth Century* (1971), p. 172.

98. Chamberlain to Hilda, 5 December 1937.

99. Chamberlain to Hilda, 9 January 1938; to Lord Weir, 15 January 1938, Weir MSS DC96/22/2; Sumner Welles, *The Time for Decision* (New York, 1944), pp. 64–6.

100. Chamberlain to Ida, 23 January 1938; Chamberlain Diary, 19 February 1938; CAB 1(38)1 and Secret Addendum, 4 January 1938, CAB 23/92.

101. Chamberlain to Sir Ronald Lindsay, 13 January 1938, PREM 1/259; to Roosevelt, 14 January 1938, Roosevelt MSS PSF 32/303.

102. Roosevelt to Chamberlain, 17 January 1938, PREM 1/259; Welles, *The Time for Decision*, p. 66; Chamberlain Diary, 19 February 1938.

103. Chamberlain to Hilda, 30 January 1938.

104. Chamberlain Diary, 19 February 1938.

105. Eden Diary, 14–21 January 1938; Harvey Diary, 15–16 February and Harvey to Eden, 18 [or 15?] January 1938, AP8/2/104; Eden to Chamberlain, 17 January 1938, PREM 1/259/55.

106. Cadogan Diary, 16 January 1938; but see Eden's account in Avon, *Facing the Dictators*, pp. 553–4.

107. Eden Diary, 14–21 January 1938; Eden to Chamberlain, 17 January 1938.

108. Harvey Diary, 3 and 7 November, 5 December 1937, 17–18 January 1938.

109. Eden to Chamberlain, 17 January 1938, PREM 1/259/55; Harvey Diary, 19–20 January 1938.

110. Harvey Diary, 22 September, 2, 15 October and 3 November 1937.

111. Butler to Brabourne, 1 January 1938, Butler MSS G8/28.

112. Eden to Chamberlain, 3 November and Chamberlain to Eden and reply, both 16 November 1937; AP20/5/12–14; Eden Diary, 8 November 1937; Harvey Diary, 3 and 16 November 1937.

113. Harvey Diary, 17 November 1937.

114. Harvey Diary, 5 and 7 December 1937; Eden to Chamberlain, 31 December 1937 and 31 January 1938, AP20/5/15 and PREM 1/276.

115. Chamberlain to Hilda, 13 February 1938; Eden at Birmingham, *The Times*, 14 February 1938; Simon Diary, 12 February 1938.

116. Chamberlain to Hilda, 30 January 1938; Chamberlain Diary, 19 February

1938; CAB 6(38)1, 19 February 1938, CAB 23/92.

117. Horace Wilson to P.J. Grigg, 31 January 1938, Grigg MSS 2/23/2.

118. CAB 5(38)9, 16 February 1938, CAB 23/92; Simon Diary, 12 February 1938.

119. Lady Ivy Chamberlain to Chamberlain, 16 December 1937, 2 January and 2 February 1938, NC1/17/5–7; Simon Diary, 12 February 1938; Ciano Diary, 22 December 1937, 1 January and 1 February 1938.

120. Eden to Chamberlain and reply, 8 February 1938, PREM 1/276/99–102; Chamberlain to Ivy Chamberlain, 3 March 1938, NC1/17/9.

121. Chamberlain Diary, 19 February 1938.

122. Ciano Diary, 17 February 1938; Simon Diary, 18 February 1938; Eden to Lord Perth, 21 February 1938, PREM 1/276.

123. Eden-Chamberlain exchange, 1, 7, 9, 13 January 1938, PREM 1/276 and AP20/6/2–7.

124. Harvey Diary, 20 January, 9, 17–18 February 1938.

125. Eden and Chamberlain Diary, both 19 February 1938; Eden to Chamberlain, 17 February 1938, PREM 1/276/83–4.

126. Horace Wilson, 'Munich', CAB 127/158, p. 15; Chamberlain Diary, 19 February 1938; Simon Diary, 18 February 1938; Eden to Lord Perth, 21 February 1938, PREM 1/276/67.

127. Report of Count Grandi, 19 February 1938, Malcolm Muggeridge (ed.), *Ciano's Diplomatic Papers* (1948), pp. 164–84.

128. Eden Diary, 17 February 1938; Chamberlain Diary, 19 February 1938.

129. CAB 6(38)1, 19 February 1938, CAB 23/92; Halifax, 'Record of Events Connected with Anthony Eden's Resignation, February 19–20, 1938', Hickleton MSS A4.410.11; Eden notes for Cabinet, 19 February 1938, AP13/1/649; Simon Diary, 19 February 1938 and appended notes; Chamberlain Diary, 27 February 1938; Duff Cooper Diary, 19 February 1938, quoted in John Charmley, *Chamberlain and the Lost Peace* (Papermac ed., 1991), p. 50.

130. Chamberlain Diary, 27 February 1938; Simon Diary, 20 February 1938; Simon to Eden, 23 February 1938, Simon MSS 84/180–82; CAB 7(38)1, 20 February 1938; Chamberlain to Eden, 20 February 1938, AP8/2/39.

131. Simon Diary, 19 February 1938 and appended notes.

132. Butler to Brabourne, 23 February 1938, Brabourne MSS Eur.F97/22B/87; Amery Diary, 21 February 1938; Halifax, 'Record'.

133. Simon Diary, 20 February 1938; Halifax, 'Record'.

134. Thomas Jones to Lady Grigg, 24 October 1937; Crookshank Diary, 10 and 14 November 1937, Crookshank MSS Eng.hist.c.359 fol. 186–7.

135. Chamberlain to Hilda, 12 September and to Ida, 16 October 1937.

136. Hilda Runciman Diary, 14 and 27 December 1937; Chamberlain to Eden, 2 January and reply 9 January 1938, AP20/6/3, 5.

137. CAB 6(38)1, 19 February 1938, CAB 23/92; Chamberlain to Hilda, 27 February 1938; to Ivy Chamberlain, 3 March 1938, NC1/17/9; Simon Diary, 18 February 1938.

138. Simon Diary, 19 February 1938.

139. Chamberlain to Hilda, 27 February 1938; Crawford Diary, 26 February 1938; Arthur Murray to Roosevelt, 20 February 1938, Roosevelt PSF 38.

140. See Gwynne and Lords Rushcliffe and Brocket to Chamberlain, 21–22 February 1938, NC7/11/31/35, 116, 233.

141. Joseph Ball to Chamberlain, 21 February 1938, NC7/11/31/10 and reply 22 February 1938, Ball MSS Eng.c.6656/9; Dawson, Channon, Headlam, Amery and Winterton diaries, all 21 February 1938.
142. Simon Diary and Chamberlain to Hilda, both 27 February 1938.
143. Crookshank Diary, 20–24 February 1938; Crookshank and Bernays to Chamberlain, 23 February 1938, and reply 24 February 1938, NC7/11/31/92, 14–16; Halifax, 'Record'; Harvey Diary, 27 February 1938.
144. Parker, *Chamberlain and Appeasement*, p. 121.
145. George H. Gallup (ed.), *The Gallup International Public Opinion Polls, Great Britain 1937–1975: Volume I, 1937–1964* (New York, 1976), pp. 8–9; 'The Eden Crisis', Mass-Observation MSS TC25/5/A; Headlam Diary, 6 April 1938.
146. Simon Diary, 27 February 1937.
147. Lord Onslow to Chamberlain, 28 February 1938, NC7/11/31/215; Amery Diary, 24 February 1938; Butler to Sir Archibald Cochrane, 24 March 1938; Butler MSS G8/97-98; Emrys-Evans memorandum to Eden, n.d., Emrys-Evans MSS 58247/78–9.
148. Ball to Chamberlain, 21 February 1938, NC7/11/31/10.
149. Butler to Brabourne, 15 March 1938, Brabourne MSS Eur.F97/22B/77.

Chapter 13: The Road to Munich, March–September 1938

1. Jones Diary, 27 February 1934; Beaverbrook to Arthur Brisbane, 20 November 1932, Beaverbrook MSS C/64.
2. Chamberlain to Hilda, 27 March 1924 and 20 March 1926; to Irwin 15 August 1926, Irwin MSS Eur.C152/17/82A.
3. Chamberlain to Hilda, 13 March and 9 July 1938; to Ida, 20 March 1938.
4. Butler to Brabourne, 31 May and 12 July 1938, Brabourne MSS Eur.F97/22B/36, 48.
5. Butler 'character sketches', n.d. [June 1939], Butler MSS G10/26.
6. Ibid.; Nicolson Diary, 18 December 1939 reporting Butler; Chamberlain to Ball, 28 October 1940, NC Letters Additional 131; Kenneth Clark, *Another Part of the Wood: A Self-Portrait* (1947), p. 271.
7. Butler to Brabourne, 17 February 1939, Butler MSS F79/98; Dunglass to Chamberlain, 28 July 1940, NC7/11/33/60.
8. Channon Diary, 4 September 1939.
9. Hilda Runciman Diary, 22 May 1937, reporting Lord Davidson.
10. Butler to Brabourne, 22 March 1938, Brabourne MSS Eur.F97/22B/73; Channon Diary, 18 March 1938.
11. Chamberlain to Ida, 23 January 1938; FP(36) 21st and 22nd Meetings of Foreign Policy Committee, 24 January and 3 February 1938, CAB 27/623.
12. 'Memorandum of Conversation [with British Ambassador]', 9 and 12 February 1938, Welles MSS 162/06; Phipps to Eden, 21 October 1936, Simon MSS 84/20.
13. Chamberlain to Ida, 13 April 1936; to Hilda, 6 February 1938.
14. Henderson, *Failure of a Mission*, pp. 116–17; *DBFP*, 2, XIX, 609.
15. Chamberlain to Hilda, 13 March 1938.

16. Ian Kershaw, *Hitler 1936–1945: Nemesis* (Penguin ed., 2001), pp. 64–6, 83–4.
17. CAB 12(38)1, 12 March 1938, CAB 23/92; Chamberlain to Hilda, 13 March 1938.
18. *H.C. Debs*, 5s, 333, col 45–52 and Amery Diary, both 14 March 1938.
19. CAB 12–13(38)1, 12 and 14 March 1938, CAB 23/92; Wilson note, 28 March 1938, PREM 1/256.
20. Chamberlain to Ida, 20 March 1938.
21. Margesson memorandum, 17 March 1938, NC7/11/31/188; Chamberlain to Hilda, 27 March 1938.
22. For the criticism see Barnett, *Collapse of British Power*, pp. 474, 505, 509–13; Trelford Taylor, *Munich: The Price of Peace* (1979), pp. 629–33; Reynolds, *In Command of History*, pp. 102–3.
23. Chamberlain to Ida, 20 March 1938; Horace Wilson, 'Munich', CAB 127/158, pp. 17–18.
24. FP(36) 26th Meeting, 18 March 1938, CAB 27(623).
25. Parker, *Chamberlain and Appeasement*, pp. 137 and 364–5.
26. FP(36) 25th–26th Meeting, 15 and 18 March 1938, CAB 27/623; Harvey Diary, 7 March 1938 reporting Halifax.
27. CAB 15(38)1, 22 March 1938, CAB 23/93. For the COS report see CAB 27/627 fol. 35–42.
28. Parker, *Chamberlain and Appeasement*, p. 138.
29. Patrick Finney (ed.), *The Origins of the Second World War* (1997), pp. 14–15; Paul Kennedy, 'Appeasement' in Gordon Martel (ed.), *The Origins of the Second World War Reconsidered* (1986), p. 156.
30. CAB 15(38)1, 22 March 1938, CAB 23/93; Chamberlain to Hilda, 27 March 1938.
31. Nicolson Diary, 29 March 1938; CAB 23(38)4, 11 May 1938, CAB 23/93.
32. *H.C. Debs*, 5s, 333, col 1393–413, 24 March 1938; CAB 15(38)1, 22 March 1938, CAB 23/93; FP(36) 25th Meeting, 15 March 1938, CAB 27/623.
33. Chamberlain to Hilda, 27 March and 9 April 1938 with extract from Henderson to Halifax; Channon and Amery Diary, 24 March 1938; Butler to Sir Archibald Cochrane, 24 March 1938, Butler MSS G8/97–8.
34. N.J. Crowson, *Facing Fascism: The Conservative Party and the European Dictators 1935–1940* (1997), pp. 90–92; Gallup, *Gallup International Opinion Polls*, p. 8.
35. CAB 11(38)4, 9 March 1938, CAB 23/92.
36. FP(36) 24th Meeting, 1 March 1938, CAB 27/623; Ciano Diary, 2, 4, 8, 17 and 21 March 1938.
37. Simon Diary, 16 April 1938.
38. ISC(32) 35th Meeting of Irish Situation Committee, 14 December 1937, CAB 27/524.
39. Chamberlain to Ida, 23 January 1938.
40. INC(38) 1st Meeting of Irish Negotiations Committee, 17 January 1938, CAB 27/642.
41. ISC(32) 38th Meeting, 24 February 1938, CAB 27/524; Chamberlain to Hilda, 13 March 1938.
42. INC(38) 1st Meeting, 17 January 1938; ISC(32) 40th Meeting, 1 March 1938, CAB 27/524 and 642.

43. *H.C. Debs*, 5s, 335, col 1094–105, 1071–9, 5 May 1938; Chamberlain to Ida, 1 May 1938.
44. Chamberlain to Hilda, 27 March and 9 April 1938; to Ida, 3 April, 1 May 1938; Harvey Diary, 13 April 1938 reporting Horace Wilson; Lloyd George to Henderson Livesey, 23 and 30 May 1938, Lloyd George MSS G/12/3/6, 9. But see Joseph Ball, 'Secret: to the Prime Minister', June 1938, NC8/21/8.
45. R.J. Minney, *No. 10 Downing Street: A House in History* (n.d.), pp. 399–401.
46. Chamberlain to Hilda, 26 June, 24 October and 6 November 1937; to Ida, 20 March 1938.
47. Chamberlain to Hilda, 30 January and 13 March 1938; Anne Chamberlain to Lady Lee, 4 January 1941, NC9/2/34.
48. Butler to Brabourne, 15 March, 11 April, 9 and 26 May 1938, Brabourne MSS Eur.F97/22B/45, 56–60, 75.
49. Eden to Baldwin, 11 May 1938, AP8/2/13A; Harvey Diary, 12 March 1938; Crookshank Diary, 12 April 1938.
50. Baldwin to Davidson, 11 April 1938, Davidson MSS 258; Dugdale Diary, 22 May 1938.
51. Harvey Diary, 19 May 1938; Chamberlain to Hilda, 9 April 1938.
52. Butler to Brabourne, 24 April and 8 July 1938; Hardinge to Brabourne, 17 May 1938, Brabourne MSS Eur.F97/22B/29, 38, 53.
53. Chamberlain to Ida, 15 May 1938; Winterton to Chamberlain, 13 May 1938, NC7/11/31/292; Winterton Diary, 12 May 1938.
54. Chamberlain to King George VI, 17 May 1938, NC7/3/24; to Ida, 15 May 1938.
55. Harvey Diary, 3 May 1938; Headlam Diary, 13 May 1938.
56. Chamberlain to Hilda, 17 May 1938; Swinton, *I Remember*, p. 146; Swinton to Chamberlain and reply, both 16 May 1938, SWIN174/2/1/17–19, 23–5.
57. Swinton to Chamberlain, 7 December 1937, NC7/11/30/125.
58. Halifax to Chamberlain, 16 May 1938; Swinton and Lady Swinton to Chamberlain, both 20 May 1938, NC7/11/31/121, 259, 263.
59. Chamberlain to Hilda and Hore-Belisha, both 17 May 1938, HOBE5/29; to Simon, 31 July 1938, Simon MSS 84/191–2.
60. Kershaw, *Hitler*, pp. 83–4, 91–3.
61. Joseph Kennedy dispatch 296, 11 April 1938, Roosevelt MSS PSF 20.
62. Chamberlain to Ida, 20 March, 16 April 1938; Henderson, *Failure of a Mission*, pp. 128–9; CAB 15 and 18(38)1, 22 March and 6 April 1938, CAB 23/93.
63. Chamberlain to Ida, 1 May 1938.
64. Chamberlain to Hilda, 18 March 1933.
65. Adamthwaite, 'Reactions to the Munich Crisis', p. 183; *DBFP*, 3, I, 164; Chamberlain to Ida, 1 and 15 May 1938.
66. Chamberlain to Hilda, 22 May 1938; *DBFP*, 3, I, 237–40, 244–5, 249–50, 264.
67. Bernays Diary, 27 May 1938; Amery Diary, 30 May 1938.
68. Simon and Cadogan diaries and Chamberlain to Hilda, all 22 May 1938; to Ida, 28 May 1938.
69. Chamberlain to Hilda, 22 May and 9 July 1938.

70. Chamberlain to Ida, 28 May 1938; to Hannon, 3 June 1938, Hannon MSS 17/1.

71. Chamberlain to Hilda, 22 May 1938.

72. Chamberlain to Hilda, 28 March; to Ida, 28 May 1938.

73. Wilson note, 22 July 1938, PREM 1/251/2.

74. Chamberlain to Ida, 12 February 1939.

75. CP 112(38), 7 May 1938, CAB 24/276; CAB 23(38)4, 11 May 1938, CAB 23/93; Chamberlain to Ida, 28 May, 18 June 1938.

76. FP(36) 30th, 33rd, 37th, 42nd Meetings, CAB 27/623–4; Watt, *How War Came*, pp. 89–90, 170–76, 271–307; Butler to Lord Erskine, 28 March 1938, Erskine MSS Eur.D596/20.

77. Chamberlain to Ida, 28 May, 18 June 1938; to Hilda, 25 June, 9 July 1938.

78. Chamberlain to Ida, 18 June 1938.

79. Chamberlain to Hilda, 9 July and to Ida, 16 July 1938; *DBFP*, 3, I, 510; Cadogan Diary, 18 July 1938.

80. Chamberlain and Wilson notes, both 22 July 1938, PREM 1/330; *H.C. Debs*, 5s, 338, col 2963, 26 July 1938.

81. Chamberlain to Ida, 16 July and 6 August 1938; Simon Diary, 3 August 1938; Chamberlain to Leslie Scott, 29 July 1938, NC Letters Additional 58.

82. *DBFP*, 3, II, 575–81, 608, 704; Simon Diary, 31 August 1938.

83. Chamberlain to Lord Halifax, 19 August and reply, 21 August 1938, NC7/11/31/123; *DBFP*, 3, II, Appendix 4; Chamberlain to Runciman, 12 September 1938, PREM 1/266A.

84. For Hitler's belief that the Western Powers were bluffing but that he was not, see Kershaw, *Hitler*, pp. 106, 109, 116, 119.

85. 'Notes of a meeting of Ministers', 30 August 1938, CAB 23/94; Inskip Diary, 30 August 1939.

86. Joseph Kennedy to Cordell Hull, 30 August 1938, Roosevelt MSS PSF 21.

87. Chamberlain to Hilda, 6 September 1938; to his wife, 2 September 1938, NC1/26/530; to Margesson, 4 September 1938, MRGN1/3/20.

88. Chamberlain to Ida, 3 September 1938.

89. Horace Wilson, 'Munich', October 1941, CAB 127/158, p. 26; Chamberlain to Runciman, 12 September 1938; Simon Diary, 29 September 1938; Wilson memorandum, 30 August 1938, PREM 1/266A/320–24, 363.

90. Charmley, *Chamberlain and the Lost Peace*, p. 95.

91. Chamberlain to Ida, 11 September 1938. For comparisons with Canning see Professor Temperley and Chamberlain to *The Times*, 28 and 30 July 1938; also Temperley, Strauss and Benn to Chamberlain, 29–30 July 1938, NC7/11/31/266, 256–7, 21.

92. Harvey Diary and Henderson to Wilson, both 9–10 September 1938, PREM 1/266A/354–8; CAB 37(38)1, 12 September 1938, CAB 23/95.

93. Simon Diary, 29 September 1938; CS(38) 1st Meeting of Czech Crisis Committee, 12 September 1938, CAB 27/646.

94. Inskip Diary, 8 September 1938; Chamberlain to Hilda, 6 September 1938.

95. FP(36) 26th Meeting, 18 March 1938, CAB 27/623.

96. Kershaw, *Hitler*, pp. 96, 101.

97. Runciman to Chamberlain, 21 September 1938, Runciman MSS 296/2/213–16.

98. Chamberlain to Ida, 11 September 1938; to King George VI, 13 September 1938, PREM 1/266A; Kennedy dispatch 893, 10 September 1938, Roosevelt MSS PSF 21.

99. Inskip Diary, 13 September 1938; Zetland to Brabourne, 16/20 September 1938, Zetland MSS Eur.D609/10/57.

100. CS(38) 3rd Meeting of Czech Crisis Committee, 13 September 1938, CAB 27/646; Chamberlain telegram, 13 September 1938, PREM 1/266A/15.

101. Kennedy dispatch 923, 14 September 1938, Roosevelt MSS PSF 21.

102. Chamberlain to Ida, 19 September 1938; Channon, Crookshank, Dawson, Headlam diaries, 14–15 September 1938.

103. Zetland to Brabourne, 16/20 September 1938, Zetland MSS Eur. D609/10/56; Inskip, Cooper, Winterton and Hore-Belisha diaries, all 14 September 1938.

104. CAB 38(38)1, 14 September 1938, CAB 23/95; Inskip Diary, 14 September 1938.

105. Zetland to Brabourne, 16–20 September 1938, Zetland MSS Eur. D609/10/57.

106. Kennedy dispatch 923, 14 September 1938, Roosevelt MSS PSF 21.

107. Inskip Diary, 14 September 1938.

108. Chamberlain to Hilda, 24 February 1923.

109. Chamberlain to Ida, 19 September 1938; Inskip Diary and CAB 39(38)1, both 17 September 1938, CAB 23/95.

110. Emrys-Evans to Eden and reply, 15-16 September 1938, AP13/1/66G–H.

111. *DBFP*, 3, II, 895–96; Kershaw, *Hitler*, pp. 111–13.

112. 'The Prime Minister's visit to Germany: Notes by Sir Horace Wilson', 16 September 1938, NC8/26/2.

113. Chamberlain to Ida, 19 September 1938.

114. Chamberlain to Baldwin, 19 September 1938, Baldwin MSS 124/126.

115. CS(38) 5th Meeting of Czech Crisis Committee, 16 September 1938, CAB 27/646.

116. Zetland to Brabourne, 16–20 September 1938, Zetland MSS Eur. D609/10/57; Inskip Diary, 17 September 1938.

117. Kennedy dispatch 950, 17 September 1938, Roosevelt MSS PSF Box 37/339; CAB 39(38)1, 17 September 1938, CAB 23/95.

118. Zetland to Brabourne, 16–20 September 1938.

119. Inskip Diary, 19 September 1938; Kennedy dispatch 960 and 970, 17 and 19 September 1938, reporting Chamberlain, Roosevelt MSS PSF 21.

120. Simon Diary, 29 September 1938; Chamberlain to Ida, 19 September 1938; *DBFP*, 3, II, 928.

121. CAB 40(38)1, 19 September 1938, CAB 23/95.

122. Ibid.; Amery and Hore-Belisha Diary, both 19 September 1938, Elliot to his wife, 18 September 1938, Colin Coote, *A Companion of Honour: the Story of Walter Elliot in Scotland and Westminster* (1965), p. 165.

123. Chamberlain to Ida and Kennedy dispatch 970, both 19 September 1938.

124. Simon Diary, 29 September 1938; CAB 41(38)1, 21 September 1938, CAB 23/95.

125. Zetland to Brabourne, 25 September 1938, Zetland MSS Eur. D609/10/63.

126. Weather Report, 22 September 1938, NC8/26/5.

127. Paul Schmidt, *Hitler's Interpreter: The Secret History of German Diplomacy, 1935–1945*, (1951), pp. 95–7; *DBFP*, 3, II, 1033 and PREM 1/266A/144–207.

128. Horace Wilson, 'Munich', October 1941, CAB 127/158, pp. 39–42; *DBFP*, 3, II, 1048 and 1058; CS(38) 10th and 11th Meeting with Appendices, 22–23 September 1938, CAB 27/646.

129. Henderson, *Failure of a Mission*, p. 157; *DBFP*, 3, II, 1073; *DGFP* series D, II, 572–3, 583; CAB 42(38)1, 24 September 1938, CAB 23/95.

130. Simon Diary, 29 September 1938; CAB 42(38)1, 24 September 1938, CAB 23/95.

131. CS(38) 13th Meeting, 24 September 1938, CAB 27/646; Cadogan Diary, 24 September 1938.

132. CAB 42(38)1, 24 September 1938; Cooper, *Old Men Forget*, pp. 234–5.

133. Halifax to Lord Robert Cecil, 22 September 1938, Cecil MSS 57084/162–3.

134. Cadogan Diary, 24–25 September 1938; CAB 43(38)1, both 25 September 1938.

135. Chamberlain's note to Halifax and reply, 25 September 1938, Hickleton MSS A4.410.3.7.2–3.

136. Crookshank and Eden Diary, 25 September 1938; Amery Diary, 24 September 1938.

137. Dugdale Diary, 19 September 1938; Elliot to his wife, 25 September 1938, Coote, *Companion of Honour*, pp. 171–2.

138. Inskip Diary, 14, 17 and 19 September 1938.

139. CAB 43(38)1, 25 September 1938; Cooper Diary, 24–25 September 1938, *Old Men Forget*, pp. 235–36.

140. *DBFP*, 3, II, 1076 and 1093; Lord Strang, *At Home and Abroad* (1956), p. 140; Simon Diary, 29 September 1938.

141. CAB 44(38)1, CAB 23/95; Cooper and Harvey Diary, all 25 September 1938; Zetland to Brabourne, 25/26 September 1938, Zetland MSS Eur. D609/10/65.

142. *DBFP*, 3, II, 1096.

143. Cooper Diary, 25 September 1938.

144. *DGFP*, D, II, 611; *DBFP*, 3, II, 1111.

145. Simon and Hankey Diary, 29 September 1938.

146. Cooper Diary and CAB 45(38)2, both 26 September 1938, CAB 23/95.

147. *DBFP*, 3, II, 1115–16, 1118, 1128–9; Henderson, *Failure of a Mission*, pp. 159–61; Horace Wilson, 'Munich', October 1941, CAB 127/158, pp. 45–50.

148. Chamberlain to Hilda, 2 October 1938; *DBFP*, 3, II, 1112.

149. Dawson Diary, 27 September 1938; Chamberlain, *The Struggle for Peace*, pp. 275–6.

150. R.H. Bruce Lockhart, *Comes the Reckoning* (1947), pp. 9, 23; *Memoirs of Lord Gladwyn* (1972), p. 75; Cooper Diary, 27 September 1938, *Old Men Forget*, p. 239.

151. CS(38) 15th Meeting, 27 September 1938, CAB 27/646.

152. CAB 46(38)1, 27 September 1938, CAB 23/95; Cooper, *Old Men Forget*, pp. 239–40.

153. Chamberlain to Hilda, 2 October 1938; Anne Chamberlain to [?], 15 December 1940, NC13/13/2/34.

154. Chamberlain to Hilda, 2 October 1938; *DBFP*, 3, II, 1158, 1159, 1161, 1192; Henderson, *Failure of a Mission*, pp. 161–4.
155. Simon Diary, 29 September 1938; Home, *The Way the Wind Blows*, p. 65.
156. Crookshank, Nicolson, Channon, Dawson, Amery diaries, all 28 September; Simon Diary, 29 September 1938.
157. Gerard De Groot, *Liberal Crusader: The Life of Sir Archibald Sinclair* (1993), pp. 141–2.
158. Chamberlain to Hilda, 2 October 1938.
159. Channon Diary, 28 September 1938.
160. Simon and Channon diaries, both 29 September 1938.
161. Chamberlain to Hilda, 2 October 1938; *DBFP*, 3, II, 1224, 1227.
162. Cadogan Diary and CAB 47(38)1, both 30 September 1938. For a detailed defence of the terms see Lord Maugham, 'Reflexions on the Munich Crisis', n.d., Simon MSS, Eng.c. 6647/281–3 published as *The Truth About the Munich Crisis* (1944).
163. Chamberlain to Hilda, 2 October 1938; Strang, *At Home and Abroad*, pp. 146–7; 'Notes of a conversation between the P.M. and Herr Hitler on 30 September', and Anglo-German Declaration, PREM 1/266A/32–46.
164. Strang, *At Home and Abroad*, p. 148; Home, *The Way the Wind Blows*, pp. 64, 66.
165. Martin Gilbert, 'Horace Wilson: Man of Munich?', *History Today*, 32 (1982), p.6. Also Colville Diary, 15 February 1940, reporting Dunglass.
166. Chamberlain to Hilda, 2 October 1938.
167. Lord Home interview in the BBC documentary, 'God Bless You, Mr Chamberlain', 23 September 1988; Home, *The Way the Wind Blows*, p. 67.
168. *H.C. Debs*, 5s, 339, col 551, 6 October 1938.

Chapter 14: Betrayal, October 1938–March 1939

1. Hilda Chamberlain, 'Review of Feiling', 1946, BC5/12/1 and NC1/15/6/1.
2. Colville Diary, 5 April 1940, reporting Arthur Rucker.
3. Bruce Lockhart Diary, 25 September 1938; Bruce Lockhart, *Comes the Reckoning*, p. 12.
4. Crowson, *Facing Fascism*, pp. 82, 98–9, 102–18. For the resolutions see NC13/9.
5. W.W. Hadley, *Munich Before and After* (1944), Chapter XIV; Cockett, *Twilight of Truth*, pp. 65, 83.
6. Henderson Livesy to Lloyd George, 22 September 1938, Lloyd George MSS G/12/3/20.
7. J.P.L. Thomas to Geoffrey Fry, 3 October 1938, Baldwin MSS 124/140–45; Amery Diary, 30 September 1938.
8. Mackintosh, *Echoes of Big Ben*, p. 147.
9. Runciman to Baldwin, 17 October 1938, Baldwin MSS 124/148; Nicolson Diary, 29 September 1938.
10. Joseph Kennedy Diary, n.d. [November 1944]; Wilhelm to Queen Mary, 1 October 1938, NC13/11/803.
11. *H.C. Debs*, 5s, 339, col 545, 6 October 1938; Chamberlain to Hilda, 15 October

1938; to Mary, 5 November 1938, NC1/20/1/186. See NC13/5–7 for a list of the gifts and the letters.

12. Wilde to Lord Kemsley, 13 October 1938, NC13/11/675; Chamberlain to Hilda, 6 November 1938.

13. Beatrice Webb Diary, 3.30 am, 1 October 1938.

14. Keynes to Virginia Woolf, 21 February 1938; to Kingsley Martin, 1 October 1938, Skidelsky, *Keynes*, III, pp. 14, 29, 37.

15. Collin Brooks Journal, 4 October 1938; Channon Diary, 30 September 1938.

16. Simon to J.A. Spender, 10 October 1938, Simon MSS 85/77.

17. Chamberlain to Hilda, 2 October 1938; to Baldwin, 2 October 1938, Baldwin MSS 124/138.

18. Chamberlain to Ida, 9 October 1938.

19. Harvey Diary, 27 February 1938.

20. Crookshank Diary, 25 September, 2 and 4 October 1938; Stanley to Chamberlain, 3 October 1938, PREM 1/266A.

21. Chamberlain to Ida, 9 October 1938; Chamberlain Diary, 3 May 1935; Butler to Brabourne, 22 March 1938, Brabourne MSS Eur.F97/22B/71.

22. Harvey Diary, 10 September 1938; Elliot to his wife, 18 September 1938; Elliot to Blanche Dugdale, 7 October 1938, Coote, *Companion of Honour*, pp. 163, 165.

23. CAB 48(38)5, 3 October 1938, CAB 23/95; De La Warr to Chamberlain, 4 October and reply, 5 October 1938, PREM 1/266A; Amery Diary, 8 October 1938.

24. Winterton, Dawson, Channon, Crookshank, Amery and Nicolson diaries and *H.C. Debs*, 5s, 339, col 48–50, all 3 October 1938; Butler to Brabourne, 12 October 1938, Brabourne MSS Eur.F97/22B/28.

25. Chamberlain to Ida, 9 October 1938.

26. Crookshank Diary, 30 September, 4 and 5 October 1938.

27. Chamberlain to Ida, 9 October 1938; Stephen Furness to Simon, 5 October 1938, Simon MSS 85/44; Amery Diary and Amery to Chamberlain, both 6 October 1938, NC7/11/31/2.

28. Chamberlain to Ida, 9 October 1938; Bernays Diary, 27 October 1938; Crookshank Diary, 6 October 1938.

29. Neville Thompson, *The Anti-Appeasers: Conservative Opposition to Appeasement in the 1930s* (Oxford, 1971), p. 189; Crowson, *Facing Fascism*, pp. 98–101; Roger Lumley to Eden, 2 October 1938, AP13/1/66P.

30. Channon Diary, 6 October 1938; Chamberlain to Ida, 9 October 1938.

31. Halifax to Chamberlain, 11 October 1938, NC11/31/124A.

32. Chamberlain to Lord Ponsonby, 21 February 1939, Ponsonby MSS Eng. hist. c.681/61.

33. Chamberlain to Mary, 5 November 1938, NC1/20/1/186; to Hilda, 15 October, 6 November 1938.

34. Chamberlain to Ida, 4 December 1938.

35. Templewood, *Nine Troubled Years*, p. 374.

36. Lord Croft, *My Life of Strife* (n.d. [1948]), p. 289; *H.C. Debs*, 5s, 339, col 58–60 and 549–51, 3 and 6 October 1938.

37. Horace Wilson to Woods [Simon's Principal Private Secretary], 1 November 1938, PREM 1/236; CAB 53(38)2, 7 November 1938, CAB 23/96.

38. CAB 48(38)5 and CAB 51(39)3, 3 and 31 October 1938, CAB 23/95–6.

39. Amery Diary, 1 November 1938; Emrys-Evans to Eden, 4 November and reply 8 November 1938, AP14/1/742-A.

40. Ironside Diary, 22 September 1938.

41. Ball to Chamberlain, 1 June 1938, NC8/21/7.

42. Elliot to his wife, 23 October 1938, reporting Hudson, Elliot MSS Acc.6721/7/1; Dawson Diary, 4 October 1938.

43. Lord Halifax, *The Fulness of Days* (1957), pp. 99–100; Hoare to Chamberlain, 5 October 1938, NC7/11/31/133; Thomas Jones to Lady Grigg, 5 October 1938, Jones (ed.), *Diary with Letters*, p. 414. Bernays Diary, 27 October 1938.

44. Crookshank Diary, 4 October 1938; Collin Brooks Journal, 5 October 1938; *H.C. Debs*, 5s, 339, col 548, 6 October 1938.

45. Chamberlain to Hilda, 15 October 1938.

46. Elliot to his wife, 26 October 1938, Elliot MSS Acc.6721.

47. Cranborne to Cecil, 16 October 1938, Cecil MSS 51087/142; Thompson, *The Anti-Appeasers*, pp. 192–4.

48. Nicolson Diary, 11 April 1938; Harvey Diary, 13 and 22 April, 31 May and 7 June 1938; Baldwin to Davidson, 11 April 1938, Davidson MSS 258.

49. 'Talk with Anthony Eden', 12 September 1938, Liddell Hart MSS LH11/1938/95; *H.C. Debs*, 5s, 339, col 77–88, 3 October 1938; Eden to Baldwin, 30 September 1938, Baldwin MSS 124/136–7.

50. Halifax to Chamberlain, 11 October 1938, NC11/31/124A.

51. A.L. Kennedy Journal, 30 November 1938.

52. Chamberlain to Ida, 9 October 1938 and to Hilda, 15 October 1938.

53. Eden to Baldwin, 15 January 1939, AP16/1/5.

54. Harvey Diary, 20 October 1938; Chamberlain to Ida, 24 October 1938.

55. Chamberlain to Hilda, 6 November and to Ida, 13 November 1938.

56. Chamberlain to Ida, 12 February 1939; Channon Diary, 23 January 1939.

57. Hoare to Chamberlain, 5 October 1938, NC7/11/31/133.

58. Chamberlain to Runciman, 20 October 1938, Runciman MSS 289/47.

59. Chamberlain to Ida, 24 October 1938; to Hailsham, 21 October 1938, NC7/11/31/119.

60. Chamberlain to Hilda, 15 October; to Ida, 24 October and 4 December 1938.

61. Chamberlain to Lord Mottistone, 16 May 1938, Mottistone MSS 5/165; to Ida and Hore-Belisha Diary, both 24 October 1938.

62. Hoare to Chamberlain, 5 October 1938, NC7/11/31/133; Warren Fisher to Simon and Wilson (for Chamberlain), 3 January 1939, Fisher MSS 461.

63. Chamberlain to Hilda, 6 November and 11 December 1938; to Ida, 4, 17 December 1938 and 12 February 1939.

64. Watt, *How War Came*, pp. 95, 208, 397; Richard Cockett, 'Ball, Chamberlain and *Truth*', *Historical Journal*, 33 (1990), pp. 131–42.

65. Chamberlain to Hilda, 28 July and 10 November 1934.

66. Chamberlain to Baldwin, 7 December 1938 and two memoranda by Ball, Baldwin MSS 174/19–27.

67. Butler to Brabourne, 14 December 1938, Brabourne MSS Eur.F97/22B/8; Chamberlain to Ida, 4 December and to Hilda, 11 December 1938.

68. Channon Diary, 19 December 1938.

69. Chamberlain to Simon, 16 and 23 December 1938, Simon MSS 85/93–5.
70. Fisher to Wilson (for Chamberlain), 17 September and to Chamberlain, 1 October 1938, Fisher MSS 2/7, 2/9 and PREM 1/252
71. J.A. Cross, *Sir Samuel Hoare: A Political Biography* (1977), pp. 289–90.
72. Harvey Diary, 29 September, 1, 4 October 1938 and 17 February 1939; Amery Diary, 30 September 1938.
73. Halifax to Brabourne, 18 November and 14 December 1938, Brabourne MSS Eur.F97/22C/11, 42–3; Andrew Roberts, *The 'Holy Fox': The Life of Lord Halifax*, (1992), pp. 125–37.
74. Chamberlain to Ida, 17 December 1938.
75. Harvey Diary, 12 October 1938
76. W. Hadley to Chamberlain, 24 December 1938 reporting Lord Camrose, NC7/11/31/118.
77. Chamberlain to Ida, 4 December 1938.
78. Robert Hudson to Halifax and memorandum, 12 December 1938, Hickleton MSS A4.410, 22A; Chamberlain's 'Memorandum of a Conversation with R.H. Hudson … 8 December 1938', PREM 1/344.
79. Chamberlain to Hilda, 11 December and to Ida, 17 December 1938; to Simon, 23 December 1938, Simon MSS 85/95, Hore-Belisha Diary, 21 December 1938, HOBE15/42; Lord Feversham to Chamberlain, 21 December 1938, PREM 1/344/11–16; Halifax to Chamberlain, 14 December 1938, NC7/11/31/125.
80. Chamberlain to Ida, 28 January 1939.
81. D.F. Clarke to Ball, 28 November 1938, Conservative Party Archive, CRD 1/7/35/15; Chamberlain to Hilda, 11 December 1938.
82. Chamberlain to Ida, 8 January 1939.
83. CAB 51(38)3, 31 October 1938, CAB 23/96.
84. A.L. Kennedy Journal, 25 October 1938.
85. *DBFP*, 3, III, 329; Chamberlain to Ida, 9 October 1938; Halifax to Chamberlain, 11 October 1938, NC11/31/124A; Ciano Diary, 6, 13, 27–28 October 1938.
86. Chamberlain to Hilda, 6 November 1938; Cadogan Diary, 14 November 1938; CAB 50(38)2, 26 October 1938, CAB 23/95.
87. Chamberlain Diary, 6 November 1938; FP(36) 32nd Meeting, 14 November 1938, CAB 27/624.
88. Chamberlain to Hilda, 6 November 1938.
89. Chamberlain to Sir Eric Phipps, 30 November and reply 1 December 1938, Phipps MSS 3/1/53, 55; to Hilda, 27 November 1938. For Army intrigues see Pownall Diary, 14, 21 and 28 November 1938.
90. Cadogan to Lord Perth, 12 December 1938, PREM 1/327.
91. Kennedy Dispatch 27, 7 January 1939 reporting Cadogan, Roosevelt MSS PSF 21.
92. Chamberlain to Mary, 9 January 1939, NC1/20/1/188; to Ida, 8 January 1939.
93. Chamberlain to Hilda, 15 January 1939; Halifax 'Rome Visit, 1939', Hickleton MSS A4.410.3.11.
94. For these conversations see *DBFP*, 3, III, 500 and PREM 1/327/48–62; Chamberlain to King George VI, 17 January 1939, NC7/3/31.
95. Ciano Diary, 11 January 1939; Denis Mack Smith, *Mussolini* (1983), p. 263.

96. Channon Diary, 15 January 1939; *The Times* (leading article), 'Return From Rome', 16 January 1939.
97. Chamberlain to Ida, 12 February 1939; Kennedy Dispatch 246, 17 February 1939, Roosevelt MSS PSF 21.
98. Chamberlain to Ida, 12 and 26 February 1939.
99. Chamberlain to Hilda and to Henderson, both 19 February 1939, PREM 1/330/41; to Lord Tweedsmuir, 7 February 1939, NC7/11/32/281.
100. Chamberlain to Hilda, 6 November and 11 December 1938; to Ida, 13 November 1938.
101. Watt, *How War Came*, pp. 30, 38–40; Sir Ivone Kirkpatrick, *The Inner Circle* (1959), p. 135.
102. Crowson, *Facing Fascism*, pp. 30–33, 108–10.
103. Chamberlain to Ida, 13 November 1938; FP(36) 32nd Meeting, 14 November 1938, CAB 27/627.
104. Butler to Brabourne, 19 November 1938, Brabourne MSS Eur.F97/22B/16.
105. FP(36) 32nd Meeting, 14 November 1938, CAB 27/624.
106. Cadogan Diary, 28–29 November and 12–13 December 1938; Chamberlain to Ida, 17 December 1938.
107. Butler to Brabourne, 14 December 1938, Brabourne MSS Eur.F97/22B/16; Harvey Diary, 2 and 4 January 1939.
108. Chamberlain to Ida, 8 January 1939; Kennedy Dispatch 27, 7 January 1939, Roosevelt MSS PSF 21.
109. Harvey Diary, 29 January 1939; Chamberlain to Hilda, 19 February 1939; *DBFP*, 3, IV, 65.
110. Chamberlain to Hilda, 5 February 1939.
111. Kennedy Dispatch 246, reporting Chamberlain, 17 February 1939, Roosevelt PSF 21; 'Message for the President and Secretary of State', 28 February 1939, Welles MSS 162/09.
112. Cadogan Diary, 17 January 1939; Inskip Diary, 23 January 1939.
113. Inskip Diary, 11 January 1939; FP(36) 35th–36th Meeting, 25–26 January 1939, CAB 27/624; *H.C. Debs*, 5s, 343, col 623, 6 February 1939.
114. Hore-Belisha Diary, 28–29 March 1939; CAB 15(39)5, 29 March 1939, CAB 23/98.
115. Chamberlain to Ida, 28 January and 26 February 1939; Kennedy Dispatch 246, 17 February 1939.
116. Chamberlain to Ida, 12 February 1939; Henderson to Chamberlain, 23 February 1939, PREM 1/330/38–40.
117. Chamberlain to Hilda, 19 February 1939 and Addendum.
118. Chamberlain to Henderson, 19 February 1939, PREM 1/330/41–2; to Hilda, 19 February 1939.
119. Zetland to Linlithgow, 29 January 1939, Zetland MSS Eur.D.609/11/24; Henderson to Chamberlain, 23 February 1939, PREM 1/330.
120. Simon Newman, *March 1939: The British Guarantee to Poland* (Oxford, 1976), pp. 79–84.
121. Kennedy Dispatch 246, 17 February 1939, Roosevelt MSS PSF 21.
122. Chamberlain to Hilda, 19 February 1939; Kennedy Dispatch 246, 17 February 1939.
123. Chamberlain to Ida, 12 and 26 February, 12 March 1939; to Hilda,

19 February and 5 March 1939; Kennedy Dispatch 246, 17 February 1939 reporting Chamberlain; Channon Diary, 7 March 1939.

124. A.L. Kennedy Journal, 17 January 1939.
125. Chamberlain to Hilda, 19 February and 5 March; to Ida, 12 March 1939.
126. Chamberlain to Ida, 12 March 1939; Halifax to Chamberlain, 10 March 1939, NC7/11/32//111 and reply 11 March 1939, Hickleton MSS A4.410.17.1.
127. Templewood, *Nine Troubled Years*, pp. 328–9.

Chapter 15: The Coming of War, March–September 1939

1. Cmd. 6115, Germany No. 1 (1939): *Final Report of the Right Honourable Sir Nevile Henderson on the Circumstances Leading to the Termination of his Mission to Berlin, September 20, 1939*, Parliamentary Papers, 1938–39, XXVII, para. 8.
2. Chamberlain to Hilda, 19 March 1939; Channon Diary, 15 March 1939.
3. King George VI to Chamberlain, 18 March 1939, NC7/3/35; Hoare to Chamberlain, 17 March 1939, NC7/11/32/128; Weir to Chamberlain, 20 March 1938, Weir MSS DC96/22/2. Channon Diary, 15 March 1939.
4. Amery Diary, 15 March 1939.
5. CAB 11(39)1–2, CAB 23/98; *H.C. Debs*, 5s, 345, col 435–50, both 15 March 1939.
6. Cadogan and Dawson Diary, both 15 March 1939; Brendan Bracken to Beaverbrook, 16 March 1939; Cockett (ed.), *My Dear Max*, p. 445.
7. Nicolson Diary, 17 March 1939; Amery Diary, 16 and 21 March 1939.
8. Sir Orme Sargent to Emrys-Evans, 16 March 1939, Emrys-Evans MSS 58238/67–8; Cadogan Diary, 20 March 1939.
9. Chamberlain to Hilda, 19 March 1939; Channon Diary, 15 March 1939.
10. Butler, *Art of the Possible*, p. 77.
11. Cmd 6106 (1939): *Documents Concerning German-Polish Relations and the Outbreak of Hostilities between Great Britain and Germany on September 3, 1939*, Parliamentary Papers, 1938–39, XXVII, pp. 5–10.
12. Dawson Diary, 17 March 1939.
13. 'Lunch with Hore-Belisha', 27 March 1939, Liddell Hart MSS LH11/HB1939/3; Kennedy to Roosevelt, 20 March 1939, Roosevelt MSS PSF 21.
14. Channon Diary, 17 March 1939; Margesson to Chamberlain, 17 March 1939, NC7/11/32/185; Colonel Tweed memorandum, 16 March 1939, Lloyd George MSS G/28/2/12.
15. CAB 12(39)1, 18 March 1939, CAB 23/98; Chamberlain to Ida, 26 March; to Hilda, 29 April 1938.
16. Chamberlain to Hilda, 19 March 1939; *DBFP*, 3, IV, 446.
17. Kennedy to Roosevelt, 20 March 1939, Roosevelt MSS PSF 21; Chamberlain to Hilda, 19 March 1939; to Mussolini, 20 March 1939; Wilson note (and Chamberlain's annotation), 19 and 21 March 1939, PREM 1/327.
18. Pownall Diary, 20 and 27 March 1939; Chamberlain to Ida, 26 March 1939.
19. *DBFP*, 3, IV, 596; Chamberlain to Ida, 26 March and 9 April 1939.
20. *DBFP*, 3, IV, 484; FP(36) 38th Meeting, 27 March 1939, CAB 27/624;

Christopher Hill, *Cabinet Decisions on Foreign Policy: the British Experience, October 1938–June 1941* (Cambridge, 1991), pp. 36–43.

21. Chamberlain to Hilda, n.d. [1 April 1939]; Cadogan Diary, 29 March 1939.
22. Hill, *Cabinet Decisions*, p. 19.
23. Kennedy dispatch 478, 14 April 1939, Roosevelt MSS PSF 21; Cadogan Diary, 29 March 1939.
24. *DBFP*, 3, IV, Appendix V; Cadogan Diary, 29 March 1939; Chamberlain to Hilda, 1 April 1939.
25. 'Germany's intentions regarding Danzig, 20 March 1939', PREM 1/331A.
26. Chamberlain to Hilda, n.d. [1 April 1939]; CAB 16(39)1, 30 March 1939, CAB 23/98; FP(36) 40th Meeting, 31 March 1939, CAB 27/624.
27. Zetland to Linlithgow, 4 April 1939, Zetland MSS Eur.D609/11.
28. Chamberlain to Hilda, n.d. [1–2 April 1939].
29. *H.C. Debs*, 5s, 345, col 2415; Nicolson and Channon Diary, all 31 March 1939.
30. Chamberlain to Hilda, n.d. [2 April 1939].
31. Hore-Belisha Diary, 28 March 1939, reporting Chamberlain.
32. Halifax note, 'Foreign Policy 1938–39', n.d., Hickleton MSS A4.410.12.1.
33. Chamberlain to Hilda, n.d. [2 April 1939].
34. Dawson Diary, 3 April 1939; A.L. Kennedy Journal, 4 April 1939; *The Times* (leading article), 'A Stand for Orderly Diplomacy', 1 April 1939.
35. Chamberlain to Hilda, n.d. [1 April 1939]; Eden to Chamberlain, 1 April 1939; Derrick Gunston to Chamberlain, 2 April 1939, NC7/11/32/77, 101.
36. Edgar Granville to Chamberlain, 3 April 1939, NC7/11/32/88; Eden to Chamberlain, 1 April 1939, NC7/11/32/77.
37. *DBFP*, 3, V, 81–2.
38. Chamberlain to Ida, 9 April and to Hilda, 15 April 1939; Kennedy dispatch 478, 14 April 1939, Roosevelt MSS PSF 21.
39. Hore-Belisha Diary, 19 April 1939; FP(36) 41st Meeting, 10 April 1939, CAB 27/264; CAB 20(39)2, 13 April 1939, CAB 23/98.
40. Chamberlain to Hilda, 15 April 1939.
41. Chamberlain to Ida, 14 March 1936 and 9 April 1939; to Hilda, 27 March 1938 and 15 April 1939.
42. Chamberlain to Hilda, 15, 29 April and 14 May 1939.
43. Chamberlain to Hilda, 14 May 1939; CAB 20 and 24(39), 13 and 26 April 1939.
44. Chamberlain to Hilda, 29 April 1939.
45. Chamberlain to Ida, 7 May and 10 June 1939; to Hilda 15 July 1939; to Daladier, 13 July 1939; Phipps to Chamberlain, 14 July 1939, Phipps MSS PHPP3/1/81–8.
46. *H.C. Debs*, 5s, 345, col 2482, 3 April 1939; Halifax, *Fulness of Days*, p. 200.
47. Channon Diary, 3 and 13 April 1939.
48. Nicolson Diary, 20 and 26 April 1939; Amery Diary, 19 May 1939.
49. Chamberlain to H.A. Gwynne, 7 January 1939, NC7/11/32/106.
50. Ernest Benn Diary, Whitsun [17 May] 1939, D. Abel, *Ernest Benn: Counsel for Liberty* (1960), p. 96. Chamberlain to Hilda, 29 April 1939.

51. Kennedy Dispatch 440, 4 April 1939, Roosevelt MSS PSF 21.
52. Hoare to Chamberlain, 2 April 1939, NC7/11/32/129.
53. See, for example, Nicolson Diary, 18 and 20 July 1939.
54. Duke of Buccleuch to Butler with memorandum, 24 April 1939, Butler MSS G10/3–10; Chamberlain to Hilda, 15 and 29 April 1939.
55. Hore-Belisha Diary, 18–19 April 1939; Weir to Chamberlain, 11 April and Wilson memorandum, 20 April 1939, NC7/11/32/294–5.
56. CAB 22(39)3, 24 April 1939, CAB 23/99; Hore-Belisha Diary, 13–22 April 1939; Hore-Belisha to Chamberlain, 15 April 1939, HOBE1/5; Chamberlain to Hilda, 15 April and to Ida, 23 April 1939.
57. Chamberlain to Hilda, 29 April, 17 June and 17 September 1939.
58. Chamberlain to Ida, 23 April 1939.
59. Nicolson Diary, 20 and 26 April 1939; Dalton Diary, 4 May 1939; Robert Brand to Dawson, 28 June 1939, Dawson MSS 81/1.
60. Dalton Diary, 7 May 1939; Harvey and Channon Diary, both 3 May 1939.
61. Chamberlain to Ida, 23 April 1939.
62. Channon Diary, 28 March 1939; Winterton to Chamberlain, 27 April 1939, NC7/11/32/300; Chamberlain to Smedley Crooke, 30 June 1939, NC Letters Additional 23.
63. Davidson to Horace Wilson, 9 May 1939 (marked 'Not Sent') and to Ball, 9 May 1939, Davidson MSS 262; Channon Diary, 4 May 1939.
64. Chamberlain to Hilda, 28 May 1939; Gallup, *Gallup International Public Opinion Polls*, pp. 9–21.
65. 'Chamberlain: A Candid Portrait', n.d. [November 1939], Butler MSS F77/3.
66. Chamberlain to Ida, 9 April, 25 June; to Hilda, 15 April, 2 July 1939; W. Blackwood to Chamberlain, n.d. [1–2 August 1939], NC7/11/32/13.
67. Hoare to Lord Erskine, 18 July 1939, Erskine MSS Eur.D596/21/62.
68. Chamberlain to Hilda, 17 June 1939.
69. Channon Diary, 20 May 1938.
70. Chamberlain to Hilda, 17 June; to Ida, 25 June 1939; FP(36) 52nd–53rd Meeting, 19–20 June 1939, CAB 27/625.
71. Lord Cranborne to Emrys-Evans, 27 June 1939, Emrys-Evans MSS 58240/17–18; Harvey Diary, 24 June 1939.
72. Murray memorandum, 21 October and Murray to Roosevelt, 13 December 1938, PREM 1/367 and Roosevelt MSS PSF 53; Roosevelt to Murray, 19 January and Murray to Chamberlain, 1 February 1939, Murray MSS 8809/105–8, 162–4.
73. Kennedy Dispatch 440 and 478, 4 and 14 April 1939, Roosevelt MSS PSF 21; David Reynolds, *The Creation of the Anglo-American Alliance, 1937–41* (1981), pp. 50–53.
74. Roosevelt to Chamberlain, 11 September and reply 8 November 1939, PREM 1/366.
75. Nicolson Diary, 7 March 1938; *Tribune*, 1 April 1938, quoted in A.W. Wright, *G.D.H. Cole and Socialist Democracy* (Oxford, 1979), p. 245.
76. Chamberlain to Ida, 26 March, 9 April 1939.
77. Chamberlain to Ida, 21 May; to Hilda, 28 May 1939; FP(36) Meeting, 27 April 1939; Ernest Benn Diary, Whitsun 1939.
78. Robert Conquest, *The Great Terror: Stalin's Purge of the Thirties* (Pelican

ed., 1971), pp. 277–312, 615–22, 645–8; *DBFP*, 3, I, 148 and IV, 183 with enclosures.

79. Chamberlain to Ida, 9 April 1939; FP(36) 44th Meeting, 25 April 1939, CAB 27/624.
80. Hugh Dalton, *The Fateful Years: Memoirs 1931–1945* (1957), pp. 237–8.
81. Hill, *Cabinet Decisions*, p. 68; Chamberlain to Hilda, 29 April 1939.
82. CAB 20(39)2, 13 April 1939, CAB 23/98.
83. Cadogan Diary, 19 May 1939.
84. Channon Diary, 15–16 May 1939; Harvey Diary, 20 May 1939; Amery Diary, 19 May 1939.
85. FP(36) 48th Meeting, 19 May 1939, CAB 27/625; Cadogan Diary, 19, 20 and 24 May 1939; *DBFP*, 3, V, 582; Chamberlain to Hilda, 28 May 1939.
86. CAB 30(38)1, 24 May 1939, CAB 23/99; *H.C. Debs*, 5s, 347, col 2267, 24 May 1939.
87. Chamberlain to Hilda, 28 May 1939; *DBFP*, 3, V, 657.
88. Chamberlain to Ida, 10 June and to Hilda, 17 June 1939; FP(36) 53rd Meeting, 20 June 1939.
89. FP(36) 50th, 53rd, 58th and 59th Meeting, 9, 20 June and 19, 26 July 1938, CAB 27/625; Chamberlain to Hilda, 15 July 1939.
90. Chamberlain to Ida, 21 May 1939; CAB 38(39)1, 19 July 1939, CAB 23/100.
91. CAB 41(39)3, 22 August 1939, CAB 23/100; Chamberlain to Hilda, 27 August 1939; *DBFP*, 3, VII, 137.
92. Parker, *Chamberlain and Appeasement*, p. 245; Frank McDonough, *Neville Chamberlain, Appeasement and the British Road to War* (Manchester, 1998), p. 85.
93. 'Foreign Policy 1938–39', Hickleton MSS A4.410.12.1. Also Strang, *At Home and Abroad*, p. 198.
94. Kershaw, *Hitler*, pp. 207–8.
95. Headlam Diary, 3 June 1939. See also Robert Brand to Geoffrey Dawson, 28 June 1939, Dawson MSS 81/1.
96. Chamberlain to Hilda, 14, 28 May 1939; Wilson to Henderson, 12 May 1939, PREM 1/331A; *The Times*, 12 May 1939.
97. Dalton Diary, 28 June 1939.
98. Chamberlain to Hilda, 15 July 1939.
99. 'The Polish request for Financial Assistance', 9 May 1939; Simon memorandum, 15 May 1939, PREM 1/357; CAB 39(39)3, 26 July 1939, CAB 23/100.
100. Chamberlain and Wilson notes, both 14 May 1939; Simon to Halifax, 24 July 1939, PREM 1/357.
101. Watt, *How War Came*, pp. 271–308, 334–6.
102. Chamberlain to Hilda, 2 July 1939.
103. Chamberlain to Ida, 23 July 1939. For these talks see PREM 1/330.
104. Chamberlain to Ida, 23 July 1939.
105. Chamberlain to Hilda, 2 July 1939; to King George VI, 3 July 1939, NC7/3/37.
106. Tennant to Butler, 28 March 1938; Butler to Halifax, 14 April and reply, 16 April 1938, Butler MSS F79/1–6, 11–13; E.W.D. Tennant, *True Account* (1957).

107. Chamberlain's 'Note of an interview with Wenner Gren, 6 June' and Wenner Gren to Chamberlain, 3 July 1939, PREM 1/328.

108. Wilson note on Tennant briefing, 24 July 1939, PREM 1/335/46.

109. For the Tennant, Gren and Bryant discussions see PREM 1/328, 333, 335; 'Notes of the conversation with Herr Hitler', 28 July 1939; Wilson note and Lord Kemsley to Dr Dietrich, both 1 August 1939, PREM 1/332.

110. Wilson note, 3 August 1939, PREM 1/330/3–11.

111. Channon Diary, 31 July; Channon and Nicolson Diary, both 2 August 1939.

112. Channon Diary, 5 May 1939; Nicolson Diary, 2 August 1939; Chamberlain to Ida, 23 July and 5 August 1939. For action against Cartland see NC7/11/32/38–9.

113. Channon Diary, 31 July 1939; Chamberlain to Hilda, 15 July and to Ida, 23 July 1939.

114. Occasional [Chequers] Diary, 4 August 1939, NC2/26; Chamberlain to Hilda, 30 July and to Ida, 5 August 1939.

115. Anne Chamberlain to Hilda, 18 August 1939, NC18/1/1113; Fishing Diary, 7–20 August 1939, NC6/3/3.

116. Halifax to Chamberlain, 19 August 1939, PREM 1/331A; Chamberlain to Ida, 19 August; to Hilda, 27 August 1939.

117. Halifax 'Record of Events before the War, 1939', entry for 21 and 24 August 1939, FO 300/317/82.

118. Hore-Belisha Diary, 21 August 1939; Chamberlain to Hilda, 27 August 1939.

119. Cmd 6106, *Documents*, No. 56; *H.C. Debs*, 5s, 351, col 8–10, 24 August 1939.

120. Channon and Nicolson Diary, both 24 August 1939.

121. Hore-Belisha Diary and to Chamberlain, 23–24 August 1939, HOBE1/7.

122. Chamberlain to Hilda, 27 August 1939; Cmd 6106, *Documents*, No. 68–9.

123. Henderson, *Failure of a Mission*, p. 261.

124. Kershaw, *Hitler*, pp. 213–15; Strang to Cadogan, 26 August 1939, PREM 1/331A/125.

125. Cadogan Diary, 28 August 1939; Harvey Diary, 27 August 1939.

126. Pownall Diary, 29 August 1939; Wallace and Hore-Belisha diaries and Halifax 'Record of Events', all 26–27 August 1939.

127. Harvey Diary, 26–27 August 1939; Chamberlain to Hilda, 27 August 1939.

128. Cmd 6106, *Documents*, No. 74–81; Cmd 6115 *Final Report*, para. 40; Henderson, *Failure of a Mission*, pp. 262–9; Watt, *How War Came*, pp. 508, 516.

129. Halifax 'Record of Events', 27, 29 August 1939; Chamberlain to Ida, 10 September 1939; Inskip Diary, 29–30 August 1939; Cadogan Diary, 29 August 1939. For the peripatetic Swede's efforts see Birger Dahlerus, *The Last Attempt* (1947).

130. CAB 46(39)1, 30 August 1939, CAB 23/100; Harvey Diary, 29 August and Wallace Diary, 30 August 1939.

131. *DBFP*, 3, VII, 525; Inskip Diary, 30 August 1939; Kennedy dispatch 1325, 30 August 1939, Roosevelt MSS PSF 21.

132. Halifax 'Record of Events', Harvey and Wallace diaries, both reporting

Halifax; Hoare Diary reporting Wilson all 31 August 1939; Channon Diary, 2 September 1939, reporting Dunglass.

133. Chamberlain to Ida, 10 September 1939.

134. Kershaw, *Hitler*, pp. 217–19.

135. CAB 47(39)1, 1 September 1939, CAB 23/100. Wallace, Inskip and Cadogan diaries, 1 September 1939.

136. *H.C. Debs*, 5s, 351, col 261; Nicolson Diary and Halifax 'Record of Events', all 1 September 1939 FO 800/317/84.

137. Halifax 'Record of Events', Harvey, Channon, Inskip, Wallace, Hore-Belisha and Simon diaries and CAB 48(39)1–2, all 2 September 1939.

138. CAB 47–8(39)1, 1–2 September 1939, CAB23/100; Cadogan and Simon diaries; *H.C. Debs*, 5s, 350, col 280–81, all 2 September 1939.

139. Pownall Diary, 2 September 1939; Amery Diary, 1 September 1939.

140. Halifax, 'Record of Events', 2 September 1939; Butler 'Events before the war', September 1939, Butler MSS G10/108.

141. Channon, Crookshank, Nicolson, Simon, Wallace, Amery, Hore-Belisha, Pownall diaries, Halifax 'Record of Events', *H.C. Debs*, 5s, 351, col 280–82, all 2 September 1939.

142. Chamberlain to Ida, 10 September 1939; Amery and Nicolson diaries and Halifax 'Record of Events', all 2 September 1939; Butler 'Events before the war', Butler MSS G10/108.

143. Halifax, 'Record of Events', 2 September 1939; Asa Briggs, *The History of Broadcasting in the United Kingdom, Volume III, War of Words* (1970), p. 78.

144. Simon to Chamberlain, n.d., NC7/11/32/231; Halifax, 'Record of Events', Simon, Wallace, Hore-Belisha, Pownall diaries, all 2 September 1939; Inskip Diary, 3 September 1939.

145. Chamberlain to Ida, 10 September 1939.

146. Inskip and Simon Diary, Halifax, 'Record of Events', all 2 September 1939.

147. CAB 49(39)1, CAB 23/100 and Channon Diary, both 2 September 1939.

148. Henderson, *Failure of a Mission*, pp. 284–5.

149. Halifax 'Record of Events' Appendix IV.

150. Winterton Diary, 3 September 1939; King George VI Diary, 3 September 1939, J.W. Wheeler-Bennett, *King George VI: His Life and Reign* (1958), p. 405.

151. Halifax, 'Record of Events', Channon, Colville, Beatrice Webb and Beveridge diaries, all 3 September 1939.

152. Nicolson and Amery diaries, 3 September 1939.

153. John Colville, *The Fringes of Power: Downing Street Diaries, 1939–1955* (1985), p. 19.

154. *H.C. Debs*, 5s, 351, col 291–2, Channon and Nicolson diaries, all 3 September 1939 – but see Wallace Diary, 3 September 1939.

155. Winterton and Pownall diaries, 3 September 1939; Tufton Beamish autobiographical notes, 2 September 1939, Beamish MSS 3/3.

156. Nicolson, Amery, Dugdale and Gordon Walker diaries, all 3 September 1939.

157. King George VI Diary, 3 September 1939, Wheeler-Bennett, *King George VI*, p. 405.

158. Chamberlain to Ida, 10 September 1939.

Chapter 16: 'The Bore War', September 1939–January 1940

1. Colville Diary, 27–28 September 1939; Gwynne to Lord Linlithgow, 25 September 1939, Linlithgow MSS Eur.F125/130/30.
2. Young, *Alec Douglas Home*, p. 59; Hoare to Beaverbrook, 1 October 1939, Beaverbrook MSS C/308.
3. Channon Diary, 4 November and 10 December 1939; Colville Diary, 27 November 1939.
4. Inskip Diary, 10 November 1939; Colville Diary, 16 December 1939; W.K. Hancock and M.M. Gowing, *History of the Second World War: British War Economy* (1949), p. 95.
5. Chamberlain to Ida, 10 September 1939; War Cabinet Conclusions, WM 8(39)18, 8 September 1939, CAB 65/1.
6. Chamberlain to Hilda, 17 September; to Ida, 22 October, 5 November 1939.
7. 'The War and Ourselves', BBC Home Service, 26 November 1939, NC7/11/32/174.
8. Boothby to Lloyd George, 10 September; Lord Davis to Lloyd George, 5 September 1939, Lloyd George MSS G5/13/10, 12.
9. Colville Diary, 28 September and 9 November 1939.
10. Chamberlain to Hilda, 17 May 1940.
11. Dalton Diary, 24–25 August and 6 September 1939.
12. Chamberlain to Hilda, 30 July 1939; Dalton Diary, 24 August 1939.
13. Hoare to Chamberlain, n.d.; Sinclair to Chamberlain, 2 and 6 February 1939, and replies 6 and 7 February 1939, NC7/11/32/131, 232, 234–7.
14. De Groot, *Liberal Crusader*, p. 151; Addison, *Road to 1945*, p. 62; Samuel to Lothian, 13 September 1939, Lothian MSS GD40/17/404.
15. Hankey Diary, 23 August and to his wife, 3 September 1939, Stephen Roskill, *Hankey: Man of Secrets, Vol. 3, 1931–63* (1974), III, p. 419.
16. Earl of Avon, *The Reckoning* (1965), pp. 62–3, 90–91, but see Inskip Diary, 8 September 1939.
17. Amery to Geoffrey Dawson, 4 September and 17 November 1939, Dawson MSS 81/13–14, 24; Eden Diary, 4 October 1939.
18. Swinton to Chamberlain, 3 September 1939, NC7/11/32/247.
19. Salisbury to Halifax, 22 September 1939, FO 800/317/33.
20. Kennedy to Roosevelt, 20 July 1939, Roosevelt MSS PSF 37/340.
21. Lord Citrine, *Two Careers* (1967), p. 16; Chamberlain to Hilda, 17 September 1939.
22. Channon Diary, 14 September 1939; Chamberlain to Ida, 13 April 1940.
23. Hoare to Beaverbrook, 1 October 1939, Beaverbrook MSS C/308.
24. Chamberlain to Hilda, 17 November 1939; Inskip Diary, 21 November 1939.
25. Churchill to Chamberlain, 2, 10, 11 and 15 September 1939, NC7/9/45–9.
26. Anne Chamberlain to Hilda, 18 April and reply 19 April 1955, NC1/15/5/3–4; Chamberlain to Hilda, 17 September and to Ida, 8 October 1939; to Churchill, 16 September 1939, NC7/9/50; Horace Wilson memorandum, 3 October 1939.
27. Chamberlain to Ida, 8 October 1939; Simon Diary, 7 October 1939

reporting Churchill; Hoare to Beaverbrook, 1 October 1939, Beaverbrook MSS C/309; Hankey Diary, 23 August 1939.

28. Chamberlain to Ida, 22 October 1939.
29. Inskip diary, 4 December 1939; Wallace Diary, 9 May 1940; Chamberlain to Hilda, 25 February 1940.
30. Violet Bonham Carter to Eden, 15 October 1939, AP20/7/67.
31. Templewood, *Nine Troubled Years*, pp. 386–7.
32. Colville Diary, 13 and 16 October reporting the No. 10 Press Secretary and Davidson; Hoare to Beaverbrook, 15 February 1943, Beaverbrook MSS C/308.
33. Hankey Diary, 23–24 August and memorandum entitled 'A War Cabinet', 24 August 1939, HNKY10/1/2–7 and PREM 1/384.
34. Chamberlain to Hilda, 26 January 1935.
35. Sir William Bridges to Wilson, 3 September 1939, CAB 21/777.
36. Dawson to Amery and *The Times*, both 4 September 1939, Dawson MSS 81/15.
37. Amery Diary, 4 September 1939.
38. Hankey to Beveridge, 6, 13 and 22 February 1940, Beveridge MSS IIb/39; Hankey's 'Six Months of War – 1939–40 and 1914–15', Ismay MSS 3/4/18A; Roskill, *Hankey*, III, pp. 427–8; Chamberlain to Hilda, 6 April 1940.
39. Richard Law to Emrys-Evans, 13 September 1939, Emrys-Evans MSS 58239/2–3; Wallace and Crookshank diaries, 3 September 1939.
40. Simon Diary, 23 September 1939.
41. Stephen Brooke, *Labour's War: the Labour Party during the Second World War* (Oxford, 1992), pp. 40–41, 45; Jeffreys, *Churchill Coalition*, p. 65.
42. *Annual Abstract of Statistics 1938–48* (1949), p. 108.
43. Beveridge Diary, 13, 18 September, 3–4 October 1939; Beveridge to Hankey, 4 September; to Horace Wilson and reply, 3, 5, 7 October 1939, Beveridge MSS IIb/39; *The Times*, 3 October 1939.
44. Addison, *Road to 1945*, pp. 65–7; Hancock and Gowing, *British War Economy*, p. 93.
45. Beveridge to Wilson, 7 October 1939, Beveridge MSS IIb/39; Violet Bonham Carter to Eden, 15 October 1939, AP20/7/67; 'Cato', *Guilty Men* (1940, Penguin Classics ed., 1998), p. 97.
46. Gallup, *Gallup International Public Opinion Polls*, pp. 23–32 Mass-Observation MSS, files TC25/5/I and TC25/6/C.
47. Sir Ian Jacob memoir in J.W. Wheeler-Bennett (ed.), *Action this Day: Working with Churchill* (1968), pp. 161, 185. Also Amery Diary, 27–29 September 1939.
48. Chamberlain to Ida, 10 September 1939; Inskip Diary, 13 September 1939; WM 12(39)9, 11 September 1939, CAB 65/1.
49. Chamberlain to Ida, 20 December 1939.
50. Nicolson Diary, 20 and 26 September; Channon Diary, 26 September 1939.
51. Chamberlain to Ida, 27 January 1940.
52. Davidson to Baldwin, 6 October 1939, Davidson MSS 265.
53. J.P.L. Thomas to Eden, 14 September 1939, AP20/7/61A; Amery to Emrys-Evans, 21 June 1954, Emrys-Evans MSS 58247/16.
54. David Roberts, 'Clement Davies and the Fall of Neville Chamberlain, 1939–40', *Welsh History Review*, 8 (1976), pp. 188–215.

55. Chamberlain to Ida, 19 November; to Hilda, 26 November 1939.
56. Amery Diary, 22 November 1939; Nancy Astor to Lord Lothian, 23 November 1939, Lothian MSS GD40/17/407.
57. Crozier interview with Bracken, 29 March 1940, Taylor (ed.), *W.P. Crozier: Off the Record*, p. 156.
58. Davidson to Baldwin, 6 October 1939, Davidson MSS 265; Colville Diary, 13 October 1939.
59. Thomas to Eden, 14 September 1939, AP20/7/61A; Wolmer to Churchill, 6 September 1939, Wolmer MSS Eng.hist.d.450/62; Richard Law to Emrys-Evans, 13 September 1939, Emrys-Evans MSS 58239/2.
60. Anne Chamberlain to Hilda, 24 October 1939.
61. Chamberlain to Ida, 23 September 1939; Channon Diary, 14 December 1939.
62. Colville Diary, 24 October 1939.
63. Hoare to Beaverbrook, 1 October 1939, Beaverbrook MSS C/308; Anne Chamberlain to Hilda, 24 October 1939; Crowson, *Facing Fascism*, p. 169.
64. R.H. Edwards [Birmingham Chief Agent] to E.W. Salt, 3 October 1939, Hannon MSS 72/1.
65. Chamberlain to Conservative National Union Executive, Central Hall, Westminster, 27 June 1940, NC4/4/1.
66. Addison, *Road to 1945*, p. 57.
67. WM 14(39)1, 13 September 1939, CAB 65/1; SWC (39/40) 1st Meeting of Supreme War Council, 12 September 1939, CAB 99/3; Chamberlain to Ida, 10 September 1939.
68. Chamberlain to Hilda, 15 October and to Ida, 22 October 1939.
69. Hankey, 'War Policy' and 'War Appreciation', 12 and 29 September 1939, HNKY11/1 and 10/3/3.
70. Chamberlain to Roosevelt, 4 October 1939, Roosevelt MSS, PSF 32/303.
71. Chamberlain to Liddell Hart, 8 March 1937; to Hore-Belisha, 29 October 1937, Liddell Hart MSS1/159.
72. Chamberlain to Joseph Ball, 26 December 1939, Ball MSS Eng.c.6656/17.
73. Chamberlain to Roosevelt, 4 October and 8 November 1939, Roosevelt MSS PSF 32/303.
74. Chamberlain to Hilda, 17 September 1939; Colville Diary, 28 September and 13 October 1939.
75. WM 26(39) and Cadogan Diary, both 25 September 1939.
76. F.H. Hinsley *et al.*, *British Intelligence in the Second World War* (4 vols, 1979–90), I, pp. 59–73; Kershaw, *Hitler*, pp. 64, 92–3, 274–6.
77. Colville Diary, 28 September 1939.
78. *Gallup International Public Opinion Polls*, pp. 24–33.
79. Wolmer to Churchill, 6 September 1939, Wolmer MSS Eng.hist.d.450/62; Harvey Diary, 11 and 26 September 1939.
80. Hancock and Gowing, *British War Economy*, pp. 96–8.
81. Chamberlain to Ida, 19 November 1939.
82. Chamberlain to Hilda, 17 September; to Ida, 23 September 1939.
83. Chamberlain to Ida, 10 and 23 September 1939; WM 17(39)9, 16 September 1939, CAB 65/1.
84. 'War Policy', 12 September 1939, para. 30–31, 35 HNKY11/1.
85. Chamberlain to Hilda, 17 September; to Ida, 8 October 1939.

86. Chamberlain to Ida, 23 September, 8 and 22 October 1939; WM 20(39)14, 19 September 1939, CAB 65/1.

87. Colville Diary, 29 October and 2 November 1939; Foreign Office notes, 30 October, 7 and 16 November 1939, NC8/29/1, 3–4.

88. Chamberlain to Ida, 10 September, 8 October, 5 November 1939; to Lord McGowan, 5 September 1939, NC7/11/32/181.

89. Hoare's 'Weekly Notes' entry for 26 September 1939, Templewood MSS XI:2; Cadogan Diary, 28–29 September 1939.

90. Chamberlain to Hilda, 1 October 1939; WM 35(39)8, 3 October 1939, CAB 65/1; Confidential Annex to WM 38(39), 5 October 1939, CAB 65/3.

91. Chamberlain to Ida, 8 October 1939.

92. Davidson to Baldwin, 6 October 1939, Davidson MSS 265.

93. Joseph Kennedy to Roosevelt, 3 November 1939, Roosevelt MSS PSF 37/340.

94. Chamberlain to Ida, 8 October 1939; to Hilda, 15 October 1939.

95. Roger Parkinson, *Peace in Our Time: Munich and Dunkirk – the Inside Story* (1971), pp. 257–8.

96. WM 42(39)8 and WM 43(39)13, 9–10 October 1939, CAB 65/1.

97. Davidson to Baldwin, 6 October 1939, Davidson MSS 265.

98. Wallace Diary, 6 October 1939; Cockett, *Twilight of Truth*, pp. 152–9; *Gallup International Public Opinion Polls*, p. 24; 'War Questionnaire', November 1939, Mass-Observation MSS TC25/5/I.

99. 'Note of an interview with Lord Halifax, 26 September 1939', Cecil MSS 51084/219; Chamberlain to Lord Tweedsmuir, 25 September 1939, NC7/11/32/288.

100. WM 9(39)5 and WM 12(39)9, WM 45(39)7, 9, 11 September, 12 October, CAB 65/1; Inskip Diary, 13 October 1939.

101. WM 45(39)7 and Annex, 12 October 1939; Wallace Diary, 11 October 1939.

102. *H.C. Debs*, 5s, 352, col 563–8 and Channon Diary, both 12 October 1939; WM 49(30), 16 October 1939, CAB 65/1; Chamberlain to Hilda, 15 October 1939; Lord Lloyd to Chamberlain, 12 October 1939, NC7/1/32/171.

103. Kershaw, *Hitler*, p. 266.

104. Chamberlain to Ida, 22 October 1939.

105. Colville Diary, 4 November 1939; 'The War and Ourselves', BBC Home Service, 26 November 1939, NC7/11/32/174.

106. Chamberlain to Hilda, 28 October and 10 December 1939.

107. Chamberlain to Ida, 8, 22 October, 5 November; to Hilda, 15 October 1939.

108. Chamberlain to Ida, 23 September, 5 and 19 November; to Hilda, 12 November 1939.

109. Chamberlain to Ida, 19 November and 3 December 1939.

110. Chamberlain to Ida, 5 November, 3 December 1939.

111. Chamberlain to Hilda, 30 December 1939; to Joseph Ball, 26 December 1939, Ball MSS Eng.c.6656/17.

112. Chamberlain to Ida, 20 December 1939; Francis Freemantle to Chamberlain, 13 December 1939, NC7/11/32/82.

113. Inskip Diary, 16 December 1939.

114. Chamberlain to Hilda, 10 and 30 December 1939; Colville Diary, 28 December 1939.

115. Colville Diary, 13 December 1939.
116. Chamberlain to Hilda, 30 May, 1 August, 26 November 1937; to Lord Weir, 15 August 1937, Weir MSS DC96/22/2.
117. Headlam Diary, 7 May 1938, reporting Lord Londonderry; Collin Brooks Journal, 23 November 1939.
118. Hudson to Halifax, 12 December 1938, Hickleton MSS A4.410.22A; Headlam Diary, 7 April 1939; Pownall Diary, 1 May, 12, 19 June and 22 November 1939.
119. Collin Brooks Journal, 23 November 1939.
120. Channon Diary, 6 January 1940; Pownall Diary, 22, 29–30 November 1939.
121. Chamberlain Diary, 19 and 24 December 1939; Pownall Diary, 29 November 1939.
122. Hore-Belisha Diary, 20–21 December 1938, HOBE5/42; Cf. 'Lunch with Hore-Belisha', 27 March 1939, Liddell Hart MSS LH11/HB1939/3.
123. Pownall Diary, 22 November, 8 and 19 December 1939; Chamberlain Diary 24 December 1939.
124. Chamberlain to Ida, 7 January 1940.
125. 'H.B.'s account to the Press (private) of his resignation and N.C.'s comments thereupon: For record only' and 'Commentary', 15 and 17 January 1940, NC8/32/1–2; Chamberlain Diary, 24 December 1939; Hore-Belisha Diary, 20 December 1939 HOBE1/7; 'Talk with Hore-Belisha', 15–16 January 1940, Liddell Hart MSS LH11/HB1940/8–9.
126. Chamberlain to Ida, 7 January 1940.
127. Halifax to Chamberlain, 23 December 1939, NC7/11/32/116–17.
128. Colville Diary, 29 December 1939 and 3 January 1940; Chamberlain to Ida, 7 January 1940.
129. Chamberlain to Ida, 7 January 1940; to Hore-Belisha, 4 January 1940, HOBE5/94; 'H.B.'s account to the Press' and 'Commentary', NC8/32/1–2; Hore-Belisha Diary, 4 January 1940.
130. Hore-Belisha to Chamberlain, 4 January 1940, HOBE5/95.
131. 'Commentary', 17 January 1940, NC8/32/2; Hore-Belisha Diary, 5 January 1940.
132. Chamberlain to Ida, 20 January 1940; 'H.B.'s account to the Press' and 'Commentary', NC8/32/1–2; Channon Diary, 6 January 1940; Hore-Belisha Diary, 5 January 1940.
133. Channon Diary, 6, 8 and 17 January 1940; Colville Diary, 8–9 January 1940. For public reaction see Mass-Observation MSS TC25/6/B.
134. Hore-Belisha Diary, 16 January 1940; Chamberlain to Hilda, 13 January; to Ida, 20 January 1940; Cockett, *Twilight of Truth*, pp. 168–9; Sir John Dill to Montgomery-Massingberd, 30 January 1940, Massingberd MSS 10/14/160/2.
135. Colville, Channon and Amery diaries, all 16 January 1940; Chamberlain to Ida, 20 January 1940.
136. Chamberlain to Ida, 20 January 1940; Colville Diary, 4 November 1939.
137. Nick Smart, *The National Government 1931–40* (1990), pp. 212–13; David Dutton, *Simon: A Political Biography* (1992), p. 287.
138. Hankey Diary, 23 August 1940; Peden, *The Treasury and British Public Policy*, p. 306.

139. J. Harry Jones, *Josiah Stamp: Public Servant* (1964), pp. 335–9.

140. Chamberlain to Ida, 20 January 1940; Colville Diary, 28 December 1939, 1–2 January, 1 February 1940.

141. Colville Diary, 4 January 1940; Channon Diary, 6 January 1940; Emrys-Evans to Eden, 7 January 1940, Emrys-Evans MSS 58242/20; Amery Diary, 5 January 1940.

142. Colville Diary, 24 January 1940.

143. Reith Diary, 27 March 1940; Chamberlain to Ida, 27 January 1940.

144. Chamberlain to Hilda, 6 April 1940; Colville Diary, 24 January, 2 February 1940.

145. Chamberlain to Ida, 20, 27 January 1940; Colville Diary, 17 and 25 January 1940.

Chapter 17: Decline and Fall, February–May 1940

1. Chamberlain to Ida, 30 March 1940; to Sir Francis Humphrys, 21 March 1940, NC7/11/33/113.

2. Thomas Jones to A. Flexner, 12 January 1940, Jones (ed.), *Diary with Letters*, p. 445; Colville Diary, 6 February 1940.

3. Colville Diary, 24 April 1940; Emrys-Evans Diary, 23 April 1940, Emrys-Evans MSS 58246/123.

4. Chamberlain to Hilda, 13 January 1940; Mackenzie King to Chamberlain (telegram), 9 January 1940; Tweedsmuir to Chamberlain, 10 January 1940, NC7/11/33/119, 177; Collin Brooks Journal, 21 January 1940.

5. Chamberlain to Ida, 2 March 1940.

6. Channon, Nicolson, Crookshank, Colville diaries, all 19 March 1940.

7. Chamberlain to Ida, 27 January and 17 February; to Hilda, 25 February, 20 April 1940.

8. SWC (39/40) 5th Meeting of Supreme War Council, 5 February 1940, CAB 99/3; Chamberlain to Ida, 17 February and 2 and 16 March 1940.

9. Chamberlain to Hilda, 13 January, 9, 25 February; to Ida, 16 March 1940; Reith Diary, 27 March 1940.

10. Richard Law to Emrys-Evans, 30 December 1939 and 1 April 1940; Emrys-Evans to Eden, 17 March 1940, Emrys-Evans MSS 58239/4, 7 and 58242/29–31.

11. Colville Diary, 26–28 March 1940; Chamberlain to Ida, 30 March 1940.

12. King George VI to Chamberlain, 25 March 1940, NC7/3/45.

13. Ben Pimlott, *Hugh Dalton* (1985), p. 272.

14. Churchill to Chamberlain, 1 April 1940, CHAR19/2/176.

15. Chamberlain to Ida, 30 March 1940.

16. Wallace Diary, 31 March and 4 April 1940; Zetland to Linlithgow, 1 May 1940, Zetland MSS Eur.D609/12/124; Crookshank Diary, 2–3 April 1940.

17. Salisbury to Emrys-Evans, 31 March 1940, Emrys-Evans MSS 58245/1–2; Watching Committee Minutes, 4 April 1940, Emrys-Evans MSS 58270/4, 7–8; Salisbury's 'Record of an Interview with Neville Chamberlain' and Amery Diary, both 10 April 1940. For its formation see Larry Witherell, 'Lord Salisbury's "Watching Committee" and the Fall of Neville Chamberlain, May 1940', *English Historical Review*, 116 (November 2001), pp. 1134–66.

18. Chamberlain to Ida, 30 March 1940.
19. Chamberlain to Hilda, 6 April 1940; Headlam Diary, 4 April 1940. For the speech see NC4/5/66.
20. Colville Dairy, 10 April 1940.
21. Chamberlain to Joseph Ball, 26 December 1939, Ball MSS Eng.hist. c.6656/17.
22. Kershaw, *Hitler*, pp. 286–7.
23. WP 162(39) 'Norway – Iron-ore Traffic', 16 December 1939, CAB 66/4; WM 122(39), 22 December 1938, CAB 65/4.
24. Colville Diary, 21, 26 and 27 March 1940; Chamberlain to Ida, 30 March 1940.
25. Ironside Diary, March 1939; SWC (39/40) 6th Meeting of Supreme War Council, 28 March 1940, CAB 99/3; Colville Diary, 4–5 April 1940; WM 77(40), 29 March 1940, CAB 65/6.
26. WM 85(40), 9 April 1940, CAB 65/6; MC(40) 17th Meeting of Military Coordination Committee, 9 April 1940, CAB 83/3.
27. Chamberlain to Ida, 27 April 1940.
28. Chamberlain to Ida, 27 April; to Hilda, 4 May 1940.
29. Davidson to Baldwin, 6 October 1939, Davidson MSS 265; C.E. Lysaght, *Brendan Bracken* (1979), pp. 170–71.
30. Chamberlain to Ida, 30 March 1940.
31. Chamberlain to Hilda, 4 May 1940; Reith Diary, 1 and 3 May 1940.
32. Halifax to Chamberlain, 'Thursday', n.d., NC7/11/33/92; Reith Diary, 14 April 1940.
33. Chamberlain to Ida, 13 April 1940; Colville Diary, 25 April 1940.
34. Chamberlain to Hilda, 6 April and to Ida, 27 April 1940; Ironside Diary, 14 April 1940.
35. Memoranda by Bridges and Wilson, both 25 April 1940, PREM 1/404.
36. Chamberlain to Hilda, 20 April 1940; Colville Diary, 17 April 1940; MC(40) 26th Meeting of Military Coordination Committee, 16 April 1940, CAB 83/3.
37. Colville Diary, 17 April 1940.
38. Wilson and Bridges memoranda, both 25 April 1940, PREM 1/404; Ironside Diary, 26 April 1940.
39. Churchill, *Gathering Storm*, p. 505; Churchill to Chamberlain, 24 April 1940, 'not sent', Martin Gilbert, *Churchill VI*, p. 267.
40. Chamberlain to Ida, 27 April 1940; Colville Diary, 24–25 April 1940.
41. Addison, *Road to 1945*, p. 91.
42. Colville and Channon diaries, both 25 April 1940; Chamberlain to Hilda, 4 May 1940.
43. Chamberlain to Hilda, 10 March 1940.
44. Chamberlain to Ida, 27 April 1940.
45. Chamberlain note and 'Defence Organisation', 30 April 1940; Churchill to Chamberlain, 30 April 1940, PREM 1/404.
46. John Charmley, *Churchill: The End of Glory. A Political Biography* (1993), p. 390.
47. Sir Ronald Wingate, *Lord Ismay: a Biography* (1970), pp. 43–4; *The Memoirs of Lord Ismay* (1960), pp. 112–14.
48. Chamberlain to Hilda, 4 May 1940; Ismay, *Memoirs*, p. 113; Churchill, *Gathering Storm*, pp. 576–8; Channon Diary, 1 May 1940.

49. Charmley, *Churchill*, p. 383.
50. *Gallup International Public Opinion Polls*, p. 33; 'Norway', Mass-Observation MSS TC25/2/D.
51. Channon Diary, 1 May 1940; Amery Diary, 24–30 April 1940; Roberts, '*Holy Fox*', p. 194; Chamberlain to Hilda, 4 May 1940; Colville Diary, 26–27 April and 3 May 1940.
52. Watching Committee minutes and Emrys-Evans Diary, both 29 April 1940, Emrys-Evans MSS 58270/10–11 and 58246/123.
53. Colville Diary, 3 May 1940; Wallace Diary, 1 May 1940.
54. Zetland to Linlithgow, 1 May 1940, Zetland MSS Eur.D609/12/124; Nicolson Diary, 30 April 1940.
55. Channon Diary, 26, 30 April, 2, 3, 5 May 1940; Emrys-Evans Diary, 2 May 1940, Emrys-Evans MSS 58246/124; Nicolson Diary, 30 April 1940.
56. Addison, *Road to 1945*, pp. 92–3.
57. Channon Diary, 26 April and 1 May 1940; Reith Diary, 1 and 3 May 1940.
58. Nicolson Diary, 30 April and 1 May 1940; Emrys-Evans Diary, 30 April 1940, Emrys-Evans MSS 58246/123.
59. Chamberlain to Ida, 13 and 27 April 1940; Percy Harris, *Forty Years In and Out of Parliament*, p. 149.
60. Reith Diary, 3 May 1940; Chamberlain to Hilda, 4 May 1940.
61. Channon Diary, 5 May 1940 reporting Dunglass; Colville Diary, 6 May 1940; Stephen Koss, *The Rise and Fall of the Political Press in Britain: Volume Two, The Twentieth Century* (1984), p. 599.
62. Chamberlain to Hilda, 4 May 1940; Colville Diary and Margesson note, both 6 May 1940, NC8/35/47.
63. Dawson, Channon and Nicolson diaries, 7 May 1940; Hankey to his son, 10 May 1940, HNKY3/44/17.
64. Amery, Colville and Emrys-Evans diaries, all 7 May 1940.
65. Colville and Channon diaries, both 7 May 1940. For an excellent account of the speeches see Addison, *The Road to 1945*, pp. 94–9.
66. Sinclair to Lord Robert Cecil, 8 May 1940, Cecil MSS 51185/217.
67. Nicolson Diary, 7 May 1940.
68. Colville Diary, 1 May 1940; Lady Eva Keyes to Churchill, 23 April 1940, CHAR19/2/94–5.
69. *H.C. Debs*, 5s, 360, col 1125 and Nicolson Diary, both 7 May 1940; Bonham-Carter Diary, 14 May 1940.
70. *H.C. Debs*, 5s, 360, col 1150; Churchill, *Gathering Storm*, p. 525.
71. Channon, Wallace, Crookshank, Emrys-Evans and Nicolson diaries, all 7 May 1940; Colville Diary, 8 May 1940.
72. Wallace Diary, 7 May 1940.
73. Amery Diary, 7 May 1940.
74. Watching Committee minutes and Emrys-Evans Diary, both 8 May 1940, Emrys-Evans MSS 58270/12–13 and 58246/125; Nicolson and Amery diaries, 8 May 1940.
75. Headlam Diary and Sinclair to Cecil, both 8 May 1940, Cecil MSS 51185/217.
76. Dalton Diary, 8 May 1940; Attlee note, n.d., Attlee MSS 1/16.
77. Emrys-Evans and Nicolson diaries, 8 May 1940; James, *Victor Cazalet*, p. 226.

78. Colville Diary, 8 May 1940.
79. Emrys-Evans Diary, 8 May 1940 and to Paul Addison, 14 April 1965, Emrys-Evans MSS 58246/126 and 58247/124.
80. *H.C. Debs*, 5s, 360, cols 1251–66; Dalton and Nicolson diaries, all 8 May 1940.
81. Amery Diary, 8 May 1940; Lord Hemingford, *Backbencher and Chairman: Some Parliamentary Reminiscences* (1946), pp. 229–30.
82. Colville Diary, 8 May 1940.
83. Channon and Amery diaries, both 8 May 1940.
84. Nicolson and Reith diaries, both 8 May 1940; Bonham-Carter Diary, 14 May 1940; Sir Herbert Williams, *Politics – Grave and Gay* (n.d.) p. 112.
85. Dalton, Channon, Nicolson, Reith diaries, all 8 May 1940.
86. Chamberlain to Ida, 11 May 1940.
87. Channon Diary, 8 May 1940; Mackintosh, *Echoes of Big Ben*, p. 153; Joseph Kennedy Diary, 9 May 1940.
88. Nicolson Diary, 8 May 1940.
89. Jorgen S. Rasmussen, 'Party Discipline in Wartime: the Downfall of the Chamberlain Government', *Journal of Politics*, 32 (1970), pp. 379–406; Addison, *Road to 1945*, p. 98.
90. Crowson, *Facing Fascism*, p. 195; Kevin Jeffreys, 'May 1940: The Downfall of Neville Chamberlain', *Parliamentary History*, 10.2 (1991), p. 373.
91. Addison, *Road to 1945*, pp. 97–8.
92. Nick Smart, 'Four Days in May: the Norway Debate and the Downfall of Neville Chamberlain', *Parliamentary History*, 17.2 (1998), pp. 215–43; idem, *National Government*, pp. 217–19.
93. Emrys-Evans Diary, 8 May 1940, Emrys-Evans MSS 58246/127.
94. Colville Diary, 8 May; Channon Diary, 9 May 1940.
95. Sir Patrick Spens to Chamberlain, 9 May 1940, NC7/11/33/162.
96. Davidson to Baldwin, 12 May 1940, Baldwin MSS 174/273–4; Colville Diary, 8 May 1940.
97. Chamberlain to Ida, 11 May 1940; Addison, *Road to 1945*, p. 98.
98. Chamberlain to Ida, 11 May 1940.
99. Robert Gower to Chamberlain, 9 May 1940, NC13/17/106.
100. Lord Hailsham to Chamberlain, 10 May; Quintin Hogg to Chamberlain, 9 May 1940, NC7/11/33/73, 108.
101. Channon Diary, 8 and 10 May 1940.
102. Butler diary notes, 13 May 1940, Anthony Howard, *RAB: The Life of R.A. Butler* (1987), p. 94.
103. Dawson Diary, 8 May 1940.
104. Smart, *National Government*, pp. 218–19.
105. Butler to Halifax, 9 May 1940, Hickleton MSS A4.410.16.
106. Chamberlain to Mary, 11 May 1940, NC1/20/1/198; to Ida, 11 May 1940; Joseph Kennedy Diary, 19 October 1940.
107. Channon and Nicolson Diary, Watching Committee minutes, all 9 May 1940, Emrys-Evans MSS 58270/13.
108. Amery, Nicolson and Emrys-Evans diaries, all 9 April 1940.
109. Hannon to Chamberlain, 9 May 1940, Hannon MSS 17/3.
110. Bernard Donoughue and G.W. Jones, *Herbert Morrison: Portrait of a Politician* (1973), p. 271.

111. Dalton, Amery and Nicolson diaries, all 9 May 1940.
112. Channon Diary, 9 May 1940; Williams, *Politics – Grave and Gay*, pp. 112–13.
113. Dalton Diary, 10 May 1940; Channon Diary, 9 May 1940; Attlee notes, n.d. ATLE1/16.
114. Francis Williams, *A Prime Minister Remembers: The War and Post-War Memories of the Rt. Hon. Earl Attlee* (1961), p. 33; Chamberlain to Ida, 11 May 1940.
115. Chamberlain to Ida, 2 March 1940. This claim is made in Jeffreys, *Churchill Coalition*, p. 26.
116. Butler to Halifax, 9 May 1940, Hickleton MSS A4.410.16.
117. Chamberlain to Ida, 11 May 1940; Joseph Kennedy Diary, 19 October 1940; Lord Moran Diary, 7 December 1947; Churchill, *Gathering Storm*, p. 523.
118. Roberts, *'Holy Fox'*, pp. 204–6; Attlee to Emrys-Evans, 31 December 1960, Emrys-Evans MSS 58247/48.
119. Chamberlain to Beaverbrook, 10 May 1940, Beaverbrook MSS C/80; A.J.P. Taylor, *Beaverbrook: A Biography* (New York, 1972), p. 410; Amery Diary, 10 May 1940.
120. Channon, Emrys-Evans and Nicolson diaries, all 10 May 1940.
121. WM 116(40), 10 May 1940, CAB 65/7; 'Sept 1939–May 1940' notes, Templewood MSS XI/2-3.
122. Dalton Diary, 10 May 1940; Williams, *Politics – Grave and Gay*, p. 113.
123. Queen Elizabeth to Chamberlain, 17 May 1940, NC18/1/1157a.
124. Nicolson Diary, 10 May 1940; Amery Diary, 13 May 1940.

Chapter 18: Epilogue, May–November 1940

1. Churchill, *The Gathering Storm*, pp. 526–7.
2. Churchill to Chamberlain, 10 May 1940, NC7/9/80.
3. Chamberlain to Ida, 11 May 1940.
4. For vast numbers of sympathetic letters on this theme see NC13/17.
5. Colville and Channon diaries, both 10 May 1940.
6. Lord Davidson to Baldwin, 12 and 14 May 1940, Baldwin MSS 174/273–4, 277; Collin Brooks Journal, 8 October 1940.
7. W.J. Brown, *So Far* (1943), p. 222; Martin Gilbert, 'Horace Wilson: Man of Munich?', p. 9.
8. Chamberlain to Mary, 11 May 1940, NC1/20/1/198.
9. Dalton Diary, 11–12 May 1940; Chamberlain to Ida and Colville Diary, both 11 May 1940.
10. Colville Diary, 10 May 1940; Davidson to Baldwin, 14 May 1940, Baldwin MSS 174/275.
11. Butler to Chamberlain, 11 May 1940; Croft to Chamberlain, 12 May 1940, NC7/11/33/35, 48.
12. Channon Diary, 13 May 1940; Davidson to Baldwin, 14 May 1940, Baldwin MSS 174/276.
13. Churchill to Chamberlain, 16 May and reply 18 May 1940, NC7/9/84–5; Chamberlain to Hilda, 17 May 1940.
14. Edward Cobb to Chamberlain, 10 May (and 7 October) 1940, NC13/17/57 and NC13/18/315.

15. Walter Liddall to Chamberlain, 13 May 1940, NC13/17/145; Cecil King Diary, 4 June 1940 reporting Lloyd George; Wallace Diary, 5 June 1940.

16. Richard Law to Lord Wolmer, 22 June 1940, Wolmer MSS Eng.hist.c. 1015/53.

17. Paul Einzig to Chamberlain, 29 June and reply 1 July 1940, NC7/11/33/80 and Einzig MSS 1/10; Paul Einzig, *In the Centre of Things* (1960), pp. 208–10.

18. Whigham telegram, 26 June and Flory interview, 27 June 1940, NC8/34/16, 19; *The Times*, 1 July 1940 for Chamberlain's broadcast.

19. Chamberlain to the National Union Executive, 27 June 1940, NC4/4/1.

20. Einzig, *In the Centre*, pp. 210–12.

21. John Martin Diary, July 1940, MART1/14; Winston S. Churchill, *The Second World War: Volume II, Their Finest Hour* (1949), p. 211; Churchill's interview with Crozier, 26 July 1940, Taylor (ed.), *Off the Record*, p. 175.

22. Crookshank Diary, 9 October 1940; Woolton Diary, 20 November 1940; Channon Diary, 23 June 1942; Jeffreys, *Churchill Coalition*, pp. 50, 54, 104.

23. Chamberlain to Hilda, 17 May and 15 June 1940. For these letters of support see NC7/11/33.

24. Templewood, *Nine Troubled Years*, pp. 432–3; Joseph Kennedy Diary, 16 May 1940.

25. Chamberlain to Ida, 11 May, 21 June and 7 July; to Hilda, 17 May, 29 June 1940.

26. Margot Asquith to Geoffrey Dawson, 11 May 1940, Dawson MSS 81.

27. Chamberlain to Ida, 25 May 1940.

28. Chamberlain to Hilda, 17 May 1940.

29. Chamberlain to Ida, 11 May, 21 June 1940.

30. Chamberlain to Hilda, 17 May; to Ida, 25 May 1940.

31. Chamberlain Diary, 9 September 1940.

32. Reith Diary, 14 May 1940; Chamberlain to Hilda, 17 May 1940.

33. Chamberlain to Ida, 7 July 1940; to Hoare, 15 July 1940, Templewood MSS XIII:17/20. Williams, *A Prime Minister Remembers*, p. 37; Sinclair to Chamberlain, 28 July 1940, NC7/11/33/156.

34. Wheeler-Bennett, *Action this Day*, pp. 49, 220.

35. Cecil King, *With Malice Towards None*, p. 50; Chamberlain to Dorothy, 18 May 1940, NC1/23/80.

36. Chamberlain to Ida, 21 June and 7 July 1940; Chamberlain Diary, 28 May, 12, 15, 25–28 June. For the correspondence with de Valera and Craigavon see PREM 1/131/2; Robert Fisk, *In Time of War: Ireland, Ulster and the Price of Neutrality* (1985), pp. 186–219.

37. WM 139–45(40) and Chamberlain Diary, 26–28 May 1940, CAB 65/13; John Lukacs, *Five Days in London, May 1940* (New Haven and London, 1999).

38. Chamberlain to Ida, 25 May; to Hilda, 15 June 1940.

39. Angus Calder, *The People's War: Britain 1939–1945* (1969), p. 104; Hancock and Gowing, *British War Economy*, pp. 216–17, 330–32.

40. Lord Robbins, *Autobiography of an Economist* (1971), p. 173; Stuart, *Within the Fringe*, p. 87.

41. Home Intelligence, 'Daily Reports on Morale', 31 May, 12, 14, 15, 18 June, 1, 3, 16 July 1940, INF 1/264; 'Cato', *Guilty Men*, pp. 13–14. For the impact of this book on Chamberlain's reputation see Dutton, *Neville Chamberlain*, Chapter 3.

42. Bonham Carter Diary, 23 May 1940; Boothby to Lloyd George, 10 and 15 June 1940, Lloyd George MSS G 3/13/22–3. For 'The BEF' and Dunkirk, see Mass-Observation MSS TC 25/2/F.

43. Chamberlain to his wife, 14 June 1940, NC1/15/4/7; to Ida, 7 and 20 July 1940.

44. Chamberlain to Hilda, 1 June 1940; Butler to Stafford Cripps, 18 June 1940, Butler MSS E3/3/146; Sylvester note, n.d., Lloyd George MSS G/24/1/154.

45. Chamberlain to Ida, 8 June 1940.

46. Chamberlain to Hilda, 1 June 1940; Chamberlain Diary, 28 May 1940; Churchill to Lloyd George, 29 May 1940, Lloyd George MSS G/4/15/48; Sylvester Diary, 29 May 1940.

47. Chamberlain to Ida, 8 June 1940; Chamberlain Diary, 5–6 June 1940; Churchill to Chamberlain and reply and Churchill note, all 6 June 1940, NC7/9/86-88.

48. Chamberlain to Ida, 8 June 1940; Cecil King, *With Malice Towards None*, pp. 47–8; Hugh Cudlipp, *Publish and be Damned: The Astonishing Story of the Daily Mirror* (1953), pp. 144–5.

49. Chamberlain to Ida, 21 June 1940; Chamberlain and Amery diaries, both 18 June 1940.

50. Michael Foot Preface to the 1998 Penguin Classics reprint of *Guilty Men*, p. vi; Addison, *Road to 1945*, p. 110; 'Public Opinion about Mr Chamberlain', June–July 1940, Mass-Observation MSS FR251, 275 and TC25/6/F.

51. Topping to Hacking, 26 June 1940 and *Socialists and Armaments*, NC8/21/19/22. For a report of Chamberlain's speech see NC4/4/1.

52. Beaverbrook to Hoare, 27 June 1940, Beaverbrook MSS C/308. See Home Intelligence, 'Daily Reports on Morale', 2 August 1940, INF 1/264.

53. William Spens to the Editor, *The Times*, 10 June 1940; Chamberlain to Ida, 7 July 1940; Beaverbrook to Hoare, 6 July 1940, Beaverbrook MSS C/308; Sylvester note, 3 July 1940, Lloyd George MSS G/24/6.

54. Chamberlain Diary, 7, 10–11, 18 June 1940; to Hilda, 15 June; to Ida, 8, 21 June 1940.

55. Chamberlain to Hilda, 14 July 1940.

56. 'Portrait of the three Chamberlains and my Eldest Sister Beatrice written for their descendants', July–November 1956, BC5/10/1.

57. Chamberlain Diary, 16 June 1940; Chamberlain to Ida, 20 July 1940.

58. Chamberlain Diary, 24, 26–27 July; to Hilda, 15 June, 27 July 1940.

59. Chamberlain Diary and Anne Chamberlain to Churchill, both 29 July 1940, NC7/9/90. For the real diagnosis see Joseph to Rose Kennedy, 2 August 1940, Amanda Smith (ed.), *Hostage to Fortune* (2001), p. 457.

60. Feiling, *Life of Neville Chamberlain*, p. 450.

61. Chamberlain to Churchill, 20 August 1940, CHAR20/1/57; to Arthur Rucker, 14 August 1940, NC8/34/47.

62. Churchill to Chamberlain, 21 August 1940, NC7/9/93; Chamberlain to Mary, 4 September 1940, NC1/20/1/201.

63. Churchill to Chamberlain, 3 August 1940, NC7/9/92; John Martin to his mother, 1 August 1940, MART1.

64. Chamberlain to Churchill, 3 September 1940, CHAR20/1/60; Chamberlain Diary, 9 September 1940; Channon and Nicolson diaries, both 17 September 1940.

65. Chamberlain to Ida, 15 September 1940.
66. Churchill to 'Mrs Neville', 20 September 1940; Chamberlain to Churchill, 22 September 1940, NC7/9/96–7; to Halifax, 23 September 1940, NC7/11/33/82.
67. Chamberlain to Ida, 15 September; Chamberlain Diary, 24 September 1940.
68. Chamberlain to Churchill, 22 September 1940, CHAR20/1/61.
69. Eden, *The Reckoning*, p. 129; Churchill to Chamberlain, 24 September and reply 25 September 1940, NC7/9/98, CHAR20/1/63.
70. Chamberlain to Hendriks, 25 September and to Halifax 23 September 1940, NC7/11/33/82 and Hickleton MSS A4.410.17.3.
71. Chamberlain Diary 30 September–1 October and to Mary, 1 October 1940, NC1/20/1/202; Churchill to Chamberlain, 29, 30 September and reply 1 October 1940, NC7/9/99–102.
72. Chamberlain Diary, 20 September and 2 October 1940; Eden Diary, 30 September 1940.
73. 'Party meeting at the Caxton Hall … 9 October 1940', Halifax to Chamberlain, 9 October and reply 11 October 1940, NC7/11/33/88–9.
74. Crookshank and Wallace diaries, 9 October 1940; Tufton Beamish 'Notes', 16 October 1940, Beamish MSS BEAM3/4; James Stuart to Chamberlain, 16 October 1940, NC13/18/927; Geoffrey Dawson to Chamberlain, 9 October 1940, Dawson MSS 81/47.
75. Feiling, *Life of Neville Chamberlain*, p. 454.
76. Chamberlain to Miss Campbell, 30 September 1940, NC7/10/24; to Halifax, 2 October 1940, Hickleton MSS A4.410.17.4A.
77. Chamberlain Diary, 4 October 1940.
78. Simon to Chamberlain, 3 October and reply 5 October 1940, Simon MSS 87/3, 5.
79. Chamberlain Diary, 6 October 1940.
80. Chamberlain Diary, 16 March 1937; Hilda Chamberlain, 'Portrait of the three Chamberlains', 1956, BC5/10/1.
81. Chamberlain Diary, 14 October 1940; Horace Wilson to Baldwin, 1 October and 10 November 1940, Baldwin MSS 174/293–4.
82. Chamberlain to Halifax and to Joseph Ball, both 28 October 1940, NC7/11/33/91 and NC Letters Additional 131; Halifax notes for statement to the House of Lords, NC13/20/19.
83. Halifax to Simon, 7 November 1940, Simon MSS 87/24.
84. Channon Diary, 10 November 1940.
85. WM 286(40), 11 November 1940, CAB 65/10; Churchill to Anne Chamberlain, 11 November 1940, NC7/9/107.
86. Channon Diary and *H.C. Debs*, 5s, 365, col 1617–19, both 12 November 1940.
87. Tufton Beamish 'Notes', 13 November 1940, Beamish MSS BEAM3/4; Andrew Roberts, *Eminent Churchillians* (Phoenix ed., 1995), pp. 193–210.
88. Channon and Colville diaries, 14 November 1940.
89. Addison, *Road to 1945*, p. 9.
90. Butler to Anne Chamberlain, 22 December 1940, NC13/2/83 and Butler MSS G11/180.
91. Dawson to R. Barrington-Ward, 23 December 1940, Dawson MSS 81/53.

92. Chamberlain to Joseph Ball, 28 October 1940, NC Letters Additional 131; to Sir George Schuster, 26 October 1940, Schuster, *Private Work and Public Causes: A Personal Record, 1881–1978* (Cambridge, 1979), p. 135; to Baldwin, 17 October 1940; Horace Wilson memoir, 'Munich', October 1941, CAB 127/158.
93. Malcolm MacDonald to Chamberlain, 8 November 1940, NC13/18/879.
94. Sir Leslie Scott to Anne Chamberlain, 16 November 1940, NC Letters Additional 72.
95. Colville Diary, 13 November 1940, reporting Dorman-Smith; Simon to C.E. Bechhofer Roberts, 13 November 1940, Simon MSS 87/27.
96. Colville Diary, 22 June 1941. See also the entry for 28 March 1941.
97. Dutton, *Neville Chamberlain*, pp. 101–24, 184–5; Donald Cameron Watt, 'Churchill and Appeasement' in Robert Blake and Wm Roger Louis, *Churchill* (1996), pp. 202, 214.
98. Paul Kennedy, *The Realities Behind Diplomacy: Background Influences on British External Policy, 1865–1980* (Fontana ed., 1981), p. 301; Bell, *Chamberlain, Germany and Japan*, p. 146; Watt, *How War Came*, p. 601.
99. Colville Diary, 2 October 1940; Geoffrey Shakespeare, *Let Candles Be Brought In* (1949), p. 205.

A Guide to Sources

Although this work draws on extensive research in over 150 collections of private papers on both sides of the Atlantic, at the heart of any biography of Neville Chamberlain must be his own vast archive deposited with those of the rest of the Chamberlain family at Birmingham University Library. Without any doubt, some of the most important sources within the Neville Chamberlain papers are his diary letters to his sisters Hilda and Ida, written with unfailing regularity every week between March 1915 and his death in 1940. The original copies of these letters can be found in the catalogue under the classmark NC18/1/1-1168, but they are also available in Robert Self (ed.), *The Neville Chamberlain Diary Letters* (4 volumes, Aldershot, 2000–2005) from which they have been quoted. All other documents from the Chamberlain papers are noted with their appropriate reference. Secondary sources are referenced in the notes and the place of publication is London unless otherwise specified.

1. Private Papers and Diaries

Birmingham University Library

Austen Chamberlain MSS	Sir Joseph Austen Chamberlain (AC).
Avon MSS	Sir Anthony Eden, 1st Earl of Avon (AP).
Beatrice Chamberlain MSS	Beatrice Chamberlain (BC).
Joseph Chamber MSS	Joseph Chamberlain (JC).
Neville Chamberlain MSS	Arthur Neville Chamberlain (NC).

Bodleian Library, Oxford

Addison MSS	Christopher Addison, 1st Viscount Addison.
Altrincham MSS	Sir Edward Grigg, 1st Baron Altrincham.
Ball MSS	Sir Joseph Ball.
Bayford MSS	Sir Robert Sanders, 1st Baron Bayford.
Brand MSS	Robert Henry Brand, 1st Baron Brand.

Crookshank MSS	Harry Frederick Comfort Crookshank, 1st Viscount Crookshank.
Dawson MSS	Geoffrey Dawson.
Griffith-Boscawen MSS	Sir Arthur Sackville Griffith-Boscawen.
Gwynne MSS	Howell Arthur Gwynne.
Maclean MSS	Sir Donald Maclean.
Milner MSS	Sir Alfred Milner, 1st Viscount Milner.
Ponsonby MSS	Arthur Augustus Ponsonby, 1st Baron Ponsonby of Shulbrede.
Sankey MSS	Sir John Sankey, 1st Viscount Sankey.
Selborne MSS	William Waldegrave Palmer, 2nd Earl of Selborne.
Simon MSS	Sir John Simon, 1st Viscount Simon.
Somervell MSS	Donald Bradley Somervell, Baron Somervell.
Wallace MSS	(David) Euan Wallace.
Winterton MSS	Edward Turnour, 6th Earl Winterton.
Wolmer MSS	Roundell Cecil Palmer, Viscount Wolmer, 3rd Earl of Selborne.
Woolton MSS	Sir Frederick James Marquis, 1st Earl of Woolton.
Worthington-Evans MSS	Sir Laming Worthington-Evans.

Borthwick Institute of Historical Research, York

Hickleton MSS	Edward Frederick Lindley Wood, 1st Earl of Halifax and microfilm consulted at Churchill College, Cambridge.

British Library

Cecil MSS	Lord Robert Cecil, Viscount Cecil of Chelwood.
d'Abernon MSS	Edgar Vincent, 1st Baron d'Abernon of Esher.
Emrys-Evans MSS	Paul Vychan Emrys-Evans.
Gladstone MSS	Herbert John Gladstone, 1st Viscount Gladstone.
Scott MSS	Charles Prestwich Scott.
Spender MSS	John Alfred Spender.

British Library: Oriental & India Office Collections

Birkenhead MSS	Frederick Edwin Smith, 1st Earl of Birkenhead, while Secretary of State for India.
Blackett MSS	Sir Basil Phillott Blackett.
Brabourne MSS	Sir Michael Knatchbull, 5th Baron Brabourne.
Curzon MSS	George Nathaniel Curzon, 1st Marquess Curzon of Kedleston.
Davidson (Indian) MSS	Sir John Colin Campbell Davidson, 1st Viscount Davidson, as Chairman of the Indian States Enquiry.
Erskine MSS	John Francis Ashley Erskine, Lord Erskine.
Hoare MSS	Sir Samuel John Gurney Hoare, 1st Viscount Templewood, while Secretary of State for India.
Irwin MSS	Edward Frederick Lindley Wood, Baron Irwin (later Earl of Halifax), as Viceroy of India.
Linlithgow MSS	Victor Alexander John Hope, 2nd Marquess of Linlithgow.
Reading MSS	Sir Rufus Daniel Isaacs, 1st Marquess of Reading
Zetland MSS	Lawrence John Lumley Dundas, 2nd Marquess of Zetland.

British Library: National Sound Archives

Rucker Interview	Interviews with Sir Arthur Nevil Rucker by Professor Brian Harrison.
Veale Interview	Interviews with Sir Douglas Veale by Professor Brian Harrison.

British Library of Political and Economic Science

Adams MSS	Vyvyan Trerice Adams.
Beveridge MSS	Sir William Beveridge, 1st Baron Beveridge.
Chapman MSS	Sir Sydney Chapman, unpublished autobiography.
Citrine MSS	Walter McLennan Citrine, 1st Baron Citrine.
Dalton MSS	Hugh Dalton, 1st Baron Dalton of Forest and Frith.

Fisher MSS	Sir Norman Fenwick Warren Fisher.
Markham MSS	Violet Markham.

Cambridge University Library

Baldwin MSS	Stanley Baldwin, 1st Earl Baldwin.
Conway MSS	Sir Martin Conway.
Hull MSS	Cordell Hull (microfilm).
Kennett MSS	Sir Edward and Lady Hilton Young, 1st Baron Kennett.
Templewood MSS	Sir Samuel Hoare, 1st Viscount Templewood.

Centre for Kentish Studies, Maidstone

Stanhope MSS	James Richard Stanhope, 7th Earl of Stanhope.
Thomas MSS	James Henry Thomas.

Churchill Archive Centre, Churchill College, Cambridge

Attlee MSS	Clement Attlee, 1st Earl of Attlee (ATLE).
Beamish MSS	Rear Admiral Tufton Beamish (BEAM).
Bower MSS	Commander Robert Bower (BOWR).
Cadogan MSS	Sir Alexander George Cadogan (ACAD).
Churchill MSS	Sir Winston Leonard Spencer Churchill (CHAR).
Colville MSS	Sir John Colville (CLVL).
Cooper MSS	Sir Alfred Duff Cooper, 1st Viscount Norwich (DUFC).
Croft MSS	Sir Henry Page Croft, 1st Baron Croft (CRFT).
Einzig MSS	Paul Einzig (ENZG).
Grigg MSS	Sir Percy James Grigg (GRGG).
Hailes MSS	Patrick George Thomas Buchan-Hepburn, 1st Baron Hailes (HAIS).
Hankey MSS	Sir Maurice Hankey, 1st Baron Hankey (HNKY).
Hawtrey MSS	Sir Ralph George Hawtrey (HTRY).
Hore-Belisha MSS	Leslie Hore-Belisha, 1st Baron Hore-Belisha (HOBE).

Inskip MSS	Sir Thomas Walker Hobart Inskip, 1st Viscount Caldecote (INKP).
Jacob MSS	Sir Ian Jacob (JACB).
Kilmuir MSS	Sir David Patrick Maxwell-Fyfe, Earl of Kilmuir (KLMR).
Lloyd MSS	Sir George Ambrose Lloyd, 1st Baron Lloyd (GLLD).
Margesson MSS	David Reginald Margesson, 1st Viscount Margesson (MRGN).
Marsh MSS	Sir Edward Howard Marsh (EMAR).
Martin MSS	Sir John Martin (MART).
Phipps MSS	Sir Eric Clare Edmund Phipps (PHPP).
Spears MSS	Major-General Sir Edward Louis Spears (SPRS).
Strang MSS	Sir William Strang, 1st Baron Strang (STRG).
Swinton MSS	Sir Philip Cunliffe-Lister, 1st Earl of Swinton (SWIN).
Thurso MSS	Sir Archibald Henry MacDonald Sinclair, 1st Viscount Thurso (THRS).
Vansittart MSS	Sir Robert Gilbert Vansittart, 1st Baron Vansittart (VNST).
Weir MSS	Sir William Douglas Weir, 1st Viscount Weir (WEIR).

Durham Record Office

Headlam MSS	Sir Cuthbert Headlam.
Londonderry MSS	Charles Vane-Tempest-Stewart, 7th Marquess of Londonderry.

Glasgow University Archives

Weir MSS (DC96)	Sir William Douglas Weir, 1st Viscount Weir, Glasgow University Archives.

Hatfield House, Hertfordshire

Chelwood MSS	Robert Gascoyne-Cecil, Viscount Cecil of Chelwood.

Quickswood MSS   Hugh Cecil, 1st Baron Quickswood.

Salisbury MSS   James Edward Hubert Gascoyne-Cecil, 4th Marquess of Salisbury.

Herbert Hoover Presidential Library, West Branch, Iowa

Castle MSS   William R. Castle.

Hoover MSS   Herbert Clark Hoover.

Stimson MSS   Henry Lewis Stimson (microfilm by courtesy of Yale University Library).

House of Lords Record Office

Beaverbrook MSS   William Maxwell Aitken, 1st Baron Beaverbrook.

Davidson MSS   Sir John Colin Campbell Davidson, 1st Viscount Davidson.

Hannon MSS   Sir Patrick Hannon.

Law MSS   Andrew Bonar Law.

Lloyd George MSS   David Lloyd George, 1st Earl Lloyd-George of Dwyfor.

Samuel MSS   Sir Herbert Louis Samuel, 1st Viscount Samuel.

Stansgate MSS   William Wedgwood Benn, 1st Viscount Stangate.

Strachey MSS   John St. Loe Strachey.

Wargrave MSS   Edward Alfred Goulding, 1st Baron Wargrave.

Liddell Hart Centre for Military Archives, Kings College, London

Dill MSS   Field-Marshal Sir John Dill.

Ismay MSS   General Sir Hastings Lionel Ismay, 1st Baron Ismay.

Liddell Hart MSS   Sir Basil Liddell Hart.

Massingberd MSS   Field-Marshal Sir Archibald Montgomery-Massinberd.

Pownall MSS   Lt-General Sir Henry Pownall.

Liverpool City Central Library

Derby MSS   Edward George Villiers Stanley, 17th Earl of Derby.

National Archives, Kew

Bradbury MSS	Sir John Swanwick Bradbury, 1st Baron Bradbury (T 170).
Cadogan MSS	Sir Alexander Cadogan (FO 800).
Cranborne MSS	Lord Cranborne (FO 800).
Eden MSS	Anthony Eden (FO 800).
Halifax MSS	Lord Halifax (FO 800).
Henderson MSS	Sir Nevile Henderson (FO 800).
Hopkins MSS	Sir Richard Hopkins (T 175).
Howorth MSS	Sir Rupert Howorth (CAB 127).
Leith-Ross MSS	Sir Frederick Leith-Ross (T 188).
MacDonald MSS	James Ramsay MacDonald (PRO 30/69).
Magnum Opus MSS	Sir Maurice Hankey, 'Magnum Opus' files (CAB 63).
Newman MSS	Diaries of Sir George Newman (MH 139/1–5).
Phillips MSS	Sir Frederick Phillips (T 177).
Sargent MSS	Sir Orme Sargent (FO 800).
Wilson MSS	Sir Horace Wilson (CAB 127).

National Archives of Scotland, Edinburgh

Lothian MSS	Philip Henry Kerr, 11th Marquess of Lothian.
Steel-Maitland MSS	Sir Arthur Steel-Maitland.

National Library of Scotland, Edinburgh

Elliot MSS	Walter Elliot Elliot.
Grant MSS	Sir Alexander Grant correspondence with Ramsay MacDonald.
Macmillan MSS	Hugh Pattison Macmillan, Baron Macmillan.
Murray MSS	Lt. Col. Arthur Murray, 3rd Viscount Elibank.

National Maritime Museum

Chatfield MSS	Sir Alfred Ernle Montacute Chatfield, 1st Baron Chatfield.

Newcastle University Library

Hilda Runciman Diary	Hilda Runciman
Runciman MSS	Walter Runciman, 1st Viscount Runciman.

Nuffield College, Oxford

Mottistone MSS	John Edward Bernard Seely, 1st Baron Mottistone.

Reading University Library

Astor MSS	Nancy and Waldorf Astor, 2nd Viscount Astor.

Rhodes House Library, Oxford

Rey MSS	Sir Charles Rey.

Franklin Delano Roosevelt Presidential Library, Hyde Park, New York

Ezekiel MSS	Mordecai Ezekiel.
Moffat MSS	Jay Pierrepont Moffat.
Morgenthau MSS	Henry Morgenthau Jnr.
Roosevelt MSS	Franklin Delano Roosevelt.
Tugwell MSS	Rexford Tugwell.
Welles MSS	Sumner Welles.

Scottish Records Office

Elibank MSS	Gideon Murray, 2nd Viscount Elibank.

Sheffield University Library

Hewins MSS	William Albert Samuel Hewins.

Shropshire Record Office

Bridgeman MSS	Sir William Clive Bridgeman, 1st Viscount Bridgeman.

Sussex University

Mass-Observation MSS	Mass-Observation, File Reports and Topic Collections.

Trinity College, Cambridge

Butler MSS   Richard Austen Butler, 1st Baron Butler.

2. Conservative Party Archives

Conservative Party Archives, Bodleian Library, Oxford.

Birmingham Conservative and Unionist Association, Minute Books, 1914–40, Birmingham Central Library.

Ladywood Division Unionist Association, Minute Books, 1914–40, Birmingham Central Library.

Ladywood Women's Unionist Association, Minute Books, 1919–33, Birmingham Central Library.

Midland Union Executive Committee, Minute Books, 1919–40, Conservative Party Archive, Bodleian Library, Oxford.

Midland Union of Conservative Associations, Correspondence, Birmingham University Library.

3. Government Records at the National Archives, Kew

BT 10	Import Duties Advisory Committee: minutes and papers
CAB 2	Committee of Imperial Defence: minutes
CAB 4	Committee of Imperial Defence: memoranda
CAB 6/109–11	Defence Requirements Committee
CAB 6/136–44	Defence Policy and Requirements Committee, 1935–39
CAB 16	Ministerial Committee on Disarmament
CAB 21	Cabinet Office: Registered Files of Cabinet Secretariat
CAB 23	Cabinet Conclusions
CAB 24	Cabinet Papers
CAB 26	Home Affairs Committee
CAB 27	Cabinet Committees
CAB 29	World Economic Conference, 1933
CAB 32	Imperial Conferences
CAB 53	Chiefs of Staff Committee

CAB 58	Economic Advisory Council: Committee on Economic Information and Committee on Financial Questions
CAB 63	Hankey memoranda: 'Magnum Opus' files
CAB 65	War Cabinet Conclusions and Papers
CAB 83	Military Coordination Committee: minutes
CAB 99/3	Supreme War Council, September 1939 – June 1940
CAB 118	Lord President's Papers
CAB 127	Private Collections: Horace Wilson and Rupert Howorth
FO 371	Foreign Office: General Correspondence
FO 800	Foreign Office Private Papers Series: Cadogan, Eden, Halifax, Nevile Henderson, Sargent
HLG 9	Ministry of Housing and Local Government: Royal Commission on London, 1921–22
HLG 29	Public Health and Local Government Legislation: Bills and Papers
HLG 30	Unemployment: Special Areas, 1920–39
HLG 40/38–9	Housing (Rural Workers) Bill
HLG 56	Rating and Valuation
INF 1	Ministry of Information
MH 57	Public Health and Poor Law Services: Public Assistance
MH 61	Commissioner for Special Areas
MH 68	Poor Law Authorities
MH 83	Bill Papers
NATS 1	Ministry of National Service: National Service Department, 1917
NSC 1	National Savings Committee: minute books
PIN 1	Ministry of Pensions and National Insurance: committees
PIN 3–4	Bill Papers: Widows and Old Age Pensions Bill, 1925
PREM 1	Prime Minister's Office: correspondence and papers, 1937–40
T 160	Treasury: Finance files
T 161	Treasury: Supply files

T 170	Sir John Bradbury papers
T 171	Chancellor of the Exchequer's Office: Budget papers
T 172	Chancellor of the Exchequer's Office: miscellaneous papers
T 175	Sir Richard Hopkins papers
T 177	Sir Frederick Phillips papers
T 188	Sir Frederick Leith-Ross papers
T 208	Sir Ralph Hawtry papers

4. Published Collections of Official Documents

Cmd 6106 (1939): *Documents Concerning German-Polish Relations and the Outbreak of Hostilities between Great Britain and Germany on September 3, 1939, Parliamentary Papers*, 1938–39, XXVII.

Documents on British Foreign Policy, 2nd Series, 1929–38, 21 volumes, ed. R. Butler, W.N. Medlicott and others (1946–85) (*DBFP*, 2).

Documents on British Foreign Policy, 3rd Series, 1938–39, 9 volumes, ed. E.L. Woodward, R. Butler and M. Lambert (1949–61) (*DBFP*, 3).

Documents on German Foreign Policy, Series D, 1938–39, 7 volumes (London, Washington and New York, 1949–56) (*DGFP, Series D*).

Foreign Relations of the United States, 1919–39 (Washington, 1934–56).

Hansard, Parliamentary Debates, House of Commons, 5th Series, 1916–40.

5. Published Diaries (Place of publication is London unless otherwise stated.)

Amery Diary	John Barnes and David Nicholson (eds.), *The Leo Amery Diaries, 1896–1929* (1980) and *The Empire at Bay: The Leo Amery Diaries, 1929–1945* (1988)
Bayford Diary	John Ramsden (ed.), *Real Old Tory Politics: The Political Diaries of Sir Robert Sanders, Lord Bayford, 1910–1935* (1984)
Bernays Diary	Nick Smart (ed.), *The Diaries and Letters of Robert Bernays 1932–1939: An Insider's Account of the House of Commons* (Lampeter, 1996)
Bonham-Carter Diary	Mark Pottle (ed.), *Champion Redoubtable: The Diaries and Letters of Violet Bonham Carter, 1914–1945* (1998)
Bridgeman Diary	Philip Williamson (ed.), *The Modernisation of Conservative Politics: The Diaries and Letters of William Bridgeman, 1904–1935* (1988)

Brooks Journal   N.J. Crowson (ed.), *Fleet Street, Press Barons and Politics: the Journals of Collin Brooks, 1932–1940* (Cambridge, 1998)

Cadogan Diary   David Dilks (ed.), *The Diaries of Sir Alexander Cadogan, 1938–1945* (1971)

Channon Diary   Robert Rhodes James (ed.), *Chips: The Diaries of Sir Henry Channon* (1967).

Ciano Diary,   Malcolm Muggeridge (ed.), *Ciano's Diary, 1937–1943* (2 vols, 1947, 1952)

Colville Diary   John Colville (ed.), *The Fringes of Power: Downing Street Diaries, 1939–1955* (1985)

Crawford Diary   John Vincent (ed.), *The Crawford Papers: The Journals of David Lindsay, Twenty-Seventh Earl of Crawford and Tenth Earl of Balcarres, 1871–1940, during the years 1892–1940* (Manchester, 1984)

Crozier Interviews   A.J.P. Taylor (ed.), *W.P. Crozier: Off the Record, Political Interviews, 1933–1943* (1973)

Dalton Diary   Ben Pimlott (ed.), *The Political Diary of Hugh Dalton, 1918–40, 1945–60* (1986) and *The Second World War Diary of Hugh Dalton, 1940–45* (1986)

Dugdale Diary   Norman Rose (ed.), *Baffy: The Diaries of Blanche Dugdale, 1936–1947* (1973)

Fitzroy Diary   Sir Almeric Fitzroy (ed.), *Memoirs* (2 vols, n.d.)

Gordon Walker Diary Robert Pearce (ed.), *Patrick Gordon Walker: Political Diaries, 1932–1971* (1991)

Harvey Diary   John Harvey (ed.), *The Diplomatic Diaries of Oliver Harvey, 1937–1940* (1970) and *The War Diary of Oliver Harvey* (1978).

Headlam Diary   Stuart Ball (ed.), *Parliament and Politics in the Age of Baldwin and MacDonald: The Headlam Diaries, 1923–1935* (1992) and *Parliament and Politics in the Age of Churchill and Attlee: The Headlam Diaries, 1935–1951* (Cambridge, 1999)

Ironside Diary   R. Macleod and D. Kelly (eds.), *The Ironside Diaries, 1937–1940* (1962)

Jones Diary   Keith Middlemas (ed.), *Thomas Jones: Whitehall Diary, 1916–1930* (2 vols, 1969) and Thomas Jones, *A Diary with Letters, 1931–1950* (1954)

Kennedy Journal   Gordon Martel (ed.), *The Times and Appeasement: The Journals of A.L. Kennedy, 1932–1939* (Cambridge, 2000)

Kennedy Diary	Amanda Smith (ed.), *Hostage of Fortune: The Letters of Joseph P. Kennedy* (2001)
King Diary	Cecil King, *With Malice Towards None: A War Diary* (1970)
Lockhart Diary	Kenneth Young (ed.), *The Diaries of Sir Robert Bruce Lockhart, 1915–1965* (2 vols, 1973, 1980)
Nicolson Diary	Nigel Nicolson (ed.), *Harold Nicolson: Diaries and Letters, 1930–1962* (3 vols, 1966–68)
Pownall Diary	Brian Bond (ed.), *Chief of Staff: Diaries of Lt-General Sir Henry Pownall, Vol. I, 1933–1940* (1972)
Reith Diary	Charles Stuart (ed.), *The Reith Diaries* (1975)
Riddell Diary	J.M. McEwen (ed.), *The Riddell Diaries, 1908–1923* (1986) and Lord Riddell (ed.), *Lord Riddell's War Diary, 1914–1918* (1933), *Lord Riddell's Intimate Diary of the Peace Conference and After, 1918–1923* (1933)
Scott Diary	Trevor Wilson (ed.), *The Political Diaries of C.P. Scott, 1911–1928* (Ithaca, NY, 1970)
Stevenson Diary	A.J.P. Taylor (ed.), *Lloyd George: A Diary by Frances Stevenson* (1971)
Sylvester Diary	Colin Cross (ed.), *Life with Lloyd George: The Diary of A.J. Sylvester, 1931–1945* (1975)
Webb Diary	Norman and Jeanne MacKenzie (eds.), *The Diary of Beatrice Webb* (4 vols, 1982–85)

6. Published Collections of Letters and Speeches

Bullitt, Orville (ed.)	*For the President, Personal and Secret: Correspondence Between Franklin D. Roosevelt and William C. Bullitt* (Boston, MA, 1972)
Chamberlain, Austen (ed.)	*Politics from Inside: An Epistolary Chronicle, 1906–1914* (1936)
Chamberlain, Neville (ed.)	*The Struggle for Peace* (1939)
Cockett, Richard (ed.)	*My Dear Max: The Letters of Brendan Bracken to Lord Beaverbrook, 1925–1958* (1990)
Freedman, Max (ed.)	*Roosevelt and Frankfurter: Their Correspondence 1928–1945* (1967)
Gilbert, Martin (ed.)	*Winston S. Churchill, Companion to Vol. 5* (3 Parts, 1979–82)
Laugharne, Peter (ed.)	*Aneurin Bevan: A Parliamentary Odyssey, Vol. I: Speeches at Westminster, 1929–1944* (Liverpool, 1996)

Morgan, Kenneth O. (ed.) — *Lloyd George Family Letters, 1885–1936* (Cardiff & London, 1973)

Muggeridge, Malcolm (ed.) — *Ciano's Diplomatic Papers* (1948)

Self, Robert (ed.) — *The Austen Chamberlain Diary Letters: The Correspondence of Sir Austen Chamberlain with his sisters Hilda and Ida, 1916–1937* (Cambridge, 1995)

idem — *The Neville Chamberlain Diary Letters* (4 vols, Aldershot, 2000–2005)

Soames, Mary (ed.) — *Speaking for Themselves: The Personal Letters of Winston and Clementine Churchill* (1998)

Taylor, A.J.P. (ed.) — *My Darling Pussy: The Letters of Lloyd George and Frances Stevenson, 1913–1941* (1975)

Index

Neville Chamberlain inevitably appears on every page of this biography. His index references thus refer only to general themes. Specific events and people are all indexed separately – virtually all of these entries relate to Chamberlain and his attitude to them. Entries for significant characters are followed by their position or relationship with Chamberlain at the time they are mentioned in the text. Full biographical details can be found in Self (ed.), *The Neville Chamberlain Diary Letters*. Short notes on the family can be found on page 453.

Abdication crisis, 256–57
Abyssinia: crisis (1935), 246–50, 255; recognition of Italian sovereignty, 272–73, 274, 284; lessons, 365
Addison, Christopher (Minister of Munitions, 1916–17; Reconstruction, 1917–19; Health, 1919–21), 53, 56, 57, 59, 62, 90–91, 116
Addison, Paul, 419, 421
Admiralty, 62, 249, 263, 270, 337, 417, 419
Agreement to Differ (1932), 166
Agricultural Party, (Norfolk NFU), 147
agriculture, 59, 102, 139, 171, 233, 263, 264, 339, 340–41, 438; rating, 92, 109, 130
Aims and Principles (1924), 102
Air Ministry, 263, 270, 301–2, 419
Air Raid Precautions, 44–45, 47, 332, 337, 355
air raids, 44–45, 56, 355, 382, 443–44
Albania, 358–59, 365
All-Party Parliamentary Action Group, 392, 421, 423
Altmark (German supply ship), 417
Amery, Leopold S. (tariff reformer and imperialist; Colonial/Dominion Secretary, 1924–29; backbench critic of NC in 1930s), 84–85, 94–95, 96, 98, 138, 143, 145, 149, 153, 167, 187, 194, 201, 202, 211, 213, 215, 272, 288, 331, 348, 380, 386, 393, 422, 423–24, 428, 429, 440, 441
Anderson, John (Lord Privy Seal, 1938–39), 106, 337, 388, 407, 408

Andros island (Bahamas), 6, 8, 22–27, 39, 61
Anglo-American Trade Agreement (1937–38), 190–91, 277, 279, 345
Anglo-German Declaration (September 1938), 1, 324–26, 332
Anglo-German Fellowship, 372
Anglo-German Transfer Agreement (1934), 250–52; Payments Agreement (1934), 251
Anglo-Italian Agreement (1938), 283–84, 288, 297–98, 306, 341–42, 359
anti-aircraft defences, 296, 318, 322, 337, 347, 354
appeasement, 3–4, 380; historiography 4, 267, 295, 450; origins/logic behind policy, 237, 240, 252, 262, 267, 272, 283, 295–97, 332; 'double policy'/buying time for rearmament, 237, 252, 267, 270–71, 294, 327, 331, 333, 340, 343, 346, 435, 449; as alternative to rearmament?, 270–71, 273, 283, 371; critics of policy, 3–4, 11–12, 230, 269–70, 313, 318–19, 324, 331–32, 361, 365; public opinion, 247, 252, 300, 317, 319, 325–26, 339; colonial restitution, 279–80, 293, 341, 371, 375; economic appeasement, 347; applied to Ireland, 298–99
Argentina, 181
Army, 50–51, 57, 59, 61, 62, 63; rearmament, 237–38, 253–54, 404, 427; expeditionary force, 237–38, 253–54, 346–47, 388, 404, 439; Territorials, 254, 347, 357, 374;

Army (cont.)
    relations with Hore-Belisha, 404–5,
    407
Asama Maru (Japanese steamer), 412
Asquith, Herbert, 49–50, 51, 385, 421
Asquith, Margot, 328, 435
Association of Local War Pensions
    Committees, 74
Astor, Nancy (Conservative MP and
    socialite), 9, 10, 264, 393
Attlee, Clement (Labour leader,
    1935–55; Lord Privy Seal, 1940–42),
    14, 115, 323, 359, 363, 385, 394, 407,
    409, 422, 424, 429–30, 436, 440, 448
Australia, 170, 171–72, 181, 191
Austrian Anschluss (1938), 153, 252,
    283–84, 285, 291, 293–94, 295–96,
    302

'Boys Brigade', 224, 240, 330
Balance of Trade Committee (1932), 159,
    164–66, 216–17
Baldwin, Stanley (Conservative leader,
    1923–37), 27, 102, 107, 446, 448;
    vacillating/weak leadership, 98,
    100, 123, 137–38, 139, 145, 196, 245,
    255, 261, 265; indolence and
    lethargy, 135–36, 147, 148, 159, 245;
    ingratitude, 147, 150, 245; poor
    judgement, 104, 229; shrewd
    understanding and appeal to
    electorate, 128, 136, 245, 261–62;
    physical and mental state, 99, 100,
    123, 137, 233, 256; compared with
    NC, 7, 12, 14, 30, 261–62, 264, 265,
    266, 300; NC's opinion of/relations
    with, 87, 93, 96, 98, 104, 110, 124,
    128, 134, 135–36, 138, 146, 148–50,
    152, 158, 181, 243, 245, 253, 256, 339,
    419
    career: as Prime Minister (1923), 87,
        138; offers NC the Treasury,
        92–93; calls tariff election, 94–97;
        party reunion and Churchill's
        return (1924), 99–100, 104; Prime
        Minister (1924–29), 106, 115, 215;
        rating reform, 124, 126, 127, 128;
        failures in Opposition (1929–31),
        137–39, 142, 145, 148; threat from
        Empire Crusade, 137–39, 141–42,
        143, 144, 147; NC plans to
        displace, 146–47, 148–50;
        formation of National
        Government, 151–52, 153, 157,

158, 160, 161; Lord President
    (1931–35), 166, 201, 181; at
    Ottawa Conference, 169, 170, 172;
    Lloyd George's return to office/
    'New Deal', 226–27, 243; Prime
    Minister (1935–37), 227, 228,
    243–44, 258, 264; uninterested in
    foreign affairs, 235, 266, 287;
    rearmament, 236–37, 239, 253;
    declining health and powers,
    243, 256; Abdication, 256–57;
    critical of NC leadership, 301,
    335; in retirement, 331, 338, 419
Balfour, Arthur (Conservative leader,
    1902–11; Prime Minister, 1902–5;
    other senior offices, 1915–29), 8
Ball, Joseph (Director, Conservative
    Research Department, 1930–39),
    139, 150, 259, 274, 284, 289, 328, 334,
    338, 364, 403, 407, 447
Bank of England, 155, 180, 251
Bank of International Settlements, 175
Barlow, Anderson Montague, 76, 231
Bartlett, Vernon (anti-Munich victor of
    Bridgwater by-election 1938), 348
Bastardy Bill (1920), 78–79
Battle of Britain, 371, 439, 443, 444
Beamish, Tufton (Chamberlainite
    Conservative backbencher), 448
Beaverbrook, Lord (proprietor, Express
    Newspapers), 106, 137, 138, 340,
    352, 430, 441; Empire Crusade,
    138–51; vendetta against Baldwin,
    139, 141, 147; alliance with
    Rothermere, 140–41; NC's opinion
    of/relations with, 139, 141, 142, 143,
    147, 148
Bedwellty, Board of Guardians, 119
Beecham, Thomas, 47
beer duty, 201, 203
Belgium, 190, 238, 397, 400, 402, 412, 434
Bennett, R.B. (Canadian Premier,
    1930–35), 146, 170, 172–73, 187, 191,
    194
Berchtesgaden, 278, 312, 343, 346
Bernays, Robert (Junior Health
    Minister, 1937–39), 288, 331
Betterton, Henry (Minister of Labour,
    1931–34), 213, 232
Bevan, Aneurin (leftwing Labour
    backbencher), 11
Beveridge, William (civil servant, social
    reformer, Director, LSE, 1919–37),
    108, 390

Birkenhead, Lord, 99–100
Birmingham City Council, 41, 194;
    Joseph Chamberlain's mayoralty,
    19, 42, 47, 87; NC's mayoralty, 2, 11,
    15, 39–49, 87, 163; Freeman of City,
    163
Birmingham Corporation Act (1919), 76
Birmingham Daily Mail, 28, 47
Birmingham Daily Post, 49, 79
Birmingham Municipal Savings Bank,
    45–46, 47, 56, 67, 75, 76–77, 91
Birmingham Small Arms Company
    (BSA), 71, 81
Birmingham, 2, 40, 47; Chamberlain
    family connection, 19, 40, 47; NC
    and city development, 40–41, 70;
    General Hospital and Dispensary,
    31–32; Birmingham Extension Act
    (1911), 40, 132; University, 21, 31,
    32, 70; Symphony Orchestra, 46–47,
    70; electoral politics, 42, 68–70,
    77–78, 86, 97, 103, 134–35, 161, 245,
    448; Liberal Unionist Association,
    32, 66, 67, 69, 80; Conservative and
    Unionist Association, 69, 77–78, 97,
    103, 352
Bledisloe, Lord, 215
blockade, 395–96, 397, 398, 401, 413
Blum, Leon (French Socialist leader),
    327
Board of Education, 122–23
Board of Trade, 161, 406, 408
Boards of Guardians (Default) Act, 119
Boards of Guardians, 110, 113, 115, 116,
    118–19, 130
Bonnet, Georges (French Finance
    Minister, 1933, Foreign Minister,
    1938–39), 303, 310, 314, 319, 378, 380
Boothby, Robert (Conservative
    backbench anti-appeaser), 223, 230,
    295, 439, 440, 441
Bracken, Brendan (backbench Churchill
    loyalist), 352, 393, 424
Bridgeman, William (Home Secretary,
    1924–29; close friend of Baldwin),
    98, 144, 145–46, 149, 161
Bridges, Edward (Cabinet Secretary,
    1938–46), xii, 15, 389, 408, 418
British Association for International
    Understanding, 338
British Broadcasting Company, 88, 380
British Council, 338
British Expeditionary Force, 237–38,
    253–54, 346–47, 388, 404, 439

British Iron and Steel Federation, 217
British Legion, 338
British Workers' League, 67, 69–70
Brocket, Lord, 362
Brooke, Henry, 221
Brooks, Collin (journalist), 329, 432
Brown, Ernest (Minister of Labour,
    1935–40), 319
Bruce, Stanley (Australian High
    Commissioner, London 1933–45),
    188
Brussels Conference (1937), 277
Bryant, Arthur, 372
Buccleuch, Duke of, 362
budgetary policy, 193, 195, 199–208,
    209–10, 212, 254–55
Budgets and Finance Bills: (1909), 50,
    90; (1924), 100; (1925), 107; (1928),
    128–29; (1931), 196, 201, 211; (1932),
    196, 199, 200, 201–2, 210; (1933),
    194, 200–201, 203–4, 205, 206, 210;
    (1934), 210–11; (1935), 211–12, 227;
    (1937), 259–60; (September 1939),
    390
Bull, William, 96
Burgin, Leslie (Minister of Supply,
    1939–40), 319, 363–64, 388, 403–4
Butler, R.A. (Under-Secretary for
    Foreign Affairs, 1938–41), 14, 220,
    289, 292, 301, 338, 345, 352, 367, 372,
    376, 422, 428, 431, 432, 448
by-elections: Mitcham (1923), 88; Abbey
    (1924), 99–100; Bromley (1930), 143;
    South Paddington (1930), 147; East
    Islington (1931), 148; St George's
    (1931), 148–50; Stalybridge (1937),
    259; West Fulham (1938), 300;
    Oxford (1938), 319, 427

Cadogan, Alexander (Permanent
    Under-Secretary for Foreign Affairs,
    1938–46), 265, 281, 285, 306, 309,
    318, 324, 352, 356, 357, 367, 380
Camrose, Lord (proprietor, *Sunday
    Times* and *Daily Telegraph*), 145, 423
Canada, 191; NC's visit (1922), 84–85;
    Ottawa Conference, 168–69, 170,
    172, 191
canal development, 74–75
Canning, George (Foreign Secretary,
    1822–27; Prime Minister, 1827), 309
'Capital and Labour' movement, 48
capital levy, 97, 100
Carlton Club revolt (1922), 84, 87, 93

Carson, Edward, 79
Cartland, Ronald (Conservative anti-
appeaser after Munich), 14, 230, 373
Caucuses oilfields, 415
Caxton Hall meeting (June 1930), 143,
147
Cecil, Lord Robert (Conservative rebel
against Lloyd George Coalition,
1919–22), 80–81, 102
Central Control Board (Liquor Trade),
43–44
'Chain Home' radar network, 397
Chamberlain (Arthur) Neville, personal
life and character: physical
appearance, 7; 'dual personality' /
reserved shyness behind austere
façade, 4, 5–9, 10, 12, 15–17, 26, 33,
34, 105, 261, 265, 300, 409, 425; lack
of sentiment, 263, 375; conceit,
vanity and arrogance, 4–5, 12–13,
52, 262, 409; provocative sneering
manner, 13–14, 115; self-sufficient
obstinacy, 10, 12–13, 36, 53, 57, 61,
203, 262, 341, 388–89, 409; physical
and mental resilience, 10, 33, 272,
280, 294–95, 300, 304, 306, 373, 409,
411–12, 442; social life, 9–10; fishing
and shooting, 10, 29–30, 84, 93, 155,
244, 274, 280, 304, 306, 308, 357, 374,
403, 442; orchids and gardening, 10,
28, 258, 349, 374; natural history, 10,
28–29, 411, 442; art, music and
books, 30, 144, 384; relations with
sisters, 6–7, 12; finances, 81–82,
103–4, 258; lack of religious faith, 20
political and leadership style:
decisive leadership, 13–14, 42,
176, 195, 209, 239–40, 261–62,
264–66, 348, 439; business-like
approach, 15, 194, 364, 392, 436;
love of administration not
politics, 14–15, 104, 137; the
'ideal' minister, 16, 88, 92–93, 95,
195, 436, 438; hard work,
efficiency and mastery of detail,
5, 7, 10–11, 16, 42, 88, 106, 114,
165–66, 195, 255–56, 262, 411, 439;
negotiating skills / the
'Chamberlain touch', 108, 110,
123, 178–79, 251–52, 299–300, 305,
313, 314; approach to policy
problems, 13, 55–57, 209, 232,
262, 341, 348, 388–89; analytical
skills / inexorable force of logic, 7,

11, 13, 15, 239, 262; constructive
vision, 12, 152, 156–57, 158–59,
209, 213; narrowness of vision,
10–13, 89, 120, 201, 262; excessive
rationality, 12, 241, 291, 317,
396–98, 402, 414–15;
authoritarianism, 14, 119, 261–62,
264–66, 292, 308, 319, 340;
intolerance / resentment towards
opposition, 4–5, 7, 13–14, 15–16,
114, 229, 232–33, 264–66, 292, 373,
384, 386, 409; self-belief and
sense of mission / indispensability,
13, 51, 262, 304, 332, 341, 348, 364,
394, 410; relations with press /
media manipulation, 48–49, 52,
58, 78, 113, 197, 221, 250, 253, 266,
289, 325, 328, 333, 338, 341;
mastery of Cabinet, 280, 300, 401;
mastery of Commons, 108, 130,
300–301; speaking style, 7, 39,
73–74, 108, 129, 197, 288, 375, 412
political relationships and personal
standing (to 1937): with
colleagues, 5, 6, 8, 11, 14, 16, 87,
201, 203, 223–24, 228, 280, 300;
with officials, 16, 62, 94, 133,
194–95; with backbenchers, 8–9,
14, 36, 87, 100–101, 114, 123, 129,
194, 197, 201, 202–3, 204, 211–12,
223, 250, 259, 289, 300–301,
331–32; with Conservative party,
123, 202, 233, 259, 264, 288, 316;
with electorate, 202–3, 211, 251,
261–62, 288, 300, 317; indifference
to cheap popularity / public
image, 8, 37, 200–201, 414;
frustration with press, 74, 409–10,
417, 427. See also these references
under Career and Record: Prime
Minister
NC's attitudes and ideas: on
Conservatism, 48, 80, 102, 160,
174, 244, 484, f.67; corporatist
cooperation of Capital and
Labour, 47–48, 69, 71, 73; state /
municipal intervention, 41, 44,
74–75, 76, 117–18, 129, 214–15,
218–20; reluctance to interfere
with private enterprise, 218–20,
230, 390; trades unions, 45, 51, 54,
56–57, 62, 70, 114; passionate
commitment to social reform and
improvement, 3, 15, 40–41, 43–44,

46–47, 70, 71, 73, 102, 105–6, 108, 129, 133, 252, 431, 446; postwar reconstruction, 47–48, 80; property owning democracy, 77, 91; imperial unity, 48, 167–68, 170–74, 190–92; the purpose of politics, 15–16; coalition government, 72–73, 80, 81–85, 100, 160, 174, 244; the House of Commons, 8, 73; revulsion against war, 72, 383, 391–92, 434

NC's career and place in history: 2–4, 39, 87, 93, 112–13, 193, 435, 444–46, 448–51; biographies of NC, vii–viii, 4; childhood and Andros, 6, 20–27, 31, 35, 39, 61; marriage and family, 33–37; businessman, 27–30, 31, 71; early indifference to politics, 39; entry to politics, 32–33, 47–48; Birmingham civic affairs and council, 2, 11, 15, 31–33, 39–49, 51, 65, 70, 221, 438; Director-General of National Service, 50–63, 65, 66–68, 79, 88, 262; repairs Birmingham/Midland Unionist party organisation, 42, 68–70, 77–78, 86, 134; Unionist backbencher, 15, 67–68, 73–86; joins Bonar Law's government, 15, 84–88; Minister of Health (1923), 89–92, 94; Chancellor of Exchequer (1923), 92–94; dislike of financial control, 92–94, 104–5; tariff election and party reunion, 94–97, 99–100; strategy towards Labour government, 97, 100–101; author of 'New Conservatism', 101–2, 104; returns to Health Ministry (1924–29), 104–37, 363; Poor Law/local government reform, 114–33; plans to be Colonial Secretary, 134, 140; depressed by 1929 defeat, 137–38; East African tour, 140; Party Chairman, 142–43, 145, 150; wants 'free hand' on tariffs, 138–40, 144–46, 160; defeats Beaverbrook's Empire Crusade, 139–51; Baldwin's heir apparent/attitude to succession, 135–36, 138, 142, 144, 145, 146–50, 195, 210, 243, 256, 258, 261; financial and political crisis (1931), 151–59;

returns to Treasury, 160–61; increasing dominance in National Government, 159, 195–96, 210, 213, 224, 232–33, 243, 264; fulfilment of father's tariff/imperial policy, 162–74, 177, 187–89, 190–91; asserts Treasury control over economic diplomacy, 175, 195; frustrations of conference diplomacy, 177, 179; balanced budgets and 'confidence', 187–89, 193, 197, 199–208, 209; plans a recovery policy, 197, 200, 204, 210, 215, 229; resists 'imaginative'/expansionist finance, 188, 200, 202, 203, 208, 223–29; NC as policy innovator, 209, 213, 214, 218, 220–24; NC and 'the managed economy', 214–18, 231; criticism of NC's economic policy, 193–94, 199, 203–4, 208–9, 214, 220–21, 223–24, 228, 229; NC defends economic policy, 211–12, 213, 214, 220, 223, 227, 228, 231; regulation of output, 111, 186, 191, 244; Abdication crisis, 256–57; National Defence Contribution, 259–60; NC's health and spirits (to 1937), 84, 176, 197, 256, 258, 261, 274

Peacetime Premiership: succeeds Baldwin, 37, 258–62; government reshuffles, 263–64, 301–2, 340, 388, 407–8, 413–14, 424, 428–29; hands-on management and discipline, 262–63, 265, 335, 373, 393; NC's abrasive partisanship, 265, 288, 300–301, 335; asserts control over foreign policy, 213, 215, 266, 271, 273, 282, 287, 292; alleged ignorance of foreign affairs, 12, 30–31, 235, 450; fear of war on three fronts and 'resource gap', 190, 236–37, 241, 243, 266–67, 271, 275, 276, 277–78, 283, 295, 362; awareness/emphasis on military weakness, 296–97, 309, 318, 319, 321, 435; belief in air deterrence, 236–37, 238, 240, 252, 253, 333; economic strength as 'fourth arm of defence', 267–69; NC's sense of urgency, 272, 273, 285, 287, 356; hopes to play off

Peacetime Premiership (cont.)
dictators, 272, 284, 297, 342;
determined to exhaust all
peaceful options, 308, 310, 311,
314, 316–17, 320, 322, 325, 327,
351, 355, 378, 381–84; convinced
of Hitler's honesty / limited
objectives, 314, 317–18, 332–35,
347–48, 354, 370; convinced war
could be averted, 348, 349, 355,
358, 361–62, 371–72, 374, 376–77;
belated preparation for war,
337–39, 340, 362–63; declares war,
2, 378–82; criticisms of NC's
foreign policy, 273, 282, 291, 295,
316, 363, 365; Cabinet attitude
and role in policy formulation,
308, 310–11, 316, 317, 318–20, 322,
336, 353, 355–57, 367–68, 374, 376,
379, 380–81; backbench reaction
to NC's policy, 297, 300, 316, 322,
335, 340, 342, 344, 348, 352, 353,
357, 363–64, 373, 379–81; public
reaction to NC's policy, 297,
300–306, 316, 317, 319, 325–26,
327–33, 335, 338, 344, 348, 358,
364, 382, 384; NC's health and
spirits as PM, 272, 280, 294–95,
300, 304, 306–7, 320, 323–24,
329–31, 336, 338–40, 348, 349,
359–60, 373–74; feeling of
isolation and melancholy as PM,
336, 339–40, 348, 359–60, 373–74
Wartime leadership: problems of
Phoney War, 383–84, 393, 394–98;
Phoney War and NC's life, 384,
411; determined to continue as
PM, 384–85, 410, 421; perceived
defects as war leader, 389–91,
396, 408, 413–15, 417, 421, 423–24;
suspicions of NC's leadership,
386, 396; criticisms of War
Cabinet, 385, 388–90, 408, 413,
427; failure to coordinate war
economy, 390, 396–97, 408, 414,
438; complacent confidence in
own judgement, 397, 402, 403,
413, 414; expects war to fizzle
out / pursues 'waiting policy',
385–86, 393–98, 401–3, 412–13,
414–15, 416; Hitler's 'peace
offensive', 398–401, 403, 413;
British war aims, 192, 400–401;
convinced Hitler 'missed the bus'

at Munich, 306, 346, 397, 403, 413,
414–15; backbench reaction to
NC's wartime policy, 392, 393,
396, 399, 401, 403, 408, 412,
414–15, 420–27; public reaction to
NC's wartime policy, 384,
391–93, 396, 401, 412, 417, 420,
429, 434, 439, 441; NC's fall, 2, 16,
420–30; party support for NC
after defeat, 426–27, 431, 432–34,
441–42, 443; Lord President, 432,
436–37, 438–39, 443; campaign to
remove the 'Guilty Men', 435–36,
439–42; hopes to return to office
after war, 443, 444; NC's health
and spirits during wartime, 272,
280, 294–95, 300, 304, 306–7, 320,
323–24, 329–31, 336, 338–40, 348,
349, 359–60, 373–74, 384, 403, 404,
407, 409, 411, 415, 419, 421–22,
425, 430, 434, 442–48; feeling of
isolation and melancholy during
wartime, 425, 430, 434–36, 440;
final illness and resignation,
442–48; refuses Garter, 445;
tributes to NC, 446–48; regrets
nothing / expects vindication by
history, 431, 435, 439, 445–46,
448–51
Chamberlain, (Joseph) Austen (NC's
half-brother), 5, 9, 24, 26, 33, 45,
51–52, 53–54, 63, 65, 67, 71, 96, 134,
141, 146, 150, 157, 283, 445;
groomed for greatness, 6, 20–21, 26,
33, 87; political career, 19, 20–21, 32,
52, 65, 163, 298; Conservative leader
in coalition, 79, 80–86, 259; rift and
reunion with Conservatives, 89, 93,
99–100; Elder Statesman, 167, 169,
249; finances, 258; death, 258, 411;
compared with NC, 5, 7, 8, 10,
20–21, 41, 50, 62, 77, 80, 83, 112–13,
215, 258, 259, 411; relationship
with NC, 6, 20, 26–27, 33, 65, 73, 74,
79, 80, 82, 83, 85, 87, 100, 163, 235,
258
Chamberlain, Anne Vere (née Cole,
NC's wife), 203, 274, 300, 308, 322,
374, 404, 444, 447, 448; marriage to
NC, 34–37; health and nerves,
35–36, 49, 51, 71, 115, 144–45;
support for NC, 34, 36–37, 40, 66,
67, 129–30, 265, 375, 376; public and
political role, 36–37, 86

Chamberlain, Arthur (NC's cousin), 258
Chamberlain, Beatrice (NC's half-sister), 48, 72
Chamberlain, Dorothy (NC's first child), 34–35, 144, 404, 453
Chamberlain, Ethel (NC's sister), 20
Chamberlain, Florence (née Kenrick, NC's mother), 20
Chamberlain, Frank (NC's second child), 28, 34–35, 144, 404, 453
Chamberlain, Hilda (NC's sister), 6–7, 12, 20, 33, 34, 51, 67, 404, 442, 446, 453, 539
Chamberlain, Ida (NC's sister), 6–7, 12, 20, 34, 113, 404, 446, 453, 539
Chamberlain, Ivy (née Dundas, Austen's wife), 283–84
Chamberlain, Joseph (NC's father), 24, 52, 67, 381; personality and character, 10, 41; death of wives/ relations with children, 6, 20–21, 26, 28; connections with Birmingham, 19, 40, 68, 103; political career, 6, 19–20, 49, 68, 298; tariffs and imperial development, 8, 20, 22, 32, 97, 162, 167, 215; final years, 32–33, 259, 349, 446; NC completes tariff vision, 162–63, 166–67, 169, 170, 173; finances, 21–22, 23, 25; compared with NC, 10, 33, 42, 89, 94, 105, 170 ,174, 215, 218, 259, 261, 288, 349, 382, 445, 446; relationship with/influence on NC, 15, 33, 41, 48, 82, 84, 87, 105, 108, 130, 133, 134, 167, 218
Chamberlain, Mary (née Endicott, JC's third wife), 26, 42, 65, 167, 453
Chamberlain, Norman (NC's cousin), 71–72, 245, 453
Channon, Henry 'Chips' (PPS to Butler, 1938–40), 323, 330, 351, 353, 364, 373, 381–82, 383, 419, 420, 425–26, 429, 430, 431, 447
Charmley, John, 308, 419
Chatfield, Lord (Minister for the Coordination of Defence, 1939–40), 337, 340, 378, 386, 388, 414, 418
Chatham House, 338
Chautemps, Camille (French Premier, 1937–38), 280, 303
'cheap money' policy, 196–97, 199, 200, 207, 212–13, 231
Chequers, 280, 281, 300, 329, 341, 349, 357, 360, 374, 384, 404, 411, 421, 435

Chester-le-Street, Durham, Board of Guardians, 119
Chevening, 10, 337
Chiefs of Staff, 235–36, 238, 240–41, 266, 268, 295, 296, 309, 311, 355, 367, 397, 414, 418, 419
Children of Unmarried Parents Bill (1921–22), 78–79
China, 213, 241–42, 275, 277
Churchill, Winston S., 4, 9, 83, 96, 112, 296, 423; Dardanelles, 417, 418; returns to Conservatives, 99–100, 104; as Chancellor, 104, 114, 117; cooperates with NC on social/ rating reform, 107, 110, 113, 121–32; in Opposition, 138–39; free trade, 138, 146, 216; competitor for leadership, 138–39, 142, 146, 148, 149; Abdication, 257; critic of NC's foreign/defence policy, 4, 11–12, 267–68, 270, 288, 295, 299, 358, 359–60, 377, 450; plotting against NC, 294–95, 330, 335, 360, 363, 387, 388, 392, 418; hopes for office, 348, 360, 363; returns to Admiralty, 192, 386–88, 391, 393, 417; and Phoney War, 387–88, 395, 400, 405, 413, 414; promotes image as War Lord, 385, 391, 393, 417, 420; and Military Coordination Committee, 414, 418–19; Norway campaign, 415, 416–19, 420, 421–23; Defence Minister?, 418–20; succeeds NC, 420–21, 424, 429–30; Conservative mistrust, 431–34, 445, 448; values NC's support, 431–32, 436, 437–38, 444–45, 447; opposes negotiated peace, 437–38; defends NC, 440–41; NC's illness and resignation, 443–45; tribute to NC, 447–48; condemns NC's failure, 4, 450; attitude and relations towards NC, 4, 8, 107, 121, 126, 128, 417, 431–37, 440–41, 443–44, 447–48; NC's opinion of/ conduct towards, 99–100, 107, 121, 123–24, 125, 127, 128, 158, 267, 338, 360, 371–72, 386–88, 417–18, 421, 436, 443, 444, 447; compared with NC, 391–92, 411–12, 432
Ciano, Galeazzo (Italian Foreign Minister, 1936–43), 283, 284, 341, 342, 377, 379
City of London, 194, 197, 198, 201, 214, 251, 259–60

Civic Recreation League, 44, 70
Cliveden, 9, 10
coal industry reorganisation, 220
Cole, Lilian (NC's aunt), 33–34, 443
Cole, Valerie (Anne Chamberlain's niece), 404
Collings, Jesse, 68
colonial appeasement, 279–80, 293, 341
Colville, John (Assistant Private Secretary to NC, 1939–40), 381, 382, 419, 420, 422, 431, 450
Colvin, Ian (*News Chronicle* Berlin correspondent, 1938–39), 356, 402
Committee of Defence Preparations and Accelerations, 333
Committee of Imperial Defence, 239, 271, 386, 389
Committee on Economic Information, 196, 200, 204, 207, 209–10
Committee on Financial Questions (1931), 197–98
conscientious objectors, 43
conscription, 43, 49–50, 51, 54, 259, 337, 339, 362, 379; of wealth, 259
Conservative Party, x, 69, 73, 160, 431, 448–49, 484, f.67; Business Committee, 141, 146, 150; Cabinet Conservative Committee, (1934–35), 244; Central Office, 69–70, 139, 142, 150, 158, 265, 300, 393, 441; Chairmanship, 2, 142–43, 145, 150, 301, 335; National Union Executive, 394, 433, 441; Central Council, 415; Party Conferences, (1923), 96; (1928), 134; (1936), 262; 1922 Committee, 202, 250, 301, 393, 399, 426–27, 441, 445; backbench Foreign Affairs Committee, 249, 266, 289, 295–96, 345, 352, 356, 364; parliamentary discipline, 265, 335 – see also Margesson
Conservative Research Department, 139, 141, 150–51, 216, 219, 221, 261, 338, 341, 445
Cooper, Duff (War Minister, 1935–37; First Lord of Admiralty, 1937–38), 8, 12, 150, 249, 254, 266, 286; critic of NC's policy, 270, 308, 311, 314, 315, 318, 319, 320–21, 322, 330, 336, 348, 364, 386, 429
Cooperative Societies, taxation, 203
co-partnership in industry, 102
Corbin, André Charles (French Ambassador, London, 1933–40), 354

cotton industry reorganisation, 216, 217, 219–20, 244, 263
Council of Action for Peace and Reconstruction, 228
Countryman, The, 29
Cranborne, Lady, 330
Cranborne, Lord (Under-Secretary for Foreign Affairs, 1935–38), 287, 288
Crawford, Earl of, 94
Cripps, Stafford (left-wing Labour MP), 253, 348, 358
Croft, Henry Page (Diehard Conservative backbencher; Under-Secretary for War, 1940–45), 198, 333, 423
Crookshank, Harry (Secretary for Mines, 1935–39; Financial Secretary, Treasury, 1939–43), 288, 323, 331, 334, 414
Crowson, Nick, 426
Cunard Line, 218–19, 224, 383
Cunliffe-Lister, Philip (Colonial Secretary, 1931–35; Air Secretary, 1935–38), 12, 94–95, 124, 128, 139, 143, 151, 156–57, 159, 161, 386; opposes NC over war debts, 181, 182, 185, 189; opposes NC's economic policy, 224, 225; critic of NC's foreign policy, 240, 270; resignation as Air Minister, 301–2
currency/exchange stabilisation, 186–87, 190
Curzon, Lord (Foreign Secretary, 1919–24), 51, 88, 93, 94, 102
Czechoslovakia, 192, 240, 285, 295; Sudeten problem, 192, 241, 279, 291, 293, 295, 302–4, 306, 319, 321–22; military vulnerability, 295–96, 312, 321; NC's 'guessing policy', 295–96, 303–4, 308, 309; French treaty obligations, 303, 310, 315; the 'May crisis', 304, 306; pressure for concessions to Germany, 296, 303, 315, 316, 322; NC negotiates with Hitler, 310–26; British guarantee of new frontiers, 311, 315, 351–52; Hitler seizes Prague, 271, 349–50

Dahlerus, Birger (Swedish intermediary with Hitler), 377, 399–400
Daily Express, 138, 143, 204
Daily Mail, 140, 204
Daily Mirror, 429
Dakar operation (1940), 444

Daladier, Edouard (French Premier, 1938–40), 303, 310, 314–15, 319–20, 324, 342, 361, 378, 379, 381, 391, 415

Dalchosnie, 29, 242

Dalton, Hugh (Labour frontbencher; Minister for Economic Warfare, 1940–42), 359, 367, 385, 409, 421, 424–25, 428, 429, 430

Danubian Conference (1932), 185

Danzig, 354, 356, 361, 370–71, 372, 373–82

Davidson, J.C.C. (Conservative Party Chairman, 1926–30), 94, 141–42, 145, 149, 363–64, 400, 431

Davies, Clement (leader, anti-Chamberlainite All-Party Parliamentary Action Group), 392, 421, 423, 440, 441–42

Dawson Committee (1920), 133

Dawson, Geoffrey (editor, *The Times*, 1923–41), 60, 341, 348, 428

De La Warr, Earl (National Labour, Lord Privy Seal, 1937–38; Education Minister, 1938–40), 297, 308, 311, 314, 318, 319, 320, 330, 337, 414

de Valera, Eamon (Irish Taoiseoch and Minister for External Affairs), 298–99, 437

Déat, Marcel, 370

Defence Loans, 239, 254–55, 260

Defence Policy and Requirements Committee, 253–54

Defence Requirements Committee, 236–40, 246, 253–54

Delamere, Lord, 140

Denmark, 415, 416

Dennis, John, 68

Derby, Earl of (War Minister, 1916–18), 42, 53, 58, 60, 61, 94

Dilks, David, vii, 95, 96, 127

Disarmament, Ministerial Committee on, 239, 240–41

disarmament, 102, 181, 232, 280, 293, 324, 344, 348, 349, 371, 400

Disraeli, Benjamin, 325

Distressed/Depressed Areas, 120, 133, 220, 221–22, 253

Dollfuss, Engelbert (Austrian Chancellor, 1932–34; assassinated), 252

'domestic competitor' principle, 170–71, 191

Dominion Office, 168

Dominions, 95, 134, 167, 168, 169, 171,

191–92; at World Economic Conference, 187–89; and appeasement, 191–92, 321–22, 327, 351, 367; war aims, 192, 400–401, 437

Dorman-Smith, Reginald (Minister of Agriculture, 1939–40), 340

Downing Street, 300, 435

Dufferin, Lord, 340

Duncan, Andrew (President, Board of Trade, 1940; Minister of Supply, 1940–41), 408

Dunglass, Lord Alec (PPS to NC, 1936–40; later Sir Alec Douglas-Home), 5, 8, 9, 292, 323, 325, 331, 419, 422, 424, 429, 430, 431

Dunkirk evacuation, 435, 439

Dunstan, Dr R., 86, 97, 103

Dutton, David, vii–viii, 4

Economy Bill (1926), 113–14, 135

Eden, Anthony (Foreign Secretary, 1935–38; Dominion Secretary, 1939–40), 3, 91, 235, 250, 265, 377; character and health, 284, 286; critical of NC's policy, 270, 282; priority on USA, 281–82, 286, 287; obstructs negotiations with Mussolini, 273–74, 281, 284–86, 287–88, 336; resignation, 282–89, 291, 330, 335, 345; hopes to return to office, 331, 335–37, 343; as rival leader, 335, 336, 349, 352, 358, 363, 364, 373; support for NC policy, 348, 358; and wartime governments, 386, 393, 407, 413, 444, 445; NC's opinion of/relations with, 250, 265, 282–89, 291, 292, 338, 345, 348, 358

Edgbaston (NC's constituency, 1929–40), 103

Edward VIII, King, (later Duke of Windsor), 256–57

Egypt, 102

Einzig, Paul (journalist, *Financial Times*), 433

Eire: see Ireland

Elizabeth, Princess, (later Queen Elizabeth II), 430

Elizabeth, Queen (wife of George VI), 257, 274, 308, 325, 430, 446

Elliot, Walter (Minister of Health, 1938–40), 224, 240, 286, 308, 315, 319, 320, 330, 333, 380, 428

Elliott's Metal Company, 27–28, 71, 81

Ellis, Geoffrey, 142
Emergency Powers Acts (1939–40), 375, 438
Empire Crusade (1929–31), 138–51
Empire Free Trade, 138, 139, 141, 143
Empire Industries Association, 99, 138, 151
Emrys-Evans, Paul (Conservative backbench anti-appeaser), 424, 426
Epstein, Jacob, 30
Evening Standard, 340
Excess Profits Duty, 259
Exchange Equalisation Account, 197–98

Fair Trade Union (1924), 99
Federation of British Industry, 191
Feiling, Keith, vii–viii, 2, 6, 256
Ferguson, Howard (Canadian High Commissioner, London, 1930–35), 168–69
Fergusson, Donald (Private Secretary to Chancellor, 1920–36), 217
Feversham, Lord, 340
Fighter Command, 439
Film Institute, 338
Financial Times, 433
Finland, 366, 403, 411, 412, 413
Fisher, Victor, 69
Fisher, Warren (Permanent Secretary to Treasury, 1919–39), 98, 181, 194, 195, 205, 225, 257, 338, 339
Flandin, Pierre (French Finance Minister, 1931, 1934), 185
Food Control Department, 53, 55, 61, 62
food taxes, 95, 138, 139, 147, 162, 164, 168, 171
Foot, Dingle (Liberal MP, 1931–45), 16
Forbes, Lord Atholl (friend and host of NC), 9, 359
Forbes, Neil, 251–52
Foreign Affairs Committee, 249, 266, 289, 295–96, 345, 352, 356, 364
Foreign Office, 175, 242, 251, 273, 285, 295, 365, 367–68; NC's disagreements/tensions with, 175, 195, 242, 265, 266, 271–72, 273, 283, 284, 321, 344, 345, 347, 365, 399, 409
Foreign Policy Committee, 271, 289, 295, 296, 345, 356, 364, 367, 368
Foreign Press Association, 345
Forestry Commission, 360
Four Power Declaration (March 1939), 354–56
'fourth arm of defence', 268–69

France, 190, 198, 218, 246–49, 295; war debts and reparations, 175–79, 181–82, 184, 185; Italian threat to, 342–43, 344, 355, 361; German threat to, 346, 355; military weakness, 266, 295, 310, 314, 342, 346, 434–35, 437; accepts British policy leadership, 280, 303–4, 314–15; British military support for, 237–38, 239, 253, 254, 285, 303, 311, 319, 320–21, 339, 342–43, 346; Czech crisis, 295–97, 303–4, 310, 311, 313, 314–15, 316, 319–20; Polish guarantee, 355, 358; Soviet alliance, 368; declaration of war, 378–81; wartime cooperation, 389, 390; NC's tour of inspection, 395, 397, 404–5; invasion and defeat, 413, 434–35, 436, 437–38, 439; NC's opinion of/relations with, 181–82, 247–48, 249, 266, 280, 319–20, 434
Franco, Francisco, 275, 344, 435
'free hand' on tariffs (1930–31), 138–39, 140, 144, 145, 160
French, Field-Marshal Sir John (Commander, BEF, 1914–15 and Home Forces, 1915–18), 45

garden cities, 75–76
Garvin, J.L. (editor, *Observer*, 1908–42; official biographer of JC), 33
Geddes, Auckland (Director of Recruiting, War Office, 1916–17; Minister of National Service, 1917–19), 53, 61, 62, 66, 94
General elections: (1918), 72–73; (1922), 77, 82–86, 95, 103; (1923), 77, 94–98, 103; (1924), 73–74, 77, 103, 106; (1929), 130–32, 134–35, 138; (1931), 154, 158, 159–61; (1935), 2, 211, 225, 227, 244–45, 253, 256; (post-Munich), 331, 334–35, 341, 348, 364; (1945), 448
General Strike (1926), 113–14
George V, King, 88, 201, 256, 274
George VI, King, 257, 274, 308, 312, 325, 351, 381, 382, 404–5, 407, 413, 430, 446
Germany, 50–51, 153, 282; reparations and debts, 174–75, 177–78, 181, 250–52; grievances after Versailles, 237, 253, 270, 278, 293–94, 302, 399; threat to British interests, 236–37, 247, 252–53, 271, 356; NC's key policy priority, 278, 284, 362; British

policy towards, 296, 305–6, 307–26, 344; leaves League, 236, 240, 250; rearmament, 246, 252, 347, 439; Rhineland, 253, 279; Spain and Italy, 246, 275, 341–42; Austria, 252, 302–3; Czechoslovakia, 295, 302–4, 306–7, 351–53; German public opinion and NC's visit to Hitler/ threat of war, 312, 315, 325, 344, 346; anti-Nazi resistance, 346, 356; internal economic weakness, 279, 306, 347, 395, 412; threat to neighbours, 353–55; wartime morale, 395, 396, 397, 403; peace feelers, 398–401, 403, 413; launches war in West, 413, 415–16, 434–35, 442, 443, 444; NC's opinion of/ relations with, 144, 251, 252, 280, 304

Gilmour, John (Minister of Shipping, 1939–40), 388, 413

Gladstone, Herbert (Liberal Home Secretary, 1905–10), 94

Gladstone, William Ewart (Liberal Chancellor of Exchequer and Prime Minister), 19, 194

'Glamour Boys' (Edenites), 328, 364, 373, 392, 403, 421, 426

Gloucester, Duke of, 407

Godesberg Conference/terms, 316, 318, 319, 324

Goebbels, Joseph (German Propaganda Minister 1933–45), 252, 266, 395

Goering, Hermann (C-in-C, German Air Force, 1933–45), 252, 279, 306, 371, 372, 374, 377, 394, 398, 399

gold standard, 159, 186–88, 196, 197–98

Gort, Viscount (Commander, BEF, 1939–40), 404–5, 407

Government of India Act (1935), 248

Graf Spee (German pocket battleship), 417

Grandi, Dino (Italian Ambassador, London, 1932–39), 272–73, 284, 285

Greater London Regional Plan, 76

Greece, 305, 359, 361

Greenwood, Arthur (Deputy Labour leader; Minister without Portfolio, 1940–42), 358, 378, 380, 385, 394, 409, 429, 430

Greenwood, Walter, 213

Gren, Axel Wenner- (Swedish industrialist; intermediary with Hitler), 372

Gretton, John, 79

Griffith-Boscawen, Arthur (Minister of Health, 1922–23), 88, 90, 91

Grigg, Edward (Conservative MP; former Private Secretary to Lloyd George), 151, 226

Guilty Men, 4, 193, 439, 441, 450

Guinness, Walter (Agriculture Minister, 1925–29), 128

Gunston, Derrick (PPS to NC, 1931–36; later an anti-appeaser), 424

Hacking, Douglas (Conservative Party Chairman, 1936–42), 301, 335

Haig, Field-Marshal Sir Douglas (Commander, BEF, 1915–19), 63

Hailsham, Lord (Lord Chancellor, 1928–29, 1935–38; War Minister, 1931–35), 135, 148, 149, 157, 166, 173, 181, 182, 185, 189, 240, 311, 319, 320, 337

Haldane, Viscount (reforming Liberal War Minister, 1905–12), 405

Halifax, Lord (Lord President, 1937–38; Foreign Secretary, 1938–40), 272, 301, 302, 317, 323, 334, 361; character and reputation, 291; support for NC, 274, 278, 282, 286, 291–92, 301, 318, 329; visits Hitler, 265, 266, 278–79, 287, 293; Eden's resignation, 285–86, 287; at Foreign Office, 272, 291–92, 295, 309; concern about Czech policy, 296, 307, 308, 309; opposition to NC's policy, 318–19, 320, 321–22, 335–36, 339–40, 345, 346, 347, 349, 359, 367; Eastern/Balkan bloc, 305, 339, 359, 370; visits Paris and Rome, 342–43; Polish guarantee, 353–58, 367, 370; Soviet alliance, 367–69; Danzig, 376, 378, 380, 381; Phoney War, 385, 386, 388, 395, 400, 405–6, 421; to succeed NC?, 352, 421, 424, 429–30; under Churchill, 432, 445, 448; proposes negotiated peace, 437–38; tribute to NC, 445–47

Hallas, Eldred (National Democratic MP for Duddeston, 1918–19), 67–68, 69

Hankey, Lord (Cabinet Secretary, 1916–38; member of War Cabinet, 1939–40), 385, 388, 389, 398, 408, 418

Hannon, Patrick, 429

Harris, Percy (Liberal Chief Whip, 1935–45), 404, 421
Hart, Basil Liddell, 395
Hartington, Lord, 302
Harvey, Oliver (Principal Private Secretary to Foreign Secretary, 1936–39), 281–82, 379
Hayes, Carlton, 328
Headlam, Cuthbert (Junior Minister of Transport, 1932–34), 202, 288, 370, 423
health: reform, 117, 120, 133; hospital service, 131. See also public health
Henderson, Arthur (Labour leader and member of War Cabinet, 1916–17), 57, 156, 385
Henderson, Nevile (British Ambassador, Berlin, 1937–39), 279, 293, 297, 308, 309, 320, 347, 352, 370, 375–76, 377, 378, 379, 381
Henlein, Konrad (leader, Sudeten German Party), 310
Herriot, Edouard (French Premier, 1932), 176, 177, 178, 179, 181
Heseltine, Michael, 231
Hewins, W.A.S. (veteran tariff reformer), 102
Highbury (Birmingham home of Joseph Chamberlain), 6, 20, 26, 28, 33
Highfield Park (Hampshire home of Lilian Cole), 443, 444, 446
Hiley, Ernest (Birmingham Town Clerk, 1908–16), 45, 53, 60, 76
Hitler, Adolf, 1, 143, 147, 236, 246, 253, 268, 270, 361, 433; NC's overtures/ appeals to, 320–21, 322, 344–46, 349, 372, 375, 377; overtures to Britain/ NC, 306, 347, 372, 375–76; Austria, 279, 302–3; Sudetenland, 279, 303–4, 306, 307, 308–10, 312–13, 316–17, 321, 327, 344; meets NC, 308, 310–12, 314, 316, 317, 318, 319, 324–25, 362; 'missed the bus' at Munich, 306, 346, 397, 403, 413, 414, 422; seizes Prague, 271, 351; Danzig and Poland, 356, 369–71, 374–82; convinced western powers would not fight, 307, 316, 369, 377–78; plans/threatens war, 302–3, 316–17, 321, 346, 369, 370, 376, 377, 391, 400, 415–16; Phoney War, 394–98; 'peace offensive', 192, 398–404; Norway campaign, 415–16; attacks France and Britain, 400–402, 430, 442–43,
444; Hitler's hatred for NC, 344, 345; NC's hatred for Hitler, 351–52, 399, 438; NC's opinions of Hitler's character and ambitions, 266, 278–80, 293, 295, 302–3, 304, 306, 307–8, 309, 310–11, 312–14, 317–18, 322, 336, 341, 343, 345, 346, 347–48, 349, 351–52, 353, 354, 371, 377–78, 383, 394–403, 412, 414–15, 431, 450; NC's inability to comprehend Hitler's recklessness, 291, 317, 396–98, 402, 414–15
Hoare, Samuel (Foreign Secretary, 1935; First Lord of Admiralty, 1936–37; Home Secretary, 1937–39; Lord Privy Seal, 1939–40), 12, 109, 139, 143, 146, 149, 157, 158, 159, 214, 263, 347, 407; Foreign Secretary, 246–50, 253; advises NC, 263, 264, 271, 334, 337, 340, 362; on NC's foreign policy, 296, 349, 364; Sudetenland, 309, 315, 319; declaration of war, 379; member of War Cabinet, 386, 387, 393, 394, 406, 407, 413; fall, 421, 424, 425, 428–29, 432; NC's opinion of/relations with, 139, 158, 214–15, 246, 339, 340, 379, 434
Hodge, John (Minister of Labour, 1916–17), 59–60, 62
Hogg, Quintin (pro-Munich Conservative victor of Oxford by-election), 231, 319, 427
Hohenlohe, Prince Max von, 399
Holland, 238, 346, 397, 400, 402, 434
'Home and Empire' Campaign (1930), 141–42
Home Intelligence Unit, 439
Home Office, 123
Home, Earl of, 331
Hoover, Herbert (US President, 1928–32), 175, 178, 184; moratorium, 175, 179
Hopkins, Richard (finance specialist; Second Secretary, Treasury, 1932–42), 206, 207, 209, 230
Horder, Lord (prominent Society physician), 443, 446
Hore-Belisha, Leslie (Transport Minister, 1934–37; War Minister, 1937–40), 232, 233, 264, 269, 295, 315, 318, 320, 338, 340, 347, 353, 355, 362, 375, 386, 404–9
Horne, Robert (former Conservative Chancellor), 89, 99

Hoskins & Company, 27, 39, 71, 81–82, 103–4, 115, 258
Hotel Cecil meeting (February 1924), 102, 106; (1930), 141
House of Lords reform, 82, 102, 221
Housing Acts: (1890), 76; (1919: Addison), 90–91, 101; (1923: Chamberlain), 88–92, 101, 110, 112, 132; (1924: Wheatley), 100–101, 111–12, 132; (1925: Chamberlain), 101, 112
housing and slums policy, 40–41, 73, 75–76, 83, 88–92, 100–101, 102, 106, 110–13, 132, 135, 221, 233
Hudson, Robert (Secretary for Overseas Trade, 1937–40), 340, 352, 371, 404
Hull, Cordell (US Secretary of State, 1933–44), 186, 190, 276
Hungary, 316
Hutchinson, Lord, 307
Hyde, H. Montgomery, vii

Imperial Conference: (London 1930), 146, 172; (Ottawa 1932), 167–74, 187–88, 190–92, 197; (London 1937), 243, 280
imperial preference and development, 48, 73, 95, 134, 138, 139, 140, 146, 154, 163, 167–74, 190–91
Import Duties Act (1932), 8, 164, 166, 167, 168, 215
Import Duties Advisory Committee, 165, 216–18
income tax, 107, 193, 203, 208, 210–11, 212, 231, 259
India, 102, 198, 248
'Industrial Army', 54–61
Industrial Charter (1947), 220
industrial court, 114
industrial democracy, 48
Industrial League, 47
industrial policy/reorganisation, 195, 215–20, 231
Industrial Reorganisation League, 219
Industrial Transference Board, 222
infant welfare centres, 43, 47, 73
inland waterways, 74–75
Inner Executive (of Cabinet), 309, 314, 315, 317, 318, 319, 321
Inskip, Thomas (Minister for Coordination of Defence, 1936–39; Lord Chancellor, 1939–40), 253, 256, 268, 283, 286, 311, 314, 319, 340, 387

Intelligence reports, 356, 374, 396, 402–3
Invergordon 'mutiny' (1931), 159
Iraq, 434
Ireland, 82, 102; Irish Home Rule, 19, 79; Irish Treaty (1921), 82, 299; Anglo-Irish settlement (1937–38), 298–99; wartime neutrality, 299, 434, 437
iron and steel industry/reorganisation, 216–18, 219–20
Ironside, General William (Chief of Imperial General Staff, 1939–40), 334, 416
Ismay, General Hastings (Chief of Staff to Churchill as Defence Minister, 1940–45), 418, 419–20
Italy: threats to British interests, 236, 271, 283, 295, 362; tensions with Britain, 266, 273–74, 275; tensions with France, 342–44, 355; potential ally against Germany, 273, 274, 283–84, 286, 306, 342, 355, 358, 359, 361; NC's efforts to appease, 237, 246, 272–75, 278, 283–86, 294, 322, 341–42, 355, 361, 435; Abyssinia, 246–50, 274, 281, 283, 284; Spanish Civil War, 273, 274, 283, 285, 297, 306; Anglo-Italian agreement, 283–84, 288, 297–98, 306, 341–42, 359; NC's visit to Rome, 252, 342–43, 348; invades Albania, 358–59; and the Axis, 341–42, 361; peace proposals (1939), 377, 379, 380; intermediary for negotiated peace, 437–38

Jackson, Stanley (Conservative Party Chairman, 1923–26), 95–96
Japan, 213, 218, 246; alliance with Britain, 241; threat to British interests, 236, 238–39, 241, 266, 271, 275, 283, 295, 362, 364–65, 412; appeasement of, 237, 241–43, 309, 435; British policy towards, 275–76, 277; in Manchuria/China, 235, 241–42, 246, 275–77
Jeffreys, Kevin, 426
John, Augustus, 30
Johnson Act (USA, 1934), 190
Jones, Kennedy, 53
Jones, Thomas, 11

Kemsley, Lord (proprietor, *Sunday Times*), 372, 405

Kennedy, Joseph (US Ambassador, London, 1937–41), 308, 343, 348, 349, 365, 377, 386, 399, 434
Kennedy, Paul, 272, 450
Kenrick, George (NC's favourite uncle and benefactor), 29, 258
Kew Gardens, 258, 384
Keyes, Admiral Sir Roger, 423
Keynes, John Maynard , 188, 200, 203, 204, 205, 208, 214, 329; Keynesian economics, 193–94, 199, 204, 206, 214, 228, 231
Kitchener, Field Marshal Lord (War Minister, 1914–16), 51
Kleist-Schmenzin, Ewald (German anti-Nazi dissident), 307, 309
Kneeshaw, J.W., 73
Knowles, Michael, 23–24
Kristallnacht, 344–45

labour exchanges, 57, 58, 59, 60, 61
Labour Party, 54, 59, 69, 211; in Birmingham, 86, 103, 134–35, 161; in the country, 106, 118, 125; Labour government (1924), 97, 100–101, 103; opposes Poor Law reform, 115, 118–19; tariffs and imperial preference, 138, 143; financial crisis and fall of Labour government (1931), 151–59; criticism of unemployment policy, 211, 229, 363; attacks NC's foreign/defence policy, 253, 255, 304, 328, 348, 359–60, 373, 435, 441; Popular Front, 343, 366; to join NC's government?, 336, 385, 413–14, 424; exploits Phoney War conditions, 393–94; critical of NC's war leadership, 403–4, 409–10, 417, 422–24; supports Churchill, 418, 422, 428–30, 432; NC's opinion of/relations with, 7–8, 13–14, 15–16, 52, 62, 69, 97–98, 113–15, 118, 125, 137, 348, 359, 364, 382, 385, 393–94, 409–10, 428–29, 432, 436, 440, 441, 449
Ladywood, (NC's Birmingham constituency, 1918–29), 9, 36, 72–73, 77, 86, 97, 103, 135
land valuation tax, 211
Lausanne Conference (1932), 175–79, 180, 181, 185, 196, 197
Laval, Pierre (French Premier and Foreign Minister, 1931–32, 1934–35), 175, 247–49

Law, Andrew Bonar (Conservative leader, 1911–21 and 1922–23; Prime Minister, 1922–23), 72, 79, 84, 87, 88, 89, 94, 95, 96, 106, 138, 448; NC's relations with, 79, 88
Law, Richard (anti-Chamberlainite, Conservative backbencher), 413, 424
League of Nations, 102, 224, 246–50, 280, 295, 368, 370; NC's view of, 247, 249–50, 294
League of Nations Unions, 247, 338
Leith-Ross, Frederick (Chief Economic Adviser), 189
Liberal Party, 19–20, 161, 211, 338; supports Labour government, 97, 99, 101, 151; defection of Simonite group, 151; free trade opposition to NC, 159–61; to join NC's government?, 336, 385, 386; NC's opinion of/relations with, 348, 435
Liberal Unionist Party, x, 99
Liddall, Walter, 433
'limited liability' policy, 235, 240–41, 254
Lindsay, Ronald (British Ambassador, Washington, 1930–39), 175, 179–80, 183–84, 189
Lithuania, 355, 356
Lloyd, Geoffrey, 135
Lloyd George, David (Liberal Prime Minister of Coalition, 1916–22), 49–50, 138, 257, 353; character and methods, 55, 62, 226, 431; Prime Minister, 50–63, 66–67, 72, 74, 79–86, 87, 334, 385, 389–90, 421; 1931 crisis, 151, 158, 159, 160; offers British 'New Deal', 188, 205–6, 208, 224–29, 243; critic of NC's foreign policy, 288, 339, 358, 363, 366, 392, 425; to join War Cabinet?, 424, 440–42; hostility to NC, 4, 11, 13, 16, 53, 54, 56, 61–63, 225, 288, 425, 440–41; NC's contempt and hatred for, 8, 49–50, 63, 79, 80, 81–84, 100, 143, 151, 188, 208, 224–28, 262, 358, 399, 440–41
Lloyd, Lord, 167, 247, 441
Lloyd-Greame, Philip: see Cunliffe-Lister
Local Authorities (Financial Provisions) Act (1921), 117, 120
local government: reform, 106, 117–32; finance, 117, 120–22, 125; Local Government Act (1929), 128–32, 133

Locarno Agreement (1925), 253, 283
location of industry, 230. See also town
   planning
London County Council, 117
London Transport Board, 228
London Zoo, 304, 411
Londonderry, Lord, vii
Looking Ahead (1924), 102
Lord President's Committee, 438–39
Lowe, Francis, 79
Lukacs, John, 438

MacDonald, James Ramsay (Labour
   leader, 1922–31; National Labour
   leader 1931–37), 12, 160; Prime
   Minister (1929–35), 153–61, 163, 164,
   165, 174, 177, 183, 204, 224–26, 239,
   264; Lord President and decline,
   227, 233, 235, 243–44, 256; dislike of
   NC, 169, 201, 203, 211, 217, 224, 256;
   NC's opinion of/relations with,
   176, 195, 203, 239
MacDonald, Malcolm (Colonial/
   Dominion Secretary, 1935–40), 192,
   286, 296–97, 319, 340, 353, 449
McKenna, Reginald (Chancellor of
   Exchequer, 1915–16; banker), 92, 95,
   408
Maclean, Donald (Liberal MP;
   Education Minister, 1931–32), 116,
   120
Macleod, Iain, vii–viii, 48, 94
Macmillan, Harold (Conservative
   backbench critic of NC in 1930s;
   later Prime Minister), 6–7, 9, 12,
   139, 203, 231, 237, 392, 425, 440, 441
Macmillan, Lord (Minister of
   Information, 1939–40), 405
Maginot Line, 320, 395, 397
Maisky, Ivan (Soviet Ambassador to
   London, 1932–43), 366
managed economy, 214–18, 231;
   managed currency, 197–99
Manchester Guardian, 262, 422
Manchuria, 235, 241–42, 246, 275–77
Man-Power Distribution Board, 51, 54
Margesson, David (Conservative Chief
   Whip, 1931–40), 224, 265, 302, 331,
   335, 353, 360, 363, 384, 389, 393, 394,
   407, 414, 421, 422, 423, 429, 433, 448
Markham, Violet (Acting Head,
   Women's Section, National Service
   Department), 13, 52, 58, 60
Mary, Queen (wife of George V), 328, 381

Masaryk, Jan (Czech Minister to Britain,
   1925–39), 330
Mason College, Birmingham, 6, 21, 26
maternity care and mortality, 43, 73,
   106, 113, 133, 245
Maugham, Lord (Lord Chancellor,
   1938–39), 319
May Committee on National
   Expenditure (1931), 154–55, 216, 217
May, George (Chairman, Economy
   Committee, 1931 and IDAC,
   1932–39), 216–17
medical services, 113, 133; reform, 117,
   120; medical education, 92; hospital
   service, 131. See also public health
Memel, 313, 354–55, 370
'mental deficiency', 113
Mersey, Viscount, 2
Metropolitan Common Poor Fund, 117,
   120
Middlemore, John, 67
Middleton, Roger, 209
Midland Concert Promoter's
   Association, 46
Midland Union, 69, 78, 82
Midleton, Lord, 79
Military Coordination Committee, 414,
   418–19
Military Intelligence, 356, 374
Military Service Acts (1918), 66
Military Training Act (1939), 43, 362–63
Milk Bill (1938), 339
Mills, Ogden (US Treasury Secretary,
   1932–33), 180–82
Milner, Lord (member of War Cabinet,
   1916–18), 48, 51, 52, 58, 59, 60, 62,
   63
Ministerial Committee on Economic
   Policy (1939), 390
Ministers of the Crown Act (1937), 258
Ministry for the Coordination of
   Defence, 414
Ministry of Economic Warfare, 390, 410
Ministry of Health, 2, 14, 79, 105–6, 213,
   232; NC's tenure in 1923, 88–92; in
   1924–29, 105–37
Ministry of Information, 405, 408
Ministry of Labour, 55, 59–60, 108, 213,
   221
Ministry of Munitions, 51, 53, 55–56, 59
Ministry of Shipping, 53, 387, 388
Ministry of Supply, 337, 339, 360, 362–63,
   390
Ministry of War Economy, 408, 413

Moley, Raymond (advisor to Roosevelt), 187
Molotov, Vyacheslav (Soviet Foreign Minister, 1939–49), 368
Mond, Alfred (Health Minister, 1921–22), 90
monetary policy, 187–88, 194, 196–99
Montagu, Edwin (Liberal MP; Minister of Munitions, 1916), 51, 54, 55
Monteagle, Lord, 34
Morgenthau Jnr., Henry (US Treasury Secretary, 1934–45), 276
Morning Post, 155
Morrison, Herbert (Labour frontbencher; Minister of Supply, 1940), 8, 409, 421, 424, 428, 429
Morrison, W.S. (Agriculture Minister, 1936–39; Duchy of Lancaster, 1939–40), 311, 319, 340, 414
Mosley, Oswald (NC's Labour opponent in Ladywood 1924; later leader, British Union of Fascists), 103
Munich conference (September 1938), 1, 3, 12, 179, 194, 295, 300, 322–23, 324–26, 346, 351, 358, 369, 370, 377, 396, 414, 426, 427, 434–35; ambivalent reactions to, 1, 295, 327–32, 335, 336, 339, 449; NC's hopes, 270–71, 327, 330, 333–34, 341; defence of, 327, 334, 346, 352, 362, 434–35, 448; another conference on Poland, 377, 379
Munster, Earl of, 407
Murray, Gilbert (Liberal intellectual; Chairman, League of Nations Union, 1923–40), 348
Mussolini, Benito, 278; Abyssinia, 246–49, 272; Spain, 275, 324; Austria, 297; at Munich, 324; Albania, 358–59; fear of war, 376, 412; negotiated peace, 437–38; relations with Hitler/Germany, 297, 306, 355, 361; Eden mistrusts, 273, 281, 284–85; NC's overtures to, 237, 246, 252, 272–75, 278, 283–85, 294, 322, 341–43, 354–55, 361; potential ally against Germany, 273, 274, 283–84, 286, 306, 342, 355, 358, 361; attitudes to NC/Britain, 275, 343; NC's opinion of/relations with, 266, 272, 278, 306, 342–43, 358–59, 361, 370

Nathan, Lord (Labour backbencher, 1937–40), 429
National Debt, 196, 207
National Defence Contribution (1937), 259–60
National Expenditure, Select Committee, 58
National Government: formation, 2, 151–61; deadlock over tariffs, 164–66; resignation of free traders, 165–66, 174; unemployment problem, 213, 220–23, 229, 253; threat from Lloyd George, 224–29; criticisms of, 193–94, 199, 223, 225, 229, 301; standing with backbenchers, 298, 300, 306, 339; standing with public, 197, 223, 224, 244, 255, 288, 297, 298, 300, 306, 338–39, 341; Cabinet reconstruction, 256, 335, 337, 384, 386, 428, 430; Churchill's government, 428, 432, 436
National Health Insurance, 108–9, 245
National Labour Party, 160, 203, 211, 428, 436
National Liberal Party, 160, 162, 174, 263
national physique, improvement of, 244
national service/conscription, 43, 49–50, 51, 54, 259, 337, 339, 362, 379
National Service Committees (1938), 337
National Service Department, 2, 13, 15, 16, 25, 50–63, 68, 262
Naval Disarmament Preparatory Conference (1934–35), 241–43
Navy League, 31
Nazi-Soviet Pact (1939), 356, 369, 374–75
Necessitous Areas Committee/grants, 92, 118, 120, 123, 124
Nettlefold & Chamberlain, 19, 21, 25
Neurath, Constantin von (German Foreign Minister, 1932–38), 293
Neutrality Acts, 266, 269, 395
News Chronicle, 173, 356
Nicolson, Harold (National Labour MP; anti-appeaser), 296, 323, 348, 375, 380, 392, 424, 430
Norman, Montagu (Governor, Bank of England, 1920–44), 180–81, 194, 201, 251, 345, 407
Norway Campaign, 411, 412, 413, 415–17, 420, 421, 423; Commons debate, 2, 421–26

Nyon Conference (1937), 275, 276

'Old Moore's Almanack', 209–10
Ormsby-Gore, William (Colonial
Secretary, 1936–38), 189, 240, 302
Orwell, George, 213
Oster, Hans, 402
Ottawa Imperial Economic Conference
(1932), 167–74, 177, 187–89, 190–92,
197

Pact of Steel (1939), 361
Palestine, 338
Panay USS, 277
Parkes, Ebenezer, 68
pauper votes, 118, 119
Peace Ballot (1935), 247
Peden, George, 209, 238
Peel, Robert, 94
pensions, 47, 106; 1925 Widows,
Orphans and Old Age Pensions
Act, 106–9, 110, 120, 132, 135; 1937
Act, 244
Percy, Lord Eustace, 139
Pétain, Henri (French Premier and
Chief of State, Vichy regime,
1940–44), 442
Plan Z (to meet Hitler), 388–89
Poland, 240, 316; mistrust of Soviets,
355, 366–67, 368; British guarantee/
aid, 192, 346, 353–58, 361, 367, 369,
370–71, 372, 375, 376; suspicions of
NC's policy towards, 362, 376, 379;
Danzig, 370–82; Hitler prepares
invasion, 1–2, 356, 370, 376, 377,
378, 395, 396, 397, 399;
reconstitution after war, 399–400
Poor Law reform, 83, 92, 106, 107, 109,
114–32; Boards of Guardians/
Unions, 92, 110, 113, 115, 116, 117,
118–19, 120, 122, 130; outdoor
relief/workhouses, 116, 117, 119–20,
130–31; Poor Law Amendment Act
(1834), 116, 129, 130
Poplar, Board of Guardians, 92, 117–18
Popular Front, 343, 348, 366
Portugal, 280
Postgraduate Medical School, London,
92
Pownall, General Sir Henry, 239, 404
Public Assistance Committees, 130
public expenditure, 199, 201–2, 203, 204,
209–10
public health, 112, 130, 132, 133, 252

public works, 188, 200, 202, 203, 204–8,
223–25, 228

Queen Mary, RMS, 218–19

Radio Luxembourg, 338
Raeburn Committee (1932), 203
Ramsbotham, Herwald, 414
Ramsden, John, 205, 220
Rasmussen, Jorgen, 426
Ray Committee (1932), 209
Reading, Lord (Liberal peer; Foreign
Secretary, 1931), 151, 159, 160
rearmament, 199, 212, 252, 267, 282, 336,
361, 401, 402; British weakness/
need for, 235–36, 240, 246, 252,
296–97, 304, 318, 332, 334; cost,
finance and spending priorities,
236, 237–39, 240, 254–55, 259–60,
267, 283, 332, 370–71; speed of
implementation, 269–70, 297, 301,
304–5, 331, 333, 346, 354; public
opinion and, 239, 252, 253, 254–55,
259, 297, 341; trades union
response, 294, 305, 335; NC
influence over scale and priorities,
235–40, 252–53, 267, 301, 318, 333,
370–71, 397, 402; NC laments social
sacrifice/economic dangers, 252,
254–55, 267–69, 318, 332, 333, 339;
double policy/appeasement buys
time for? 237, 255, 267, 270–71, 294,
296, 304, 327, 333–34, 340, 346,
361–62, 371, 435, 449; successful
outcome, 346, 348, 354, 398, 415,
439–40; criticisms of programme,
269–70, 331, 334, 339, 396
Reconstruction Committee, 78
Red Star Line, 219
regional policy, 213, 214, 220–23, 229–32
Reith, Lord (former Director-General,
BBC; Minister of Information,
1939–40), 408, 421, 422
rent restrictions policy, 73, 89–92, 97, 106
reparations, 174–79, 180, 184
Rey, Charles, 59
Reynaud, Paul (French Premier, 1940),
416, 430
Rhineland remilitarisation (1936), 255,
360
Ribbentrop, Joachim von (German
Ambassador, London, 1936–38;
Foreign Minister, 1938–45), 258, 293,
312, 314, 345, 347, 355, 372, 381

Riddell, Lord (Chairman, *News of the World*, 1903–34), 55, 56
Road Fund, 232
Romania, 353, 355, 359, 361, 366, 367, 368
Roosevelt, Franklin Delano (US President, 1933–45), 349, 395; war debts, 183–85, 186, 189–90, 206; torpedoes World Economic Conference, 186–88; New Deal, 206–7, 208, 223–24, 225; 'quarantine' speech, 276–77; peace conference proposal, 192, 281, 284, 286, 287; pledges US aid in wartime, 269, 365–66, 395, 399; NC's opinion of/relations with, 187, 189, 190, 207, 208, 281, 284, 286, 287, 328
Rothermere, Lord (proprietor, Associated Newspapers), 140–41, 143–44, 146, 147
Royal Air Force, 236–39, 253–54, 270, 374, 397, 398, 439
Royal Commissions: Mesopotamia, 65; London development, 76; Poor Law, 116, 130, 132; National Health Insurance, 120; Unemployment Insurance, 153; Location of Industry, 76, 231
Royal Horticultural Society, 411
Royal Navy, 50, 321, 322, 338, 374, 417, 437, 439
Royal Oak, HMS, 383
Rucker, Arthur (Principal Private Secretary to NC, 1939–40), 327, 409
Rugby School, 6, 20–21, 26, 39, 449
Runciman, Hilda (wife of Walter), 194
Runciman, Walter (National Liberal MP; President, Board of Trade, 1931–37; Lord President, 1938–39), 226, 227, 263, 287, 328; tariffs, 160–61, 164, 165, 166, 172; opposes NC over war debts, 176, 178, 181, 185, 189; critical of NC's economic policy, 203, 217, 218–19, 224; rift with NC, 263–64; mission to Czechs, 307, 310, 314; returns to office, 337, 340
rural housing, 113, 132, 221

Salisbury, Lord (Conservative grandee; founder, Watching Committee, 1940), 135, 141, 414, 418, 420, 421, 423, 424
Salter, Lord, 3

Samuel, Herbert (Liberal leader, 1931–35; Home Secretary, 1931–32), 13, 159–61, 165–66, 174, 233
Sandys, Duncan (Churchill's son-in-law; Conservative anti-appeaser), 348
Sankey, Lord (Lord Chancellor, 1929–35), 159, 160, 161, 166
Saxe-Coburg, Duke of, 347
Schuschnigg, Kurt von (Austrian Chancellor, 1934–38), 284, 293–94
Scottish National Housing Company, 112
Select Committee on National Expenditure, 58, 92
Sellor, Rosalind Craig, 33
Serving Member's Committee, 424
Shanghai, 275, 277
Shea, Ambrose, 21–22
shipping industry, 218–19
Siegfried Line, 395
Simon, John (leader, National Liberal Party; senior member of National Government), 55, 151, 160, 174, 220, 224–25, 265, 323; Foreign Secretary (1931–35), 176, 186, 225, 232, 235, 242, 243, 246; Chancellor of Exchequer (1937–40), 263, 264, 407–8; Eden's resignation, 282–83, 286, 287, 288–89; Czech crisis, 307, 308, 309, 315, 317, 320, 322, 331, 352; Polish crisis, 367, 379; declaration of war, 380, 408; Phoney War, 386, 400, 406–8, 418; fall of, 421, 424, 428–29, 432, 439; NC's opinion of/relations with, 243, 244, 246, 263, 339, 424, 445–46, 449; support for NC, 311, 319, 324, 331, 340
Simpson, Wallis (later Duchess of Windsor), 256–57
Sinclair, Archibald (Scottish Secretary, 1931–32; Liberal leader, 1935–45), 174, 348, 358, 363, 373, 386, 387, 394, 418, 421, 422–23, 424, 429, 436, 440
Skidelsky, Robert, 193
slums and 'reconditioning', 40–41, 75–76, 83, 112–13, 124, 132, 213
Smart, Nick, 426
smoke abatement, 92, 106
Smuts, Jan Christian (Deputy Premier, South Africa, 1932–39), 188, 206
Snowden, Philip (Chancellor of Exchequer in Labour and National Governments, 1924, 1929–31), 100, 108, 155, 156, 159, 160, 164, 165, 174, 195, 201, 211, 214, 216

Soviet Union: Czech crisis, 316, 319, 320; Four Power declaration, 354–56; Anglo-French alliance? 192, 319, 331, 354, 366–69; NC mistrust of, 355, 366–69, 371; Nazi-Soviet Pact, 356, 369; war with Finland, 403, 412

Spanish Civil War, 266, 273, 274–75, 283, 343, 435

Special Areas Acts, 220, 222–23, 229–32

Spencer, Stanley, 30

Stalin, Joseph, 355, 381

Stamp, Lord (Chief Economic Adviser), 390, 407–8

Standstill Agreement (1931), 251

Stanhope, Lady Eileen, 444

Stanhope, Lord (friend and host to NC; First Lord of Admiralty, 1938–39), 9, 10, 319, 337

Stanley, Edward (Dominion Secretary, 1938), 336

Stanley, Oliver (Minister of Labour, 1934–35; President, Board of Education, 1935–37; Trade, 1937–40; War Minister, 1940), 224, 286, 288, 296, 297, 311, 314, 315, 318, 319, 320, 322, 330–31, 347, 352, 380, 405, 408, 423

Statement relating to Defence: (1935), 252; (1937), 255

steel housing, 110–13, 132

Steel-Maitland, Arthur (joint Chairman, Birmingham Conservative and Unionist Association with NC; later Minister for Labour, 1924–29), 69, 80

Sterling Area/bloc, 187–88, 191, 200

Stevenson, Frances, 225

Stevenson, James, 53, 56

Stewart, Percy Malcolm (Commissioner for Special Areas, 1934–36), 229–30

Stimson, Henry (US Secretary of State, 1929–33), 175–76, 179–80

Straightforward (Birmingham Conservative newspaper), 78

Strang, William (Head, Central Department, Foreign Office, 1937–39), 312, 319, 324–25

Strathcona, Lord, 340

Sudeten German Party, 302, 309–10

Sudetenland, see Czechoslovakia

sugar beet subsidy, 233

Sunday Times, 372, 405

Supreme War Council, 391, 404, 412, 416

Sweden, 206, 412, 415–16

Swinton, Lord, see Cunliffe-Lister, Philip

Tanganyika, 280

Tariff Reform Committee, 32

Tariff Reform League, 99

tariffs, 8, 32, 48, 73, 79, 82, 94–97, 98–99, 101, 102, 134, 138, 151, 154, 156, 157, 184; Empire Crusade, 137–51; triumph of tariff reform, 159–67, 215; and industrial reorganisation, 195, 215–18; basis for economic recovery, 196, 207, 211–12, 215, 231

taxation, 154, 156, 157, 179, 188, 198, 201, 203, 209–10, 211–12, 338

Taylor, A.J.P., vii, 199

Temperance Legislation League, 44

Tennant, Ernest, 372

Territorial Army, 254, 347, 357, 374

Thatcher, Margaret, 11, 231, 389

therapeutic substances regulation, 106, 112

Thomas, J.H. (Dominion/Colonial Secretary, 1930–36), 138, 159, 160, 161, 165, 166, 168–69, 172, 187, 240, 242

Thomas, J.P.L. (PPS to Eden, 1937–38, 1939–40), 287, 348

Tientsin, 277, 365

Tilea, Virgil, 353

The Times, 29, 101, 141, 197; supports Keynes' expansionist ideas, 201, 203, 204, 208, 221; and appeasement, 343, 358, 363; critical of NC's war leadership, 389, 408

Topping, Robert (Director-General, Conservative Central Office, 1930–45), 142, 143, 148–49

town planning, 40–41, 75–76, 112; Town Planning Act (1909), 40

trade unions, 45, 51, 54, 56, 57, 62, 70, 83; political levy to Labour, 102, 114; in building trade, 110–12; General Strike, 113–14; rearmament, 259, 305, 335; conscription, 337, 362; war effort, 393

Trades Disputes Act (1927), 114

Trades Union Congress, 48, 294, 337, 362

Treasury, 2, 45, 77, 264; Municipal Savings Bank, 45–46; Poor Law/rating reform, 124–25, 127; 'Treasury view'/balanced budgets, 134, 193–94, 199–208, 224, 225; NC's innovative contribution as

Treasury (cont.)
    Chancellor, 3, 208–9; scepticism
    about NC's industrial/regional
    policy, 214, 216, 217–18, 229–30;
    rearmament, 236, 267–69; asserts
    control over economic diplomacy,
    175, 195; NC's opinion of/relations
    with, 194, 198, 217
Treaty Ports (Eire), 299
Truth, 338, 407
Tryon, George (friend and host of NC;
    Postmaster-General, 1935–40), 9,
    414
Turkey, 305, 361, 434

U-boats, 383, 417
'Under-Secretary's Plot' (1940), 441
'Under-Secretary's Revolt' (December
    1938), 340, 404–5
unemployment, 97, 107, 116, 120, 130,
    132, 193, 199, 205–6, 213, 219,
    220–24, 225, 228, 229–32, 253, 390
Unemployment Act (1934), 232–33
Unemployment Assistance Board, 213,
    221, 232
unemployment insurance/benefits, 83,
    110; NC's pressure to cut, 145, 153,
    156; restores 1931 cuts, 210–11;
    reforms 1934–35, 232–33
Unhealthy Areas Committee (1919–20),
    75–76
Unionist Business Committee, 79
Unionist Propaganda Society, 78
Unionist Reconstruction Committee,
    78–79, 81
Unionist Social Reform Committee, 105
Unionist War Committee, 79
Unionist Workers' League, 77
Unitarianism, 20
United Empire Party, 140–41, 143, 148
United States of America, 246, 298;
    British war debts to, 174–76, 178–94,
    206, 208, 241; power of Congress,
    184, 185, 241; economic policy and
    position, 186, 199, 206–7, 208,
    223–24; World Economic
    Conference, 185–87, 241; Anglo-
    American Trade Agreement, 190,
    191, 277, 279; Neutrality Acts, 266,
    269, 366; NC's hope of US support
    in Far East, 241, 276–77, 281, 365;
    NC's hope of support in Europe,
    295, 346, 349, 365–66, 433, 434; USA
    attitude to NC, 242–43, 276; NC's

opinion of/relations with, 179, 180,
    182, 187, 190, 206–7, 241, 276–77;
    NC's desire to 'educate', 182, 184,
    185, 276, 277, 327

Vansittart, Robert (Permanent Under-
    Secretary for Foreign Affairs,
    1930–38; Chief Diplomatic Adviser,
    1938–41), 7, 181, 248, 265, 273–74,
    278, 285, 307, 309, 340, 347, 356
Versailles, Treaty of (1919), 237, 253,
    278, 293–94, 302, 399
Vince, Charles, 67

Walker, Patrick Gordon, 327
Wallace, Euan (Transport Minister,
    1939–40), 414
War Cabinet (1939–40), 384, 415, 416,
    418; composition, 385–87, 389–90,
    427; reform, 388, 413, 423;
    Churchill's War Cabinet, 432, 436,
    437–38, 440–41, 443, 444, 448
war debts, 174–90, 206, 208, 224, 232,
    241
War Loan/Bonds, 45; conversion
    operation (1932), 196–97, 200
War Loan Investment Act (1916), 46
War Office, 53, 58, 59, 62, 253–54, 404–5,
    408, 419, 427
war pension, 47, 71, 74
War Profits, Select Committee, 74
Wardlaw-Milne, John, 364
Washington Naval Treaty, 243
Watching Committee, 414, 418, 420, 421,
    423, 424, 428
Watt, Donald Cameron, 16
Ways and Communications Bill (1919),
    74
Webb, Sidney and Beatrice (Fabian
    social reformers and socialists), 116,
    119, 131, 329, 381
Wedgwood, Josiah (Labour
    backbencher), 423, 425
Weir, Lord (industrialist; Air Ministry
    adviser, 1935–39), 9, 110–12, 253,
    270, 362
Wenner-Gren, Axel (Swedish
    industrialist; intermediary with
    Hitler), 372
West Ham, Poor Law Union, 118–19,
    120, 122
Westbourne (NC's Edgbaston home),
    28, 258
Westminster, Duke of, 274, 374

Wheatley, John (Labour Minister of Health, 1924), 90, 100–101, 108
White Star Line, 218, 224
Whitley Councils, 71
Wiedmann, Fritz, 306
Wilhelm II, Kaiser, 328
Wilson, Horace (special adviser to NC, 1937–40), 257, 272, 282, 285, 292, 308, 309, 311, 314, 320–21, 322, 325, 340, 345, 354, 361, 362, 363, 368, 370, 371, 372, 376, 380, 389, 393, 405–6, 407–8, 418, 427, 432, 446, 448
Windsor, Duke of, see Edward VIII
Winterton, Viscount (Chancellor, Duchy of Lancaster, 1937–39), 301, 308, 311, 314, 315, 318, 319, 320, 324, 330, 381
Wise, Roy (Conservative backbencher), 427
Wohltat, Helmut, 371, 372
Wolmer, Viscount (Conservative backbench critic of NC during 1930s), 230, 348, 373
Women's Army Auxiliary Corps, 59

Women's Institute, 338
Women's Unionist Association (Ladywood), 77
Wood, Arthur (NC's fishing companion), 29, 210
Wood, Kingsley (Air Secretary, 1938–40), 269, 302, 334, 386, 405–7, 414, 418, 424, 428, 429–30, 444
Workers' Union, 70
workhouses, 116, 117, 119–20, 130–31
World Economic Conference (1933), 171, 184, 185–89, 194, 206, 241
Worthington-Evans, Laming (War Minister, 1924–29), 130

Young, Edward Hilton (Health Minister, 1931–35), 232–33
Younger, George (Conservative Party Chairman, 1917–23), 94

Zeppelins, 44–45, 56
Zetland, Lord (Secretary for India, 1935–40), 1, 311, 314, 319, 414